Internatio

"A page-turning record of th
War's zenith. . . .Von Tunzelmann artfully mixes the ambitions, love lives, drug use, grievances, deceptions and miscalculations of these men and a host of lesser characters with grand historical themes. . . . A remarkably gripping popular history."

– *Kirkus Reviews* (starred review)

"A thoroughly entertaining and well-documented account of the Cold War intrigue that swirled around the Caribbean in the late 1950s and '60s. Von Tunzelmann makes familiar material fresh by addressing it from the oft-overlooked perspective of the regional actors. In so doing, she illuminates how despots in backwaters manipulated the fears of the Soviets and Americans to garner endorsement for their predation."

– Montreal *Gazette*

"Suitcases full of cash, torture chambers, gunboats, coups, dictatorship and revolutionary fervor spill out of these pages. . . . The story would be action-packed enough on its own, but as von Tunzelmann shows, the region was also buffeted by the Cold War, transformed into an arena of mistrust and dangerous gambles, the largest of which was the Cuban missile crisis. . . . She captures the missile crisis as a frightening and real dance of knives in a dusty Caribbean cockfighting square."

– *Washington Post*

"Von Tunzelmann has strong gifts as a popular, narrative historian and is able to dig up many vignettes of life and politics in the age of the Caribbean despots. . . ."

– *Globe and Mail*

"*Red Heat* deftly juggles the stories of three countries – Cuba, Haiti and the Dominican Republic – and their relationship with the superpowers, where things were not as they seemed."

– *The Guardian*

"North American readers will not be shaken by the villainy of Communists. . . . This book, however, levels the playing field, documenting the covert terrorism of the CIA in the post–Second World War era, revealing the extent to which men who believe themselves to be good (i.e. 'our side') will go to secure their power."

– *Winnipeg Free Press*

"[An] excellent history. . . . The impact and legacy of the Cuban revolution of 1959 is a familiar tale, and here it forms the framework of the book, but an intertwined account of the more frightening developments in neighbouring Haiti and the Dominican Republic, superimposed on the strategic cold war battle between John Kennedy and Nikita Khrushchev, brings many events into unusual and fruitful focus."

– *The Observer*

"*Red Heat* is thorough in scope and quite readable. . . . The American experience in the Caribbean apparently did not teach us how dangerous it can be to make war on an idea. That was true with regard to Communism in our backyard in the 1960s, and it is true today, as we engage other ideologies on more distant battlefields."

– *Sunday New York Times Book Review*

"*Red Heat* somehow manages to combine the intricate and vital details, with a compelling and fantastical story. . . . Von Tunzelmann moves seamlessly from high-office political chess manoeuvres and the intricacies of men in suits in Washington or Santiago, to the sweat on the backs of unwashed and exhausted guerrilla forces following Fidel and Che through mango groves, carrying ammunition for their next terrorist strike."

– *Spike Magazine*

"An impressive attempt to capture the tumultuous events that shook the post-war Caribbean and has left it reeling."

– *Metro*

RED HEAT

CONSPIRACY, MURDER, AND THE COLD WAR IN THE CARIBBEAN

ALEX VON TUNZELMANN

EMBLEM
McClelland & Stewart

Cloth edition published 2011
Emblem edition published 2012

Emblem is an imprint of McClelland & Stewart Ltd.
Emblem and colophon are registered trademarks of McClelland & Stewart Ltd.

Library and Archives Canada Cataloguing in Publication

Von Tunzelmann, Alex, 1977–
Red heat : conspiracy, murder, and the Cold War in the Caribbean / Alex von Tunzelmann.

ISBN 978-0-7710-8614-4

1. Cuba–Politics and government–1959-1990. 2. Castro, Fidel, 1927–.
3. Guevara, Che, 1928-1967. 4. Dominican Republic–Politics and government–1930-1961.
5. Trujillo Molina, Rafael Leónidas, 1891-1961.
6. Haiti–Politics and government–1934-1971. 7. Duvalier, François, 1907-1971. 8. Cold War.
I. Title.

F2183.V66 2012 972.905'2 C2011-904431-5

We acknowledge the financial support of the Government of Canada through the Canada Book Fund and that of the Government of Ontario through the Ontario Media Development Corporation's Ontario Book Initiative. We further acknowledge the support of the Canada Council for the Arts and the Ontario Arts Council for our publishing program.

Printed and bound in the United States of America
Designed by Meryl Sussman Levavi

McClelland & Stewart Ltd.
75 Sherbourne Street
Toronto, Ontario
M5A 2P9
www.mcclelland.com

1 2 3 4 5 16 15 14 13 12

In memory of J. B. Dyhouse

"I hope to God you know what you are doing there. Oh, I know your motives are good, they always are. . . . I wish sometimes you had a few bad motives, you might understand a little more about human beings. And that applies to your country, too, Pyle."

—Graham Greene, *The Quiet American*, 1955

★

In our countries, people like voodoo practitioners and cannibals are as potent in affairs of state as any trained diplomat. They know how to fight and survive in our political jungles. Outsiders—like the Central Intelligence Agency, with all its trained personnel, equipment and lavish budget—do not.

—Arturo Espaillat (former director of intelligence, Dominican Republic), 1963

CONTENTS

★

IV. FALLOUT

RED HEAT

UNITED STATES
OF AMERICA
FLORIDA
West Palm Beach
Miami
Key West
Gulf of Mexico
Havana
PINAR DEL RIO
Presidio Modelo
ISLE OF PINES
Playa Girón
Bay of Pigs
Santa Clara
Cienfuegos
Sierra del Escambray
Trinidad
Camagüey
CUBA
from Tuxpan, Mexico
Cancún
MEXICO
Route of the Granma, 1956
CAYMAN ISLANDS
GRAND CAYMAN
JAMAICA
Caribbean
HONDURAS
0
100
200
300 miles
0
100
200
300
400
500 km

The Northern Caribbean, 1961

THE SECRET WAR

★

THE PLOT WAS AIMED AT NEW YORK: THE MOST FAMOUS CITY IN THE richest nation on earth, and the most sought-after prize for any anti-American terrorist. Reports said it was put into motion by a cell of fanatical young men, who saw the United States, with its interventionist foreign policy, as the world's oppressor.

A series of sensational attacks had been planned to hit almost simultaneously across the northeastern United States, with vast and indiscriminate loss of life. The targets were chosen because they were symbols of American wealth or the American military. New York was going to burn, and the world was going to watch.

That morning, New York was saved. The date was 17 November 1962. The fanatical young men were Cubans. They had planned to bomb Macy's, Gimbel's, and Bloomingdale's department stores during the Christmas rush and, simultaneously, to hit military installations and oil refineries. It was announced to the press that agents of the Federal Bureau of Investigation picked them up just in time, mostly from a costume jewelry business, and also broke up what it claimed was a "sabotage school" run by Cubans who had been linked to their country's representation at the United Nations. From Washington, Attorney General Robert F. Kennedy issued a statement praising the FBI. From Havana, Prime Minister Fidel Castro claimed that the arrests were "without foundation."[1]

History has few perfect parallels. On 11 September 2001, when a different group of anti-American fanatics did pull off an even more dramatic act of terror in New York City, there were plenty of differences between their fundamentalist Islamic ideas and those of the Cuban communists forty years before. But 17 November, coming just a fortnight after the Soviets had agreed to remove missiles from Cuba, had some similar themes. The United States' attempts to promote its own brand of freedom, democracy, and free market capitalism had offended third-world ideologies. They rallied around an icon of anti-Americanism—in 2001, Osama bin Laden; in 1962, Fidel Castro. Both men were the sons of privileged families. Both became revolutionaries. Both drew their strength from their oppositional position to what is sometimes (and not only by its critics) called the American empire, though others prefer the term *American hegemony*: the political ambitions, military adventures, and economic programs of the United States abroad. Both of their movements—fundamentalist Islam and communism—served the same purpose in a crude but effective type of American domestic politics. They could be portrayed simply and powerfully as an ultimate evil bent on the destruction of the United States. Against them, the nation could be rallied.

On that basis, both attacks would attract the attention of conspiracy theorists, some of whom asked whether the impression made on the general public was so beneficial to the American government's aims that it might have staged the attack itself. In the case of 17 November, the shocking thing is that the conspiracy theorists may well have been right. The Joint Chiefs of Staff had suggested in March 1962 that they could stage a terrorist campaign in Miami and Washington, and blame it on the Cuban government. There is no question that they were prepared to kill civilians in the process. Ideas put on paper included sinking boats full of real refugees fleeing from Cuba to Florida, and attempting to assassinate Cuban exiles. "Exploding a few plastic bombs in carefully chosen spots, the arrest of Cuban agents and the release of prepared documents substantiating Cuban involvement also would be helpful," the chairman of the Joint Chiefs wrote.[2] Repeatedly, Robert Kennedy himself suggested staging terrorist attacks on American military and diplomatic bases in Cuba and the Dominican Republic, and claiming that they were the work of Fidel Castro, to justify an all-out invasion of the sovereign state of Cuba.[3] As these plots have come to light, it has looked increasingly like the official story of the supposedly "Cuban" attempted bombing of New York cannot be taken at face value. The question that must be asked about 1962 is not whether it is feasible that the government of the United States might have resorted to such techniques—evidently, it might—but what could have been going on among the palm trees on a couple of islands in the Caribbean to provoke a superpower to such extreme action.

In October 1962, John F. Kennedy and Nikita Sergeyevich Khrushchev would take their nations to the brink of a nuclear holocaust, a war of unimaginable destruction. The crisis was provoked by a band of bearded guerrillas, mostly in their twenties and early thirties. Two and a half years earlier, these guerrillas had improbably assumed control of a modestly sized island, previously notable in the American consciousness for cocktails, casinos, and pretty girls. They had allowed the Soviet Union to place nuclear warheads within striking distance of Washington, D.C. Never in its history had the United States been so threatened. Never had the world come closer to nuclear war.

For thirteen days, the possibility that the world might end veered terrifyingly close. The bombings of Hiroshima and Nagasaki at the end of World War II had shown all too clearly what nuclear war looked like. A blinding flash of white light. Then the slow, ominous billowing of a mushroom cloud. For miles around, buildings, trees, all structures flattened into rubble. Close to the center of the blast, nothing remains but the shadows of human forms, their entire living bodies incinerated in a second by a flash of intense heat. Tens of thousands die instantly. Farther away, victims are blinded, scorched, and have the skin ripped off their flesh. In the weeks that follow, those who were close to the blast develop radiation sickness. They cannot eat. They bleed internally. Their hair falls out in clumps. Tens of thousands more die. In the years afterward, survivors experience high rates of leukemia and cancers of the organs. The total killed by the bombing of Hiroshima and Nagasaki is estimated at between 150,000 and 400,000.

These two bombs—the Little Boy at Hiroshima, and the Fat Man at Nagasaki—were considered to have been relatively inefficient. By 1962, the Soviet nuclear arsenal in Cuba alone was thousands of times more powerful than the Little Boy or the Fat Man. The American nuclear weapons ranged against the Soviet Union in Europe and on the mainland of the United States were more powerful still. If even a small number of these instruments of death was used, it is no exaggeration to estimate that millions would die, millions more would suffer, and the world would never be the same again.

In Cuba, parents rubbed olive oil into their children's skin, believing it would repel napalm. In Texas and Virginia, gun stores sold out of rifles—bought not to fight invading Soviets, but to defend rural properties against potential refugees from bombed cities. In London, Trafalgar Square filled up with demonstrators shouting "Hands off Cuba!" Police manhandled them into vans. In Chile and Bolivia, there were riots. In Venezuela, saboteurs blew up an American oil pipeline. In Prague, demonstrators smashed the windows of the American embassy. Shops across the Soviet bloc ran out of salt and cooking fat, as people panic-bought supplies for a nuclear winter. Housewives at the American military base at Guantánamo Bay, in Cuba, were told to tie their pets up in the yard, leave their house keys on the dining room table, and stand outside with their children, awaiting the buses that would evacuate them. "For some strange reason I felt compelled to defrost the refrigerator," remembered one, "although I made a mess of the job by allowing the drain to run over and spilled the water all over the floor. I poured a little over a quart of milk into a pan and put it out for the cat. I hope my cat will be able to forage a living. . . . I felt as if I were enacting some terrible, compulsive dream. I cried, of course."[4] Unknown to her, to the Pentagon, and to the president of the United States, nuclear cruise missiles were being maneuvered into position amid the trees, just fifteen miles from the base's perimeter.

The story of the Cuban Missile Crisis, as it is usually told, is not a story about Cuba. The real object at stake, it has been argued by some historians, may not have been Cuba at all, but the control of Berlin.[5] All the important events are presumed to have taken place in Washington or Moscow. What went on in Havana is widely considered to be irrelevant. The story of the Cuban Missile Crisis is not even a story about events. There was no fighting on the ground or at sea. No nuclear missiles were ever fired. War did not break out. It is a story about nothing happening.

While it may have been possible, from an American or a Soviet perspective, to believe that nothing happened, in the Caribbean plenty did. The missile crisis went down in American history as just thirteen days. From a Caribbean perspective, though, it was just one battle in an extraordinary secret war that spanned decades. George W. Bush's War on Terror was not the first time the United States declared war on an idea. In the 1950s, under the shadowy direction of the Central Intelligence Agency, it went to war against communism. This was not just a "cold war," a frosty standoff that never came to a fight. This was a real war. Dollars were spent. People were killed. Governments fell. To an incredible extent, the American public was at the time none the wiser.

This secret war was waged all over what was then called the third world: in Southeast Asia, in Africa, in Latin America. But it was in the Caribbean nations of Cuba, Haiti, and the Dominican Republic that it found its most sensitive and, for the inhabitants of the United States, most dangerous battleground: "only ninety miles from our shores," as John F. Kennedy often said.[6] That closeness mattered. When things went wrong in these nations, the exiles washed up in Florida, or flew to New York. They formed large, distinct communities, which have exerted significant influences on the nation's life as a whole—including, in the case of south Florida's Cubans, holding the balance of power in presidential elections.

Cuba, Haiti, and the Dominican Republic were the largest nations among the Caribbean islands, and the only fully decolonized republics. During the 1960s, several former British colonies, including Jamaica and Trinidad and Tobago, would also achieve independence. But their long histories of close relations with Britain, and continuing relationships with that power after independence, kept them largely out of Washington's Cold War purview. They were not the battlegrounds of this war.

The histories of Cuba, Haiti, and the Dominican Republic are by no means identical, but they share a few important factors. All were occupied and run by the American military during the early twentieth century. When the Cold War reached its zenith, each had brought forth a distinctive dictator. Cuba had Fidel Castro, a headstrong nationalist who became the world's longest-enduring communist head of state. The Dominican Republic had Rafael Trujillo, a capricious psychopath, who established perhaps the most effective authoritarian state ever seen in the western hemisphere—one usually defined as right-wing, though more accurately it had no ideology. Haiti had François Duvalier, a buttoned-down, bespectacled doctor with interests in embezzlement, torture, and the dark side of Haiti's syncretic religion, Vodou, whose regime defies belief of any kind. The United States would conspire to overthrow Fidel Castro, Rafael Trujillo, and François Duvalier, and to murder the first two.

Behind the Caribbean's paradise image of white sand beaches, lush jungles, and warm, clear seas lurks a gruesome human history. It is rooted in genocide, slavery, imperialism, and piracy, and these roots have shaped it well into the modern age. The passions and atrocities of the ancient world are often recalled. Graham Greene, one of the most perceptive observers of the Caribbean in the middle years of the twentieth century, wrote that François Duvalier's Haiti was best understood as a classical tragedy, "nearer to the Europe of Nero and Tiberius than to the Africa of Nkrumah." Fidel Castro studied closely the leadership styles of Julius Caesar and Alexander the Great; his code name among the Cuban revolutionaries, Alejandro, was his own middle name, but he used it as a tribute to the ancient Macedonian general. Arturo Espaillat, Rafael Trujillo's security chief, described his master's rule as "absolute as that of any Roman emperor. I thought of Caligula, the mad Caesar. Caligula once appointed a horse to be consul of Rome. Trujillo certainly could have announced that a horse was to be named president of the Dominican Republic, and Dominicans would have accepted it."[7]

This is a story of the machinations and the blunders of superpowers, and the brazen daring of the mavericks who took them on. It is a story of the rise of the politics of fear, and of the extraordinary things that even outwardly respectable governments have been prepared to do in their quests for control. It is a story of how the United States and the Soviet Union acted out the world's tensions in the theater of the Caribbean, attempting to use Cuba, Haiti, and the Dominican Republic as puppets. What neither superpower had bargained on was that their puppets would come to life. The result was tyranny, conspiracy, murder, and black magic; it was poverty, violence, and a new model of global interventionism that still dominates American policy. For this story is a prologue to later American-led interventions, covert and overt, all over the world, including those in Laos, Cambodia, Vietnam, Chile, El Salvador, Grenada, Honduras, Panama, Kuwait, Afghanistan, Iraq, and Pakistan. The precedent is not merely figurative, but literal. The *Small Wars Manual* of the United States Marine Corps, used in many of these operations, was written on the strength of the marines' experience in the Caribbean.[8] What happened in Cuba, Haiti, and the Dominican Republic during the middle years of the twentieth century would not just change the Caribbean. It would change the world.

PART ONE

IN SEARCH OF MONSTERS TO DESTROY

1

THE ENTRAILS

★

On the north coast of Cuba's Isle of Pines stands the Presidio Modelo, a panopticon prison. There are four large, drum-shaped cell blocks and a round refectory, all painted the color of butter, on a wide, desolate, grassy plain that leads down to the Caribbean Sea. The cells are open to the elements. Winds whip across the flat scrub, as do hurricanes, in season. When the sun blazes down, a thick, exhausting heat simmers back off the rocky ground. Blizzards of flies and mosquitoes swarm around, and biting ants teem over every surface. Behind the drums is a low-rise isolation block, where special prisoners were kept. It was here, in 1953, that a young lawyer called Fidel Castro began to read the history of revolutions.

Fidel had been sent to this island prison after his failed attack on a barracks of the Cuban dictator Fulgencio Batista. Twenty-seven years old, beardless, and a passionate nationalist, he was facing the prospect of a stay in the Presidio Modelo that, if he took no amnesty, would last well into his forties. He had no intention of taking an amnesty, for that meant negotiating with Batista. But staying true to his principles pained him. "In many of the terrible moments that I have had to suffer during the past year," he wrote to a friend, "I have thought how much better it would be to be dead."[1]

Life was hard for the prisoners in the panopticons. Had Fidel, over six feet tall and broad as an ox, been forced to cramp himself with another man into one of the tiny cells, he would barely have had room to stand up or lie down. But Fidel was not kept in the panopticons. He was kept alternately in the relative comfort of the infirmary or in the isolation block, along with his brother Raúl and a small band of comrades. The reason for his comfort was his family connections. His brother-in-law was one of Batista's ministers. The reason for his isolation was that he could not keep his mouth shut. When Batista had visited, Fidel had organized his fellow prisoners into an impromptu choir, singing out a rebel anthem at the fuming dictator until he went away.

Fidel's cell, with limewashed walls, a high ceiling, and granite floor, was relatively cool and hospitable. He was permitted to read, cook, and even smoke the occasional cigar from the fancy Havana firm of H. Upmann—then also the favorite brand of John F. Kennedy, a young senator from Massachusetts. His mood swung between despair and ebullience, the latter when he contemplated revolution.

Fidel read stacks of French, Russian, and English literature, and the works of Freud. "But my attention is really focused on something else," he wrote. "I have rolled my sleeves up and begun studying world history and political theory."[2] Among a broad selection of works that he acquired was Marx's *Das Kapital*. He claimed at the time that it made him laugh, and later admitted he had never managed to get through the whole thing. With history, he fared better. He considered Julius Caesar "a true revolutionary," became obsessed with Napoleon, and admired Franklin D. Roosevelt. But his hero remained the nineteenth-century Cuban poet and patriot José Martí. Fidel also read of the first flowering of glory in the islands, post-Columbus: what he described as the "very moving" story of the Haitian revolution.[3]

★

The history of Cuba, Haiti, and the Dominican Republic is a repeating cycle: plunder, oppression, a flash of hope, and a slide into disappointment. The first iteration was its conquest by the Spanish, who arrived in the wake of Christopher Columbus's voyages. They sought gold, found little, and drained it fast, but in seeking it brought war, disease, and slavery to the native Taino and Ciboney people. The islands' chieftains led heroic revolts against the European conquest. Yet within a remarkably short space of time—little more than half a century—the Hispaniolan Taino, and most of the Cuban Taino and Ciboney, would be dead. Their civilizations were wiped off the earth.

Sugar would make the Caribbean's fortunes, and its arrival began the second iteration of the cycle. But the farming and refining of sugarcane is punishing work, made tortuous by the heat. No free man would willingly do it. And so, having worked one race to death, the Europeans imported a new race so that they could work that one to death, too. The first African slaves arrived in the Caribbean just ten years after Columbus. Those who made it off the boats alive were put to work for twelve hours a day, six days a week. On the seventh day, they were forced to grow their own food, or otherwise starve. Conditions were squalid, disease was rife, and beatings and abuses were universal.

The West Africans enslaved in Hispaniola and Cuba died just as quickly as had the Taino and Ciboney. But these deaths troubled the Europeans little. Dead African slaves could be replaced with live African slaves. It cost money, of course, but not a great deal; and the supply seemed to be inexhaustible. Though the first few white voices of protest began to be raised in the second half of the sixteenth century, they were widely viewed as a lunatic minority.[4] Slavery was endorsed by the church on biblical authority, by governments on economic and social authority, and by the market itself.

Cuba and the eastern two-thirds of Hispaniola, now known as Santo Domingo, grew rich off the whip-scarred backs of slaves. But the French, who had taken control of the western third of Hispaniola and called it Saint-Domingue, perfected the slave economy. Saint-Domingue was acclaimed as the Pearl of the Antilles. Its plantations accounted for two-fifths of French foreign trade. It became the world's premier producer of sugar, its profits per acre double those of most Caribbean lands, and its slave population twice that of its nearest rival, Jamaica.[5]

In Saint-Domingue alone, slavery is estimated to have killed 1 million people.[6] More yet lived lives of misery. Though this may not have concerned the plantation owners morally, it did concern them practically. There were a great number of mistreated human beings in Saint-Domingue, and they were very angry.

A revolution broke out in North America. A regiment of black slaves and freedmen from Saint-Domingue was sent to fight in the ensuing war of independence, and saw action against the British at Saratoga and Savannah. When its men returned, they brought with them the idea that a people need not put up with being dominated. And so, on the night of 14 August 1791, a ceremony was held during a thunderstorm in the northern woods of Bois Caïman. A priestess, Roumaine, cut the throat of a black pig and drained its blood, mixing it with gunpowder. Those present drank the potion. An offering was made of the pig's entrails, to affirm a pact between those present and the *loas*, or spirits, of their Vodou religion. A priest, Boukman, declared that all whites must die. "We must not leave any refuge," he declared, "or any hope of salvation."[7]

Eight days later, drumming was heard all over the north of Saint-Domingue. It heralded fire attacks on plantations of cane, cotton, and coffee. By September, over one thousand plantations had been burned, and tens of thousands killed. The United States wanted the French out of the Caribbean, and sent arms and supplies to the black army. This move was strategic, not idealistic. Like the French, white Americans did not see black Haitians as human beings of equal worth to themselves. As President John Adams noted of the Haitians in 1799, "Independence is the worst and most dangerous condition they can be in for the United States."[8]

"There was Napoleon acting like Caesar, as if France were Rome," wrote Fidel Castro, a century and a half later, "when a new Spartacus appeared, Toussaint L'Ouverture."[9] Born into slavery, Toussaint had ascended to the prestigious position of livestock steward. He had learned to read and, like Fidel, had looked to Caesar's commentaries for his political and military education.[10] When he joined the revolution he was already forty-five years old. His physical stamina—on an ordinary day, he rode 125 miles on horseback—and exceptional abilities as a strategist and a leader ensured a swift rise. By 1800, Toussaint had wrested control of Saint-Domingue. He declared independence and the end of slavery, and annexed the Spanish side of Hispaniola, Santo Domingo.

In February 1802, Napoleon sent his brother-in-law, General Charles Leclerc, to retake Hispaniola. Leclerc publicly promised that French rule would in the future be free, equal, and fraternal for all. At this, many of Toussaint's best generals defected to the French. Toussaint was defeated by May, trapped in June, and put on a ship to France.

There was no trial. There was only imprisonment high in the Alps—a climate to which Toussaint did not adjust—and a meager prison diet. The greatest slave leader in history was found dead the following spring, his small, cold body huddled sadly by the fireplace in his cell.

In July came Napoleon's treachery. Slavery, which had been outlawed in 1794, was restored across the French Empire. At once, every black and many mulatto soldiers and officers who had fought for the French turned against them. If slavery were to be reimposed, Leclerc told Napoleon, "I shall have to wage a war of extermination."[11] Instead, an epidemic of yellow fever killed most of the French troops, including Leclerc himself. The tattered remains of the French army were defeated finally by the black general Jean-Jacques Dessalines on 18 November 1803.

On the first day of 1804, Dessalines declared independence and renamed the country Haiti, after its Taino name, Ayiti, land of mountains. "I have given the French cannibals blood for blood," he said. "I have avenged America."[12]

"What a small place in history is given to the rebelling African slaves who established a free republic by routing Napoleon's best generals!" Fidel Castro wrote, back in his cell on the Isle of Pines. "I am always thinking about these things because I would honestly love to revolutionize this country from one end to the other! I am sure this would bring happiness to the Cuban people. I would not be stopped by the hatred and ill will of a few thousand people, including some of my relatives, half the people I know, two-thirds of my fellow professionals, and four-fifths of my ex-schoolmates."[13]

★

The revolution in Haiti created shock waves across the world's slaveholding nations. At the beginning of 1806, the United States Congress banned trade with Haiti.[14] With the battle continuing on Dominican soil between the Haitians and the various colonial interests on the Spanish side of the island, the sugar industry collapsed on both sides of Hispaniola. But European powers and the United States still required sweetness. Gigantic cane plantations sprang up all over Cuba, with a corresponding increase in slave numbers.

In white-ruled Cuba, the United States saw opportunity. Thomas Jefferson was one of many early American statesmen who expressed interest in adding the island to the Union. This did not imply that all its people would be treated as equal American citizens. Jefferson thought that non-European peoples had much further to go before they would be "capable" of enjoying liberty. No hope at all was held out for African slaves or Native Americans, and only little for Latin Americans, who were "immersed in the darkest ignorance, and brutalized by bigotry & superstition." Still, Jefferson hoped that "light will at length beam in on their minds and the standing example we shall hold up, serving as an excitement as well as a model for their direction may in the long run qualify them for self-government."[15]

As secretary of state, John Quincy Adams agreed that the role of the United States was to serve as an example of freedom, not a crusader. In a famous address to the House of Representatives on Independence Day, 1821, he declared proudly that the United States "goes not abroad, in search of monsters to destroy. She is the well-wisher to the freedom and independence of all. She is the champion and vindicator only of her own."[16] Two years later, he notified the Spanish government of Washington's formal interest in acquiring Cuba.

American politicians still considered themselves opposed to empires, which they associated with their own oppression by the British. Paradoxically, though, they sought to expand the territory of the United States, and to establish political primacy across the Americas. At the end of that year, President James Monroe announced to Congress that, while the United

States would not interfere in existing European colonies, it would henceforth view any effort on the part of European powers to extend their domains in the western hemisphere, including "any interposition for the purpose of oppressing them, or controlling in any other manner their destiny," to be "the manifestation of an unfriendly disposition toward the United States."[17] This Monroe Doctrine would become a central plank of American foreign policy, well into the Cold War and beyond.

★

The Haitian revolution had created its flash of hope, and Caribbean history was due a slide into disappointment. The villains were the French. In 1825, the restored king Charles X sent warships to encircle Haiti's coastline. France considered that the land—and the slaves—had been French property. Emancipation had stolen that property. Now it demanded reparations: 150 million francs, in gold.

There could have been no more flagrant breach of the Monroe Doctrine. Haiti had declared and maintained its independence, existing free from European rule for a generation. The demand was an interposition by France, with the intent to oppress Haiti and control its destiny. Yet it was not considered an unfriendly act against the United States, as undoubtedly it would have been in any of the white-ruled republics. The Monroe Doctrine did not apply to states whose independence the United States had not acknowledged, and the United States had refused to afford the black republic the dignity of recognition. And so the American government placidly looked on while French warships, acting for the French crown, extended their colonial power in the western hemisphere.

The ransom demanded from Haiti was ten times its annual national revenue. But, with the guns of the French Caribbean fleet pointed at Port-au-Prince, Haiti's president was forced to agree that the former slaves should compensate their masters. To make the first payment—30 million francs—Haiti was obliged to take on loans covering the full sum from Parisian banks. Interest of 20 percent on this loan—6 million francs—was demanded in advance. To pay that, the treasury was emptied.

For the first liberated Latin American nation, formal independence on 11 July 1825 did not signify the beginning of freedom, but the end of hope. The chains were not cast off; they were soldered back on. Even after it was reduced to 60 million francs in 1838, the debt was an impossible sum. During the nineteenth century, slavery would be outlawed all over Europe and in the United States. Compensation was paid to slave owners—but by the governments that outlawed slavery, not by the slaves themselves. Yet the French government continued to insist that its own ex-slaves in Haiti pay for their liberty. The slavery reparations would not be paid off until 1947.[18]

★

In 1848, 1854, and 1859, explicit offers to purchase Cuba were conveyed from Washington to Madrid. On several more occasions, implicit offers were made, requesting the island as surety on loans made to Spain. Meanwhile, in Hispaniola, the complicated tensions between French speakers and Spanish speakers, rich and poor, former freeman and former slave, had only intensified. Strict race lines had crept back into society, and were defined by the precise proportions of black and white in seven generations of a person's ancestry. Foreigners could rarely detect the all-important differences between a *noir*, a *sacatra*, a *griffe*, a *marabou*, a *mulâtre*, a *quarteron*, a *métis*, a *mamelouc*, a *quarteronné*, and a *sang-mêlé*. Partly, this was because they were not always detectable by sight: as the black leader Jean-Jacques Acaau observed, "Nèg riche se mulat, mulat pauvre se nèg"—a rich black was a mulatto, and a poor mulatto was a black.[19] Nonetheless, these categories correlated strongly to a person's station in life, prospects, and politics. A lighter skin brought with it many privileges. Wedged deep in every political, economic, or social argument in Hispaniola was the splinter of racial hatred.

The Spanish side of Hispaniola eventually won its independence from Haiti in 1844, becoming the Dominican Republic. But Haitian incursions continued. Though both Haiti and the Dominican Republic would be inhabited and ruled by a mixture of whites, blacks, and mulattoes, Haiti continued to be associated with radical black former slaves, while the Dominican Republic attempted to present itself as more conservative and, essentially, more white. Successive Dominican leaders tried to persuade external powers to colonize their territory, to defend against Haitian invasion. They appealed to France and the United States, but it was Spain that returned as the imperial master by invitation on 18 March 1861. That same day, civil war broke out in the United States, meaning the former republic's northern neighbor had more pressing matters to attend to than the Monroe Doctrine.[20] In 1865, following the end of that war, the Spanish abruptly granted the Dominican Republic its independence again.

At the end of 1868, President Andrew Johnson recommended that both the Dominican Republic and Haiti be annexed. The project rolled over to the subsequent administration of Ulysses S. Grant. His representative was sent to Santo Domingo with a treaty of annexation, which was signed on 29

November 1869. But it failed to achieve the two-thirds majority in the United States Senate that was required, and so the Dominican Republic dropped out of the American embrace. It descended into chaos, and fell under the rule of a tyrant.

★

In 1868, mill owner Carlos Manuel de Céspedes declared Cuba's independence from Spain. The subsequent war continued for ten years. Céspedes freed the slaves in the territories he held. He was suspicious of the United States' interest in his cause, and was fully aware that it had ambitions to annex or purchase Cuba. He recommended drily that the Cuban revolutionaries reject American assistance, and go in search of "other, more disinterested friends."[21] When the Cuban rebels accepted defeat in 1878, four years after Céspedes's death, some refused to sign the surrender. The return of Spanish rule meant the restoration of slavery.

The third iteration of Caribbean history had begun. Banks and corporations of North American or European origin mushroomed in all three countries, and put themselves energetically to plunder. National debts were bought up and speculated upon. Enormous loans were made to governments, usually on poor terms. Swaths of land were gathered up under foreign ownership or control. The wealth that was created—and there was plenty of it—was retained by small, white- or light-skinned elites, and often channeled out of the countries themselves.

It was in Cuba that the next flash of hope appeared. Among the many patriots forced into exile by Spanish rule was José Martí. In the early 1880s, Martí had moved into politics, and developed an unusual ability to unite Cubans regardless of their race or class under the banner of nationalism.

In a pattern that would be emulated consciously by his ardent follower Fidel Castro many years later, Martí had toured the United States, raising funds from the exile community and setting up the Cuban Revolutionary Party in 1892. Three years later, he disembarked on the shores of Oriente, Cuba's wild, impoverished southeastern province, to begin the revolution. He was killed in battle soon after the landing. Martí had often warned against any alliance with the United States, but did so most poignantly on the day before he died. "I have lived inside the monster," he wrote, in lines often quoted later by Castro, "and know its entrails."[22]

Attacks on American property provoked President William McKinley to send the USS *Maine* to Havana in January 1898. It docked in the harbor and, on the evening of 15 February, was spectacularly blown up. The explosion, subsequent investigations have revealed, was probably an accident. But it was blamed on Spain, and it fed an enormous public appetite in the United States for war.[23]

On 16 July, the Spanish surrendered to the United States at Santiago de Cuba. The Spanish-American War had cost $200 million, and the lives of 3,254 Spaniards and 224 Americans in battle, as well as those of 5,000 more Americans from disease in the poorly managed military camps. As part of the peace deal, the United States acquired control of the Philippine Islands and Guam, far away across the Pacific. It had also taken the opportunity to annex Puerto Rico, which had won its own self-government from Spain the previous year. This had been, according to Secretary of State John Hay, "a splendid little war."[24]

The Cubans who had fought for their independence were not permitted to enjoy that splendor. Cuban guerrilla forces were prevented by the Americans from entering Santiago for the surrender ceremony. At the end of 1898, Cuba was legally transferred out of Spanish ownership and into theoretical independence, under American stewardship, without the signature of a single Cuban.[25] So began yet another slide into disappointment.

The United States established a military government in Cuba. Its rule was not without benefits. Progress was made in the fight against yellow fever; roads and bridges were improved; water and sewage systems were introduced, as were modern communications of telephones and telegraphs; schools were organized. There was also a massive increase in private American investment. As American interests came to own more and more of Cuba, the American government and public opinion came to believe ever more strongly that it was their land by right.

On 2 March 1901, the United States amended the Cuban constitution. The Platt Amendment gave Washington the right in perpetuity to interfere, including active participation in Cuban finances, domestic policy, foreign policy, and sovereignty, and granted the United States land of its choice for naval bases. There was an outcry in Cuba, where the convention on the constitution refused to accept it. There was also an outcry in the United States, where several senators protested vociferously. But the senators were in a minority, and the convention had no bargaining chips. Until the Platt Amendment was accepted, the occupying forces simply refused to leave. And so, on 22 May 1903, the constitution and the amendment were accepted, and the United States took possession of its new naval bases at Bahia Honda and Guantánamo Bay.[26]

In 1901, Theodore Roosevelt became president of the United States.

Roosevelt, a hero of the war in Cuba who had ridden with the Rough Riders at the Battle of San Juan Hill, believed it to be his job in Latin America, as he put it, to "show these Dagoes that they will have to behave decently." In order to show them, he proposed to "speak softly and carry a big stick."[27]

In response to a request from the Dominican Republic, which was being pressed for debt repayments by European powers, Roosevelt tinkered with the Monroe Doctrine. John Quincy Adams's warnings against seeking out monsters to destroy had long been forgotten. Now, Roosevelt said, "the Monroe Doctrine may force the United States, however reluctantly, in flagrant cases of such wrongdoing or impotence, to the exercise of an international police power."[28] This Roosevelt Corollary decreed that the United States would intervene in Caribbean and Central American national affairs: not merely in the case of defending those nations' sovereignty against European imperialism, but also if the nations were unable to pay their debts.

The American presence in the region grew rapidly. In 1903, the United States established a protectorate in Panama, with a view to building a canal through the slender isthmus separating Central from South America. Panama itself had been severed from Colombia as a result of overwhelming American aid to secessionists. American naval bases were established at Key West, Guantánamo, Samaná Bay, the Môle St.-Nicolas, Puerto Rico, the Virgin Islands, the Corn Islands of Nicaragua, and Fonseca Bay, all to defend the Panama Canal. The American naval presence was now so strong in the region that any unfriendly Caribbean government could be defined automatically as a threat to American national security.[29]

Roosevelt seized control of Dominican customs in 1905 but, when asked if he would annex it, declared that he was no more keen to absorb that state "than a gorged boa constrictor would be to swallow a porcupine wrong end-to." American troops also returned to Cuba from 1906 to 1909. An American was brought in to head the Cuban government: Minnesotan lawyer Charles Magoon, former governor of the Panama Canal Zone. "The day is not far distant when three Stars and Stripes at three equidistant points will mark our territory: one at the North Pole, another at the Panama Canal, and the third at the South Pole," declared Roosevelt's successor, William Howard Taft, in 1912. "The whole hemisphere will be ours in fact as, by virtue of our superiority of race, it already is ours morally." During Taft's administration, the marines returned again to Cuba and the Dominican Republic, and the National City Bank of New York commenced a takeover of Haiti's national bank.[30]

On 27 October 1913, the new American president, Woodrow Wilson, promised that "the United States will never again seek one additional foot of territory by conquest."[31] In practice, his administration would test the limits of that pledge. It would invade the Dominican Republic and Haiti and establish in both countries pro-American military governments, and intervene in the internal affairs of Cuba, Mexico, and Nicaragua in the name of protecting American interests.

In 1915, the largely American-controlled Haitian national bank refused to advance any further funds to the Haitian government, with the expressed purpose of forcing it to request American assistance or face intervention. The government fell, and the American admiral William Caperton personally accompanied Washington's preferred candidate for the presidency, General Jean Vilbrun Guillaume Sam, to Port-au-Prince.[32] But the fury in Haiti against American impositions had now reached the boiling point. The country would demonstrate what it could do to a patsy of the United States.

A powerful anti-American faction, led by Rosalvo Bobo, began a revolt. In response, Sam imprisoned several hundred hostages. He left orders that they should be executed the moment the first shot was heard, and fled with his family to the French legation. Stephen Alexis, later Haiti's ambassador to the United Nations, was in a cell at the prison when the first shot was heard and, therefore, when the massacre began. Within moments, he could hear the blows of saber sticks and clubs. A young boy who screamed was dragged from his cell by a guard, who expressed his displeasure by removing the boy's teeth one by one with pliers and gouging out his eyes before killing him. The prison was awash with blood and littered with heaps of entrails. Between 160 and 200 were slaughtered.

When news of this atrocity filtered out, a crowd gathered outside the French legation, demanding Sam. The president was reduced to crawling around on all fours, lest he be seen and attacked through a window. Finally, on the second day, eighty men smashed their way in. Sam hid in a bathroom, but the mob was soon outside the door. Finally, he opened it, with the resigned words: "Gentlemen, finish me." He was dragged by the feet down the stairs, through the salon, and onto the gravel driveway. He reached out, and one attacker smashed his hand with a cane. Another dealt three heavy blows with a machete. The last split Sam's head open. His body was thrown over the wall, where it was torn to pieces. One observer was rushed at by a man who held Sam's freshly severed hand in his mouth. What was left of the United States' favored candidate was paraded around Port-au-Prince until it was reduced to nothing, apart from the head, which was impaled and displayed in the city.[33]

This was too much for the American administration. That afternoon, Caperton moved the USS *Washington* into the harbor at Port-au-Prince, and the American occupation began. The Americans rejected Rosalvo Bobo as president. Instead, Caperton put Philippe Sudré Dartiguenave in power. Two days after Dartiguenave's election, which was conducted under the auspices of the United States Marines, the new president was informed that his recognition by the occupying forces was conditional on signing a treaty giving the United States control over his customs and excise as well as the police force. There was a delay while the Haitian legislature objected, during which the United States stopped all funds to the country. The Haitian government had no choice but to give in.[34]

The United States similarly occupied the Dominican Republic in 1916, after it looked like the wrong government might be elected. Washington assumed direct rule. Americans reformed the tax system, civil service, post office, and schools as they saw fit, and set up a constabulary. They departed in 1924, but the United States officially maintained its customs receivership until 1941, and only relinquished its other fiscal controls on the Dominican government in 1947.[35]

In Cuba, Haiti, and the Dominican Republic, occupation meant economic, judicial, military, and cultural control of a high degree. President Wilson insisted on land ownership reforms in the Dominican Republic to benefit American-owned plantations. Meanwhile, American-run police control was greatly strengthened, and political censorship was introduced. The Dominican poet Fabio Fiallo was accused of writing articles against the American occupation. He was subjected to a trial and a three-year prison sentence.[36] Cuba, meanwhile, fell into a spiral of corrupt governments, whose falls prompted repeated American interventions; each American intervention simply installed another corrupt government.

Herbert J. Seligmann, an American journalist, wrote a searing critique of the occupation in Haiti, accusing it openly of machine-gunning unarmed civilians and imposing "actual slavery"—forced labor—on the black population. The first ethnic group to be described by United States troops as "gooks" were not the Vietnamese in the 1960s. The slur had originated in the Philippines, and was now transferred to black Haitians. "I have heard officers wearing the United States uniform in the interior of Haiti talking of 'bumping off' (i.e., killing) 'Gooks' as if it were a variety of sport like duck hunting," wrote Seligmann.[37] Fifteen thousand Haitians revolted under the guerrilla leadership of Charlemagne Péralte in the 1910s, before he was assassinated by a marine. To prove he was dead, the Americans allowed Péralte's body to be photographed. It was depicted nude except for a loincloth, held up against a board by a rope slung under the armpits and across the chest, with the head dropped to one side, the arms hanging loose, and a flag draped behind the head. The resemblance to the crucified figure of Jesus of Nazareth was striking.[38] The marines had not realized what the effect of such an image would be on the Haitian people, steeped as they were in the visual symbolism of Vodou and Catholicism. The anti-American guerrilla immediately became an icon.

★

In 1917, the first communist revolution brought Lenin to power in Russia. It provoked immediate unease in the United States, and particularly in a young lawyer called John Foster Dulles. That year, his uncle, the secretary of state, sent him to Panama, Nicaragua, and Costa Rica to report on the situation there. Dulles recommended that, in view of the worrying leftist examples of the Russian and Mexican revolutions, Washington back Costa Rica's right-wing dictator.[39] Thirty-five years later, when he himself was secretary of state, Dulles would find his fellow Americans more receptive to his fears about Moscow's influence in Latin America.

In the early 1920s, the extent of communism in Latin America was minuscule, but the extent of anti-Americanism was considerable, and growing. The imposition of tariffs and financial meddling by the United States was widely blamed for the "dance of the millions," a boom and bust in the Cuban sugar industry between 1919 and 1921 that wrecked the island's economy. During the 1920 presidential campaign in the United States, there was much criticism of the occupations in Congress and the press. The *Nation* pointed out that for the last four years there had been no president, no cabinet, and no parliament in the Dominican Republic. "There is a censorship so dictatorial and so humorless that *the word 'Liberty' is stricken out from the program of the Teatro Libertad*," it said. "By official order of the United States authorities it is now plain 'Teatro.' And this in the name of America, while we were fighting to make the world safe for democracy!"[40]

★

In the thirty years or so since Cuban independence, the United States created effective protectorates in Cuba, Panama, the Dominican Republic, Nicaragua, and Haiti, annexed Puerto Rico and the Virgin Islands, took over customs and excise duties in four countries, established naval bases across the Caribbean region, increased its investments abroad from between $200 million and $300 million to $4 billion, and built and controlled the

Panama Canal. Between 1898 and 1934, United States Marines were sent to Cuba and the Dominican Republic four times each, and to Haiti twice. They had also been dispatched to Guatemala once, Panama twice, Mexico thrice, Colombia four times, Nicaragua five times, and Honduras seven times.[41]

By the latter half of the 1920s, the results of American occupation in these countries were plain to see. Some were exemplary. Transport, communications, education, health, sanitation, and public works had been improved almost across the board. Others were not. In all three countries, the attempted establishment of American-style democracy had been a shambles. Repeated violations of sovereignty had fueled parasitical political cultures, more interested in appeasing Washington than their electorates or subjects. The gap between rich and poor had widened in all the countries, with wealth concentrated in the hands of an elite that was largely foreign and white. Attempts to train Cubans and Dominicans for political or civil service had been minimal. Attempts to train Haitians had been nonexistent. The focus of training had been on national constabularies, whom the United States Marines had taught to enforce order by any means necessary—providing current and future dictators with a prefabricated means of control.

Cuba could not maintain order or sustain democratic government. The Dominican Republic was weak and chaotic. In December 1929, President Herbert Hoover himself publicly voiced concerns about the future of the American occupation in Haiti. The American journalist Edwin L. James noted with sadness that, by the middle 1920s, "the United States of America is the most unpopular nation on the face of the earth."[42]

Though many individual Americans working in or with the Caribbean were well-intentioned, perceptive, and capable, this could not compensate for the imperious attitude of the government in Washington. Sovereignty was ignored. Dictators were supported. Money from these poor countries filled the yawning coffers of Wall Street. In a nation that had a powerful sense of its own identity as a trailblazer for freedom from colonial rule, there was widespread squeamishness about using the word "imperialism" to describe this process. Complex arguments were constructed about how the United States was essentially different in character or morality from the European powers, and therefore its activities were not—could not be—imperialist. Some put it that imperialism was the control of one nation's territory, economy, and culture by another, and the United States did not control territory. But private American landholdings or land control in Cuba, Haiti, and the Dominican Republic were enormous (in 1920, American companies owned two-thirds of Cuban land);[43] the United States government intermittently ruled the nations directly as if they were subject possessions; and the marines arrived and stayed as Washington saw fit. "The United States does not undertake first to consult the Cuban Government if a crisis arises requiring a temporary landing somewhere," said Secretary of State Philander Knox bluntly when the Cuban government complained about marines turning up uninvited to crush a black political movement.[44]

"I have a feeling that imperialism is very much like an open window," observed the British politician Philip Guedalla in 1927. "If you open it, it is fresh air. If the other fellow opens it, it is called a draught. Of course I realize that America is quite unlikely to annex any territory; but what you call protecting nationals when it happens in Mexico, you frequently call imperialism when it happens somewhere else."[45] The world had entered a new era. European empires had gone, or were in decline. The United States had become a global power of immense and increasing importance. In the Caribbean it had created dependencies, nations not admitted to the Union that nonetheless were obliged—by force of arms, if necessary—to accept American dominance of their economies, foreign policies, legal systems, constitutions, cultures, and even political thoughts.

It was a system under which ambitious Cubans, Haitians, and Dominicans had two options: submit, or accept near-certain death in fighting American dominance. Whether it was called an empire or not, the thirty-year de facto rule of the American military and American finance in these countries signaled that a fourth cycle of plunder and oppression had begun. But a new generation had grown up with that system all around them, and they had new ideas about how to manipulate it. In the Dominican Republic, the first of these men was already poised to seize power.

2

GOOD NEIGHBORS

★

THE VILLAGE OF SAN CRISTÓBAL SITS ON THE MOUTH OF THE NIGUA River, just eighteen miles down the Dominican Republic's coast from the capital, Santo Domingo. In it, on 24 October 1891, Rafael Leónidas Trujillo Molina was born. It is not recorded who gave him that striking middle name, after the ancient king of Sparta: supposedly the first defender of Western civilization, who in his last stand kept back the hordes surging from the east. Trujillo's Cuban paternal grandfather was the corrupt head of Havana's police force, on the run in Santo Domingo for just long enough to impregnate his Dominican grandmother while spying for the Spanish. His maternal grandfather was also Dominican; his maternal grandmother, Haitian. As a child, he adored her. Later in life, he would obscure her memory. The line of blackness running through his ancestry would come to appear to him not as a source of pride, the noble inheritance of an enslaved people who had risen up to defeat Napoleon, but as a stain.

Little may be verified about Trujillo's youth, though a sense of misbehavior lingers around it. His father and he were suspected of cattle rustling, and it has been suggested that he served one or more prison sentences, for stealing, forgery, and theft. No proof exists. The Supreme Court of the Dominican Republic, which housed such records, burned down in 1927. He had six brothers and four sisters. Petán, a brother slightly younger but just as swaggering, soon became along with Rafael the most notorious gangster in San Cristóbal. In his teens, Rafael married a local girl, Aminta Ledesma, and had a daughter, Julia. Just a year into her life, Julia fell ill. Her father sought a doctor, but was stranded on the wrong side of a river bloated by the rains. While he frantically tried to cross, the baby died. A second daughter was born, named Flor de Oro (Flower of Gold), and cherished.[1]

In 1915, there were rebellions in support of Horacio Vásquez, leader of the National Party. A few troublemakers were rounded up and sent before Jacinto Peynado, the minister of justice. Peynado remembered one, a toothless youth clad in rags. He let him off, pausing only to ask his name. "Rafael Leónidas Trujillo, from San Cristóbal," came the reply. After the rebellion, Trujillo joined a gang called the "44," specializing in petty thievery, blackmail, and menacing, and also took a straight job as a watchman on a sugar estate, which required similar skills. It provided him with a lucrative sideline managing cockfights, the Caribbean sugar industry's most popular form of entertainment.[2] While the spectators shouted their bets, two roosters flew at each other, necks ruffed, wings arched, spurs forward. They clashed in midair, scratching and gouging, until one dropped. The victor was left pecking a lump of broken feathers in the dust. Trujillo controlled the takings. Whichever bird lost, he always won.

Two years later, he enrolled in the Dominican national guard, then trained by the occupying forces of the United States Marines. "He thinks just like a marine!" exclaimed his American superiors, on more than one occasion.[3] The most commonly praised of his skills was an aptitude for persuading detainees to confess. The marines taught him the methods: these included looping a rope around the subject's head, and slowly twisting it tighter and tighter until the pressure became unbearable. He was sent to the east of the country to fight rebels and proved adept at that, too. During one patrol, Second Lieutenant Trujillo kidnapped a peasant family to use as a human shield. For three days, he kept them locked in a church. On each of those days, he raped their seventeen-year-old daughter. She was left covered in blood, sobbing in her mother's arms. The marines were obliged to investigate, but Trujillo's lawyer put it to them that "three times implies consent." He was acquitted.[4] Three years later, he was promoted to the rank of captain.

In 1924, a new Dominican parliament chose Horacio Vásquez as president, and the United States withdrew its occupation. Arturo Espaillat, later the head of Trujillo's secret police, remembered that even thirty-five years later "Trujillo always thought of himself as basically a Marine Corps officer—and 'damned proud of it.'"[5] He was never a Marine Corps officer, but he was rising rapidly up the Dominican ranks. Vásquez made him a colonel and appointed him chief of police. In 1927, when the police were turned into a national army, Trujillo became its commander. He divorced his long-abandoned wife and married a member of the landed gentry, Bienvenida Ricardo. The marriage was not a success. In 1929, Trujillo's first son, Rafael Leónidas Jr., known as Ramfis, was born to a businesswoman, María Martínez. Ramfis was recognized by Trujillo as his son and heir, and would be legitimized by his parents' marriage following his father's second divorce in 1935.

General Trujillo appeared to have no political interest. But President Vásquez's star was dimming. Trujillo's headquarters, the Ozama Fort, was a sixteenth-century castle at the river's mouth in Santo Domingo. Some political prisoners kept in its cells recruited the general to their cause.

Later, one of his eulogistic biographers would ask when Trujillo had first thought of becoming president.

"When I first began thinking at all, as a child," replied Trujillo.

"And when did you first decide definitely that you would be president?" asked the biographer.

"The same day I began thinking about it," said Trujillo.[6]

On 26 February 1930, the capital put up no resistance when the rebel troops marched in.

"Trujillo is the head of a band of gangsters," Charles Curtis, the American minister to Santo Domingo, wrote to the State Department. "Can't you persuade Al Capone to offer him more money than he is making here to come to the United States as his instructor?" The State Department ignored his warnings, and told him to mediate a settlement. The civilian leader of the coup, Rafael Estrella Ureña, would be provisional president until elections could be held a few months later. Neither Vásquez's former vice president, nor Trujillo himself, would contest that election.[7]

Everyone kept his side of the bargain, except Trujillo. On 18 March, he announced his candidacy for president. Estrella Ureña threw himself on the mercy of the Americans, begging Curtis to declare publicly that the United States would not recognize Trujillo. The general, he said, had been so persuasive behind the scenes that no other candidate dared present himself.

The election had little to do with freedom or democracy. In early April, private houses and businesses in Santiago de los Caballeros linked to anti-Trujillo interests were ransacked. In Barahona, there were murders. Political leaders were shot at in their cars near Moca. Two bodies were found in a summer house at San José de las Matas, high in the mountains. One was the leader of the opposition National Party. He had been shot multiple times, slashed at so fiercely that his nose had been severed, and decapitated. The other was his young, pregnant wife, who had been shot twice in the belly. The offices of the newspaper that reported this grisly find, *Listín Diario*, were raided by Trujillo's supporters a few days later.[8] An air of menace hung over the country, the expression of the army's sentiments in favor of Trujillo's ascension. On polling day, his soldiers manned the booths. There were no opposition candidates, but, should anyone attempt to write one in, the troops had orders to shoot. Turnout was low, and Rafael Leónidas Trujillo Molina was elected president of the Dominican Republic.

Disregarding Estrella Ureña's dire warnings and Curtis's concerns, the State Department decided it would recognize the new president, telling Curtis that it was set on "scrupulously avoiding even the appearance of interfering in the internal affairs of the Dominican Republic."[9] If American interests were to be preserved, stability was required. A strongman was the ideal candidate.

On 3 September, a devastating hurricane hit Santo Domingo straight on. Of the city's ten thousand buildings, only four hundred were left standing. Two thousand were dead. Tens of thousands were homeless. Trujillo declared a state of emergency. He cleared streets and coordinated aid. He also used the opportunity to suspend constitutional rights, extend his powers, and dispose of some opponents. As the fires of the mass cremations crackled in Plaza Colombina, those who looked on whispered that the pyres contained some bodies of politicians and activists who had not died in the storm.[10]

Trujillo passed a law that allowed him to take the country's privately owned salt monopoly into "government" hands. Within a decade, some estimates would suggest that salt alone gave him a private income of $400,000 a year, in a country where the average per capita income was then $200. Officially, most of his business ventures went under the radar, though they were no secret among Dominicans. Over the years, the president would accumulate a controlling stake in or absolute control of the national oil company, cement manufacture, ironworks, brewery, milk, meat, navigation, aviation, and motoring industries, and factories making fruit juice, chocolate, sacking, and rope. He even made a fortune off a common weed from the Dominican jungles, after planting a phony article in an American magazine about "Pega Palo—The Vine That Makes You Virile."[11]

American investment poured into the newly stable Dominican Republic, with its business-friendly policies. The Dominican Congress declared Trujillo "Benefactor of the Fatherland." His son Ramfis, three years old, was appointed a colonel in the army, "taking into account his services."[12] His daughter, Flor de Oro, married the debonair young Porfirio Rubirosa, one of her father's aides. Trujillo granted him a diplomatic post. At this Rubirosa proved surprisingly adept, becoming an international playboy and the most visible face—apart from the Benefactor himself—of the Dominican Republic. He played polo, attended parties, and married rich women. After his five-year marriage to Flor, he wed the movie star Danielle

Darrieux, followed by two heiresses, Doris Duke and Barbara Hutton. Flor consoled herself with a further six husbands. Rubirosa's ambassadorial skills did not even stretch to charm. They consisted solely of sexual mystique, centered on what Truman Capote described with relish as "a purported eleven-inch" masculine endowment.[13] Thanks to Rubirosa's exploits, the image of the Dominican Republic in the world's press became so glamorous that it was hard to believe life in Santo Domingo could be anything other than a cocktail party.

Life in the Dominican Republic was something other than that, and there were rebellions. One civilian plot to ambush Trujillo in his car involved among several Dominicans a businessman, Oscar Michelena, and an Italian honorary consul, Amadeo Barletta. It was discovered. The Dominican conspirators were tortured and killed, aside from Michelena, whose Puerto Rican origins prompted the State Department in Washington to rescue him. Before it did so, he was taken to a beach and flogged into unconsciousness with a cat-o'-nine-tails. "Trujillo doesn't use leather," said Michelena; "these were steel cables laced together and knotted at the end."

He woke up in an airless cell, six feet by two, teeming with rats. There was no furniture but a bucket, which was not emptied until it overflowed. "This was done purposely," remembered Michelena, "it was part of the torture." He remained there for three months.[14]

Barletta, too, was imprisoned. But he had friends in high places. A month later, Benito Mussolini personally informed the State Department in Washington that, were Barletta not freed, he would send a warship to shell Santo Domingo. It was one of the few occasions on which Trujillo met an even bigger bully than himself. Barletta was released five days later and fled to Cuba.

★

In Cuba, another corrupt, vicious dictator, Gerardo Machado, was falling from power. Machado fled the other way from Barletta, from Cuba to the Dominican Republic. It was reported that his luggage included thirty-three suitcases filled only with cash. Trujillo put him up in a fortresslike house outside the capital, and stated publicly that the Cuban ex-dictator was not there.

Machado's flight sparked weeks of arson and assassinations in Cuba. People flooded through Havana with hammers, smashing up the stone reliefs of Machado's face that he had placed on public buildings. A few months earlier, Sumner Welles, a friend of the new American president

Franklin Delano Roosevelt, had been sent to the island to supervise the situation. The two key figures to emerge were Sergeant Fulgencio Batista, an obscure army officer, who had taken control of the military headquarters in Havana; and Ramón Grau, a leading figure in the opposition to Machado, who took over as president. Welles described both Batista and Grau as "extremely dangerous radicals, possibly Communists."[15] Though not, by any normal definition, a communist, Grau was left of the American center. He attempted to redesign the structure of Cuba's economy to remove American controls. Washington withheld recognition of his administration. But the parallel rise of Batista, Grau's fellow noncommunist, was rapidly building up steam. Five hundred army officers, concerned by his discreet consolidation of power, barricaded themselves in the Hotel Nacional. On 2 October, he attacked. Two hundred officers were killed, mostly after they had surrendered.

Five days later, Welles met Batista and deduced that he was pro-American. In mid-November, another counterrevolution led to three days of fighting in Havana among the army, students, and the government. In December, Welles advised Batista to take over and impose stability. By the middle of January, Grau found himself on a ship, sailing into exile, and Batista and Washington agreed on a placeholding president.[16]

On 29 May 1934, Roosevelt abrogated the Platt Amendment, the source of much Cuban mistrust of Americans. This act was part of his Good Neighbor policy, a deliberate break with aggressive interventionism to refocus on reciprocal trade and investment. Roosevelt gave up several treaties privileging American interests in the region, withdrew troops, and promoted a new doctrine of nonintervention in Latin American affairs. He even turned up in person to end the occupation of Haiti, becoming the first American president to visit that country while in office. Though he had made a few regrettable statements about Haiti in the past, including calling its people "little more than primitive savages," he received a cordial welcome.[17]

Ten thousand Haitians assembled on the docks to watch the marines sail away. As the ships disappeared from view, riots broke out. Telephone lines were cut. Bridges were destroyed. The new president, Sténio Vincent, declared martial law and suspended the constitution.[18] Under the circumstances, it was difficult to conclude that the protracted period of American guidance had done much for Haiti's political culture or stability.

Nonetheless, Roosevelt's attempt to change the United States' image made a positive impact. When he toured Argentina, Brazil, and Uruguay in 1936, hundreds of thousands of people turned out to cheer him.[19] The Good Neighbor policy had made the United States popular in Latin America.

★

With much folderol, an escort of bodyguards toting submachine guns, and a spotless wardrobe of elaborate uniforms—designed by his own hand—Trujillo descended upon Port-au-Prince in November 1934. Norman Armour, an American diplomat, could not conceal his amusement. "Even at the receptions and dances, when the Generalissimo takes the floor, as he has done on occasion, to tread the light fantastic," Armour wrote to Sumner Welles, "he is followed around the room by his officers with hands pointedly resting on an ominous bulge in their hip pockets."[20] They were not just pleased to see him.

Publicly, Trujillo made nice with the Haitian regime, then headed by the corrupt and authoritarian Sténio Vincent. Privately, he preferred the company of Elie Lescot, Haiti's ambassador to the Dominican Republic; and of the powerful commander of the Haitian national guard, Démosthènes Calixte. Behind the scenes, he began channeling money to Lescot. In public, Trujillo and Vincent resolved a boundary dispute, and agreed on a treaty of friendship. The foreign secretary of the Dominican Republic submitted their names for the Nobel Peace Prize at the end of 1935. The Nobel Committee did not find the case persuasive. It was just as well, for the harmony between the Dominican Republic and Haiti was about to be destroyed.

The Massacre River is named after a last stand by buccaneers in 1728. Its shallow, silvery waters divide the town of Ouanaminthe in Haiti from Dajabón in the Dominican Republic, one of three main crossing points on the border. In September 1937, Trujillo's soldiers began an unusual operation around Dajabón. Dressed as peasants and armed with handfuls of parsley, they would approach black people and ask, "What's this?"

The Spanish word *perejil*, meaning "parsley," is difficult for Creole-speaking Haitians to pronounce. If a person answered in a Creole accent, "pelegil," the soldier would whip out a machete or bayonet, and hack the presumed Haitian to death.

At first, such stories seemed to be isolated incidents. True, there had long been a feeling against Haitian immigrants, legal and illegal, in the Dominican Republic. Though many came every year to cut sugarcane—a task not relished by native Dominicans—they were blamed for everything from malaria to stealing to sorcery. One of Trujillo's slogans was "Desafricanazar las fronteras"—de-Africanize the border. But few predicted that this meant genocide. On 1 October, a story spread that dozens had been killed at the town of Banica. It was widely dismissed as a rumor. The next day, a motorcade arrived at Dajabón. Trujillo himself emerged from his gleaming Packard outside the church, and addressed his people. "I came to the border country to see what I could do for my fellow countrymen," he told them. "I found that Haitians had been stealing food and cattle from our farmers here. I found that Dominicans would be happier if we got rid of the Haitians." He stamped his foot for emphasis. "I will fix that. Yesterday three hundred Haitians were killed at Banica. This must continue!"[21]

That night, the orders were carried out. Trujillo's officers had been told not to waste their bullets, so few Haitians were spared a slow death at the blade of a machete or the blunt end of a club. In the dark, hundreds of men and women plunged into the Massacre River and raced for the other side, splashing desperately through the waist-deep waters, clutching their babies and terrified, screaming children. But Trujillo's troops had been ordered to kill, not to repatriate. Behind them, soldiers waded in, machetes flashing in the moonlight. Mutilated black bodies piled up on the bridge linking Dajabón and Ouanaminthe, so many that Trujillo's men had to heave them off into the water at regular intervals. For days, the river ran red with the blood of the butchered. In Ouanaminthe and surrounding villages, thousands of the injured lay gasping and dying on mud floors, while locals struggled to improvise what little aid they could.[22]

The frenzy spread. In Santiago de los Caballeros, almost two thousand black men, women, and children were forced into a barracks, where they were beaten to death, or close enough. The army trucks on which their broken bodies, some still breathing, were piled to be taken away and dumped in the sea left thick trails of gore behind them on the roads. Trujillo's soldiers tied people together in groups, then, one at a time, decapitated them. Piles of severed heads were seen on the roads out of Dajabón. Between two and five days after the massacre had started, and with just as little warning, it stopped.[23]

The first small report appeared three weeks later, on 21 October, in the *New York Times*. Four days later, the newspaper had a fuller account, estimating the number of killed and wounded at three hundred. This was immediately denied by the Dominican consul in Washington, in a joint statement with Elie Lescot, Trujillo's paid friend, now Haiti's minister to the United States.

Ten days later, the State Department summoned Lescot, who still denied it. Behind the scenes, he was engaged in a bitter struggle with Georges Léger, the Haitian foreign minister, who demanded that the facts be admitted. Quentin Reynolds of *Collier's* magazine went to the Dominican Republic to investigate, and was received by Trujillo over lunch with Lanson champagne of the excellent 1928 vintage. "Yes, it is true," said Trujillo. "A few Haitian farmers crossed the border up North and tried to steal some goats and cattle from our farmers. There was a fight—very regrettable—and several were killed on both sides."[24] In person, Trujillo's charm reminded Reynolds of Ernst Röhm; but, when he got to Ouanaminthe, Reynolds thought instead of a higher-ranking Nazi. "With Hitler it was the Jew," he wrote; "with Trujillo it was the Haitian."

Léger took matters into his own hands and went to see Sumner Welles, now undersecretary of state. His allegations were shocking: at least one thousand Haitians were dead, and perhaps as many as five thousand. Horrified, Welles confronted Lescot, who reluctantly confirmed that it was so. Finally, Haiti was obliged to do as its own foreign minister demanded, and seek mediation from the United States, Cuba, and Mexico. Trujillo cabled to Roosevelt, pleading that he had no idea what was vexing the Haitian government.[25] Soon afterward, Sténio Vincent announced that the confirmed death toll now stood at eight thousand.

Trujillo took out a full-page advertisement in the *New York Times*, declaring his innocence. Eventually, though, he was obliged to accept a process of mediation. Before the end of 1937, the *Times* revised the death toll up to twelve thousand. An authoritative final count was never made, but estimates of the numbers really murdered during what became known as the Parsley Massacre range from seventeen thousand to thirty-five thousand—between a quarter and half the total number of Haitians in the Dominican Republic.

Soon afterward, some details emerged of a plot sponsored by Trujillo to remove Vincent from the Haitian presidency, in favor of Démosthènes Calixte.[26] Some wondered whether the Parsley Massacre was part of this plot. But the purpose of the massacre was more broadly to send a message, most obviously to the Haitians, but also to Dominicans, Americans, and the world, that Trujillo must be feared. He was capable of doing anything. He might do anything, at any time, for any reason, if it pleased him to do it. And he would get away with it.

For get away with it he did. The inter-American mediators settled on compensation of $750,000. This was not a great sum in any case, valuing as it did each Haitian life at between $21 and $44. It was reported that Trujillo paid the first installment of $250,000 in 1938, and handed out

$25,000 in cash to politicians in Port-au-Prince. None of the money ever reached the victims or the bereaved, and the rest of the compensation was never paid. The American congressman Hamilton Fish III, who led the outcry in the United States and in November 1937 called the Parsley Massacre "the most outrageous atrocity that has ever been perpetuated on the American continent," was invited to the Dominican Republic. There, the Benefactor subjected him to a remarkable charm offensive, and defanged him completely. Just two years later, Ham Fish, now known cozily in the Dominican Republic by the literal translation of his name, "Jamón Pescado," welcomed Trujillo to New York. At the Biltmore Hotel, while crowds outside shouted "Down with Trujillo!" Fish declared to the beaming dictator and a large invited audience of American investors, "General, you have created a golden age for your country." He also created a golden age for Jamón Pescado: $25,000 left Trujillo's personal account at the National City Bank of New York, and at the same time an account at the same bank was opened with a deposit of $25,000 in the name of Hamilton Fish. Trujillo only pushed it too far in 1945, when he proposed to change the name of Dajabón to Ciudad Roosevelt. The American embassy objected, and the suggestion was dropped.[27]

There is some evidence—not especially conclusive—that the State Department put pressure on Trujillo not to stand for president in the election of 1938 owing to the Parsley Massacre.[28] This presented little inconvenience. Trujillo announced he was returning to private life, and filled the ballot paper with his placemen. On the day of the elections, *Listín Diario* proclaimed, "People! Vote for the candidates of the Dominican Party, Peynado and Troncoso, suggested by the Honorable President Trujillo!"[29] Jacinto Peynado, the man who as minister of justice had shown mercy to a destitute young Trujillo, duly received 100 percent of the vote, and was recognized by the United States.

Peynado put up a neon sign outside his own house reading DÍOS Y TRUJILLO. It was, as the Spanish-born Dominican academic Jesús de Galíndez acidly noted, a declaration of his submission to higher powers, though in reverse order.[30] The "new" administration promoted Trujillo's son Ramfis, then nine years old, to brigadier general. Trujillo theoretically retired. He took an apartment on Park Avenue in New York City with his wife and son. But soon after he arrived came the attack on Pearl Harbor. On behalf of the Dominican Republic, Trujillo, not Peynado, declared war on Germany and Japan. He hastened back to his homeland, and reclaimed overt power.

Trujillo's control over the Dominican Republic was now absolute. He renamed the capital, Santo Domingo, Ciudad Trujillo. Three provinces were renamed Trujillo, Trujillo Valdez (after his father), and Benefactor. The country's highest mountain, also the highest in the Caribbean, became Pico Trujillo. After 1933, every new building had to include a plaque glorifying his name. After 1940, all public letters and documents had to bear two dates: that of the normal calendar, and that of the new calendar marking the Era of Trujillo. He had splendid stables, splendid kitchens, and the best yacht in the Caribbean, the *Ramfis*, with an all-American crew. To satisfy his prodigious sexual appetite, there was on his staff a lavishly paid official whose full-time job it was to procure beautiful women, preferably virgins, to be offered to him. Credible estimates suggest that he worked his way tirelessly through many hundreds of conquests, perhaps thousands. Women who resisted were fired from their jobs and slandered in the public press. Their fathers or brothers were sometimes beaten up or imprisoned until the women "consented."[31] His sexual exploits earned him the nickname "the Goat" to complement his official titles: His Excellency Generalissimo Doctor Rafael Leónidas Trujillo Molina, Meritorious Son of San Cristóbal, Father of the New Fatherland, Benefactor of the Fatherland, Restorer of the Financial Independence of the Republic, Loyal and Noble Champion of World Peace, and Maximum Protector of the Dominican Working Class.

As for the Dominicans living in the nation that was now, in effect, Trujillo's private estate, they risked dishonor, torture, and death if they did not submit. Trujillo stationed snipers outside foreign embassies, and had them shoot anyone attempting to run in to seek asylum. Even in murder, this immaculately attired tyrant cultivated a certain gentlemanly charm. The widows of the victims of his many political assassinations would often receive a personal letter of condolence and a cash payment. Sometimes, they would even be invited to the palace where, in their presence, Trujillo wept for their slain husbands.[32]

★

The Caribbean was not a major theater of the Second World War. Trujillo had allowed Nazi agents to operate freely until 1939, and neither he nor Batista was keen to accept the Jewish refugees that Roosevelt tried to persuade them to take on. On the condition of American funding, Trujillo eventually agreed to accommodate between 50,000 and 100,000 European Jews, though nowhere near that number ever arrived. Instead, he was presented with political refugees from the Spanish Civil War. He accepted a number of these before realizing they included a proportion of known subversives and communists.[33]

The Spanish exiles did represent a genuine, if not especially large, importation of European communist thought to the Americas. Trujillo cracked down on it fast, and banned further refugees. There had been another, more organized importation of communism to Cuba by Comintern, the Soviet agency set up to promote Marxism-Leninism in the third world. Comintern had funded a Cuban communist party in the 1920s, but Machado and then Batista had eliminated it.

By 1940, though, Batista had become concerned with legitimacy. He held something approximating a free election, and signed along with a cross section of Cuban politicians a new democratic constitution. During the following four-year term, he admitted two communists—Blas Roca and Carlos Rafael Rodríguez—to his cabinet. At this stage, to be communist was not to be anti-American. "The Cuban people need and desire close and cordial relations with the United States because they will derive innumerable advantages from these," wrote the Marxist-Leninist Roca in 1943.[34]

Outside the Dominican Republic, the Caribbean trend was toward progressive politics. In Puerto Rico, Luis Muñoz Marín's Popular Democratic Party won the 1940 election, and promised—and delivered—reform. But in Haiti, the desire for liberation took its own, uniquely racialized form.

Barred from politics, most Haitians channeled their hope into a strong religious feeling. Vodou, passed down from African slaves and evolved into a unique Haitian form, was the majority religion. But it was repressed by law, propaganda, and occasional government anti-Vodou drives. Vodouists compensated by matching forbidden loas to permitted Catholic saints. So Damballa, the snake loa, became St. Patrick, who drove the snakes out of Ireland; Papa Legba, the guardian of crossroads and holder of the "key" to the spirit world, became St. Peter, with his crossed keys; Erzulie, the chaste loa of love and femininity, became the Virgin Mary. For Haitians, there was no contradiction in practicing Vodou alongside Catholicism, with a sincere belief in each.

During the 1930s, ideas of negritude—pride in a distinctly African identity—spread to Haiti. Along with this went a rehabilitation and celebration of Vodou. Jean Price-Mars, a distinguished Haitian intellectual staunchly opposed to the American occupation, published a treasure trove of Vodou fables, proverbs, and songs, *So Spoke the Uncle*, in 1928, boosting the religion's visibility and its reputation. A local version of negritude, known as noirisme, had already attracted Price-Mars's less distinguished follower, François Duvalier.

Duvalier had been born in 1907, only a few streets away from the National Palace. His father was a teacher. His mother worked in a bakery, and later went mad. He was raised by an aunt. He had been educated, but stood out neither academically nor socially. In person, he was introverted to the point of being a loner.

During his teens, Duvalier had started to associate with fellow ethnology enthusiasts Louis Diaquoi and Lorimer Denis. In 1932, they would name themselves Les Griots, after a West African word for a bard. Denis and Duvalier (Diaquoi died in 1932) developed the idea that culture and psychology were biologically defined characteristics. A person's character and behavior, so they argued, were results not of experience, but of race. Therefore, whatever the influence of European and North American cultures on Haiti had been, Haitians of "pure" black African descent were temperamentally and morally different from mulattoes or whites.[35]

Duvalier published pseudoscientific theories about race, and trained as a doctor. He did not involve himself with politics. "François was the only one of his generation who never knew the inside of a prison," remembered one of his friends.[36] At the very end of 1939, at the church of St.-Pierre in Pétionville, the diminutive black doctor married a tall mulatto nurse, Simone Ovide. None of the guests would have predicted that this unremarkable couple would ever amount to anything more than they already were.

In 1943, Duvalier joined an American-funded public health clinic at Gressier, near Port-au-Prince. He was selected to spend two semesters at the graduate school of public health at the University of Michigan, but failed the course on account of his poor English.[37] Returning to Haiti, he set up another clinic under an American banner in Cabaret, a village up the coast from Port-au-Prince. His three daughters, Marie-Denise, Simone, and Nicole, were born during the 1940s. A son, Jean-Claude, would follow in 1951.

When he returned from the United States, Duvalier renewed his acquaintance with Lorimer Denis, now assistant director of the government's Bureau of Ethnology, under Jean Price-Mars. Denis affected the air of a Vodou *houngan*, or priest, always carrying his *coco macaque* (a traditional cane) and wearing a hat, even indoors. Some found this style irresistibly amusing, but Duvalier was impressed. Denis introduced Duvalier to a rising black politician, Daniel Fignolé, and persuaded him to join their party, the Workers' and Peasants' Movement (MOP). "Duvalier was like the female egg that needs a male to make it produce," said one of their friends. "In this case Denis was the male."[38]

Despite the leftist ideals of the MOP, the union of Duvalier and Denis did not bring forth socialism. In 1948, the pair published *The Class Problem Throughout Haitian History*. The dominance of the mulattoes, they argued, was caused by a fundamental inequality of race, not of class. The struggle, therefore, was not a class struggle, but a race struggle. The men they saw as Haiti's greatest liberators, including Toussaint L'Ouverture and Jean-Jacques Dessalines, had been black. The time had come now for black Haitians to reassert themselves over the mulattoes—by force, if necessary. (Duvalier did not allow the fact that his own wife, and by extension his children, were mulatto to temper his rhetoric.)

By this time, Trujillo's old friend Elie Lescot was president of Haiti, but the two had fallen out. In 1943, the Benefactor gave some Haitian mercenaries $30,000 and some lend-lease weapons from the United States to kill Lescot. When this attempt failed, Trujillo tried a different tactic: he published all the private correspondence that had passed between him and Lescot since 1937. It showed that Lescot had embezzled large amounts of public money, taken Trujillo's bribes to cover it up, and for almost a decade acted as a Dominican puppet.[39] Lescot's career was over. In the ensuing election, a moderate black candidate, Dumarsais Estimé, won. François Duvalier was offered a post in the new government as director of public health. He accepted, and shortly afterward cut his ties with the MOP. Meanwhile, Trujillo busied himself trying to have Estimé poisoned, hoping for an excuse to invade Haiti.[40]

In March 1946, James Byrnes, the American secretary of state, wrote to President Harry S. Truman that Rafael Trujillo was "the most ruthless, unprincipled, and efficient dictator in this hemisphere." It was neither Lescot's fall, nor Trujillo's plans to invade Haiti, that had disgusted Byrnes, so much as the Benefactor's constant claims of being a friend to Washington: "His regime is completely unsavory and we should scrupulously avoid even the appearance of lending him any support."[41] But Washington did continue to support him, with diplomatic recognition and military cooperation. American investors continued to make fortunes in the Dominican Republic. For many Latin Americans, though, Trujillo had ridden roughshod for too long. It was time to take up arms.

★

During 1947, an invasion force swelled its ranks in Cuba, planning a strike directly at Trujillo. Calling itself the Caribbean Legion, the force was supported by the governments of Venezuela and Guatemala, and tolerated by that of Cuba.

A young Cuban activist, Carlos Franqui, was among the hundreds who signed up from all over Latin America. He was in distinguished company from across the political spectrum. The Legion was led by anti-Trujillo Dominicans, including a rising star of the exiled opposition, Juan Bosch. The Cuban president, Ramón Grau, supported it; the leader of the opposition, Carlos Prío, was involved; among the legionnaires was a senator, Rolando Masferrer, who had fought in the International Brigades during the Spanish Civil War, but was now in the process of moving from the left to the extreme right. Rómulo Betancourt, the future president of Venezuela, was also on board.

Nonetheless, when Franqui arrived at the recruitment post in Antilla, he was not impressed. It was all "gangsters drinking whiskey and conflicts, immorality, ambitions." Among his fellow recruits was a young student from the University of Havana, Fidel Castro. "I blame myself as the man who gave him his rudimentary training in military affairs," said Rolando Masferrer late in life, after spending many years trying to kill Fidel. "He was in charge of a platoon of men and behaved very discreetly."[42]

Fidel came from Mayarí, deep in the ruralities of Oriente province. His father, Angel Castro, was a Spaniard, who fought as a conscript in the 1898 war and afterward worked on the United Fruit Company's railways. By 1930, Angel had become a landowner, with thousands of acres of sugar plantation. He had married a schoolteacher and produced two children, Pedro Emilio and Lidia, but his more meaningful relationship was with the family cook, Lina Ruz. That couple would eventually have seven children, and were married after Angel's first wife died. Their sons were Ramón, Fidel, and Raúl.[43]

"We were considered rich and treated as such," Fidel admitted later. "I was brought up with all the privileges attendant to a son in such a family." He was a badly behaved child. When he was just five or six, his parents sent him away to school with his brothers in the provincial capital of Oriente, Santiago de Cuba. "It all seemed extraordinary to me: the station with its wooden arches, the hubbub, the people," he said later. "I wet the bed on the first night."[44]

Young Fidel could usually be found in the middle of a fight. Once he bit a priest, and became the school hero. The Castro brothers were split up. Ramón went into practical training, and Raúl was sent to military school. Fidel threatened to set fire to his parents' house if he were not permitted to continue academic study. Evidently, they believed him, for he was sent to the Dolores Jesuit school in Santiago. He was not yet ten years old. These pedagogic enterprises would make a deep impression. Ramón would grow up to be a farmer; Raúl would become a consummate military man; and Fidel, though he would become an atheist, would always retain a markedly Jesuitical streak.[45]

In his teens, Fidel's height shot up to six foot two, and his frame bulked out. He was named Cuba's best school athlete. On his matriculation at the University of Havana in 1945, this country boy immediately challenged the president of the student federation to a fight. It is not known who won. In Havana during the 1940s, student politics were violent. Beatings were common; murders not unknown. Subsequently, plenty of claims have surfaced that Fidel was involved in those murders, but scant evidence.[46]

Though full of bluster—he once rode a bicycle headfirst into a wall, to prove his machismo—Fidel became famous on campus not for his muscle, but for his unusual charisma when he spoke. Those who met him one-on-one, though, encountered a very different creature from the witty, confident young man on the platform. In private, Fidel was soft-spoken, shy, and unsure of himself. He had many acquaintances, but few close friends. Some who have known him say that only his brother Raúl and his longtime companion Celia Sánchez ever became real confidants.

In the spring of 1947, Eduardo "Eddy" Chibás and Roberto Agramonte founded the Cuban People's Party, generally known as the Ortodoxos. It was reformist and anticorruption, though decidedly bourgeois. Owing to the communists' cooperation with Batista, most members, including Chibás himself, were fiercely anticommunist.[47] Fidel joined the same year. He also became a member of the student Revolutionary Insurrectionist Union. Despite its name, it was actually the moderate choice: he rejected the left-wing Revolutionary Socialist Movement. Both groups joined the Caribbean Legion.

Cuba was then enjoying an interlude of democracy. The Ortodoxos believed firmly in democratic change. In 1947, any young Latin American looking for a revolution to get mixed up in turned to the Dominican Republic. And so Fidel, like many other idealists, enlisted, and traveled that September from Havana down through the miles of plantations that flanked Cuba's spine to Antilla. From there, they sailed to Cayo Confites, a tiny, flat sand strip with nothing on it but a clump of coconut palms, some long, tough grass, and a variegated collection of Latin American subversives attempting to train themselves to be guerrillas.

"I spent three months living outdoors on a sandy key waiting for the signal to leave," Fidel would later write. "I was on the spot, ready to go into the fight against Trujillo." But Trujillo's information network was well connected, and he realized what was happening. He made a plea to the

United States. The United States put pressure on Grau's administration. At the last minute, the Cuban navy turned up to stop the Legion's ships. Fifteen hundred members of the Legion were taken prisoner. Fidel lashed his machine gun and ammunition belt to his back, leaped over the ship's rail into the shark-infested waters of Nipe Bay, and swam several miles back to the mainland. He was the only legionnaire to escape.[48]

★

In the spring of 1948, Fidel was among four Cuban students sent to a congress of Latin American university associations in Bogotá, Colombia. There, on 7 April, Fidel met the popular progressive liberal leader Jorge Eliécer Gaitán. He was impressed, and they arranged another meeting for two days later. It was not to be. That morning, Gaitán was murdered. As the news spread, riots broke out across the city.

"People were wrecking streetlights; rocks flew in all directions," Fidel remembered. "Glass store fronts were shattering." And, where there was trouble, again there seemed to be Fidel at the center of it. He ambled into a police station to stock up on equipment, furnished himself with a tear gas gun, and moved on to the officers' quarters. Blithely, he sat down on a bed and pulled on a pair of army boots, ignoring the officer next to him screaming, "Not my boots! Not my boots!" In his boots, Fidel stomped down to the courtyard and shoved his way to the front of a queue that had formed for guns.

The rioting continued for three days, and became known as the Bogotazo. Fidel spent a couple of those days rampaging around Bogotá, though according to his own recollection he fired only four of the sixteen bullets that came with his gun. Later rumors that he went on a killing spree are unsupported by evidence. A thorough investigation at the time by London's Scotland Yard—the agency requested by the Colombians—found no evidence that the Cubans had committed any crime during the Bogotazo, except for looting arms and stockpiling them in their hotel rooms. Further rumors, later given undue prominence, that the Bogotazo was started by communists were scotched by American diplomats. The small Colombian communist party joined in the rioting, as did virtually every other political group in Colombia, but the dynamic of the conflict was Liberal versus Conservative. Eventually, Fidel and his colleagues found their way into the Cuban embassy, and were evacuated to Havana.[49]

On 12 October 1948, Fidel married Mirta Díaz Balart, a fellow student. It was a love match, and neither family approved. Mirta's father was a government official, close to Batista. Her brother Rafael had been leader of

Batista's youth faction. Fidel and Mirta honeymooned in New York City, thanks to Batista himself, who gave them $1,000 as a wedding present.[50] During the honeymoon, Fidel supposedly bought the copy of *Das Kapital* he would later read on the Isle of Pines, though his reading tastes at the time were politically and culturally eclectic. The following year, the couple had a son, Fidel, known as Fidelito.

Legend has it that the senior Fidel's pitching for the University of Havana baseball team attracted attention from American scouts, including those of the Pittsburgh Pirates and the New York Giants. In 1949, the Giants allegedly offered Fidel Castro a contract, complete with a signing bonus of $5,000. History might have taken a very different turn had he accepted, but he did not. "We couldn't believe he turned us down," said a negotiator for the Giants. "Nobody from Latin America had ever said 'no' before."[51]

★

In Haiti, Estimé's government had fallen, and the public health minister François Duvalier fell with it. The new regime was headed by Major Paul Magloire, a relatively personable pro-American military dictator. Duvalier offered the first hint of a harder side to his mild-mannered character when privately he pledged to Estimé that he would "take care of Magloire and his clique."[52] Estimé did not ask him to follow the threat through. Subdued again, Duvalier returned to private life, and to his work with the American health mission.

Another casualty of Estimé's fall was Clément Barbot, a handsome young official who had lost a minor position at the Ministry of Agriculture. Duvalier found him a job with the mission, and the two struck up a friendship. Duvalier coached Barbot, who had had only four or five years of schooling, to improve his reading. He also taught him some English.[53]

Haiti was enjoying something of a renaissance. Development funds poured into the country, largely from the United States. Cosmetic improvements were made, and celebrities followed: Noël Coward, Truman Capote, Irving Berlin. In their wake, tourists flocked to Port-au-Prince to admire the pink blaze of the bougainvillea, the rickety gingerbread houses, the cockfights and domino tournaments in the streets, and the Vodou ceremonies specially arranged for their entertainment. The rum was cheap, and the brothels were even cheaper. In the background, though, there were political arrests without trial, restrictions on press freedom, closures of schools considered "subversive," and abrogations of constitutional rights.[54]

Meanwhile, the United States engaged in the Korean War. The sense that there was a global enemy, communism, and that it was the duty of the

United States to fight it, was made a reality. In 1947, President Harry S. Truman had declared the Truman Doctrine, arguing that it must be "the policy of the United States to support free peoples who are resisting attempted subjugation by armed minorities or by outside pressures."[55] Though the original speech was carefully phrased, it was clear that by "outside pressures" Truman referred to the Soviet Union. In the United States, a unique horror of communism took hold and stuck. Partly, this was for good reasons: Stalinism trampled upon many of the values Americans held most sacred, including life, liberty, and the pursuit of happiness. But the prospect of a new global enemy also created opportunities for vested interests, including the military, the industries around the military, and the intelligence services. During World War II, these interests had wielded great power. After the war, they would be reluctant to let it go.

In the same year, the CIA warned that "Communist undercover penetration" of Latin America, directed by Moscow, was at an advanced stage. At the behest of the United States, most Latin American countries signed the Pact of Rio de Janeiro. This made the Monroe Doctrine multilateral: an attack against any one state from outside the hemisphere was considered an attack against all states within the hemisphere, and they would come together to fight it.[56]

"Soviet policy in South America subjects the Monroe Doctrine to its severest test," said John Foster Dulles that year. "There is a highly organized effort to extend to the South American countries the Soviet system of proletariat dictatorship." The idea that Soviet masses were marching on Latin America would become an unquestioned and enduring fundamental of American foreign policy. In 1947, though, fears of the Soviet Union extending its red tentacles over Latin America were a fantasy. Lenin had believed that it was possible for the third world to skip the capitalist stage of development and become communist, but Stalin, then in complete control of the USSR, doubted it. He neglected Comintern, the agency set up under Lenin to preach communism to the third world, and finally disbanded it in 1943. During its existence, it achieved no notable results. Stalin's lack of interest was particularly pronounced when it came to the western hemisphere. "Latin America is a collection of U.S. satellites," he had sneered dismissively in 1946. In 1951, he would add that it constituted "the obedient army of the United States."[57]

Likewise, Soviet-style communism held little appeal for Latin Americans. Though they were by no means homogeneous, there were certain common factors in many Latin nations that predisposed them against communism.

Latin Americans, especially poor Latin Americans, tended to be very religious; communism entailed a rejection of religion. Most Latin American societies had low levels of industrialization; Marxism and Stalinism depended on the existence of a large industrial proletarian class. Converting the military to communism was a crucial factor in that ideology's success in the USSR and China; but in much of Latin America, the military was already in a position of privilege. Communism did hold some appeal for a small contingent of bourgeois intellectuals; but the cultural, racial, and sometimes linguistic gap between those intellectuals and the masses in Latin America was even wider than it was in much of the rest of the world.

But there existed in most Latin nations, especially those in the Caribbean and Central America, a historical antipathy toward the United States. Its privilege was visible, and contrasted starkly with widespread poverty in Latin America. Its frequent political, military, cultural, and economic interventions had not always been welcome. When the American government began to clamor about communism as its ultimate enemy, that ideology did acquire some countercultural cachet.

Dictators like Rafael Trujillo in the Dominican Republic—along with Anastasio Somoza in Nicaragua, Carlos Castillo Armas in Guatemala, Marcos Pérez Jiménez in Venezuela, and others—realized that the United States' fear of communism could be exploited. Posing as strong men ordering back the red tide gave them legitimacy and purpose. The more communists they could drum up, and the more credible they could make them, the more financial and military support they could shake out of Washington's pockets.

If communists did not exist, the dictators were happy to invent them. In 1944, Trujillo created a Popular Socialist Party (PSP), and shipped in exiles to manage it. The PSP obediently declared itself Marxist-Leninist-Stalinist, and ran against him in the 1947 election. This allowed Trujillo to argue that the only significant opposition to his administration came from communists. After the election, the PSP was accused of terrorism, and its members were thrown in jail. Trujillo appeared to deal decisively with this pantomime "threat" by outlawing all communist or anarchist groups. From then on, Trujillo ensured that rebellions against his regime were always defined as communist.[58]

Meanwhile, the influential diplomat George Kennan toured Latin America and decreed that the fight against communism should be the priority in the region. The United States, he said, should not object to "police repression by the local government," were such action aimed at rebuffing the

Soviets.[59] Kennan's arguments made a deep impression in Washington. The Good Neighbor policy had come to an end.

★

In August 1951, Eddy Chibás, the leader of Cuba's Ortodoxos, was presenting his popular radio show one Sunday as usual. Following a lengthy oration about a corruption scandal, he finished on the words: "This is my last wake-up call!" Listeners heard two loud bangs. Chibás had shot himself twice in the gut. His bizarre suicide was claimed as a political act. At his funeral, Fidel Castro stood among the guard of honor.[60]

The democratic governments of Ramón Grau and Carlos Prío had disappointed many Cubans. Both were characterized by gangsterism and corruption. On 10 March 1952, Fulgencio Batista entered the military headquarters, Camp Columbia, with a pistol in his hand, just three months before elections were due to be held. Seventy-seven minutes later, he was in charge. Batista called his new regime "disciplined democracy," and canceled the elections.[61] The ousted president, Prío, fled to Mexico.

Fidel Castro, then a partner in a Havana law firm, had been a congressional candidate for the Ortodoxo party. Like many, he was outraged by Batista's coup. He attempted to file legal pleas against it, accusing Batista of sedition, among other offenses. He had little hope of success, but meant to prove a point. "If I had failed to follow the course of the law," he said later, "how could I have been justified in doing what I had to do? How would I have been better than the dictator?"[62]

Six days later, the Ortodoxos met at the tomb of Eddy Chibás in the grand necropolis of Havana's Colón Cemetery. Fidel leaped atop the stone and cried: "Eduardo Chibás, we have come to tell you that we will prove worthy of your sacrifice and we will never halt in the struggle to set the nation free."[63] But nothing happened. No one rose up.

In Havana, the American ambassador reminded the Cuban minister of state, Miguel Angel de la Campa, of Batista's past links with communists, and implied that these were preventing the United States from recognizing his government. "I asked whether we might expect these close relations would continue," wrote the ambassador. "Dr. Campa said that the Provisional Government and he himself would do what could be done under the law to eliminate the freedom and privileges which the Communists were now enjoying in Cuba." Batista severed diplomatic relations with the USSR, and the United States granted him recognition.[64]

★

In 1953, Dwight D. "Ike" Eisenhower was inaugurated as president of the United States. Senator Joseph McCarthy's domestic crusade against communism was still charging forward. In private, Eisenhower deplored the "hysterical folly" of McCarthy's efforts. In public, he felt obliged to restate his detestation of communism frequently.[65]

Ike had wanted John McCloy as his secretary of state but, owing to internal party politics, ended up with John Foster Dulles. He also made Foster's brother, Allen, director of the CIA. The Dulles brothers were both lawyers by training. Foster, a devout Christian, saw the world in terms of good and evil. The battle between good and evil that most exercised him was the one between the "free world" and communism. Blunt and awkward, he had a long roster of compulsive habits, which alarmed some of his colleagues: these included twirling a pencil in his ears or nostrils while thinking, stirring whiskey with his finger, and a mysterious urge to chew candle wax.

Allen, too, deplored communism, but his perception of the world accommodated shades of gray. While Foster assumed the style of an apocalyptic preacher, Allen was regularly described as a "gentleman spy": affable, smooth, and loyal. Women, especially, found him easier to get on with, and he enjoyed their company to the fullest. When McCarthy's reign of fire whipped through the State Department and the CIA, Allen protected his people. Foster did not.[66]

Though Ike was more inclined to Allen's line on communism than to Foster's, he did believe that the Soviets were building a power base in the third world, and that the security and way of life of the United States depended on containing and defeating that threat.[67] Nowhere in the world was that task more pressing than in Latin America. Whether or not Latin America was widely communist, it was certainly volatile. While two brothers took over the fight against communism in Washington, two very different brothers, in Cuba, were about to begin their revolution.

3

QUACKING LIKE A DUCK

★

ON 25 JULY 1953, HARVEY WELLMAN OF THE UNITED STATES STATE Department invited Aurelio Concheso, the Cuban ambassador, to meet him in Washington. The Americans wanted an anticommunist law in Cuba, to match the one already instigated by Trujillo in the Dominican Republic. Concheso agreed to look into the matter, though he warned it would be difficult to go to the lengths the United States desired, such as having teachers dismissed on grounds of their political opinions. "He said that some might criticize such action as another example of the 'Batista tyranny,'" reported Wellman.[1] Neither Wellman nor Concheso was aware that the very next day would be the foundation date of what would become the most significant communist revolution in the western hemisphere. Then again, Fidel Castro did not know that, either—and he was leading it.

From Havana, Fidel had assembled a national network of revolutionary Ortodoxos. An estimated 150 cells had been created by the middle of 1953, with some twelve hundred members. Eventually, this organization would come to be known as the 26 July Movement, after the date of its first attack. Fidel insisted on strict moral discipline. Members did not drink, and his second-in-command, Abel Santamaría, advised the movement's female members to guard their reputations against sexual impropriety.[2]

Fidel had grown close to Abel while his brother, Raúl, had gone to Vienna that February to attend the World Youth Congress. On the trip, Raúl met delegates from eastern Europe, and took up their invitation to venture behind the Iron Curtain. He traveled to Bucharest and Prague. According to intelligence reports held by the State Department in Washington, Raúl had traveled "not as a delegate but as an anti-Communist private citizen, at his own expense, and while there made a speech critical of communism."[3] The most important aspect of his visit—though one recognized by no one at the time—was the friendship he struck up during the journey back with Nikolai Sergeyevich Leonov, a young KGB recruit on his way from Prague to Mexico. When their ship docked at Havana, Leonov made Raúl give him the negatives of all the photographs taken of him during the crossing. He did not, at that stage, trust the Cuban to end up on the Soviets' side.[4]

On his disembarkation, Raúl was arrested. The police confiscated his diary. The local chief took it to Melba Hernández, a member of Fidel's movement, to try to convince her that Raúl was a crackpot. "How can you believe all that?" he asked. "Look at the way this diary describes the Socialist world! As a heaven on earth! I've never come across a heaven here."[5]

Raúl's diary does not necessarily contradict the State Department's intelligence and Leonov's caution. Several months would elapse before he joined Socialist Youth, the Cuban junior communist party, in June. He may simply not have made up his mind when he returned to Cuba. Fidel stayed loyal to the Ortodoxos. He spent the summer in the tiny apartment at the corner of Calle 25 and Calle O in the center of Havana occupied by Abel and his sister, Haydée, planning an attack on Batista's regime.

This put Raúl on the horns of a dilemma. Socialist Youth was not allied to the Ortodoxos, and to join Fidel and Abel would be a conflict of interest. But his loyalty to Fidel would prove more powerful than his newfound communism. On 24 July, Raúl broke his allegiance to Socialist Youth and followed his brother south to Santiago de Cuba. "It was wrong," he admitted later, "but I had only belonged to the Party for a month and a half and did not have a very keen feeling of belonging."[6]

Fidel had told his network to meet in a farmhouse in Siboney, rented by one among them on the pretext that he meant to start a chicken farm. The movement was, by communist standards, bourgeois. Most of the men who met at Siboney were young, white, middle-class, and highly educated; Haydée and Melba, the two women in the group, also fitted this description. One notable exception was Juan Almeida, a mulatto bricklayer.

Before dawn on 26 July, Fidel told them of his real plan. He meant to stage a full assault on the Moncada Barracks in the center of Santiago, to coincide with a simultaneous attack by a smaller group on a garrison at Bayamo. Once these had been taken, a manifesto would be read out over the radio, followed by a recording of Eddy Chibás's final broadcast, Beethoven's *Eroica*, and Chopin's Polonaise in A flat.[7] This, it was thought, would persuade the Cuban people to rise up. The steps in between taking Moncada and full-blown national revolution were vague, but those present seem to have agreed that the point was to land a blow, not to fell the dictator. It was a suicide mission. "Not everybody will have a death like this," Haydée's fiancé, Boris Luis Santa Coloma, remarked with pride.[8]

"You adhered voluntarily to The Movement," Fidel told them. "And today you must take part voluntarily in the attack. If anyone is not in agreement, now is the time to withdraw."[9] Of the 150 or so present, nine or ten opted out. The rest put on army uniforms over their clothes.

Fidel and Abel had a squabble over deployment, each arguing that the other's life was more valuable to the movement and, therefore, that he should be given the safer role, leading the group that would set up the field hospital. Fidel won—putting himself in the frontal assault on the barracks. Just before five, a convoy of cars left Siboney for the short drive to Santiago.

★

The Moncada Barracks was a custard-yellow compound just outside the colonial center of Santiago. It occupied a square, with the civil hospital opposite on one side, and the Palace of Justice, then the tallest building in town, on another. Fidel's plan was for the main convoy to head straight to the front gate, opposite the Palace of Justice. The men in the first car would disarm the sentry, allowing the main column—led by Fidel in the second car—to swarm in behind them. Meanwhile, Raúl's group, led by Léster Rodríguez, would set up a machine gun on the roof of the Palace of Justice, to provide cover, and Abel would lead a group of soldiers and medics, including Haydée and Melba, to take over the hospital.

At 5:17 AM, the first car, containing Renato Guitart, Jesús Montané, and Ramiro Valdés, drew up at the front gate. The three leaped out. "Attention! The general is coming!" barked Valdés, unhooking the chain across the entrance. For an instant, the sentries were fooled. It was a long enough instant for the attackers to snatch their guns. As the sergeant of the guard reached for his alarm bell, the first shot was fired. It hit him, though he slumped against the bell anyway and rang it. Guitart ran into the barracks in search of the radio station, from which he was to broadcast the manifesto.

Montané and Valdés gave the signal for the rest of the column to move in. Just as the cars began to accelerate, an army patrol jeep turned unexpectedly into the street. Unlike the sleeping soldiers in the barracks, the men in the jeep were ready and alert. The lieutenant leaped out and raised his pistol at Fidel's car.

Fidel, at the wheel, shouted, "Take care of the lieutenant!" Gustavo

Arcos, in the backseat, leaned out of the car with his rifle. As he did so, Fidel stamped on the accelerator. He hit the curb; the car jumped, and the rear door slammed hard into Arcos, knocking him back. The lieutenant fired, and hit him. Arcos tried to crawl back into the car, but the soldiers in the jeep had readied the machine gun mounted upon it. A volley of bullets tore through Fidel's car and into Arcos.

Meanwhile, Raúl and the sniper group had entered the Palace of Justice. Its half-asleep sergeant answered the door to them unawares, still doing up his trousers. At gunpoint, they forced him back into the lobby. Then, the first shots were heard from Moncada.

"What's happening?" asked the sergeant.

"Batista has fallen," snapped Raúl. Slight, blond, and baby-faced, he looked younger than his twenty-two years. But he was, according to those who knew him, even tougher than his brother. He shot the lock off the stairs to the roof, and they all trooped up to survey the scene.

The picture below was one of chaos. Guitart lay dead at the door of the radio station. Arcos was being carried into a car—he was alive, though filled with bullets. Montané and Valdés had control of the sleeping quarters, complete with fifty-five prisoners, but the rest of the garrison's men were now in the fight. Rebels were dotted around the scene, behind cars and walls, taking potshots at soldiers. Fidel was crouched by the army jeep, waving frantically to signal the men through the main gate. In a daring maneuver, a group of them ran straight across the open parade ground and up the steps on the outside of the barracks to what they had identified as the armory. When they got inside, it turned out to be the barbershop.

From the roof of the Palace of Justice, the rebel snipers were able to shoot the occasional soldier. But their main target—the sandbagged machine gun on the roof of the officers' mess—was out of sight. They descended to the top floor and tried to fire out of the windows, but still could not hit the main gun.

Better armed and better trained, Batista's forces soon regained the upper hand. The rebels realized that they were losing. Fidel sent messengers to the hospital and the Palace of Justice, but they were captured. The snipers could see what was going on, and decided to make a run for it. As they reached the lobby, a police van screeched to a halt outside. Its five occupants jumped out and hammered on the door.

Raúl flung the door open, snatched the sergeant's pistol, and turned it on him. Taken by surprise, the policemen were easily arrested. Raúl ordered them into a small office and barricaded them in.

The shooting outside had stopped, and for some time the snipers debated what they should do next. Finally, one simply put down his rifle, took off the uniform he wore over his civilian clothes, and walked out. Raúl followed, but headed in a different direction, toward the railroad tracks. The others dispersed into the city.[10]

Abel's group had set up a base in the civil hospital. But they, too, could see that the battle was over. Abel took the two women aside. "We are lost," he admitted. "You and I know what is going to happen to me and, possibly, to all of us." To comfort Haydée, he added, "Don't you realize that Fidel will live, that Fidel really must not die, that Fidel will stay alive and he is now retreating into the hills?"[11] Soldiers stormed in. The rebels were arrested, and, moments later, the women could see Abel being dragged out into the yard. The soldiers were beating him with the butts of their guns.

The survivors of all three groups had scattered, and around sixty managed to escape. Eight were dead, and eight wounded. The rest were taken to the military prison. There, they were beaten and abused while their guards attempted to extract information about the extent of the conspiracy.[12] The journalist Robert Taber later interviewed the rebel Jesús Montané, formerly an accountant, and asked how he had felt when he was in the cell, his torturer preparing to castrate him. "For us, to die for *la patria* is a satisfaction," Montané explained. Then, as an afterthought, he added, "Luckily, an officer intervened at that moment."[13] Taber was unable to comprehend how a man could be so indifferent to his own castration, let alone death. But within Cuban culture, Montané's willingness to sacrifice his body or even his life for his political cause was part of a long tradition. José Martí had done it. Eddy Chibás had done it. Fidel would eventually coin the slogan *Patria o muerte*—homeland or death—and mean it literally.

Haydée and Melba were locked in a cell, and overheard a guard saying, "That one with the two-tone shoes, he's for it!" The man with the two-tone shoes was Haydée's fiancé, Boris Luis Santa Coloma. He had escaped the attack on the barracks but, when he heard Haydée was trapped at the hospital, returned to save her. Instead, he had been captured. While Haydée and Melba sat powerless, he was tortured within their earshot. Finally, he achieved that rare and glorious death he had anticipated that morning.

The two women were transferred to the basement of the prison. Haydée whispered to Melba, "If Abel isn't here, that means they've killed him." Together, they walked through the dark, hands clutching each other, peering desperately into each cell as they were marched past. When they reached the last one, and Abel was not in it, Melba felt Haydée's hand go limp.[14]

"I do not remember anything else clearly," said Haydée, "but from that moment on, I thought of nobody but Fidel. . . . So long as Fidel was alive, Abel, Boris, Renato and the others were not dead. They would live in the person of Fidel who would make the Cuban Revolution and would lead the people of Cuba to their destiny.

"The rest was a haze of blood and smoke: the rest belonged to death."[15]

★

On the hot, dusty railroad tracks outside Santiago, Raúl Castro was trudging north. He walked all day, and that night slept in a field of sugarcane. The next morning, he arrived at Dos Caminos de San Luis, went to buy bread, and was arrested. He explained to the officers that he had gone to Santiago for the carnival, but had run out of money and was obliged to walk home. It took the police thirty-six hours to establish his real identity.[16]

Fidel, meanwhile, fled with the rump of his rebels back to the chicken farm at Siboney. He announced that he was heading into the Sierra Maestra, the mountains to the west. Those who wanted to come with him were welcome. Eighteen did. They went up into the Cordillera de la Gran Piedra, pursued by soldiers.

Most of the outlaws were quickly captured. Soon, only three remained free, Fidel among them. On the first day of August, he was sleeping with the other two in a palm-thatched hut outside a farm. Soldiers crept into the hut, and bound their hands before they woke. Several wanted to shoot Fidel then and be done with it, but the commander of their platoon refused to let them. He ordered the three captives to be taken to the civilian jail in Santiago, not the military jail. This intervention almost certainly saved Fidel's life.

Of the hundred or so prisoners taken from among the Moncada attackers, fifty-nine were murdered after their arrests. To that total may be added several of the men who simultaneously attacked the garrison at Bayamo. Two were found hanging by the side of a road, and three at the bottom of a well.[17]

Back in Washington, Aurelio Concheso, the Cuban ambassador, seemed unconcerned. He told the State Department that the attack on Moncada Barracks had strengthened Batista's administration, for "it had shown that the armed forces are solidly behind the Government, which would handle promptly and efficiently any attempted revolution."[18] Neither Concheso nor the State Department made any connection between this revolutionary act and communism, for the good reason that there was none.

The Moncada attack came in for much criticism from across the wide spectrum of Batista's opposition. This included a stinging comment from the Popular Socialist Party (PSP), Cuba's communist party. "We repudiate the putschist methods of the action in Santiago de Cuba and Bayamo, which are characteristic of bourgeois political factions," it said in an official statement. "The heroism shown by the participants in these attacks is false and sterile, for it is guided by mistaken bourgeois conceptions." Batista later attempted to blame the attack on communists. This made the PSP hate Fidel even more.[19]

In the wake of Moncada, hundreds were arrested. The trials started at the end of September. After two days of Fidel taking the stand, which he used to detail at length the tortures meted out to his coconspirators, it was announced that he had fallen ill and would no longer be appearing. Melba Hernández concealed a note from Fidel in her hair, and dramatically unfurled it in front of the court. In it, Fidel confirmed that the army was preventing him from appearing. The judges ordered that he be safeguarded, and again his life was saved.

Herbert Matthews of the *New York Times* later remarked to Juan Almeida that Fidel's ability to survive situations of extreme danger must indicate great good luck.

"No! no!" replied Juan, "no suerte, testículos!" (Not luck, balls!)[20]

In mid-October, after the mass trials had been concluded, Fidel was tried alone in a heavily guarded makeshift courtroom. He defended himself. Instead of refuting the charges, he put forward a critique of Batista's regime. Later, he would reconstruct this from memory, and publish it. Though Fidel polished his words for publication, the substance seems to reflect what was said. "I do not fear prison, as I do not fear the fury of the miserable tyrant who took the lives of seventy of my colleagues," he concluded. "Condemn me. It does not matter. History will absolve me."[21] He was sentenced to fifteen years' imprisonment on the Isle of Pines.

★

At the end of 1953, Dwight D. Eisenhower wrote to a senator privately that he believed "the work of the Soviet Communist Fifth Column does indeed constitute an international conspiracy." His government, he said, was "determined to use every appropriate means to counteract it." Equipped with an understanding of the armed forces that would be matched by no subsequent president, Ike resisted military and civilian pressure to commit too much to what he would call the "military-industrial complex," lest it come to be more powerful than the government.[22] But a careful balance had to be maintained. This concept of a global conspiracy called "international communism" was of vital importance, for it legitimized the United States' fight against communism; and the United States' fight against communism was a major plank of its government's legitimacy with its own electorate.

The Soviet Union had shown no significant interest in Latin America for a decade. According to the limited sources available, the KGB made no payments at all to communist parties in Latin America between 1943 and 1955.[23] Yet if the United States wanted to use the 1947 Pact of Rio de Janeiro to fight communism, it had to demonstrate that the communism in question had originated and was being managed outside the western hemisphere. There was no legal basis for opposing Latin American communism if Latin Americans had come up with it of their own accord. And so the view came to be taken that, as the Republican senator Alexander Wiley told Congress in 1954, "there is no Communism but the Communism which takes orders from the despots of the Kremlin in Moscow. It is an absolute myth to believe that there is such a thing as homegrown Communism, a so-called native or local communism."[24]

Not only was it difficult to prove that communism was being imported from outside the hemisphere, it was difficult to prove that it existed within the hemisphere except as a tiny minority. Few leading Latin American politicians described themselves as communists. "Many times it is impossible to prove legally that a certain individual is a communist," admitted the diplomat Richard Patterson in 1950, "but for cases of this sort I recommend a practical method of detection—the 'duck test.' The duck test works this way: suppose you see a bird walking around in a farm yard. This bird wears no label that says 'duck.' But the bird certainly looks like a duck. Also, he goes to the pond and you notice that he swims like a duck. Then he opens his beak and quacks like a duck. Well, by this time you have probably reached the conclusion that the bird is a duck, whether he's wearing a label or not."[25] By the logic of the duck test, a regime that looked dubious to the Americans could be considered communist, even if it did not consider itself communist and had no links to the USSR or China. But while the State Department may have had no problem identifying ducks, its ability to identify communists was unproven. The question of what a communist actually was seems hardly ever to have been raised. In the era of McCarthy, it was patriotic to presume that communists were anti-American, antifreedom, and bent on massive clandestine infiltration of the western hemisphere.

Rafael Trujillo, meanwhile, was an expert at identifying communists. He identified scores of them each year. Asked whether every single one of his opponents could really be a communist, he confirmed: "Yes, they are all Communists. No patriotic Dominican who loves his place of birth would try to overthrow its stable, beneficial government except Communists."[26]

The deafening chorus of quacking from Ciudad Trujillo soon reached the ears of John Foster Dulles, who in early 1953 signed a bilateral military assistance agreement with Trujillo. The Benefactor came to the United States at the beginning of 1953, and met President Truman. He returned two months later, and met President Eisenhower. Repeatedly, he proposed a pan-American fight against communism. The State Department had heard rumors that Trujillo planned to expropriate American businesses in the Dominican Republic, and proceeded with caution; yet still it proceeded, and Trujillo received arms, fighter jets, and a military assistance team.[27]

★

Though Trujillo staged his own duck hunt in the Dominican Republic, it was in Guatemala that the United States would first try its hand at the sport. Jacobo Arbenz Guzmán had been elected president of Guatemala in 1951. Over 90 percent of that country's farmable land was under the control of large landowners or foreign corporations. Arbenz proposed reform. Each landowner would be permitted a certain acreage. Over that, unused land would be expropriated by the Guatemalan government, and redistributed to the landless peasants who made up over half the population. Between 1952 and 1954, Arbenz redistributed 1.5 million acres to 100,000 poor families. Compensation was offered to the previous landowners. The United Fruit Company had been the largest landowner in Guatemala, and lost 400,000 acres. Arbenz offered it $1.2 million. It demanded $30 million. Both Allen and Foster Dulles had had decades-long associations with United Fruit, as advocates and advisers.[28] Much has been made of these links subsequently, perhaps too much. From its headquarters in Foggy Bottom, a few blocks from the White House, the CIA had begun to draw up contingency plans for the overthrow of the Guatemalan government in 1951, the year before Arbenz's program of agrarian reform began.

The right wing in Guatemala, like Rafael Trujillo in the Dominican Republic, had learned how to exploit American fears of communism. During the 1930s, under Jorge Ubico, anyone who spoke out against the interests of the landed elite in Guatemala was in danger of being labeled a communist. At one point, Ubico even described Roosevelt's New Deal as "communistic activities."[29] In fact, Arbenz's land redistribution was not communist by Moscow's definition, nor Marx's. A communist would have nationalized the land. Arbenz did not. He transferred it from large and often foreign private landowners to small domestic private landowners.

This was democratization of stakeholding, a centrist policy that would a decade later be supported by the State Department in other parts of Latin America.[30]

Among the many political parties with which Arbenz cooperated was the communist Guatemalan Workers' Party (PGT). In a population of around 3 million, the PGT claimed just five thousand members. "Yes, Guatemala has a very small minority of communists," William Prescott Allen, a friend of Eisenhower's, told the president, "but not as many as San Francisco."[31] Undaunted, the CIA began to search for links between the PGT and their presumed masters in Moscow. The agency's exhaustive investigations established that the grand total of the party's financial dealings with the Soviet Union amounted to a bill for $22.95 for Marxist literature, which the Guatemalans had ordered from a Moscow supplier. But when the Guatemalan parliament observed a minute's silence upon Stalin's death in March 1953, there was a serious case of the jitters in Foggy Bottom.[32]

A new ambassador, John E. Peurifoy, was chosen. Echoing Teddy Roosevelt, he cabled back to Washington, "I have come to Guatemala to use the big stick." To the House of Representatives, he soon confirmed that Arbenz "talked like a Communist, and if he is not one, Mr. Chairman, he will do until one comes along."[33] Eisenhower authorized the destabilization of Arbenz, and Allen Dulles put the plans in motion. They were managed by the CIA agents Tracy Barnes and Jake Esterline, who would later work on the Bay of Pigs invasion, and by E. Howard Hunt, later involved in both the Bay of Pigs and the Watergate break-in.

The CIA attempted to bribe Arbenz, who declined. It planted articles in Chilean newspapers, alleging that his ministers were communists; then, it presented these to the American press as evidence of Latin American opinion. It planted a cache of "Soviet" weapons on the Nicaraguan coast. It sponsored the bombing of bridges, military bases, and private property. It sent out instruction manuals for terrorism, describing in detail and with diagrams how to make bombs. In Honduras, it trained an invasion force under Colonel Carlos Castillo Armas. With Castillo Armas, it drew up a death list of fifty-eight Guatemalan politicians and leaders who were thought to lean to the left.[34]

In March 1954, Foster Dulles attended an Organization of American States (OAS) conference in Caracas, and spoke out against "international communism." The Guatemalan foreign minister, Guillermo Toriello, took him on, at one point baldly asking, "What is international Communism?"

"It is disturbing that the foreign affairs of one of our American Republics are conducted by one so innocent that he has to ask that question," Dulles replied. But Toriello, as even Dulles himself admitted, won the point and the debate. The United States, said Toriello, was "cataloguing as 'Communism' every manifestation of nationalism or economic independence, and desire for social progress, and intellectual curiosity, and any interest in progressive or liberal reforms."[35]

With rumors of an imminent invasion swirling, Arbenz did inquire about help from the Soviet Union. Though it was supportive of his aims, it had no intention of getting involved. Instead, in a one-off deal, he ordered arms from Czechoslovakia. In May 1954, they turned up: so old that some apparently bore Nazi insignia. Many were useless. Nonetheless, Foster Dulles was outraged, and Jack Peurifoy declared that the United States was at war. Eisenhower ordered a naval blockade, which was indeed an act of war. This alarmed some of the United States' own allies. Britain and France both made noises about supporting Guatemala in its appeal to the United Nations. Ike made it clear that, were they to do so, he would support the appeals brought against them by Egypt, Cyprus, Indochina, and Algeria.[36]

Castillo Armas's invasion of Guatemala was defeated. But the Guatemalan army was disquieted by the United States' opposition to the democratic president, and its officers decided to act before another invasion could be mounted. On 27 June, Arbenz was ousted by the army. In early July, the American ambassador installed Castillo Armas as president. For Guatemala, there followed forty years of oppressive military rule.

★

The coup created a shock wave of anti-American feeling across Latin America. It made a particularly deep impression on an Argentine doctor, just turned twenty-six, who had arrived in Guatemala that January. During the upheaval, Ernesto Guevara was forced to seek refuge in the Argentine embassy.[37]

Guevara had grown up in a mildly dysfunctional middle-class family, who divided their time between the cosmopolitan center of Buenos Aires and the jungles of Misiones. From infancy, he was afflicted with asthma. Triggered by a complex set of allergies and sensitivities, the little boy would fall into paroxysms of wheezing. Unable to breathe, he would panic. Panicking, he would be still less able to breathe. Though treatment was available, and the family could afford it, attacks were severe, frequent, and unpredictable. All sorts of preventative rigors were tried. Bedclothes and carpets were changed. Pets were withdrawn. Various diets were imposed. Specks of dust were meticulously removed. Ernesto was kept indoors. None of this had much effect on the asthma, but it did produce a child who seized any opportunity to run wild, gorge himself, and roll around in the mud.[38]

His mother, Celia de la Serna, a woman of ardently rebellious character, was not at all sorry to see her son turn out this way. Intelligent though he was, Ernesto spent much of his youth getting into fights, skipping school, and from the age of fourteen or fifteen industriously bedding the family maid. His friends watched Ernesto's first sexual encounter through the bedroom keyhole. Every now and then, he paused in his exertions to take a reviving blast on his asthma inhaler. The spectacle reduced them to helpless laughter.[39] In the years to come, Guevara would have to interrupt battles, as well as lovemaking, to attend to his asthma. It never dampened his enthusiasm for either pursuit.

After school, he pursued medicine and began to develop an interest in politics. The works and life of Marx and Lenin appealed to him from an early age, as did Jawaharlal Nehru's *The Discovery of India*. He affected a slovenly style of dress, wearing grubby secondhand clothes and boasting that he almost never washed himself or them. Even this could not put off a growing band of female admirers. "The truth is, we were all a little in love with Ernesto," remembered one female friend.[40] Two years before he was due to finish medical school, he too fell in love. It went badly. He was persuaded by his friend Alberto Granado to run away for a while, touring Latin America on a motorcycle. Just as the young Nehru had discovered a real India by traveling the length and breadth of the vast subcontinent, so Guevara would discover a real Latin America: at once grand, seductive, and beautiful, and starving, underdeveloped, and oppressed.

Granado later remembered a day at Machu Picchu, the citadel of the Incas high in the Peruvian Andes, then a little-visited site. Granado basked on the "sacrificial" rock, while Ernesto made maté, the Argentine tea to which he was addicted. At length, Granado talked of the future: of how they might transform the lives of Latin America's poor masses, of winning elections so they could institute agrarian reform, literacy, education, revolution.

Ernesto grinned. "Make a revolution without firing shots?" he said. "Are you crazy?"[41]

He returned to finish medical school, qualified, and went on the road again. By 1953, he was in Bolivia, where he met an exiled Argentine lawyer, Ricardo Rojo. Rojo remembered Ernesto as a scruffy young man, though he displayed "monumental unconcern" about this fact and would unabashedly wander into the bar of the ritzy Sucre Palace Hotel in La Paz in his dirty trousers.[42]

"Things are happening to Guatemala, *viejo*," Rojo told him. "An important revolution is going on there; it's something you've got to see."

Ernesto was persuaded. Then he proposed a wager: he bet his companions that the underpants he was wearing, the only ones he had owned for the last two months, were so filthy that they would stand up by themselves. Disbelieving, Rojo accepted. "Guevara took off his trousers," he remembered. "Before our eyes was a piece of underwear that looked like a bricklayer's work pants, the fabric was so stiff and its color so incredible. He removed this also, and we had to give up. Guevara had won the bet. His shorts stood upright, and their owner promised that he would soon teach them to mark time."[43]

Guevara and a group of friends traveled to Guatemala by hitching a lift on a United Fruit Company steamship. On the way, he paused in Costa Rica, where several icons of the Latin American left were in exile, including Rómulo Betancourt of Venezuela and Juan Bosch of the Dominican Republic. Guevara met them. He approved of Bosch, "a literary man of clear ideas and of leftist tendency," but not of Betancourt. Guevara asked Betancourt whether he would support the United States or the USSR in a war. Betancourt replied with a clear declaration for *los yanquís*—the Yankees.[44]

Ernesto continued on to Guatemala. There, he met Hilda Gadea, a Peruvian, whose strict far-left politics attracted him. Together, they read Marxist literature, and she introduced him to the study of the Chinese revolution. In March 1954, Ernesto called on Hilda and found a birthday party in progress. She was dancing, which surprised him. "I didn't realize you were so frivolous," he sniped. Then he passed her a handwritten note. It was a poem, proposing marriage.

"It impressed me profoundly," remembered Hilda, "but I could hardly show great enthusiasm as he was telling me that he had had an affair with a nurse."

"I confessed about the fuck with the nurse," admitted Ernesto. "I gave her a new ultimatum, but the abundance of these meant that it didn't have much effect."[45]

Hilda declined to marry Ernesto, but she kept the poem. "Through it he told me that he did not desire beauty alone but more than that, a comrade."[46]

Ernesto, when washed and brushed for his official photograph, was as handsome as a movie star; he could—and did—have plenty of beautiful women. Hilda was plump and squat. Her grumpy expression in most photographs obscures whatever charms she may have had. Later, a Cuban friend would ask him bluntly why he had carried on with such an "ugly" woman. Ernesto gallantly defended her, before adding slightly less gallantly that even ugly people could be good in bed.[47] But he emphasized again to his friend that Hilda had been a great *compañera*—a comrade. Ernesto sought a revolutionary partner, with whom he could discuss his growing obsession with politics. His rocky affair with Hilda was not one of history's great love stories. For the moment, though, it was the closest he could get to fulfilling a deeper need.

Linking into the local political groups, Guevara befriended a group of Cuban exiles, veterans of the failed attack on the Moncada Barracks. From them, he first heard the name Fidel Castro. The Cubans were amused by Guevara's characteristically Argentine speech, peppered with the word *che*—meaning something like "mate" or "buddy." It is used casually to grab the attention of a familiar friend, but develops an edge of impertinence if said to a figure of authority. Guevara used it with everyone. The Cubans called him "el Che." It stuck.

Contrary to some subsequent mythmaking about his alleged militia activities in Guatemala, Che did not fight in the revolution.[48] Instead, he joined an emergency medical ward and wrote his first political article, "I Saw the Fall of Jacobo Arbenz." No copy survives, but according to Hilda it was an outline of how guerrilla warfare could be used to make revolution. The closing words, she remembered, were "The struggle begins now."[49] But for Che, threatened by Castillo Armas's bloody purges, this particular struggle ended with him shut away in the Argentine embassy, kicking his heels.

After the operation ended in Guatemala, the CIA agent David Atlee Phillips remembered filing the agency's documents when he came across a single piece of paper mentioning an Argentine doctor. "I guess we'd better have a file on him," he remarked, offhandedly.[50] A few years later, the file on Che Guevara would be one of the fattest in the CIA archives.

★

In August 1954, Trujillo dramatically withdrew from his status as a delegate to the United Nations, claiming to have been appalled by its leftist bias during his attendance over the winter of 1952–53. The United Nations, he declared, "is a center where, in all or in the majority of its offices, Communist ideology prevails."[51] It was astute of him to have noticed. During the winter of 1952–53, he had only been in a United Nations building for the duration of one afternoon, and attended no meetings.

In October, Trujillo returned to the United States, and made as many statements as possible to the press about his expertise in dealing with communist infiltration. He offered to consult with the government and to share his files. Paid advertisements appeared in the New York press lauding his status as the foremost anticommunist in the western hemisphere. He had a pamphlet printed and circulated throughout the hemisphere, including in the United States itself. It named a number of democratic leaders of Latin America, including Governor Luis Muñoz Marín of Puerto Rico and President Pepe Figueres of Costa Rica, as procommunists.[52]

In Haiti, President Paul Magloire took Trujillo's endeavors as inspiration. He had recently become suspicious of the political machinations of the former public health minister, François Duvalier. Magloire told the American health mission that employed him that Duvalier was using the job as a front for illicit political activities. Duvalier was fired and went into hiding, next door to his family's gingerbread house on the Ruelle Roy. In 1955, he moved across the street, to the house of a priest, Jean-Baptiste Georges. In order to keep the move clandestine, he dressed as a woman. It is hard to imagine that the drag version of Duvalier would have attracted less attention, but nonetheless the maneuver was carried out in full Cold War covert style. He was picked up in a car, driven all around Port-au-Prince to throw off any possible tail, then dropped in a back street to sneak into Georges's house. He lived there for six weeks and met Luckner Cambronne, the treasurer of the student center next door. He spent much of his time reading and writing. According to his close friend Clément Barbot, the book Duvalier most commonly reread was Niccolò Machiavelli's *The Prince*. So often did he leaf through his tattered copy that, eventually, it fell apart.[53] With Machiavelli as their inspiration, Duvalier, Barbot, and Cambronne plotted.

In January 1955, Magloire was invited to the United States for an official visit and stayed at the White House with President and Mrs. Eisenhower. In New York, he was given a ticker-tape parade. "Since the decree against Communism nineteen years ago no red infiltration has been noted," he assured the press. "Basically, the people of Haiti are immune to Communism because the goods are well distributed among everybody." Magloire himself had recently distributed $50,000 for some fancy gold uniforms for his palace guard, and spent five-figure sums entertaining the likes of Héctor Trujillo and Anastasio Somoza in Port-au-Prince. The average Haitian income was then around $25 a year.[54]

The State Department was under no illusions as to the democratic pretensions or human rights records of the likes of Rafael Trujillo and

Paul Magloire, nor of any other dictators it supported. By the beginning of 1955, these included Alfredo Stroessner in Paraguay, Fulgencio Batista in Cuba, Anastasio Somoza in Nicaragua, and Manuel Odría in Peru. Its sense of hemispheric security then depended on stability, not progress. John Foster Dulles made it clear to his State Department officials that they should "do nothing to offend the dictators; they are the only people we can depend on."[55]

To prove Dulles's point, the vice president, Richard Nixon, embarked on a Caribbean tour. He began in Cuba, where he embraced Batista, and compared him fulsomely to Abraham Lincoln. The atmosphere between the Americans and Batista's coterie, said Philip Bonsal, a member of Nixon's party, was one of "intimate cordiality." In the Dominican Republic, Nixon praised "this great country and its illustrious ruler." He embraced Trujillo, and presented him with a signed photograph of President and Mrs. Eisenhower. In Haiti, Nixon took a break from dictators to meet a peasant woman walking by with a donkey. "Tell this *cocoyé* [coconut] to let me go on my way," she said, in stout Creole. "She says she is happy to meet the Vice President of the United States," stammered the interpreter, in English. "What is the donkey called?" Nixon asked. This was lost in translation, both linguistic and cultural. "He is crazy," replied the woman. "It is called a donkey." She unleashed a stream of invective. Defeated, the interpreter moved the official group on.[56]

★

Fidel whiled away the months in the isolation unit of the Presidio Modelo, in the middle of a grassy plain on the Isle of Pines, waging his own small war against ants, flies, and mosquitoes. Raúl was forced to share a cell with him, and had no peace. "I have heard enough of Fidel for a lifetime," he said afterward.[57] The twenty-seven men in the unit set up a school, which Fidel named the Abel Santamaría Ideological Academy. He taught political economy and public speaking. He tried to learn English. He read *Vanity Fair*, *Les Misérables*, and the Dean of Canterbury's *The Secret of Soviet Strength*. He tried Marx and Lenin, too. "Marx and Lenin each had a weighty polemical spirit, and I have to laugh," he wrote. "It is fun, and I have a good time reading them. They would not give an inch, and they were dreaded by their enemies: two genuine prototypes of the revolutionary."

His brother Ramón, and a centrist political ally, José Miró Cardona, sent him cigars. Others sent him food, and he cooked spaghetti with squid, cheese omelets, ham with guava jelly. "I am always arguing with them not to send me things, but they don't listen," he said. "When I sit outside in my shorts in the morning and feel the sun and the sea breeze, I think I am on a beach and later, here, in a small restaurant. They will make me think I am on vacation! What would Karl Marx say about such revolutionaries?"[58]

Thanks to a mischievous prison censor, one of Fidel's letters to his wife, Mirta, was switched with one of the letters he had meant for Naty Revuelta, his glamorous mistress. "I love you and I am always thinking of you," read one such missive to Naty. "I would gladly offer my life for your honor and well-being."[59] Mirta was deeply hurt. The letters to her were less passionate. She took a job at the Ministry of the Interior. Fidel refused to believe she would work for Batista, and threatened to launch a libel suit against the newspaper that printed the story. But it was true, and it ended their marriage.[60]

On principle, he refused to ask for an amnesty. Nevertheless, in May 1955, he received one. As part of an attempt to sanitize himself, Batista released a bevy of political prisoners. Fidel had sworn to accept no clemency, but in the end was kicked out of prison.[61] Haydée and Melba met him as he walked down the grand steps outside the Presidio Modelo's neoclassical front. On the ferry back to the mainland, Fidel officially named his group the 26 July Movement (shortened to M-26-7). In Havana, he was met by the national committee of the Ortodoxo Party, along with almost every politically inclined student at the university.

Fidel was offered positions in the party, but he declined. "All doors to a peaceful political struggle have been closed to me," he wrote. "Like Martí, I think the time has come to seize our rights instead of asking for them, to grab instead of beg for them." He would leave Cuba. At that stage, he did not know where he was going. Of one thing he was sure: "There is no going back possible on this kind of journey, and if I return, it will be with tyranny beheaded at my feet."[62]

4

COMRADES

★

IN NOVEMBER 1955, RICARDO ROJO WAS INVITED TO A HOUSE PARTY IN Mexico City by his friend Che Guevara. When they arrived, it was packed with young people shouting about politics. So many were present that some had to sit on the floor. The air was steamy with the sweat of hot-blooded youth and the dizzying fug of cigar smoke. The noise, Rojo remembered, was "deafening." Guevara grabbed his arm and leaned into his ear: "Come on, let's go shut ourselves in the kitchen. It's the one place where we can talk." Together, they pushed their way through. In the kitchen, they found Fidel Castro leaning over a hot stove, boiling a vat of spaghetti. Never taking his eye off the pasta, Fidel expounded his plan to invade Cuba.[1]

Che had left Guatemala for Mexico and, after a close brush with Castillo Armas's regime, Hilda had followed. On their reunion, he again proposed marriage. This time, she accepted—but not for long. A photographic negative of a young girl in a bathing suit fell out of a book of his, and she called off the engagement.[2] When her fury subsided, they moved in together. Then, one summer night in 1955, Che brought a new friend back to their house: Raúl Castro.

Little impressed Hilda, but Raúl did, with a fulsome espousal of communism. Meanwhile, Che, serious of mind, radically left-wing, and strikingly handsome, proved immediately fascinating to Raúl. But the person they really had to meet, Raúl emphasized, was his brother. Soon afterward, Fidel arrived in Mexico. Raúl first introduced him to Che at a friend's house at eight o'clock one evening. When the sun came up the next morning, the three young men—Fidel was then twenty-nine years old, Che twenty-seven, and Raúl twenty-four—were still talking.

"We are in complete accord," Che told Hilda afterward of Fidel; "it's only someone like him I could go all out for." Hilda's place in his affections had been superseded. Between Fidel and Che, said Fidel's then girlfriend, there had been "an intense flare of light."[3]

Two months before the party at which Fidel boiled spaghetti, he had legally obtained an American tourist visa and traveled overland to Texas. From there he had embarked upon a fund-raising tour, visiting Connecticut, New Jersey, New York, Pennsylvania, and Florida. He experienced few problems with the authorities, except for a brief detention by the FBI in Union City, New Jersey. Publicly and repeatedly, he proclaimed his new slogan: "In the year 1956, we will be free or we will be martyrs."[4] The tour raised $9,000.

In Mexico, this money allowed the men to train on a ranch outside the city, shooting turkeys. As Fidel had captured Che's heart on their first meeting, he also captured Alberto Bayo's. Bayo had cut his teeth alongside Francisco Franco as a Spanish officer in the Moroccan war. When war came to Spain itself, he fought Franco. Afterward, he went to Latin America, and trained men for various guerrilla struggles. Fidel, he wrote, "subjugated me. I became intoxicated with his enthusiasm."[5] He gave up his job, sold his business, and followed this Cuban messiah.

Bayo trained the men rigorously. His star pupil was Che, the toughest of the captains, and one of the sharpest shots in the forty-strong group. But the leadership of a Spaniard and an Argentine did not sit well with the Cubans, and there were incidents of insubordination. One of these was serious, and resulted in a court-martial and a death sentence, called for by Fidel and Raúl. Eventually, Fidel relented. The man was pardoned. In a separate incident, a spy identified inside the group was court-martialed, and received the same sentence. This time, the execution was carried out by one of the rebels. The body was buried in a field on the ranch.[6] Fidel was proving to be a ruthless and unflinching leader.

Soon, Hilda realized she was pregnant. Che married her, though without enthusiasm. "For another guy it would be transcendental; for me it is an uncomfortable episode," he wrote in his diary. "In the end, she gets her way—the way I see it, for a short while, although she hopes it will be lifelong."[7] He wanted Raúl or Fidel to be a witness, but Jesús Montané took on the role, to avoid the Castros having to make their whereabouts public to the authorities. Raúl attended the ceremony, and Fidel joined them afterward for the party. The following March, Hilda gave birth to a girl, known as Hildita. Che had wanted a boy, but both he and Fidel were enchanted by this new human, despite her sex. "This girl is going to be educated in

Cuba," boasted Fidel. "My communist soul expands plethorically," Che wrote to his mother; "she has come out exactly like Mao Tse-tung."[8]

★

At the beginning of 1956, a group of Cuban army officers planned a coup. They were betrayed, and the attempt defeated. Though this prompted a predictable crackdown, it did not cause undue concern in the Cuban government, in Washington, or among foreign investors in Cuba. Fulgencio Batista's regime, though undemocratic and repressive, was presiding over a boom. The island had the highest income per capita in Latin America, save for Venezuela. Its economy was growing fast. It had more television sets, motor cars, and telephones per person than any other Latin American country. New mansions and casinos were constantly being added to Havana's panoply. Ginger Rogers, Frank Sinatra, and Elvis Presley topped the billing at the casinos and nightclubs. At night, the city blazed with neon.

But Havana's glitter distracted observers from a country divided. Cuba had wealth, but most Cubans did not. Away from the tourist traps, Havana was a maze of miserable slums. In the countryside, the sugar season provided a few months' grueling work. Out of season, any work was hard to find. Between 1950 and 1958, the gross national product grew by just 1 percent. While Cubans may have been wealthy by the standard of Latin Americans, their average income per capita was still only about one-third that in Mississippi, the poorest American state; and Mississippi's was half of the United States' average.[9] Only one in ten of the rural Cuban population ever drank milk, and only one in twenty ever ate meat.[10]

The French writer Jean-Paul Sartre visited Batista's Havana and, like most visitors, was seduced by its earthly delights. "I had misunderstood everything," he later admitted. "What I took to be signs of wealth were, in fact, signs of dependence and poverty. At each ringing of the telephone, at each twinkling of neon, a small piece of a dollar left the island and formed, on the American continent, a whole dollar with the other pieces which were waiting for it."[11] Americans owned the telephone and electricity monopolies. The American government owned the nickel mines at Nicaro, Cuba's largest plant operation. American gangsters moved in, too: Meyer Lansky and Santo Trafficante were among those investing in new casinos, brothels, and illegal drug operations. "Violence became the arbiter of the nation's politics," wrote Philip Bonsal, later to become American ambassador to Cuba; "the gunman, on both sides of the fence, took the place of the politician." Between a fifth and a quarter of governmental expenditure went on bribery and corruption. Batista accumulated a personal fortune estimated at between $60 million and $300 million.[12]

The American ambassador to Cuba in 1956 was Arthur Gardner, a Republican businessman who had allowed himself to become a close friend of Batista's. Gardner actively obstructed the reporting of the true picture. "The only time we really got any good political reporting out of Cuba was when he was away," remembered Terrence Leonhardy, who worked on Cuban affairs at the State Department at the time. The ambassador, he said, "would not sign anything going out of the Embassy that was at all adversely critical to the regime."[13] The potential for a revolution barely registered in the United States.

The same was true in the Soviet Union. Nikolai Leonov had by then become the KGB resident in Mexico City, and enthusiastically renewed his acquaintance with Raúl Castro. It pleased him to discover that Raúl had a much increased interest in Marxism, and a new best friend, Che Guevara, who was supportive. With Fidel Castro, he was less impressed. The man's charisma was apparent, but he was, Leonov concluded, no communist. All of this was communicated carefully back to the KGB headquarters in Moscow, where it was received with displeasure. Leonov was recalled to Moscow and reprimanded for establishing contact with the Cubans without the proper authorization. According to Sergo Mikoyan, the son of Khrushchev's deputy Anastas Mikoyan and a close friend of Leonov's, the KGB had heard from the Cuban communists that Fidel was "bourgeois." Leonov was ordered to end the relationship.[14]

Nonetheless, the Soviet Union's interest in the third world had begun to revive. Largely responsible was the mercurial new first secretary, Nikita Sergeyevich Khrushchev. In February 1956, Khrushchev used the Twentieth Party Congress to make his "secret speech," denouncing Stalin as a murderer, a torturer, and a tyrant. The first reports of this shocking break with Soviet tradition reached Allen Dulles two weeks later. Many in Washington believed it to be a feint. At the same congress, Khrushchev sounded another note of change: "The new period in world history which Lenin predicted has arrived, and the peoples of the East are playing an active part in deciding the destinies of the whole world." Those newly freed by the ending of empires "need not go begging for up-to-date equipment to their former oppressors. They can get it in the socialist countries, without assuming any political or military commitments."[15] From Moscow's viewpoint, the portion of the third world with potential still lay to its east, in Asia. It did not even occur to Khrushchev to look west.

Khrushchev had been born in poverty in 1894. His father was a serf, until Russia's captive class was emancipated in the late nineteenth century. Young Nikita's parents could not afford to further his education beyond four years of school in their Ukrainian village, and as a teenager he became a metalworker. In 1915, he found himself working alongside Czech prisoners of war, and invited them back to his lodgings for tea and jam. With the Czechs, he pursued disparate interests in mechanical drawing and pan-Slavism. He joined the Bolshevik Party a few months after the October Revolution, and in 1919 went into the Red Army.

In 1921, famine struck much of the Volga and Ural regions. An estimated 5 million would die. Khrushchev's wife succumbed to typhus, leaving him a single father of two young children. In 1924, he met Nina Petrovna. They would live together for the rest of his life, though their marriage was only registered forty years after they met. He moved to Moscow, to train at the Industrial Academy. Among his contemporaries was Stalin's wife, Nadezhda Sergeyevna Alliluyeva. Nadya attempted to remain incognito, but Khrushchev sought her out. "I drew a lucky lottery ticket when it happened that Stalin observed my activities through Nadezhda Sergeyevna," he later acknowledged. He admitted that it was probably that friendship that saved him from the executions that awaited many of his contemporaries.[16]

Khrushchev rose through the ranks of the party, and during the Second World War was at Stalingrad. After the war, he returned to Moscow, and in 1953 found himself at Stalin's bedside with Georgy Malenkov and Lavrenty Beria, watching the old monster slip away. When Stalin stopped breathing, he was given artificial respiration. "Can't you see the man is dead?" snapped Khrushchev. "What do you want? You won't bring him back to life." Beria smirked and called for his car, driving off to take control of the security forces in what he hoped would be the beginning of his coup. But it was Malenkov who replaced Stalin and, in early 1955, Khrushchev who replaced Malenkov. The coup took place behind closed doors. Malenkov was obliged at a meeting of the Supreme Soviet to accept the blame for agricultural failings and "resign." Foreign diplomats in the audience detected a smile on Khrushchev's face and deduced that he was now the leader. The CIA, too, was taken by surprise. The first President Eisenhower heard of it was on the wire services.[17]

Khrushchev had been seen as a hard-liner, criticizing Malenkov for being too soft on Western capitalism. But in power he backed away from belligerence. He believed, as Lenin had said in his later years, that "peaceful coexistence" with capitalist nations was possible. The obvious benefits of socialism and communism would, he thought, soon entice the world's workers to make revolution everywhere, without the need for Soviet military intervention.[18]

Alarmed by the tripling of the defense budget during the Korean War, Eisenhower sought to replace the costly standing army with a cheaper nuclear deterrent. To avoid any appearance that the budget cut was a sign of weakness, he had Foster Dulles use the Geneva Conference of 1955 to raise the specter of "massive retaliation," should the Soviets attempt to invade the United States or its allies. Eisenhower still hoped for some disarmament; that, after all, would allow him to cut spending even further. But Dulles's warlike language inevitably raised the stakes. During the Suez Crisis in October 1956, Nikolai Bulganin, the Soviet foreign minister, would for the first time threaten to use nuclear weapons against the United States' allies, Britain and France.[19]

Khrushchev's "secret speech" had meant to draw a line under the worst excesses of Soviet rule, and move toward a moderate and inclusive future. Instead, it was disastrous for communist unity. Cominform, the organization of international communist parties formed by Stalin to extend Soviet foreign policy across the Eastern bloc, was disbanded by its own members two months later. That autumn, Mao Tse-tung would deride Khrushchev for lacking "revolutionary morality," and imply that he was not a true Marxist-Leninist.[20] Though in the United States politicians would continue to talk about "international communism" as an entity until as late as 1964, the cracks that would widen into the Sino-Soviet split had already begun to show.

★

In Mexico, Fidel's guerrillas did not escape the attention of the authorities. At the end of June 1956, twenty of them—including Fidel and Che—were imprisoned following a police sweep, and faced an array of charges ranging from plotting Batista's assassination to overstaying their visas. While Fidel was in prison, Batista tried Trujillo's ploy, and claimed publicly that his opponent was in league with the communists. Fidel wrote an article for a Cuban magazine rejecting the claim as "absurd" and pointing out, accurately, that the person who had links with the Cuban communist party was Batista.[21] Though he was under pressure from his supporters to produce a written manifesto for M-26-7, Fidel resisted. He was drawing support and funding from an unusually broad ideological base, and had no intention of alienating any part of it. "Not even Raúl or Che could ever guess exactly what was on Fidel's mind," remembered Carlos Franqui. "He was inscrutable."[22]

With Fidel carefully peddling all things to all men, Che nearly blew it by blabbing to his Mexican interrogators. He was a communist, he told them, and believed in armed revolution across Latin America. He even had Nikolai Leonov's card with him. When Fidel found out, he was apoplectic. Though Che usually bowed to Fidel's instructions without question, on this occasion he does not seem to have been sorry. His mother, too, had been critical of his communist revelations in a letter; he replied to her now in defiant terms. "I am not Christ or a philanthropist, old lady, I am all the contrary of a Christ," he wrote. "I fight for the things I believe in, with all the weapons at my disposal and try to leave the other man *dead* so that I don't get nailed to a cross."[23] Carlos Franqui visited the prison, and found the two men's moods vastly different. "Fidel was desperate," he wrote. "He paced back and forth like a caged lion." Che, meanwhile, was insouciant, stripped to the waist and playing ball with another prisoner.

In prison, Fidel and Che had to share a cell, and sleep side by side. According to Franqui, they had both been studying Stalin's *The Fundamentals of Leninism*. The three had a heated argument, Che defending Stalin and Franqui attacking him. "A revolution must have only one leader if it is to remain whole and not be defeated," Fidel observed, thoughtfully. "One bad leader is better than twenty good ones."[24]

Fidel was released on 24 July. Che remained in prison. Despite their disagreement, his ardor for the Cuban had not diminished. He used up the prison stationery writing lyrical poetry to Fidel.[25]

Outside, Fidel began to work for Che's release. Conscious that he was being a burden, Che told him not to waste his energies. The invasion of Cuba was important. An Argentine languishing in prison was not. To his surprise, Fidel replied, gruffly, "I will not abandon you."[26] Their fight was over. A revolutionary pact had been sealed.

★

In Haiti, Paul Magloire's dictatorship had coasted for a time on the prosperity brought by the postwar boom in the United States. With wealth and glamour making an unprecedented appearance in Port-au-Prince, it was possible to restore and, for a while, maintain public order. But the mysterious disappearance of aid money after Hurricane Hazel in 1954 (Haitians called the new mink coats draped over the shoulders of government ministers' wives *les Hazels*) had made the administration's corruption all too apparent. In 1956, the good times began to sour.

As the boom faded, discontent increased. Strikes were called by students and laborers. Early that year, agents working for François Duvalier—still in hiding—contacted exiled former Cuban president Carlos Prío. Prío was now based in Miami, and was positioning himself as the insurgent paymaster of the Caribbean. The two made a deal. Prío would provide Duvalier with his support (to the tune, apparently, of $20,000) to topple Magloire and seize the presidency of Haiti. When Duvalier was president, he would allow Prío to set up bases in Haiti from which he could attack Batista. Prío sent a young Cuban student politician, Temístocles Fuentes, to Haiti. At Duvalier and Clément Barbot's direction, Fuentes reportedly masterminded the terrorist campaign that soon began across Haiti.

Magloire's term of office was supposed to end on 15 May 1956. Like many dictators, he preferred not to abide by that, and in office he remained. Two days later, riots broke out across the country. Repression was swift and violent. Large numbers of rebelling students and teachers from the Lycée Toussaint L'Ouverture in Port-au-Prince ended up in the hospital.[27] That summer, the sounds of explosions, gunfire, and screaming regularly rang out across the capital. Markets and other public places were targeted. Kidnapping gangs terrorized the roads. Magloire arrested dissidents, imposed censorship, and banned all political broadcasts and meetings. Publicly, François Duvalier released a statement condemning all acts of terrorism. The fact that he was behind the campaign would not become known for many years.[28]

The climax came at the end of 1956. On 5 December, politicians Louis Déjoie and Duvalier were among those who called publicly for Magloire to remove the ban on political meetings and other censorship. With massive demonstrations pressing at the gates of the National Palace and a general strike in full swing, Magloire realized he was beaten. He packed his suitcase with a haul of cash alleged to be somewhere near $20 million, and fled.[29]

★

In September 1956, Carlos Prío was waiting impatiently at the Casa de Palmas, an elegant, Spanish-style hotel in downtown McAllen, Texas. The man he was to meet finally arrived: Fidel Castro, just turned thirty, six feet two inches of bravado wearing an unflattering mustache. This time, Fidel had not risked applying for a visa. At Reynosa, on the Mexican border, he had simply stripped naked, plunged into the Rio Grande, and swam to the United States. On the northern shore, some friends met him and furnished him with dry clothes.

Prío left with his pockets $50,000 lighter. Fidel had no qualms about taking money from a man he had publicly castigated for corruption. "Pinching $50,000 from a son of a bitch is not theft," he said afterward. "It's a good deed."[30] Prío was prepared to give it. Or, perhaps, to pass it on. A well-placed KGB official later alleged that, though Fidel did not know it, the money came from the CIA.[31] Certainly, this would make sense of why Prío was dispensing substantial cash sums to so many disparate and unreliable Caribbean rebels, in return for which he seemed to be receiving no clear guarantees of personal benefit.

Reports of tension and repression continued to emerge from Cuba. In October, Batista's head of military intelligence was murdered. The dictator accused Prío. A target for retaliation was chosen: nine young Cubans, who had been seeking asylum in the Haitian embassy for the past few weeks. The next day, Batista's chief of police marched on the Haitian embassy, burst in, and opened fire. Seven youths were killed, though one managed to get a bullet into the chief of police before he died. The remaining two were taken to the hospital. Ernestina Otero, who worked in the Havana bureau of the *New York Times*, saw them laid out on tables awaiting the doctor. A Cuban army officer pushed past the medics. "Never mind the doctor!" he snarled. He drew a knife, and slashed both of their throats. There was an outcry in Haiti. Temístocles Fuentes went public at a Port-au-Prince student association to condemn the attack.[32]

The news from Havana stoked the revolutionary fervor among the Cubans training in Mexico. Fidel was now set on mounting an invasion of his homeland before the end of the year. This decision was not popular. Frank País, the young leader from Santiago whom Fidel had left in charge of the Cuban network, tried in two separate visits to talk him out of it, insisting that M-26-7 at home was not yet ready to provide full support. Alberto Bayo despaired at Fidel's public proclamations on the matter. Though the authorities did not know exactly what he was planning, everybody knew he was planning something. In November, one of Batista's colonels alleged that Trujillo and Prío had paid Fidel 200,000 pesos to stage armed actions in Pinar del Río.[33]

In reality, Trujillo had offered Batista a military alliance. Batista had replied that he did not want to be seen publicly to associate with Trujillo, but would be happy to accept secret gifts.

"That shitty sergeant!" Trujillo snapped—for he considered Batista's modest military rank to be a sign of intolerable effeminacy. "I'm going to oust the bastard!"[34] Consequently, he had money and munitions smuggled to Miami and distributed to various Cuban rebel outfits. There was never a formal link between Trujillo and Fidel Castro, but some of the Dominican dictator's munitions would find their way to M-26-7.

Fidel could not be persuaded to delay the invasion. Though this dogmatism was not out of character, his determination to get away and begin the potentially suicidal fight may have been strengthened by two upsets in his private life that autumn. His planned marriage to a Cuban exile was called off at the same time that his first wife, Mirta, was marrying again. Then, at the end of October, his father died. Father and son had been close, but not friendly. They had fought constantly over politics. Raúl was seen to be upset by the news. Fidel never spoke of his father's death, focusing instead on the mission.[35]

The focus worked and, in November, Fidel finally published the manifesto of M-26-7. It promised a return to the 1940 constitution, free elections, agrarian reform, and a free press. There was nothing in it that marked any development toward communism, or even socialism, as Che himself acknowledged. "That was the result of a very long process," he told an American journalist years later.[36] For now, the revolution was democratic. The purpose was established; the boat would sail; the men would go; and if they did not succeed in becoming free, they would accept martyrdom.

"My dear daughter, my little Mao, you don't know what a difficult world you're going to have to live in," Che said to the infant Hildita before he left. "When you grow up this whole continent, and maybe the whole world, will be fighting against the great enemy, Yankee imperialism. You too will have to fight. I may not be here any more, but the struggle will enflame the continent."[37]

★

On a rainy night in Tuxpan, a sleepy port in the Mexican state of Veracruz, M-26-7 assembled. "A silent embrace among the weeds at the river's edge was the only greeting between men who hadn't seen one another for a long time," said one of them, Faustino Pérez.[38] Through the dark, the figures of men could just be seen, busily loading a fourteen-man yacht with rifles, machine guns, ammunition, maps, compasses, blankets, food, medical supplies, and two thousand gallons of fuel, even filling the bilge space. This was what Prío's money—or, possibly, the CIA's—had bought: the *Granma*, named for its previous owner's grandmother. Hopefully, she had aged better than the boat. It had only a twelve-hundred-gallon tank, insufficient for the journey. Its gears were too badly worn for high speeds. Its radio could only receive. Finally, the men piled in: eighty-two of them, crammed into every available space. Another fifty could not fit and had to stay behind.

One engine was started up—the noise was being kept down to avoid unwanted attention—and the *Granma* slowly chugged out of the harbor. When they reached open water, the men burst into song. Their odyssey had begun.

A few hours later, some must have wished it had not. A massive storm hit the *Granma* full on. The tiny yacht bounced up and down on monstrous Caribbean waves. Frantically, the men scrambled for antinausea pills; they could not be found, and soon the guerrillas were slumped in corners, groaning, awash with vomit. The bilge pump broke, and water poured in. Glancing down, Faustino realized that the planks of the deck at his feet were submerged. Frantically, the weakened men began to bail it out with buckets. For once, said Faustino, even Fidel "seemed worried." But the men bailed hard, and someone managed to fix the bilge pump. Soon, when Faustino looked down at his feet, he could once again see planks.

The crew survived the storm, but the trials had not finished. Much of the food they had brought was ruined. Che had no medicine for his asthma, and was seized by a violent attack. Fidel allowed himself to be slightly impressed by the Argentine's stoic refusal to complain.[39] They were also miles off course. The plan had been to reach the south of Cuba by 30 November, when Frank País's group in Santiago would stage a simultaneous uprising. But the day came, and they were still at sea. Over the one-way radio, they could hear that Frank's uprising had begun without them. After more than a day of fighting, it was crushed.

In the very early hours of 2 December, the *Granma* neared the coast of Cuba. The pilot, Roberto Roque, leaned over the ship's antenna, craning his neck to search for sight of land. He fell. Fidel ordered the searchlight turned on, and after forty-five minutes, the half-dead Roque was pulled back in by the Dominican helmsman. Roque was not the only man suffering. All were dehydrated and weak from lack of food. Several had vomited themselves into exhaustion. Some could barely walk.[40]

In the first light of dawn, the *Granma* ran aground near the edge of a mangrove swamp off Playa las Coloradas, miles from their intended destination. "It wasn't a landing," remembered one guerrilla; "it was a shipwreck." Faustino added: "Our plans had failed completely. Fidel looked angry."[41]

The men loaded up their small landing dinghy with boxes of ammunition and heavy weapons, and heaved it over the side. The dinghy dipped; the bow went underwater, and within moments it glugged down to the seabed, lost.

Between the men and the beach were a few hundred yards of mangroves. The twisted, thorny branches loomed out of muddy water, forming a natural barricade as effective as barbed wire. On foot, the men began to wade through, navigating this obstacle course through water that, at some points, came up to their necks. Many times, they tripped over underwater roots, invisible beneath the silted sea. If they grabbed branches to steady themselves, thorns ripped through their skin. Saltwater stung in the wounds. Fidel ordered them to ditch anything not required for combat, and so all cooking equipment, extra clothes, and blankets were surrendered to the mangroves. "Before our anxious eyes," remembered Faustino, "we could see only more mud, more water, more mangroves."[42]

After three or four hours, the men had almost reached the shore. Just at that moment, a plane appeared in the sky. Frank's uprising in Santiago had put Batista's air force on high alert, and the wreck of the *Granma* was a visible marker. The plane flew low over the mangroves, and opened fire with its machine guns. Unable to run, the men hid as best they could amid the branches. They did at least succeed in that: after a few passes, the plane flew off.

The exhilaration of combat had restored Fidel's usual boundless optimism. "Look," he said, with a dismissive flick of his hand at the disappearing plane, "they are terrified, because they know we have come to destroy them."[43]

When the men reassembled on the shore, Che remembered, they were "disoriented and walking in circles, an army of shadows, of phantoms, walking as if moved by some obscure psychic mechanism."[44] By day, they slept. By night, they walked, heading through sugar plantations inland toward the mountains. They ate sugarcane from the fields, and accepted the hospitality of local peasants. On 5 December, just after dawn, they had set up camp in a valley near Alegría del Pío. Che was leaning against a tree, eating his ration of half a sausage, and chatting to Jesús Montané about their respective children. Then came a blast of automatic fire.

The men scattered, plunging into the high, dense cane on the only side of the valley from which bullets did not seem to be emanating. "I felt a hard blow on my chest and sharp pain in my neck," Che remembered. "I was sure I had been fatally wounded." Meanwhile, another revolutionary, blood pouring from his mouth and nose, began firing into the trees at the unseen enemy, shouting, "They've killed me!" Che heard one voice plead weakly that they should surrender, answered immediately by the bellow of a young rebel named Camilo Cienfuegos, who had joined the *Granma* at the last minute: "Nobody surrenders here!"—followed, as Che remembered, "by a four-letter word."[45]

Flat on the ground, Che gasped, "I'm fucked." Faustino glanced at his fallen comrade, blood welling from the bullet wound in his neck, and told him it was nothing. Che felt otherwise. "Everything seemed lost, and I suddenly started thinking about the best way to die," he said later. "I remembered an old Jack London story in which the hero, knowing he will freeze to death in the cold wilderness of Alaska, leans against a tree trunk and gets ready to die with dignity."[46]

Juan Almeida found Che in this state, preparing for death, his shirt red and soggy with blood. Ignoring the Argentine's protests, he grabbed him and physically dragged him out of the Alaskan wilderness and back into the Cuban sugarcane.

In the tall, thick cane, heavy leaves flapping about, it was impossible to tell whether another man a few feet away was friend or foe. For two hours they fought, hand to hand. Eventually, the army set fire to the cane fields. The rebels had to flee. As they ran, they realized with horror that many of their wounded colleagues remained in the burning fields, unable to crawl out.

The survivors dispersed into the forest, and lost each other. Fidel was with Faustino and Universo Sánchez. Raúl had another small group. Juan Almeida and the wounded Che were with three more. Camilo had two with him. Fernando Sánchez Amaya had six. Fourteen others surrendered to the army back at the battlefield, and were summarily shot. Three men split from Sánchez Amaya's group and also surrendered; they, too, were shot.[47]

Fidel himself later admitted that, between the Moncada attack and the *Granma* landing, "revolutionary struggle in Cuba in the face of a modern, well-equipped army seemed to many people to lack any prospect for success. . . . The crushing defeat and total dispersal of the inexperienced guerrilla detachment by Batista's troops on December 5, 1956, seemed to confirm entirely those pessimistic forebodings." Back in Havana, Batista could again relax in his baroque palace. He released the news that Fidel and Raúl Castro had been killed.[48]

It is disputed exactly how many of the eighty-two men on the *Granma* survived Alegría de Pío: probably between fifteen and twenty-two, but they have passed into Cuban lore with apostolic resonance as the Twelve. They were ragged, exhausted, and in some cases wounded. They had lost everything, except their hunger for a fight.

The Sierra Maestra is a remote region, with little in the way of roads or infrastructure to provide contact with the outside world. Its sparsely populated, thickly forested mountains suit those who prefer not to be found. The men drank water from streams, and spat out the bugs. Che used the pump of his asthma vaporizer to siphon moisture out of porous rocks. They ate snake, sugarcane, cactus, prickly pear, and the occasional tortoise—hard to find, but easy to catch. Soon, Che's group encountered Camilo's. The two men had not known each other before the *Granma*; Camilo was a fearless, sparky, and unfailingly good-humored art-school dropout from Havana, who had worked in the United States for a spell before joining Fidel's movement just in time to sail. The two hit it off immediately. Che would later call Camilo "the greatest guerrilla chief that this revolution produced . . . a perfect revolutionary and a fraternal friend."[49] Che adored Fidel, but their relationship was never equal. Fidel commanded, militarily and personally. Che adored Camilo, and Camilo adored him back, as a comrade, a friend, a brother.

Slowly, like drops of mercury, the small groups found each other again, and reassembled into a whole. Finally, from a hilltop, Fidel spotted the last few—Che, Camilo, and their band—coming to complete the handful of straggling survivors. "Batista's fucking had it now!" he crowed delightedly, as his total troop numbers doubled to around sixteen limping, half-starved men. But when Che told him the story of their days since the ambush at Alegría, his joy turned to rage. They had left most of their guns with a peasant and lost them. Fidel gave Che a stinging, public rebuke. Che was mortified. One biographer has suggested that his distress might have provoked the serious asthma attack he suffered that night. The following day, Fidel confiscated Che's treasured pistol and instead gave him what he called "a bad rifle."[50]

Life in the mountains was tough, and on no one more than Che. On top of his neck wound, asthma, and Fidel's intermittent wrath, he came down with malaria in January. Every day brought a new struggle for food, water, shelter. They began to recruit local peasants to the cause. Camilo would test their hardiness by barbecuing a cat on his alcohol burner and offering it as Sierra cuisine. More than one potential recruit presented with this dish realized that he did not have the stomach for a guerrilla existence. It was rare that the guerrillas had the chance to wash. This, at least, was not a problem for Che. "Our noses were completely habituated to this type of life," he bragged; "the hammocks of guerrilla fighters are known for their characteristic, individual odor."[51]

Aside from survival, the men had two main aims: recruiting and training locals, and skirmishing with Batista's troops. Though the population often sympathized with the Twelve, few joined up. It has been estimated that only 1 percent of the peasants in the Sierra Maestra—that is to say, five hundred people—joined the rebels, and most of them only in the last months of 1958.[52] The key to their survival in 1957 was not numbers but a brilliant piece of media manipulation. Fidel invited a yanqui journalist, Herbert Matthews of the *New York Times*, to their camp. At this point, Batista was still claiming that the Castros were dead.

Matthews arrived, and Fidel told the men to look sharp. "I looked at myself, then at the others," wrote Che, "shoes falling apart, tied together with wire; we were covered with filth. But we put on an act; we filed off in step with me in the lead." Matthews spent three hours talking to Fidel, while Che and Raúl paraded by with column after column of lean, smart troops. At one point, a soldier interrupted the interview, running up to Fidel to inform him that the second column had sent a message. Profoundly impressed, Matthews filed a sensational piece about Fidel's direction of the Cuban resistance and his impressive force of well-drilled fighters.[53]

Matthews had been duped. Fidel's entire force then numbered just eighteen men. The line about the "second column" had been a bluff, and Raúl and Che had marched the same group past him several times. This was an old trick of Rafael Trujillo's, though Fidel may not have realized it. In 1938, Trujillo had invited FDR's son, James Roosevelt, to an enormous army parade. "Look closely," he had whispered, mischievously. "You'll see the same units coming round a second time."

In Havana, Batista scoffed at Matthews's interview and announced that the journalist had made the whole thing up in his hotel room. If it were real, he said, the *Times* would have printed a photograph of Matthews with Fidel. The very next day, the *Times* did just that.[54]

Though much of it was unwitting fantasy, Matthews's report precipitated a real change in the political climate. Inspired by the story of the mountain guerrillas, underground revolutionary groups began to form all over Cuba. A few weeks later, another journalist, Jules Dubois of the *Chicago Tribune*, interviewed Batista, and was treated to a lengthy tirade on Fidel's alleged communism. The proof, Batista said, was that "he killed six priests in Bogotá during the Bogotazo." Dubois pointed out that no priests had been killed during the Bogotazo. Undaunted, Batista sent him some clumsily forged documents to "prove" the charge.[55]

Batista's renewed determination to get rid of Fidel earned him a new lease of patronage from an unexpected source: Rafael Trujillo. The

Benefactor stopped trying to "oust the bastard," and again lavished gifts upon him: planes, supplies, men, and money. Along with them, he sent his newest and most beloved aide: Johnny Abbes García, head of the Dominican Military Intelligence Service (SIM).

Abbes, who was described by an OAS election observer in the Dominican Republic as "the regime's Iago," enjoyed an extraordinary rise to power during the course of 1956.[56] Having shown early promise in his childhood hobby of gouging out the eyes of chickens, he later developed a passion for torturing human beings. He secured a minor position in Trujillo's palace, and engaged in what was widely said to be a physical affair with Trujillo's half brother Nene. In spite of their political differences—Abbes affected to be on the far left, and anti-American—Trujillo recognized in him a soul mate.

Abbes claimed to have experience of Fidel Castro. While he had been working as a freelance torturer in Mexico in 1955, a stint with the police had given him the chance to spy on the Cuban rebels. Trujillo set Abbes the task of removing Fidel, while also renewing and expanding the power of the SIM within the Dominican Republic. Soon, the SIM's trademark Volkswagen Beetles would be an ominous feature of daily life in Ciudad Trujillo. La Cuarenta, a prison near the capital, became its torture house.[57]

"I would say that out of every one hundred young [Dominican] people who were fifteen years old in 1956, ninety-nine would have dreamed of being Fidel Castro," said Juan Bosch, Trujillo's leading opponent in exile. "He still lives in the hearts of nearly all Dominican young people and all the parties." Bosch was speaking in 1964, as a sharp critic of Fidel and an admirer of the United States, long after Fidel had cast aside the principles of constitutional democracy he espoused in the manifesto of 1956. But the fact that Fidel was no democrat, Bosch said, did not bother Dominican youth. "They thought democracy was Trujillo, Batista, and Perez Jimenez, and the entire corrupt spectacle of Latin American dictatorship. The word democracy is associated in Latin America with the worst political periods of our countries because those dictators always spoke in the name of democracy, and because in the United States itself . . . they were referred to as the rulers of the free world."[58]

Bosch had hit on the secret of Fidel's success. Latin American politics—and Caribbean politics in particular—had its own language. Democracy was dictatorship. The free world was a prison. Communism was just a word people used when they wanted the attention of Washington. Ideology of any sort was largely irrelevant to political life. Batista could invite communists to join his cabinet, and then become a violent anticommunist.

Trujillo could label all his enemies communists, torture them, throw their mangled bodies into the sea to be ripped apart by sharks, and then promote the most open far leftist in the Dominican Republic, Johnny Abbes, to be his right-hand man. Political life in Cuba, Haiti, and the Dominican Republic was a cockfight. For any politician landing in the dust, the only thing that mattered was to survive for as long as possible. Fidel Castro understood this. If communists were useful to his cause, he would recruit them. If corrupt right-wing politicians offered him money, he would take it. He was sincere in his nationalism: his idolization of José Martí was genuine and profound, and he did, unquestionably, love Cuba. Everything else was open to negotiation. Had it been any other way, his name would long have been forgotten.

This was Caribbean politics. Fidel Castro spoke the language. So too, it would shortly transpire, did François Duvalier. But, as would be demonstrated repeatedly over the coming years, neither the Eisenhower administration nor its successor could make any sense of it at all.

PART TWO

CUBA LIBRE

5

"A LOT OF FUSS BY A BUNCH OF COMMUNISTS"

★

AT LUNCHTIME ON 13 MARCH 1957, A GROUP OF EIGHTY STUDENTS AND activists leaped out of vehicles outside Fulgencio Batista's palace, set back from Havana's seaside promenade. They charged across the lawns and into the building, spraying bullets, hurling grenades. The guards, eating lunch, were taken by surprise.

The attack had been organized by the Revolutionary Directorate, led by José Antonio Echevarría, and by the Spanish Civil War veteran Carlos Gutiérrez Menoyo. Echevarría had a pact with Fidel Castro, but was just as well placed as he to be a future leader of Cuba. In some quarters, particularly the Auténtico party, he was preferred. To fund the operation, the Directorate had turned to the leader of the Auténticos, and Castro's and François Duvalier's patron, Carlos Prío. They had also received arms sent by Rafael Trujillo, still playing for both sides in the Cuban conflict.

At the palace, the attackers surged through the ornate rooms and up the staircases, firing pistols and throwing bombs. One hurled a grenade through what appeared to be an open door into a glass- and wood-paneled chamber. In fact, it was one of the palace's many trompe l'oeil features, an optical illusion painted on a flat wall to look like another room. The grenade bounced off the solid wall and rolled back to the attacker's feet. Fortunately for him, it failed to explode.

Drenched in their own blood, a small group of men led by Faure Chomón made it to Batista's office. They shot the lock off the door, but the dictator had managed to flee through a side room, apparently just moments before. Chomón ran and escaped out through the landscaped gardens of Zayas Park. "I ran like a deer," he said, "feeling missiles landing all around me." He reached the fountain at the center of the park, the bullets whistling past him gouging out chunks of cement. He hurled himself to the ground and scrambled over the low wall around the fountain. "My shirt was sticking to my body with sweat," he remembered. "All I could smell was gunpowder, blood, and death."[1] Chomón had three bullets in his body, but he escaped. Forty or fifty attackers were killed, including Gutiérrez Menoyo. Many of the survivors would be tortured and murdered.

Batista's tanks rolled around Zayas Park, which was bordered by many of Havana's luxury hotels. Guests flattened themselves on the floors while bullets peppered through the windows and tank shells exploded the furniture. The civilian victims included an American tourist, shot by one of Batista's snipers when he ventured onto his hotel balcony to photograph the action.[2] Another casualty was the Ortodoxo party president, who may not even have been involved in the attack. It was rumored that Echevarría had planned to make him provisional president, and so he was arrested. The next morning, his body was found near a lake in one of Havana's country clubs.

But the most significant victim, from the point of view of Cuba's future, was young Echevarría himself, shot and killed at the radio station from which he had intended to broadcast news of the revolution. Thanks to a bullet fired by an agent of Batista, Fidel Castro's most credible rival for the future leadership of Cuba was gone.

Though he would later claim the attack as part of the story of his revolution, Fidel's first reaction was to criticize it. From the Sierra Maestra, he submitted a disapproving essay to an upmarket Havana weekly, *Bohemia*, and it was published. Philip Bonsal, later American ambassador to Cuba, ascribed his negative tone to what he called Fidel's "congenital dislike of competition."[3] If so, he should have been pleased. The competition was over.

★

In Haiti, the opening months of 1957 had been characterized by strikes, riots, lootings, shootings, beatings, and bombings, largely directed at business and government. In early March, a false rumor spread that the popular politician Daniel Fignolé had been arrested. Rioters descended on the Champs de Mars park in the center of Port-au-Prince, marauding through buildings including the police station and National Palace. A month later, two policemen were killed when their investigation of a terrorist bomb factory in Martissant triggered an explosion. According to the factory chief, he had been commissioned by François Duvalier and Clément Barbot.[4]

The hot, dusty streets of Port-au-Prince were filled with rioters. The army turned artillery against civilians, and at one point a bomb was dropped from an airplane, though it did not explode. The following day, 26 May, Fignolé became president, promising democracy. "He bravely picks a cabinet," said a Pathé news announcer, over footage of a serious-looking Fignolé at his desk. "For how long is a question mark."[5] The answer was just nineteen days.

Fignolé's mistake was to appoint Antoine Kébreau head of the armed forces. Kébreau was a friend of two significant figures in the equation: François Duvalier and Rafael Trujillo. He also had ambitions of his own. On 14 June, Kébreau's officers marched directly into the council chamber and apprehended the president.

"This meeting is adjourned," Fignolé announced calmly, and put his hands up.

"Ti-Coc, you're shit," remarked the arresting officer, using Fignolé's Creole nickname, Little Cockerel.[6] Fignolé was driven to Bizoton, where his family and possessions had already been collected onto a boat, and shipped off to exile in Miami.

Rumors of Fignolé's disappearance spread. Some even suggested that he had been murdered. On the evening of 16 June, his supporters smashed and looted what was left of Port-au-Prince. Kébreau's troops opened fire on citizens, and a full-scale war broke out between the government of Haiti and the people.

Even in a nation used to high levels of public violence, the sight the next morning was grotesque. People had been literally ripped apart. The city's stray dogs were seen lapping up pools of human blood from the streets. The fire service had to be dispatched to hose it away. Most thought the official death toll of fifty fell far short of the truth. Unofficial estimates ran to at least five hundred dead, and perhaps twice that.[7]

The United States refused to recognize Kébreau's military junta, and eventually the general realized he would have to hold some sort of election. The straight-talking American ambassador, Gerald Drew, doubted the sincerity of such an act. "He's only doing it to get recognition," he said. "We don't want to recognize the bastard."[8] The election was fixed for 22 September 1957. The nominations were Louis Déjoie, a Stetson-wearing, well-connected mulatto planter with strong American links; Clément Jumelle, Paul Magloire's black finance minister and anointed successor; and François Duvalier. Kébreau and the military supported Duvalier by default, for they would support neither a mulatto nor a Magloirist. He was the only candidate permitted to campaign unmolested.

★

On the evening of 12 March 1956, Jesús de Galíndez, a Spanish-Dominican academic, had been lecturing as part of his Latin American history course at Columbia University, New York. Galíndez left Columbia at 9:20 PM, and went for coffee opposite the university with two students. A few minutes before ten, he left with a student, who drove him to the subway sixty blocks south, at the corner of Eighth Avenue and Fifty-seventh Street.[9] Thirteen days before, he had handed in his doctoral dissertation: a well-researched critical account of the rule of Rafael Trujillo.

From the subway, Galíndez vanished. Immediately, it was suspected that one of Trujillo's secret services was responsible. Indeed, there was no other credible suspect, though a few Trujillistas would later claim unconvincingly that Galíndez had been killed by the CIA. Galíndez's students and colleagues took up the story, and it was mentioned by President Eisenhower in press conferences. An extensive police investigation found nothing.

In December 1956, it was reported blandly in the Dominican press that the abandoned car of an American pilot, Gerry Murphy, had been found next to a slaughterhouse in Ciudad Trujillo. Murphy was from Oregon, and that state's representative and senator began to clamor publicly about links between his murder and Generalissimo Trujillo.

On 12 March, it turned out, Murphy had flown a twin-engine aircraft from Amityville, Long Island, to West Palm Beach, Florida, and thence to Monte Cristi, in the Dominican Republic. The only two witnesses to the cargo put on board were Murphy and a night watchman. The watchman told investigators that the cargo was a man on a stretcher, who could not move and had to be carried aboard. This, it seemed, was Jesús de Galíndez. The watchman died of a heart attack before he could testify.

In West Palm Beach, a mechanic who refueled the plane also said that he saw a body, lying either dead or unconscious, on a stretcher in the cabin. Six days before this mechanic was due to testify, he went on a hunting trip in a light private plane. It crashed, and he, too, conveniently died.

Murphy himself had been allowed to live for a while after this mysterious flight. He had made several trips to the United States and Cuba with large sums of cash and explosives for Trujillo's purposes. Then he had begun to talk.[10]

When Murphy's car was discovered, the Dominican regime announced that Octavio de la Maza, another pilot, had just hanged himself with a mosquito net noose suspended from a shower head in prison. He had left a note. It said that Murphy had made a sexual advance upon La Maza, which La Maza resisted. The two had engaged in a struggle on the sun-drenched cliffs. During the fight, Murphy fell to his death. La Maza had been unable to live with the guilt, and had committed suicide.[11]

The story was full of holes. The FBI quickly showed that the handwriting in the note was not La Maza's. The shower head in his cell was found to be loose, and unable to support the weight of a body. Mosquito nets were not issued to Dominican prisoners. Ramfis Trujillo, the Generalissimo's handsome, twenty-seven-year-old wastrel son, had been a close friend of La Maza's. He did not believe it, either, and the incident provoked one of the regular fallings-out between father and son.

Trujillo went to the length of using a public ceremony, in which he was being decorated by two foreign governments in front of a gilded array of Dominican luminaries, to deny it. Ramfis sat in the front row of the chamber, staring hard at the floor, while his father spoke. "It is untrue, *absolutely untrue*, that the government ordered the death of Captain de la Maza," he said, beating his hand against the arm of his chair to emphasize the words. "Why would it do such a thing?" Ramfis stayed silent and brooding.

"You saw that cynical performance?" said a government minister afterward over drinks with a trusted colleague. "That man is the past master of dissimulation! That whole scene was for Ramfis, because one of his best friends was killed."[12]

By May 1957, the *New York Times* was openly connecting Trujillo to the disappearances of Galíndez and Murphy. In response, Dominican consulates filled American newspapers with advertisements proclaiming the Generalissimo's anticommunist credentials. The SIM, Johnny Abbes's intelligence service, alleged that Galíndez had been a Soviet spy during his time in New York. *El Caribe*, one of Trujillo's newspapers, alleged that he was a communist. Arturo Espaillat alleged that he had been in the employment of the CIA. In fact, Galíndez had been born in Spain to a Basque family. He was part of the wave of Spanish Civil War exiles who had fled to the Dominican Republic, but he was a Basque nationalist and Christian democrat, not a communist.[13]

By getting rid of Galíndez, Trujillo may have hoped to prevent the truth from being published. It was too late. Just three days before Galíndez disappeared, his dissertation had been submitted to a publisher. *La Era de Trujillo* became an immediate best seller across Latin America, and even today remains one of the best accounts of Trujillo's rule.

Trujillo was obliged to rent a crowd to demonstrate outside the White House in his support, and engaged a number of public relations experts, including Franklin Delano Roosevelt Jr. Roosevelt's offices were besieged by exiled Dominican and Puerto Rican demonstrators.[14] But Trujillo had still not blotted his copybook enough to estrange himself completely from the United States government, which maintained a guided missile tracking station in the Dominican Republic, nor from the American business community, which approved of both the stability he enforced and his staunch opposition to communism. Cordial relations between the United States and the Trujillo regime continued.

★

"We have struck the spark of the Cuban revolution," announced Fidel Castro, standing atop Cuba's highest mountain, Pico Turquino.[15] He was speaking to Robert Taber of CBS. The resulting documentary, *The Rebels of the Sierra Maestra—Cuba's Jungle Fighters*, premiered on American television on 19 May 1957. Wealthy Cubans decamped to Miami to watch it. To their disappointment, the South Florida station WJTV did not screen its usual CBS content at the appropriate time. WJTV said that its commercial contracts obliged it to pull Taber's much-anticipated documentary in favor of a repeated episode of *Lassie*. It was rumored that Batista had bought the time slot and blocked the program.[16]

For the past few months, Fidel and his men had been raiding army posts and sugar mills for weapons and supplies, and recruiting locals to their cause. Taber estimated that there were around one hundred guerrillas in Fidel's group when he visited, though half of those were members of the urban underground who had joined only the week before. The first female recruit was Celia Sánchez, a tough, birdlike young woman, who had for the past few years been one of M-26-7's best organizers in Oriente. Between Celia and Fidel, an extraordinary relationship soon formed. She is often described as his lover, but their bond seems to have been more profound than that. Celia became Fidel's domestic companion, confidante, and assistant from 1957 until her death in 1980. Through all of Fidel's subsequent relationships with women—and, though he kept them fiercely private, there were many, including one that produced five children—Celia remained a constant presence. Alongside Raúl, she was the only person who was ever able to form anything like an equal, reciprocal emotional relationship with Fidel. She was probably the closest friend of his life.

The men and women called each other *compañero*—a word that translates approximately as "comrade," but is free from the communist overtones of *comarada*. The men among them grew beards, and vowed not to shave until Cuba was free.[17] As a result, the Cuban public called them *barbudos*—the bearded ones. Fidel insisted his compañeros abide by a strong code of moral conduct and justice. Rebels collected taxes from the population, and used them to set up free schoolrooms and medical clinics. They paid for any supplies they took. Stealing from or abusing locals was punished. One of Fidel's first acts in the Sierra Maestra was to apprehend two bandits accused of rape and murder, try them, and on their conviction by a rebel court execute them. "We lined up very few people before firing squads, very few indeed, during the entire war," he said later; "we did not shoot more than ten guys in twenty-five months."[18]

On 28 May, the rebels staged their biggest operation yet, against a military post at El Uvero, on the rocky southern shore of the Sierra Maestra. The post was staffed by around seventy soldiers. According to Robert Taber, eight rebels were killed, along with about thirty soldiers. A cache of weapons and ammunition was taken. Fidel hailed it as a victory. Che did, too, noting with pleasure that after a march of ten miles and nearly three hours of fighting in the hot sun, "our bodies gave off a peculiar and offensive odor that repelled anyone who came near."[19]

Batista sent five thousand soldiers to rout out the guerrillas, and bombed the jungly slopes. But the guerrillas were difficult to hit. The bombs often killed civilians, and blew up their homes and farms. This did nothing for the regime's image. The American writer Warren Miller was in Havana during those early months of 1957. As he traveled around the city, he noted that "every sign bearing Batista's name was gouged and stained with flung filth."[20]

Washington was increasingly dissatisfied with its ambassador to Cuba, Arthur Gardner. As Bob Stevenson of the State Department put it, "He was just buddy-buddy with Batista, pictures of him with his arms around him, doing an abrazo and whatnot."[21] In July, Gardner was swapped for a financier, Earl Smith. Smith was thought to have better bipartisan links than Gardner, and the State Department sent him to be briefed by Herbert Matthews in New York so he could hear Fidel Castro's side of the story. Nonetheless, like Gardner, he was a wealthy Republican businessman with no diplomatic experience. The job in Cuba was not suited to the amateur, as Smith discovered the day he turned up in Havana to hear that three bombs had just been found in the grounds of the Hotel Nacional.

Six days later, he presented his credentials to Batista. "He impressed me as being a tough guy with bull-like strength and exuding a forceful, agreeable personality," Smith remembered. "Here was an extraordinary example of a virile man of the soil and of mixed antecedents, who had projected himself from a simple sergeant to the Presidency of his country."[22]

Smith tore himself away from the dictator's virility to travel down to the other end of the island, where he was supposed to accept the keys to the city of Santiago de Cuba.

On 30 July, the day before Smith arrived, Fidel Castro's ally and the leader of the urban underground, Frank País, was discovered in what was supposed to be a Santiago safe house by police. He was with another M-26-7 leader. The two men were chased, captured, tortured, and driven to a quiet street, where each was shot in the back of his head. It was announced that they had been killed in a shootout.

The city's people rose in fury, declaring a general strike. Despite this, Smith's ceremony went ahead. He was taken to the town hall, which faced onto Santiago's elegant cathedral square, Céspedes Park. Two hundred black-clad women had assembled, shouting: "Liberty! Liberty!" Their group was called the Mothers of Santiago, prompting Smith to observe prissily: "Many were too young to have been mothers of grown sons. They were obviously recruited for the occasion." It did not seem to occur to him that the name might be symbolic.

A few women managed to break through the cordon toward Smith. The police smashed at them with clubs. Some were knocked to the ground. Others were manhandled, dragged off, thrown into police wagons. Smith later claimed to have been "appalled" by the brutality of the police, but his first comment to the press betrayed another view: "I think it unfortunate that some of the people of Santiago de Cuba took advantage of my presence here to demonstrate and protest to their own government."

Over lunch, it was discreetly pointed out to him that this statement could imply approval of police methods. And so, afterward, he made another: "Any form of excessive police action is abhorrent to me. I deeply regret that my presence in Santiago de Cuba may have been the cause of public demonstrations which brought on police retaliation. I sincerely trust that those held by police as a result of their demonstrations have been released."[23]

This statement was still as mild as Smith could make it, but after years of Arthur Gardner the words "excessive police action," and the notion that such a thing might be abhorrent to a representative of the United States, sounded radical. Fidel's guerrillas in the mountains cheered when they heard it. Members of M-26-7 in New York hoisted a Cuban flag from the crown of the Statue of Liberty, where it flew for half an hour before the police took it down.[24] Batista was furious. His aides lobbied to have Smith recalled.

But the fuss died down, for it soon became apparent that Smith's rookie mistake would not be repeated. "They say that his wife used to play bridge with some of these Cuban ladies who were pro-Batista," said Terry Leonhardy of the State Department, "and she'd come home and he'd be sound asleep and she'd write him a note and say, 'You've got to get away from this liberal crowd and get over on Batista's side.' "[25] Soon, Washington's ambassador would again be doing an abrazo and whatnot with Cuba's dictator.

★

Haiti's election on 22 September, for a president, twenty-one senators, and thirty-seven deputies, was perhaps the freest and fairest in its history up to that point, though that was not saying much. Fourteen hundred polling booths were set up, each permitted to collect a maximum of fifteen hundred votes.

Each willing peasant or slum dweller's vote could be bought for two gourdes (forty cents). Inside the booth, an election worker clipped the nail of the voter's little finger, and dipped that finger in red ink, in an attempt to prevent repeat voting. But packing the nail with soap beforehand kept it long, and the red ink could be scrubbed off; so the enterprise continued. Four Déjoie supporters were arrested in Port-au-Prince for buying votes, but the greater effort seems to have been on Duvalier's side. On the remote Île de la Gonâve, where the voting population had been only 13,302 in the last census, 19,304 votes were cast—just 463 of them for Déjoie. Voting was even more popular in La Tortue, where 900 registered voters managed between them to cast 7,500 votes. A fight broke out in Jacmel, where troops were observed to be swapping Déjoie ballots for Duvalier ones. One person was killed.[26]

After the polls closed, Duvalier praised the military, which had supported him, and which would be allowed to help tabulate the final results. "The people present the sad spectacle of black misery in the heart of riches," he said. "This nation has sufficient wealth, but it is not properly distributed. It is the wretched condition of the masses which drove Dr. Duvalier into politics."[27]

By the time the army had finished counting, Duvalier had won a two-thirds majority from an electorate mostly so illiterate they could not read the names on the ballot paper. Déjoie had a majority only in Port-au-Prince, where he retained the support of the business community and the elite. When Duvalier's victory was declared, this community shut its shops. Duvalier used a decree from Kébreau's regime that, during a general strike, police could break into private premises and requisition their wares without compensation. But instead of the police, he summoned up his *cagoulards*, or hooded men. The cagoulards were drawn from among the poorest and most disaffected of Haiti's young black male population. They were organized and trained by Clément Barbot. This unofficial militia toured Port-au-Prince, using electrical saws to cut through the steel shutters of shops, ransacking them, and leaving them to the looters whom they openly encouraged. The shopkeepers would not attempt a shutdown again.[28]

From Washington's point of view, the neatly dressed and mild-mannered Duvalier had looked like a slightly dull middle-class conservative. "It was hard to believe he would not be open to our efforts since he was the only Latin-American dictator with some U.S. education," wrote Edwin Martin, the assistant secretary of state for inter-American affairs. (In a footnote, Martin added, "Not counting Pentagon sponsored training for several of the military ones.")[29] Duvalier seemed proud to claim American support, which he had, vocally, from an Episcopal bishop and from a senior development official. The one voice consistently raised against him was that of Ambassador Drew, who had expressed serious concerns to the State Department throughout his rise to power—though little attention had ever been paid to them.[30]

The first clear warning sign came almost immediately after the election. The wife of Shibley Talamas, an American citizen living in Haiti, went into labor after the strict curfew. Talamas ventured out to find an obstetrician. He was arrested. While he sat in a cell, his daughter was born. He was released temporarily to see her, on the condition that he would surrender afterward. Talamas visited his wife and child, and then went to the American embassy. The embassy asked the Haitian police for an assurance that he would be well treated. It was provided. Talamas duly surrendered, and was transferred to the military prison, Fort Dimanche.

At Fort Dimanche, Talamas was questioned about the murder of a sentry and four soldiers by Déjoie supporters a few hours previously. During the interrogation, he was savagely beaten, so much so that parts of him were literally reduced to pulp. When they had finished, his interrogators took him to the civilian prison. The duty officer pointed out that Talamas could not be interned, for he was now a corpse.

Outraged, American embassy officials demanded to see the body. It was shown to them, in its mangled state. With a straight face, the doctor assured them that Talamas had died naturally of a heart attack.

The United States suspended three technical aid programs and demanded a $100,000 indemnity from the Haitian government.[31] But Duvalier was not personally blamed. At a cost of $150,000 to the Haitian state, he engaged the New York public relations firm run by John Roosevelt—a conscious imitation of Trujillo's employment of John's brother, Franklin D. Roosevelt Jr.—to manage his administration's image.[32]

On 2 October, Duvalier held his first press conference. He was asked why he had been elected, and replied, with a smile, "The peasants love their Doc." He spoke about democracy, national unity, and the redistribution of wealth, but was careful to point out that this last went hand in hand with "an economic democracy." This indicated that he was no leftist. Redistribution, he implied, was a matter for the market. Further, he expressed a hope that, "like Puerto Rico," Haiti would soon become the "spoiled child" of the United States.[33]

Cash was the first need. Duvalier accepted a loan of $4 million from Batista, the man he had promised to help overthrow, secured against $7 million in deposits held privately by Haitian laborers in Cuba. This money did not pass through a Haitian government account. Nor was it ever paid back. Various intermediaries between Batista and Duvalier skimmed off $1 million, and Duvalier kept the rest. There was something in the deal for Batista, too: Duvalier would deport to Cuba any of his enemies hiding in Haiti. This started with Temístocles Fuentes, Duvalier's own terrorism manager, and the rest of Prío's people. As Arturo Espaillat, Trujillo's security chief, put it: "Some they dumped in prison, others into the sea. That was the end of Duvalier's flirtation with the Cuban revolutionary movement." Pleased, Batista decorated Duvalier with the Order of Carlos Manuel de Céspedes. Duvalier then invented the Grand Cross of Toussaint L'Ouverture to bestow upon Batista. Rolando Masferrer, head of Batista's private army, visited Port-au-Prince to reassure Duvalier that switching sides was wise, for Fidel Castro would soon be smoked out of the mountains of Oriente.[34]

For more money, Duvalier turned to Trujillo. The two signed a deal to send thirty thousand Haitian cane cutters to the Dominican Republic every year until 1963, which Duvalier altered the constitution to set as the end of his term. A joint American-Dominican inquiry that year found that Haitian contractors were paid $15 a head for "recruiting" cane cutters. Once in the Dominican Republic, the laborers were obliged to send half of their wages back to Haiti in dollars. This did not reach their families. It went straight to Duvalier, netting him an estimated $6 million to $8 million a year.[35] The laborers were threatened with violence if they left before the end of their contracts. It is paradoxical that a self-declared champion of black supremacy would choose to profit from an enterprise not far removed from slavery, but he did. Like Fidel Castro, François Duvalier understood from the very beginning that power was more important than ideology in Caribbean politics. But Fidel Castro, though ruthless, was a patriot, a man with a profound sense that it was his mission to save the Cuban people. Behind Duvalier's horn-rimmed spectacles and unblinking gaze, there was a void.

Within the first month of his presidency, Duvalier had hundreds of people who had publicly opposed his election arrested and imprisoned. These included a journalist, Pierre-Edouard Bellande, who managed to smuggle out the story of an eight-day hunger strike in which he had participated. There was a fuss, and Duvalier was obliged to release Bellande. But the affair was not forgotten. On the night of 5 January, Bellande's sister-in-law, the feminist activist Yvonne Hakim-Rimpel, was at home with her husband and eight children. Masked cagoulards broke into the house. Two of her daughters were beaten and dragged into the street. Yvonne was kidnapped, bundled into a car, and driven off into the night.

The car drove Yvonne to a lonely field in Delmas, a suburb of Port-au-Prince. She was shoved out and faced a group of men: she counted nine. These included Elois Maitre, a baker, and François Duvalier himself, in military uniform. The cagoulards who had brought her stripped her in front of this council and proceeded, one by one, to rape her. It is not clear whether Duvalier was among the rapists. Finally, she was beaten almost to the point of unconsciousness, and kicked into a ditch.

Above her, she heard Duvalier's voice: "Now finish her off."

"Let me," insisted Maitre. A gun cocked. Yvonne felt bullets thud into the earth beside her. Later, she would wonder whether he had saved her life deliberately. "She's as dead as she'll ever be," said Maitre. "Come on, men. Let's get out of here."

There followed a long silence, in which Yvonne did not dare to move. Finally, she crawled out of the ditch. Searching the field, she found her torn nightgown and one slipper with which to clothe herself. In great pain, she limped to a nearby house and banged on the door. A peasant woman opened it. She took one look at Yvonne, bruised, dazed, and covered in dirt, and screamed, "Zombie! Zombie!" The door slammed in her face.

Yvonne limped to another house. This time, the inhabitant feared earthly repercussions. "Go away! You're putting me into terrible danger!" Another door slammed. Yvonne collapsed by the side of the road. Fortunately, she was found by an acquaintance, who drove to a hospital and wisely registered her under a false name. She stayed in the hospital for three months, guarded twenty-four hours a day by her family.

Another of Yvonne's brothers-in-law, Antonio Rimpel, was Duvalier's finance minister. The family begged him to intervene. "There's nothing I can do," he said, and advised that they all stay quiet about what had happened.[36]

From among the cagoulards, Barbot began to organize a more formal militia. The men—and occasional women—who joined it would be known as the Tontons Macoutes. Tonton Macoute (Uncle Knapsack) was a Vodou bogeyman, said to snatch naughty children and bundle them into a sack. Dressed in dark blue denim, with pistols on their hips and dark glasses permanently obscuring their eyes, the Macoutes played up to rumors that they were zombies, mute killing machines raised from the dead by Duvalier's magic.

Duvalier denied in an American radio interview that the Macoutes existed. "I have never heard them mentioned, except in the American press," he said. "They do not exist in reality." But exist they did. Their proud master, Barbot, had business cards printed describing himself as the chief of secret police—though, on realizing that this spoiled the secret, he soon stopped giving them out.[37]

★

On 5 September, there was a naval mutiny at the Cuban port of Cienfuegos. Batista sent in the army with tanks, and the air force bombed the city. "The slaughter which occurred was incredible," wrote Ruby Hart Phillips of the *New York Times*. "Houses were strafed, innocent people in the streets were killed."[38] Some pilots refused to bomb civilian areas, and released their bombs into the sea. They were court-martialed and sentenced to six years' imprisonment each. Batista imposed blanket censorship, and prevented American journalists from reaching the town. Estimates of the civilian death toll stood between one hundred and four hundred.

The excesses of the Batista regime were beginning to deter tourists, but substantial numbers still flocked to Cuba, including a young senator from Massachusetts, John F. Kennedy. At Christmastime 1957, Kennedy and his fellow senator George Smathers went to Havana to visit Earl Smith, a friend of the Kennedy family and sometime beau of Kennedy's mother, Rose. Like so many other tourists, they had a wonderful time in this tropical playground, drinking daiquiris, smoking cigars, and enjoying the nightlife. "Kennedy wasn't a great casino man," remembered Smathers, "but the Tropicana nightclub had a floor show you wouldn't believe."[39]

John Fitzgerald Kennedy, known as Jack, had grown up as the second son in a large and privileged Boston family, under the rule of a tirelessly ambitious duumvirate: Joseph and Rose Kennedy. After Jack, there were seven more children. Were it not for a series of untimely deaths, the family might have produced four presidents in a single generation—for Joe Jr. was meant to be set on that path, and in later years both Bobby and Ted would come close to clinching the Democratic nomination.

The Kennedy patriarch, Joe Sr., made little secret of his preference for his eldest son, Joe Jr., but all the children were coached for success. "We don't want any losers around here. In this family we want winners," said Joe Sr. But while Joe Jr. thrived, Jack ailed. At various points, he was diagnosed with scarlet fever, appendicitis, hepatitis, agranulocytosis, leukemia, anemia, and bouts of hives that required hospitalization. Some of these diagnoses turned out to be false alarms, but a large proportion of his youth was spent in captive isolation, convalescing.[40]

Jack intended to follow Joe to the London School of Economics, but again his health failed him. After only three weeks, he returned to the United States. He enrolled at Princeton, but after six weeks had to be hospitalized again. The following year, he tried Harvard. Friends remembered him gulping down pints of raw cream on doctors' orders, but he remained skinny and fragile.

Jack wanted to be a journalist. His father had different ideas, as the historian John Wheeler-Bennett noted on meeting the family in 1938. "I'll tell you about these boys," Joe Sr. had said in front of his brood as if, Wheeler-Bennett thought, they could not hear him. "There's young Joe, he's going to be president of the United States; and there's Jack, he's going to be a university president; and there's Bobby, he's the lawyer."[41]

In 1940, Jack published his Harvard thesis on the failures of British policy to prevent the Second World War. Titled *Why England Slept*, it became an instant best seller, and abruptly alerted Joe Sr. to his second son's value. Suddenly, Jack mattered. At the end of that year, the bombing of Pearl Harbor dragged the United States into World War II. Joe Jr. wrote to his father peevishly announcing his intention to join the Navy Air Corps: "As far as the family is concerned, it seems that Jack is perfectly capable to do everything, if by chance anything happened to me."[42]

Jack's health would have barred him from service had his father not pulled a few strings. In August 1941, he joined the navy. Two years later, his patrol torpedo boat was in the South Pacific when a Japanese destroyer rammed it. The impact broke the boat in two, killing two men and leaving the rest clinging to the wreckage in a dark and dangerous sea.

Jack ordered his men to swim for a nearby island. The ship's engineer had been badly burned and was too weak to make it. Jack took the ties of the man's lifejacket between his teeth, and dragged him for five hours until they reached the shore. The men were presumed missing in action, and were stranded on the island for five days before they were rescued. When they were, Jack became a national hero.[43]

A few weeks later, at his father's birthday party, Joe Jr. was heard to weep in anguish at being surpassed again by his younger brother.[44] In August 1944, he volunteered to pilot a plane filled with explosives over a missile launch site in France. He was to switch the plane to remote control before reaching the site, then parachute out. Over the Suffolk coast, the explosives were accidentally triggered. Joe Jr.'s plane blew up, killing him and his copilot instantly. His body was never found.

The formidable engine of the Kennedy family now rumbled into life behind Jack, and he was maneuvered into Joe's designated profession: politics. He was twenty-nine when he made his debut on the national stage, entering the House of Representatives in the place that, had that plane not exploded, would have been Joe's. Jack was thirty-five when he graduated to the Senate, and forty-two when he announced he was running for president. His campaigns were bankrolled by immense reserves of family money.

Tagging along with Jack was one of his younger brothers, Bobby, who had become a lawyer as his father decreed. Bobby was eight years younger than Jack, and the seventh of the nine Kennedy children: a small noise in a big family, and one who compensated by becoming loud. Though vocal in his opinions—which, during the 1950s, were conservative and even McCarthyite—he was thought by most of his contemporaries to lack Jack's intellectual sophistication and easygoing wit. "Bobby was the most vulnerable human being I have ever known," wrote one journalist who knew him well. "He was also the most outraged."[45]

Bobby saw Jack, flaws and all, as a hero. Sold though Jack was as the embodiment of uncorrupted, youthful vigor, there were sides to him that were carefully hidden from the public. He had eventually been diagnosed with Addison's disease, a serious endocrine disorder that can cause exhaustion, physical weakness, and mood swings, and was subjected to a series of risky operations. A range of supplementary medical conditions required regular attention.

His high-profile marriage to Jacqueline Bouvier had been in trouble from the honeymoon, which he had suggested that she leave early so he could spend a few days enjoying himself. Jack's infidelity was compulsive and perpetual. When Jackie was scheduled for a Cesarean delivery of their first child, he left on a sailing trip with a group of friends. The baby was stillborn. It was three days before Jack could be contacted on his yacht, and, in the meantime, Bobby stepped in to arrange the burial. Even when Jack heard the news, he saw no reason to rush to his wife's side, and had to be ordered to do so by his furious father. For the first but not the last time, Jackie threatened divorce.[46]

Though Kennedy was seen as a rising political star by 1957, his opinions were not entirely clear. His voting record in the House of Representatives was a mix. "His political philosophy was very unformed," said Theodore Sorensen, his speechwriter. "He acknowledged that himself, I believe. So that to some extent I was writing on a clean slate."[47] In the early days of the Cuban Revolution, like many Americans, he expressed approval of Fidel Castro. "From the beginning many, including Senator Kennedy and others argued that Castro was a new Bolivar," Eisenhower remembered. "Now, along with this, all of us hated the government of Batista, who had been a dictator and had used the methods of a Hitler to retain his power. All this was a confusing situation. We did know that one man, Che Guevara, and Castro's brother, Raul Castro had both been into Communist areas, and we were pretty certain they were Communists. But all the time the problem was, is this a Communist movement, or is it an actual liberation of a country?"[48]

That was the question of the day. On 12 July 1957, Fidel had released the Manifesto of the Sierra Maestra, calling for civil liberties, free elections, redistribution of barren lands with compensation for their owners, literacy, and industrialization. It was marginally left of center, but a long way from being communist. In October, at Fidel's direction, a Liberation Council was established in Miami consisting of M-26-7; the Ortodoxos; Prío's Auténticos; the Revolutionary Directorate, now led by a recovering Faure Chomón; and various student and trade unions. The communists of the PSP were not invited. In December, Fidel abandoned the Liberation Council over various policy squabbles. His action was prompted not by ideological differences, but by the growing sense that M-26-7 was powerful enough to go it alone.[49] Inside the movement itself, there was considerable anticommunism. M-26-7's leader in Miami was Felipe Pazos, a centrist economist. Carlos Franqui, later the movement's official biographer, wrote at the time: "Our differences with the Communists [PSP] are insurmountable; it's better that way, for they are contaminated with the 'Soviet virus.' And the Cuban people are right in not supporting them, not merely because of their ideology but because of their history."[50] Most of all, Fidel himself consistently rejected communism. "I have never been and am not a communist," he declared. "If I were, I should have the courage to say it." He told an American journalist that nationalization was "a clumsy instrument." In front of a Spanish journalist reporting for *Paris-Match*, he went further: "I hate Soviet imperialism as much as Yankee imperialism! I'm not breaking my neck fighting one dictatorship to fall into the hands of another."[51]

Communist views were accurately ascribed to Raúl and Che. "They attack me personally, just as they do Che," Raúl wrote to Fidel; "as for you, on the other hand, they say they don't believe you're a Communist." A letter Raúl wrote to Che was intercepted by the regime, and read out on a pro-Batista radio show. Raúl confessed to Fidel that the letter had been intercepted, hoping to preempt a familiar dressing-down from his older brother. "I didn't talk about Stalin or any other damn thing in it," he protested.[52]

Raúl was summoned to Fidel's camp to receive the dressing-down anyway. "When he gets here I'll shoot him!" Fidel shouted. "I don't care a fuck if he *is* my brother! I'll shoot him!" Celia Sánchez talked him down, and managed to convince him that shooting Raúl was not necessary. Nonetheless, when Raúl arrived, Fidel forced him to promise never to write to Che about politics again.[53]

The State Department asked Homer Bigart, a *New York Times* journalist visiting Fidel in the Sierra Maestra, to sound out M-26-7. He detected a general sense of unease among the revolutionaries about Che's politics. Che told Bigart he was a liberal, and added various criticisms about American imperialism. Bigart asked Fidel why he allowed Che, a foreigner and an extreme leftist, to remain in the movement. Fidel replied that Che's medical skills had initially been an asset, and he had turned out to be a skilled fighter and leader. "He stated flatly that he, Castro, was the supreme commander of the movement. Hence, he added, it really made little difference what Guevara's political beliefs were, since Castro determined policy."[54]

In Mexico, Raúl and Che had openly declared their communism. Now, Fidel was keeping them on a tight leash. Cubans had lived with communists in their government for almost two decades, and were not unduly troubled by their existence as a minority party. But few in M-26-7 wanted to risk a confrontation with the United States, and all knew how sensitive its government was to the slightest whiff of leftism. Raúl and Che were Fidel's two most reliable lieutenants. From a strategic point of view, it would have been madness to purge them, as Bigart apparently suggested. At the same time, Fidel knew their politics could damage his own reputation. The best policy was to shut them up: though, between Che's uncontainable honesty and Raúl's bullish independence, that was never easy. Raúl, too, publicly denied that he was a communist, and claimed to be a follower of José Martí like his brother. When it was put to him that Batista claimed the Castros were communists, Raúl snapped, "What does surprise me is the attention that is given to this matter, when everyone knows he doesn't do anything but repeat stupid accusations like a parrot."[55]

Batista devoted much time to telling Earl Smith that Fidel was a communist and part of an international conspiracy. The inexperienced Smith, who was not aware that this was what right-wing Latin American dictators routinely said about their opponents, credulously reported everything Batista told him back to Washington, where it was followed up.[56] "We were urged to leave no stone unturned in the effort to ascertain Castro's Marxist-Leninist proclivities—or lack of them," remembered Wayne Smith, then in the State Department's Bureau of Intelligence and Research. "We found no credible evidence to indicate Castro had links to the Communist party or even had much sympathy for it. Even so, he gave cause for concern, for he seemed to have gargantuan ambitions, authoritarian tendencies, and not much in the way of an ideology of his own."[57] That assessment was accurate, and would go a long way to explaining Fidel's past and future behavior.

Fidel was exasperated by the communist rumors, including a particularly far-fetched one in a British magazine that claimed the Soviets were sending him troops in submarines. "The magazine is very badly informed," he wrote, tongue in cheek. "The Russian reinforcements are received by means of remote-controlled intercontinental projectiles, and moreover, the little Russian dog 'Laika' is on the Sierra Maestra, and they haven't mentioned that." The American consulate in Santiago judged that Fidel was more outlaw hero than political icon: "his exploits were considered to be those of a latter-day Robin Hood." His adventures thrilled the town's youth, and even provided "vicarious pleasure to older and less daring Santiagueros."[58] It was widely feared by Fidel's own supporters that their bourgeois, militaristic leader might, were he given the chance, impose a right-wing dictatorship.

On 13 February 1958, the United States threw a sop to Batista. Carlos Prío was belatedly imprisoned in Miami on an old charge: conspiracy to violate American neutrality by funding armed expeditions operating from American territory. Though they had taken his money, the rebels in the Sierra Maestra had no affection for Prío. But with every removal of a figure from the center or right of the Cuban opposition, and every gesture that looked supportive of Batista, the United States shifted the Cuban rebel movement a little farther to the left.

★

At first, the need to establish control had obliged François Duvalier to keep the official army on his side. But as his Tontons Macoutes grew stronger, this need shrank away. General Kébreau, who a few months earlier could credibly have been called the most powerful man in Haiti, had been displaced. This truth eventually dawned on him when Duvalier gave an interview to the *New York Times* on 5 March 1958, declaring that he himself was "constitutionally and in fact" commander in chief of the armed forces.

A week later, Kébreau was on the road to Pétionville when, in the distance, he heard a thirteen-gun salute. He deduced that this signified the appointment of a new head of the armed forces. Immediately, he turned his car and headed for the Dominican embassy by a back road. Four days later he appeared in Ciudad Trujillo, enjoying the hospitality of Rafael Trujillo. The Generalissimo gave him a medal and a Mercedes-Benz car, and addressed him as "President Kébreau," in the hope he would go back and stage a coup.[59]

That same month, Duvalier gave the most public demonstration yet of his aptitude for terror. Bel-Air was one of Port-au-Prince's most deprived slums. It was also a traditional base for supporters of a former president, Daniel Fignolé—once Duvalier's ally, and now his enemy. There was a shrine at the corner of the Rue du Peuple and the Rue des Remparts, with a wooden cross and a large bronze statue of a cockerel. Every week, local people came to worship at the spot.

One day in March, without warning or explanation, a man turned up to hack the statue and the cross off their bases and haul them away. When he was gone, a team of workmen turned up and dug an enormous pit on the site, ten feet deep. They left policemen to guard it.

As night fell, the locals retreated into their homes. At 10:00 PM, soldiers arrived to redouble the guard. All around Bel-Air, locals peeped at the former shrine through the cracks in their rickety houses. Finally, three trucks drove up. According to Albert Salas, a local resident who was watching, they were full of men, women, and children—dozens of them, including uniformed police officers. Every one was tightly bound and gagged.

The trucks backed up against the pit. Men in civilian clothes jumped out and began shoving and dragging the passengers into the deep hole.

Even through the gags, their muffled screams could be heard. When it was full, another team of workmen arrived, and began shoveling clods of earth back over the living bodies. Slowly, as the pit filled up, the screams became softer and softer, until they could not be heard at all. Cement was poured and leveled over the top, until the pit was smoothed over. At last, the man who seemed to be in charge walked to the center of the wet cement and plunged something down. It was the old wooden cross.

Duvalier ordered the event, but no one knew why. The victims of this massacre were never identified. Perhaps it was simply a demonstration of power; but many wondered whether it was also a sacrifice to malignant spirits.[60] A Catholic priest declared the spot to be satanic. Duvalier had deliberately created the impression that he was using Vodou for evil ends: what Haitians called *magie noire*, black magic. Most of Haiti's population was deeply religious, and this made a profound impression.

In the middle of all of this, General Lemuel Shepherd Jr., the chairman of the Inter-American Defense Board, visited Haiti to meet Duvalier. Shepherd recommended to the State Department that efforts should be made to retrain the Haitian army to perform police functions, with the United States Marines in an advisory capacity. At the end of March, Duvalier's foreign minister arranged to send three army officers to the United States, to begin negotiations for an American military mission in Port-au-Prince.[61]

★

In Cuba, rebels cut electric cables, pulled down telephone poles, and burned factories. The urban underground was setting bombs on a daily basis. The State Department received an inquiry from George H. W. Bush, then merely president of the Zapata Offshore Company, who was worried about Cuban rebels attacking his oil rig.[62]

On 12 March, Fidel declared "total war," and said he had columns moving out from the Sierra Maestra. Raúl was sent east to the Sierra del Cristal, the mountains surrounding the area in which the Castro brothers had grown up, to set up a second front. Juan Almeida and Che were put in command of further columns.

In total, Fidel still commanded only around two hundred guerrillas, and the heaviest weapon wielded by Raúl's sixty-five troops was a .30-caliber Browning automatic rifle.[63] Against this, Batista had forty thousand well-armed and -supplied men. Worse still, Fidel's supply network was patchy and disorganized. He wrote to Che that he was desperately short of bullets, but some of the restocks he had requested had been sent to Almeida by mistake, and the rest had been lost. "This is a complete fuck-up," he complained. "When you're ready to attack, they tell you the bullets are a thousand miles away."[64] He had also called a general strike, to be focused in Havana, on 9 April. In response, Batista suspended constitutional guarantees.

This routine act seemed to prompt a surprise reaction on 14 March, when the United States announced a suspension of arms sales to Batista's government. Foster Dulles was in the Philippines at the time. The chief of inter-American affairs, Dick Rubottom, was on vacation. Both opposed a suspension. It has been suggested that in their absence Bill Snow, Rubottom's deputy, made the decision on his own.[65] Arms sales had been delayed, though not cut off, for the previous few months. According to State Department documents, seven requests from Batista were still pending, of which four had been recommended for approval. These included ammunition for Batista's navy, specifically said to be for controlling "small boats which are suspected of carrying arms to rebel groups, including that of Fidel Castro."[66]

This mention of Fidel's group was significant, for arms were supposedly being supplied under the Military Assistance Program (MAP). This program granted ordnance and training to foreign leaders for the alleged sole purpose of external defense. Military aid to Batista's regime under MAP had risen from $400,000 in 1953 to $3 million in 1958. But the mention of Fidel makes it clear that American arms were being sold to Batista in the knowledge that they would be used to defend his regime against internal dissent. The suspension was justified partly by the belated enforcement of MAP terms.[67]

Batista did not have to buy his weaponry from the United States. "The United States sells them to Somoza and Trujillo," Fidel said on Radio Rebelde, the guerrilla radio station. "Somoza and Trujillo sell them to Batista."[68] That was not entirely fair; the United States had, at the same time, stopped granting licenses to sell arms to the Dominican Republic.[69] It was true that Batista still bought arms from Trujillo, and Trujillo smuggled them from the United States. But the arms stoppage did have a psychological effect. Good relations with Washington had been a crucial reason that the army and business leaders had continued to tolerate Batista. With relations deteriorating, that base began to fall away.

Fidel's general strike was supposed to represent a united coalition against Batista, including the Revolutionary Directorate, Prío's Auténticos, and M-26-7. Again, Fidel refused to accept the support of communist labor leaders.[70] Nonetheless, unity proved elusive. The rebels in Havana suspected that the rebels in the mountains were hoarding weapons, and at the last minute the Auténticos pulled out.[71] The urban underground's network turned out to be less reliable than it had thought. "There never really was a revolution, anyway," Batista told American journalists, as the coalition fell apart, "just a lot of fuss by a bunch of communists." They asked about Fidel Castro. "We must kill him," the dictator said. "He cannot be allowed to live."[72]

The ninth of April came, and with it some shutdowns and disorder. Forty youths were killed in street fighting. But Batista's intelligence service, and the police, had prepared an efficient response. By sunset, public order had been restored, without much inconvenience to the regime. Cuba had not come to a standstill, as the rebels had hoped. The great national uprising had flopped.

Fidel Castro had staked much on the strike. To Celia, he wrote angrily, "I am the supposed leader of this Movement, and in the eyes of history I must take responsibility for the stupidity of others, and I am a shit who can decide on nothing at all."[73] The day after the strike, a *New York Times* reporter found out that not only had the communists stood aloof from Fidel's strike, but they had actually helped sabotage it for Batista. Asked why, one replied: "Well, you didn't see any Communists getting killed yesterday. We keep our heads."[74]

"I expected a Waterloo," joked Batista afterward, "but what happened was a Dunkirk."[75] Batista's allegory would turn out to be more accurate than he intended. The Allies did indeed lose at Dunkirk. But, though they lost that battle, they went on to win the war.

6

"THE MINDS OF UNSOPHISTICATED PEOPLES"

★

IN THE FIRST FEW YEARS OF HIS LEADERSHIP, NIKITA KHRUSHCHEV had championed the third world, touring India, Burma, and Afghanistan, and supporting Egypt in the Suez Crisis. In May 1958, partly as a response, Dwight D. Eisenhower's administration decided to send their man to tour Latin America.[1] The man they chose was the vice president, Richard Nixon.

"The CIA had warned that although the Communist Party had been officially suppressed in most South American countries, I might have to face occasional demonstrators," Nixon wrote.[2] There were small protests against his presence in Uruguay, Argentina, and Colombia. In the Peruvian capital, Lima, there was a larger one. Crowds at San Marcos University shouted, "Go home, Nixon!" and "Death to Nixon!"

Nixon shouted back. Remembering the events in his memoirs, he wrote, oxymoronically, "I had full control of my temper as I lashed out at the mob." They responded by throwing rocks, one of which hit a secret service man in the face. "You are cowards," bellowed the vice president, as he was dragged away by his handlers; "you are afraid of the truth!" When he reached his hotel, he was confronted by a man he described as "one of the most notorious Communist agitators in Lima." The man spat at him. "I felt an almost uncontrollable urge to tear the face in front of me to pieces," Nixon confessed. Spotting that the vice president was again in full control of his temper, his security men pulled him aside. "I at least had the satisfaction of planting a healthy kick on his shins," wrote Nixon. "Nothing I did all day made me feel better."[3]

But it was in Venezuela, where a decade-long American-sponsored dictatorship had come to an end just months before, that the protests were most dramatic. As soon as Nixon and his wife alighted from their plane at Caracas, demonstrators yelled, "Get out, dog!" and "We won't forget Guatemala!" The Nixons proceeded to the terminal, and the vice president felt a light spattering of rain. He glanced up, and realized the crowd gathered on the observation deck above was spitting on him and Mrs. Nixon: "I saw Pat's bright red suit grow dark with tobacco-brown splotches."[4]

The Nixons were transferred to a car, inside which the embarrassed foreign minister of Venezuela offered his handkerchief. "Don't bother," snapped Nixon. "I am going to burn these clothes as soon as I can get out of them." The minister groveled. "If your new government doesn't have the guts and good sense to control a mob like the one at the airport," Nixon told him, "there soon will be no freedom for anyone in Venezuela."

The official party was supposed to drive to the Pantheon, where Nixon was to lay a wreath on the tomb of the liberator of Latin America, Simón Bolívar. But in the suburb of Catia the car was brought to a halt by a crowd several hundred strong, who began to beat it with wooden clubs and sections of iron pipe. Stones smashed against the reinforced glass windows, sending splinters flying through the interior. The foreign minister was hit in the eye by a shard. He moaned, and bled copiously. Another shard nicked the skin of Nixon's temple. A secret service agent drew his revolver, but Nixon remembered telling him not to shoot: "Once a gun went off the crowd would go berserk and that would be the end of us."[5]

Twelve terrifying minutes later, Nixon's wrecked car finally drove out of the mob. A block before the Pantheon, the driver abruptly swerved into a side street. According to *Time* magazine's report, "Nixon could see a mob of 3,000 rioters, mostly high school students, waiting for him."[6] The wreath-laying was abandoned, lest it turn into another funeral. Nixon's car sped back to the residence of the American ambassador.

Eisenhower ordered a rescue mission, and one thousand American troops assembled at Guantánamo Bay for "Operation Poor Richard." Venezuela's junta sent four hundred of its own soldiers to guard the ambassadorial residence. The next day they accompanied the vice president through streets heavily fogged with tear gas back to the airport. He was put back on a plane and evacuated to Puerto Rico.[7]

Nixon blamed the trouble on what he called "the international Communist conspiracy." An official in the State Department reported to Foster Dulles that "the pattern of organization and of slogans in all cases points to Communist inspiration and direction, as do certain of the intelligence reports."[8] In fact, the CIA found no evidence that the Soviet Union had been connected in any way to the events in Lima or Caracas, and Allen Dulles sharply disagreed with Nixon's statement that it did. It is hard to imagine that the crowd of three thousand schoolchildren described by *Time* were all Soviet-indoctrinated Marxist-Leninists. Perhaps it was possible even for noncommunists to dislike Dick Nixon. In Cuba, the writer Carlos Franqui—a committed anticommunist—wrote proudly that "the Venezuelans had not forgotten Pérez Jiménez with his North American medals."[9] Both Venezuela's fallen dictator, and Peru's, had been awarded the Legion of Merit by Eisenhower.

By the time Nixon arrived back in Washington, his opinion of Latin Americans had taken on the tenor of Teddy Roosevelt's. On 22 May, he told the National Security Council that "the southern continent" appeared to be moving as one toward democratic government. "Normally we would hail such a development," he told them, "but we should realize that such a development may not always be in each country the best of all possible courses, particularly in those Latin American countries which are completely lacking in political maturity." He claimed to have spoken to all the "new political types," and observed that not one among them was upper-class or wealthy. This, it seemed, was a problem. "Being the kind of men they are, they are very naive about the nature and threat of Communism, so much so that their attitude is frightening. They regard the Communists as nothing more than a duly-constituted political party."[10]

Foster Dulles developed this idea at a later meeting of the National Security Council. He pointed to the electoral college system in the United States as evidence that the Founding Fathers had believed that even Americans required guidance in the safe practice of democracy. "Unlike ourselves, many of the Latin American states are leaping ahead to irresponsible self-government directly out of a semi-colonial status," he explained. "This presents the Communists with an ideal situation to exploit." According to the minutes, Dulles then "launched into a vivid account of the skill with which the Communists operate in this field and stated that we were hopelessly far behind the Soviets in developing controls over the minds and emotions of unsophisticated peoples."[11] Allen Dulles attempted to take issue with his brother's argument, but Eisenhower moved the conversation on.

Ike observed thoughtfully that there was a problem with the "use of the term 'capitalism,' which means one thing to us, [but] clearly meant to much of the rest of the world something synonymous with imperialism." He suggested to the National Security Council that "we should try to coin a new phrase to represent our own modern brand of capitalism."[12] Nicer words for capitalism were soon found. By calling it "free enterprise," the "free world," or simply "freedom," it was possible to reframe the debate so that the concentration of capital in private hands appeared to be a token of liberation, rather than, as Marx and his followers saw it, the cause of oppression.

After Nixon's trip, several senators argued that military aid to Latin America should be stopped. Supporting dictators, they argued, had damaged the reputation of the United States. John F. Kennedy disagreed with these senators, and said that such aid was necessary to maintain American influence over the Latin American armed forces. He conceded that it was "down the drain in a military sense," and had no practical use against the Soviets.[13] As usual, Rafael Trujillo was alert to any threat to his own comfortable arrangement. On 8 June, he funded a lengthy report in the *Herald Tribune* on the delights of the Dominican Republic. One article was titled "No Time for Communism"; it dusted off the aged story of the arrival of refugees from the Spanish Civil War in the Dominican Republic, alleging that they had been "thoroughly indoctrinated propagandists," deliberately sent "by the boatload" to cause mischief. With pride, it concluded that Trujillo's regime refused to tolerate them.[14]

François Duvalier, too, sought to present himself as a champion of anticommunism. Before his election, he had enjoyed the support of a few communists, including the intellectuals René Depestre and Jacques Stephen Alexis. But he had always rejected the idea of a class struggle in favor of a race struggle, and now he positioned himself firmly to the right. A bomb factory exploded at Mahotières. It was claimed as an anti-Duvalier plot, though some said it was a setup, planned by Duvalier himself. It allowed him to ban the May Day trade unions rally—the beginning of a crackdown on the unions that would see them broken within two years—and on 2 May to declare a state of siege. His opponents in the last election, Louis Déjoie and Clément Jumelle, were branded outlaws. Jumelle had already gone into hiding. Déjoie now absconded to the Mexican embassy. Duvalier then offered the United States a missile base on Haitian soil. The communists were thoroughly alienated. Both Depestre and Alexis would become fierce opponents of Duvalier in exile.[15]

At the same time, Duvalier sent three officers to Washington to continue negotiations for a United States Marine mission, and to purchase weapons. The Department of Defense was keen, but Gerald Drew, the American ambassador in Port-au-Prince, was not. "I find myself . . . increasingly repelled by the thought of a mission here when the jails are crammed with political prisoners," he wrote; "when defeated candidates . . . are beaten, tortured and hounded into exile; when a restrained opposition press has been ruthlessly snuffed out of existence; and when masked night riders . . . operate from their headquarters in the National Palace."[16] Drew advised that the United States should demand better behavior from Duvalier if it gave him military assistance. The Department of Defense ignored him, and offered Duvalier a full fifty-man mission, to arrive that June.

★

In Cuba, despite the public cessation of arms sales to Fulgencio Batista, arms kept arriving. The Department of Defense had sent three hundred rocket heads to Batista before the sales suspension. They were the wrong ones, and did not fit Batista's rockets. The error was discovered after the suspension, and Batista requested the correct heads. Someone in the Department of Defense seems naively to have assumed that returned merchandise would not violate the suspension. Batista received a new set of rocket heads.

The evidence suggests this was a genuine mistake. It may well have been, but it was compounded by Washington's slowness to react when Batista began bombing Cuban civilians with the arms it had sent. It was no secret that he was using American weapons, and the United States' silence on the matter looked like complicity.

"When I saw the rockets that they fired on Mario's house, I swore that the Americans are going to pay dearly for what they're doing," an exhausted and miserable Fidel Castro wrote bitterly to Celia Sánchez. "When this war is over, I'll start a much longer and bigger war of my own: the war I'm going to fight against them. I realize that will be my true destiny."[17]

With American bombs exploding all over the country, it was difficult for even the most pro-yanqui Cuban to maintain a positive view. Ambassador Smith was not helping. To the rebels, his support of Batista looked like proof that the United States was on the side of the dictator. In fact, Smith was at odds with most of the staff of his own embassy, but neither the State Department nor the Cuban rebels knew this. Anti-Americanism ballooned. In an impassioned letter that week, Raúl Castro reported that he had heard an officer of Batista's army during a skirmish shouting, "Advance, you cowards, it doesn't matter if a hundred of you die, we survivors will be able to have more girls to rape in Bayate!"

Raúl was outraged. "Almost all of them are drunk, perhaps some are on marijuana, and they're a bunch of crooks!" he wrote. "They rape, murder, and rob. Their planes hurl firebombs, delivered to them by the Yankees, from their naval base at Guantánamo, as has happened these past few days, and the Yankees order Trujillo and Somoza to give arms to Batista. While here, the cream of our youth die with a miserable rifle in their hands. These monstrous crimes must be revealed to the entire world."[18]

A week and a half after sending this letter, Raúl's patience ran out. On the evening of 26 June, his Second Front stormed the premises of the Moa Bay Mining Company. They took ten American and two Canadian engineers captive, and vanished back into the hills. The next evening, they struck again, ambushing a bus just outside the Guantánamo Bay base. Raúl now held forty-three Americans and three Canadians, including eleven marines and thirteen other naval personnel. The kidnappings coincided with M-26-7's release of the requisition form for the rocket heads to the press.[19]

The attacks seem to have been planned independently by Raúl and the radical guerrilla Vilma Espín, then his girlfriend and later his wife. Fidel neither knew nor approved. He found out when the Cuban government announced the news on the radio on 28 June, and refused to believe it. When it was confirmed, he was furious.

Park Wollam, the American vice-consul at Santiago, was authorized to contact the rebels directly. On 29 June, having been assured by Batista that the Cuban air force would cease bombing while American hostages were held, he traveled by jeep into the hills. Messages had to be sent ahead to ensure safe passage through rebel checkpoints. At one, the message had not arrived. Wollam was briefly held up by men with shotguns. "He didn't speak Spanish until the moment I told him he was under arrest," remembered Manuel Fajardo, a rebel.

"That is very serious, that is very serious. Do you know what you are doing?" asked Wollam. Fajardo replied that he did, and that what was even more serious was that Wollam's government was still selling arms to Batista. They argued for a while, until, according to Fajardo, "I brought him a bottle of Bacardi, and we began to talk in a more friendly way."

Wollam asked about the rebel army's ideology, and Fajardo confirmed that they were revolutionary nationalists. What, asked Wollam, would Fajardo do if the Soviet Union sent him weapons?

"I told him that I would take arms from Russia without reservations," said Fajardo, "and from him, too, if he sent any."[20]

Eventually, Wollam was permitted to continue. He had reached a wooden Baptist church when he noticed a Cuban plane in the sky. Having received Batista's guarantee, he thought nothing of it—but the plane opened fire with its machine guns. A service had been in progress at the church. The faithful scattered for cover. Wollam plunged into a pigsty.

"Call them off!!!!" he scrawled shakily on his yellow notepad. "Keep other planes out of area. . . . These were some near misses. If we get hurt—it is this! . . . For the safety [of] all [and] any Americans, if nothing else—get them stopped?"[21] Finally, the plane disappeared, and Wollam forwarded his note to Moa. It was relayed to Smith, who relayed it to the Cuban government. The raids were, for the moment, stopped.

Wollam emerged from the pigsty and continued his journey, meeting several hostages at houses along the way. They had been well fed, and given beer, rum, and cigars. Their captors had taken them on jeep tours to show them bomb damage, and had allowed them swimming excursions. Several expressed their sympathy with the rebel cause. The commander at Guantánamo Bay was affronted by his fellow Americans' readiness to get into the Caribbean spirit, and said crossly that hostages ought not be "enjoying life" and "drinking beer." The following day, Raúl kidnapped six more from a United Fruit Company operation and the Nicaro nickel plant.[22]

Though the captives were enjoying life and drinking beer, the publicity for M-26-7 in the United States was terrible, and Fidel was mortified. Allen Dulles thought that the kidnappings were probably an attempt to force an American intervention. He did not recommend that course, but the part of the documents in which he suggested other strategies to ensure the hostages' release remains classified. At a press conference on 1 July, he said, "I can't think of anything that would be worse than, in effect, to pay blackmail to get people out."[23]

That day, Wollam met the man and woman responsible. Raúl and Vilma turned up in a jeep, and talked with the vice-consul for four hours. They settled on two demands: that the American base at Guantánamo Bay would not be used in any way to aid Batista's forces, and that no more arms be supplied to Batista. Both of these were already in theory American policy. Wollam accepted. Raúl told him to send for a helicopter: five hostages would be released immediately. At the last minute, he slipped Wollam a third demand in writing, asking for an American delegate to be embedded with the Second Front to monitor Batista's use of American military aid. Wollam took the note without comment. Smith would later refuse this request, on the grounds that it would violate Cuban sovereignty. He also cabled to Washington, "Wollam says he is sure there are Communists in the group," which was a considerable exaggeration of what Wollam had told him. Later, he was obliged to admit that the released Americans "describe Raul Castro's men as extremely religious, anti-Communist and ultra super-nationalist."[24]

On 3 July, too late to make much difference, a press release was issued by the American government admitting the accidental dispatch of the rocket heads to Batista over a month before. The same day, Fidel broadcast an appeal to his own brother on Radio Rebelde. The North Americans must be released, he said. It was their government, not the citizens, who sold weapons to Batista. Raúl did not comply. The following day, 4 July, Raúl's Second Front threw an American Independence Day party. There was a hog roast and a baseball game, which was interrupted during the seventh inning by another air raid. (Batista's guarantee had, apparently, expired again.) The score stood at Rebels 10, Invited Guests 4.[25]

Raúl continued to seek direct negotiations with the Americans. He wrote to the American embassy, and asked that the State Department publicly declare its adherence to his two initial terms: the use of Guantánamo and the cessation of all arms sales. If Smith met him to talk, he said, he would release all the remaining hostages. Smith refused point-blank. When it was suggested that Fidel be brought in to reason with Raúl, Smith protested that a United States Navy helicopter would have to be used to bring the brothers together—and that would upset Batista.[26]

By 9 July, Raúl and Vilma had released all the civilians, except for one Canadian. The enlisted men were still held. The American chief of naval operations, Arleigh Burke, protested to the Joint Chiefs of Staff that American prestige was being impugned, and concluded, "I consider that the damage will be almost irreparable if strong measures are not taken now to secure the release of our personnel."[27] Despite his advice, the United States still refrained from intervention. Instead, Wollam returned to the hills to negotiate with the rebels, and Fidel sent four of his men from the Sierra Maestra to the Sierra del Cristal—a march of eight days—to convey the direct order to Raúl to release all his hostages. On 18 July, the final few walked free. According to Ruby Hart Phillips, the *New York Times* correspondent in Havana, "almost all of the kidnapped men returned as confirmed *Fidelistas*."[28]

Batista had begun to feel his time was running out. He put on weight, and spent long tracts of time obsessively playing canasta. Meanwhile, his troops continued their campaign against civilians. Villages that were thought to be cooperating with the rebels were burned. Suspect individuals, some little more than children, were hanged as "examples." Their bodies were left on public view. "The tragedy of Cuba is that its youth is fighting and dying against Batista," wrote Allan Stewart of the State Department to his colleague Bill Snow. "If an Army officer or soldier is killed, three, four or more youths are found shot to death the next morning beside a road outside the locality where the attack against the soldiers occurred. This has become standard procedure. Consul Wollam says that the youth of Santiago have taken to the hills to fight with Raúl Castro."[29] Stewart estimated that two to three thousand troops were now under Raúl's command. The truth was probably short of one-tenth of that, but the twelve thousand government troops and air force now spread across both Sierras seemed unable to root them out.

In an attempt to invoke American protection, Batista's army asked the United States forces at Guantánamo Bay to relieve the Cuban guard at Yateras, the waterworks for that military base. The commanding officer was reluctant. To do so would break the agreement made between Park Wollam and Raúl Castro, and in any case Raúl had ordered his rebels to leave Yateras alone. Three weeks later, Batista forced the situation by removing the Cuban guard. So sensitive was the decision to send marines to take over that it went all the way to Foster Dulles himself. According to the State Department's Terry Leonhardy, who took the matter to Dulles, the latter looked at the order and said, "Well, there's only one thing to do." He authorized it, but added, "Not in uniform."

"Well, this was violating our sacred inter-American agreements, sending troops into any part of Cuba," said Leonhardy. On 28 July, the marines went into place. Fidel found out immediately, and made it public. In the United States, there was an outcry. Fidel requested that Washington withdraw its forces in exchange for a renewed rebel promise that there would be no mischief at the waterworks. Four days later, the marines returned to Guantánamo Bay.[30]

Fidel's consistent appeals to negotiation with the Americans, rather than armed action, were at odds with his private fury at American policy, and with his characteristic lack of restraint. To avoid confrontation was a sensible military and political strategy; but there may have been more to it than that. Tad Szulc, one of the journalists most closely connected to the rebels, reported the rumor that during 1957–58 the CIA sent $50,000 to Fidel's organization in Santiago. The money probably passed through vice-consul Robert Wiecha, a CIA agent, who was in contact with Raúl Castro and, like Wollam, stayed with him in the Sierra del Cristal. It has also been suggested that Interarms, an American-based company sometimes used by the CIA, sold arms to pro-Castro groups in the United States. Fidel had been happy to take Carlos Prío's money, which may have been the CIA's anyway. There is no reason to think he would not have been similarly happy to take the CIA's directly. At some time around the middle of 1958, a delegation from the Cuban communist party, the PSP, visited Moscow, and informed the Soviets that Fidel Castro was an undercover

American agent.[31]

Asked at a conference in 1992 whether it was true that the CIA had supplied his movement with weapons, Fidel was noncommittal. "I really have never heard a word about that, but I think they would have been right to give weapons to the 26th of July Movement," he said. "They would have been defending a just cause. So if they didn't, I'm very sorry about that, and if they did, well, I would like to take this occasion to thank them."[32]

In the absence of CIA documentation, these allegations cannot be proved; but they are not far-fetched. "Fidel was deeply concerned about American intervention," said the journalist Andrew St. George, who spent weeks in the Sierra Maestra and knew Fidel and Che well. "He wanted channels opened. He really wanted a CIA man up there with him. He offered to provide coded radio facilities."[33] Fidel asked St. George to pass a message to the American government, asking for an observer to be embedded with his men. As far as is known, none was. But several CIA agents in Cuba did want to make contact with Fidel, and provide support. "A combination of arms and money would probably be best," suggested Al Cox, head of the paramilitary division. Robert Reynolds, in charge of the CIA's Caribbean operations desk, remembered years later, "My staff and I were all Fidelistas."[34]

This did not imply any incipient left-wing sympathies on the part of the CIA. By 1958, the CIA had lost control of the Cuban Bureau for the Repression of Communist Activities (BRAC), which Allen Dulles had encouraged Batista to set up in 1955. BRAC was making suspiciously few arrests—which, the *New York Times* correspondent Ruby Hart Phillips thought, was because the PSP had struck a secret deal with Batista in which it pledged to oppose Fidel Castro. Instead, against the CIA's direction, Batista used BRAC against M-26-7, and licensed it to use violence in its interrogations.[35]

In the Caribbean of the Cold War, it was impossible to apply the dictum that an enemy's enemy was a friend. Friendships and enmities shifted too fast and too fluidly. But if Batista was making deals with the communists—whatever nonsense he had managed to sell to Ambassador Smith—the CIA may well have concluded, as many did, that Fidel Castro was Cuba's best hope for anticommunist democratic leadership.

★

Late on the night of 28 July 1958, a fishing boat called the *Mollie C* sailed from the Florida Keys to a Haitian beach northwest of Port-au-Prince. Its occupants, posing as tourists, aimed to overthrow François Duvalier.

They were led by a former Haitian army captain, Alix Pasquet. With him were two former lieutenants: his brother-in-law Philippe Dominique and Henri Perpignand. All were mulattoes. There were also five white American mercenaries, retained at a cost of $2,000 each, including three former deputy sheriffs from Miami and Buffalo. The operation was supposed to be backed by sixteen men in Miami, who would fly weapons and ammunition to the Dominican Republic in a private plane. Arturo Espaillat, Trujillo's head of security, later alleged that most of the men in Miami were Cubans, and members of M-26-7.[36] Whatever the truth, Miami customs officials had grown suspicious. The plane stayed on the ground.

In the dark, the eight seaborne invaders began unloading their weapons. But a local peasant had tipped off the police, and soon three men arrived in a jeep. There was a brief firefight on the beach. One American mercenary, thirty-four-year-old Arthur Payne of Dade County, Florida, was shot in the leg. The three Haitian policemen were all killed. The invaders took the jeep and hijacked a local tap-tap, one of the rickety but cheerfully painted trucks that served as informal national public transport. This one was blue and called Ma Douce Clairemène, a motto on it reading "In Spite of All, God Is the Only Master." In a convoy with the jeep, it rattled off for Port-au-Prince.

At Arcahaie, the jeep broke down, but Ma Douce Clairemène kept going, with all of the invaders crammed inside. News of their arrival had been spread by the police. The soldiers at the Dessalines Barracks in Port-au-Prince were on high alert. But nobody expected Ma Douce Clairemène. Pasquet, dressed in his old army uniform, told the guards he was bringing in five *blanc* invaders he had just taken prisoner. The tap-tap was given permission to drive straight into the barracks.

The invaders barged into the headquarters and shot the day officer, sergeant of the guard, and officer of the guard. Fifty groggy soldiers, who had been fast asleep, were taken prisoner. To Pasquet's surprise, the armory was empty. Duvalier had moved its contents to the basement of the National Palace shortly after his election.

Hearing gunfire, Duvalier telephoned the commandant of the barracks. Pasquet answered. "This is Alix Pasquet. There is no general here." He asked for the caller's name, title, and rank.

"President of the Republic and Supreme Chief of the Armed Forces," replied Duvalier. Then, according to Duvalier's own recollection, Pasquet—whom he called "the little maniac"—demanded that he present himself unarmed at the barrier of Dessalines Barracks, waving a white flag.[37]

Duvalier hung up the telephone, took up his gun, jammed a steel helmet on his head, and gathered his loyal forces. He also took the opportunity to make an arrangement for his own asylum at the Colombian embassy, in case things went wrong. Afterward he joined his defense corps at the barracks, including Clément Barbot with the Tontons Macoutes.

Inside the barracks, Henri Perpignand felt in the mood for a cigar. He sent a soldier out to purchase some of Régie du Tabac's *splendides*. The soldier was apprehended by one of Duvalier's officers, who asked him how many invaders were inside. Was it the three hundred they feared? More? The soldier replied no—eight.

Duvalier led his troops into battle, storming the barracks with the Haitian army and the Tontons Macoutes. Each of the invaders met a grisly end. Pasquet was the first, his head blown clean off by a well-aimed grenade. The wounded Payne wrapped himself in a mattress and screamed, "I am a journalist, I am a journalist," as an attacker opened fire point-blank with a machine gun. Perpignand tried to hide, but was quickly retrieved from a chicken coop and beaten to death. The Americans were shot. Afterward, their mutilated bodies were dragged through the streets.[38]

"Excellence," one of Duvalier's aides was heard to say, "if this were President Hippolyte, the town would be on fire now."

For once, Duvalier was not in the mood for a purge. "*Eh bien, mon cher*," he replied, with a faint smile. "Other times, other customs."[39]

Though the American embassy avoided commenting publicly on the invasion, Ambassador Drew reported again that the country was moving toward dictatorship. The State Department questioned whether it was really a good idea to send a marine mission to Haiti. The presence of American troops might stabilize things; but it might also make the United States look like it was supporting another dictatorship.[40]

Duvalier sent Louis Mars, his foreign minister, to meet Eisenhower in Washington. Mars assured the president that the mission would help bring stability to Haiti. Furthermore, he said, Haiti would fund it. This was important, for, under the terms of the Military Assistance Program, missions intended to police internal security could not be funded by the United States. The State Department was reassured. Duvalier and Drew initialed an informal agreement pledging "to take all reasonable and necessary measures to allay current political tension in order that the assignment of USMC [United States Marine Corps] mission personnel to Haiti would not be construed as intervention by the United States in the internal affairs of the Republic of Haiti."[41] Furthermore, Duvalier accepted the offer of an American consultancy firm to survey his government, at a cost to the Haitian state of $338,000. This sign of positive cooperation impressed the State Department, though it would result in nothing more than yet another lengthy report that would lie on desks, unread. The United States granted a $4.3-million loan, to help Haiti pay back a debt to the Ex-Im Bank run up on a previous American development project in the Artibonite Valley. It also gifted $3.5 million of budgetary assistance. All of this money went directly to Duvalier, making him, in a very real sense, the "spoiled child" of the United States he had wished to become.[42]

"I have mastered the country," Duvalier proclaimed. "I have mastered power. I am the New Haiti. To seek to destroy me is to seek to destroy Haiti herself. . . . No earthly power can prevent me from accomplishing my historic mission because it is God and Destiny who have chosen me."[43] He made no attempt to conceal his dictatorship. But he was an obedient dictator—one of those who, in the words of John Foster Dulles, the United States could depend on.

★

During the summer of 1958, Earl Smith bombarded the State Department with a series of poorly researched telegrams. He insisted that Batista would hold honest elections that November, and all would be well. He maintained that Fidel had no real support, and that M-26-7 would never take power. The only opposition to Batista, he repeatedly stated, came from communists and other extremists.

Smith's superiors in Washington were not convinced. They resisted his suggestions that they restart arms sales to the Cuban government. Instead, Batista managed to buy some pieces from Britain. There was a public outcry in Britain and Cuba, and this enterprise was stopped. Incredibly, Smith at this point personally approached the British ambassador in Havana to plead for him to restore arms sales to Batista.[44] Had the State Department known that the representative of the United States was freelancing as a procurer for the armed forces of another country—and one to which it had suspended sales—he would surely have been recalled immediately.

As Batista's elections approached, Smith's missives to the State Department became more eccentric yet. He reported that between 80 and 85 percent of M-26-7 were communists. He reported that Fidel had "a syphilitic inheritance." He reported the opinion of a candidate that "both Fidel and Raul are mentally unbalanced. When Raul was attending Havana University there was talk that he was homosexual."[45] That last is a rumor that has refused to die; but, even were it true, it is hard to see how Raúl's sexual preferences would have been relevant to Fidel's chances of victory. What he did not report, and what was far more important, was that Batista's support was collapsing, and that, with many pro-Castro political parties declining to participate, there was no chance of the upcoming elections solving anything. Batista was obliged to manufacture his own opposition from the fringes. Rumor had it that he was prepared to pay anyone who would stand against him.[46]

The American embassy in Havana was capably staffed. Apart from Smith himself, almost all seem to have understood that Batista was no longer acceptable to the Cuban people, and neither would be any puppet successor. Smith's reaction to this difference of opinion was to censor it. Like Arthur Gardner before him, he refused to allow subordinates to send communiqués to Washington unless he approved them first; and, as one of them said, "Smith approved very little."[47]

At the end of October, Allen Dulles belatedly informed the National Security Council that it was unlikely elections could be held at all in the parts of Cuba most strongly influenced by the rebels. Fidel, he said, had threatened to kill candidates who did not withdraw from the race. According to the minutes of the meeting, Foster Dulles then "commented facetiously that this could provide President Eisenhower with a good idea." There was much laughter, but Allen reminded the council of the serious truth: that the Cuban government would win its election, and that the victory would not be accepted.[48]

Allen Dulles was right. Despite some attempts by Batista's army at harassing people to the polls, few Cubans were interested in voting. Just 5 percent turned out in Santiago.[49] Batista's candidates, Andrés Rivero Agüero for president and Gonzalo Güell for prime minister, duly won.

A civil war was now in full swing between the government of Cuba and its coalescing opposition. Power and telephone lines were cut. Trains were derailed. Molotov cocktails were thrown. The rebels bombed the Havana Hilton and attempted to bomb the Coca-Cola bottling plant. In the Dominican Republic, Trujillo read reports of the Cuban rebel underground's terrorist campaign, and thought of the munitions he had sent to Miami for them two years beforehand. "My dynamite, there goes more of my dynamite," he muttered sorrowfully.[50]

That autumn, Fidel sent three columns, headed by Che, Camilo, and Jaime Vega, to the center of the island, to interrupt the supply chain from the bases in Havana to Oriente. Vega's column was ambushed by government forces, but the other two made it intact. Meanwhile, Fidel and Raúl advanced from the Sierras toward Santiago.

The guerrillas saw little action apart from sabotage and a few skirmishes. Their impact was largely romantic. In practice, the urban underground and civil resistance—less glamorous than Fidel's barbudos, but more numerous and better placed—carried out much of the struggle. Batista's army, meanwhile, had been weakened by years of internal corruption. As the government's image weakened and the rebels' reputation strengthened, its morale collapsed. Batista's troops were so demoralized that journalists observed they often avoided fighting the rebels altogether, and usually surrendered if they met them.[51]

Eisenhower sent Bill Pawley, an anticommunist millionaire with strong connections both to Batista and to Trujillo, to try to persuade the Cuban dictator to step aside. Batista refused to do so unless he was allowed to say that the American government had requested his retirement. Pawley was not authorized to offer that, and so the mission failed.[52]

News of the worsening situation in Cuba spread quickly to Haiti and the Dominican Republic. Trujillo begged the United States to aid Batista, arguing that the alternative was communism. On 7 November, Foster Dulles reassured the Dominican foreign minister that the United States was perpetually grateful for Trujillo's anticommunist leadership in Latin America.[53]

That month, there was a disastrous upset. Trujillo's son Ramfis had been sent to the Command and General Staff School at Fort Leavenworth, Kansas, run by the United States Army. Gossip columns soon brimmed over with Ramfis's exploits. Away from his long-suffering wife and small children, Ramfis indulged in a string of dates with actresses, most notably Kim Novak, then starring in Alfred Hitchcock's movie *Vertigo*. He wafted around Los Angeles, casually disbursing massive sums on Mercedes-Benz cars, chinchilla furs, and diamonds. Questions were raised in Congress about how this profligacy squared with the $1.3 million in aid recently given to the Dominican Republic.[54] He baked himself in the sun on the deck of his yacht, sailing up and down the Californian coastline. He spent very little time in Fort Leavenworth, Kansas, studying battle command, military strategy, or army leadership. When it came to graduation, General Ramfis Trujillo duly failed.

"Ramfis had never been told no in his whole life and was furious," remembered Henry "Hank" Dearborn, American ambassador to the Dominican Republic. "Trujillo was furious and considered it a slight." Trujillo's newspapers unleashed torrents of criticism about the alleged shortcomings of the American military program. Ramfis's sister, Flor de Oro, told an American officer that her brother had developed an "anti-American complex." He no longer wanted to buy American arms, so his San Isidro air base was being kitted out with European equipment. Moreover, he now refused to eat hamburgers. The National Security Council in Washington was informed that the flunking of Ramfis had done serious damage to Dominican-American relations.[55]

The elder Trujillo looked elsewhere for support. In December, wearing one of his flamboyant self-designed uniforms, he drove to the border at Jimaní, where he was to meet François Duvalier. In a well-rehearsed demonstration of insouciance, Duvalier was two and a half hours late, leaving the Dominican dictator—as usual, on time to the minute—to wait in the sweltering heat, his pale makeup slowly melting to reveal his real, darker color. On Duvalier's arrival, though, Trujillo swallowed his anger, for the matter up for discussion was important. The only political entity standing physically between a potentially Castro-controlled Cuba and Trujillo's Dominican Republic was Duvalier's Haiti. Though Haiti's internal security was strong, its armed forces were almost comically inadequate. The Americans could not be relied upon. Trujillo wanted Duvalier to allow the Dominican navy and air force to patrol Haitian waters and airspace.

Duvalier did not like the idea of Trujillo breathing down his neck, but he liked the idea of Castro turning up even less. The Haitian and Dominican leaders agreed not to tolerate exiles or communists planning subversion missions in their states. Clément Barbot and Johnny Abbes, who had arranged the meeting, toasted the deal with champagne.[56]

★

"I heard you telling Fidel that you were going to take Santa Clara and I don't know what the hell else," Che said jovially to Camilo over the radio on 6 December, "but don't butt in there because that's mine."

"As far as that business about Santa Clara, okay, fine, we are going to make plans for later on, and we are going to do them together," replied Camilo. "I want to share some of the glory with you, because I'm not ambitious."[57]

That winter, the Cuban revolutionaries fought almost constantly. Che's front moved up the island, capturing towns from Batista's forces. He was heading for Santa Clara, the last major city on the central highway before Havana. These were thrilling days; and the thrill was enhanced by the fact he had fallen in love. Aleida March was an undercover militant from Las Villas. On the run from the police, she had taken refuge in Che's camp. At first, she thought he looked old—which was unfair, for he was only thirty to her twenty-four—as well as "skinny and dirty," which was undeniably true.

One night just before Christmas, Che's troops massed to attack the town of Cabaiguán. Aleida stayed in the camp, but awoke in the middle of the night. She wandered out and sat by the roadside. A jeep pulled up, with Che driving.

"What are you doing here?" he asked.

"I couldn't sleep," she said.

"I'm going to attack Cabaiguán. Do you want to come along?"

"Sure," she replied, and got into the passenger seat beside him. "And from that moment on," she said later, "I never left his side—*or* let him out of my sight."[58]

Che did, eventually, tell her about Hilda and Hildita, though he said that he had separated from his wife on his departure from Mexico. He did not seem to Aleida to have been in love with Hilda: "I think that was not really the feeling that had brought them together."[59] Though it was convenient for her to think it, this was probably true. In any case, he was in love with Aleida—passionately so.

On 23 December, Allen Dulles addressed the National Security Council. "The Communists appear to have penetrated the Castro movement, despite some effort by Fidel to keep them out," he told them; "we ought to prevent a Castro victory." Eisenhower was shocked. This was the first time a conclusion had been reached on the influence of communism in the Castro movement, and the first time he had been told a Castro victory ought to be prevented.[60] At the same time, the rebels in Cuba saw that their victory was no longer preventable anyway. "The war is won," Fidel wrote gleefully to Che on 26 December, "the enemy is collapsing entirely."[61]

But Che's moment was still to come. On 28 December, he launched his audacious attack on Santa Clara. The city was defended by thirty-five hundred well-trained soldiers, and Batista's air force. Che had just three hundred worn-out men and women. News came through to the rebels that an armored train was bringing more of Batista's troops from Havana.

Che's rebels removed a section of track near the army headquarters. The next day, the train chugged into view as expected. It headed for the barracks, and hit hard ground. The engine toppled and derailed. Three carriages fell over. Rebels leaped up from all around, shooting and throwing Molotov cocktails. Within hours, the troops inside the besieged train surrendered. Che seized six bazookas, five mortars, fourteen machine guns, a cannon, six hundred automatic rifles, and one million rounds of ammunition. Delighted, he had his girlfriend pose with the remains of the train: "Aleida, I'm going to take a picture of you for history."[62]

Still, on 30 and 31 December, the State Department was wondering about a "third force" that it could back to take over from Batista in place of Fidel Castro.[63] It seems extraordinary that such an idea could still have been considered realistic, but the American response had again been hampered by its ambassador. Earl Smith claimed to have informed Dick Rubottom at the Office of Inter-American Affairs on the morning of New Year's Eve that Batista, Güell, and others would leave within twenty-four hours. Documents show the undersecretary of state, Christian Herter, being informed at 4:00 PM.[64] Either way, Smith's colleagues would tell a different story. Back in Washington shortly after the events of that December, Terry Leonhardy of the State Department, and Bob Stevenson, who had been in the embassy in Havana, wrote a report on what had happened. Smith came in for his debriefing and took issue with Stevenson's assertion, based on the telegrams sent, that Batista's departure had been a surprise.

"That isn't the way it happened at all," Smith said. "I knew Batista was leaving three days before he left."

Taken aback, Stevenson and Leonhardy pointed out that no such information was in the telegraphic traffic.

"Well," replied Smith, "I didn't think it was important at the time."

Smith admitted that his secretary had been looking for an apartment to rent, and the Cuban foreign minister, Güell, offered his. "I didn't think anything about it," he told the astonished Stevenson and Leonhardy. The secretary went to see the apartment, where she found Güell and his wife frantically packing for a swift departure. She reported this obvious sign of trouble to Smith, who reported it to no one at all.

"Can you imagine?" exclaimed Leonhardy, recounting the story years later. He summed up the ambassador's conduct as "pretty pathetic."[65]

On New Year's Eve, Batista ate his last Cuban meal of chicken and rice. Seventy close associates and their wives were invited for coffee after dinner at Camp Columbia, a low-key New Year's Eve party. Few knew that Batista was leaving, but the atmosphere was heavy nonetheless. At one in the morning, Batista's wife remarked on the chill, and left the room to change her dress. The guests took the hint and left.

An hour later, Batista resigned. He boarded a plane, along with his wife, his son Jorge, Dr. and Señora Güell, Andrés Rivero Agüero, and a few other officials. According to Graham Greene, there was a dramatic scene on the tarmac. Esteban Ventura, Batista's police chief, turned up and pulled a gun on his ex-president, demanding to get on the plane. Ventura, famous for his white suits and a series of extrajudicial slayings, served as the model for Captain Segura in Greene's *Our Man in Havana*—though Segura was a considerably more affable character. Ventura did indeed get on the plane, and it took off. The combined haul of its passengers from the national coffers has been estimated as high as $350 million, but the exact figure has never been established. When officials broke open Batista's personal safe deposit boxes in Havana soon afterward, they recovered $20 million in cash.[66]

David Atlee Phillips, the CIA agent who claimed to have started Che's file in Guatemala, was now based in Havana. He had been enjoying a final glass of New Year's Eve champagne on his lawn when he saw an aircraft fly overhead and out over the sea. No flight was scheduled at four in the morning. He telephoned his CIA case officer, and told him, "Batista just flew into exile."

"Are you drunk?" asked the case officer.

"Feeling okay," mumbled Phillips. "If Batista's not aboard I'll eat your sombrero."[67]

The sombrero was safe. A couple of hours later, the plane touched down in the Dominican Republic, Batista handing out $1,000 cash bonuses to the pilot and copilot as he disembarked. Trujillo had not been expecting Batista, and was severely displeased. As he saw it, he had paid good money for Batista to stay in Havana and defeat Castro.

The situation was worse yet, for Batista had not brought Johnny Abbes with him. Trujillo had sent Abbes to Havana to aid the fight against Fidel Castro. The last thing he wanted was for Fidel to discover his pet mercenary lurking in Cuba with blood all over his hands. A complicated operation would have to be mounted to get Abbes out. The disgraced Batista was not invited, as most distinguished visitors were, to one of Trujillo's estates, and was instead obliged to hole up at the Hotel Jaragua with his entourage. There, the sullen Captain Ventura devoted his energies full-time to the slot machines.[68]

Meanwhile, Fidel Castro, Celia Sánchez, and a clutch of rebels were celebrating New Year's Eve at Palma Soriano, near Santiago. Among the revelers was, by his own claim, the aging Hollywood actor Errol Flynn. Flynn was notorious at the Bodeguita del Medio, a restaurant near Havana's cathedral, for his tall tales of joining the fighting in the Sierra Maestra. "If so, his was a fast trip up and back," remarked Wayne Smith, an American embassy staffer, "for the corner table was rarely unoccupied." Flynn announced at a press conference that he had been wounded in the leg by a strafing government plane. In fact, the injury he displayed for the cameras was a bruise he had sustained when getting out of a jeep, painted over with red nail polish to make it more photogenic.[69]

The next morning, over coffee at a sugar mill, news reached the rebels that the war was over, and they had won. It was as much a surprise to them as to anyone. Though Fidel had been confident of an eventual victory, there had been no decisive battle. Geographically, Fidel himself was almost as far away from Batista's headquarters in Havana as it was possible to be while remaining in Cuba. Against the dictator's enormous and well-equipped army, navy, and air force, he still commanded only eight hundred scrappy rebels. None of this mattered. The government had collapsed. The army had disintegrated. Batista had bolted, and left the door to power swinging wide open behind him. Fidel Castro was the most famous name among the Cuban rebels. By default, then, he had just won the Cuban revolutionary war.[70]

7

"NOT RED, BUT OLIVE GREEN"

★

"TRUJILLO NEXT!" SHOUTED FIDEL CASTRO, AS HE DROPPED COINS INTO a collection box proffered by a Dominican exile group on the day of his triumphal entry into Havana. Rafael Trujillo had already announced that he was levying a special tax to raise $50 million for a national defense fund, in response to Fidel's victory. It was a miserable day in Ciudad Trujillo, but Havana rejoiced. "Except for the prisoners awaiting trial, every man was a brother," wrote Warren Miller; "there was never any place, except perhaps Paris on liberation day, so full of hope and glory as Cuba then."[1]

When the news broke of Batista's unexpected flight a week before, Fidel had gone to Santiago to claim his victory. The rebels were welcomed by cheering crowds, and by the army. Meanwhile, five hundred miles away in Havana, the general public went on the rampage. They tore through hated ministries, American-owned stores, and a newspaper plant belonging to Rolando Masferrer, the head of Batista's private army, the Tigres. At the Capri Hotel, a crowd arrived with axes to hack apart the slot machines. The Hollywood actor George Raft, who had made his name in the 1930s playing hard-boiled gangsters, was now a partner in the Capri alongside Santo Trafficante and Meyer Lansky, who were hard-boiled gangsters in real life. Raft squared himself up in the entrance to the gaming rooms, fixed the ax-wielding mob with a steely glare, and snarled, "Yer not comin' in my casino." The mob thought the better of it, and moved on to loot the Hotel Nacional instead. Someone also burned down the house of Fidel's former brother-in-law, Rafael Diaz Balart. Later that month, in New York, Diaz Balart would found La Rosa Blanca, the first organization dedicated to fighting the Castro administration.[2]

An M-26-7 militia drove around Havana with a loudspeaker, telling looters to stop or they would be shot. "This was something new in the history of Havana," noted Ruby Hart Phillips, the *New York Times* correspondent who had also lived through the revolution of 1933: "a volunteer group determined to keep order and protect property." Roxanna Smith, the wife of an American official (Vice-Consul Wayne Smith, rather than the ambassador, Earl Smith) went to her neighbor Sonia Mullin's apartment to watch the celebrations. Hearing the popping and banging of fireworks, the ladies opened the glass doors to the balcony and leaned over, remarking on how cheerful it all was. Their rapture was broken by a military attaché who lived upstairs, shouting, "For God's sake, Mrs. Mullin, get down on the floor; that's gunfire."[3]

Fidel's bearded rebels, the barbudos, began arriving in the capital. Che Guevara was stationed in La Cabaña Fort, across the bay from Havana proper. Camilo Cienfuegos took Batista's stronghold, Camp Columbia. According to many observers, the presence of the rebels—who refused to drink alcohol, spoke politely to the people, and announced their intention to respect the rule of law—had a remarkable effect. The looting and violence stopped. All crime stopped. "For a week, the entire island, six million people, lived by the honor system," wrote Warren Miller. "Burglary and theft virtually came to a halt that week, and no crime of violence was committed." Batista's policemen either had gone into hiding or were imprisoned. The Boy Scouts volunteered to direct Havana's traffic, and were obeyed with civility by Havana's notoriously irascible drivers. Wherever the barbudos went, they were cheered. "One had the feeling that they would not hesitate to shoot a Batista supporter," said Ruby Hart Phillips, "but he would be shot with the greatest courtesy."[4]

Not everyone loved the rebels. Earl Smith had to steel himself to visit his departed friend Batista's beloved Camp Columbia. "In the commandant's office was Camilo, with his romantic beard, looking like Christ on a spree," remembered Carlos Franqui, "his boots thrown on the floor and his feet up on the table, as he received his excellency the ambassador of the United States."[5]

Che's wife, Hilda, arrived in Havana in that first week of January with their small daughter, Hildita. For two years, she had waited for her husband, keeping faith with his memory, receiving occasional letters, but rarely knowing for sure whether he was alive or dead. Brimming with anticipation, she went to see him. Straight away, with his usual blunt honesty, he told her that during the last two weeks, in the course of the campaign at Santa Clara, he had fallen in love with another woman.

Hilda was shocked and deeply hurt. Seeing her pain, Che added, "Better I had died in combat."

She looked at him for a moment, speechless, then told him that no, she was happy he was alive. He had a new society to build, and a continent to liberate. "For all this, I prefer you to live."

"If that's how it is, then it's all right," he replied: "friends, and comrades?"

"Yes," she managed to reply.[6]

Hilda granted a quick divorce. Che would marry Aleida March on 2 June. The forlorn Hilda took a job in the same building as Che and Aleida, seemingly in the hope that she might win her ex-husband back. This made nobody happy, and eventually she was transferred to a less visible role in another department. She never remarried, and would remain in Havana, looking after Che's daughter and working for his revolution, until her death in 1974.

Fidel, meanwhile, embarked on a six-day procession from Santiago to Havana, accompanied by five thousand compañeros and fans. He arrived on 8 January, and almost the entire population of the city turned out to meet him, hurling confetti, waving the red and black flags of M-26-7, and shouting "Viva Fidel!" Though his face revealed exhaustion—since his victory, he had hardly eaten or slept—Fidel managed to smile. He spoke briefly from the balcony of the presidential palace to the thousands outside. When the time came to leave, Fidel asked the crowd to let him pass. Normally, soldiers would have pushed them back. Instead, they drew aside. "Many politicians in Cuba had been able to arouse the people, to awaken their passions," wrote Phillips, "but never before had I seen such respect and awe."[7]

From the palace, he drove to Camp Columbia. There, he addressed another enormous crowd, and the nation beyond it via television and radio. Earl Smith described his speech as "sincere, rambling, forceful, received with great enthusiasm."[8] At once thrilled and exhausted, he seemed for a brief moment, uncharacteristically, to lose his thread. He turned to Camilo Cienfuegos, standing by his side.

"Am I doing all right, Camilo?" he asked, earnestly.

"You're doing fine, Fidel," replied Camilo, with a grin.

The crowd burst out laughing. "You're doing fine, Fidel" would become one of the revolution's most enduring slogans. Someone released white doves, and one landed on Fidel's shoulder.

In Washington, Foster Dulles recommended to Eisenhower that they recognize the regime put in place by Fidel Castro. The president installed by Castro, Manuel Urrutia, and the prime minister, José Miró Cardona, were both seen as sensible, progressive men. More sensible men had been put in charge of the treasury, the national bank, and foreign affairs. A sensible woman had been put in charge of social affairs. There were no barbudos in evidence. "The Provisional Government appears free from Communist taint and there are indications that it intends to pursue friendly relations with the United States," wrote Dulles. "Soon," concluded a newsreel announcer, "Cuba can begin the big task of returning to normal."[9]

★

Warren Miller and his wife traveled from Havana to Varadero, a resort set along a spit of white sand arching out into the turquoise waters of the Caribbean. There, they found a cluster of Americans, waiting for the casinos to reopen. "Drawn to each other by a common language and nothing else," he remembered, "we sat on the beach and listened to the sound of gunfire from the city of Matanzas across the bay, where executions were being held."[10]

The trials of Batista's villains had begun on 2 January, and the executions almost as quickly. There was a public appetite for revenge. Newspapers were filled with photographs of the torture devices used by Batista's police, and of bodies being dragged from the wells and sewers in which Batista's men had dumped them. On 14 January, Park Wollam reported from Santiago that scores of accused Batistianos had already been tried, convicted, and executed. Many of the defendants had, he admitted, been "thugs and assassins of the worst type," mostly members of the torture squads and Rolando Masferrer's Tigres. Fidel ensured that tribunals were set up, which was an improvement on the lynch mobs that had run riot after Machado was deposed thirty years earlier.

But the barbudos were working through trials so fast, and with such enthusiasm, that it was inevitable mistakes would be made. Wollam identified the case of the Santiago police chief, who had been praised by Fidel himself in a speech on 2 January and was credited with converting many of his own officers to the rebel cause. During a trial the following week, he had been accused by two defendants of collaborating. By the fourteenth, he too had been tried and shot. "This hurried 'justice' and the possible slighting of judicial procedures is usually blamed on Raul Castro, who is the command figure here," Wollam wrote.[11] Later, accusations would emerge that Raúl had ordered seventy prisoners to be executed without trial, immediately after the capture of Santiago.[12]

In Varadero, Miller spoke to one American man who was going to Matanzas to see an old friend, a policeman, face the firing squad. "He had been in the habit of leaving his victims strung up along the highway, their testicles in their mouths, as an object to others," wrote Miller of the policeman. According to his American friend, the policeman had not done this for sadistic reasons, but as a warning: "He had only wanted to spare people pain."[13] Hard as it was to summon up sympathy for such characters, some Cubans did question whether the trials were fair or dignified. There were protests in the United Nations, the Organization of American States, and in the international press.

Fidel dismissed the international protests, arguing that those organizations had never raised objections to Batista's lengthy catalog of atrocities. But the spectacle of the trials and executions, televised in Cuba and shown on newsreels across the world, was grim. Thousands of people packed Havana's Sports Palace stadium to watch Batista's officers be accused, shamed, and convicted. "Kill them!" shouted the crowd, and "*paredón, paredón*" (to the wall, to the wall), calling for death by firing squad. In the first two weeks of January, around two hundred people were executed. On 19 January, the prime minister, Miró Cardona, resigned, ostensibly on grounds of ill health.[14] Later, in exile, he would become one of the leading critics of the Castro government.

Fidel invited several American congressmen to observe the trials. On 21 January, they saw Fidel give a four-and-a-half-hour address to half a million people in Havana. At one point, Fidel asked who in the crowd approved of the "shooting of the assassins." There was a tremendous roar, and a forest of hands sprang up to assent. Fidel carefully avoided overt criticism of the United States in his speech, though he did at one point mention the bombings of Japan at the end of the Second World War. "And when all is said and done the total of assassins we shoot will not be more than four hundred," he said, "which is about one assassin for every thousand men, women and children assassinated in Hiroshima and Nagasaki." It was not obvious how this equation justified his government's actions. Afterward, Fidel met an American embassy official at the Havana Hilton, and reassured him that he hoped the United States and Cuba could work together. He had intended no hurt by his speech, but "it was necessary in a public rally of that sort to express certain points of view."[15]

According to White House figures, the total tried and executed by the Cuban government during 1959 would stand at just over 600. Fidel Castro put it at 550.[16] Trujillo, Duvalier, and Batista had all found it necessary to dispose of substantial numbers of political opponents to consolidate their authority. None of them had bothered with the legal formality of trials. But Fidel was aiming to be something better than Trujillo, Duvalier, or Batista. That week, he told one American journalist that he expected to "withdraw from the limelight soon."[17] He accepted that he would have a permanent role as the figurehead of the movement, but did not want to be head of state. (He could not be, anyway: the Cuban constitution set the minimum age for a president at thirty-five, and he was thirty-one.) Were he to be killed, he said, Raúl would take over as leader of M-26-7 and its new, unofficial committee, the Office of Revolutionary Plans and Coordination, which was in effect functioning as a parallel government.

On 23 January, Fidel left for Venezuela. He met Rómulo Betancourt, soon to take over as president, and privately requested a massive $300-million loan and discounted oil. Detecting youthful inexperience, Betancourt declined. But Jake Esterline, the CIA's station chief in Venezuela, was not so quick to write Fidel off. "I saw—hell, anybody with eyes could see—that a new and powerful force was at work in the hemisphere," he said, observing the cheering crowds that assembled to greet the Cuban hero in Caracas. "It had to be dealt with."[18]

★

Earl Smith hated Fidel, and Fidel hated him. Eisenhower was reluctant to let Smith go, and Undersecretary of State Christian Herter politely agreed with the president that the ambassador "had done a creditable job despite a couple of 'bloopers' which were not too surprising in view of the complexities."[19] Smith's colleagues at the embassy in Havana were less forgiving. One accused him of creating a "poisonous" atmosphere. Another said flatly that he had become "an apologist and defender for Fulgencio Batista." The United States Information Service officer in Havana actually blamed him for Castro's victory, pointing out that if he had been a "real pro" he could have used his close relationship to persuade Batista to step aside earlier, before Castro was in place to take over.[20] Smith was duly replaced with Philip Bonsal, the serving ambassador to Bolivia, a perceptive man with a track record of dealing calmly with unusual Latin American regimes.

In subsequent years, it came to suit Fidelistas and anti-Fidelistas alike to suggest that Fidel had been a secret communist all along. According to this view, to which Earl Smith subscribed and which Fidel himself, for very different reasons, later attempted to promulgate, the Cuban Revolution was a conspiracy. Fidel from his earliest days had been waiting for the opportunity to barge dramatically out of the red closet. At best, this theory is based on a misreading of history; at worst, it is based on a deliberate desire to obscure the truth. Until the last few months of 1958, the PSP, Cuba's actual communist party, and M-26-7 had been trenchantly opposed to each other. The PSP was publicly and privately critical of Fidel, and he returned fire. As far as the Soviet administration in Moscow was concerned, the only information it had on Fidel came through the junior KGB agent Nikolai Leonov or the PSP. The former had assessed him definitively as a noncommunist, and the latter had alleged that he was a bourgeois American stooge in the employment of the CIA.[21] Only at the very end of 1958—on 27 December—had the Kremlin first shown any interest in the Cuban revolutionaries, to the extent that it considered sending them a small number of German rifles left over from World War II.[22] This was, of course, too late to make any difference to the revolutionary war effort.

"When Fidel Castro achieved victory," remembered Nikita Khrushchev, "we in the USSR, to put it plainly, still didn't know what political direction the victors would take. We knew that in the movement headed by Castro some individual Communists were participating, but the Communist Party of Cuba as a whole was not in contact with Castro. . . . The situation was very unclear."[23] Fidel, meanwhile, was a nationalist and remained a nationalist. He was also an opportunist, taking money from the right and manpower from the left. He knew that both Che and Raúl had established and nurtured contacts with the PSP during 1958. At the beginning of 1959, he, too, opened secret lines of communication with that party, among many other organizations, with the intention of consolidating his popular base.[24] Fidel suggested casually to the PSP that he would consider the Soviet Union as a potential ally against the United States, if it was required. "This did not mean that he intended to become a Marxist-Leninist," said Wayne Smith, of the American embassy in Havana. "Other Third World leaders had turned to the Soviets for help without converting to Moscow's faith. Nasser had done it. So had Sukarno."[25] What Fidel needed was comprehensive support. He would take it wherever he found it.

The Eisenhower administration perceived this accurately.[26] Bill Wieland, director of Caribbean Affairs at the State Department and its most astute Cuban analyst, saw that Fidel held the key to whether the radicals or the moderates would eventually win the Cuban power struggle. He recommended that the United States focus on gently influencing the man himself. "This will require forbearance in the face of ill-considered statements and policies which Castro is likely to continue to make in the present euphoria which surrounds him," wrote Wieland, "as well as persuading him by friendly and sympathetic contacts that the rancors which either events or anti-US persons have induced Castro to feel against the US are no longer justified, if they ever were."[27] Wieland also noted that Fidel had actually made some moves in the field of labor organization directed at cutting down communist influence. "Ironically, Fidel Castro stands as a possible bulwark against Communism," wrote Ruby Hart Phillips at the time.[28]

By the time Wieland was recommending overtures to Fidel, though, the PSP was making headway on the spot. Blas Roca and Lázaro Peña, old-time communists who had served under Batista, returned to Havana's political circles. Fidel could not be persuaded by the Americans to stop tolerating the PSP, pointing out that both the United States and its ally Britain had legal communist parties, and there was no reason Cuba should not follow suit.[29]

At the same time, a delegation from the Cuban government had arranged a meeting at the United States Treasury to request a stabilization fund. At the National Security Council meeting on 12 February, Eisenhower resisted, saying that he did not think Washington could stabilize the currency until Cuba had stabilized its government. According to the minutes, "Allen Dulles pointed out that the new Cuban officials had to be treated more or less like children. They had to be led rather than rebuffed. If they were rebuffed, like children, they were capable of doing almost anything."[30]

Meanwhile, in Havana, the barbudos tore apart the Dulles brothers' notorious Cuban creation, the Bureau for the Repression of Communist Activities. After the revolution, the American-trained colonel in charge of this torture agency had fled the country. He would later be employed by the American government, screening Cuban exiles in Florida for their political opinions. That March, though, the barbudos captured his second-in-command, José Castaño. Castaño was tried, convicted, and sentenced to death by firing squad.

The CIA station in Havana contacted Andrew St. George, an American journalist who knew Fidel and Che well from the Sierra Maestra, and asked him to intervene with Fidel to save Castaño's life. St. George could not find Fidel, but called on Che. He found him in bed, suffering an asthma attack. Under the present tense circumstances, St. George explained, it might be diplomatic to spare the friend of the yanqui spooks.

"In the mountains," said Che, struggling to get the words out in between wheezes, "we learned nothing about diplomacy."

St. George spent most of the day trying to talk Che around. It was no good. Che insisted Castaño's sentence must be carried out. "Tell them my answer exactly as I tell you," Che said, and sent him away.

Returning to the American embassy, St. George was greeted by a crowd of officials.

"Well, what did he say?" asked the CIA station chief.

"Che said to tell you that if he didn't shoot him for a Batista thug he would shoot him for an American agent," replied St. George.

For a moment, the Americans were silent. Finally, the station chief spoke. "This," he said, "this is a declaration of war."[31]

According to St. George, the Havana CIA station—which, up to this point, had contained several Fidelistas—now turned implacably against the Cuban Revolution. The very next morning, Castaño was shot.

★

Three political factions appeared to be competing for control of the Cuban Revolution. First, there was the center-right government Fidel had installed, which wanted conservative policies and close relations with the United States. Second, there was the moderate center left, which included Fidel himself, proposing various shades of reform.[32] Third, there was the radical left wing, which saw the revolution as an opportunity to do something completely different.

Che Guevara and Raúl Castro led the radicals, but neither had control of Fidel. In fact, there were numerous reports from the beginning of 1959 that he had become openly hostile to their cause. "Do you know what I'm going to do with Che Guevara?" Fidel had told a shocked dinner party in the city of Cienfuegos during his tour from Oriente to Havana. "I'm going to send him to Santo Domingo and see if Trujillo kills him. As for my brother Raúl, I'm going to send him to Europe as a minister or diplomat or ambassador." Notably, when Fidel appeared in public, the lieutenant at his side was never Che, hardly ever Raúl, and almost always Camilo—widely seen as one of the moderates. When Fidel anointed Raúl as his successor, the State Department received a secret report that "Camilo Cienfuegos was hopping mad."[33]

Allegiances in Cuba were complex, and unclear. Bob Stevenson, of the American embassy in Havana, remembered around this time a delegation of barbudos, led by Camilo and Juan Almeida, asking for permission to travel to the United States. "These guys showed up in their clean fatigues, with their beards trimmed, neat, and they went through the ceremony very nicely, laid the wreath on the Tomb of the Unknown Soldier," Stevenson said. "It went very well. The 'why' of that always puzzled us. We never knew why we never got any word, what they wanted, really." It was, he thought, an attempt by the moderates to open a dialogue with the United States.[34]

There were two big questions. First, whether Fidel really would step away from politics, as the rumors had suggested; second, if he did not, whether he would fall in line with the conservatives or the radicals. The first question was answered in the negative at the beginning of February, when Fidel assumed the role of prime minister, vacated by Miró Cardona. It was widely said by Fidel's critics that he must have planned this all along, and it was taken as evidence of his unstoppable lust for power. But had he wanted power, he could have taken it straightaway on 1 January, just as legitimately, with less risk.

A more subtle and satisfactory explanation was hit upon by Phil Bonsal, the new American ambassador. "I did not achieve any intimacy or friendship with Castro," he wrote.

> I do not believe he has any friends in the commonly accepted meaning of that word. My definition of friendship does not cover the master-servant relationship that exists between him and the men and women in his personal entourage. He is not lacking in charm or versatility of personality. His mental and physical gifts are phenomenal. He was, in my time, a vigorous practitioner of such normal sensual pursuits as eating, smoking, drinking, and sex. But he seemed to derive from these activities none of the human sociability that usually accompanies them. Castro achieves intimacy only when he addresses the masses in the Plaza de la República or over television. It is only then when he experiences that flow of ideas and sentiments characteristic of real personal ties between human beings.[35]

Since his student days, Fidel had been famous for the power of his speaking. But it was only when he arrived in Santiago on 1 January 1959 that he was able for the first time to address a crowd of thousands. In Havana, it had been hundreds of thousands. On television, it was millions. Something electric happened when Fidel spoke to a crowd. Bonsal was right: it was a form of intimacy, for him and for his audience. No one could have predicted the power of this relationship, on both sides, nor its longevity. Perhaps inevitably, Fidel was prone to take the adoration and the affirmation he received from Cuban crowds as a mandate for office. More than that, though, he began to see the crowd as an incarnation of the ideal of Cuba itself—proud, passionate, defiant, revolutionary. When the crowd applauded him, he believed that it *was* Cuba, sanctioning whatever political actions he was taking. The most important relationship of Fidel's life would not be with any of his wives, girlfriends, or children, nor with Celia, nor with Raúl, and certainly not with Che. It would be with the crowd.

So Fidel would have power. But the second question, of what he would do with it, remained. His first acts as prime minister showed that he was far from sold on the radical line. He organized a conference to determine government policy in February, inviting the cabinet, the chiefs of the rebel army, and members of M-26-7—a broad political group. It quickly descended into violent fighting between civil and military interests, the latter advocated strongly by Raúl Castro. Fidel took the side of the civilians, and launched into a vicious attack on his own brother in front of the five hundred people present. "After the performance he has given here," Fidel said, "*el compañero* Raúl would do well to rip off his major's insignia and leave as a buck private."[36] Raúl burst into tears and stormed out.

Raúl was not defeated. The PSP reported to Moscow that he and Che had been forced to conceal the extent of their communist links from Fidel, but now they were growing bolder. The State Department noted in early February that "certain elements" in the Cuban administration, "especially the Argentine Communist-liner Major 'Che' Guevara," were planning active support of revolutionaries aiming at Haiti and the Dominican Republic, among other nations.[37]

Caribbean exiles poured into Havana. Two Haitians, the pro-American Louis Déjoie and the communist poet René Depestre, arrived just days after Castro's victory. Though these men were theoretically from opposite sides of the political spectrum, their opposition to François Duvalier brought them together. Depestre met Che and introduced him to Déjoie.[38]

Déjoie was permitted to use the Havana Hilton, the new government's requisitioned headquarters, to hold a press conference denouncing Duvalier. Raúl and Che arranged for him to make a speaking tour of Oriente, drumming up support for an invasion of Haiti. Both the State Department in Washington and Rafael Trujillo suspected that this was a prelude to a Cuban invasion of the Dominican Republic.

Though Che and Raúl egged the Haitians on, Fidel insisted to Déjoie's men that his government's attitude was: "Revolution, yes; occupation, no." He had no interest in invading Haiti for any purpose of conquest, but he supported the overthrow of dictators across Latin America. The Haitians received arms from the Cuban government. They were also approached by private arms dealers from the United States. Lyonel Paquin, a cousin of the Haitian opposition leader Clément Jumelle, remembered the attitude of the private dealers: "We could get any amount of cash for one collateral item, the gambling casino concession after victory."[39]

According to information received by the State Department, Raúl and Che set up two training camps for Haitian exiles: one about fifty miles south of Havana, and the other in Oriente. Camilo told Déjoie that Radio Progreso, a Cuban station, would broadcast political programs in Creole three nights a week across the Windward Passage to Haiti.[40] The black Republican Val Washington complained to the State Department that Raúl and Che were attempting to paint Duvalier as a dictator and "had sold this line to most of the correspondents of the U.S. negro press who had visited Cuba." State Department officials recommended that he try to get a "balanced" set of facts to the press, to counter this "distorted image." Their real concern, as they admitted, was that publicity about the dictatorship in Haiti might fuel the fires of invasion. Showing an enthusiasm for Duvalier's regime unusual outside the ranks of paid lobbyists, Val Washington finished the meeting by reminding the State Department that Duvalier needed more aid from the United States.[41]

Duvalier sent agents to Cuba to assassinate Déjoie. They were apprehended. Questioned, they blurted out that the Haitian embassy was supposed to pay them $10,000 for each of four Haitian targets in Havana. Duvalier attempted to make up for this gaffe by sending gifts of medical supplies to Cuba, and pardoning a few political prisoners. Sensing that Duvalier needed reminding which side he was on, Trujillo sent a navy corvette to Port-au-Prince, on the pretext of showing solidarity with Haiti. He also started a foreign legion, to defend the whole island of Hispaniola.[42]

The specter of a wider confrontation loomed. In January, a new detachment of seventy United States Marines, Navy, and Coast Guard arrived in Haiti to train Duvalier's army. In accordance with the American Military Assistance Program (MAP), this mission was supposed to train the army to resist external aggression, but to stay out of internal disputes and any form of politics. Nevertheless, according to Robert Heinl, the commander of the marines in Haiti, they had been specifically instructed by a State Department deputy undersecretary that "the most important way you can support our objectives in Haiti is to help keep Duvalier in power so he can serve out his full term in office, and"—here the deputy undersecretary paused—"maybe a little longer than that if everything works out. Good luck."[43]

The question was raised internally in the State Department of whether communist participation in the government of Haiti should be exposed. Despite his shift to the right, Duvalier's administration still included several figures with left and far-left backgrounds. Indeed, during those early months of 1959, his government contained significantly more leftists than Fidel Castro's. But the State Department's John Calvin Hill, one of the most vocal critics of Fidel at the time, was reluctant to apply the same treatment. "In this context, it would be very much to our disadvantage to undertake activities which might have the tendency to give an impression that the Duvalier Administration is riddled with Communists and thus make it more vulnerable to opposition elements," he wrote. "Our policy is based on the assumption that the Communists do not participate in the Duvalier Government, at least in any appreciable way, although we have our doubts re the political background of some individuals."[44] Hill was explicit about the reasons for not wanting to expose Haitian communism: the United States was giving financial support and a marine mission to Haiti. A government that accepted American influence could get away with much more than one that did not.

On 11 April Clément Jumelle, the main opposition leader still remaining in Haiti, died at the Port-au-Prince residence of the Cuban ambassador, Antonio Rodríguez Echazabal. Five days earlier, Jumelle, suffering from uremic poisoning, had hauled himself onto Rodríguez's patio and collapsed. Rodríguez dragged him inside, and summoned specialists from Cuba to treat him, but it was no use. Jumelle expired.

Jumelle's body was wrapped in white linen and hidden in a blue Ford car before Rodríguez telephoned the funeral parlor. When Duvalier's men turned up to collect it, Rodríguez directed them to a decoy stretcher. Meanwhile, the blue car drove the real body to a clinic on the Rue Magny owned by Jumelle's brother. There, its organs were removed and taken away to be interred in a secret location. The corpse was returned.

Jumelle's funeral was arranged for the next day, 12 April. As the cortège drove up Avenue Charles Sumner to the Sacré-Coeur church, sirens were heard. A black van swerved in front of the cortège and blocked its path. The door slid back, and a band of armed Tontons Macoutes leaped out. Some plunged into the crowd, swinging coco macaques. Others, with submachine guns, held up the mourners. With the widow Jumelle howling terrible curses, the Macoutes knocked the wreaths off the coffin, snatched it, and carried it off. It was taken to the National Palace.

As the story was told, Duvalier meant to use Jumelle's organs in a Vodou ritual. This was the reason Jumelle's family had removed them. It may have suited Duvalier to avoid contradicting this story, for it added to his own legend. In any case, the body was returned to Jumelle's grieving family in a sealed coffin. They refused to accept it without identifying it, so the Macoutes who delivered it took it away again and buried it themselves. Afterward, the family arranged for it to be dug up. Inside was the corpse of a stranger. Jumelle's body was never found.[45]

"All popular movements will be repressed with utmost rigor," Duvalier said. "The repression will be total, inflexible, and inexorable." At the same time, he was careful to make several statements about the importance of Haitian-American relations.[46] It was clear that trouble was coming between Cuba and Haiti. It was equally clear that, bizarre though Duvalier's behavior might be, the United States had already taken his side.

★

There was a new mystery in Cuba. Che Guevara had disappeared. "There are so many conflicting reports as to the health, whereabouts and activities of Guevara that it might be warranted to undertake a special effort to get at the facts," reported John Calvin Hill. "He is variously reported to be suffering from TB and/or other maladies, to be secretly training exiles and to be off with some girl friend. The only point of agreement seems to be that he is at Tarara Beach or ranch near Habana."[47] Other rumors suggested that Fidel might have had him arrested. According to Che's friend Ricardo Rojo, he was in voluntary political reclusion. "He thought Castro would compromise the course of the revolution by trusting the United States," Rojo wrote. "He frankly told him so and immediately retired to his house with his iron guard. While Castro worked out the problem, Guevara and his friends remained confined and came out only when the head of the revolutionary government renounced his temptation."[48]

Che himself soon released an open letter: "I wish to explain to the readers of *Revolución* that I am ill, that I did not catch my illness in gambling dens or spending nights in cabarets but by working more than my system could endure, for the Revolution." He was ill; but the house at Tarará was also used for secret meetings. Che's most important allies, Raúl Castro and Camilo Cienfuegos; his close Sierra aide Ramiro Valdés; and the PSP's Victor Piña met there to set up a secret service. Meanwhile, regular meetings with the PSP continued at Fidel's villa in nearby Cojímar.[49]

With Che out of sight, Fidel showed no sign of distancing himself from the United States. In fact, he did the exact opposite and applied for a visa so that he might accept an invitation to address the American Society of Newspaper Editors in Washington, D.C. "I inquired whether we could not refuse him," remembered Eisenhower, who had been outraged by the Cuban executions and was increasingly suspicious that Fidel might be a communist. "Advised that under the circumstances this would be unwise, I nevertheless refused to see him."[50]

Fidel may not have been in Ike's good books, but he arrived to adulatory crowds. To most Americans, he was still the brave young hero of the

Sierra Maestra. On arrival, he looked almost overwhelmed by the attention, though he could not suppress a bashful smile. He had been warned by police not to mingle with the crowds, but this he ignored, and plunged in. "The report later that hired gunmen may have plotted to assassinate him does not completely restrain his enthusiasm," noted one newsreel announcer.[51] Outside Fidel's hotel, there was another large crowd. A small boy dressed as him—complete with stick-on beard—was hoisted aloft, waving a Cuban flag.

Eisenhower found a pressing golfing engagement in Georgia to attend. In his stead, the Cuban met the new secretary of state, Christian Herter, and the vice president, Dick Nixon. Nixon spent three hours with him. "I talked to him like a Dutch uncle," he told Bob Stevenson afterward. "What do you think? Do you think I did any good?"

"To be honest," replied Stevenson, "I'd like to think that you did, Mr. Vice President, but my honest opinion is that you probably didn't."

Nixon stood up, and clapped his hands on his thighs. "That's what I think, too."[52]

He translated his frustration into contempt. "Whatever we may think of him he is going to be a great factor in the development of Cuba and very possibly in Latin American affairs generally," he wrote to Eisenhower. "He seems to be sincere. He is either incredibly naïve about communism or under communist discipline—my guess is the former, and as I have already implied his ideas as to how to run a government or an economy are less developed than those of almost any world figure I have met in fifty countries."[53] Nixon informed the White House, the State Department, and the CIA that there was no point trying to understand Castro or to reason with him. The best thing to do, he said, would be to train up Cuban exiles—at this point, he can only have meant Batistianos—and send them to remove him from power.[54] Thereby Nixon gave a spin to the wheels on what would become the Bay of Pigs invasion.

Fidel was adamant with his retinue that they were not to ask the Americans for money. "Look, Rufo," he said to his treasury minister, Rufo López-Fresquet, "I don't want this trip to be like that of other new Latin American leaders who always come to the U.S. to ask for money. I want this to be a good-will trip."[55] When they returned to Cuba, he added, they could start talking about accepting American aid.

Dignified though this strategy may have been, it confused the Americans. They offered the Cubans a $25-million standby loan, only to be told by López-Fresquet, "Thank you very much, but we don't want it."[56]

The plan backfired. Fidel's refusal to take American aid was seen within the State Department as evidence that he was planning another allegiance—and that could only be with the Soviet Union.

Fidel was invited to lunch at the Statler Hotel with Herter and Rubottom. Celia Sánchez made a heroic effort to get him there on time, a previously unknown phenomenon. As it turned out, he was early. His car had to drive around the block a few times so he would not arrive before his host.[57] He turned up with a dozen armed barbudos, who stationed themselves in the dining room until one of Herter's aides convinced Fidel that it might be more friendly without them. Afterward, the atmosphere warmed up. "There was a lot of kidding, a lot of jokes," remembered Bob Stevenson, who was present. "Castro has a sense of humor and so did Herter and Rubottom, and they were making cracks back and forth."

Fidel continued to New York, where he had accepted an unusual secret engagement. The CIA had requested an interview, through Rufo López-Fresquet. Washington was thought to be too conspicuous a venue, which is why it had been set up outside the capital. The CIA man spent three hours alone with Fidel in his hotel suite. He emerged exhausted, but happy, and asked López-Fresquet for a drink. "Castro is not only not a Communist," he confirmed, "but he is a strong anti-Communist fighter."[58]

Stevenson heard a report during the trip that things were going so well, Fidel was considering working out a deal with the United States. Raúl Castro heard it, too, and flew into a rage. He and his brother had an argument over a long-distance telephone line. "Raúl must have been worried that Fidel was being seduced by 'the Americans,' because the older brother, in an effort to calm him, repeated that he knew 'them' too well for that to happen," remembered López-Fresquet. Then Raúl told him that some Cubans he had been training had launched an invasion of Panama, and Fidel lost his temper. He told Raúl he would not return to Havana until after 1 May, to avoid having to address that day's leftist labor rally.[59]

So concerned was Raúl by his brother's possible conversion that he flew from Havana to Texas to continue the argument. "They had a big fight in the hotel room down in Dallas as he was leaving here, and I think that was in an FBI report," said Stevenson. "I think it's probably true. He [Fidel] may have wavered a little bit, because he did get a good reception, no doubt about it."[60]

On leaving the United States, Fidel went to a meeting of the Organization of American States (OAS) in Buenos Aires. There, he proposed that the United States fund a $30-billion development program for Latin America and that the OAS create a common market. It may have been an audacious sum to demand, but it was another indication that he wanted to work with American involvement. At the same time, Phil Bonsal was in El Salvador at a regional meeting of American ambassadors. He described Fidel as eccentric, but claimed "that he could probably be handled" with the judicious application of patience and economic aid. Fidel, Bonsal continued, was "a terrific person, physically and mentally, he was far from crazy . . . not living on pills and . . . not a communist."[61] Robert Hill, the ambassador to Mexico, disagreed in the strongest terms, contending that Castro was already in league with Moscow and Peking.

He was not, but he was keeping his options open. In April, Castro appealed to the International Monetary Fund (IMF) and the World Bank, both bastions of American capitalism, for help. As always, the IMF demanded credit restraint and something close to a balanced budget, which would increase unemployment, preclude agrarian reform, and reduce the pot available for popular measures like cheap electricity, telephone calls, and transport. The IMF also insisted on a free exchange rate, currency devaluation against the dollar, and the ending of controls over imports and exports—all of which would strengthen American wealth in Cuba.[62]

In 1958, two-thirds of Cuba's exports and imports had been exchanged with the United States.[63] In addition to one-third of the sugar industry, American interests controlled all Cuba's nickel resources, the electricity and telephone companies, and a substantial proportion of the railroads, cement plants, manufacturing, banking, oil refining, and resorts and casinos, as well as the illicit industries of drugs and prostitution.[64]

The American embassy knew some nationalization was coming. Fidel had already taken over the administration of the American-owned Cuban Telephone Company and lowered the rates to pre-1957 levels. He had also lowered private rents. Outside the specific sectors affected, the business community did not object. The average Cuban's spending power was increased, and cheap utilities benefited businesses as well as individuals. "To find through quiet diplomacy formulas that would be equitable and would not interrupt the flow into Cuba of private capital for many much-needed purposes seemed to me a promising possibility in those hopeful early days," Phil Bonsal admitted.[65]

On 17 May, Fidel Castro passed an agrarian reform law. It was intended to diversify the island's agricultural production, and to break up big landowning estates in favor of smaller, local farmers. "The Agrarian Reform Law was a tremendous jolt," gloated Che. "The great monopolies also cast their worried look upon Cuba; not only has someone in the little island of the Caribbean dared to liquidate the interests of the omnipotent United

Fruit Company, legacy of Mr. Foster Dulles to his heirs; but also the empires of Mr. Rockefeller and the Deutsch group have suffered under the lash of intervention by the popular Cuban Revolution."[66]

Bob Stevenson, of the State Department, disagreed. "Cubans, for example, the Castro Cubans, say that the S really hit the fan in U.S.-Cuban relations when they passed their agrarian reform law, but that's absolute nonsense," he said. "We never questioned their right to pass an agrarian reform law. . . . All we say is that they [the proprietors] should receive prompt, adequate, and effective compensation."[67]

Compensation was offered. It came in Cuban currency bonds, to mature in twenty years, at 4.5 percent interest. The bonds were based on land values assessed for tax purposes before Batista's fall. It was widely known that American proprietors had been permitted to assess the value of their lands at a very low rate, which naturally limited the compensation they could claim now. But American companies that had engaged in that particular scheme were hardly in a position to complain.[68] Cuba's agrarian reform law, like Guatemala's, was not communist. Private holdings, up to 995 acres, were permitted to individuals and corporate entities alike. Larger holdings, up to 3,316 acres, were permitted under certain circumstances.

"Our revolution is neither capitalist nor communist!" protested Fidel Castro on television on 21 May. "We have been placed in a position where we must choose between capitalism which starves people, and communism which resolves the economic problem but suppresses the liberties so greatly cherished by man. . . . Our revolution is not red, but olive green, the color of the rebel army that emerged from the heart of the Sierra Maestra."[69] But increasingly it looked like he must make a choice, and make it soon. The question remained: what would Fidel do?

★

On 24 May 1959, John Foster Dulles died of cancer. In his last days, though it was hard for him to talk, he vouchsafed to Allen his final thoughts. They were focused on the great battle between good and evil. Allen recorded them.

> The ambitions of the Soviet leadership were not limited like those of the tsars of old to reaching out for warm waters and free oceans. The Soviets sought not a place in the sun, but the sun itself. Their objective was the world. They would not tolerate compromise on goals, only on tactics. And, as each advance was consolidated into the communist system, there was to be no turning back, no choice for the people enslaved.

> A Grand Alliance of the free nations could meet and turn back this threat. In power, moral, economic, as well as military, we of the Free World, if united, stood head and shoulders over the communist world. But would we have the steadfast purpose and the understanding, the skill and the fortitude, to use our strength wisely, meaningfully, successfully? And how could our people here in the United States be brought to understand the issues, their responsibilities and the need for American leadership anywhere, maybe even everywhere, in the world?[70]

Ironically, Foster's sense of an inexorable communist advance and capitalist collapse resembled Karl Marx's theory of history. But it related little to reality. Khrushchev spoke frequently of his desire to demonstrate in the Soviet Union progress that the world would wish to follow. So far, though, the glittering delights of life under communism were not apparent to many people. Since June 1953, fifteen thousand people had been leaving East Germany through Berlin every month. The Soviet Union had fallen disastrously behind in the arms race against the United States. It was also in the process of falling out with China, its most significant and substantial ally: Mao sneered at Khrushchev's poetic aspirations toward "peaceful cooperation" with capitalist states.[71] If the Soviets really were bent on world domination, they were making a poor job of it. But by predicating his foreign policy on inevitable conflict with the left, extending friendship to almost any regime on the right, however deplorable, and defining communism as the ultimate anti-Americanism, John Foster Dulles helped create the conditions for a far more virulent spread of communism than Khrushchev's hazy ideas of Soviet progress ever did.

The same day that Foster Dulles died, François Duvalier collapsed. His physician, Jacques Fourcand, diagnosed a diabetic coma, and administered a massive dose of insulin. It nearly killed him. In fact, Duvalier had suffered a heart attack. The high dose of insulin caused the glucose level in his blood to plummet. He became hypoglycemic, and then did fall into a coma.

Clément Barbot noticed something had gone wrong. Swiftly, he called in a second opinion. The second doctor said to Simone Duvalier that he thought Fourcand was trying to kill the president, and told Barbot to administer glucose to counter the insulin. Barbot did so personally, and then contacted the American ambassador. A United States Navy cardiac team was immediately sent over from Guantánamo Bay to save the Haitian dictator's life.[72]

Duvalier remained in the coma for nine hours before finally emerging. But he was still critically ill. News of his illness was suppressed for a fortnight. In his place, Barbot took over. The chief of the Tontons Macoutes was now in charge of Haiti—with the United States military already in place to support him.

8

"OUR REAL FRIENDS"

★

ANTONIO RODRÍGUEZ ECHAZABAL WAS A CUBAN REVOLUTIONARY OF the 1930s vintage, and a consummate tough guy. Having fought the dictator Gerardo Machado, he moved to Port-au-Prince and set up a butcher's shop. Since François Duvalier's victory, he had run Radio Freedom from his shop, broadcasting anti-Duvalier messages. Once, he had had the support of Rafael Trujillo. Now, Fidel Castro saw in the unmellowed butcher ideal material for a diplomat, and so Rodríguez became the Cuban ambassador to Haiti.

Rodríguez displeased his Haitian hosts, and the Dominicans across the border. In May 1959, a live grenade was thrown into his car, apparently by one of Trujillo's agents. The quick-thinking Rodríguez tossed it back out, killing his would-be assassin. On 6 June, he was again in his car with a companion when it was ambushed by Tontons Macoutes armed with submachine guns. He ducked behind the armored panel he had prudently installed in the driver's door, pulled out his own pistol, and fired back. More than fifty bullet holes were later counted in the chassis. Rodríguez escaped with a few scratches.

This attack on its ambassador provoked the government of Cuba to lodge a formal complaint with the government of Haiti. Rodríguez flew to Havana to tell Fidel Castro the story in person. A few days later, he returned, with four new bodyguards: heavily armed, heavily bearded Cuban revolutionaries. Crowds assembled to admire this remarkable sight whenever Rodríguez went shopping. Port-au-Prince lit up with rumors that Castro's next step might be a full invasion.[1]

"Haiti is in a terrible position," a Brazilian diplomat told Dick Rubottom. "It is right in the middle between Cuba and the Dominican Republic and there is good reason to fear that an attempt might be made to strike at the Dominican Republic by invading through Haiti."[2] By the summer of

1959, Haiti, under the caretaker rule of Clément Barbot, was in turmoil. Bombs exploded in casinos and at public festivals. There was an attempt to kill the interior minister. Someone disinterred the corpse of Duvalier's father, who had died a few weeks before his son became president, cut out the heart, and defecated on the mutilated body.[3]

On 16 June, the United States Marine adviser Captain Charles Williamson was accredited to the presidential guard in Port-au-Prince and was invited to meet the recuperating president. Williamson was shown up to Duvalier's quarters on the second floor of the east wing of the National Palace, and found the president reclining in an easy chair, clad in pajamas and a dressing gown, his bare feet propped up on a stool. He was reading a Wild West adventure novel by the popular author Max Brand. Duvalier was in fine spirits, even telling jokes while Williamson passed on the marines' apparently sincere wishes for his speedy recovery. "Contrary to all rumors, the President is quite alert and far from physically infirm or mentally incompetent," wrote Williamson. "He seems to be very well disposed toward the Marines and the work they are doing."[4]

It had been expected, almost universally, that once Barbot had accustomed himself to power he would never hand it back to Duvalier. There had even been rumors that he had already received payment from Rafael Trujillo, through their shared friend Johnny Abbes, to arrange a coup.[5] But Barbot's loyalty to Duvalier was absolute. He had proven himself willing to kill for the president. Those who knew him well believed he would die for him, too.[6] In July, when Duvalier returned to public life, Barbot stepped down. Soon, he would wish he had not.

After Duvalier resumed power, he seemed to become even more brutal. Peepholes were made in his torture chambers, to allow him to observe discreetly. Sometimes, he was in the room itself, while men and women were beaten, tortured, and plunged into baths of sulfuric acid. But his interest may have been as much or more in feeling a frisson of control over the fear and suffering of others as it was in the spectacle. Yvonne Hakim-Rimpel, who had been beaten and raped in front of him at the beginning of 1958, was arrested again by the Macoutes and interrogated in a cell. "Who was responsible for beating you that night?" her interrogator asked. "Was it the government? Do you think it was *Duvalier*?" At that moment, she glanced at a tiny hole in the wall and noticed a gleam of light reflecting off a pair of spectacles. She replied that she did not know who had attacked her, but it was not soldiers or government officials, and definitely not Duvalier.[7]

According to some, the worst torture of all was just to be kept in

Fort Dimanche, the military prison built by the Americans during the occupation—now reserved mainly for political prisoners. Crammed into tiny cells, the inmates had to sleep in shifts. They were fed with gruel, slopped directly onto the floor. Each was rationed one glass of drinking water a week. Beyond that, every day they were given a one-minute hosepipe shower in untreated water, and had to gulp down as much as possible. Almost every day, someone died, if not from torture or dehydration then from malnutrition, infection, waterborne disease, or one of the maladies spread by the vermin that swarmed over walls, floors, and bodies. The dead were left to decompose for days, side by side with the living, until finally the guards would trundle up with the same cart they used for distributing gruel, lug the corpse onto it, and wheel it away to be dumped in the mass graves outside.

By the middle of 1959, Duvalier's behavior began to worry close associates, including Clément Barbot, Jacques Fourcand, General Gérard Constant, and an American physician, Elmer Loughlin. Many blamed it on his heart attack or on the treatment he had received. During a coma, any process that reduces blood flow to the brain may result in permanent damage. Such brain damage may be associated with a reduction in cognitive or physical ability, but neither of those was observed in Duvalier. It is unlikely to have triggered psychopathy.[8] It is true that he had no empathy with human suffering. It is true that he behaved impulsively. It is also true that he seemed to have no moral compass. But these behaviors were present prior to the illness. As for Duvalier's political mind, if anything, it had sharpened. It is possible, though, that something about the brush with death made Duvalier psychologically determined to exert control.

More than once, Barbot and Loughlin went independently to American officials to warn them about Duvalier's dangerous mental state. Their concerns were dismissed. Duvalier's government was considered constitutional, stable, and anticommunist. It continued to enjoy American support.[9]

★

At dusk on 14 June 1959, a plane with Dominican markings took off from Cuba and touched down in the Cordillera Central, Dominican Republic. Inside were fifty-six guerrillas. They soon encountered a local garrison. There was a fight, and the invaders were defeated. Thirty or forty survivors fled. Rafael Trujillo launched what he called a "rabbit hunt" to find them.

Six days later, two yachts filled with more guerrillas were escorted by

Cuban frigates to Great Inagua, in the Bahamas. From there, the yachts headed for the north coast of the Dominican Republic. Dominican intelligence had infiltrated this second wave. Before they landed, the yachts were blasted by mortar fire and bazookas from the shore. Trujillo's planes, directed by his son Ramfis, commander of the air force, zoomed low over the yachts and shot rockets. Both boats were blown to splinters. The sapphire waters around them were filled with bobbing bodies. A few survivors managed to swim to the shore, and escape into the forest. The army used napalm to get them out.[10]

Ramfis Trujillo and Johnny Abbes were in charge of the response to the invasion, and it was they who made the decision to execute all prisoners who were taken alive. The Cordillera Central prisoners were bound hand and foot, loaded onto planes, and flown to San Isidro, the national air headquarters. When the plane doors opened, the bound men were kicked out onto the runway, twelve feet below. Ramfis personally led the tortures and murders that followed. In local slang, the word for "bird" also meant "homosexual." Ramfis took one invader up in a plane. "You're a bird," he said; "let's see if you can fly." The man was thrown out of the hatch.[11] Only 4 of the 225 or so invaders survived.

The invasion had been led by the Dominican Enrique Jiménez Moya, and the Cuban Delio Gómez Ochoa. Both were friends of Fidel Castro, and former officers in M-26-7. Jiménez was killed in Trujillo's rabbit hunt. Gómez was taken prisoner. It was soon announced that he had died in his cell of a heart attack.

The invasions revealed the existence of an impressively large domestic underground opposition to Trujillo. Members of prominent families were involved; some were even friends of Trujillo's younger children, Ramfis, Rhadamés, and Angelita.[12] This was intolerable, and so Trujillo denied it. Instead, he blamed the invasion entirely on Fidel Castro. In reality, though it was plain to see that Fidel had supported the invasion in every possible way, the force had consisted of Dominicans, Cubans, Venezuelans, Spaniards, Guatemalans, and Americans—not unlike the Caribbean Legion that had attempted to topple Trujillo a decade before.

If he were to claim the invasion as Cuban, Trujillo realized that he needed Gómez after all. The Cuban guerrilla unexpectedly recovered from his "fatal" heart attack. "Again and again, Delio was hauled out of his cell and temporarily installed in a hotel suite so that he could tell foreign correspondents how grateful he was for Trujillo's boundless mercy," remembered Arturo Espaillat. "That boy really made a production out of it!"

Gómez was tortured, but managed to avoid any further incidents of death. Meanwhile, Trujillo threatened Cuba with air strikes.[13]

The American government was concerned on Trujillo's behalf. Dick Rubottom warned Christian Herter that the "Cuban" invasion violated the principle of nonintervention, "which is a corner stone of the inter-American system."[14] The attacks, he said, could precipitate all-out war in the Caribbean. The United States could not permit such an intervention.

On 8 July, with a straight face, Rubottom told a meeting of Latin American diplomats that 180 years of history proved that the United States had always deplored dictators and supported representative governments. "However, we cannot allow individual groups of 'liberators' to pass judgment on the governments of particular countries and to undertake from bases in other countries to launch attacks aiming to oust violently the governments they dislike," he said. "This amounts to anarchy. It is a shame and a mistake for anyone to imply that our abhorrence of this sort of behavior constitutes support for or protection of the despotic or dictatorial governments being attacked."[15]

If individual groups passing judgment on the government of one country from another was the problem, then Trujillo was just as guilty as Castro. Over the preceding few months, as the State Department knew, a force had been assembled by Trujillo in the Dominican Republic to invade Cuba, under the command of a former Batista police chief.[16] Trujillo commenced another major arms-buying spree from European dealers, and hired more mercenaries for his foreign legion. He also had the Cuban embassy in Ciudad Trujillo ransacked. The Cuban government severed diplomatic relations on 26 June. On 2 July, Trujillo went to the OAS, claiming that a joint Cuban-Venezuelan invasion force of three thousand men and twenty-five aircraft was preparing in Cuba for an imminent invasion of his country.

Trujillo's complaints were not welcomed. Venezuela and Cuba both refused to admit any visiting inspectors, on the grounds that, as an illegitimate ruler, Trujillo had voided his right to representation.[17] Rubottom attempted to persuade the Venezuelan ambassador that international communism was involved, and the OAS should take the threat of invasion seriously. The Venezuelan ambassador responded coldly that a week had passed since Trujillo's appeal, and therefore the invasion was obviously not as imminent as all that. Rubottom then tried to convince him it was urgent on grounds of saving François Duvalier. "One of the most disturbing things is the terrible position of little Haiti, caught between the two tigers," he said. "After a series of Government changes and internal strife in the past 18 months the freely elected government of Duvalier deserves a chance to straighten things out. While the Duvalier Government may not be a paragon of excellence it at least offers some promise of stability."[18]

The allegations of communism within M-26-7 had not died down. On 17 July, Fidel resigned as prime minister, telling a press conference—including a pensive Raúl, sitting in the front row—how affronted he was to be called a communist by those inside and outside Cuba. He decried Urrutia, the moderate president he had installed, as a traitor. Crowds assembled in Havana demanding Urrutia's resignation, which was swiftly received. On 23 July, Fidel resumed the prime ministership, celebrating by playing in a charity baseball game. He appointed a new president, Osvaldo Dorticós, an upper-middle-class lawyer who had helped to draft the Agrarian Reform Law. Behind the scenes, unknown to most of the Cuban administration as well as the wider world, Fidel was still keeping his options open. That same month, he sent his intelligence chief, Ramiro Valdés, to Mexico City, for a secret meeting with the Soviet ambassador and a representative of the KGB.[19]

Trujillo had no hope with the OAS, but another opportunity presented itself. William Morgan was an American mercenary who had led a guerrilla force known as the Tigers of Espesura in the Sierra del Escambray during the Cuban Revolution. His longtime collaborator was Eloy Gutiérrez Menoyo, whose brother, Carlos, had organized the failed Revolutionary Directorate attack on Batista's palace in 1957. Morgan and Gutiérrez Menoyo had made a deal, apparently financial, with Raúl Castro to fight alongside M-26-7. After the victory, they had gone to Trujillo, telling him that the Castros had declined to pay. Now, they were more than happy to turn on Fidel. For a fee of $1 million, they would invade Cuba.

It is a measure of Trujillo's desperation that he forked over the first $500,000 immediately. He also put Johnny Abbes on the project. The invasion would strike at Trinidad, a pretty colonial town on Cuba's west coast. Trinidad was adjacent to the Sierra del Escambray, Morgan and Gutiérrez Menoyo's old territory, and a plausible base for guerrilla warfare. Little attempt was made to keep the plans secret. By May 1959, as one Dominican agent wearily reported to his senior officer, "General, they're talking about Morgan's counter-revolution in every Cuban bar on Flagler Street"—the center of Miami's Cuban exile community.[20]

During the first two weeks of August, preparations continued. Abbes and Morgan indulged in extensive planning conversations over uncoded radio. Morgan constantly asked for more money. Trujillo shook funds out of wealthy Cubans in Miami. He also harassed Batista, still loitering miserably in Ciudad Trujillo. Batista declined. "Then the Old Man let it be known that he was on the verge of having Batista hauled bodily from his Hotel Jaragua suite and dumped in the sea," remembered Arturo Espaillat. "Batista suddenly saw the light."[21] Batista matched Trujillo's commitment of $1 million.

On 12 August, Morgan's voice crackled over the radio to Trujillo: "Trinidad is ours! Don't let us down! We need men, guns, supplies."

Trujillo sent an exploratory plane to Cuba, with a cargo of munitions. When it returned, its crew reported that, flying overhead, they had heard machine-gun fire and explosions from Trinidad. They had landed nearby to unload the munitions. They were greeted by Cuban troops shouting, "Viva Trujillo!" and "Down with Castro!"

Gutiérrez Menoyo radioed Trujillo next: "We hold Trinidad and the airport," he said. "We are ready to begin and we will win."

"What do you need?" asked Trujillo.

"More planes, machine guns," came the reply.

"And what else?" asked the Benefactor. "Go ahead, tell me. You deserve the best."

Shyly, Gutiérrez Menoyo continued: "Well, with your permission, Generalissimo, I have always admired your uniform, with the medals and the tri-cornered hat. I would like to enter Havana in a uniform like that. But I feel too ashamed to ask for it, though it is something I would like very much to have."[22]

Delighted, Trujillo took note of Gutiérrez Menoyo's measurements, and prepared a full invasion force.

"But Chief," said Espaillat, "Castro and Morgan are luring us into a trap."

Trujillo gave him a look. "What's the matter, General, lost your guts?"

"No, Chief, but I haven't seen any blood," said Espaillat. "I haven't seen any corpses—just words and dramatics, a stage show. Show me some blood and I will go."

"You'll soon see plenty of blood," snarled Trujillo. But most of his men agreed with Espaillat, and would not go. Trujillo finally agreed to send a first strike force of just ten men, with hundreds held back for the next wave.

When the ten landed, they were met not by Morgan and Gutiérrez Menoyo, but by Fidel Castro and three thousand barbudos. Fidel had been watching from the shadows, much amused, when his troops shouted "Viva Trujillo!" to fool the first plane. The Dominican captives were paraded on television, and the radio conversations between Abbes and Morgan—which Cuban intelligence had recorded—were played for all to hear. Before the whole of Cuba, and the whole of Latin America beyond, Trujillo had been trounced. The Cubans threw a fiesta, at which everyone wore tricornered Trujillo hats made out of paper.

It is still not clear whether Morgan had planned this from the beginning, or whether he was caught red-handed by the Cubans and forced to turn double agent. Briefly, he seemed to be in Fidel's favor and was allowed to retire to the Cuban countryside to run a frog farm. In 1961, though, he would find himself before a firing squad. Gutiérrez Menoyo would serve twenty-two years in jail. To Espaillat's astonishment, Trujillo did not execute Johnny Abbes. "It had been taken for granted that he would be 'accidented,'" he wrote. "I think the Old Man was so embarrassed that he wanted to forget about the whole thing."[23]

In Ciudad Trujillo, Batista had reached the end of his tether. The United States had prevaricated about offering him asylum on its own territory. Finally, he had simply applied for a visa at the American embassy alongside all the other potential migrants and visitors, sponsored by Senator Edward Dirksen of Illinois.[24] This prompted a desperate flurry by the State Department to find somewhere else to send him. Liechtenstein, Holland, Ireland, and Andorra were tried. Eventually, the United States managed to persuade Portugal's dictator to accommodate Batista in Madeira. At the end of August, he finally fled from Trujillo's clutches—a few million dollars poorer, but alive.

Meanwhile, in Cuba, Fidel's popularity showed no signs of abating. In the summer of 1959, the movie star Ava Gardner, who had been vacationing in Haiti, took a suite at Cuba's Hotel Nacional. She cut a glamorous figure. Jack Ruby, an obscure nightclub operator in town on dubious business with associates of the mafioso Santo Trafficante, would remember for the rest of his life the day he breakfasted beside her in Havana. A few years later, he would achieve infamy as the murderer of Lee Harvey Oswald—and scores of conspiracy theorists would wonder whether gazing upon an actress was really the most important thing he had done in Havana in the summer of 1959.[25]

Gardner asked to meet Fidel, and was invited to the nearby Havana Hilton. Fidel, Raúl, and Che had their offices in the former VIP suite at the top. She was taken up and introduced. Earnestly, Fidel told her his plans for Cuba. "She spoke very highly of Castro when she got back," a friend of hers remembered. "Said he was full of good ideas." She asked him if he hated Americans. He replied no, only Richard Nixon.

Though she remarked upon his trailing boot laces and unmatched socks, Gardner found Fidel strikingly attractive, and sent him a series of notes after their meeting. She had a reputation as a gentleman killer. Alongside a string of high-profile boyfriends and husbands, her conquests had allegedly included John F. Kennedy, a decade earlier. Nineteen-year-old Marita Lorenz, who would later write a lurid and erratic memoir about her alleged affairs with Fidel and the Venezuelan dictator Marcos Pérez Jiménez, and her involvement with the CIA, claimed at the time to be Fidel's girlfriend. According to her story, she intercepted Gardner's notes.

After a day of heavy drinking, Gardner turned up at the Hilton and pounced upon Lorenz in the lobby. "So you're the little bitch who's hiding Fidel!" she said. Lorenz dived into an elevator. Gardner pursued, catching her and slapping her hard across the face. The nearest guard drew his pistol on the Hollywood star, and the matter was swiftly resolved.

One thing Fidel was not short of was macho young men. He "fixed up Ava Gardner with an aide," Marita said, "who was to satisfy her in a suite at the National Hotel, compliments of Cuba."[26] History does not record which barbudo fulfilled this revolutionary duty.

★

On the night of 12 August, a small ship from the southern port of Baracoa in Cuba brought thirty men into Haitian waters near Cap des Irois. They were wearing the uniforms and carrying the arms of Fidel Castro's army. They were led by Henri d'Anton, an Algerian Frenchman by birth, who had married into the Déjoie family, spoke Creole, and had lived in Haiti for some years. D'Anton had joined Fidel in the Sierra Maestra. It was rumored that he had been sent to Haiti by Che Guevara himself.[27]

D'Anton hijacked a sailing boat to land on Haitian shores. The anchor—a rusty engine block—was thrown overboard, and the skipper paid off in Cuban cigars. Few shots needed firing to take the village, and its inhabitants were thereafter presented with Déjoieist propaganda and informed of their liberation. The thirty men made for the Massif du Sud.

News spread quickly to Port-au-Prince. First Lieutenant William Bonthron of the United States Marines was sleeping off a bout of malaria when he was woken by someone shouting that the Cubans had invaded. Years later, he remembered thinking, "Wow, a chance to go to war."[28]

That it was not, for the marines were under strict orders from their embassy to restrict their contribution to advising the Haitians. They attended Haiti's council of war, directed the crisis management operation, and suggested air and seaborne responses. Some of them accompanied the Haitian army to Jérémie, where it was widely rumored their help spilled over from the advisory into the practical. The mission chief, Robert Heinl, personally accompanied Clément Barbot.

There were two major skirmishes between the Cubans and the Haitians, in which many of the former were killed or wounded. Barbot publicly offered 500 gourdes ($100), four times the average annual income, for each dead Cuban turned in. Over the next ten days, most were retrieved. Four men were brought in alive, tied together with a rope, and flown to Port-au-Prince. A large crowd gathered at the airport, hoping to see replicas of Ambassador Rodríguez Echazabal's grizzly barbudos. When the plane door opened, out were shoved four nervous youths, barely a trace of fluff on their faces. "Look, they are children," hooted a voice from the crowd.[29]

In a book he later wrote on Haiti, Heinl flatly denied any practical involvement on the part of his men, but then claimed, "The U.S. Marines involved are probably the only United States troops to have engaged in ground combat with the forces of Fidel Castro."[30] These two assertions seem to contradict each other. It is not clear how far American involvement went. None of the countries involved wanted to admit its role. For Cuba, it was a failure. For Haiti, it was an embarrassment. For the United States, if troops did engage, it could have been a war.

After the invasion had been defeated, Barbot invited the marines' logistics adviser, Lieutenant Colonel Thomas Tighe, to his house. Over drinks, Barbot said smoothly that some in the army felt the marine mission had not helped as much as it could have. Tighe agreed, but reminded Barbot of the possible ramifications in the United States were they to do so.[31] At the same time, Haiti formally requested American patrols of its waters and airspace, and offered a military base to the United States. The request and the offer were declined.[32]

There were plenty of good reasons for the United States to be cautious in Haiti. During that same month, Duvalier banned a teacher's union on the grounds that it had allegedly been infiltrated by communists, and ordered two French priests to leave the country because they left his name out of prayers. Late in the afternoon of 18 August, there was a silent vigil for the departing priests in Port-au-Prince's cathedral attended by a congregation of over one thousand. Midway through, Clément Barbot burst through the doors at the head of a band of Tontons Macoutes, armed with submachine guns and coco macaques, and wearing steel helmets. The Macoutes stormed the cathedral, beating worshippers. Outside, the police arrested sixty of the wounded.

By the end of the summer of 1959, Duvalier had terrorized, imprisoned, and tortured much of his opposition out of existence. One evening, he sent trucks to the Vodou heartland outside Port-au-Prince, between Croix-des-Missions and Croix-des-Bouquets. Vodou *houngans* and *mambos*, male and female priests, were kidnapped at gunpoint and ordered into the trucks. They were driven back into the capital, to the National Palace, and were taken into the ornate Salon des Bustes. On the stroke of midnight, Duvalier swept in, unaccompanied, draped in the crimson robes of the Secte Rouge, a legendary Vodou society supposedly devoted to cannibalism and other wickednesses. "Never forget," he intoned, "that I am the supreme authority of the State. Henceforth, I, I alone, I am your only master."[33] That was all; he swept out again, and the houngans and mambos were sent off into the night.

No Haitian leader before Duvalier had understood the potential of Vodou. Though largely clandestine, following waves of persecution and intolerance, Vodou remained the social glue across much of the country. Houngans and mambos were important figures in the community, often functioning as elders, leaders, doctors, teachers, and judges, as well as priests. Duvalier drew Vodou out of the closet, gave it respect, and legitimized its position. This was a populist and genuinely liberating gesture, which did give him a groundswell of legitimate support, especially among poor black Haitians.[34] But he also manipulated public belief in Vodou as a means of control. The religion is based on ideas of balance. It may be used for good or evil, depending on the practitioner's intent. Duvalier worked with the evil. He dressed in the manner of Baron Samedi, the Vodou loa of the dead, in a smart, dark suit, occasional top hat, and dark glasses. He cultivated an eerie stillness of manner, designed to enhance the impression. It was said that in private he would sit in his bath, wearing only the top hat, in order to speak with spirits, and that he used goat entrails to predict the future. In an echo of the names of the Vodou loas known as Papa Guédé and Papa Legba, he called himself Papa Doc.

There can be no answer to the question of whether Duvalier himself was sincere in his Vodouism, or whether he was using it cynically for political ends. He seems never to have spoken or written unguardedly about it. There are inconclusive hints. In one State Department report from 1959, Val Washington, who had recently met Clément Barbot, alleged that Duvalier had helped cement the bond between himself and his chief Macoute when he "pointed out to Barbot the absurdity of some of the latter's superstitious Voodoo beliefs which Barbot had absorbed as a child."[35] But Duvalier and Barbot, like many Haitians, were conscious that Vodou should not be spoken about openly in front of most Americans—and impressing the Americans was the highest priority.

"In Haiti we are striving to achieve democracy," Duvalier told an audience of civilian volunteers and United States Marines at a rally that October. "The next two years will see many things accomplished. . . . There has been an Army, but I have created a new Army, an Army dedicated to the youth of the country."[36] He meant the Tontons Macoutes. As he spoke into the microphone, his family and the presidential guard arranged around him, lightning flashed in the sky above the National Palace, and thunder echoed around the mountains that ring Port-au-Prince. Charles Williamson, one of the marine commanders present, noted with wonder that the setting "seemed to have been staged." The implication in the speech was correspondingly monumental: Duvalier made it clear that he wanted the marines to train the Macoutes. Williamson himself would later deny that he had any connection to the Macoutes, but did acknowledge that he was often seen with Macoute officers. In Port-au-Prince, he was nicknamed "TTM blanc" (white Macoute). Eventually, all the United States Marines would be called "TTM blancs."

The head of the army was alarmed at the closeness between the marines and the Macoutes, and sent an officer to give Williamson a pistol to protect himself. Williamson thanked the man, but declined on grounds of American neutrality. Anyway, he joked, in the event of a shootout, he would prefer a submachine gun. The officer gave him a cold stare, and told him one had already been set aside for him. It was delivered to his house that evening, along with a sackful of loaded magazines.[37]

★

On 15 September, Nikita Khrushchev arrived in the United States. He had been invited by mistake. Eisenhower had asked the diplomat Bob Murphy to invite him only if progress were made at a meeting of foreign ministers in Geneva. Murphy misunderstood, and invited him without conditions. Pleasantly surprised, Khrushchev accepted. In private, Ike was embarrassed; but this apparently conciliatory gesture on the part of the American administration was praised in the international press.[38]

Photographed together at Camp David, the two leaders, with their bald heads, protruding ears, and single-breasted suits, looked remarkably alike. They discovered some shared interests. Both enjoyed cowboy movies, and Khrushchev happily confirmed that Stalin had watched dozens of them, too, afterward reviewing the politics of each western from a critical Marxist viewpoint.[39] But neither was at ease. Khrushchev was alternately impressed and repelled by the wealth and productivity he saw. At a party on New York's Upper East Side, he met a selection of big shots, including Averell Harriman, Dean Rusk, John D. Rockefeller III, and John Kenneth Galbraith. Their human appearance took him aback: "By no means did they have faces like pigs, as depicted in posters from our civil war era. They didn't look at all like the capitalists you see in such caricatures." But he found them aggressive and closed-minded, and that reminded him very much of those capitalists. "I think that mainly they were trying to dishearten me, to create the impression that the situation was hopeless, with no way out," he remembered. "Perhaps they wanted to make a united front with the government, so that we would accept the conditions they were trying to dictate to us."[40] In Hollywood, he was introduced to some of Twentieth Century Fox's actors, including Frank Sinatra, Gary Cooper, and Elizabeth Taylor; Ronald Reagan refused to turn up. "I could tell Khrushchev liked me," purred Marilyn Monroe. "He smiled more when he was introduced to me than for anybody else."[41] Khrushchev made a point of telling the glamorous party about his childhood laboring in coal pits.

After the party, he had been scheduled to visit Disneyland, but disappointment was in store. The Los Angeles police said that his safety could not be guaranteed without forcing everyone else to leave the park, and so he would not be allowed to go. In front of Hollywood's finest, he protested. Was there cholera in Disneyland? Was it full of bandits? Frank Sinatra whispered to David Niven, who was sitting next to Khrushchev's wife, Nina: "Screw the cops! Tell the old broad you and I'll take them down this afternoon."[42] But Sinatra was not allowed, either, and so Khrushchev was instead driven around aimlessly for the afternoon in a limousine, simmering with resentment. It was a poor substitute for Mr. Toad's Wild Ride.

Neither Eisenhower nor Allen Dulles took to Khrushchev's rambunctious style. When the Soviet premier told them the CIA and KGB should ally—"We should buy our intelligence data together and save money. We'd have to pay the people only once"—they did not see the joke.[43] Over lunch with Nixon and Eisenhower on 26 September, one of Ike's advisers said Khrushchev became "personally insulting" and "almost violent."[44] Eisenhower was surprised to note that the wives of the Soviet party were "feminine even though Communist," but otherwise was confirmed in his prejudices. He found Khrushchev unpredictable and belligerent. Though there was a last-minute thaw, prompted by a cheerful day at Gettysburg in which Khrushchev said nice things about Ike's cows, the trip was not a success.[45]

While Khrushchev was in the United States, the Soviet Presidium had considered the question of providing military aid to Cuba. The foreign minister advised strongly against. Such a move, he argued, would antagonize Washington. It was Khrushchev personally who, on his return, overturned that decision. The visit had not gone well. Clearly, antagonizing Washington was something the Soviet premier was now prepared to risk. Warsaw Pact weapons were dispatched to Havana.[46]

In October 1959, a Soviet cultural delegation arrived in Havana. It was led by the press correspondent Aleksandr Ivanovich Alekseyev. Fidel was not told that the delegation was a front for the KGB, nor that Alekseyev had previously been the KGB resident in Buenos Aires, but it was clear from his reaction to Alekseyev's arrival that he knew this was a line of communication straight to Moscow. When he first met Fidel, Alekseyev brought vodka and caviar. "What good vodka, what good caviar!" Fidel exclaimed. "I think it's worth establishing trade relations with the Soviet Union!" He proposed that Anastas Mikoyan, Khrushchev's deputy, should visit Cuba. Then, to Alekseyev's astonishment, he claimed that Marx and Lenin were his intellectual guides. "At that time," Alekseyev said, "we could not even imagine that [Fidel] knew Marxist theory."[47]

Alekseyev's recollection is the earliest credible evidence of Fidel explicitly aligning himself with communism. A turning point had been reached. There were several reasons, and probably the least important was the ideological influence of Raúl and Che. Fidel had resisted his brother's politics for six years, and Che's for three. He had remained a trenchant nationalist and constitutionalist, even in the loneliest days in the Sierra Maestra, when those two men became his most trusted compañeros; even when they were almost his only compañeros. As Alekseyev hinted, Fidel's "conversion" was probably pragmatic. The most important factor was his relationship with the United States. Since the day of his victory, he had been dancing around Uncle Sam: one minute whispering private entreaties, the next slinging public insults. For any Caribbean leader, the United States was too big to ignore. Those who ingratiated themselves sufficiently with it could survive. Trujillo had, for many years. Duvalier was warming up to the same strategy. Everyone knew what happened to those who did not. Che Guevara had seen it in Guatemala.

Fidel, like all would-be reformers in Latin America, was in a precarious position. If he accepted American help, he risked becoming a puppet. If he refused American help, he risked being toppled. The surprise granting of military aid by the Soviet Union did not change this game overnight. All that was offered was a few conventional weapons; not political support, not economic aid, not military defense, and certainly not a nuclear deterrent. Fidel might also have felt less secure had he known how little support he had in the Presidium beyond Khrushchev himself. Nonetheless, any deal with the Soviets represented a potential counterbalance to American domination. Fidel seized it.

In October, Major Huber Matos, the military commander of Cuba's Camagüey Province, resigned, claiming that a purge of anticommunists was under way. He was immediately accused of planning a coup. According to the Cuban treasury minister Rufo López-Fresquet, Matos had been building a support base among the peasants in Camagüey—but to fight against Raúl, who had just been promoted to minister for the armed forces, and for Fidel. "At first in a roundabout way and later more pointedly, the major told me that a Communist conspiracy was taking place," López-Fresquet remembered. "Matos believed Castro was not involved and did not know its extent and gravity. Raúl, I was informed, was the leader of the cabal and, in Matos's opinion, was prepared to kill his brother if need be."[48]

In fact, by that month, the Castro brothers had drawn closer together. Fidel sent Camilo Cienfuegos to place Matos under house arrest, and to assume control of Camagüey. In December, Matos would be sentenced to twenty years' imprisonment for conspiracy, sedition, and treason. Sensing the change in climate, some former Fidelistas began to leave, even from high government positions. In Washington, this was taken as a sign that Fidel was losing support. But the State Department was ill informed about the expanding working-class movement in Havana and around the country.

Throughout 1959, Fidel was building an enormous power base, at a social level too low for the CIA to notice. The base was constructed on ideas of national liberation, and its enemy was *el imperialismo yanquí*. Many middle- and upper-class Cubans may have been put off by this confrontational rhetoric, but most Cubans were not. The United States government was not aware of how much ordinary Cubans resented it, and consistently underestimated Fidel's appeal. "Here is a country that you would believe, on the basis of our history, would be one of our real friends," said Eisenhower at a press conference on 28 October. "I don't know exactly what the difficulty is."[49]

★

One day in October, Hilda Gadea went to pick up her daughter, who had been visiting Che. As she was leaving, Camilo Cienfuegos arrived. He picked Hildita up, and she pulled his beard.

"Does it hurt?" she asked.

"No," he replied with a laugh, "because I am very strong."

"How is it that you have such a long beard?" she asked.

"Because every day I pull on it a little," he said, "look, like this!" Hildita giggled and pulled his beard again.[50] Her mother, too, was charmed by the smiling young man. It was with a shock that, a few days later, she heard he was dead.

On 28 October 1959, the Apache six-seater plane in which Camilo was returning from Camagüey to Havana disappeared. Camilo had been piloting himself. He had one aide with him. Raúl rushed into a cabinet meeting, and told Fidel. Fidel sent for a map, and told Raúl to investigate.

Three hours passed before Raúl returned, with the news that there had been an atmospheric disturbance on Camilo's route. Now, Fidel seemed worried. The brothers spread out large military maps of Cuba over the cabinet table, and tried to work out where he might have crashed.[51] An extensive search was mounted, but neither the plane's wreckage nor either of the two bodies was ever found.

Conspiracy theories flourished. "The rumor was that Castro had ordered his death," said Wayne Smith, of the American embassy in Havana. "He was not the type to follow Castro's orders blindly, and it was believed that he was unsympathetic to the Communist control of the 26th of July Movement."[52]

"There's the general feeling that Cienfuegos was kind of sympathetic with Matos," added Smith's colleague, Bob Stevenson. "[Matos] was anti-communist, but he wasn't disloyal to the revolution. Cienfuegos may have intended to come back with that message, which wasn't the message Castro wanted. At any rate, his plane disappeared when he left Matos' place, and no one ever knew what happened to him. We suspected at the time that he might have been shot down."[53]

The French embassy passed on to the Americans a secret memorandum, reporting that Camilo and two aides (rather than one) had been seized aboard the plane, murdered, and buried alongside the plane on a farm in Camagüey. The site, reported the French embassy, was afterward guarded by a militia.[54] No evidence has ever emerged to support these allegations. Rufo López-Fresquet, then Fidel's treasury minister but soon to leave for exile in the United States, was ambivalent about the possibility that Camilo had been murdered. Though he did not rule it out, and noted that Camilo "was too popular for Fidel's peace of mind," he also pointed out that political differences were unlikely to have caused a rift. Camilo's brother, Osmani, was a communist, as was his best friend, Che Guevara.

Though Camilo was not, he never seemed to have political arguments with anybody. Furthermore, López-Fresquet said, "I remember how, during my trip to Camagüey in September 1959, he had landed his plane in the middle of a cane field, taking no precautions whatever."[55] Among the barbudos, Camilo was legendary for his recklessness.

"Who killed him?" asked Che, in the introduction to his later treatise, *Guerrilla Warfare*. "The enemy succeeded in killing him, because there are no safe airplanes; because pilots cannot acquire all the experience necessary; because, overburdened with work, Camilo wished to be in Havana quickly. His own character killed him, too. Camilo did not measure danger; he used it for a diversion, mocked it, lured, toyed and played with it. With his guerrilla fighter mentality he would not postpone a plan on account of a cloud." Che was devastated by Camilo's death. For many years, he had planned to call his first son Ernesto—or possibly Vladimir, in a tribute to Lenin.[56] When that son was born, in 1962, he chose instead to call him Camilo.

Whatever had happened to Camilo, Fidel's anti-American drive showed no sign of slowing down. The American ambassador, Phil Bonsal, later recalled that it was in November 1959 that he gave up any hope of compromise with Fidel. The State Department's National Intelligence Estimate noted that Che had moved from the Agrarian Reform Institute to replace Felipe Pazos, the centrist president of the National Bank. This appointment, it said, had "brought forth a spontaneous expressing of public lack of confidence in the government's financial policy. Depositors withdrew at least $50,000,000 of savings from banks."[57]

The journalist Herbert Matthews wrote to the former secretary of state Dean Acheson that a crucial point had been reached. There was, he thought, still time to avert falling out with Cuba. He suggested that an extension of investment support from the United States might give Fidel the option to stay within the American fold. Acheson disagreed sharply. "It seems to me," he concluded, "that the whole situation is a mess and that it is going to be a lot worse before it is any better."[58]

Though before October 1959 it might have been possible to turn things around, the question of what Fidel would do was now settled. The departure of moderates from his government, the trial of Matos, the overtures to the KGB, and the increasing fear of and hostility toward the United States had all coalesced into a victory, behind the scenes, for the Cuban radicals. What Fidel would do had become what Raúl was already doing. A Research Institute report in the State Department's files from August 1959 argued that, with both the armed forces and the land reform apparatus under his control, Raúl was the engine of change in Cuba. "The widely-disseminated image of Raul as the smaller, less handsome, less able, less effective brother is totally misleading in appraising Cuba today and tomorrow," it said. "This does not mean that Fidel Castro has lost importance. He remains genuinely the Messianic leader, the mouthpiece of the Revolution's promise of improvement for the Cuban masses. But in his distaste for the details of implementing the ideals, he has allowed Raul to pull many of the strings of actual government."[59]

Fidel still may not have adhered in any meaningful way to communism. He would not declare himself to be a Marxist-Leninist for another two years. But Raúl was a communist, and Raúl was in a position of immense power. As the moderates and the professional classes began to leave Cuba, his armed forces would be obliged to assume more of the administrative roles of the Cuban state. As they did that, more moderates would leave.

"There is an element of pathos in the relationship between the towering figure, and personality, that is Fidel, and the underdeveloped physique of his younger brother," said López-Fresquet. "Fidel acts rather like a father to Raúl—a strict father. In my presence, Fidel scolded Raúl on several occasions."[60] What observers less commonly saw was that the relationship between the two brothers was a symbiosis: a head and a heart. Raúl was a skilled organizer, capable of consultation and inclusion, strategic and practical in his thoughts and deeds; but he loathed the limelight, and had no ambition even to be a fully public figure, let alone an icon. Fidel was the exact opposite.

Though he was unpredictable, fiercely puritanical, and controlling, Fidel was not the crackpot that many in the United States government assumed he was. Fidel's passion, his intensity, and his fearlessness resonated with a very different narrative; one that was barely perceived in Washington, except for that brief reference to his "Messianic" role in the Research Institute's report. Fidel saw himself, and was seen by his admirers, as a liberator and a deliverer. Much in the story of the Cuban Revolution (the "twelve" men who survived the *Granma* landing, the strong moral code, the emphasis on justice, the strict simplicity of the leaders' lifestyles—even the flowing beards) resonated with the Christian gospels and the style of the early church. The language Fidel used often recalled that of Jesus of Nazareth—though Fidel spoke of *patria* (homeland), where Jesus spoke of the kingdom of God. But the story of Jesus is incomplete without opposition, without those who feared his power and sought to destroy him. In order to make his own narrative work, Fidel needed a villain willing to persecute him until the bitter end. Into that role, quite unwittingly, stepped the United States.

Fidel had long foreseen a break with the United States, but he would come to regret the swiftness with which he had forced it. "I came to power with some preconceived ideas about the United States and about Cuba's relationship with her," he would admit years later. "In retrospect, I can see a number of things I wish I had done differently. We would not in any event have ended up as close friends. . . . Still, even adversaries find it useful to maintain bridges between them. Perhaps I burned some of these bridges precipitately; there were times when I may have been more abrupt, more aggressive, than was called for by the situation." Philosophically, he added, "We were all younger then; we made the mistakes of youth."[61]

★

For three decades, Rafael Trujillo had been loyal to the United States. Now, he sensed that the tide was turning against him. During an interview for an American television show, he said that everything the United States had done since the days of Roosevelt had been wrong, and its government was made up of *pendejos* (literally, pubic hair; the implication is "suckers"). This presented his ambassador, simultaneously translating, with a challenge of etiquette (he thought for a while, before settling on "fools").[62] Spurred on by the anti-Americanism of his son, Ramfis, and of his aide Johnny Abbes, Trujillo did the unimaginable.

Literally overnight, on 12 January 1960, La Voz Dominicana stopped broadcasting its usual violent incitements and slurs against Castro and praise for the Americans. At the same time, the more radical Radio Caribe—run by Johnny Abbes—started broadcasting twenty-four-hour propaganda from Soviet wires, lambasting the "despicable gringo government" of the United States.[63] Trujillo sent Abbes to Czechoslovakia to seek Soviet support for the Dominican Republic.

"He was getting angry with us and in order to bother us and maybe change our minds about him, he was threatening to be chummy with the communists, which was ridiculous," remembered Hank Dearborn, the American ambassador. "But he sort of waved this in our faces—if you don't like me I will go over to Castro. Of course Castro had no desire to get in with Trujillo, so from that side there wasn't anything. But Trujillo was making all these motions to join hostile forces against us with anyone he could find. And with some success. It did bother Washington."[64] Under an agreement signed in 1951, the United States had a guided missile tracking station in the Dominican Republic. Legally, the agreement was unbreakable for ten years. Eisenhower raised the question of moving the station, but this was judged to be impractical.[65]

In June, Dick Rubottom had deplored the Cuban-supported armed attempt to invade the Dominican Republic and topple Trujillo as a violation of the OAS principle of nonintervention, amounting to anarchy. In December, his approving initials appear on a document in the State Department's archives that implies that the United States was doing exactly the same thing. At the beginning of that month, the American ambassador in Ciudad Trujillo reported that an invasion force was massing in Venezuela, and that it would soon receive a clandestine landing of arms. "These arms will come from Venezuela and also there is the possibility of a shipment from the United States," he wrote. "It is altogether possible that December 20, 1959 has been marked as the date for revolt. As I have heretofore pointed out, if it does not develop during the month of December there exists the pressing necessity of disbanding the organization for the time being in order to avoid detection."[66]

Revolt did not develop during the month of December. There are no other references to this particular coup attempt in the American archives. On 21 January, just twenty-four hours before it was supposed to get under way, Trujillo discovered an assassination plot against him, orchestrated by the 14 June Movement (1J4), which had risen from the ashes of the Cuban-supported invasion seven months before. He ordered a police crackdown, a purge, and a smattering of extrajudicial killings.[67]

Another shock was in store. The Catholic church had long been a bulwark of Trujillo's power. He had lavished generous subsidies and privileges upon it, and it had responded with solid support. But a new papal nuncio, Archbishop Lino Zanini, arrived in October 1959.

Juan Perón, then exiled in Ciudad Trujillo, warned his friend Trujillo that Zanini had appeared in Buenos Aires shortly before the Catholic church had turned against him. "It was that man who caused my downfall," he told Trujillo. "Wherever that man puts his foot, he causes disturbances. Watch yourself carefully."[68]

Perón left the Dominican Republic soon afterward. At the beginning of 1960, he was, in absentia, proven right. Zanini ordered the five bishops in the Dominican Republic to cut all ties with the regime. Prayers in the Dominican Republic, traditionally including the line "You are requested to pray for the health of Trujillo, the Benefactor of this country, and for his brother [Héctor], the President," now continued, "and for all those who are suffering in the prisons of the country and their afflicted families." So radical and thrilling was this that many churchgoers stayed for a second service to hear it again.[69]

"It was the first time I had ever seen the Old Man rattled," remembered Arturo Espaillat, Trujillo's head of security. "The rest of the official family was in a state of shock."[70] It was noted by Trujillo's secret services that Zanini was friendly with Hank Dearborn, the American ambassador. Trujillo began a bizarre campaign of harassment against the nuncio. On one occasion, he issued fake invitations to upwards of one thousand officials, requiring their attendance at a reception at the nunciature. At the prescribed time, Zanini was mobbed by this enormous crowd, with Trujillo at the head of it, innocently waving his own fake invitation. Undeterred, on 3 February, the bishops published an open letter asking Trujillo to release forty political prisoners, and calling upon him to respect human rights.[71]

Trujillo stepped up the pace. Churches were attacked with stink bombs during services, and, in some cases, with real bombs. In La Vega, the town's prostitutes were rounded up and driven into the church, where they were obliged to dance to loud music of a nonsacred character. Johnny Abbes's secret police harassed the clergy. Finally, Trujillo summoned a *jettatore*—a Vodou magician said to have the power of the evil eye. "I am designating you Secretary of the First Class in the Embassy at the Vatican," he told him. "You will have every facility, and you will have only one paramount duty: Your responsibility is to use your powers in such a way as to kill the Pope."[72] The evil eye failed on this occasion. The pope survived until 1963. All Trujillo succeeded in doing was to make himself look to the Americans like a liability.

★

Fifteen hundred miles to the north, a less whimsical attempt at dislodging a world leader was on the table. On 11 December 1959, the CIA's deputy director for plans, Dick Bissell, recommended to Allen Dulles that consideration ought be given to "the elimination of Fidel Castro." Dulles toned this down in the draft of the proposal that would go to Eisenhower a month later, making the subject "the removal from Cuba of Fidel Castro."[73] At the beginning of 1960, Dulles rejected an explicit proposal from J. C. King, the CIA's western hemisphere chief, to kill Fidel.[74] Instead, he pushed for a milder campaign of industrial sabotage and propaganda.

On 13 January, Dulles presented Eisenhower with his proposal. "Allen, this is fine, but if you're going to make any move against Castro, don't just fool around with sugar refineries," the president said. "Let's get a program that will really do something about Castro."[75] And so, against Dulles's instincts, the plan was aimed at really doing something about Castro.

Che Guevara, writing his field instruction manual *Guerrilla Warfare* at around this time, speculated accurately that the capitalists were planning "physical elimination by means of an assault on the old 'crazy fellow,' Fidel Castro, who has become by now the focus of the monopolies' wrath. Naturally, measures must be arranged so that the other two dangerous 'international agents,' Raúl Castro and the author, are also eliminated."[76] J. C. King agreed: "Unless Fidel and Raul Castro and Che Guevara could be eliminated in one package—which is highly unlikely—this operation can be a long, drawn-out affair and the present government will only be overthrown by the use of force."[77] According to the mainstream of CIA thought, though, Fidel was the only Cuban leader who mattered. Neither Raúl nor Che was believed to have anything approaching his charisma, and neither was thought capable of maintaining power.

The plan would therefore focus on overthrowing Fidel, by means of sabotage and the promotion of counterrevolutionary activity in Cuba. It began the very next week, on 18 January 1960. Dulles delegated responsibility to Dick Bissell, who got to work on recruiting twenty or thirty Cubans. They were to be trained in guerrilla warfare. Then, they would themselves recruit and train a larger group of around two hundred men.[78]

On paper, Bissell's plan stopped short of an assassination. But there was "a drug, which if placed in Castro's food, would make him behave in such an irrational manner that a public appearance could well have very damaging results to him." Dick Nixon loved this idea. Some even more eccentric strategies were vetoed before the politicians saw them, such as "the Dripping Cuban." The Cuban in question, trained by the CIA, would stagger from the waves onto a Turkish beach, and claim he had just jumped from a Russian prison ship. Aboard, he would tell the world, were thousands of innocent Cubans, kidnapped by the wicked Castro, who was sending them to Siberia to work as slaves to the communists.[79]

At the same time, Eisenhower's administration, led in this decision by Christian Herter and Dick Rubottom, formally decided that Trujillo needed to be removed from office. It was generally agreed that he had so enfeebled political life in the Dominican Republic that after his death there would be chaos—and chaos, the State Department now believed, brought forth communism. Rather than face that, the United States had to act urgently to prevent what it called "a domino effect of Castro-like governments" in the Caribbean.

Unlike Castro, Trujillo did not need to be killed. Instead, the plan was to persuade him to leave nicely. Various dignitaries were dispatched to Ciudad Trujillo to charm the Generalissimo. Assuming correctly that the Americans might also be trying to bolster the Dominican opposition, Trujillo rounded up scores of intellectuals, professionals, and businessmen, and accused them of sedition. Assuming incorrectly, though logically, that the Americans believed him to be even worse than Fidel Castro, he considered taking Fidel out himself. "Those bastards want to use me as the instrument to pull down Castro," he told his advisers, "and I'll do it because Castro is no friend of mine. But I know also that they want to pull him down in order to pull me down afterward."[80]

On 26 January 1960, less than a fortnight after instructing the CIA to get Fidel, Eisenhower publicly announced a policy of nonintervention in Cuba. The United States, he said, respected Cuba's right to enact social revolution. The following day, Fidel replied with a note affirming that friendship between the United States and Cuba was "indestructible."[81] In fact, his intelligence network in Miami and Washington was sufficiently strong that he found out within days that Eisenhower was planning his downfall.[82]

No longer were Latin America's dictators "the only people we can depend on," as Foster Dulles had once argued. The lesson from Batista's fall appeared to be that dictators created the conditions for radicalism and anti-Americanism, and those might lead to communism. As a result, the United States finally turned against despotism. But it would turn against it with the means of despotism itself: conspiracy, terror—and murder.

9

"A CRUSADE TO SAVE FREE ENTERPRISE"

★

IN FEBRUARY 1960, DWIGHT D. EISENHOWER SET OFF ON A GOODWILL tour of Latin America, including Puerto Rico, Brazil, Argentina, Chile, and Uruguay. Throughout, he maintained the line that the United States was in favor of freedom and progress, and that its policy would continue to be based on "a policy of non-intervention and mutual respect."[1] He was well received, except in Argentina, when his route had to be changed to avoid large crowds of demonstrators shouting, "Viva Castro!" and "Death to Ike!"

Unlike Nixon's trip two years earlier, Eisenhower's was acclaimed as a success; but the president himself was shaken by the deprivation that he saw. "I could not at the time reveal what was shaping up in my mind—that the private and public capital which had flowed bounteously into Latin America had failed to benefit the masses, that the demand for social justice was still rising," he wrote. One particular sign he saw held up along his route disturbed him. It read, WE LIKE IKE; WE LIKE FIDEL TOO.[2]

That same month, a Soviet trade delegation, led by the deputy leader Anastas Mikoyan, arrived in Havana. Fidel and Mikoyan viewed a Soviet expo, at which Mikoyan invited the Cuban to look through a microscope and admire Soviet progress. The irony was not intentional, but Fidel noticed it. "In front of Mikoyan, Castro belittled everything we saw at the exhibit," remembered Rufo López-Fresquet, who toured it with him; "he was sincerely unimpressed by the Russian products."[3]

Fidel and Raúl took Mikoyan to a hunting lodge in the Cuban countryside. The men spent the days catching fish from a lagoon, and the evenings cooking it on campfires while the frogs croaked and the mosquitoes whined. As the light died away, they consumed the island's three great crops, puffing on Cuban tobacco and drinking *cafecito*, the piping hot combination of Cuban sugar and Cuban coffee in almost equal proportions. Finally, they fell asleep on the concrete floor, wrapped in army coats and blankets. This bucolic re-creation of guerrilla life bowled Mikoyan over. "Yes, this is a real revolution," he told the KGB's Nikolai Leonov, who had joined the trip as his interpreter. "Just like ours. I feel as though I've returned to my youth!"[4]

There was serious business, too. Mikoyan offered to buy 425,000 tons of the sugar harvest, at a price below the world market rate. He also offered a loan of $100 million: $20 million in convertible currency, and the rest in Soviet goods. As the American ambassador Phil Bonsal noted, this was not a great deal for Cuba.[5] Its purpose appeared to be to create a market for overproduced Soviet goods, on which the Cubans would pay 2.5 percent interest. As for the sugar purchase, in the late 1950s, the Soviet Union had regularly bought half a million tons of sugar from Cuba annually, but Batista had been able to demand the world market rate. A few months earlier, the USSR had offered to buy 500,000 tons from Castro at a slightly better rate. Even that deal was considered so shoddy that the then-chairman of the National Bank, Felipe Pazos, had refused to accept it, and this one was worse.[6]

Most of the Soviet leadership did not see potential in Cuba, but it did see how popular the Cuban Revolution was in the rest of the third world. Aspiring revolutionaries from Dakar to Dhaka seldom pinned pictures of the dour, gray faces of the Presidium to their walls, but in Fidel and his young barbudos they saw heroes. When Mikoyan was photographed with the Cubans, the fusty old Soviet Union unexpectedly began to look, in the word of the day, hip. Nobody could have been more surprised than the Soviets themselves. "Cuba forced us to take a fresh look at the whole continent, which until then had traditionally occupied the last place in the Soviet leadership's system of priorities," wrote Nikolai Leonov.[7]

Though the sugar deal and the loan were on poor terms, the State Department had made up its mind before it saw the evidence. At the end of February, John Calvin Hill wrote a memo that, he said, was "making a case that the Castro regime represents a new phase of international Communist intervention. You will note that it will be necessary to have the researchers flesh out this skeleton with a lot of substantiating facts which, I believe, are available."[8] But there were still signs that Fidel had not entirely given up on the United States. On 29 February, the Cuban government sent a note to the American embassy naming a negotiating team who were ready to travel to Washington, to discuss all disagreements and look for solutions. It attached only one condition. While the negotiations were going on, the United States should take no unilateral action against

Cuba's government or economy. According to the vice-consul in Havana, Wayne Smith, "the U.S. government was in a foul and suspicious mood" owing to Mikoyan's visit, and refused the condition.[9]

Unmarked planes, taking off from Florida, were regularly bombing Cuban sugar mills and other industries. On 18 February, one exploded in flight over Matanzas. Fidel announced afterward that the pilot had been carrying identification naming him as Robert Ellis Frost, an American citizen. The CIA was funding all sorts of schemes in Miami, and Fidel's suspicion that the bombings were among them does not, in retrospect, look misplaced. At the time, the negative press generated by these flights worried the State Department. A junior official noted, "I feel that it is of the utmost importance that every available resource be used to insure that air incursions of this kind do not depart from U.S. soil."[10] But the CIA was not answerable to junior officials of the State Department.

In such an environment, it is not surprising that the dramatic event of 4 March was also blamed on the CIA. *La Coubre* was a French-owned vessel, moored in the harbor at Havana. That afternoon, its crew was in the process of unloading its cargo: some seventy-six tons of grenades, artillery shells, and ammunition, which Fidel had bought from Belgium. Suddenly, there was a colossal explosion. The deck blew apart, hurling debris and bodies high into the air. The shells combusted. The pier at which the ship was moored was destroyed. Windows across Havana smashed. A plume of dark smoke rising from the harbor could be seen from miles away.

Fidel drove over immediately. As he ran from his car toward the ship, dozens of hands shot out of the crowd, grabbed him, and held him back. "Damn it, you're suffocating me!" shouted Fidel, trying to wrest himself free. But the hands were just in time. A volley of tracer bullets, triggered by the explosion, whizzed past him as he was dragged backward.[11] Raúl Castro almost had to arrest his own brother to get him off the dock. Che turned up soon afterward, and began to organize the medical response. Fidel took a helicopter up to survey the damage.

Whether or not the CIA was responsible for the fate of *La Coubre*, its agents must have been tantalized by the fact that Fidel almost flew too close. As the helicopter moved in for a closer look, a second massive explosion ripped through *La Coubre*'s hull, buffeting the helicopter back. Fidel, as usual, escaped unscathed. Many of the paramedics, troops, laborers, sailors, and wounded people from the first explosion still on the dock were not so lucky. A total of around one hundred people had been killed and more than two hundred injured.[12]

In 1898, the explosion of the USS *Maine* in Havana's harbor had provoked the United States to enter the Cuban War of Independence. The parallels were not lost on the Cuban propaganda machine. Within hours, a government-issued news sheet hit the streets, accusing the United States of terrorism and sabotage. Fidel told the KGB's Aleksandr Alekseyev that he was "absolutely certain" the United States had been behind the explosion.[13] Following its pattern of anti-Cuban activities at the time, the CIA is not an implausible suspect, but there is no conclusive evidence it was involved. Other conspiracy theories include an elaborate one circulated at the State Department suggesting it was the work of French terrorists, in retaliation for Cuba's support of Algeria at the United Nations.[14]

The following day, Fidel held a public funeral on Havana's main thoroughfare, Calle 23, for victims of the attack. It was attended by half a million people. The normally lively Cubans were silent and somber.

During Fidel's four-hour speech, a photographer from the newspaper *Revolución*, Alberto Korda, was taking pictures. At around 11:20, Che Guevara briefly appeared by the side of the podium. He was wearing his black beret, and its metal star picked up the light. As he watched Fidel speak, his handsome features were set in an expression that spoke of great emotion, barely restrained. For only a moment he remained there, silhouetted against the light sky and the wilting fan of a palm leaf. Korda snapped a couple of frames on the end of a roll of film. The resulting image was rejected by the editor of *Revolución*. Korda hung up the only print in his home, and called it "Heroic Guerrilla."[15]

It would be several years before that photograph became world famous, but the passion and determination in Che's face hints at how powerfully this presumed act of terrorism against them had affected the Cuban leaders. The *Coubre* explosion, according to Bob Stevenson, changed everything. "From then on, there was really no talking. Ambassador Bonsal kept trying, but they really weren't ready to talk seriously."[16] As far as the Cubans were concerned, the United States had just declared war.

★

In March, Christian Herter was obliged to tell Eisenhower that the "latest National Intelligence Estimate does not find Cuba to be under Communist control."[17] Interviewed after his presidency, Eisenhower agreed, noting that Fidel would not declare himself a Marxist-Leninist until the end of 1961. Nonetheless: "The actions of Castro after January '59 when he got into Havana, became those of a dictator and [*sic*] the Communist type," he said.[18] Fidel Castro was quacking like a duck. A fortnight after *La Coubre*, the CIA presented Eisenhower with Bissell's new plan to bring down the Cuban government. An offshore radio station was to be set up, broadcasting anti-Castro propaganda. Simultaneously, funding and supplies were to be directed to dissidents within Cuba. Finally, a paramilitary invasion force was to be recruited and trained. On 17 March, Eisenhower bestowed his presidential approval.[19]

Two days before that, Nikita Khrushchev had sent his first personal message to Fidel Castro, through Aleksandr Alekseyev. Khrushchev assured Fidel of "our sympathy and fellow-feeling," and announced that his speeches and articles were to be published in Russian—which, according to Alekseyev, "visibly moved" the Cuban leader. Khrushchev concluded that Fidel could purchase whatever arms he wanted from Czechoslovakia "and, if necessary then directly from the Soviet Union." Still, Fidel held the Soviets at arm's length. He told Alekseyev that it was too early to allow the Soviets to reopen an embassy in Havana.[20]

"I believe that Castro is gambling for much more than just the dictatorship of Cuba," wrote the State Department's Bill Wieland to his hawkish colleague John Calvin Hill at the end of March. "I believe that he regards himself as the father of a new ideology. . . . His confused doctrine of Castro-humanism will take him to a position of world prominence as a radical agitator of under-developed areas." Wieland warned that Fidel "is ready, even eager to risk his life, and willing to hold Cuba up as a ready sacrifice to intervention."[21] Wieland was ignored, though his memorandum was perhaps the most accurate and prophetic assessment of the situation to appear in the State Department's archives up to that point. Hill could not be moved from his focus on getting rid of Fidel. "What do we do about or with Castro if he is run out of Cuba before he is completely discredited?" he wrote to Lester Mallory, a fellow official, in April. Mallory replied, "Let him go to Moscow & if not give him to Trujillo by mistake."[22]

That option might not be available for long. The State Department had just drawn up a document titled "U.S. Plan for Trujillo's Retirement." General Edwin Clark sent Eisenhower a memorandum on it. "Trujillo is a man of great pride with great love for his country, his people and his family," Clark wrote on 13 April. But the great danger was that if Trujillo fell, "hostile outside elements"—meaning Fidel Castro—might invade.[23] As the Policy Planning Staff noted, an active role in Trujillo's downfall could be a neat thing for the United States to have: "the political damage resulting from a U.S. involvement in Cuba could be minimized by our first or simultaneously helping overthrow a hated dictator."[24] The next day, Undersecretary of State Douglas Dillon pointed out again that if Trujillo were removed, "our anti-Castro campaign throughout Latin America would receive a great boost."

Eisenhower was convinced. That day, 14 April, he approved an initiative "actively to bring about the early overthrow of Trujillo provided that we can make prior arrangements with an appropriate civil military leader group in a position to and willing to take over the Dominican Government with the assurance of United States support."[25] Trujillo had to go: not because he was a genocidal tyrant, a murderer, a torturer, a rapist, an embezzler, a blackmailer, and an enemy of freedom and democracy in all its forms, for he had been all of those things for decades and Washington had never tried to topple him; but because his exit would legitimize the United States' pursuit of Fidel Castro.

★

On 1 May, one of the U-2 spy planes that Eisenhower had authorized to fly regularly over the Soviet Union disappeared. Ike had long feared "losing a bird," as the CIA put it. The regular breaches of Soviet airspace by American U-2s could be defined as an act of war. The CIA's Dick Bissell assured Allen Dulles that, had the plane crashed or even been shot down, the pilot could not have survived.[26]

Four days later, the Soviet Union announced that it had shot down an American plane. Eisenhower ordered that no one should comment, with the exception of the State Department, and Dulles got to work on an official statement. Before he had finished it, the president apparently gave a conflicting order through his press secretary, James Hagerty. As a result, the National Aeronautics and Space Administration (NASA), which had been involved in the missions, announced that one of its weather-research planes had gone down near Turkey. "We didn't like this at all," remembered Douglas Dillon, then working with Dulles on the statement, "because it was a cover story that had been 'canned' way ahead, and it was obviously way wrong, because we knew the damn thing had gone down near Smolensk in Central Russia, 1000 miles or more from the area mentioned by NASA."[27]

Two days later, with much fanfare, Khrushchev introduced to the Supreme Soviet one Gary Powers of Pound, Virginia. "I deliberately refrained from mentioning that we have the remnants of the plane—and we also have the pilot, who is quite alive and kicking!" he said. "We did this quite deliberately, because if we had given out the whole story, the Americans would have thought up another fable." He ridiculed NASA's story about weather research. "The whole world knows that Allen Dulles is no great weatherman!"[28]

"That it had to be such a boo-boo and that we would be caught with our pants down was rather painful," admitted Ike. In the Oval Office on 9 May, he said that he wanted to resign.[29] Dulles was furious with Powers. The kit of every U-2 pilot contained a suicide pill or pin, which he had neglected to use. Dulles, too, offered his resignation, but it was rejected. "Hagerty persuaded the President that he couldn't allow Allen Dulles to take all the blame, because it would look like the President didn't know what was going on in the government," remembered Dillon.[30]

Despite his comedy performance in front of the Supreme Soviet, Khrushchev was hurt, personally and politically. He told the British prime minister Harold Macmillan of his disbelief that "his *friend* (bitterly repeated again and again) his friend Eisenhower had betrayed him."[31] A conference in Paris that month, meant to discuss a nuclear test ban treaty, was ruined. Khrushchev canceled his invitation for Eisenhower to visit the USSR. Ultimately, though, all this may have done him more damage than it did Eisenhower. "From the time Gary Powers was shot down in a U-2 over the Soviet Union, I was no longer in full control," Khrushchev would say in 1969; "those who felt that America had imperialist intentions and that military strength was the most important thing had the evidence they needed." Others, including Anastas Mikoyan, would argue that Khrushchev's "inexcusable hysterics" over the incident had lessened his standing in the Presidium.[32]

In the middle of this scandal, on 7 May 1960, Cuba and the USSR finally established formal diplomatic relations. But the first Soviet ambassador sent to Cuba, Sergei Kudryavtsev, was a disaster, slipping furtively around Havana in a bulletproof vest and refusing to go anywhere without a full bodyguard. Fidel considered him a coward and told Alekseyev he behaved as arrogantly as "one of Batista's generals."[33] Meanwhile, Fidel had taken to calling Alekseyev "Alejandro." It was the Spanish version of his name, Aleksandr, but had also been Fidel's own code name in the Sierra Maestra. This was a high accolade. Alekseyev, and the KGB, remained his main line of communication to Moscow.

★

In May, the left-wing National Union of Haitian Students held its first congress. The official theme was segregation and colonialism, which meant a lot of speeches bitterly critical of the United States. The congress was roundly assessed as the most left-wing and anti-American public event that had ever taken place in the country. François Duvalier permitted it with the specific intent of shocking the American ambassador, and creating the sense that a communist threat existed in Haiti. He wrote long letters to Washington, emphasizing that his government was threatened with collapse because the United States was not sending enough aid.[34]

On 21 June, Duvalier gave a public speech at Jacmel, aimed at the softest part of Washington's anatomy. The Cri de Jacmel (Cry of Jacmel) was a powerful appeal to the American government for "a massive injection of money," and a thinly veiled threat to turn to the Soviet Union if it did not pay up.

"Two great poles of attraction lure groups of people and associations of countries to a pilgrimage," Duvalier said. "Observing and living in such an international context, in the era of national independence . . . we need solid ground to make a choice." He did not want Haiti to become another Cuba, he implied, but there was only so much he could do. "Communism has established centers of infection. . . . No area in the world is as vital to American security as the Caribbean."[35]

When asked to clarify just how much of a "massive injection of money" was required, Haitian officials quoted figures ranging between $150 million and $300 million. The American embassy in Port-au-Prince pointed out that since Duvalier's accession Washington had given him $21.4 million, to no avail.[36] Nonetheless, Duvalier would receive a boost the following month, when Eisenhower added 25 percent to Haiti's sugar quota, cut from Cuba's. (Rafael Trujillo received a similar boost: the Dominican Republic gained from the Cuban sugar quota cut, too. Meanwhile, the Soviet Union stepped in to buy all 700,000 tons of Cuba's surplus sugar.)[37]

The fuss in Haiti was overshadowed just three days later, when someone tried to kill Rómulo Betancourt. The president of Venezuela was due to drive through Caracas for Army Day. A green Oldsmobile was parked on a street along the route, containing a remote-control electronic bomb with the power of sixty-five kilos of TNT. Shortly after 9:00 AM, Betancourt drove past. The remote detonator clicked. The bomb blew up. The force of the explosion was so great that Betancourt's Cadillac was blasted fully to the other side of the road, where it burst into flames. One officer in the Cadillac, and one bystander hit by the car as it landed, were killed. Betancourt survived, though his hands were badly burned.[38]

There was no mystery as to who was behind the attempt. Rafael Trujillo's radio station, La Voz Dominicana, prematurely announced Betancourt's death as soon as the bomb went off. "Now we're rid of that fairy," chuckled Trujillo, before he realized that Betancourt had in fact survived.[39]

Trujillo had nurtured a personal hatred of Betancourt for many years, and had probably been behind a brazen attempt in 1951 to stab him with a poison syringe on a busy street in Havana. In April 1960, Betancourt had publicly stated that any resolution of the Cuban situation depended on the resolution of the more pressing situation in the Dominican Republic.[40] Trujillo had responded with a colorful campaign to discredit the Venezuelan president, dwelling on the false implication that Betancourt was homosexual, and portraying him as a footstool for the Americans.[41] He and Abbes had been planning the assassination for several months.

Four days after Betancourt's close shave, Dick Rubottom met J. C. King, the CIA's western hemisphere chief. The CIA offered to provide "a small number of sniper rifles or other devices for the removal of key Trujillo people," which would be given to the opposition. Rubottom liked the suggestion, and the CIA went ahead with the planning—though the mission would have to be approved by Eisenhower before weapons could be sent. Under American occupation, private citizens in the Dominican Republic had not been permitted to bear arms. Trujillo had continued that policy. The twelve rifles proposed by the CIA, complete with telescopic sights and five hundred rounds of ammunition, were therefore a sought-after commodity. There was no confusion about the target. As Dearborn wrote to Rubottom, his opposition contacts were interested only in "the assassination of their principal enemy."[42] That meant Trujillo.

In a meeting of the National Security Council, Dearborn said that "if he were a Dominican he would favor killing Trujillo." Days later, Eisenhower said in another such meeting that "it appears impossible to shake the belief of Latin America that the Trujillo situation is more serious than the Castro situation. Until Trujillo is eliminated, we cannot get our Latin American friends to reach a proper level of indignation in dealing with Castro."[43]

At an OAS summit in Costa Rica shortly afterward, condemnation of Trujillo was unanimous. The OAS voted to sever all diplomatic relations with the Dominican Republic. Even Luis Somoza's Nicaragua voted against Trujillo, its old ally. "Well, what do you expect," Trujillo remarked with a shrug. "They don't need me now."[44] Christian Herter tried to match the unanimous vote against Trujillo with a vote for multilateral action against Castro. But the OAS was not convinced by American arguments, and Cuba went uncensured. Fidel accused the United States of using the condemnation of Trujillo "as a pretext to attack us," and pointed out that not only had Trujillo emerged from an American occupation, but Washington had supported him for thirty years.[45]

At home, Eisenhower tried to remove the extra sugar quota reallocated from Cuba to the Dominican Republic's account, to starve Trujillo of funding. In this he faced the implacable opposition of the chair of the Senate Agricultural Committee, Senator Allen Ellender of Louisiana, who along with Senator James Eastland of Mississippi was one of Trujillo's great admirers.

"I wish there were a Trujillo in every country of South and Central America," said Ellender during the debate.

"Is it not true that the same group in the State Department that had a hand in delivering Cuba to Castro desire to overthrow Trujillo?" asked Eastland.

"I would not be at all surprised," replied Ellender.[46]

Eisenhower was furious. He knew Trujillo had been bribing American legislators. If there were a congressional mandate to buy Dominican sugar, he said, he would rather risk impeachment than honor it.[47]

Trujillo halfheartedly responded to all this criticism by removing Héctor, his brother, from the nominal presidency he then occupied, and replacing him with a pliant, bookish politician, Joaquín Balaguer. Ambassador Dearborn reported that Trujillo would continue to dominate the scene "whether he is President or dogcatcher."[48] As the American attitude hardened, Dearborn took on the role of CIA station chief, liaising with the underground resistance. "We were using all these weird means of communication because we didn't want to be seen with each other," he remembered. "Things like notes in the bottom of the grocery bag, rolled up in cigars, etc." In December, Eisenhower added his presidential approval to the CIA's plan to supply weapons to the anti-Trujillistas.[49] "We didn't always give them what they wanted," said Dearborn, "but they knew that if they got into power that we would be supporting them."[50]

★

At the end of June, Aleksandr Shelepin, the chairman of the KGB, passed to Nikita Khrushchev a startling assessment of American policy. "In the CIA it is known that the leadership of the Pentagon is convinced of the need to initiate a war with the Soviet Union 'as soon as possible,'" it said. The United States, it continued, believed the Soviet defense capability was growing, and might soon match its own. Before that happened, there was a window of opportunity in which the United States could strike and be sure of winning. "As a result of these assumptions, the chiefs at the Pentagon are hoping to launch a preventive war against the Soviet Union."[51]

This assessment was based on a misinformed report by an unidentified

NATO liaison officer with the CIA. Khrushchev was horrified. Faced with what he believed could be imminent annihilation, he stepped up the rhetoric. On 9 July, he told an audience of Soviet schoolteachers that Soviet missiles could hit the United States long-range. The example he used was a United States attack on Cuba: "Figuratively speaking, if need be, Soviet artillerymen can support the Cuban people with their rocket fire, should the aggressive forces in the Pentagon dare to start intervention against Cuba."[52]

In reality, Soviet missiles and propulsion systems were not yet sufficiently advanced to hit targets in the United States. Khrushchev hoped, by his bluster, to put the Pentagon off attacking him. In Washington, there were varying estimates of Soviet missile capability: the army and navy thought it was low, the air force thought it was high, and Allen Dulles hedged his bets in the middle. A year later, satellite pictures would prove that the lowest estimates were the most accurate.[53] For the meantime, though, the United States government was not considering a preemptive strike—Eisenhower had ruled one out decisively in 1954—and would have been shocked to find out that Khrushchev thought it was. The Soviet leader's words were taken as an inexplicable burst of aggression.

That same month, Raúl Castro went to Czechoslovakia to buy weapons. In Prague, he impressed the locals with his determination to sleep with his boots on, his appetite for blond prostitutes, and his Marxism-Leninism. He continued to Moscow, where he thanked Khrushchev for his speech offering to defend Cuba, albeit figuratively, from an American attack. He requested that KGB officers be dispatched to Havana to train the Cuban intelligence service.[54] On 21 July, Raúl and Khrushchev issued a formal joint declaration that the USSR could prevent American armed intervention in Cuba.

The Soviets were delighted with Raúl. Following his visit, the KGB signaled a change in its attitude toward Cuba by switching the code name for the file it kept on the Cuban government. Until August 1960, it was *Youngstye* (Youngsters). From then, it became *Avanpost* (Bridgehead).[55]

During this drama, Fidel Castro was nowhere to be seen. It was announced that he was on his sickbed. Allen Dulles observed that "while Castro was probably ill, he also appeared to be in temporary retirement, perhaps because he was not sure of the line he should take."[56]

Perhaps that was the reason. At around the same time, Jean-Paul Sartre noticed that Fidel was finding the expectations of the Cuban people hard to handle. Sartre accompanied Fidel and Che on a tour to Holguín. Thousands of fans packed a sports stadium. It was Fidel's first public event of the day, though that afternoon he would have to fly back to Havana and do two more just the same. Every day was like this. Everyone in Cuba wanted to see Fidel, hear his voice, and touch his combat fatigues.

Fidel rose to speak, but he was visibly exhausted and his voice was hoarse. He spoke for only a few minutes. When he sat down, there was a sense of disappointment in the crowd. Then, Sartre remembered, a row of children at the front of the stadium began to wail. Two of them, a boy and a girl aged eight or ten, clambered up onto the platform and grabbed Fidel's ankles.

Fidel lifted the sobbing boy by his armpits. "What do you want?"

"Come home with us," cried the boy. "Come to the village."

"Is something going wrong?"

"Everything is fine, Fidel. But come over to our place!"

Fidel promised that he would return. He tried awkwardly to leave the platform, urged on by his barbudos. "But he didn't leave," said Sartre; "he seemed intimidated."

The boy was still bawling. "But I tell you I will come," Fidel pleaded.

By now, all the children were crying, screaming, and pressing themselves bodily against Fidel's platform. He looked overwhelmed. The hundred or so soldiers present could not clear a passage through the crowd. Stuck, Fidel took a straw hat proffered by a child and put it on his head. "I call attention to the fact because it is rare," said Sartre. "Castro detests demagogic parades and disguises. He made a symbol of the act because there was no act to do. The straw hat was quickly taken off." He handed it to Che, who briefly put it on, and then gave it to Sartre himself. Finally, Fidel, at a complete loss, literally fled, bounding up over tiers of seats to escape from the howling masses who wanted by seeing him to experience some sort of uplifting magic.

"I am happy that they surround me and jostle me," he told Sartre's companion, Simone de Beauvoir, after another such incident. "But I know that they are going to demand what they have the right to receive and what I don't have the means of giving them."[57]

At the end of July, newsreels reported that Fidel's doctors had ordered him to take "absolute rest, mental and physical" for an unspecified period of time. In his stead, Raúl was in charge. "If you think I'm radical," Pathé news quoted Fidel as saying, "wait till you see my little brother."[58]

★

The American ambassador in Port-au-Prince always held a party on 4 July. In 1960, one of the VIP guests was François Duvalier's closest aide, the chief of the Tontons Macoutes, Clément Barbot. After the Cri de Jacmel speech, Barbot had mentioned again to a cabinet minister that, in his view, "Duvalier has gone mad."

At the ambassador's party, he collared Lieutenant Colonel Thomas Tighe of the marines. Barbot told Tighe that, while he was not superstitious, he did occasionally listen to the predictions of an elderly peasant sage. The sage had recently told him that something would happen to Duvalier that July, and he would not leave the palace alive. If that happened, Barbot said, he, Barbot, would take over.[59]

Ten days later, Barbot attended another embassy party: this time, the French, celebrating Bastille Day. On his way home, his car was stopped at a roadblock by presidential guards. He was put under house arrest for six hours, during which he tried to escape by having himself wrapped up in a sack of dirty laundry. He was discovered, and interrogated. Afterward, he was sent to Fort Dimanche.[60] There was no trial, and no term of imprisonment was set. He would remain there for eighteen months.

Duvalier reacted to correct Allen Dulles's suspicion, expressed to the National Security Council, that "the Duvalier regime was drifting Leftward. . . . The government had been attacking the U.S. and was pro-Castro."[61] He had student leaders arrested by the Tontons Macoutes and charged with communist conspiracy. He abolished all youth groups on the basis that they might be communist, including that well-known hotbed of Marxism-Leninism, the Boy Scouts. The French archbishop, François Poirier, was arrested. The Macoutes did not even give him time to collect his false teeth. He was marched out of his palace wearing just his underpants and a cassock, and shoved aboard a plane to Miami with one dollar in his pocket. Duvalier announced that Poirier and "communist priests" had given $7,000 to help agents from Cuba and Moscow infiltrate the student movement. The Vatican excommunicated Duvalier for his treatment of Poirier, and Haiti's students went on strike. Undeterred, Duvalier sent the Macoutes to take registers in classrooms, and jailed and tortured the parents of anyone who joined the strike.[62]

Duvalier's hard line worked. At the end of the year, the United States would announce a new $11.8-million grant of aid and budget support for Haiti. It also sent a new ambassador, Robert Newbegin, who notified the State Department that Duvalier required extra military support, including a helicopter platoon. The lesson for Duvalier was obvious. This was the way he was supposed to behave.[63]

★

In August 1960, Dick Bissell of the CIA put into action a plan to kill Fidel Castro. The question of what, if anything, Eisenhower knew about this remains difficult to answer. Especially since the U-2 incident, the CIA had prioritized "plausible deniability"—the idea that the president should not be obliged to know about activities that were so grossly illegal that they might bring down his administration. Under this policy, the CIA operated through euphemisms—"removal" being one of them, and "elimination" another—which were never fully translated for the president. It also began to take presidential silence as consent: so, if the president did not actively stop a policy, it would continue.

Owing to the CIA's deliberate vagueness around the president, it has been considered feasible that Eisenhower authorized the assassination attempts against Fidel Castro, and simultaneously against the Congolese leader Patrice Lumumba, without entirely realizing that he had done so. This possibility seems remote. The president had talked on the official record about the "elimination" of Rafael Trujillo, and authorized the supply of weapons to Trujillo's enemies. Eisenhower was a five-star general, used to the language of war—and he was no fool. Bissell plainly thought he was acting with presidential approval: "if you had asked Eisenhower what he was thinking at that moment he probably would have said, 'I sure as hell would rather get rid of Lumumba without killing him, but if that's the only way, then it's got to be that way,'" he said. "Eisenhower was a tough man behind that smile."[64]

That August, Bissell ordered Robert Maheu, a former FBI agent, to contact the Mafia, looking to take out a hit on Fidel Castro. Fidel had few fans in the mob. It had lost $100 million a year when he took its Cuban casinos, brothels, and drug trade away. Maheu talked to John Roselli, a small-timer from Las Vegas. Roselli brought in Sam Giancana, a big-timer, and don of Chicago. Giancana brought in Santo Trafficante Jr., the boss in Florida. Trafficante had been based in Havana before the revolution, and tried to tough it out there afterward. Fidel threw him in jail. He was released a few months later, and fled to Tampa. Gossip among the Cuban exile community suggested that Trafficante had been released so that he could run the drug trade for Fidel's benefit. Then again, gossip in the exile community suggested almost anything if it reflected badly on the Castro brothers.

At the CIA's expense, Giancana and Roselli were accommodated in a smart hotel in Miami Beach, and left to plot. An assassin was sought in Havana. Giancana proposed to slip poison pills into Fidel's drink, though Bissell preferred that he be shot by a marksman.[65] Jake Esterline, now director of operations for the CIA's Cuban task force, had to authorize five- and six-figure dollar payments from the agency to Giancana and Trafficante. "I thought it was absolutely amoral [*sic*] that we involve ourselves for the record in anything of that sort," he later said; though, with reservations, he continued to involve himself. Bissell, too, later came to believe that involving the Mafia had been a mistake, partly for moral reasons, and partly because it made the operation so insecure. Nevertheless, he admitted, "My philosophy during my last two or three years in the agency was very definitely that the ends justified the means, and I was not going to be held back."[66]

Bissell told Dick Nixon he would need a Cuban invasion force of five hundred men, rather than the two dozen then training in Panama. This request was granted. Esterline persuaded the Guatemalan dictator Miguel Ydígoras to lend them a base camp, known as Trax. At the end of September, the CIA began to drop weapons to counterrevolutionary groups in Cuba. In the same month, the Cuban secret service caught three CIA agents red-handed with electronic surveillance equipment, drilling through the ceiling of the New China News Agency. The men's cover story—that they were tourists—did not wholly explain this particular sightseeing endeavor, and all three were imprisoned.[67]

With these shady events going on all around him, Fidel arrived in New York for the opening session of the United Nations. He and his entourage of guerrillas, numbering around fifty, checked into the Shelburne Hotel. Outside, protesters had gathered, waving placards that read FIDEL COMMIE, GO HOME! A rival crowd of supporters chanted, "Viva Fidel!" Scuffles had to be broken up by the police.

The Shelburne's manager, Edward Spatz, was in a state of nervous tension already at the prospect of receiving his Cuban guests, whom he had only agreed to accept at all on receiving a request in writing from the American government. After the Cubans had settled into their rooms, he demanded $10,000 from Fidel as a surety against bills and damage. Fidel offered $2,000, which Spatz refused. Insulted, Fidel walked out. He would be more insulted yet by the rumors then spread about his entourage's behavior. It was said that the Cubans caused a hullabaloo of the sort even rock 'n' roll bands had not yet perfected in 1960. Allegedly, drunken rages had been entered into, furniture had been broken, guns had been pulled on staff, and chickens had been slaughtered in bedrooms. These stories seem to have had little basis in fact.

In a convoy of public taxicabs, the Cubans decamped to the United Nations. Fidel claimed they would sleep in Central Park if necessary. "We are mountain people," he said. "We are used to sleeping in the open air." New York missed out on that spectacle, which doubtless would have been memorable. Instead, the Cubans were accommodated in Harlem, in the Theresa Hotel on Seventh Avenue and 125th Street, occupying four floors of the rickety old hotel. Fidel loved the place immediately, and in a moment of expansion took all its service staff to dinner. Celebrities including Allen Ginsberg and Malcolm X turned up to meet the Cuban hero. Curious locals milled around outside, hoping to catch a glimpse of the barbudos. MAN, LIKE US CATS DIG FIDEL THE MOST, read one placard. HE KNOWS WHAT'S HIP AND WHAT BUGS THE SQUARES.[68]

The day after Castro's arrival in New York, Nikita Khrushchev had arrived by ship with a collection of Eastern bloc leaders and dignitaries. He turned up to meet Castro at the Theresa. "We enclosed each other in an embrace," remembered Khrushchev, and then admitted: "I use the term 'enclose' provisionally, keeping in mind my height in contrast to Castro's. He bent over me as though covering my body with his." To reporters, Khrushchev joked that he did not know if Castro was a communist, but he himself was certainly a Fidelista.[69] Hours later, at the UN, the two men reprised their public display of affection for the benefit of the delegates, and then set out to bug the squares in the chamber as much as possible. During the three-week session, Khrushchev was repeatedly reprimanded for his histrionics. At one point, he took off his shoe and banged it on the desk when the delegate from the Philippines criticized Soviet policy. The chairman broke his gavel trying to bring the session back to order.[70]

★

On five thousand acres of former coffee plantation in the heavy, wet summer heat of Guatemala, American officers were training Dick Bissell's invasion force of Cuban exiles. From Florida, squads of six men at a time were being dispatched to fishing villages on Cuba's north coast. The idea was that they would create cells locally, and make contacts with the underground resistance movement against Castro. It did not go well. "I think that every team we sent was picked up within a few days," Bissell admitted.[71] Worse still, by the end of October, Bissell began to realize that no organized or even coherent underground resistance movement existed within Cuba. The CIA's Tracy Barnes commissioned a covert poll assessing support for Fidel's government, and found it to be overwhelming. The poll, which conflicted with what the CIA wanted to find and with what anti-Castro exiles in Miami were telling it, was discarded.[72]

A joke then current in the CIA said that there were three ways of ensuring that a message was sent all the way across Cuba as quickly as possible: telephone, telegraph, and tell-a-Cuban. The last of these was proving to be remarkably effective. At one point, an FBI agent in Miami contacted the Coral Gables CIA station and advised its staff to start withholding details of their plans from the Cubans, for news of an imminent assassination plot against Castro and an invasion of Cuba was being discussed volubly in every café in town.[73] The CIA made matters worse by setting up a general council of Cuban political leaders, which functioned as a forum for gossip and feuds. Liberal Cuban exiles refused to join, and the CIA had to merge it with another, even larger political council, to try to prevent it from becoming a refuge for Batistianos. This did not help. "They were constantly fighting and it took the full time of several people to keep them sorted out," Bissell said.[74]

Eventually, the political council produced a leaflet to distribute in the wake of the planned invasion. It vowed to return all seized property to its original owners—which would mean booting out thousands of peasants to whom Castro had given land and homes. Bissell read it with horror, and told the council, "If this piece is published, it will kill any counterrevolution." The State Department agreed. No longer did the CIA trust the Cuban politicians it was planning to install as a government. Bissell complained that "we had to go through hoops negotiating them into writing a more attractive, sexier political manifesto."[75]

The Miami leaders begged to go to Guatemala so they could get to know the invaders. The CIA let them, despite the danger that such a tour might lend itself to individual canvassing by political hopefuls. As it turned out, that was not the problem. The invaders loathed the politicians on sight. On one or two occasions, Americans had to step in to prevent particularly unpopular Miami Cubans from being hurled into the swamp outside Trax. Years later, Bissell summed up the operation so far simply: "It was a mess."[76] Yet in Guatemala and in Miami, without unity or direction, the mess staggered on; and more and more people came to know about it.

★

Earlier that year, Ian Fleming, the author who had created James Bond, went to a dinner party in Georgetown hosted by the presidential hopeful, John F. Kennedy. Kennedy had long been a fan. In 1957, his wife, Jacqueline, had given a copy of *From Russia with Love* to Allen Dulles, saying, "Here is a book *you* should have, Mr. Director."[77] From then on, it had become a tradition that Dulles and Jack Kennedy would exchange copies of Bond novels as they appeared, Dulles adding comments in the margins. The director of the CIA was not present at this particular dinner party, though at least one other agency official was.

Over dinner, Kennedy asked Fleming what James Bond would do to get rid of Fidel Castro. Fleming replied that Bond would drop leaflets saying that the fallout from American nuclear tests provoked a strange reaction in men with facial hair, reducing them to sexual impotence. All barbudos would immediately shave off their beards, and the revolution would be over.

The next day, this discussion filtered back to Allen Dulles, who apparently took it seriously. He telephoned to set up a private meeting with Fleming. To his disappointment, the author had already left the country. Shortly afterward, the CIA agent David Atlee Phillips remembered being told of a box of cigars, impregnated with a strong depilatory, that would be given to Fidel and would make his beard—indeed, all his body hair—fall out.[78] The agency also developed a thallium powder, which could be dusted on his shoes to the same effect.

Jack Kennedy had been a critic of Foster Dulles's aggressive foreign policy for many years. In the 1950s, he had taken a progressive line on Latin America. "If we persist in believing that all Latin-American agitation is Communist inspired—that every anti-American voice is the voice of Moscow—and that most citizens of Latin America share our dedication to an anti-Communist crusade to save what we call free enterprise for the Free World," he had told a Democratic audience in San Juan, Puerto Rico, at the end of 1958, "then the time may come when we will learn to our dismay that *our* enemies are not necessarily *their* enemies, and that our concepts of progress are not yet meaningful in their own terms." He had expressed strong support for the principle of nonintervention. He had described Fidel Castro as "part of the legacy of Bolívar," the great liberator of Latin America. But as Cuba went leftward, and Eisenhower's administration appeared to be taking little action—for the general public knew nothing of the planned Mafia hits, nor of the men training in Guatemala—Kennedy saw a chink in the Republicans' armor. "We have allowed a soft sentimentalism to form the atmosphere we breathe," he said at the beginning of 1960. "And in that kind of atmosphere, a diffuse desire to do good has become a substitute for tough-minded plans and operations—a substitute for strategy."[79]

Kennedy's drift to the right may have been prompted by a shove from his father. On the night in July that his son achieved the presidential nomination, Joe Kennedy dined at the New York apartment of Henry

Luce, publisher of the right-leaning magazines *Time* and *Life*. Luce told Joe that he understood that Jack had to run to the left on domestic policies to secure the vote in northern cities. But when it came to foreign affairs, there must be no weakness in fighting communism. The well-informed journalist David Halberstam reported the conversation: "There's no chance of that, Joe Kennedy had guaranteed; no son of mine is going to be soft on Communism. Well, if he is, Luce answered, we'll have to tear him apart."[80]

No tearing apart would be necessary. "The Russian leaders must understand that we are men who are committed in every fiber of our being not merely to protect our nation but also to struggle for the cause of freedom on the world scene," wrote Jack Kennedy, in an article (unusually, not ghostwritten) published just a couple of months later; "that we are not men who can be pressed, by blackmail or by force, to accept the transfer of territories and people to Communist rule." In Salt Lake City, he characterized the Cold War as "a struggle for supremacy between two conflicting ideologies: Freedom under God versus ruthless, godless tyranny."[81] He stepped up his attacks on Eisenhower for being soft on communism and allowing a missile gap to open up. During the campaign, he was informed by Dulles that there was no missile gap—or, rather, that there was, but to the United States' advantage. He did not allow this fact to get in the way of his story, and continued to berate Eisenhower publicly over its supposed existence.[82] And in October, he switched from his previously easygoing line on Fidel Castro to fierce opposition, announcing suddenly that he advocated American intervention in Cuba.

Within government circles, Kennedy's opponent Dick Nixon had championed such an intervention since meeting Fidel Castro in Washington a year and a half before. But the plan to intervene was top secret, and as vice president he was unable to mention it publicly. Kennedy, who theoretically did not know about it, could. "For the first and only time in the campaign, I got mad at Kennedy—personally," Nixon admitted. "I understand and expect hard-hitting attacks in a campaign. But in this instance I thought that Kennedy, with full knowledge of the facts, was jeopardizing the security of a United States foreign policy operation. And my rage was greater because I could do nothing about it."[83]

Nixon believed that Allen Dulles had secretly briefed Kennedy on the covert operation, and lost his temper at the CIA director during a meeting of the National Security Council when he would not admit it.[84] Dulles insisted that he had not. He had visited Kennedy at Hyannis Port on 23 July to brief him about foreign policy concerns, but this was normal practice with presidential candidates. Officially, Dulles first briefed Kennedy about the Cuban invasion plans on 18 November, ten days after the election. But Dick Bissell did have a secret meeting with him around the beginning of October; and Bobby Kennedy, in a 1964 interview, insisted that his brother had known about the training of Cuban exiles by the CIA in Central America before the election.[85]

Dulles may not have been responsible. The Democratic governor of Alabama, John M. Patterson, claimed to have told Kennedy of the plan at a hotel in New York that autumn. He had authorized Alabama's air national guard to travel to Central America and train Cuban exiles, and had worked out what was going on. "I made him promise," Patterson said, "that he wouldn't breathe a word, and I told him what was going on . . . that the invasion was imminent and if it occurred before the election, I believed Nixon would win. I recall watching him very closely. I couldn't read him. He heard me out and thanked me."[86]

On 19 October, the Kennedy campaign issued a statement saying that the "non-Batista democratic anti-Castro forces in exile" were "fighters for freedom" and should be aided by the United States.[87] Bound to secrecy, Nixon was forced into a position where his only option was to call Kennedy's idea—which mirrored precisely what he had been promoting in secret for the past year and a half—irresponsible and even illegal. To his disgust, he earned plaudits from the left-wing press.

Meanwhile, the Eisenhower administration banned most exports to Cuba, leaving the country's economy hanging. Campaigning for Kennedy in the South, Lyndon Johnson, Kennedy's vice presidential candidate, played to the gallery. David Halberstam remembered Johnson's reply to the question of what he would do about Cuba. "First he'd take that Castro fellow and wash him. (Cheers.) And then shave him. (Cheers.) And then spank him. (Wild cheers.)"[88]

But the firm hand of Washington was dispensing something worse than a spanking. In the last year of Eisenhower's presidency, the CIA had taken steps to kill at least three world leaders, or would-be leaders: Castro, Trujillo, and Patrice Lumumba. There were only weeks left before a new American president would be sworn in, and the race between Kennedy and Nixon was too close to call. With the candidates publicly swapping positions on Cuba, no one could be sure what would happen under a new administration. The fate of all these men, and their nations, was poised on the brink.

PART THREE

COCKFIGHT

10

REGIME CHANGE

★

IN NOVEMBER 1960, BILL PAWLEY, AN AMERICAN FORMER AMBASSADOR who for thirty years had been a close friend of Trujillo's, was sent to Ciudad Trujillo by President Eisenhower. Pawley was one in a series of emissaries sent to persuade the Dominican strongman to step aside, and it was his second try. In his suite at the Ambassador Hotel, he suggested to Trujillo that it was time for him to retire, offering the Generalissimo a permanent place to live in the United States, complete with his entire family, and the carefully bred cows and horses that he was widely said to love more than them.

Trujillo became emotional. The masklike face, usually composed, crumpled. Tears spilled down the pale-powdered cheeks. "You can come in here with the Marines," the dictator said, raising a finger for emphasis, "and you can come in here with the army, and you can come in here with the navy or even the atomic bomb, but I'll never go out of here unless I go on a stretcher."[1]

A few months before, Trujillo had claimed repeatedly to the American ambassador that he had a personal letter from Richard Nixon, saying that were he elected he would do anything in his power to keep the Benefactor in place in the Dominican Republic.[2] Now, though, Trujillo's frustration with the Eisenhower administration transferred itself to Nixon. In the presidential election then under way, the dictator supported the young senator from Massachusetts, John F. Kennedy.

The race in the United States coincided with a high point of hysteria about the implications of nuclear strategy, and the potential for a new world war. Tolerance and compromise were out. Hawkish posturing against the Soviet Union suited the Republican Dick Nixon perfectly; as 1960 went on, the Democrat Jack Kennedy began to adopt it, too.

Kennedy's increasingly hard line on foreign policy, though it may have pleased his father and Henry Luce, alienated many on the center and left in his own party. "The military were the tough guys, and they always looked on the liberals as being muddle-headed, creeping socialists and all that sort of thing," said the Democratic congressman Chester "Chet" Bowles, one of Kennedy's foreign policy advisers. "And so a lot of the liberals went to Washington with a strong desire to prove that they weren't that; they were just as tough as anybody."[3]

By late 1960, it seemed like Kennedy would say anything and do anything to win the election. In private, he felt the strain. A series of televised debates with Nixon was proposed. Jack engaged the services of Max Jacobson, a fashionable but dubious New York physician, and, just before the first debate, took a shot of a drug cocktail called "joy juice." According to one of Kennedy's biographers, Jacobson's recipe "usually included methamphetamines, steroids, calcium, monkey placenta and procaine."[4] As expected, it gave him a buzz of energy and elation. It also made him feel "out of control," and for that reason he decided not to make Jacobson's drugs into a habit. For the time being, at least, he did not.

Whether it was the joy juice or natural talent, Kennedy shone in the first of the televised debates. His good looks and charm, against Nixon's deficiencies in both, made him more telegenic. The Kennedy message—a lot of nonspecific aspirations for an American future, and scaremongering about the American present—translated well to television. It was simple, emotive, and direct. It put Nixon on the defensive, and Nixon was at his worst when he was defensive. Famously, the Republican had refused to wear makeup for the debate. A sheen of sweat was soon visible on his face, making him appear nervous and sickly. The British prime minister Harold Macmillan observed that, during the broadcast, Nixon had looked like "a convicted criminal" against Kennedy's "rather engaging undergraduate." Rose Kennedy's response was sharper: "I felt so sorry for Nixon's mother."[5]

While the day of voting in the United States did not approach the scale of fraud common in Haitian elections of the time, there were some unfortunate similarities. "There is no doubt that there was substantial vote fraud in the 1960 election," Nixon wrote in his memoirs. "In one county in Texas, for example, where only 4,895 voters were registered, 6,138 votes were counted. In Chicago a voting machine recorded 121 votes after only 43 people had voted; I lost this precinct, 408–79."[6]

Rumors of bribery and even Mafia involvement later surfaced, partly through Judith Campbell, a wealthy socialite then romantically involved both with Jack Kennedy and with the Chicago Mafia boss, Sam Giancana.

Giancana had already had a run-in with Bobby Kennedy, who had interrogated him in 1959 during his courtroom crusade against the Teamsters and the Mafia. The FBI kept tabs on Campbell's liaisons, substantiating at least some of her story in the face of the predictable denials from Kennedy loyalists. Campbell later said that she set up meetings in which Giancana's support for Kennedy was assured. She alleged that Giancana had votes bought for Kennedy in West Virginia, and that he helped carry Illinois—which Kennedy would win by just a few thousand votes.[7]

In a contest so close, it mattered. That evening, Jack's campaign team set up camp in Joe Kennedy's house to watch the results on television. Early indications of a Kennedy landslide soon turned out to be mistaken. As the results were called, Nixon made greater and greater inroads into the Democrat's lead. The atmosphere in the Kennedy compound was thick with tension. At midnight, Eisenhower's press secretary telephoned with the news that Nixon would concede. The celebrations ceased abruptly when, an hour later, he telephoned again to say that Nixon would not. According to Jack's press secretary, Pierre Salinger, the candidate himself was the only person in the house who did not lose his temper. Instead, he walked back to his own house and went to bed.[8]

Minnesota provided the decisive result in Kennedy's favor early the next morning. The new president-elect was in his bath when the unshaven Salinger and Ted Sorensen turned up. In his bath he remained, while the excited aides perched on the side and gabbled. Finally, at lunchtime, Nixon admitted defeat. By the count, he had won 34,108,157 votes to Kennedy's 34,220,984—though that translated into 219 votes to Kennedy's 303 in the electoral college. John Fitzgerald Kennedy would become the thirty-fifth president of the United States of America. His mother, Rose, queen of the backhanded compliment, wrote of her son's victory: "Jack's career . . . should be an inspiration to young men who have had years of perplexity and self-doubt before deciding who they are and what they want to become."[9]

A few days after the election, the CIA's Jake Esterline sent a report to his superior Dick Bissell on the progress of the Cuban invasion. "Our original concept is now seen to be unachievable in the face of the controls Castro has instituted," Esterline said. "There will not be the internal unrest earlier believed possible, nor will the defenses permit the type of strike first planned. Our second concept (1,500–3,000 man force to secure a beach without airstrip) is now also seen as unachievable, except as a joint Agency/DOD action." When he sent the report, Esterline remembered thinking, "Goddamn it, I hope Bissell has enough guts to tell John Kennedy what the facts are."[10] It was not a question of guts. Eisenhower banned the CIA from discussing with the president-elect the details of the plans to topple Fidel Castro.

Three days later, on 18 November, Bissell and Allen Dulles went to meet Jack Kennedy in Palm Beach. The agency men were discreet—too discreet. By the end of the meeting, far from being made aware that the plans were unauthorized and had been recommended for substantial revision, Kennedy took away the false impression that Eisenhower had already ordered an invasion of Cuba.

★

On 19 December 1960, the USSR and Cuba signed a joint communiqué in which Cuba aligned itself with the domestic and foreign policies of the USSR. In Havana, a joke current at the time—and told with affection—went like this:

> Do you know why Fidel can't pass his driving test?
> No, why can't Fidel pass his driving test?
> Because he drives only on the left, goes through red lights, and doesn't know how to put the car in reverse.[11]

The Soviet pioneer spirit was everywhere in Cuba. At Playa las Coloradas, Soviet filmmakers tried to persuade Fidel to reenact his slog through the mangrove swamp. (Fidel told them to employ an actor. He had done it once, he said, and that had been enough.) Che Guevara had filled the National Bank with Marxist economists. True to Moscow's bureaucratic style, meetings with him would often be scheduled for two or three o'clock in the morning. In the small hours, his reception desk would usually be manned by a young barbudo, his cap tipped forward onto his nose, his eyes closed, and a large, lit cigar dangling out of his mouth as he snored gently. "I am first of all a doctor," Che told Jean-Paul Sartre when the French writer walked past the sleeping guard to meet him in the middle of one night, "then somewhat of a soldier, and finally, as you see, a banker."[12]

That winter, the American writer Warren Miller traveled around Cuba and saw what the CIA and the State Department did not want to: that support for the revolution was wide and deep.[13] American intelligence reports confirmed this repeatedly, one in December 1960 pointing out that "organized opposition appears to lack the strength and coherence to pose a major threat to the regime, and we foresee no development in the internal political situation which would be likely to bring about a critical shift of popular opinion away from Castro."[14] Dick Bissell later described these reports as "unwelcome."[15] They were discarded.

Though in the United States Cuba was seen as being not free, many Cubans disagreed. In Havana's Cathedral Square, Miller and his wife encountered two boys, aged about twelve and fourteen, full of questions about life in the United States.

"Tell me," said the elder one, "in New York could you stand up anywhere and say you were a socialist. I could. I could say it right here, now. I could say I was a Communist if I wanted to say such a thing. I could say I was against the revolution—but of course, no one would like me if I did. I can say anything. But if I *do* something against the revolution, such as throwing a bomb or some other such brutal act, then it's *to the wall*."

The younger boy asked about the Ku Klux Klan, and Miller made a brief comment. "I guess you'd really be beaten up if you said a thing like that back home," said the boy. "Why don't you stay here where you can really be free?"

"I assure you I will not get beaten up," replied Miller.

"Because you are white," replied the twelve-year-old, piercingly. "Only because you are white."

For many ordinary Cubans, race equality, class equality, public order, and a meal on the table at the end of the day felt like meaningful liberation—and those things were being delivered. "How delicious this freedom is," a waiter at a hotel in Holguín told Miller, and explained that it was liberating to walk around the town without fear of being shot arbitrarily by a death squad. Miller opined there was more to freedom than that—a free press, for instance. "Forgive me," said the man, "but I must tell you something that clearly you do not know. We do not know what a free press is, so how can we miss it? We never had it. Never, never, never."[16]

Not everybody loved the revolution. Che Guevara was driving in Havana with his friend Ricardo Rojo, and they pulled up at a traffic light. The driver in the car next to them turned, and gave Che a horrible scowl. Guevara smiled placidly at Rojo. "Look," he said, "this guy belongs to the middle class, which Fidel still thinks he can count on."[17]

The Cuban government was well aware that the United States was planning an invasion. On 2 January 1961, Nikita Khrushchev was invited to a reception at the Cuban embassy in Moscow. "Alarming news is coming from Cuba at present, news that the most aggressive American monopolists are planning a direct attack on Cuba," he said. Eisenhower's ambassador to the United Nations accused the Cubans of "crying wolf" over this possible invasion for the last six months, and claimed they were "fast making themselves ridiculous in the eyes of the world."[18]

That same day, Fidel gave the United States forty-eight hours to reduce its embassy staff in Havana from what he counted as three hundred (80 percent of whom, he said, were spies) to eleven—matching the number at the Cuban embassy in Washington. Eisenhower asserted that there were eighty-seven staff, not three hundred, and that more than half of them were Cubans. "But this message from Castro was the last straw," he remembered. "We broke off diplomatic relations with Cuba immediately."[19]

Opportunistically, François Duvalier used the moment to inform the Americans he had broken relations with Cuba after the 1959 Cap des Irois invasion. This was not entirely true: a Haitian consulate had still operated in Cuba since then. But the president of Haiti, like the leaders of Cuba and the Dominican Republic, was nervous. He was under pressure again domestically, from a general strike and a terrorist campaign. Though he dispatched the Tontons Macoutes to kill the students who were behind the unrest, the bombs kept coming.[20] It was a bad time to look weak. At the moment of transition between presidencies, Eisenhower was cleaning up—and no one knew what Kennedy would bring.

On 3 January, Eisenhower told his national security advisers that he would move against Castro before he left office in a fortnight, if Castro provided a "really good excuse." "Failing that," he added, "perhaps we could think of manufacturing something that would be generally acceptable." At the same meeting, Christian Herter advocated staging a fake Cuban attack on Guantánamo Bay, to justify an American invasion. Ike also emphasized the need "to do as much as we can and quickly about Trujillo."[21] The next day, the United States actually joined with Cuba to vote in the OAS for expanded economic sanctions on the Dominican Republic. Dominican radio and press sources began a concerted counterattack on Eisenhower, and the American consulate in Ciudad Trujillo was picketed.[22]

While Kennedy was putting his administration together, Nikita Khrushchev made a speech about what he called "wars of national liberation" in Cuba, Vietnam, and Algeria. These wars, he argued, were just, and revolutionaries across the third world must be supported. The message he intended was that this support should be moral. Actual involvement in war—conventional as well as nuclear—should be avoided by the superpowers, which should aim for peaceful coexistence with each other. Khrushchev had been prompted to speak by Chinese criticisms that the Soviets were not doing enough for world revolution. His statements rejecting nuclear war, and supporting peace with the West, were intended for Peking's ears.

In Washington, though, they were disastrously misheard. Jack Kennedy ordered his foreign policy team to study the Soviet leader's words, and concluded that they constituted an open threat to wage guerrilla war on the United States. The team did not see the speech in context of the divisions within the communist world, for, as Kennedy's adviser Arthur Schlesinger later admitted, they did not understand that there were divisions in the communist world.[23] On the contrary, Adolf Berle—the only one of Kennedy's advisers who had any real knowledge or experience of Latin America—argued that the communist threat was now greater than "the Nazi-Fascist threat of the Franklin Roosevelt period," and said that the Soviets and the Chinese had already agreed to carve up Latin America for "revolutionary seizure." The CIA, he said, was predicting that "eight countries may go like Castro in the next few months."[24] Kennedy was briefed at the beginning of January that "obviously Castro is a more far-reaching threat to us than Trujillo—though our indecision about Trujillo compromises our moral position."[25]

On 10 January, the *New York Times* published a front-page article headlined "U.S. Helps Train an Anti-Castro Force at Secret Guatemalan Base," complete with a map. The story was not new: the *Nation* had broken it the previous November. The Guatemalan press had been reporting that there were CIA training camps in their country for a month before that. The *Times* piece, though, was the most prominent exposé yet. The operation's cover had been comprehensively blown. "I decided that we should say nothing at all about this article," said Eisenhower.[26] But with details of the Cuban invasion now public, and Castro and Trujillo still resolutely alive and in power, it looked increasingly like Eisenhower would bequeath an ambitious and teetering structure of secret plots to Kennedy.

Only one of the leaders Ike had apparently approved for "elimination" was actually killed during his presidency. On 17 January, in the breakaway Congolese state of Katanga, Patrice Lumumba was tortured for five hours and then murdered. Though the CIA may have encouraged his killers, it did not do the deed. Lumumba was killed by his domestic enemies, Joseph-Désiré Mobutu (later known as Mobutu Sese Seko, Africa's premier kleptocrat) and Moise Tshombe. But the CIA was still assisting assassinations. On the last day of Eisenhower's administration, Hank Dearborn was informed that he would soon receive the long-promised weapons from the CIA, intended for Dominican dissidents who were planning to kill Trujillo.

That same day, Kennedy met Eisenhower in the Oval Office. Eisenhower mentioned the anti-Castro Cuban guerrillas training in Guatemala, and emphasized that this project should be "continued and accelerated." He added that Kennedy might find it necessary to "handle" the Dominican Republic at the same time.[27]

The following day, Washington, D.C., was struck by a blizzard. The town was blanketed under eight inches of snow. Along the Mall, bonfires smoldered among the swirling white flakes, lit to keep the paths clear. The snow delayed the start of the evening's inauguration balls, but so ebullient was the mood that nobody seemed to mind.

Rarely had the capital been so studded with stars. The revelers included Bette Davis, Frank Sinatra, Laurence Olivier, and the sometime object of Ramfis Trujillo's affection, Kim Novak. A satisfied Henry Luce, who had been given no cause to tear Jack Kennedy apart during election season by any softness on communism, was awarded a prime seat with the president's parents, Joe and Rose. The composer Leonard Bernstein wrote a fanfare for the occasion. Late that night, he was at one of the parties. He spotted a lady of his acquaintance dancing with a gentleman, and rudely cut in to request the next dance. Only then did he glance at the gentleman, and realize he had just ousted the new president.

Jack Kennedy "did look pale for a moment," Bernstein later told a researcher for the John F. Kennedy Presidential Library, "but he got over it, and it didn't injure our relationship. He was very sweet about it."

"He didn't make any quips?" asked the researcher.

"No, but the girl was furious," replied Bernstein. "She made lots of quips. That was fun, that evening, I must say."[28]

From a domestic point of view, the administration put together by Jack Kennedy was broad, including figures from the right and the left. From a Latin American point of view, it was shallow. Aside from Adolf Berle, there were no familiar faces. The strongest choices for the all-important role of secretary of state were vetoed. Adlai Stevenson, the former Democratic nominee and popular party elder, was the obvious candidate; but Kennedy saw him as a rival. The experienced diplomats Chet Bowles and David Bruce were out; both were considered too liberal, and Bruce too old. Kennedy's fellow upper-crust Bostonian, McGeorge "Mac" Bundy, was a Republican—to choose him would offend Stevenson too much. The civil rights oppositionist Bill Fulbright, Joe Kennedy's preferred man, was also too far right. Fulbright later met Joe Kennedy in Palm Beach. According to the journalist David Halberstam, Joe commiserated with Fulbright for missing out on becoming secretary of state; but, he explained, "the

NAACP, the Zionists and the liberals had all screamed bloody murder about the appointment." Halberstam added, "The senior Kennedy decided that a man with enemies like that could not be all bad, and when Fulbright returned to Washington he found a case of Scotch waiting for him."[29]

In the end, the position went to Dean Rusk, the least known and least offensive candidate: a moderate man, and one whose experience was limited to the Far East. Franklin D. Roosevelt Jr. lobbied to become his head of inter-American affairs—a position Jack's brother Bobby Kennedy had also had his eye upon. Rusk telephoned Adolf Berle to ask what he thought. "I told him it would be fatal," Berle remembered. The younger Roosevelt, he said, had accepted a retainer of $50,000 from Rafael Trujillo.[30] Chet Bowles became undersecretary of state, and Stevenson was sent as ambassador to the United Nations.

More important than any of these appointments, though, was the appointment of Bobby Kennedy as attorney general. The attorney general of the United States does not normally have much to do with foreign relations; but Bobby was not a normal attorney general. Though Lyndon Johnson was Kennedy's vice president, Bobby would act as a deputy president. The flagrant nepotism of this appointment was much decried in the press, but, according to Rose Kennedy, "their father thought it was a perfect idea." Bobby himself felt some embarrassment, though not enough to prevent him from accepting. "I started in the Department as a young lawyer in 1950," he would tell groups of aspirant young lawyers in the Department of Justice. "The salary was only $4,000 a year, but I worked hard. I was ambitious. I studied. I applied myself. And then my brother was elected President of the United States!"[31]

"In the first place, if you want to understand Jack Kennedy's presidency, you have to realize that he never had any really deep or broad management experience," said Chet Bowles. "The campaign had been organized with great skill and capacity, largely by Bob Kennedy and the various people he brought in. Management in Jack Kennedy's mind, I think, consisted largely of calling Bob on the telephone and saying, 'Here are ten things I want to get done, why don't you go ahead and get them done.'"[32] Under Eisenhower, the National Security Council, its planning board, and its operations coordinating board had held regular meetings, bringing together the cabinet, the CIA, and the Pentagon. The Kennedys found these cumbersome, and canceled the meetings. They were indeed cumbersome. But removing them whisked away a safety net from underneath foreign policy and operations, at the same time as a new administration was brought in that already lacked foreign policy experience, especially when it came to Latin America. At a moment when the United States was mired in some of the most dangerous and controversial Latin American operations in its history—planning a secret invasion of the sovereign state of Cuba, and putting out hits on the leaders of Cuba and the Dominican Republic—this was a serious risk.[33]

Jack Kennedy had expressed his hope to build a foreign policy that was "not merely anti-Communist but is rather for freedom, that seeks not merely to build strength in a power struggle but is concerned with the struggle against hunger, disease, and illiteracy that looms so large in the minds and the lives of the people in the southern half of the globe."[34] But there was already a power struggle in the Caribbean, and he was obliged to engage with it—and engage with it quickly, despite a crisis in faraway Laos that would preoccupy his foreign affairs team during those first few weeks of 1961.

Cuba and the Dominican Republic were the top priorities. Haiti was a secondary concern. There, the ambassador Robert Newbegin told Kennedy, they were faced with two "sorry alternatives." There was no strong opposition to Duvalier, and, were he to fall, a power struggle might ensue among equally unsavory individuals. "Such a situation might well tempt Castro or Trujillo to intervene in such a way as to jeopardize our national interests, possibly even forcing military intervention," Newbegin wrote. He concluded that "we have little choice but to follow our present course of maintaining friendly and helpful relations with the Duvalier government."[35]

On 24 January, a lengthy letter from Papa Doc himself landed on Kennedy's desk, demanding, in the most flattering terms, lavish aid if freedom and democracy were to be preserved in Haiti. "You are assuming the leadership of the government of the greatest modern State at a time when the world is threatened with explosion," Duvalier wrote. "In the face of the recriminations of some, and the aggressive actions of others, the dynamic attitude, tact, and political sense that characterize you are the best guarantees of peace the maintenance of which depends on the wisdom with which you will carry out your difficult mission."[36]

The situation in Haiti was obviously dire—it was "a kind of political and social cesspool," said Dean Rusk—but, more than that, the State Department feared its very direness might provoke uncontrollable change. "We felt that the Duvalier regime in Haiti constituted an open invitation to attempts to establish a Castro-type dictatorship in that country," Rusk continued. "Many Americans felt that Batista had prepared the way for Castro in Cuba and that the same thing could happen in Haiti."[37] Meanwhile, his attempt at charm over, Duvalier alarmed the marine mission in Port-au-Prince by bringing rural Tontons Macoutes to the capital. The mission's commander, Robert Heinl, noted that if it came to a fight, it would henceforth be impossible to defend the army against the Macoutes, even with American arms.[38]

Within Washington, Adolf Berle was a lone voice pushing strongly for regime change in Haiti, warning that Duvalier's government "might dissolve in anarchaic [*sic*] most anytime." Instead, he proposed to establish contact with members of the Haitian opposition, "to draw together the elements from which an alternative government would be constructed. This should be done by someone outside of State where possible."[39] But most of the State Department considered Haiti beyond redemption. Berle "was just out of touch with reality," said Bob Stevenson of the Office of Inter-American Affairs. "There was no future for mulattos in Haiti. The blacks had taken over and they were going to stay in power. But he had this idea that somehow we could put these 'democratic' mulattos that he'd known, who were decent fellows, labor union leaders for the most part, we could put them in power."[40] Though Stevenson may not have realized it, plenty of the "decent fellows" in opposition were black—including Daniel Fignolé, the most credible and popular contender for the presidency in exile—and many of Duvalier's victims were black. But his comments indicated the State Department's lack of interest in extending a policy that would be, as Kennedy proposed, not merely anticommunist, but for freedom, to the Haitian people. They were, it seemed, simply the wrong color.

On 28 January, Kennedy reviewed in full the CIA's plans for Cuba. Allen Dulles told the new president that the island was "now for practical purposes a Communist-controlled state."[41] Kennedy authorized the CIA to continue the political plans, including propaganda and sabotage. He asked the Joint Chiefs of Staff to provide an assessment of the invasion plan within the week. The plans laid before him included at least two separate plots to assassinate Fidel Castro, Raúl Castro, and Che Guevara, though the language in which these were expressed was typically vague.

Where Eisenhower apparently spoke Allen Dulles's cryptic language, Kennedy did not. Dulles was an old friend of the president's family, but he and Jack failed to strike up the sort of discreet rapport that had existed between Ike and him. The two frequently misunderstood each other. One small but illustrative example was that Kennedy, like much of his generation, had a habit of saying "yeah" while Dulles was speaking, in response to points he made. Too late, said Dulles, "I learned that Kennedy had intended to express, not understanding or assent, but only,

'Yes, I'm listening.'"[42] He did not reveal what may have been authorized by these unthinking presidential yeahs.

Six days later, there was another misunderstanding. The Joint Chiefs of Staff returned with a damning assessment of the CIA's Cuban invasion plan. The assessment had put the operation's chance of success at 30 percent. "Despite the shortcomings pointed out in the assessment," the report's executive summary read, "the Joint Chiefs consider that timely execution of the plan has a fair chance of ultimate success."[43] This was formal military language that Eisenhower would have understood. *Fair* was only one step up from *poor*, and the chance it implied was less than even. Both Dick Bissell and Jack Kennedy, apparently, read *fair* to mean "reasonable" or "decent"—implying that its chances were better than even. Had they read beyond the executive summary, they would have been warned that the invasion required strong and united Cuban counterrevolutionary political leadership; that there was a high chance of American backup being sought by the invaders if things did not go according to plan; and that American intervention would be unavoidable, "regardless of the international consequences," if the provisional government they founded was anything less than solid.

The Joint Chiefs of Staff left for the Caribbean. There, they were hosting a two-week event for Latin American military men. The guests included Jean-René Boucicaut of the Haitian army; Anastasio "Tachito" Somoza of Nicaragua, the son of the former dictator Anastasio "Tacho" Somoza, brother of the current dictator Luis Somoza, and a future dictator himself; and Alfredo Ovando Candia and René Barrientos, the head of the Bolivian army and air force, respectively, who would later take over as joint dictators of their country. The first week, in Puerto Rico, included demonstrations of precision flight by USAF Thunderbirds, a naval review, an amphibious landing, a tour of a nuclear submarine, and a weekend for everyone in San Juan's casinos at the American taxpayer's expense. The second, in Panama, featured a mass parachute drop, as well as a show of tanks, weapons, aircraft, artillery, and communications equipment.[44]

If these were to be its friends in Latin America, the Kennedy administration's early promises of liberty had been too ambitious. Less than a week into Kennedy's presidency, an internal State Department memorandum expressed discomfort with framing the plan to attack Trujillo as well as Castro as opposition to dictatorship in general. Instead, it suggested "redefinition of the 'dictatorship' target" to avoid "the concomitant disadvantage that the Somoza Government in Nicaragua, the Stroessner Government in Paraguay, and perhaps even the Duvalier regime in Haiti might all be brought down as well." If Kennedy's policy was genuinely to be for freedom, it was impossible to see how bringing down any of these governments would have been a disadvantage. "To reduce the foregoing possibility," the memo continued, "it might be highly useful in our future output to speak not of 'dictatorship' but rather of 'aggressive dictatorship' or 'interventionist dictatorship.'"[45] The sheep were thereby sorted from the goats. Dictators were now unacceptable only when their excesses spilled over their own borders.

There was another problem, too. When it came to getting rid of Trujillo, Jack Kennedy was proving squeamish. Rumors abounded about the connections between Joe Kennedy and Rafael Trujillo. "He did have, and I was unhappy about it, the presence of certain friends, the Palm Beach set, who were intimately and intricately aligned with Trujillo," remembered Adolf Berle of Jack Kennedy. "And this made it difficult for him to believe, I think, in the Dominican situation exactly what form of life he was dealing with. The underside of the Dominican Republic is the last word in sheer horror. But the Trujillos, when you meet them, and I have, are pleasant, good-mannered men to meet. The fact that they murder their enemies or torture them doesn't usually come up over coffee cups."[46]

Igor Cassini was a gossip columnist, and a friend of the Kennedy family. His brother Oleg was a fashion designer, who had produced Jackie Kennedy's new wardrobe as first lady.[47] Igor Cassini had introduced Jack and Jackie to Porfirio Rubirosa, Rafael Trujillo's former son-in-law and the Dominican Republic's playboy ambassador to the United States. He also introduced them to the aging Rubirosa's then wife Odile Rodin, his fifth: a much younger French actress, whose charms intrigued Jack. "Only once did I see Jackie lose her composure because of another woman," said Lem Billings, another close friend of Jack's. "It was over Odile Rodin."[48] While the Kennedys and the Trujillos may not have been intimately associated, there were few degrees of separation between them.

At the beginning of 1961, Rubirosa instructed Cassini to tell the president's father, Joe Kennedy, that the Dominican Republic was filling up with communists. If Trujillo fell, he said, the Dominican Republic would become another Cuba. The only hope was to reinstate full American support. "Trujillo and his staff considered Cassini to be our agent," confirmed Arturo Espaillat, Trujillo's security chief. "He was hired because he was a friend of the Kennedys and other powerful financial-political figures."[49] Indeed, in 1963 Cassini would plead nolo contendere to his indictment by a federal grand jury for representing the Dominican government without registering as an agent.

"Cassini said that he had a close relationship with Trujillo and Trujillo was—I don't know whether, willing to get out, but at least willing to make adjustments in the Dominican Republic, and he said he could talk to him and try to work and develop this," remembered Bobby Kennedy.[50] Cassini suggested that a personal meeting be set up in a yacht off the Dominican coast between Joe Kennedy and Rafael Trujillo. The State Department did not like that idea, and another plan began to form. Jack Kennedy would send a more neutral emissary: his old friend Senator George Smathers.

Smathers arrived in Ciudad Trujillo at the same time as diplomat Bill Pawley, this time on an unofficial visit, and the banker Charles "Bebe" Rebozo, a close friend of Dick Nixon. Both Pawley and Rebozo had enjoyed long associations with Trujillo. Smathers tried to ditch them, but they insisted on accompanying him to see the Benefactor. Reluctantly, the ambassador Hank Dearborn took this odd collection of his compatriots to meet Trujillo. Smathers sat down with Trujillo and his brother, Héctor. The former impressed him as "a very, very interesting character," carefully arranging a .45 pistol on the desk—pointed at him—before they started to talk.[51] Undeterred, the senator proposed that the Trujillos take up a Batista-like exile, perhaps in Morocco or Portugal, with what he euphemistically called a "trust fund."

"Generalissimo," said Smathers, "you have the opportunity to be a great hero in this hemisphere. You have the opportunity to be one of the few dictators, one of the only dictators, who was ever able to turn his country into a democracy during his lifetime. If you would do that you would really be a hero to your people and to the hemisphere."

Years later, Dearborn remembered, "I sat there thinking, 'Oh lord, you don't know who you are talking to.'"

"Senator," replied Trujillo silkily, "I don't know what you are talking about. I am just a citizen in this country. I don't have any public office. We have a president, an executive, a legislature, a supreme court just like your country. I really don't know what you are talking about."[52] Smathers spent two days with Trujillo, and got nowhere.

Prompted, perhaps, by Rubirosa's tall tales of incipient communist revolution, Kennedy hesitated over a plan to eliminate the windfall sugar quota, worth $22.6 million, reallocated from Cuba to the Dominican Republic that year. It had been suggested in Washington that, without this, Trujillo's regime might collapse.[53] Dean Rusk pointed out that Trujillo had a private fortune estimated at $500 million, and was unlikely to be troubled by such a loss. Furthermore, he insisted, "The underground opposition to Trujillo composed of business, student and professional people is believed to be predominantly anti-communist."

In that same memorandum, dated 15 February, Rusk notified Kennedy that close contacts had been established with numerous leaders of that opposition. He reassured him that these leaders believed in free enterprise, sought close links with the United States, and had already agreed to prevent "communist and subversive agents" from returning to the Dominican Republic. "No financial assistance has been given to these underground leaders," he wrote, "but the CIA has recently been authorized to arrange for delivery to them outside the Dominican Republic of small arms and sabotage equipment."[54] Several members of the administration maintained that neither Kennedy nor they knew that the men they were arming were planning an assassination. It is hard to see how anyone could have been in doubt after reading the dispatches sent by Hank Dearborn, in which he openly stated that the men saw "liquidation as the only way to accomplish their ends." "Political assassination is ugly and repulsive," he wrote, "but everything must be judged in its own terms."[55]

Meanwhile, the plot to kill Fidel Castro was not progressing well. The CIA had developed a poison pill, which could be dissolved in water. In early February, it supplied at least six of these to Sam Giancana, who, along with Santo Trafficante and Johnny Roselli, remained its main Mafia contact. The fact that Judith Campbell, still Giancana's girlfriend, was being put up at Washington's Mayflower Hotel in a room reserved by Jack Kennedy's secretary in the early months of 1961 added a certain spice to the proceedings.[56] Campbell would later claim that she again acted as a messenger between her boyfriends over details of the Castro assassination plot.

Robert Maheu, the CIA liaison officer formally dealing with these mafiosi, emphasized that Fidel's murder should take place "before—but preferably at the time of—the invasion." Dick Bissell later admitted that "assassination was intended to reinforce the plan. There was the thought that Castro would be dead before the landing."[57] Giancana had persuaded Fidel's secretary, Juan Orta, to administer the poison pill. But Orta was losing access to Castro, and had started to think the better of being involved. At the beginning of April, he fled to the Venezuelan embassy in Havana. Instead, Giancana and Trafficante contacted Tony Varona, a Miami-based Cuban exile linked to the gambling industry. Varona said he could provide plenty more Cubans willing to murder Fidel. He was given his poison pills, and told not to let them near hot liquids. He put them in the refrigerator. They froze solid, stuck to the freezer coils, and were rendered useless.[58]

At the beginning of the year, Ricardo Rojo visited a metalworks with Che Guevara. In the car, Che lit a cigar, and gestured toward a polished wooden box for Rojo. Rojo opened it, and swore. The box was filled not with cigars, but with a dozen hand grenades, their safety pins neatly lined up.

"What's wrong?" he asked.

"These are what we use here," Che replied. "A revolutionary's life is hard, it's always hanging from a thread. There are gangs of saboteurs, trained by the CIA, looking to assassinate the heads of the revolution. In case of attack there's no better weapon than a hand grenade aimed well, precisely placed in the middle of the group. Better still, if your nerves are strong enough and you can hold on to it several seconds after pulling the safety pin, the effect can be devastating."[59]

Nonchalantly, he drew another real cigar out of his shirt pocket, and handed it to the stunned Rojo.

The Cuban preparations for war went much further than a few novelty gift boxes of hand grenades. By the spring of 1961, the Revolutionary Army comprised 32,000 troops. In addition to that, Raúl Castro had created a nationwide militia, which American intelligence estimates correctly noted was at least 200,000 strong.[60] Though these irregulars were, for the most part, neither well trained nor well armed, they were patriotic, loyal, and motivated to fight any yanqui invasion. With the island's population standing at around 7 million, one in every thirty-five people was a militiaman or -woman. These civilians formed a network of information contacts and a rapid reaction force across the entire island. Cuba was ready for war.

★

On 11 March, Kennedy called Dulles and Bissell to the White House, to discuss the Cuban invasion plan. The CIA men explained that it would begin with bombing raids on the town of Trinidad. There would follow an amphibious landing by Brigade 2506, the Cubans training in Guatemala. The brigade would set up a beachhead. If defeated by Castro's forces, they would retreat into the nearby Sierra del Escambray, and join up with the anti-Castro guerrillas who were still hiding out there.

This plan, devised by Jake Esterline, was strikingly similar to the Trinidad invasion plan presented to Rafael Trujillo by William Morgan and Eloy Gutiérrez Menoyo two years before. It was also informed by Esterline's experience in Guatemala.[61] At first glance, it was not far-fetched. Cuba is a long, thin island, and cutting it in half from Trinidad was an obvious way to invade. The peaks of the Sierra del Escambray rise up just behind Trinidad, and would provide some cover for guerrillas.

Even in the form Esterline put it together, though, the plan would have been unlikely to succeed. "The assumption was that the Castro regime was not sufficiently well emplaced in Cuba to be able to withstand the kind of popular revolt that might be triggered by such a landing by these refugees," said Dean Rusk. "I suppose they had in mind something of Castro's own experience. They had landed with a rather small group and had triggered a general reaction throughout Cuba."[62] But the Castro regime was extremely well emplaced, complete with its massive irregular militia, its army, and its overwhelming popular support that the CIA and State Department seemed determined to ignore.

Kennedy fretted, and tinkered. He set down three conditions required of the operation. First, American military forces must be kept out of combat. Second, the operation's goal must be to trigger an internal revolt against Fidel Castro. Third, plausible deniability had to be maintained: the American government must be able to distance itself from what was happening. This last was the most important. It needed to be "less obvious" that the United States was involved. Trinidad was too visible a target; the operation must be shifted to somewhere "quiet." The air strikes, he feared, might also be too attention-grabbing.[63]

Allen Dulles admitted, in the unpublished draft of a memoir, that the CIA deliberately avoided telling Kennedy that they expected to break all three of his conditions. "We felt that when the chips were down—when the crisis arose in reality, any action required for success would be authorized rather than permit the enterprise to fail," Dulles wrote. "I have seen [a] good many operations which started out" like this one, he noted elsewhere, "insistence on complete secrecy—non-involvement of the U.S.—initial reluctance to authorize supporting actions. This limitation tends to disappear as the needs of the operation become clarified."[64] The president's concerns were being humored, but ignored.

Later, Esterline would assert that he had wanted to delay the operation at this point. "I really thought that what we were doing should stop and that this new administration coming in should have time, in an orderly manner, have time to develop their own options and think about how to deal with this problem," he said in 1996. "I put that forward to Bissell in writing and I got nowhere. I was told that it was not good to be that way and that we would go ahead and develop and continue with our plans that would be put to this new administration. I was very uneasy about it because I just . . . it was such a hairy thing to begin with."[65]

Just two days after meeting Bissell and Dulles, Kennedy launched his plan to aid Latin America—the most ambitious, and the most positive, American effort at outreach to that region since the days of the Good Neighbor policy. On 13 March, Jack and Jackie Kennedy hosted a reception for 250 people in the White House, to announce the foundation of the Alliance for Progress. Kennedy reasoned that Latin America's problems—problems that were causing revolution and communism—originated in poverty, inequality, and underdevelopment. The Alliance aimed to create the conditions for democracy and stability. It was, Kennedy told the reception, about "completing the revolution of the Americas." Billions of dollars would be invested in industrialization, education, and the reform of property, tax, judiciary, and electoral systems. "Let us once again transform the American Continent into a vast crucible of revolutionary ideas and efforts," Kennedy said, "a tribute to the power of the creative energies of free men and women, an example to all the world that liberty and progress walk hand in hand. Let us once again awaken our American revolution until it guides the struggles of people everywhere—not with an imperialism of force or fear but the rule of courage and freedom and hope for the future of man."[66]

It was a great and noble idea, and many people claimed to have thought of it first. Several Eisenhower aides complained that this was little more than a reinvention of the program they had begun with the Social Progress Trust Fund and the Inter-American Development Bank. But Kennedy's Alliance went farther than they ever had. It set firm targets for economic growth and modernization, and envisaged a total budget of $100 billion over ten years: $80 billion from the Latin American nations themselves and $20 billion from the United States. Teodoro Moscoso, the Puerto Rican coordinator of the operation, put a sign on his desk saying: PLEASE BE BRIEF. WE ARE 25 YEARS LATE.[67]

Far from being an Eisenhower plan, the Alliance for Progress bore a notable similarity to the proposal made by Fidel Castro at the OAS conference in Buenos Aires in 1959, in which he had called for a United States–sponsored $30-billion aid program over ten years, and the creation of a Latin American common market. In 1959, the American government had ridiculed this idea. By 1961, it felt differently. So did Fidel Castro. On the same day Kennedy announced the Alliance for Progress, a guard was killed in a sabotage attack on an oil refinery in Santiago de Cuba. As usual, the Cubans suspected American involvement.[68]

That month, the British prime minister, Harold Macmillan, met Jack Kennedy. The two leaders became close. They had a family connection, as well as a political sympathy: Macmillan's wife was the aunt of the Marquess of Hartington; Hartington had been married to Jack's favorite sister, Kathleen, before being killed in the war. In March 1961, though, Macmillan detected in the American president bullishness and naïveté. Privately, he predicted, "That young man is going to do something foolish about Cuba."[69] The very next month, he would.

11

"ONE OF THE MOST RIDICULOUS THINGS THAT HAS EVER OCCURRED IN THE HISTORY OF THE UNITED STATES"

★

ON 15 MARCH, TWO DAYS AFTER THE ALLIANCE FOR PROGRESS HAD been announced, Jack Kennedy was briefed on the new, updated Cuban invasion plan. It was no longer aimed at Trinidad, but at a beach called Playa Girón, sixty miles up the coast, on the outside of an inlet known as the Bay of Pigs. National Security Adviser Mac Bundy, previously skeptical, was impressed. The CIA, he wrote to Kennedy, had "done a remarkable job of reframing the landing so as to make it unspectacular and quiet, and plausibly Cuban in its essentials." He did point out, though, that there was "unanimous agreement" about the need to take out Fidel Castro's air force with air cover. "My own belief is that this air battle has to come sooner or later, and that the longer we put it off, the harder it will be," he wrote. He recommended one strike by six to eight B-26s, "some time *before* the invasion."[1]

Dick Bissell afterward maintained that the need for air cover as "an absolute prerequisite for success" was clear to the CIA, Joint Chiefs of Staff, and the military commanders of the operation itself, and insisted that this was repeatedly stated to Kennedy. "Kennedy found the new arrangement still too noisy," he said. "He asked repeatedly whether the air strikes were necessary; in effect, he wouldn't take yes for an answer."[2]

The Bay of Pigs was in the Zapata Swamp, a wetland on Cuba's south coast. There was no significant town closer than Cienfuegos, forty miles away along circuitous roads through dense jungle. The Sierra del Escambray was farther yet, its foothills rising at least ten miles beyond Cienfuegos. Amid the Zapata vegetation, crocodiles and snakes flourished, but humans did not. Those few who lived there worked in the small-scale production of charcoal. The revolutionary government had built roads, provided education, and raised the standard of living of the peasantry. Fidel and Raúl had built personal followings in the Zapata area, each visiting many times. Fidel had even spent Christmas Eve there with local families in 1959.[3]

Within the CIA, there was concern about the refocusing of the operation at the Bay of Pigs. Jake Esterline studied the area on a map. "I thought to myself, it does look very secure," he remembered, "no one is going to get in there very easily but how are we going to get any more recruits, how are we going to expand this front because there is nobody there except alligators and ducks."[4] At the beginning of April, David Atlee Phillips entered the war room to see on the map a large red cross over Trinidad, and new markings aimed at the Bay of Pigs. "I thought I was victim of an April Fool trick of the meanest kind," he said. The new location, he argued, was too far from the Sierra del Escambray, and the swamp too perilous.

"How will the Brigade take the beach, and hold it?" he asked.

"The first ships to land will carry tanks," said Jack Hawkins, the colonel in charge.

"Tanks!" exclaimed Phillips. "We're going to mount a secret operation in the Caribbean with tanks?"

"That's right," said Hawkins. "A company. Three platoons of five each, and two command tanks."[5]

Later, Bissell would admit that little thought had been given to how invaders might operate in the swamp, as opposed to the mountains for which they had been trained. If the Castros' army overwhelmed the beachhead, it was, he said, "rather lightheartedly assumed" that they would still be able to escape, turn guerrilla, and retreat into the Sierra del Escambray—at least fifty miles away, through difficult terrain teeming with Castro's fighters. "The president was thus left with an impression that a less than disastrous option would be available in the event of an initial lack of success."[6]

"I think the reason why we get all this crap from Bissell—melting into the Escambray and all that rubbish—was that Bissell believed the operation would have to succeed, no matter what," said Arthur Schlesinger, years later. "That is because once the invasion started, if it appeared to be faltering, then Kennedy would send in the marines. But Kennedy had no such intention. Kennedy would go to great lengths to avoid escalation of a crisis, especially a military crisis."[7]

By the end of March, operational security had fallen apart. Schlesinger told the president that he had just spoken to a journalist who had spent ten days in Miami. The Cuban exiles there told him they had been "systematically hopped up" over the preceding weeks by their American contacts, in preparation for an invasion of Cuba. "I listened to all this deadpan,"

Schlesinger wrote to Kennedy. "Obviously if an enterprising magazine writer could pick all this up in Miami in a couple of weeks, Habana must be well posted on developments."[8]

On the same day, Chet Bowles found out what was going on, and wrote to Dean Rusk, outlining the illegality of an invasion and dire risks to American prestige. He pleaded with Rusk to persuade Kennedy to call it off. "Those most familiar with the Cuban operation seem to agree that as the venture is now planned, the chances of success are not greater than one out of three," he wrote. "I realize that this operation has been put together over a period of months. A great deal of time and money has been spent and many individuals have become emotionally involved in its success. We should not, however, proceed with the adventure simply because we are wound up and cannot stop." From the other political wing of the Democrats, Bill Fulbright agreed, writing to Kennedy that the invasion "is in violation of the spirit and probably the letter as well, of treaties to which the United States is a party and of U.S. domestic legislation." He continued: "To give this activity even covert support is of a piece with the hypocrisy and cynicism for which the United States is constantly denouncing the Soviet Union in the United Nations and elsewhere. This point will not be lost on the rest of the world—nor on our own consciences for that matter."[9]

"We believe that the Central Intelligence Agency has no intelligence at all," Fidel told a group of workers preparing for Havana's May Day celebrations on 8 April. "They should be called the Central Agency of Yankee Cretins."[10] When they had finished laughing, he confirmed that the Central Agency of Yankee Cretins was about to mount an invasion of Cuba. He did not know exactly where, when, or how it would strike, but would prepare for any eventuality. His most reliable commanders were sent out to the provinces: Raúl to Oriente, Che to Pinar del Rio, and Juan Almeida to Santa Clara.[11]

Meanwhile, the CIA's last-ditch plan to kill Fidel before the invasion collapsed. A date had been picked at the beginning of April, when Fidel was supposed to attend a boxing match at Havana's Sports Palace. The CIA station in Coral Gables, Florida, had planned to supply a bazooka to one of the groups of Cuban exiles. The exiles would sneak back into Cuba. During the fight, the bazooka would be used to knock out the tall, bearded figure just outside the ring. As it happened, there was such bitter political infighting between the Cubans in Miami that the CIA could not work out to whom the bazooka should be given. It stayed in the box, and the attempt was canceled.[12]

On 7 April, Adlai Stevenson had been briefed in the sketchiest possible terms by the CIA's Tracy Barnes. Barnes told him only that the United States had given some training and financing to a Cuban-run clandestine operation—indicating nothing about an invasion. Even so: "Look, I don't like this," Stevenson told Schlesinger the following day. "If I were calling the shots, I wouldn't do it. But this is Kennedy's show."[13] The White House counsel, Ted Sorensen, raised his concerns with Kennedy. He remembered the president's response: "'I know,' [Kennedy] replied with some irritation, 'that everyone is worrying about getting hurt (he used a more vulgar term).' Then he went on to indicate that he felt it was now impossible to release the army that had been built up and have them spreading word of his action or inaction through the country."[14]

Gerry Droller, a CIA agent who went by the pseudonym Frank Bender, was busy reassuring the Cuban brigade that the United States had their back. "Frank told Pepe [San Román, the brigade commander] and me," remembered Erneido Oliva, one of the invaders, "that the Marines were not going with us to invade Cuba, but they would be close to us when we needed them."[15] Meanwhile, in Washington, Kennedy was insisting on the opposite. On 12 April, he lost his cool in a meeting with his advisers over the question of the marines backing up the Cuban brigade. "The minute I land one marine, we're in this thing up to our necks," he shouted. "I can't get the United States into a war and then lose it, no matter what it takes. I'm not going to risk an American Hungary. And that's what it could be, a fucking slaughter."[16] Still, though, he did not reach for the brakes.

★

On 8 April, François Duvalier held another of his democratic elections. This one merged the houses of parliament into a single fifty-seven-member National Assembly. It had not been touted as a presidential election, and most voters thought nothing of the fact that at the top of every ballot paper were the words *République d'Haïti, Dr. François Duvalier, Président de la République*. There was no box to cross next to the name.

Out of an estimated 1 million voters, 1,320,748 votes were cast, despite a low turnout. When the results were announced, it would be announced with them that, following an overwhelming result of 1,320,748 votes to zero, Duvalier would remain president for a second term, from 1963 to 1969. The act of returning the ballot paper with Duvalier's name still on it had, according to the government, constituted a vote for him. "My enemies can only reproach me with one crime—of loving my people too much," remarked Duvalier. "As a revolutionary, I have no right to disregard the voice of the people."[17]

No one could be in any doubt that the Haitian election was a travesty. But the United States would continue to recognize Duvalier as Haiti's president, and to support him with military assistance, aid, and loans. The whole world's eyes were about to turn to Cuba.

On 11 April, Dean Rusk seemed confident. He returned from a meeting, and told Chet Bowles, "Don't worry about this. It isn't going to amount to anything."

"What do you mean, 'amount to anything'?" asked Bowles.

"Well, it just won't amount to anything," Rusk repeated.

"Will it make the front page of the *New York Times*?" asked Bowles.

"I wouldn't think so," said Rusk.[18]

On 14 April, the day before the first strike was due, Kennedy told Bissell to cut the number of planes involved. Bissell had planned on using sixteen B-26s. Kennedy told him to make it "minimal," so he halved that. It was decided at the very last minute that it would be best if these looked like spontaneous defectors from inside Cuba, and so the B-26s were painted to look like those of the Cuban air force. David Atlee Phillips found himself sending a series of cables to the air base in Nicaragua, telling the "flying actors," as he called them, what to wear and say, and how to make their planes look realistically combat-damaged. The strike was said to have been triggered by a mysterious radio message: "Alert, alert! Look well at the rainbow! The fish will be running very soon!" This was no code, but a piece of nonsense made up by Phillips as a cover.[19]

The next morning, a Saturday, the operation began. Eight planes were sent to attack three Cuban airfields. The raids caused some damage, and killed a few people on the ground; but their main achievement was to warn Fidel Castro that the invasion was about to start. Afterward, one plane landed in Miami. Its pilot—impersonating a member of the Cuban air force—claimed that he was a "defector," covering his face from the cameras with a baseball cap. The cap was not a regulation piece of a Cuban pilot's uniform. Nor had the machine guns on his plane been fired. Unlike Castro's B-26s, which had plastic noses, his had a solid metal nose.[20]

Adlai Stevenson, the American ambassador to the United Nations, was immediately called upon to explain the air strike. David Atlee Phillips watched Stevenson on television, showing pictures of the "defecting" plane in Miami, and claiming that its Cuban air force markings proved the United States was not involved. Phillips was impressed by Stevenson's acting, until "a chill moved through my body," he wrote. "What had we done? *Adlai Stevenson had been taken in by the hoax!* Had no one bothered to tell our Ambassador at the United Nations of the deception involved in the air strike?"[21] The full details of the operation had been kept away from both Stevenson and Dean Rusk on Kennedy's orders. "I was taken by surprise when I learned that these were not genuine defections but were feigned, that they were, in fact, a part of the Bay of Pigs operation," said Rusk.[22] By Sunday morning, the press had noticed the problems with the pilot's clothes, his plane, and his story, and worked out that the "defector" was lying.

That same weekend, in Ciudad Trujillo, the American diplomat Bob Murphy arrived on Kennedy's orders for a secret meeting with Rafael Trujillo. The meeting had been arranged by Porfirio Rubirosa, and Murphy was accompanied by Igor Cassini. Kennedy, it seemed, still hoped to talk Trujillo down. For his part, Trujillo saw the meeting as a prelude to further negotiations with Jack, or at least Joe, Kennedy in person.[23]

As usual, Trujillo insisted that he was not a dictator. He reassured Murphy that it was his intention to step back in line with American interests, but insisted that the State Department was out to get him. He believed this was because he had been trying to tell them for many years about Fidel Castro's communist links, and the department had refused to listen. Now, he had been proven right. "They will never forgive me for that," he told Murphy.

Murphy recommended to the State Department that it take Trujillo back under its wing and restore full American support. Mac Bundy put a stop to that idea, pointing out to Kennedy that it would undermine the Alliance for Progress. On the day Murphy left the Dominican Republic, 16 April, Trujillo emphasized to him again that the United States needed all its allies in Latin America to come together to combat the Cuban problem.

"Well, pretty soon there won't be any Cuban problem," Murphy replied. "Castro is a dead duck."[24]

On the contrary, this particular duck was still quacking. That day, Fidel held a ceremony to honor those killed by the first strike. He gave a mocking speech, full of spitting rage about "miserable gringo imperialists" and "millionaire parasites." He read out some of the Associated Press's dispatches, implying that the attacking planes were spontaneous defectors from the Cuban air force, and mocked them, too. "They [the Americans] have fabricated a complete story, with details and names, scheming up everything," he said. "Hollywood would never have come up with something like this, ladies and gentlemen!" He continued, alleging that the United States "organized the attack, planned the attack, trained the mercenaries, supplied the planes, supplied the bombs, prepared the airports—everyone knows it."

Castro was right. But the most significant point in his speech came a minute or two later. "What they cannot forgive," he said, "is that we have made a socialist revolution right under the very nose of the United States!"[25] There was riotous applause. For the first time, Fidel had publicly described his revolution as socialist.

Meanwhile, in Washington, there was a final meeting, which included Kennedy, Dulles, the chairman of the Joint Chiefs of Staff Lyman Lemnitzer, Rusk, Berle, Fulbright, and the assistant secretary of state Tom Mann. Only Fulbright expressed any reservations. It was agreed that the landing would go ahead.

Though the operation was now in motion, the debate about the second air strike—planned for dawn the next morning—continued. Adlai Stevenson, already shamed at the United Nations, insisted that another strike would make his position impossible. Rusk had never wanted air strikes anyway, and now Mac Bundy agreed with him that another round would be a political disaster. At nine o'clock that night, Rusk telephoned Kennedy to persuade him to call off the next strike. It would be obvious to all, Rusk said, that the second strike would not have come from Cuban defectors, but had taken off from Nicaragua, where the dictator Luis Somoza had allowed them the use of an airfield. This had not occurred to Kennedy, who had somehow formed the false impression the second strike would be launched from the beachhead in the Bay of Pigs. "I'm not signed on to this!" he shouted into the telephone.[26] He called the strike off, hung up, and paced around his bedroom, with a rising sense of horror that he was not in control.

Charles Pearre Cabell, deputy director of the CIA, insisted "that it was now physically impossible to stop the over-all landing operation," and pointed out that the cancellation of air strikes would have a serious effect.[27] Rusk called Kennedy again at four thirty in the morning with Cabell's final request to get the strikes back on, supported by Bissell. Kennedy refused. Afterward, he could not sleep. He and Jackie sat up until the sun rose.

Bissell admitted that neither he nor Cabell was firm enough with Kennedy about the danger posed to the operation if the second strike were canceled. When they informed the planners of the president's decision, tempers were lost. "Goddamn it, this is criminal negligence," yelled Jack Hawkins, slamming his hand into the table. Jake Esterline added, "This is the goddamnest thing I have ever heard of." In the command tent on the Nicaraguan airstrip, the American general in charge of the second strike threw his cap on the ground, shouting, "There goes the whole fuckin' war!"[28]

Dulles later took the blame: "I should have said, "Mr. President, if you're not willing to permit us to . . . substantially immobilize the Cuban air force (which was a very small and crotchety and defective air force at that time), the plan to get this brigade ashore with its equipment and supplies is a faulty one."[29] But Dulles was not even there. Some months before, he had accepted an invitation to the convention of the Young Presidents' Organization in Puerto Rico that weekend. He argued, limply, that canceling this engagement would look suspicious, and to the golf courses of Puerto Rico he went. Before he left, he established a telephone code. If he called and said that he had caught "three marlin today," the officer in Washington was to reply with congratulations to confirm that it was going well. No code was set for the eventuality that it was not going well.

In his stead, Robert Amory, the CIA's head of intelligence analysis, was left on duty in the CIA offices. He had not been involved in the operation's planning and was not officially supposed to know about it—though he did, through office gossip. Before Dulles departed, Amory asked what he should do if anything came up with the operation.

"You have nothing to do with that at all," Dulles snapped. "General Cabell will take care of anything."

On 16 April, Amory came in to work, still seething with irritation over being sidelined. He opened a few cables; then, according to his own recollection, "I said, 'Screw 'em.' "[30] He went home, and played five sets of tennis. On the day Kennedy canceled the air strikes, the CIA had almost no hands on deck.

★

The fourteen hundred counterrevolutionaries who approached the Bay of Pigs in the early hours of 17 April believed that they were acting with the support of the United States and of a higher power yet. "There was also a very strong Catholic undertone to the whole brigade," remembered Alfredo Durán, one of its members. "So much so, that our emblem was a cross surrounded by a Cuban flag. The brigade was a crusade."[31]

It was around midnight when three Cuban militia groups, at Playa Girón, Playa Larga, and Punta Perdiz, each noticed lights out to sea. Seven ships were approaching. The map on which Esterline and Hawkins had replanned the operation had not indicated coral reefs, and analysts had concluded that the shadows on aerial photographs were clouds or seaweed.[32] But beneath the smooth, dark sea, coral reefs there were. The first landing craft ran aground on them, eighty yards offshore. One of its red marker lights accidentally started flashing. As the men onboard climbed out and waded toward the beach, a Cuban jeep drove up to meet them. Alerted by the red light, the local militia thought it was dealing with a lost fishing boat, and had come to warn it to avoid the reefs. As it turned to park, the jeep's headlamps illuminated the school of frogmen approaching the soft white sand. The leader of the invading group, the CIA's David Gray, opened fire.[33] For all Kennedy's emphasis on plausible deniability, the first man to engage Castro's troops at the Bay of Pigs was an American.

Though Castro's 339th Militia Battalion, stationed inland at the Australia Sugar Mill, comprised only five hundred men, there were troops all over the Zapata area. When the fighting began, local militia units radioed to the 339th. The 339th relayed the news to Point One, Fidel's command base in Havana.

The first wave of Brigade 2506 began to make its way inland. Meanwhile, one of the ships, the *Houston*, was sunk by one of Fidel's jets just inside the bay. This rendered an entire battalion useless, along with its cargo—which, according to Cuban reports, included food and drinking water, gasoline, light arms ammunition, explosives, and one and a half tons of white phosphorus.[34] Many of its 130 men seemed to be paralyzed with shock. A CIA officer paddled up to the *Houston* in a dinghy, shouting, "Get off, you bastards, it's your fucking war!" Soon afterward, the Cuban air force also sank the *Rio Escondido*, a freighter that carried most of the invaders' fuel and all of their signaling equipment. Two further ships turned back, insisting they would only continue with American naval and air support.[35]

Early that morning, Fidel telephoned his local commander, José Ramón Fernández, to mobilize the defense. Fernández called for his jeep to be filled up and summoned four officers to accompany him. Minutes later, the telephone rang again.

It was Fidel. "What are you doing?"

"I'm just finishing getting dressed, Commander," replied Fernández. Fidel hung up, and Fernández began to assemble everything he needed. Ten minutes later, Fidel rang again.

"Why are you still there?"

As Fernández headed south, Fidel continued to call the field telephone in his jeep every ten minutes. Finally, when Fernández reached the Australia mill, Fidel told him to take the village of Pálpite, on the only road out of the Bay of Pigs toward Havana. Fernández scanned his map.

"Commander, there's no Pálpite on my map."

"Look more carefully. It has to be there."

"Commander, it's not here."

Finally, a militiaman standing next to Fernández pointed to a spot on his map marked Párrite.

"OK, where is this Pálpite?" Fernández said to Fidel. "Is it between where I am now and Playa Larga?"

"That's the one. Take it!"

A battalion from the Matanzas Militia Leadership School arrived at the mill shortly afterward. Fernández sent it straight on to Pálpite, through the swamp. Many of the troops had not completed the necessary training to use their weapons. Some were taught how to fire their arms while in trucks on the road to Pálpite. Fidel sent a fighter plane to cover the battalion as it made its way through the trees. In a matter of hours, Fernández took Pálpite. He called Fidel back with the news.

"Wonderful!" crowed the irrepressible commander in chief. "They may not realize it, but they've lost the war."[36]

The Cuban troops attempted and failed to take Playa Larga, and had regrouped in Pálpite when Fidel himself arrived. He ordered a second attack on Playa Larga that evening, which was also beaten back. During the fighting at the Rotunda, a traffic circle just outside Playa Larga, Erneido Oliva ordered his men to fire white phosphorus grenades from their mortars at Fidel's troops. White phosphorus sticks to human skin, causing swift, deep burns. "The shouting of the enemy at that moment was just like hell," he remembered. "Everything was on fire. . . . It was like a curtain, completely covered with white phosphorus."[37]

By this point, reports were coming in about a second landing near Havana, at the old American base of Bahía Honda. Fidel could not risk a direct attack on the capital, and so he went himself. But it was a diversionary attack—eight ships manned by the CIA, filled with a cargo of special effects equipment. They set off a sound and light show and a sequence of electronic signals, designed to make this look like a second invasion.

Fidel had claimed the bombing raids on Cuba from Florida, and the *Coubre* explosion, as examples of covert action on the part of the United States. In both cases, there had been doubt on the part of the international community that he was right. The Bay of Pigs invasion, on the other hand, had been preceded by months of news reports in Spanish, English, and Russian that suggested the CIA was planning just such a thing. The Soviets had not yet committed large-scale military aid to Cuba, but they were watching the Bay of Pigs closely. During the invasion, Nikolai Leonov was in Moscow, liaising with Vladimir Semichastny of the KGB. The two discussed what was happening every two to three hours, and maintained on the wall of Semichastny's office two maps of Cuba. One showed the course of events from American newspapers, radio, and television, the other from Soviet agents in Cuba.[38] The results would have appeared to confirm that the Cuban government was a more reliable source than the Americans.

"Disclaimability, in a technical sense meaning the suppression of hard evidence of U.S. government sponsorship, was taken seriously by all concerned and insisted upon as a policy at a significant cost in operational effectiveness," Dick Bissell admitted years later. "It was not appreciated that the operation was bound to be universally attributed to the U.S. government, regardless of hard evidence, and that all efforts to maintain technical disclaimability would buy little or nothing in the form of political advantage or more favorable world opinion. . . . Anyone reading the *New York Times* should have known better."[39] Washington's denials only made matters worse. It was obvious that the American government was lying. This lent credibility to everything Fidel had previously claimed about the machinations of yanqui imperialism.

"Let us answer with fire and sword the barbarians who scorn us and seek to return us to slavery," Fidel told the nation. "They come to take away the land that the revolution gave to the peasants and cooperativists; we fight to defend the land of the peasants and cooperativists. They come to take away the people's factories, the people's sugar mills, the people's mines; we fight to defend our factories, our sugar mills, our mines. They come to take away from our children and from our peasant women the schools that the revolution has opened up for them everywhere; we defend the schools of our children and of the peasantry. They come to take away from black men and women the dignity that the revolution has returned to them; we fight to maintain the supreme dignity of each and every human being.

"*Viva Cuba libre! Patria o muerte! Venceremos!*" (Long live free Cuba! Homeland or death! We will win!)[40]

★

At eight o'clock on the morning of 18 April, Fidel's troops retook Playa Larga. The invaders were being forced back to a small area between San Blas and Playa Girón. The American carrier *Essex* was nearby in international waters, with two thousand marines aboard. It was not there on Kennedy's direction. According to the CIA's Jake Esterline and Sam Halpern, the order to have the marines stand by was given on his own authority by the chief of naval operations, Admiral Arleigh Burke.[41] The Pentagon, like the CIA and the members of Brigade 2506 themselves, assumed that Kennedy would not allow the operation to fail.

Back in Washington, Mac Bundy wrote to Kennedy, "I think you will find at noon that the situation in Cuba is not a bit good." He recommended that Castro's air force be eliminated, "by neutrally-painted U.S. planes if necessary."[42] Soon afterward, Kennedy received a message from Nikita Khrushchev. The Soviet premier wrote that it was "a secret to no one" that the United States was behind the invasion of Cuba. "We will render the Cuban people and their government all necessary help to repel armed attack on Cuba." Kennedy's reply accused Khrushchev of being "under a serious misapprehension in regard to events in Cuba," and restated boldly what was by now a glaring lie: "the United States intends no military intervention in Cuba."[43]

That evening, Kennedy held a congressional ball at the White House. During the dinner, Admiral Burke met with representatives of the CIA. It was a memorable sight: a roomful of men done out in white tie and tails, or full dress uniforms, and amid all this finery a collection of dejected faces. "They are in a real bad hole because they had the hell cut out of them," remembered Burke. "They were reporting, devising and talking and I kept quiet because I didn't know the general score. Once in a while I did make a little remark like 'balls.'" The president arrived. Both Bissell for the intelligence agency, and Burke for the Pentagon, begged him to commit American forces. Kennedy insisted that he did not want the United States involved.

"Hell, Mr. President, but we *are* involved," Burke rejoined. "Can I not send in an air strike?"

"No," replied Kennedy.

"Can we send a few planes?"

"No, because they could be identified as United States."

"Can we paint out their numbers or any of this?"

"No."

". . . if you'll let me have two destroyers, we'll give gunfire support and we can hold that beachhead with two ships forever."

"No."

"One destroyer, Mr. President?"

"No."[44]

Two hours later, Kennedy was still in the Oval Office, along with his advisers Arthur Schlesinger, Mac Bundy, Dick Goodwin, and Pierre Salinger. The men, subdued, talked gloomily of the options available to mitigate their failure. Kennedy read a message received from Pepe San Román, the brigade commander, who had sailed ten miles out to sea to radio for help: "Do you people realize how desperate this situation is? Do you back us up or quit? All we want is low jet cover and jet close support. . . . I will not be evacuated. Will fight to the end if we have to."[45]

Something about these words finally changed the president's mind. At three o'clock in the morning, Kennedy agreed to send six unmarked planes to provide cover for the brigade's B-26s. Suddenly and without warning, the president, in his shirt sleeves, stood up and walked out of the doors into the night, alone, tears streaming down his face. "We could see him occasionally passing by the windows," Salinger remembered. "It was a picture of loneliness."[46]

When Kennedy awoke the next morning, he was informed that the air cover had been sent—but the military planners had forgotten the one-hour time difference between Cuba and Nicaragua. When the brigade's B-26s arrived, the unmarked American planes were still sitting on the aircraft carrier.[47]

On the morning of 19 April, Fidel Castro's local militia commander José Ramón Fernández was about a mile from Playa Girón when he spotted two American destroyers moving toward the coast. According to Fernández, they stopped in Cuban waters, and one began to lower boats.

Fernández sent a message to Fidel, telling him another landing was under way and he needed two more battalions of infantry and tanks. Meanwhile, his troops gathered along the shore, watching the destroyers with a growing sense of belligerence. "Everyone wanted to fire," Fernández remembered.[48]

Fernández had been given no orders in the event he encounter the United States Navy. Carefully, he lined up his artillery, and ordered his men to fire only on the small boats. It was a wise decision. Had he fired on American ships—even in Cuban waters—the conflict would doubtless have escalated, complete with all the air strikes and marine support that the Pentagon was bursting to unleash. As Fidel immediately realized when he was told about the destroyers' approach, they had been sent to evacuate the men of Brigade 2506.

Thanks to Fernández's restraint, an all-out war was avoided. The ground fighting finished that afternoon. Almost the entire brigade—around twelve hundred men—was taken prisoner alive by Cuban troops.

Fidel Castro had returned to the Bay of Pigs, and was touring the houses serving as field hospitals for the invaders. In one lay Enrique Ruiz-Williams, one of the brigade's commanders, on the edge of delirium with almost seventy wounds on his body. Even through his haze, Williams recognized Fidel. He had stowed a pistol under his mattress. He reached for it, though neither he nor those around him could remember later whether he had managed to draw the gun and it failed to go off when he pulled the trigger, or whether he had simply made the gesture.

Fidel did not flinch. "What are you trying to do," he said, "kill me?"

"That's what I came here for," replied Williams. "We've been trying to do that for three days."

Fidel took the news with equanimity. A militia police captain gave Williams a friendly pat. "Take it easy. Take it easy. You're in bad shape."

The door of the house had been blown out during the bombing. Fidel reached down to pick it up, and uncovered the body of one of Williams's comrades. "This man is dead," Fidel observed. He indicated the rest of the prisoners. "These men can't stay here," he said. "Take them to Covadonga and put them in the hospital."[49]

Fidel had survived yet again. Che Guevara almost did not. In distant Pinar del Rio, he was hiding out in a cabin near the coast, awaiting another fight. A shot rang out close by, and Che tasted blood in his mouth. "Get him!" he yelled. "But no," he remembered later, "it was my own pistol. It had dropped to the floor cocked, along with the double belt I've always worn loosely. It went off when it struck the ground. The bullet hit my cheek, but if it had strayed one centimeter, it would have torn into the base of my brain."[50] But for one centimeter of a bullet's trajectory, the CIA might have had something to celebrate following the Bay of Pigs operation after all.

The atmosphere back in Washington was grim. Jack and Bobby Kennedy spent much of the day on the telephone to their father. When Rose Kennedy asked Joe how he was feeling, Joe replied that he felt he was "dying." Dick Nixon saw Allen Dulles, who had returned from Puerto Rico and looked so careworn that Nixon asked if he would like a drink. "I certainly would—I really need one. This is the worst day of my life!" said Dulles. "Everything is lost. The Cuban invasion is a total failure." As the full extent of the failure became apparent in the CIA's war room, David Atlee Phillips observed the agency men around him. One was "white with remorse and fatigue," one "held one hand across his face, as if hiding," one "scratched his wrists viciously; blood stained his cuffs and darkened his fingernails," and one simply "vomited in a wastebasket."[51] It had been, as the president had so succinctly predicted on 12 April, "a fucking slaughter."

"I was assured by every son of a bitch I checked with—all the military experts and the CIA—that the plan would succeed," Kennedy told Nixon, who came to see him in the Oval Office on 20 April. The president paced around the Oval Office, cursing the CIA, the Joint Chiefs, and members of the White House staff. Nixon advised him to invade Cuba. At this, Kennedy demurred, pointing out that Khrushchev might attack in Berlin if he did. "It really is true that foreign affairs is the only important issue for a President to handle, isn't it?" Kennedy remarked. "I mean, who gives a shit if the minimum wage is $1.15 or $1.25, in comparison to something like this?"[52]

That same day, Kennedy also attended a cabinet meeting, which descended into recriminations. Bobby Kennedy was, by all reports, the angriest, though Chet Bowles reported that the president, too, was in "what I felt was a dangerous mood."[53] The Washington journalist David Halberstam reported the rumor of the day: afterward, Bobby had "jammed his fingers into Bowles's stomach and told him, that he, Bowles, was for the invasion, remember that, he was for it, they were all for it (the story did not originate with the Bowles people, either)."[54] The story did not, and Bowles deliberately covered it up in his mild-mannered memoirs. "They felt badly hurt, they wanted to retaliate, they wanted to strike back," he remembered in a 1970 interview, still reluctant to talk. "I don't want to mention anybody by name, like Bobby."[55] But he did, in his own notes, record his serious concern about the vulnerability of Bobby and other members of the administration to the influence of the military and the CIA. "What worries me is that two of the most powerful people in this administration—Lyndon Johnson and Bob Kennedy—have no experience in foreign affairs, and they both realize that this is the central question of this period and are determined to be experts at it," he wrote. "The problems of foreign affairs are complex, involving politics, economics and social questions that require both understanding of history and various world cultures."[56] Without these tools, Johnson and Bobby were ill equipped to make decisions—but they would be doing so anyway.

Bobby Kennedy had not been closely involved in the planning of the Bay of Pigs. As soon as the beachhead fell, though, he wrote a memorandum to his brother, emphasizing that they must not go soft on Cuba. Some Soviet arms were already on the island, and he stressed the need to get these out, urgently. The best way to do so would be to convince other Latin American nations that Cuba threatened their security: for instance, "if it was reported that one or two of Castro's MIGs attacked Guantanamo Bay and the United States made noises like this was an act of war." The situation might get worse, he added. "If we don't want Russia to set up missile bases in Cuba, we had better decide now what we are willing to do to stop it."[57]

Bobby's style did not sit easily with his colleagues. He was, said Mac Bundy, "not always constructive, and sometimes ferocious. I mean, Bobby is capable of dealing with bureaucrats in a way that you wouldn't deal with a dog." But the president felt that aggression was exactly what was needed to reassert his control. "I made a mistake in putting Bobby in the Justice Department," Jack told Arthur Schlesinger. "He is wasted there. . . . Bobby should be in CIA. . . . It's a hell of a way to learn things, but I have learned one thing from this business—that is, we will have to deal with CIA."[58] Jack did ask Bobby to take over the CIA, but, according to Bobby's recollection, he turned the job down on the grounds that as a Democrat and the president's brother it would not look good.[59] Sam Halpern, a CIA agent closely connected with the Bay of Pigs operation who would remain on the Cuba team afterward, later argued that Bobby assumed the role unofficially anyway. "Bobby took a real close look at CIA," he said. "He decided that the best way to handle the CIA was not to destroy it, but for him to take it over and run it and use it as his own facility. And this is what actually happened."[60]

On 21 April, Jack Kennedy abandoned plausible deniability at last, and took the blame. "There is an old saying that victory has a hundred fathers and defeat is an orphan," he told a press conference. "I am the responsible officer of this government."[61] For this he received much credit, in the press and from the public. In a meeting at the White House, Lyndon Johnson blamed the CIA. "Lyndon, you've got to remember that we're all in this, and that when I accepted responsibility for this operation, I took the entire responsibility on myself," replied the president. "We should have no sort of passing of the buck or backbiting, however justified." As one biographer pointed out, those last two words reveal something of Kennedy's real feelings.[62]

Taking responsibility, for Kennedy, did not involve resignation. "If this were a parliamentary government, I would have to resign and you, a civil servant, would stay on," Kennedy told Bissell. "But being the system of government it is, a presidential government, you will have to resign." The career of Allen Dulles was similarly ended. In 1965, Dulles wrote an article for *Harper's* magazine, titled "My Answer to the Bay of Pigs," arguing that the CIA had not misled Kennedy, and it was the White House's hesitation that was responsible for the disaster. To the magazine's disappointment, he pulled it just before publication. His wife explained that he did so "because there was so much more in his favor he could have said, if he had been at liberty to do so, that the material [in the article] was inadequate."[63]

Taking responsibility did not involve changing policy, either. On 22 April, Bobby Kennedy was at a cabinet meeting, "slamming into anyone who suggested that we go slowly and try to move calmly and not repeat previous mistakes," remembered Bowles. Bobby insisted that the harassment of Fidel Castro must be stepped up, not down. Bowles would soon be fired.[64] The Kennedy administration closed its ranks. As for the CIA itself, just a fortnight after the failure at the Bay of Pigs, it commissioned a new plan for covert action against Cuba.[65]

Meanwhile, the Cuban government gleefully released details of the invading force: "194 ex-military personnel and henchmen; 100 owners of large landed estates; 24 large property owners; 67 landlords of buildings; 112 large merchants; 179 idle rich; 35 industrial capitalists; and 112 lumpens."[66] As one Cuban exile snarled to Arturo Espaillat, "Did the U.S. Government really expect to get rid of Castro with those yacht club boys?"[67] Espaillat noted respectfully that this was unfair to Brigade 2506. But the exile was right that Washington had underestimated Fidel Castro.

In addition to the men of the brigade, the Cuban government arrested thousands of people in the days just before and after the invasion. Some estimates have gone as high as 100,000, though, if it were so many, most must have been released almost immediately.[68] About 100 were eventually executed. This crackdown helped break the back of the domestic Cuban opposition. "If the Bay of Pigs fiasco had any lasting result," said Wayne Smith, formerly of the American embassy in Havana, "it was the destruction of the anti-Castro underground, which never recovered from the blows it received in April 1961."[69] The captured invaders were taken to a sports stadium, where Fidel spent four days shouting at them live on television. Such was the power of his performance that, during a high point, one of the prisoners forgot himself and applauded. The footage was rebroadcast around the world.[70]

The fate of the prisoners would take almost two years to resolve. Initially, Fidel offered to trade them for five hundred tractors and $30 million in capital relief. The United States refused, and the prisoners stayed in Cuba. "We were not mistreated; we were not tortured; we were not beaten," remembered Alfredo Durán, one of the captured invaders, of the first few months in Fidel's custody. "We were fed and those who needed medical treatment were given medical treatment." Later, conditions deteriorated. The men were given little food, and kept in overcrowded huts. Sometimes, when there was particular tension between Cuba and the United States, they would be taken out and harassed. Nonetheless, "I expected worse treatment than I received," said Durán. "I was pleasantly surprised that we were really not beaten up, or worse."[71] Neither Trujillo nor Duvalier was ever so hospitable to invaders. In a halfhearted attempt to curry favor with the Kennedy administration, Trujillo did offer Delio Gómez Ochoa and Pablito Mirabal, the only veterans of the Cuban-supported invasion

GETTY IMAGES

Fidel Castro (smoking cigar) and Che Guevara, in the Sierra Maestra, Cuba.

BETTMANN/CORBIS

"Do nothing to offend the dictators; they are the only people we can depend on": director of the CIA Allen Dulles (left) and Secretary of State John Foster Dulles (right).

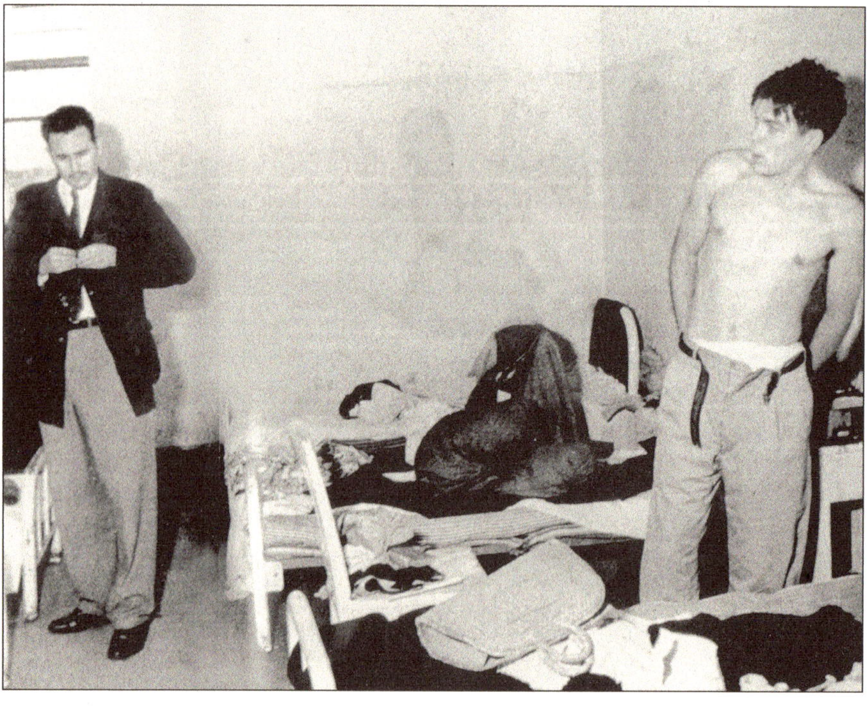

GETTY IMAGES

"I will not abandon you": Fidel Castro and Che Guevara (shirtless) sharing a cell in a Mexican prison, 1956.

BETTMANN/CORBIS

BETTMANN/CORBIS

Caribbean dictators: Vice President Richard Nixon meets American allies Fulgencio Batista (top, right) in Cuba and Rafael Trujillo (middle, right) in the Dominican Republic. François Duvalier (bottom, in hat and spectacles), seen with his wife, Simone Ovide, was elected to the presidency of Haiti in 1957 and immediately expressed his wish to become the "spoiled child" of the United States.

BETTMANN/CORBIS

GETTY IMAGES

Cuba's Jungle Fighters: filmed for American television. Fidel (center) and Raúl Castro (left, in helmet) rally their troops in the Sierra Maestra.

GETTY IMAGES

TIME & LIFE PICTURES/GETTY IMAGES

Both Rafael Trujillo (left, in white suit) and François Duvalier (in car) had good reason to fear the Cuban Revolution.

TIME & LIFE PICTURES/GETTY IMAGES

"There was never any place, except perhaps Paris on liberation day, so full of hope and glory as Cuba then": on New Year's Day 1959, the victorious Fidel Castro is mobbed by cheering crowds.

BOB HENRIQUES/MAGNUM PHOTOS

In their Barbudos (bearded ones) shirts, Fidel Castro (top, left) and Camilo Cienfuegos (top, center) take part in a charity baseball game.

TIME & LIFE PICTURES/GETTY IMAGES

Fidel encouraged his compañeros to wed for the sake of respectability: Raúl Castro (above) married the radical guerrilla Vilma Espín, with whom he had become notorious for kidnapping Americans; Che Guevara (right) married another guerrilla, Aleida March.

BETTMANN/CORBIS

AP/PRESS ASSOCIATION IMAGES

"We enclosed each other in an embrace. I use the term 'enclose' provisionally, keeping in mind my height in contrast to Castro's": Nikita Khrushchev meets Fidel Castro, New York City, 1960.

PCPPERFOTO/GETTY IMAGES

"A struggle for supremacy between two conflicting ideologies: Freedom under God versus ruthless, godless tyranny": Bobby (left) and Jack Kennedy, heading for office. Jack became a Cold War hawk during the 1960 presidential campaign.

GETTY IMAGES

Advertising holidays in revolutionary Cuba, in Miami, Florida, 1960.

BETTMANN/CORBIS

"All popular movements will be repressed with utmost rigor": François Duvalier prepares for a Cuban invasion of Haiti (left), and the Tontons Macoutes march past the National Palace, Port-au-Prince (below).

BETTMANN/CORBIS

AFP/GETTY IMAGES

"The fact that they murder their enemies or torture them doesn't usually come up over coffee cups": Dominican dictator Rafael Trujillo (right) and his son Ramfis (left), friends of the United States with strong connections to the Kennedy family.

PRENSA LATINA/REUTERS/CORBIS

"*Viva Cuba libre! Patria o muerte! Venceremos!*": Fidel Castro addresses his troops during the Bay of Pigs invasion, April 1961.

TIME & LIFE PICTURES/GETTY IMAGES

"I was assured by every son of a bitch I checked with—all the military experts and the CIA—that the plan would succeed": Jack Kennedy (left) tried to explain the Bay of Pigs disaster to former president Dwight D. Eisenhower (right), but Eisenhower "hit the ceiling."

CORNELL CAPA © INTERNATIONAL CENTER OF PHOTOGRAPHY/ MAGNUM PHOTOS

"Roughest thing in my life": Jack Kennedy meets Nikita Khrushchev in Vienna, June 1961. Kennedy's doctor repeatedly injected the ailing president with a drug cocktail he called "joy juice" during the summit.

BETTMANN/CORBIS

He "obviously yearns to be relieved of cares which keep him from less serious pursuits": Ramfis Trujillo holds a press conference after his father's assassination.

BETTMANN/CORBIS

"A series of offensive missile sites is now in preparation on that imprisoned island": John F. Kennedy signs the order for a naval quarantine of Cuba during the missile crisis, October 1962.

BETTMANN/CORBIS

According the Cuban Ministry of the Interior, there would be 637 attempts to assassinate Fidel Castro between 1959 and 1999.

AP/PRESS ASSOCIATION IMAGES

"The people present the sad spectacle of black misery in the heart of riches": Papa Doc's model town of Duvalierville, after construction.

AP/PRESS ASSOCIATION IMAGES

"Duvalier is not a communist, a democrat, or anything else. He is an opportunist": Clément Barbot (right), former chief of the Tontons Macoutes, on the run with his brother Harry (left).

TIME & LIFE PICTURES/GETTY IMAGES

November 22, 1963: in the morning, President and Mrs. John F. Kennedy arrive in Dallas, Texas, on Air Force One (left). That afternoon, Kennedy would be assassinated. In the evening, Lyndon B. Johnson takes the oath of office aboard the same plane (below). On his left is the president's widow.

CORBIS

BETTMANN/CORBIS

"We are going to have to really set up that government down there, run it and stabilize it. . . . This Bosch is no good": Lyndon Johnson embraced Dominican president Juan Bosch in public but secretly worked against him.

Pro-democracy insurgents take to the streets in Santo Domingo, Dominican Republic, 1965. To their surprise, they would find themselves at war with the United States.

THOMAS HOEPKER/MAGNUM PHOTOS

TIME & LIFE PICTURES/GETTY IMAGES

"There has been a democratic awakening in our national consciousness": Francisco Caamaño, unlikely leader of the Dominican revolution.

TIME & LIFE PICTURES/GETTY IMAGES

Raúl Castro (left) and Che Guevara (right), 1964. Once the closest of allies, the two fell out when Raúl grew closer to the Soviet Union and Che to China.

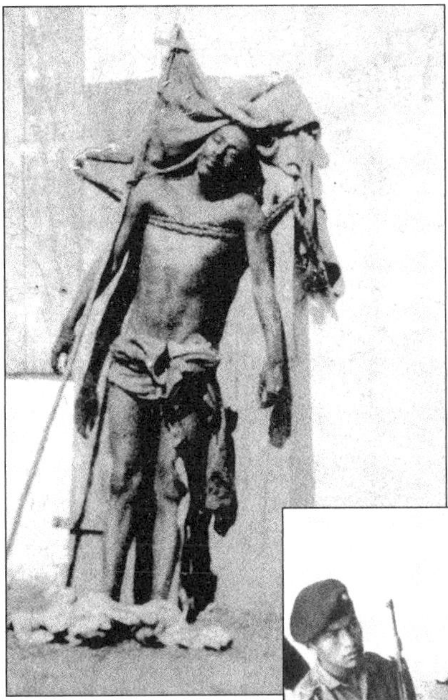

NATIONAL ARCHIVES, NWCS-S, 127-N-521221

The body of Haitian guerrilla Charlemagne Péralte, killed by a United States marine in 1919. This photograph, taken by the marines, seemed to many Haitians to recall the crucifixion. It became a religious icon.

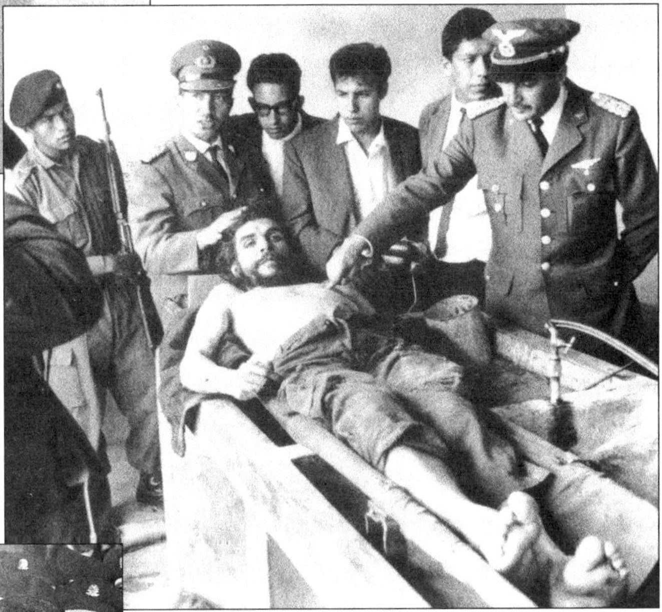

BRIDE LANE LIBRARY/POPPERFOTO/GETTY IMAGES

"The Christ of Vallegrande": the assassins of Che Guevara pose with his corpse, Bolivia, 1967. As in the case of Péralte, this photograph of a slain anti-American guerrilla became an icon.

BETTMANN/CORBIS

Jean-Claude "Baby Doc" Duvalier and his mother, Simone, mourn the passing of Papa Doc in 1971. In 1986, when Baby Doc was removed from office, his personal wealth was estimated at $450 million, and his mother's at $1.15 billion.

BETTMANN/CORBIS

A United States marine in Santo Domingo during Operation Power Pack, 1965.

of the Dominican Republic in 1959 whom he had not yet tortured to death, in exchange for Bay of Pigs prisoners. Fidel declined.[72]

Meanwhile, the men of Brigade 2506 themselves felt betrayed by everyone. Fidel went on several occasions to visit Pepe San Román, the brigade commander. Fidel was sometimes friendly, sometimes angry.

"San Román, what kind of guy are you?" he asked, tugging his own beard. "I don't understand you. I don't understand what kind of people you are." He said he had always tried to be friendly, and offered a compliment: he believed, he said, that some of the invading brigade had fought valiantly. San Román asked why he had not said that during their trial, and the two were soon embroiled in a furious argument.

Eventually, Fidel shouted, "San Román, you don't deserve to live."

"Major," replied Pepe, "that is the only thing that we agree about. I don't want to live any more. I have been played with by the United States and now you are playing with me here. I am tired of being played with. Kill me, but don't play with me any more."[73]

Fidel did not kill him. Eventually, at the end of 1962, the United States accepted a worse deal than the one it had initially rejected, exchanging $53 million in food and medical supplies for the remaining men of Brigade 2506. "I put those men in there," Jack Kennedy told Dick Goodwin, justifying the payout. "They trusted me. And they're in prison now because I fucked up. I have to get them out."[74]

There were those who blamed Eisenhower for allowing a faulty invasion plan to be designed in the first place. At this, according to Dick Nixon, Ike "hit the ceiling." "I would never have approved a plan without adequate air cover," he told Nixon. On 22 April, Eisenhower met Kennedy at Camp David, and informed him in short terms that not only had the operation been a military disaster, but it had been worse: it had let Khrushchev see he was weak. "I just took their advice," Kennedy pleaded, meaning the CIA and the Chiefs of Staff. After leaving the meeting, the new president was visibly shaken.[75]

A few days later, he sought an audience with another five-star general, Douglas MacArthur, at New York's Waldorf-Astoria Towers. MacArthur did blame Ike, his old rival and sometime subordinate officer. "All the chickens are coming home to roost and you are living in the coop," MacArthur said, gruffly. "Eisenhower should have done something about Cuba sooner."[76]

★

Havana's May Day celebrations, just days after the Bay of Pigs invasion, took the form of a victory party. There was a parade of the 339th Militia Battalion, the Revolutionary National Police, and three tank companies, in addition to marching companies of industrial laborers, health-care workers, shoe shiners, and others the Castro administration considered to be productive and underappreciated. A Cuban band played a jazz version of the "Internationale," the communist anthem. A sign in the crowd made a mnemonic from the name Kennedy: KU KLUX KLAN, ENGREÍDO, NEGATIVO, NOCIVO, ENRIQUECIDO, DIABÓLICO, Y . . . ETC., ETC. (Ku Klux Klan, Conceited, Negative, Noxious, Rich, Diabolical, And . . . etc., etc.)[77]

"We must talk of a new constitution," said Fidel. "Yes, a new constitution, but not a bourgeois constitution, not a constitution corresponding to the rule of an exploiting class over other classes. What we need is a constitution corresponding to a new social system, one without the exploitation of man by man. That new social system is called socialism, and this constitution will therefore be a socialist constitution."

There was applause.

"If Mr. Kennedy does not like socialism, well, we do not like imperialism! We do not like capitalism!"

There were shouts of agreement.

"We have as much right to protest the existence of an imperialist and capitalist system ninety miles from our shore as he feels he has the right to protest over the existence of a socialist system ninety miles from his shore."[78]

Fidel had abrogated the 1940 constitution. (Though he promised a new one, none was forthcoming. The constitution commission would sit for three years, from 1965 to 1968, with no result.)[79] Cuba was now officially a socialist state. That Cuba would seek an alliance with the Soviet Union was now inevitable. Thanks to the invasion, the United States had made it politically impossible for Fidel to consider rapprochement, even if he wanted to. Since his earliest days of student politics, the only consistent element in his message had been die-hard nationalism. The defense of Cuban sovereignty was the one thing on which he could never compromise.

The invasion had also made it politically impossible for the Soviet Union not to come to the defense of Cuba. Its credibility with the rest of its third-world allies depended on its resolve in the face of what they all saw as American imperialism. Khrushchev realized this and, as a direct consequence of the Bay of Pigs, began plans to arm Cuba. "Although the counterrevolutionaries were defeated in the landing, you would have had to be completely unrealistic to think that everything had ended with that," he remembered.[80]

Not only had the Bay of Pigs failed to achieve its objectives, it had achieved precisely the opposite of its objectives. It increased the power of Fidel Castro's government and armed forces, struck a fatal body blow to the Cuban opposition at home and in exile, and, for the first time in history, made aggressive Soviet military involvement in Latin America a fully fledged fact. As Fidel Castro himself put it a few days after the invasion, "It was one of the most ridiculous things that has ever occurred in the history of the United States. And they have only themselves to blame."[81]

The shock waves created in the Bay of Pigs rolled out across the CIA and the State Department. "As I said to the Attorney General the other day, when you are in a fight and knocked off your feet, the most dangerous thing to do is to come out swinging wildly," wrote Jack Kennedy's adviser Walt Rostow to the president on 21 April. "Clearly we must cope with Castro in the next several years. . . . But let us do some fresh homework. . . . Vietnam is the place where—in the Attorney General's phrase—we must prove that we are not a paper tiger. . . . We have to prove that Vietnam and Southeast Asia can be held."[82]

In the weeks after the Bay of Pigs, remembered Mac Bundy, Kennedy "did go through a process of saying that there must never be another Cuba." General Max Taylor made a chart of Cold War strategy, which the president pinned up in his bedroom. In any other form of democratic government, Kennedy reiterated, this time to Mac Bundy, he would have been out of office if he had authorized the Bay of Pigs. No British prime minister, he thought, could have survived such a scandal. Bundy replied that he was not so sure about that.

"Well, at least I've got three more years," said Kennedy. "Nobody can take that away from me."[83]

12

THE DEATH OF THE GOAT

★

LATE THAT APRIL, RAFAEL TRUJILLO WAS SAILING THE WATERS OFF Barahona in his yacht, the *Angelita*. A group of aides was with him but, despite the party and the salty air, he was in a bad mood. He turned to the group with a menacing smile and said, "Which one of you will be the Judas who will betray me?"

There was a chorus, almost in unity: "What's that, Chief?"

"Yes, you heard me," Trujillo replied. "Yes, one of you will betray me."[1]

It was true, though he could not have known it. At least one of the men on the *Angelita* that day was involved in the conspiracy to bring him down. The man's name has not been recorded; nor has his reaction to Trujillo's eerie words.

The conspiracy was in two parts, an action group and a political group. The action group was overseen by a public administrator, Tony Imbert, and a private construction contractor, Salvador Estrella. There were six more in it, including Antonio de la Maza, the brother of Octavio de la Maza, whose "suicide" had been a key event in the case of the Galíndez disappearance. The political group had at its helm Trujillo's childhood friend General Juan Tomás Díaz, supported by the secretary of state for the armed forces, General José "Pupo" Román, and by a wealthy landowner, Luis Amiama Tió. Many of the conspirators were wealthy former Trujillistas. Pupo Román was married to Trujillo's niece.

In the days after the Bay of Pigs, the CIA was thrown into chaos over whether to continue with the assassination of Trujillo. Some wanted him dead; some still believed that he could be charmed out. Either way, the timing looked bad. On 19 April, the same day the Bay of Pigs failed, Hank Dearborn, the American consul in Ciudad Trujillo, had received a new consignment of submachine guns from the CIA. He was supposed to wait for authorization before passing them on to his opposition contacts. On

25 April, he was told by the CIA to keep hold of the weapons, on the grounds that "filling a vacuum created by assassination [is] now [a] bigger question than ever [in] view [of] unsettled conditions in [the] Caribbean area."[2] The agency had thought that, by May, the Cuban Revolution would be over. It was not. If Trujillo fell now, Washington's worst fear might be realized. Fidel Castro might invade the Dominican Republic, and there might be another Cuba.

Meanwhile, the diplomat Bob Murphy and the gossip columnist Igor Cassini were still advising Kennedy to offer "friendly guidance" to Trujillo, and bring him back into the fold. Mac Bundy had to warn Kennedy off. "At the risk of misunderstanding, I think I ought to add that if the public were to know that Igor Cassini is providing public relations help to Trujillo, your own personal position as a liberal leader might be compromised," Bundy wrote on 2 May. "I cannot help thinking that your own position should be fully disengaged from any venture of this sort."[3] Nonetheless, the advice of the State Department was sought on whether the Dominican dictator could still be offered asylum in the United States. "I believe it was a mistake ever to agree to this," wrote an officer of the State Department, "and that it would be a serious error ever to permit it."[4] The national security report handed to Kennedy on 8 May concluded firmly that any gentle alternative to the short, sharp shock of overthrow was now too much of a risk. The best course of action, it advised, was "outside coordination of an inspired internal uprising combined with invasion by outside Dominican led forces."[5]

It was, as one top-secret State Department report pointed out, "highly desirable" for the United States to be identified with democratic opposition to Trujillo. To be seen to help overthrow him, though, would go too far. Worse yet, Trujillo might survive the attempt. Then the United States would be seen to fail again, "and following on the recent Cuban experience U.S. prestige would plummet." The conspirators were professing pro-American sentiments, but it was not clear these could be trusted: "we might find ourselves in the position of having created a Dominican Castro." Furthermore, it added, "it may be mentioned that Castro-Communist control of the Dominican Republic would almost certainly lead to a similar takeover in Haiti."[6]

From Haiti, François Duvalier's antics continued to needle the State Department. On 22 May, Papa Doc had himself inaugurated again, following the phony election of a month before. To Washington's irritation, he appropriated USAID trucks to bring peasants to Port-au-Prince for the celebration.[7]

The American ambassador, Robert Newbegin, was recalled to Washington for consultation. The economic and military aid that the United States was pouring into Duvalier's accounts was clearly doing nothing to improve Haiti, but Haitian officials were threatening to withdraw their support from the United States in the OAS if that aid were stopped. So soon after the Bay of Pigs, losing another ally in the OAS was not something the United States needed. Newbegin returned to Haiti on 29 May, and told the marine mission commander, Robert Heinl, to fake a back injury so he, too, could go to Washington for discussions with the State Department and Department of Defense. Heinl was flown to Guantánamo Bay for "medical treatment," and spirited away to Washington.

In Washington, the discussions focused on the likelihood of Haiti becoming communist. Duvalier had several figures in his government whom the American administration considered suspiciously left-wing, including Hervé Boyer, Clovis Désinor, and the brothers Paul and Jules Blanchet. A State Department official complained that Duvalier tolerated communists, for he "thinks they're tame."[8] In fact, they were. Though Boyer and Jules Blanchet, at least, had flirted with leftist ideas in their younger days, Duvalier had set up all his ministers with comfortable, well-paid positions, complete with luxury mansions, cars, and almost limitless opportunities for graft. They were bought off—and bought off in such a way that their privileges depended on Duvalier's patronage. There were brave Haitian politicians who could not be bought off, who maintained genuine interests in addressing the inequalities and problems of their nation; but they either had already left the country, or were forced underground. The reason Duvalier took a particular interest in maintaining ministers with known leftist backgrounds may have been that he was playing a version of Rafael Trujillo's old game. If the alternative to him appeared to be communism, he could be confident of American support.

At times like this, though, Papa Doc felt the need to remind the Americans of just how anticommunist he was. Jacques Stephen Alexis, an acclaimed novelist and Haiti's best-known communist in exile, was one of those politicians who could not be bought off. In April, he had traveled from Moscow to Cuba. He sailed forth from Baracoa with four other pro-Soviet communists, and landed in the northeast of Haiti. They attempted to interest local peasants in joining their cause, without success. Instead, they were soon captured by the Tontons Macoutes, who found $20,000 in cash and some Marxist literature on them. The five invaders were tied together with a rope and dragged out to a field at the Môle St.-Nicolas, where the Macoutes rounded up some local street children to throw stones at them. Alexis's eye was ripped clean out of its socket by one well-aimed rock. Reports said that he was still alive when he was taken to Fort Dimanche afterward—but after he disappeared into that prison, he was never seen again.[9]

Under the circumstances, Washington thought it best to keep Duvalier in power. New plans were drawn up for dealing with the aftermath of any possible coup in Haiti, but full American economic and military support remained in place.[10]

★

Hank Dearborn, the American consul in the Dominican Republic, had two typewriters. One he used to type his usual correspondence. The other was a secret machine, for CIA communications only. If a CIA message fell into the wrong hands, even an analysis of the precise quirks of his official typewriter could not link it to the consulate. Toward the end of May, he used the CIA typewriter to tap out the full details of the conspiracy to kill Trujillo, and sent it back via the agency's network, to be shown to the State Department.[11]

On 25 May, Kennedy told Dearborn that he could tell his conspirators that they would have American military support—unless power was seized by "unfriendly elements." If the unfriendly elements got in, he was to support pro-American groups and call on the United States and the OAS for help. Four days later, Kennedy sent a conspicuously prudent message, stating clearly that though the United States wanted to be seen to be helping to remove Trujillo, "we must not run the risk of U.S. association with political assassination."[12]

The message has the ring of one written for posterity. It is certainly convenient that this last-minute hard evidence of Kennedy's plausible deniability was one of the few communications to survive the purge of correspondence that Dearborn was ordered to complete before he left Ciudad Trujillo, and that a copy of it seems to survive in every relevant State Department file. "I must soon again reduce our files here," Dearborn had cabled cheerfully to the State Department earlier that month. "It is amazing how quickly items collect with which I literally would not wish to be caught dead."[13]

Dearborn did not conceal his own role from history. "I knew they were planning to do it, I knew how they were planning to do it, I knew, more or less, who was involved," he remembered. "Although I was always able to say that I personally did not know any of the assassins, I knew those who were pulling the strings. I knew everything except when. The only reason

I didn't know when was because they didn't know either. There had to be a certain set of circumstances when they could put their plan into action."[14]

At 7:00 PM on 30 May, a spy in Trujillo's garage reported to the conspirators that Trujillo would be visiting his twenty-year-old mistress that night. It was a regular trip he made, always along the coastal highway, always in an inconspicuous car (a light blue 1957 Chevrolet), and always unscheduled. It was the time when he was least defended. This was the set of circumstances the assassins had been awaiting.

Imbert, La Maza, Estrella, and another conspirator, García Guerrero, armed themselves with revolvers and pistols. La Maza brought a sawed-off shotgun and two semiautomatic rifles. Some of these weapons are said to have been those supplied to their group by the CIA.[15] They got into a car, and drove to the Agua Luz Theatre, on the road to San Cristóbal. There, from eight o'clock, they lay in wait for Trujillo's Chevrolet.

Trujillo was enjoying his customary stroll along George Washington Avenue, which ran along the edge of the capital above the sandy, tree-lined coves of the beach and the glittering expanse of the Caribbean Sea. He was joined that night by the loyal Arturo Espaillat. During the walk, by chance, they saw Pupo Román. Trujillo beckoned him over. On a whim, he asked Román to take him on an impromptu inspection of San Isidro air base, ten miles away. The two men got into a limousine, and drove off. "I have often wondered how Roman felt when he was taking that last ride with the man he had betrayed," Espaillat wrote afterward.[16]

Espaillat went for a drive with his wife, and then to El Pony restaurant. Soon afterward, Trujillo returned, and excused Román. The dictator called for his Chevrolet. Only his chauffeur accompanied him. Around ten o'clock, the Chevrolet cruised past the Agua Luz Theatre. Imbert's car revved up, and swung behind it.

Trujillo's car drove out of the city along rocky coral cliffs, past the Cattle Fair and El Pony. When it reached a quiet stretch of road, Imbert's car accelerated, and overtook Trujillo's. The dictator's driver heard automatic fire. He turned. There were shards of glass on the seats behind. The Benefactor had been hit.

"Please stop. I'm wounded," cried Trujillo. "Take the machine guns. We have to fight."

The car was equipped with three machine guns, but Trujillo looked too badly wounded to use one. "It's better to turn back," the driver said. "There are too many of them."

"No," howled Trujillo, "make a stop now. We have to fight."

The driver braked. Ahead of him, Imbert's car screeched around 180 degrees. Trujillo lurched out of the car, blood spreading from a wound in his back, his revolver cocked. He stumbled into the beam of the headlights, firing wildly into the dark. La Maza and Imbert, covered by their coconspirators, sneaked around the back of the dictator's car.

In El Pony, Espaillat was ordering colas when he heard gunshots. He leaped into his car and drove the route he knew Trujillo would have taken. Less than a minute later, according to his memoirs, he arrived on the scene. Trujillo's Chevrolet was stopped in the middle of the four-lane highway. Gunfire was blasting from out of the darkness. In the center was Trujillo, wounded, staggering, but still standing in the light of the car's headlamps. He raised his revolver, and fired for the last time. A volley of bullets exploded back at him, and Trujillo gave a little, high-pitched yelp. He crashed to the ground.[17] After thirty-one years, the Era of Trujillo had finally come to an end.

As the men on the highway bundled the Benefactor's small body into the trunk of La Maza's car, Espaillat turned around and drove back to Pupo Román's house. Not suspecting that Román was part of the conspiracy, he blurted out the full story. Román, he noted, "quivered visibly."

"Have you told anybody else?" the general asked. "Are you sure he's dead?"

"Of course, I'm sure he's dead," replied Espaillat. "You're in charge now. Come on, let's get busy."

Román hesitated. "He should have shot me," Espaillat admitted later.[18] Instead, Román followed him into the night.

Hank Dearborn had been at a charity event hosted by the Chinese ambassador at a country club. About 11:00 PM, he was driving back along the ocean highway into Ciudad Trujillo with a CIA man when they ran into a roadblock. Every car was being stopped and searched. People were standing in the road, while the police sifted through car trunks and shook out rugs.

"Bob, this is it," Dearborn said to his companion. "I am sure this is it."

The Americans were sent along another road, and drove straight to the embassy, in which Dearborn had been living for the previous year. As they walked in, a telephone was ringing. Dearborn picked it up.

"It is over," said Luis Amiama Tió's voice, "he is dead."[19]

Dearborn went to cable the message to Washington. Meanwhile, the assassination group had planned to take Trujillo's body to Pupo Román, to prove he had been killed. This would have triggered the political group's role in the coup. When they telephoned his house, though, his wife told them that Espaillat had got there first. The murderers left the car with

Trujillo's body in the trunk at the home of Juan Tomás Díaz, just two blocks from the American consulate. It was found at five o'clock that morning.

A blanket of censorship descended. From Washington, though, Jack Kennedy's press secretary, Pierre Salinger, immediately announced the news of Trujillo's death—before the Dominican Republic had done so. The breach of diplomatic tact was bad. The implication that the United States may have known in advance because it was involved was far worse. From Cuba, Che Guevara promptly released a statement alleging exactly that. Later, when the Dominican government released its own statement, it too would say that the initial investigation suggested that "the assassination was backed by a political conspiracy involving a foreign government." Jack Kennedy was away in Paris—and he was livid.[20]

★

President Kennedy's trip to Paris was a stop on the way to a crucial summit in Vienna. He was to meet face-to-face with Nikita Khrushchev. Much seemed to hang on the meeting, and the Americans were nervous. "In my judgment, Khrushchev thought he was dealing with rather a weak figure," said Bobby Kennedy, "because if he [Jack Kennedy] wasn't weak he wouldn't have gone through the Bay of Pigs. He [Khrushchev] didn't permit the Bay of Pigs at the time of [the 1956 uprising in] Hungary, and he felt that if you got into a problem like Cuba that you would have just wiped them all out and ended it."[21] This was a widely held opinion in Washington, but it was wrong. Soviet intelligence sources assessed Kennedy as a lightweight, but Khrushchev himself had been optimistic about the possibility of a fresh start after the disaster of Eisenhower's U-2 incident.

During and after the Bay of Pigs operation, Kennedy had been made to feel like he was not up to the job. When he arrived in a gray and damp Vienna for perhaps the most crucial meeting of his career so far, he was physically and emotionally drained. On a state visit to Canada in May, he had felt a sudden sharp pain in his back when lifting a shovel during a tree-planting ceremony.[22] Kennedy's back had been a source of trouble for many years, and though he had managed to hide it from the Canadians, he had been in agony ever since. Kennedy's lifelong ill health was becoming more difficult to conceal. A retinue of doctors was kept on hand to tend to him.

The quantities in which the president took various drugs has not been made fully public, but several of those he took regularly are known to have serious side effects on mental health. The steroid cortisol can cause depression and psychosis. In large quantities, the antidiarrhea medication paregoric causes sedation; the effects of sedation are worsened if paregoric is taken with phenobarbital and other analgesics and sedatives, as Kennedy was taking it. The sleeping pill Tuinal has subsequently been withdrawn from the market owing to its use as a recreational drug, with physical and psychological side effects. It has been argued that all the decisions Kennedy would make as president were rationally explicable, and could not be ascribed to his drug use.[23] That may be; but it is physiologically impossible that the drugs did not affect his thought processes. The combination of long-standing physical debilities with heavy steroid use would put any patient at very high risk of developing clinical depression, and a high risk of psychotic episodes. The drugs would also have had a sedative effect. Dependency on opiates, barbiturates, and analgesics following long-term use is common. A patient in Kennedy's condition and undergoing his treatment regimen would require constant medical attention to keep him functioning, both physically and psychologically.[24]

Kennedy's personal life, too, had suffered since the election. With the privileges of presidential security and a discreet press protecting his reputation, Jack's infidelity had reached a feverish pitch. Kennedy warned his staff that he would develop migraines were he not supplied with a "piece of ass every day." Aides hustled convenient women into his private quarters at the White House.[25] Though Jackie Kennedy did her best to ignore her husband's behavior, she was certainly aware of it. The first lady found herself responsible for preserving the family's wholesome image. But the stress, the misery, and the loneliness were hard to bear, and she began to exhibit the symptoms of depression. Jack's response that May had been to call in Max Jacobson, the quack who had injected him with a metham phetamine cocktail during the election campaign. By the time the two of them were to fly to Paris and Vienna, both Kennedys felt they required the services of "Dr. Feel Good": Jack for his physical pain, and Jackie for her heartbreak. Jacobson was summoned to the White House, and, for the first time during his presidency, Kennedy took a shot of joy juice.

For the sake of discretion, Jacobson was flown to Europe on a commercial flight. Nonetheless, Kennedy took another shot just before he boarded Air Force One. In Paris, both Kennedys received uppers and downers from Jacobson to cope with their schedules. Now, in Vienna, twenty minutes before his first meeting with Khrushchev, the president took another of the doctor's methamphetamine injections. Jacobson was directed to wait in an anteroom, in case Jack could not get through the meeting without another.[26]

Khrushchev appears to have found the experience of meeting Kennedy in the flesh constructive, and even pleasant. "I was generally pleased with our meeting in Vienna," he wrote. "Even though we came to no concrete agreement, I could tell that he [Kennedy] was interested in finding a peaceful solution to world problems and in avoiding conflict with us."

The Soviet leader treated Kennedy to some of his trademark humor. "I joked with him that we had cast the deciding ballot in his election to the Presidency over that son-of-a-bitch Richard Nixon," he remembered. "When he asked me what I meant, I explained that by waiting to release the U-2 pilot Gary Powers until after the American election, we kept Nixon from being able to claim that he could deal with the Russians; our ploy made a difference of at least half a million votes, which gave Kennedy the edge he needed."[27] The subject of Fidel Castro came up, and Khrushchev emphasized that, by Moscow's definition, Fidel was still not a communist.[28] But he warned that American policy might well make him one. According to the American record of the meeting, "Khrushchev said that he himself had not been born a Communist and that it was capitalists who had made him a Communist."[29]

Jack Kennedy's experience of the summit was so radically different from this convivial version that it is hard to believe that the two men were in the same meetings. From the American camp came stories of an implacable Khrushchev haranguing and bullying his counterpart, accusing him of imperialism, shouting, threatening war over Berlin, and all but breathing fire. If it is difficult to reconcile Khrushchev's and Kennedy's memories into a single coherent image, it must be borne in mind that one of the two men had been medicated with perception-altering drugs during the summit, and the other, as far as is known, had not.

It is also possible that the different versions reflect a fundamental lack of understanding between the two men. Kennedy was the living embodiment of all the privilege and sophistication Khrushchev had found so painfully intimidating when he had visited the United States. Then, he had hidden his insecurity by becoming loud and domineering. He did so again now; and, by doing so, made the already nervous Kennedy feel yet weaker and more contemptible. Jack remarked afterward to Bobby that talking to Khrushchev was "like dealing with Dad." Jack thought that Khrushchev was "completely unreasonable, and that he was tough, and he [Kennedy] had to be as tough," said Bobby. "And I think it was a shock to him that somebody would be as hard and definitive, definite, as this." Though the administration publicly promoted an image of Kennedy having bested Khrushchev, in private many admitted that he had put in a "weak performance," as the assistant secretary of state for inter-American affairs, Edwin Martin, put it.[30]

At the end of the summit, Washington's most senior journalist, James "Scotty" Reston of the *New York Times*, asked for and was granted a secret meeting with Kennedy. Unusually, Kennedy was wearing a hat when he arrived in the designated room at the American embassy. Reston remembered the president slumping onto a sofa, pushing the hat forward over his eyes, and sighing.

"Pretty rough?" asked Reston.

"Roughest thing in my life," replied Kennedy. He continued: "he just beat hell out of me. So I've got a terrible problem. If he thinks I'm inexperienced and have no guts, until we remove those ideas we won't get anywhere with him. So we have to act." On the spot, he told Reston he would increase military spending and send another division to Germany, both of which he did. Finally, the president said that the United States needed to show the world that its power was still credible, and concluded, "Vietnam looks like the place."[31]

★

Back in Ciudad Trujillo, Fidel Castro had not invaded, and no Dominican Castro had emerged. According to an OAS observer, Johnny Abbes was "running the show now."[32] The president, officially, was Joaquín Balaguer, though he was still in the pocket of the Trujillo family. On the day Trujillo was killed, Ramfis Trujillo had been in Paris—though for no reason connected to Jack Kennedy's visit. Believing that he would have to catch a connecting flight back to the Dominican Republic via Miami or New York, the United States government flagged Ramfis's name for an immediate travel ban. Ramfis simply chartered an Air France plane and flew back directly. He was greeted by his mother, Doña María, in hysterics. When she had seen her husband's body, she had thrown herself at it, wailing and sobbing.

Now, it was Ramfis's turn. He was shown into the room. Keeping his distance from the body, he looked at it for a while without comment or expression. Eventually, he left, his features set in cold determination.[33]

In the days that followed, Ramfis and Johnny Abbes set themselves two main tasks. The first was to seize control. The second was to find the men who had killed Rafael Trujillo and punish them. All but two would be caught, and subjected to the darkest fancies of their captors' imagination. Both Ramfis and Abbes had very dark imaginations. The unfortunate Pupo Román was taken to Kilometer 9, a torture house near San Isidro. His eyelids were sewn open, electrified rods were pushed into his genitals, and he was doused in acid. He had to endure days of agony before they finally allowed him to be killed.[34]

Jack Kennedy, Dean Rusk, and Mac Bundy, the three most senior officers of the American administration in a foreign policy capacity, were all in Europe. In their absence, Chet Bowles was acting secretary of state. Bowles met with representatives of the CIA, as well as defense secretary Robert McNamara, Dick Goodwin, Adlai Stevenson, and the inevitable Bobby Kennedy, and tried to decide what to do.

"Bobby put on very heavy pressure for the U.S. to move in," remembered Bowles. "I thought this was a very dangerous thing to do. We just had the fiasco of the Bay of Pigs, I didn't want to have another one."[35] The CIA insisted that Dominicans would rally to an American invasion. Bowles pointed out that, whether they did or not, such a thing would be illegal. This did not deter Bobby, who suggested that they blow up the American consulate in Ciudad Trujillo, and blame it on the Dominicans—then send in the marines.[36] Bowles instead suggested putting the fleet about thirty miles offshore. From that position, they could wait and see what happened.

According to the journalist David Halberstam, Bobby then "unleashed a cascade of insults about Bowles's being a gutless bastard, which made some of the others in the room wince." That afternoon, he leaked the story of Bowles's supposed gutlessness to the press. Exasperated, Bowles telephoned Jack Kennedy in Paris.

"Am I acting secretary or is your brother?" asked Bowles.

"You are," said Jack.

"Well," said Bowles, "will you call your brother and let him know that?"[37]

Jack called Bobby off. A United States Navy task force of nearly forty ships was sent to patrol the Dominican coast, but not to invade. A contingency plan for an invasion by the marines was drawn up, but never used. "I have often wondered what ex-Marine Trujillo would have thought of that!" exclaimed Arturo Espaillat.[38]

The day of the Benefactor's funeral came. Schools handed out bands of black cloth for students to tie around their arms. "I walked out of the lesson, ripped it off, and tore it into little pieces," remembered one future Dominican politician, who was an eleven-year-old pupil in a school at La

Romana at the time. "I refused to go back to school until the mourning period had ended, because I could not stand to wear that thing."[39] The American consul, too, excused himself. "I didn't dare go to the funeral because I was afraid I would have to call in the Navy which was just over the horizon—the biggest naval force since World War II was sitting just over the horizon—and didn't want to go away from my communications," remembered Dearborn. Speculation soon mounted among the Dominicans about what his absence meant. With Ramfis and Abbes still on a murderous rampage, speculation among the Dominicans was something with which the State Department was not comfortable. The decision was made abruptly to pull Dearborn out. He and his colleagues had to pack at high speed. "Evelyn Cotterman who was the Admin. Officer's wife, was helping us around the bedrooms," he remembered. "I had my shirt, tie, shoes and socks on but couldn't find my pants. I said, 'Evelyn where are my pants?' She said, 'Oh, my god, I packed them.' They had to go back down to the car outside and unpack my pants so that I could leave the country with dignity."[40]

Jack Kennedy, too, was returning to Washington, still in a fragile state. That week, he was photographed on crutches for the first time during his presidency. He was seen to be loaded onto Air Force One by a crane, and unloaded by a forklift truck.[41] Nonetheless, in the crucial meeting on the Dominican Republic on 7 June, he was firm. "There are three possibilities, in descending order of preference," he said: "a decent democratic regime, a continuation of the Trujillo regime or a Castro regime. We ought to aim at the first, but we really can't renounce the second until we are sure that we can avoid the third."[42] Through Balaguer, Ramfis had expressed a willingness to respect civilian authority. But, Dearborn emphasized, all Ramfis's promises of amnesties and free elections, and even his pledge to fire Johnny Abbes, were classic Trujillo moves, and would have no bearing on the structure of his regime. Bobby Kennedy disagreed. Having vowed to be a democrat, he said, Ramfis should be given a chance.[43]

Bob Stevenson, now deputy director for Mexico and the Caribbean at the State Department, remembered clearly that Bob Murphy and Igor Cassini were still in the Dominican Republic, negotiating between the Kennedys and the Trujillos. "They were going down, apparently, as special emissaries from old Joe Kennedy, as best we could figure out," he said. Stevenson raised his concerns with the White House. They may have found their way back to Bob Murphy, for he soon turned up in Stevenson's office.

"I don't like what you're doing in the Dominican Republic," Murphy said to Stevenson. "You fellows better change your mind. You seem to be taking a line that's very hostile to Ramfis Trujillo. You're pushing that line. I don't like it, and you'd better cut it out."

"He got very threatening," Stevenson remembered. "I knew Bob Murphy as a very powerful guy, so I was pretty darn nervous."

Murphy attempted to convince Stevenson that American diplomats were spreading lies about Ramfis. One had suggested that, after a party, Ramfis had taken some of his friends into a cold storage room and shown them the bodies of five of his enemies, suspended from the ceiling on meat hooks.

"Mr. Ambassador, I did see that story in an intelligence report, and it seemed to be very well documented," Stevenson replied, carefully. "Would you mind telling me how you're so sure it isn't true?"

"Why, I asked Ramfis and he told me it was completely false," said Murphy.

Stevenson was right. The story was documented.[44] Asked whether he thought the president's softness on the Trujillos had something to do with Joe Kennedy's agenda, Stevenson replied, "I think that must have been the case, and it didn't, of course, last very long, but it was a little sticky for two or three months."[45]

In the Dominican Republic, Ramfis's vengeance showed no sign of abating. He even arrested Arturo Espaillat, who had been a loyal supporter. "I had always considered words like 'human rights' to be something invented by liberals to hinder my operations," Espaillat admitted. "However, I had found that being in solitary confinement was not conducive to continuing one's enthusiasm for dictatorship."

In Paris, Ramfis had been reading about sleep deprivation tortures. Espaillat was kept in a cell without a bed. There was an office chair, and bright lights were permanently on. On the first night, despite the glaring lights, he dozed for a few minutes. This displeased his captors, and they replaced the chair with a straight-backed, less comfortable model. "A day later and my guards could keep me awake only by beating me with sticks," he remembered. "Two days of near-delirium passed." He was permitted to doze for fifteen minutes, up to four times a day. "The walls began to shimmy and I would fall face forward out of my chair when the floor suddenly seemed to dissolve. Strange monsters began to slither through the room," he said. "I could no longer think, only feel in a vague sort of way. The monsters grew larger and my whole cell faded into a shimmering fog. And then I blacked out completely."[46] When he woke up, he was released without charge and without explanation. He recovered enough of his senses to leave the country immediately.

Ramfis Trujillo may have been an accomplished torturer, but he was no politician. Behind him loomed the horrible eminence of his wider family. All ten brothers and sisters of Rafael Trujillo lived on ill-gotten gains: some channeled from their late brother's empire, some of their own making. Most of them sustained an income from dubious property deals and embezzlement. At least two brothers and one sister also grew rich from the Caribbean's prostitution industry. Amable Trujillo was one of the region's foremost human traffickers. Despite his wealth, his hobby was stealing cars. Héctor was the weakest-minded of the brothers, and had served as Rafael Trujillo's proxy president in the past. Though he was arguably the least criminal, he was also the most easily manipulated. Now, he was being manipulated again, by the man who had assumed the position of wickedest brother after Rafael's death: Arismendi Trujillo, known as Petán. During his brother's rule, Petán had carved out a feudal kingdom for himself amid the mountains near Bonao, complete with the exercise of *droit de seigneur*, and personally administered pistol whippings of his enemies.[47] Now, he began to build up his private army, known as the Cocuyos de la Cordillera (Fireflies of the Mountain Range), from among the peasants he ruled. This provoked anguish among the other Caribbean leaders. Rómulo Betancourt of Venezuela visited the Dominican Republic in June, and reported that the successor regime was even worse than Trujillo himself. He joined the many Caribbean voices telling the American government that it was more urgent to get rid of the Trujillos than to get rid of Fidel Castro—"hardly a well-considered position," sniffed Edwin Martin, head of inter-American affairs.[48]

The United States sent a new consul to the Dominican Republic: John Calvin Hill, the State Department's liaison officer with the CIA on Latin American affairs. The State Department considered that he had done "superb work in Guatemala during the fall of Arbenz." Hill was told to promise military support if there was any invasion from Cuba. Furthermore, he was to encourage Balaguer to bar exiles returning from Cuba, deport "Communists and pro-Castro elements," and shut down the Popular Dominican Movement (MPD), the communist party.[49] In reality, as John Bartlow Martin, an American journalist, observed at the time, the "MPD has virtually no popular following and is a puppet on Ramfis' string." It had been established by Rafael Trujillo as a communist front. Still, Ramfis protested that the MPD was a strong opposition party, and was full of genuine reds. Balaguer backed him up, telling the American consulate that the MPD was now run by "communist agents acting on orders from Cuba."[50]

Further evidence was added. Members of the MPD obligingly made leftist speeches, which Balaguer ensured the American consulate heard about. The Dominican flag outside the Palace of Justice was replaced with the red and black flag of the MPD. On 7 July, the offices of Radio Caribe were burned down. This, too, was blamed on the MPD. Ramfis told John Martin that communists were now forming activist groups, and that one had already attacked an American company. "The truth is that this attack was made by a gang of thugs sent out by the Government itself," Martin noted.[51] Petán and Héctor Trujillo earnestly told Hill that the communists were on the verge of rioting. This, Hill saw through: "It may well be that this element [Pétan and Héctor] has considered instigating pro-Communist riots as they have reportedly also several times considered staging mob attack on this office to give pretext [for] imposing martial law," he wrote from the American consulate.[52]

The Trujillo family made what was, in its own terms, an effort to impress the Americans with its commitment to decent democratic government. Petán even disbanded his private army. "General Arismendi Trujillo in full uniform and pistol on hip just walked into my office, delivered letter to me saying 'cocuyos de la cordillera' had been returned to their agricultural pursuits, and jovially asking that his 'good friend' whom he admired very much—President Kennedy—be informed of this," Hill reported, in a state of some shock.[53]

The day after Petán's visit, Hill went to Boca Chica, to see Ramfis in his villa. Ramfis was tickled by the thought of his gun-toting uncle barging into the American consulate, but was otherwise despondent. Hill thought him shy, awkward, and rambling. He accused sundry Dominican politicians of being communists and moaned a lot about his own situation: "when anything good is done, Balaguer gets credit; when something tough is done, I get blame." Hill believed that Ramfis was working on the "transition towards democracy," though observed that he "obviously yearns to be relieved of cares which keep him from less serious pursuits." In conclusion, he told the State Department: "Although he has responsibilities he is scarcely prepared to bear—and doubtless trying to put best foot forward to US—would be difficult to suggest concretely how he should do better in situation in which he finds himself."[54] He could have started by not torturing or killing any more people; but that he would not do.

★

In Haiti, François Duvalier had been thrown into a frenzy by Trujillo's assassination. "While Trujillo lived, Duvalier was comfortable," noted John Bartlow Martin. "After Trujillo fell, Duvalier became uneasy." Though Papa Doc was not personally sorry to see Trujillo dead, the image of a dictator being gunned down by a cabal of his closest supporters haunted him. He became obsessed with gathering all possible information on Trujillo's last days, sending spies to the Dominican Republic and scrutinizing press accounts. In secret, he issued an order to the Tontons Macoutes. If he were assassinated, or died in suspicious circumstances, they should set fire to Port-au-Prince, and kill all the white people they could find.[55]

Duvalier knew that he needed to show improvement. Soon, he settled on a project. He announced his intention to build a great new city: Duvalierville. The spot chosen was an existing town called Cabaret, north up the coast from Port-au-Prince.

Luckner Cambronne, a close friend of Duvalier since their days together in the political underground, was put in charge of collecting funds through the new National Renovation Movement. Cambronne set the level of expected contributions from Haiti's businessmen at $5,000 for those based in Port-au-Prince, and $1,000 for those in rural areas. Anyone who did not relish the idea of a house call from the Tontons Macoutes was well advised to pay up. Government workers, the military, and elected officials were also expected to pay monthly contributions. Tollbooths were set up on Haiti's potholed roads. The owners of telephones—which had not worked since the early 1950s and would not work again until 1972—were charged an extra tax of several hundred dollars. Even schoolchildren were menaced by denim-clad Macoutes until they contributed ten cents each. One foreign diplomat judged that "Duvalier is at war with the commercial and productive classes of Haiti."[56]

None of this endeared Duvalier to the State Department, but Haiti was, it still feared, a tempting prospect for Cuba to invade. Edwin Martin, the head of inter-American affairs, admitted that Fidel Castro showed no real interest, and judged that this possibly "reflected a wise decision that a communist Haiti would be more of a liability to his cause than an asset."[57] Even so, this fear was allowed to dictate American policy. Immediately after Trujillo's assassination, Dean Rusk had cabled the State Department from Paris to warn them to back off any disruption of Duvalier's regime.

"Haiti is the cesspool of the Western Hemisphere, under a dictator whom we abhor," he wrote. But the United States should try to help, for Duvalier "just might have moments when he yearns to be a decent man." So bad, in fact, was Duvalier, that Rusk admitted that if Haiti did go the way of Cuba, "we ourselves cannot in good conscience say that this could be worse for the Haitians however damaging to the US and cause of freedom in the Americas."[58]

In the Dominican Republic, too, the facts did not support the level of hysteria in Washington about a possible communist takeover. According to a secret State Department report of that summer, titled "Castro/Communist Penetration in the Dominican Republic," active Castro sympathizers were "numerically insignificant," and most people accused of such sympathies were actually mild left-wingers. "Known Dominican Communists are few," it admitted, "perhaps numbering no more than 15 or 20." From this, it leaped to suggest that a failure of the moderate opposition to the Balaguer-Ramfis regime would "open the way for more leftist leadership, including Castro/Communists, who will win popular support away from the moderates."[59]

The State Department had been hoodwinked by the central myth of the Cuban Revolution: that twelve undercover communists had stolen an entire island from a well-armed pro-American dictator. But there were not just twelve of Castro's men; the *Granma* survivors had been able to link into a large and well-connected island-wide underground. They were not undercover communists; most of them had not been communists at all. And they had not stolen the island; Batista and his army had given it to them. All the decisive facts of the Cuban Revolution were ignored, and with them all its real lessons. It was now believed—absurdly, but sincerely—that a group of communists barely numerous enough to make up a football team would be capable of taking over entire nations in the blink of an eye. Communism, it seemed, was uncontrollably powerful. It had to be found, and it had to be stopped.

★

Ironically, a real global communist strategy for the third world was at that moment being drawn up for the first time. In Moscow on 24 July, Aleksandr Shelepin, the chairman of the KGB, sent Nikita Khrushchev a proposal for a new campaign against "the Main Adversary"—the United States. The plan, according to KGB sources, aimed actively to encourage armed uprisings by national liberation movements across the third world. By doing so, the Soviets hoped to force the West to overreach itself. Thereby, it aimed to "tie them down during the settlement of the question of a German peace treaty and West Berlin."[60]

Two days later, Havana celebrated 26 July with a visit from cosmonaut Yuri Gagarin. Soviet flags fluttered in the Caribbean breeze. Model Sputniks were towed through the streets. Colossal portraits of Lenin, Fidel Castro, and Gagarin hung side by side. The Cubans, with their experience of Latin American revolutions, would be drafted to help with the new strategy against the Main Adversary. Manuel Piñeiro, known as "Barbaroja" (Redbeard), had fought with Raúl Castro in the revolution. Now, he was put in charge of exporting that revolution across Latin America. Together, Barbaroja and Che Guevara sat up late into the sticky nights of a Cuban summer, poring over maps and waving cigars. For the KGB, the first priority was Nicaragua, in which Sandinista rebels were hoping to overthrow the Somoza dictatorship. Between November 1961 and January 1964, the KGB would send a reported $25,200 to Nicaraguan guerrillas, through the residency in Mexico City.[61]

On 4 August, Jack Kennedy approved the CIA's new covert program on Cuba. Its initial budget of $5,360,000 dwarfed the sums the KGB was spending. It would provide propaganda, finance, and paramilitary support for anti-Castro groups across Latin America, as well as extra intelligence gathering and the infiltration of Cuban security services by the CIA. There was provision for "a low key sabotage and resistance program." More ambitious sabotage activities would await the authorization of a new special group on Cuba.[62] But there would be more ambitious activities. The president had had enough of looking weak.

At midnight on 12 August, without warning, the border between East and West Berlin began to close. Over the next few days, East German forces built a barbed wire barrier down the middle of the city, to be replaced later that year by a concrete wall.

"Berlin is the testicles of the West," Khrushchev said. "Every time I give them a yank they holler."[63] Khrushchev had made the decision to put up the Berlin Wall as part of his new strategy against the Main Adversary. The Cold War may have been focused on Berlin—but, if Khrushchev's strategy went according to plan, it would be fought in Latin America.

★

In August 1961, two men arrived for an inter-American conference on development and the Alliance for Progress at the Atlantic coast resort of Punta del Este in Uruguay. The serious-faced C. Douglas Dillon, Jack Kennedy's treasury secretary, stepped off a United States Air Force jet in a neat suit and tie. Che Guevara, chairman of the National Bank of Cuba, sauntered into the meeting rooms wearing olive green combat fatigues, his unruly black hair falling in his eyes, and a cigar in his hand.

On arriving in Uruguay, Che suffered a severe asthma attack. He told his friend Ricardo Rojo that, on his recent visit to Peking, the same thing had happened when he was in conference with Mao Tse-tung. As Che had gasped to fill his lungs, fearing his heart would stop, a shocked Mao had recommended acupuncture. It did not help. "Do you see?" Che said to Rojo. "This damn asthma has resisted even the Chinese, and they're just about impossible to resist."[64]

Che's presence at the conference added the sort of thrill sometimes missing from regional fiscal policy development summits. He suggested Latin America's dictators turn their military barracks into schools. He bragged that, by 1980, Cuba's per capita income would exceed that of the United States. "You do not believe us," he told his audience. "Very well. But we are here to propose competition, gentlemen. Give us a chance to live in peace, give us a chance to develop peacefully, and then let us get together 20 years from now and see who sang the song of the siren." When Dillon proposed a resolution to reduce import restrictions, Che seconded it with a courteous flourish—provoking giggles from the other delegates. Dillon was not amused, and emphasized that American aid was reserved for the "free world," not for countries "under domination of communism."[65]

At the behest of the United States, Peru proposed a resolution that indirectly condemned the Cuban Revolution. It was blocked. "Cuba is your problem," a Brazilian delegate, exasperated by the American obsession with the island, told Jack Kennedy's adviser Dick Goodwin. "We have nothing to do with Cuba. They don't even speak Portuguese."[66] The main result of the conference was the Declaration of the Peoples of America, a commitment to the ideals of Kennedy's Alliance for Progress.

During one session, Che noticed Dick Goodwin smoking a cigar. "I see Goodwin likes cigars," he remarked loudly to an Argentine delegate. "I bet he wouldn't dare smoke Cuban cigars."

Goodwin replied that he would love to smoke Cuban cigars, but Americans could no longer purchase them. In his memoirs, though, he admitted that there was a lively smuggling trade in Punta del Este: Cuban barbudos were off-loading boxes of *habanos* to hotel clerks at a great profit, and the hotel clerks were selling them for even greater profits to the American delegation.

The next day, a mahogany box of the finest Cuban cigars arrived at Goodwin's room, with a note in Spanish.

"Since I have no greeting card, I have to write," it said. "Since speaking to an enemy is difficult, I extend my hand." It was signed by Che Guevara.[67]

After the last session had ended, Goodwin attended the birthday party for a Brazilian delegate. He was informed that Che would arrive later. At two in the morning, Che turned up—"still garbed in the well-pressed olive-drab combat fatigues that he had worn throughout the conference and that had helped make him the romantic hero of the Punta del Este girls, who gathered around him admiringly every time he walked through the streets," noted Goodwin, with a hint of jealousy. The men and their interpreters retreated into a private room to talk.

Che began by thanking the American for the Bay of Pigs invasion.

"You're welcome," replied Goodwin.

Before it, Che explained, the revolution's hold on the country "had been a bit shaky." Now, it was strong.

Goodwin suggested that the Cuban government might return the favor by attacking Guantánamo Bay.

"Oh, no," Che replied, with a laugh. "We would never be so foolish as that."[68]

Soon he and Goodwin were joking back and forth. "Although he left no doubt of his personal and intense devotion to communism, his conversation was free of propaganda and bombast," wrote Goodwin to Kennedy afterward. "He spoke calmly, in a straightforward manner, and with the appearance of detachment and objectivity." Che told him that the Alliance for Progress was a fine idea, but it would fail. The changes proposed might unleash forces of revolution that the United States could not control. As for Cuba's own problems, he admitted them freely. There was sabotage against the government. There was hostility from the bourgeoisie. There was the Catholic church ("here he shook his head in dismay," Goodwin noted). The trade restrictions with the United States made it difficult to source spare parts for Cuban industry. Furthermore, despite his boasts at the conference about Cuba's future development, he acknowledged that development had been accelerated too rapidly. Though Goodwin did not record Che going into detail, this was true. The influx of Marxist economists to Cuba since 1960 had presided over a sharp decline in production. Within months of the Punta del Este conference, shortages in Cuba would oblige Fidel to introduce food rationing.

"He then said that they didn't want an understanding with the U.S., because they know [*sic*] that was impossible," Goodwin wrote. "They would like a *Modus vivendi*—at least an interim *modus vivendi*."

"Of course, it is difficult to put forth a practical formula for such a modus vivendi," Che told him. "I myself know how difficult it is, because I have spent a lot of time thinking about it. However, it is better and easier for Cuba to propose such a formula, because your country has public opinion to worry about, whereas we can accept anything without worrying about public opinion."

Che offered concessions. Though expropriated properties could not be returned to Americans, Cuba was prepared to pay for them in trade deals. Though Cuba would be a one-party system, its government was prepared to hold free elections. The Cuban government would guarantee not to attack Guantánamo Bay: "At this point he laughed as if at the absurdly self-evident nature of such a statement." He indicated that the Cubans might be willing to discuss reining in the activities of the Cuban Revolution abroad. He also suggested that Cuba was prepared to agree not to form any political alliance with the Soviet bloc, though "this would not affect their natural sympathies."[69]

Both men came away from the meeting—which lasted until six in the morning—with an unexpected sense of friendship. Years later, Che would tell an interviewer that Goodwin was the one American he had met whom he genuinely liked. Goodwin, too, remained oddly fond of the guerrilla bureaucrat. "He had humor and courage, intellectual gifts, and an unmistakable tenderness of spirit," he wrote. "I understood that he also contained ruthlessness, self-defeating stubbornness, and a hatred strong enough to cripple the possibilities of practical action. It is the paradox of the revolutionary that such divergent feelings must coexist in the same man."[70]

Those four hours were the only time that a member of the Kennedy administration and a member of the Castro administration ever attempted to negotiate face-to-face.[71] Cuba made overtures, but they were rebuffed. Goodwin's warm record of the meeting serves as a tantalizing hint of just how much better things might have gone between the two countries had Jack Kennedy, like his hero Winston Churchill, preferred jaw-jaw to war-war.

13

THROWING A HEDGEHOG DOWN UNCLE SAM'S PANTS

★

In October and November 1961, work began in Washington on the Cuba Project, also known as Operation Mongoose. Its aim was "to bring about the revolt of the Cuban people." The CIA and the State Department were no longer in any doubt that the majority of the Cuban people accepted Fidel Castro's government, and, as one CIA memorandum admitted, "substantial numbers support it with enthusiasm."[1] That was not the point.

A policy group was set up to run Mongoose, with the anonymous name Special Group (Augmented), or SGA. It encompassed the Special Group, an Eisenhower-era committee charged with oversight of the CIA's covert action adventures, which included the director of the CIA (a role that conservative Republican John McCone had just taken over from Allen Dulles), various members of the cabinet, and the chairman of the Joint Chiefs of Staff. The most significant augmentation to this group came in the form of Bobby Kennedy. Mongoose would be Bobby's pet, and his obsession.

Major General Edward Lansdale was recalled by Jack and Bobby Kennedy from Vietnam to join the Cuba Project. Both Kennedys, Lansdale remembered, had developed a vendetta against Fidel Castro. "But Bobby felt even more strongly about it than Jack," he said. "He was protective of his brother, and he felt that his brother had been insulted at the Bay of Pigs. He felt the insult needed to be redressed rather quickly." Rafael Quintero, a Cuban exile member of Brigade 2506, became a friend of Bobby's after the Bay of Pigs and joined the Cuba Project. "He mentioned this to me often and was very clear about it: he was not going to try to eliminate Castro because he was an ideological guy who wanted to do right in Cuba," Quintero said. "He was going to do it because the Kennedy name had been humiliated."[2]

Almost every day, Bobby liaised with the CIA's covert activity staff. "Bobby is a wild man on this," remarked Dick Bissell. Sam Halpern, a CIA agent assigned to Operation Mongoose, agreed. "Maybe their father convinced them to, you know—don't get mad, get even. I mean . . . to put Bobby in charge of the operation and this—well, this boy, really, this hot-tempered boy—to try to run it and do the personal bidding of his brother. Unbelievable. A lot of people got bloody noses at the Bay of Pigs, but not very many went off the deep end like the Kennedys did."[3]

In 1967, many of the Cuba Project's records were deliberately destroyed. Among the early plans of which records have remained were Operation True Blue, to set up transmitters in Florida to denounce Fidel's regime with slogans like "Rise up against the pig Castro." There was Operation Free Ride, in which one-way air tickets to Mexico City or Caracas (not, it was emphasized, to the United States) were to be dropped over Cuba. In Operation Full-Up, a biological contaminant would be squirted into Soviet jet fuel supplied to Cuba. Operation Good Times called for a photograph of an obese Fidel to be faked, complete with "two beauties" and a table heaped with fine food. ("This should put even a Commie Dictator in the proper perspective with the underprivileged masses," remarked the Department of Defense, with satisfaction.) Bobby Kennedy's favorite idea was chalked up as Operation Bingo, in which a fake attack on Guantánamo Bay would be staged to give the president an excuse to launch a full-scale invasion.[4] Another plan called for an airdrop all across Cuba of lavatory paper printed with the faces of Fidel Castro and Nikita Khrushchev. Yet another suggested orchestrating a full-scale fake Second Coming, during which the "messiah" would publicly declare that Fidel was the Antichrist.

On the University of Miami's campus, a new headquarters for the project was set up, with the code name JM/WAVE. Its annual budget of $50 million, along with its staff of three hundred Americans and thousands of Cubans, would make it the biggest CIA station in the world. "I remember that period so vividly," said Ray Cline, the CIA's chief analyst. "We were so wrapped up in what the president wanted. Bobby was always extremely emotional, and he always acted as though he occupied the Oval Office, and he really did in a way. He was perpetually on the CIA's case about the Cubans."[5]

The CIA was prepared to go to extraordinary lengths to discredit Fidel Castro—including staging acts of terrorism in American cities, and even starting a war with another Caribbean nation in his name. "We could develop a Communist Cuban terror campaign in the Miami area, in other

Florida cities, and even in Washington," suggested one memo. "A 'Cuban-based, Castro-supported' filibuster could be simulated against a neighboring Caribbean nation. It is possible to arrange an incident that will demonstrate convincingly that a Cuban aircraft has attacked and shot down a chartered civilian airliner."[6]

The day-to-day activities of Operation Mongoose were more mundane acts of terrorism and sabotage. Factories and sugar mills were blown up. Shipments to and from Cuba were interfered with. At one point, the CIA persuaded a German company to produce ball bearings that were off-centered, to damage Cuban machinery. "We were doing almost everything you could dream up," admitted one agency official. Though a great deal of effort was put into these, in retrospect even the men who ran the operation would realize they had been counterproductive. "Well, just going in, blowing up a mine, or blowing up a bridge," said Bobby Kennedy, evasively, when asked to describe the projects. "You know, some of them were, ended in disaster, and people were captured, and tried, and confessed, and . . . it wasn't very helpful." Quintero, who was sent back to Cuba undercover to organize projects like this, was harsher. "Planting a stupid bomb in a car in the middle of nowhere—it wasn't going to pay off," he said. "It was just stupid because it alerted Castro's security people and did not hurt the government even a little bit."[7] Furthermore, Quintero added, the situation in Cuba had changed since the Bay of Pigs. What anti-Castro resistance there had been then had been all but stamped out. Of those few who remained, many now hated the American government even more than they hated Fidel.

Quintero found this out firsthand at the end of 1961. He made a dangerous journey into the mountains in Cuba to meet an anti-Castro guerrilla contact. He took with him a radio. It was a gift, he told the guerrillas. If they stood their positions and radioed a message, they would receive weapons drops from the Americans.

As soon as the word *Americans* escaped Quintero's lips, the atmosphere changed. The guerrilla in charge turned to the others, indicated Quintero, and snarled, "Kill this son of a bitch."

"Because now we were the enemy," said Quintero. "Before we were comrades, now we were the enemy. That fast, it happened that fast. I had to run for my life."[8]

Even those people in Cuba who devoted their lives to ousting Fidel Castro did not want American help, but this did not deter the Cuba Project. At the beginning of 1962, Sam Halpern was ordered to send a message to every CIA station in the world, stating, "By presidential directive, Cuba is the number one priority." Thereby, he commented, "Vietnam goes down the list to almost nothing. Everybody has to concentrate on things having to do with Cuba. That will give you some idea of the atmosphere in our shop after the Bay of Pigs. Cuba was the be-all and end-all. And of course, 'Cuba' was a code word for 'get rid of Castro.' "[9]

Interviewed in the mid-1960s by his friend John Bartlow Martin, Bobby Kennedy was reticent about the aspect of the project that aimed to "get rid of Castro."

"Any direct assassination attempt to, on Castro?" asked Martin.

"No," replied Bobby.

"None tried?"

"No."

"Contemplated?"

"No."[10]

This was not true. Agents of the CIA expended much time and effort coming up with imaginative ways to kill or injure Fidel Castro. In addition to inventing several cigar-based death traps, including soaking the tobacco leaves in botulinum toxin, the CIA fixated on another of Fidel's hobbies—diving. There was a poison diving suit, impregnated with fungus spores that would cause a skin disorder. There was a poison aqualung, with the mouthpiece of its breathing apparatus rerouted to release tuberculosis bacilli into his mouth. The head of the CIA's Cuban task force, Desmond FitzGerald, wondered if they could make an exploding seashell for the Cuban leader to pick up. At this, reality briefly intruded. One of the CIA agents in the room asked how they would make Fidel choose the right shell: "Put a flashing neon sign on it and have it play Beethoven's Fifth?"[11]

Outlandish though these ideas were, the plot to kill Fidel was anything but a joke. According to the Cuban Ministry of the Interior, there would be 637 attempts to assassinate Fidel Castro between 1959 and 1999. Not all of these could be traced back to Washington, but plenty could. In 1975, Fidel estimated that the CIA had tried to murder him twenty-four times.[12] ZR/RIFLE was the CIA's code name for the operation dedicated to what was termed "executive action"—the murdering of Fidel Castro, and ideally also of Raúl Castro and Che Guevara. It was run by Bill Harvey, a foul-mouthed, pistol-toting veteran agent who could drink two double martinis and one single at lunch every day, and still turn up to the office in the afternoon neither shaken nor stirred.[13] Hard living was not thought to disqualify a man from making life-or-death decisions at the top levels of the administration. In November 1961, some of Jack Kennedy's friends, staying over at the White House after a party, witnessed Max Jacobson giving the president an injection of amphetamines just to get over a hangover.[14] Dr. Feel Good's ministrations had, by then, become something of a habit.

How much Bobby Kennedy knew about the assassination plots, and how much Jack Kennedy knew, has been the subject of controversy. The president's public line was unambiguous: "We cannot, as a free nation, compete with our adversaries in tactics of terror [and] assassination."[15] Even after it began to emerge in the 1970s that the CIA had outdone more or less every adversary in tactics of terror and assassination, Kennedy loyalists maintained that it was impossible that the president or the attorney general could have known about such activities. Mac Bundy said the idea that either brother was involved in assassination plots was "totally inconsistent with what I knew of both of them." Toeing the same line, Bob McNamara said it would have been "totally inconsistent with everything I knew about the two men." Arthur Schlesinger agreed. Dick Goodwin remembered Kennedy telling him in October 1961 that assassinating Fidel Castro could not be considered. "We can't get into that kind of thing," he said. "Or we would all be targets."[16]

But get into that kind of thing they did. Even if the story told by Judith Campbell that she passed messages about "the elimination of Fidel Castro" between Sam Giancana and the president is discounted as unprovable, there was plenty of careless talk going around.[17] "We used to sit around the White House all the time thinking how nice it would be" if leaders like Castro "didn't exist," admitted Bundy.[18] McNamara once openly suggested that Fidel Castro should be killed. In November 1961, the journalist Tad Szulc interviewed Jack Kennedy in secret. "What would you think if I ordered Castro to be assassinated?" asked the president. Shocked, Szulc replied that he would oppose it, morally and on grounds that it would not solve the problem of Cuba. Kennedy quickly assured him that he agreed, and was just testing him.[19]

Plausible deniability was still in place. There were things that the president was relieved from the duty of knowing. It is theoretically possible that the Kennedys were in late 1961 unaware of the continuing plots to kill Fidel Castro, Raúl Castro, and Che Guevara. But it is not very likely. Jack Kennedy knew, because he had read and responded to Hank Dearborn's dispatches, that the CIA had been mixed up in the murder of Rafael Trujillo—even if on the record he called it off, he knew it was far too late to make any difference. His comments to Szulc reveal that he knew the same option was on the table for Fidel Castro. Furthermore, he authorized

Operation Mongoose to oust the Cuban government. The archives bring forth no evidence that Fidel was to be offered, as Trujillo once was, a comfortable retirement in the United States or Europe. No smooth-talking millionaire businessman was sent to tempt him with cattle ranches or trust funds. Jack Kennedy authorized, and Bobby Kennedy micromanaged, a secret terrorist campaign, on a massive scale and at an unprecedented cost. They were capable of being involved in that. It is, therefore, hard to see how being involved in assassination plots would have been "totally inconsistent" with their characters.

"The question which concerns me most about this new Administration is whether it lacks a genuine sense of conviction about what is right and what is wrong," Chet Bowles had written after the Bay of Pigs. "The Cuban fiasco demonstrates how far astray a man as brilliant and well intentioned as Kennedy can go who lacks a basic moral reference point."[20]

★

In the summer of 1961, a new crisis was brewing in the Dominican Republic. It would be known as the Crisis of the Wicked Uncles, after Jack Kennedy referred casually but accurately to Ramfis Trujillo's family by that epithet.

Joaquín Balaguer and Ramfis Trujillo appeared to be trying to form a coalition. Both were making noises that they thought the Americans would want to hear. Ramfis had held a press conference to declare himself pro-American, anticommunist, and in favor of elections—"democratic in fact as well as in name"—to be held the following year.[21] For all the talk of democracy, the Trujillo family was reconsolidating its power behind the scenes. Petán Trujillo—Ramfis's wickedest uncle—was muscling his way to the fore.

In September Kennedy sent John Bartlow Martin, a journalist who had written some of his campaign speeches, to the Dominican Republic as his personal emissary. Martin soon reported back that, in his opinion, the United States must support Ramfis and Balaguer through their transition policy. Of Ramfis, he said, "we pretend we don't want him, but actually we need him." Balaguer, too, was a regrettable necessity; "but in view of his record we must never really trust him. We should accept him with grave hidden reservations, and not get stuck with his 'democratization' window dressing. In fact, I'd prefer the word 'democracy' was never used again down there."[22]

Kennedy, still soft on the Trujillos, agreed with Martin's recommendations, and wanted to give the Ramfis-Balaguer coalition a chance. The State Department disagreed strongly. "We believe that the US, by unintentionally identifying itself with an unpopular cause through its transition policy, is seriously jeopardizing its long-term interests in the Dominican Republic," it concluded. "A continuation of present trends will increase the likelihood that a successor government will be Castroist."[23]

By the fall of 1961, there was widespread public unrest and rioting. Government troops attacked civilians with clubs and, on at least one occasion, opened fire with machine guns on protesting crowds as they occupied Calle Espaillat.[24] Scores were killed. At the center of all of this was Ramfis Trujillo, the playboy prince, a man equipped with none of the intellectual or moral gifts that his situation required. On one side of him, Balaguer was pushing for a broad political coalition and a public move away from Trujillism. On the other, his wicked uncles were dragging him toward the darkest reaches of dictatorship.

Ramfis's mother, Doña María, now in Paris, took the side of the uncles. "Your father always thought you were a coward," she wrote viciously to her son, after Balaguer criticized the old Trujillo regime at the United Nations and Ramfis failed to object. "You dishonor your family name."[25] Hopelessly confused, Ramfis gave another press conference and announced, "If I were a politician in this country, I would be a leftist."[26]

This was, of course, nonsense. Ramfis had been told that joining Balaguer's coalition was his only chance of maintaining power. He had been persuaded that he needed to represent the left, in order to balance out Balaguer's right-wing links. He had also been persuaded to plunge the knife into his own family. Now, he caved in to the request of a State Department officer dispatched by Kennedy to Ciudad Trujillo, and ordered his uncles to leave. Petán and Héctor were sent to Jamaica. "You are a coward, a traitor, you allow your father's brothers to be driven from the country," raged Doña María.[27]

Meanwhile, Jack Kennedy tried a last-ditch scheme to help out the Trujillo family. Despite their thorough discrediting inside the State Department, he was still listening to the questionable advice of Bob Murphy and Igor Cassini. They had suggested that the president have a rich friend organize an American syndicate to buy out all the Trujillo properties in the Dominican Republic. This, Murphy and Cassini suggested, would liquidate the family's claims and allow them to leave permanently. On 3 November, Kennedy took the plan to Teodoro Moscoso, the head of his Alliance for Progress, and asked him what he thought.

Moscoso thought it was an appalling idea. The Dominican people, he explained, considered that the Trujillo properties had been stolen from them. Selling their national patrimony to the Americans was likely to create an explosion. "I think the president did not very much take to my suggestion because I believe he felt that in the balance of convenience it was better to suffer a misunderstanding on the part of the people of Latin America or the Dominican Republic rather than continue to suffer the presence of the Trujillos in Latin America," Moscoso remembered, diplomatically. "I told the president that he had to take the broader view, that what he did in the Dominican Republic would have hemisphere-wide repercussions."[28] Reluctantly, Kennedy dropped the plan.

In Ciudad Trujillo, Ramfis slowly realized that he had been set up. By agreeing to become the Dominican Republic's pantomime leftist, he had not, as he hoped, secured a place in a future coalition. Instead, he had stepped straight into the role of sitting duck that Balaguer had neatly prepared for him, and started quacking. Soon, a new villain would be needed. Ramfis could now be portrayed not only as a Trujillista, but as a Castroite. By getting rid of him, any politician could immediately appear both as a national hero to the Dominicans, and as a mascot of decent democracy to the Americans. In a panic, Ramfis abruptly resigned on 14 November. He retreated to his villa at Boca Chica, and telephoned his wicked uncles in Jamaica, telling them to "come at once." Then he summoned some girls, and devoted himself to a three-day partying binge.

The very next day, Petán and Héctor Trujillo arrived back in the Dominican Republic. Kennedy could not ignore this. A fleet of United States Navy warships set a course for Ciudad Trujillo, packed with a landing force of eighteen hundred marines.

It was now so obvious that the party was over that even Ramfis worked it out. In his last few hours in the Dominican Republic, he visited the surviving captive assassins of his father, who had endured the last few months being routinely tortured. In his presence, he had them all tortured one last time, and killed. Their bodies were thrown to the sharks. Ramfis boarded his yacht with an alleged $90 million in cash, and the embalmed body of his father in a refrigerated unit below deck.[29] The Swiss *National-Zeitung* conducted a sober and thorough investigation into the total Trujillo haul the following year, and came up with the figure of $800 million—around half in cash, and half in stocks and bonds, mostly in Swiss bank accounts and European holding companies.[30] It was quite a price for the Dominican Republic to pay; but at last Ramfis was sailing off into a Caribbean sunset, never to be seen in his homeland again.

On 18 November, Dean Rusk announced that the United States would not "remain idle" if the wicked uncles attempted to seize power, and that he was "considering the further measures that unpredictable events might warrant."[31] By that evening, the American fleet could be seen from Ciudad Trujillo. The commander of the Santiago air base, General Pedro Rodríguez Echevarría, backed the United States, and sent his planes to drop leaflets all over the country demanding the immediate departure of Héctor and Petán Trujillo. Without the support of the armed forces, the Trujillos realized they had no hope. Finally, they too left the country. Public celebrations broke out, and the thousands of statues of Trujillo and his family that still stood across the island were hauled down or defaced.

In Ciudad Trujillo—swiftly renamed Santo Domingo—Balaguer clung to power at the head of a seven-man council of state. Riots soon resumed. By early December, they were aimed not only at Balaguer, but again at the United States. Rumors spread that visas might be given to former Trujillistas. The American consulate had to be closed as a mob swarmed it, smashing the windshields of its staff's cars.[32]

On 16 December, Kennedy sent a personal message to Balaguer, telling him to go now, or "his prestige and his position in history will be damaged or even destroyed." The United States would not recognize a new government until Balaguer was out of the picture. "We suggest that the President make it clear that the announcement of his final solution was not forced on him by others," said Kennedy, "but was arrived at [by] his own free will and after careful thought for the welfare and future of his country." Balaguer gave in, and the American consul was authorized to congratulate him on exercising his own free will in the appropriate manner. When the consul did so, Balaguer smiled, and remarked, "After all, it was President Kennedy's plan."[33]

The new council was installed, but lasted only two weeks before it collapsed and was replaced by a junta, headed by General Rodríguez Echevarría. That lasted just two days before it was forced out by American pressure. Balaguer and Rodríguez Echevarría were sent into exile. A new council was installed, including, at the controversial suggestion of the American negotiators, Tony Imbert and Luis Amiama Tió, the two remaining assassins of Rafael Trujillo, who had been in hiding until the departure of the last of his family.[34] The journalist John Bartlow Martin appealed personally to Bobby Kennedy for a crack at the ambassadorship, and got it.[35] The United States' enthusiasm for amateur ambassadors had not, it seemed, worn off, even after the disasters of Arthur Gardner and Earl Smith.

"If you blow this one," Jack Kennedy told Martin jokingly as he left, "you'd better not come home."[36]

★

On 7 November 1961, François Duvalier officially created the Volunteers for National Security (VSN). The VSN was a new name for the Tontons Macoutes, but Duvalier was still pretending that the Tontons Macoutes had never existed. When the British ambassador went to the Haitian foreign minister to complain about the atrocities committed by the Macoutes, he was deported for saying the words "Tontons Macoutes" out loud.[37]

Duvalier requested that the American government arm his VSN to improve internal security. The outgoing American ambassador to Haiti, Bob Newbegin, warned Dean Rusk off: "State and Defense may care [to] consider in event there is in future some revolt against Duvalier regime whether we wish to be in position of having given this regime weapons with which to quell it."[38]

A new ambassador, Raymond Thurston, arrived in Port-au-Prince on 2 January 1962. Duvalier used the occasion to make a speech criticizing American policy in the Caribbean. He questioned whether Jack Kennedy was serious about implementing the Alliance for Progress, for it had not kept its promise of economic aid to Haiti. That afternoon, he made a song and dance about meeting a Polish trade delegation at the National Palace.

This provoked anger in Washington. The Alliance for Progress did not want to fund Duvalier. "Behind this was the idea that, after all, the Alliance for Progress has high goals," explained Thurston, "and it's bad enough that you're here with a dictator type, but if the aid itself is misused, then we're really blushing."[39]

A few days later, Duvalier backed up his words with a characteristic act of provocation. In the Artibonite Valley, an American loan had financed a development project. Duvalier sent his men to steal all its earth-moving equipment. They moved some of it to Duvalierville, and the rest to a site he had chosen for an airport.

The State Department did not know what to make of Duvalier. "Our record [of understanding his behavior] wasn't very good," admitted Edwin Martin, "as we could never agree on whether his unpredictability was the result of astute planning to keep us off balance or just impulsive actions by an irascible, flighty man. It sometimes seemed that he enjoyed nothing so much as to watch our confusion." Thurston agreed: "Everything that Duvalier's involved in there's an ambiguity in. It's the nature of the man, the way he operates."[40]

A week later, on 17 January, Thurston interviewed Katherine Dunham, an American anthropologist living in Port-au-Prince. Dunham was an astute and sympathetic observer of Vodou, and not given to exaggeration. She told him that there were rooms set aside for ceremonies in the National Palace, and that Duvalier had recruited large numbers of magicians and clairvoyants. Duvalier had become obsessed with consulting clairvoyants on the timing and implementation of every act. "Furthermore," Thurston cabled to the State Department, "she said she understood that there had been ceremonies performed in the palace involving the hearts of two of his political opponents."

Dunham was convinced that Duvalier was not just releasing such stories for political effect. Moreover, he "thought he was the reincarnation of Emperor Dessalines," Thurston continued. "What disturbed her now was that she understood Duvalier's clairvoyants were telling him that the time was near when he would have to kill all the mulattoes and whites in Haiti. She was afraid he was taking this advice seriously, and with his growing militia and his contacts with the Houngans she was afraid there might be real trouble. Her conclusion was that the real threat to Haiti was not communism; it was mau-mau."[41]

Duvalier's interest in ethnic cleansing was reported to the embassy by several reliable sources. A USAID anthropologist also said that month that he had heard Papa Doc fire himself up with talk of race massacres. Colonel Heinl, the head of the marine mission, was informed that Duvalier had repeated the order to the Tontons Macoutes he had given after Trujillo's assassination: that, in the event of his death, they should burn Port-au-Prince, and kill every white person they could find.[42]

Four days after Thurston sent his report to the State Department, indicating credibly that the president of Haiti was a genocidal maniac buffeted by the whims of sorcerers, came another OAS conference at Punta del Este, Uruguay. This time, Che Guevara was not present to enliven the proceedings. That would be left to the Haitian delegation.

The United States had hoped to use this conference to exclude Cuba from the OAS and place region-wide sanctions on selling arms to Fidel Castro. A two-thirds majority of the OAS countries was required. In securing this, the United States faced considerable opposition. Six nations—Argentina, Bolivia, Brazil, Chile, Ecuador, and Mexico—were minded to abstain. That left twelve that could be relied upon to vote with the United States. But there was one more nation, which presented a wild card. If it abstained or voted against the American resolution, the United States would not get its two-thirds majority. Cuba would stay in the inter-American system. The wild-card nation was Haiti.

"Oh, boy," Raymond Thurston remembered thinking, "they've really got themselves in a nice little position." René Chalmers, the Haitian foreign minister and head of its delegation, delivered on 27 January a passionate pro-Castro address, promising Haiti's vote to Cuba.

Afterward, Chalmers went to see Dean Rusk, who was representing the United States, in the lobby of the San Rafael hotel. Haiti, he explained, was very poor, and had no choice but to vote with anyone who would give it aid. Duvalier had issued clear instructions. The price of Haiti voting with the United States would be a $2.8-million loan, ostensibly to fund his new airport and a road construction project. The loan would come without conditions, and go through Duvalier's accounts.

Rusk was under no illusions that this money would disappear. But ousting Cuba from the OAS was his priority. He did not reply to Chalmers then and there, but later sent word that future aid would indeed be considered, depending on how Haiti chose to vote. Duvalier would get his money. A fictional expenses claim in the name of Dean Rusk was circulated inside the State Department:

> Breakfast—$1.85;
> Lunch with the Haitian Foreign Minister—$2,800,000.00.[43]

Rusk's report was sent to Thurston. In his dealings with the Haitian government forthwith, "I was told to take a very open and generally optimistic attitude," Thurston remembered, bitterly. "I can appreciate heavy pressures [at] Punta del Este," he cabled to Rusk, "but am frankly surprised at price we seem willing to pay in response [to] blatant blackmail tactics [by the] Duvalier government."[44]

"They tell me that I bribed the Haitians," Rusk remarked to him, later. "That was just diplomacy."[45] Whatever he called it, the real price for Cuba's exclusion from the OAS was paid by the Haitian people. Subsidized again by the United States government, Papa Doc continued to do exactly what he pleased with their nation.

★

In September 1961, the Soviets tried to look tough by resuming atmospheric nuclear testing. "Fucked again," said Jack Kennedy, privately. Publicly, he chose the moment to reveal the information that years of U-2 flights had gleaned: the United States had at least twice as many intercontinental ballistic missiles as the Soviet Union.[46]

The situation was even worse for the Soviets than the United States realized. As Khrushchev was informed by one of his top military men in February 1962, Soviet technology was so behind that if the Americans fired even one missile at Moscow, they could not fire back. "Before we get it ready to launch," he had said of their best missile, "there won't be even a wet spot left of any of us."[47] Meanwhile, Kennedy had sped up the American military's missile programs. In December 1961, the United States government published a pamphlet on how to prepare a fallout shelter in the event of a nuclear attack. The following spring, the Department of Defense began to build shelters for more than 60 million people. At the beginning of 1962, Khrushchev tried to set up a meeting with Kennedy and Harold Macmillan in Geneva, to discuss slowing the arms race or even stopping it altogether. Macmillan was game; but Kennedy, remembering the roasting he had suffered in Vienna, refused to take part.[48]

Like the fragile lizard that puffs out a frill to scare off predators, Khrushchev believed that his best tactic to stop the Americans from attacking the Soviet Union was to appear as big and dangerous as possible. He bragged that the Soviet Union was churning out missiles like sausages from a machine.

"How can you say that, since we only have two or three?" asked his son, Sergei.

"The important thing is to make the Americans believe that," his father replied. "And that way we prevent an attack."[49]

It was a risky strategy, and counterproductive. Rather than backing off, the American government only became more aggressive. But it does go some way toward explaining Khrushchev's decision in early 1962 to station nuclear missiles in Cuba.

The State Department had been watching the movement of Soviet weaponry into Cuba since the revolution. Arms had been sold by the Soviets to the Cubans, but they were conventional weapons, in modest quantities. In February 1961, the State Department investigated whether there might be nuclear weapons in Cuba—though it concluded that such a possibility was very unlikely.[50]

In late September 1961, Park Wollam, the former American vice-consul now attached to the Cuba desk at the State Department, reported that six Soviet atomic scientists were in Cuba.[51] If he was right, their visit must have been speculative, or unrelated to Cuba's defense. Khrushchev would not raise the question of sending missiles for another seven months. Nonetheless, such reports worried the American government. On 22 January 1962, the State Department released a statement, claiming that "as a bridgehead of Sino-Soviet imperialism within the inner defense of the Western Hemisphere, Cuba under the Castro regime represents a serious threat to the individual and collective security of the American republics and by extension to the security of nations anywhere in the world opposing the spread of that imperialism."[52]

The split between the Soviet Union and China had become public in late 1961, but this would not stop the State Department talking about them as if they were still a unified force. In any case, the statement sounded like it was building toward war. Khrushchev approved an expansion of military aid to Cuba.[53]

On 1 December 1961, Fidel Castro attended a party at the Soviet embassy in Havana. Afterward, he went to the offices of the communist newspaper *Hoy*, and publicly came out as a Marxist-Leninist. He claimed to have always been one, in secret: "Of course, had we said from Pico Turquino that we were Marxist-Leninists, we might possibly never have been able to descend to the plains below."[54]

Fidel, like the State Department, was building the myth of the Cuban Revolution. Though this speech was seized on by his critics to "prove" that Earl Smith, Fulgencio Batista, and Rafael Trujillo had been right in saying that Fidel had been an undercover communist all along, it was not accurate. It was meant to impress the Soviets. In fact, it embarrassed and annoyed them, for they were uneasy about taking on Cuba when the first signs were appearing that the island's economy might be failing.[55] Soon afterward, Fidel would revert to admitting that M-26-7 had not been a communist movement. Still, he apologized for the various uncharitable things he had said about the Cuban communist party, the PSP, before and after coming to power, and that did improve his relations with Moscow. Despite Fidel's short attention span for anything doctrinaire, he had been doing a relatively good job of cooperating with the PSP—though its proposed unification with M-26-7 seemed subject to endless delays.

But Fidel continued to bicker with the communist leadership in Cuba. He considered them tainted by their previous allegiance to Batista. He was irritated by their overbearing attempts to regulate or manage him—not least because most of them were old enough to be his father. "He was not a party communist," remembered Adolfo Rivero, a member of the PSP. "Nothing of the sort. He didn't fit with our ideas, which were then very rigid, of what communism was. Sometimes it was more vocal or less vocal, but there was always a lot of discontent inside the PSP with Fidel."[56] Finally, in March 1962, Fidel snapped. Publicly, he turned on Aníbal Escalante, the former PSP secretary charged with merging the PSP and M-26-7, accusing him of "sectarianism and dogmatism."

"Escalante gradually began to take over all important positions," Che explained. Worse still, he had promoted his friends: "Some of them reached leadership positions and enjoyed various privileges—beautiful secretaries, Cadillac cars, air-conditioning, keeping the warm Cuban atmosphere outside."[57] In reality, the problem was neither the prettiness of the secretaries nor the unpatriotic coolness of the air-conditioning. The problem was that Fidel could not cope with being told what to do. Disgraced, Escalante fled the country. The PSP was purged, with two thousand of its six thousand members thrown out. Officers of the Cuban administration, most notably Che, loudly expressed their admiration for Mao Tse-tung.[58]

The prospect of Cuba switching its allegiance from Moscow to Peking horrified Khrushchev. "Politics is a game, and Mao Tse-tung has played politics with Asiatic cunning," he wrote later, "following his own rules of cajolery, treachery, savage vengeance, and deceit." Something dramatic had to be done to deter both the vengeful Mao and the vengeful Kennedy. In April, the answer occurred to Khrushchev: "What if we throw a hedgehog down Uncle Sam's pants?"[59]

The hedgehog he had in mind was in the form of nuclear missiles. "If we installed the missiles secretly, and then the United States discovered the missiles after they were poised and ready to strike, the Americans would think twice before trying to liquidate our installations by military means," he explained. "If a quarter or even a tenth of our missiles survived—even if only one or two big ones were left—we could still hit New York, and there wouldn't be much of New York left." But he did not seriously intend to fire the missiles. "The main thing was that the installation of our missiles in Cuba would, I thought, restrain the United States from precipitous military action against Castro's government."[60]

That threat did exist. On 7 May, Bobby Kennedy and FBI director J. Edgar Hoover met with officers of the CIA, to discuss a wiretapping case. During the briefing, it was revealed by the CIA officers that the Mafia had been paid by the United States government to assassinate Fidel Castro.

Bobby reacted with fury, and Hoover with disbelief. "I expressed great astonishment at [the Mafia link] in view of the bad reputation of Maheu and the horrible judgment in using a man of Giancana's background for such a project," Hoover noted in a carefully preserved memo. In fact, he had known about the involvement of the Mafia in the CIA's anti-Castro plans since the Eisenhower administration. The point of this memo may have been to "prove" on the record that the Kennedys had no personal knowledge of the plots.[61]

The CIA assured Bobby and Hoover that the Mafia connection was not being pursued further. Nonetheless, the CIA general counsel, Lawrence Houston, noted that Bobby did not rule out further contact with the Mafia. Bobby wrote his own memo afterward, warning the CIA "never again in the future [to] take such steps without first checking with the Department of Justice." He did not warn it never to take such steps at all. Houston left the meeting with the sense that Bobby knew more than he was letting on.[62]

Soon afterward, Bobby Kennedy had lunch in a private room at the Carlyle Hotel in New York with one of Jack's closest friends, Lem Billings. "Bobby seemed in an excellent mood that day," Billings remembered. "He spoke and even laughed about the Mafia's involvement in trying to do away with Castro. He remarked that when the CIA had recently told him of renewing its ties to the mob, he'd done a better job of feigning shock and anger than Burt Lancaster. 'Of course, I knew,' he said. 'I'm the guy who developed the goddamn plot. But Hoover, he's a whole other ball game. He deserves a fucking Oscar.' "[63]

The Mafia plots had been initiated in 1960, under Eisenhower. Bobby did not create them, but he did know the Mafia was involved in the Cuba Project. He had received a memo from Edward Lansdale in December 1961, suggesting that Operation Mongoose use "certain of our own criminal elements . . . who have operated inside Cuba with gambling and other enterprises" to fight Fidel.[64] By the time the Church Committee investigated the assassination plots in 1975, Bobby would be dead. Less than a week before Johnny Roselli testified to the committee, Sam Giancana was frying sausages at his home in Oak Park, Illinois, when he was shot in the back of the head, and then another six times in the face. A year later, Roselli's decomposed body was found in an oil drum off North Miami Beach. Both mafioso murders remain unsolved.[65]

"It was made abundantly clear to everyone involved in the operation that the desire was to get rid of the Castro regime and to get rid of Castro," said the CIA's director of covert activity, Richard Helms. "No limits were put on this injunction." Bobby's supporters still refused to believe it. "To the extent that Bobby was involved in anything," argued Dick Goodwin, "it would have been like Henry II asking rhetorically, 'Who will free me of this turbulent priest?' and then the zealots going out and doing it." High-ranking CIA officials disagreed. "Where Castro and Cuba were concerned,

Bobby Kennedy went further than Henry II," one said, "and everybody covered up for him."[66]

Edward Lansdale suggested that Operation Mongoose would launch its new invasion strike, and remove Fidel Castro, in October 1962. The fact that Khrushchev also picked that date to move Soviet nuclear missiles into Cuba may not have been a coincidence. There is evidence that the Soviets had seen the CIA document.[67] If the Americans did try to invade Cuba, they would get more than they had bargained for.

★

On the night of 19 May, Marilyn Monroe rushed late onto the stage at Madison Square Garden, wrapped in white fur. She dropped the coat to reveal her monumental figure dripping with sparkling rhinestones. As the audience roared approval, she sang a breathy "Happy Birthday" to the guest of honor, John F. Kennedy. Afterward, he took the podium and remarked, "I can retire from politics after having had 'Happy Birthday' sung to me in such a sweet, wholesome way." The president and the movie star later disappeared together into a private house party on the Upper East Side. Bearing in mind the time difference between New York and Moscow, and the reported lateness of the birthday celebrations, the president may well still have been admiring Monroe's sweet, wholesome charms when, on the morning of 20 May 1962, Khrushchev told the Soviet foreign minister Andrei Gromyko that he had thought of placing missiles in Cuba.[68]

A week later, the Presidium met at Nikita Khrushchev's dacha and, over tea and pastries, informed a delegation that it was being sent to Cuba to tell Fidel Castro that he would be receiving nuclear weapons.

"The only way to save Cuba is to put missiles there," said Khrushchev. Kennedy, he added, was too sensible to start a nuclear war, so the point was solely to deter any American invasion. "So try to explain it to Fidel."[69]

Two days later, the Soviet delegation headed for Cuba. Marshal Sergei Biriuzov, head of the missile forces, explained to Fidel that the weapons were a deterrent. They would let the United States know that if it took on Cuba, it would be taking on the mighty Soviet Union. Furthermore, by rebalancing the missile race, they would increase the security of the entire Soviet-oriented world.

Fidel asked how many missiles they meant to send. Forty-two, said Biriuzov. Fidel replied that he was grateful for the offer, but that accepting nuclear missiles would damage the image of the revolution in Latin America. It would also aggravate the United States. Surely this was not necessary, he inquired, for did the Soviet Union not already have hundreds of missiles capable of hitting the United States from its own territory? The Soviet delegation brushed that question off.

Fidel and Raúl disappeared for consultations, and soon returned with an answer. "If this will strengthen the socialist camp and also—and this is in the second place—contribute to the defense of Cuba," Fidel said, "we are willing to accept all of the missiles that may be necessary—even 1,000, if you want to send us so many."

Speaking in 1992, he emphasized: "I had never viewed missiles as things that might someday be used against the United States in an unjustified attack, for a first strike. I remember that Khrushchev kept repeating that he would never launch a first nuclear strike."

At the beginning of July, Raúl Castro went to Moscow for two weeks. "I wanted him to ask Khrushchev a single question," Fidel remembered: "what would happen if the operation were discovered while it was in progress?"[70]

The Soviets who met Raúl remembered him as being on edge when he presented his brother's suggestions. "He was in a state of tense expectancy," said Vitali Korionov, a Central Committee adviser, who stayed up all night with him drinking Armenian cognac. "[As if thinking] 'What is going to happen now?' Because the Cuban comrades understood how this could end."[71]

The Cubans repeatedly suggested that the missile deal be made public. The United States had a clutch of agreements with countries like Turkey, Italy, and Britain, to station missiles in their territories. The Soviets could have copied those treaties word for word and applied them to Cuba, and it would have been awkward for the United States to argue that they were doing anything unacceptable.[72] But Khrushchev would not be talked out of slipping the missiles into Cuba behind the back of the United States. It was he who insisted that the deal be kept secret.

★

During the summer of 1962, the focus of the United States' war against communism in the Caribbean was split between Cuba and Haiti. On 18 May, Colonel Heinl, the marine commander in Haiti, recommended that "certain military equipment" be prepositioned in Guantánamo Bay, in case there was trouble in Haiti. Raymond Thurston was recalled to Washington for a review of the administration's policy on Haiti with the State Department, the Department of Defense, and the CIA.[73]

The plan was still to get rid of Duvalier in May 1963, when his theoretical term of office ended. The reasons given in that meeting were that some of his aides "are ultra-nationalist, anti-U.S. and have communist backgrounds," and that Duvalier himself was "unaware or indifferent to the possibility of ultimate communist rule." Finally, "A US role in dislodging Duvalier would, of course, help us with other democratic forces in the Caribbean area and be another significant step in upsetting the old 'friendly to dictators' picture which still prevails although lessened by the DR events."

There was trouble in Haiti, but it was not linked with communism. The Tontons Macoutes were operating with impunity, terrorizing everyone from the lowliest peasant up to the commanders of the army. It was the latter group that had begun to grow restive, and had been telling the American embassy that Duvalier should be felled.

The CIA and the FBI had drawn up a dossier of names from which they intended to select a successor government. The Kennedy administration planned to withdraw recognition on 16 May, the day after Duvalier's term came to an end, and persuade its Latin allies, such as Venezuela and Colombia, to follow suit. "This complete severing of relations on the part of the US and others would make his fall almost inevitable," it concluded.[74]

In the meantime, aid was held up. Dean Rusk's $2.8-million airport loan was called into question. Duvalier invited Aleksander Bekier, the Polish chargé d'affaires from Mexico City, to Port-au-Prince. "There is also speculation Bekier visit connected with Duvalier seek support elsewhere in view cooling off US-Haitian relations," reported Thurston. "Speculation probably has some foundation." It was a common Duvalier trick, and—if it followed the usual pattern—was aimed at upsetting the Americans, rather than at forming a genuine alliance with the Soviet bloc. Upset the Americans it did. The following month, shipments of arms to Haiti were halted. Soon afterward, Thurston reported the rumor that for three months Duvalier had been "making arrangements behind iron curtain [to] obtain arms."[75]

Increasingly, the marines had picked up on the fear within the army about the rise of the Tontons Macoutes. It was to the army that the Americans now looked for a hero. Colonel Heinl and the local CIA station chief began to do the rounds of the military men they hoped would topple Papa Doc. They invited General Gérard Constant to the American embassy, and offered to help him stage a coup—complete with the support of Heinl's marines.

"I'd rather have my arm chopped off," Constant replied.[76]

Back in Washington, Edwin Martin despaired of finding a leader for the coup: "we were not impressed with current military unrest as offering a satisfactory candidate since we felt they were more immediately concerned with the threat of the TTM than with the defects in the Duvalier regime which worried us."[77] What worried the Americans was the chimera of communism, and no amount of emphasizing by Haitians that the cause of the current unease was the takeover of their country by the very real, and very frightening, Tontons Macoutes would divert the Kennedy administration from that focus. It continued to labor under the illusion that there were hordes of communists on both sides in Haiti—clawing their way up inside Duvalier's administration, while simultaneously massing their ranks outside it to take over should he fall.[78]

On 1 August, Thurston again recommended readying a response from Guantánamo. "In past few days there have been rumors of impending coup by Haitian military with date mentioned as early as August 3–5," he reported to Rusk. The United States withdrew its USAID mission, on the grounds that Duvalier had rejected the conditions it wanted to place on economic support. Meanwhile, it turned its attention to another potential coup leader, General Jean-René Boucicaut, whom Edwin Martin remembered was "known to us as an enthusiastic plotter." On 8 August, Boucicaut told Heinl frankly that he was planning a coup against Duvalier, to be launched in October.[79] That afternoon, he met Duvalier and spoke out against the buildup of the Macoutes. He was promptly fired, and, by sundown, he and his wife had fled into the Venezuelan embassy.

The following day, General Constant admitted to Thurston that he, too, had been involved in Boucicaut's plan. Meanwhile, Tontons Macoutes poured into Port-au-Prince from the provinces, "presumably for showdown with armed forces within next 48 hours," as Heinl wrote to Rusk.[80] The marine commander recommended "immediate concentration of appropriate fleet units . . . in international waters" off the Haitian coast.

Kennedy sent fewer ships than Heinl wanted. A carrier was readied at Guantánamo Bay to evacuate American citizens from Haiti. Two United States Navy destroyers were sent to the international waters off Port-au-Prince. "There has been no publicity in connection with the foregoing activity and there will be none other than to answer queries to the effect that this is a routine training operation," said a note in Kennedy's national security file. The Haitian coast guard soon sighted the destroyers, and there was a squabble with the American embassy over exactly what constituted international waters.[81] The Tontons Macoutes were sent to round up the usual suspects, including Clément Barbot.

Barbot had survived eighteen months of imprisonment in Fort Dimanche, and had been released to the comfort of house arrest that summer. With American ships offshore, and a band of Macoutes on their way to arrest him, he slipped away. Duvalier spread a false rumor that he had been shot and killed. It was believed in the National Palace that Barbot was actually hiding out in the home of an American official.[82] This was plausible: Barbot had long nurtured American links. It is the first, though by no means the last, hint in the archives that the American search for a man to topple Duvalier pointed to the former chief Tonton Macoute himself.

With Duvalier's crackdown, the moment of maximum opportunity had passed. American ships lingered; but, with only the tremulous Constant left in play as a possible coup leader, nothing happened. Alarming rumors continued to circulate. By the beginning of September, the CIA was reporting information claiming that Duvalier would take money from the Soviet bloc to set up communist bases in Haiti, and that he had offered Fidel Castro bases in the event of an American invasion of Cuba.[83] In the absence of an alternative to Duvalier, these rumors did exactly what he had doubtless hoped, and pushed the Americans back to the negotiating table. Aid was restored, including the $2.8-million airport loan. "All is now well once again between powers that be in Washington and those in National Palace here," Thurston reported, with an edge of resentment, on 30 September.[84]

Constant was dismayed by the ending of the crisis. It had, he told Thurston, presented the best chance yet of ousting Duvalier. But the American government was amenable to sitting back and waiting until May 1963 came around. In the meantime, it had other things to worry about. Something unusual was happening in Cuba.

★

Through the hot, rainy Cuban summer, Soviet technicians transported equipment along potholed dirt tracks. They drained swamps, chopped down trees, irrigated dry land, built hangars and warehouses, and installed electricity and running water. On 7 August, hundreds of Soviet "tourists" marched in lines of four off a ship onto the dock at Havana. All were young and fit, and they only seemed to be wearing two different types of sports shirts and khaki trousers. The American government was deluged with reports on this activity, from its own observers and from civilians.[85]

Back in June, the Pentagon had stated that there would be two options in the event of a Soviet military base appearing in Cuba: accept the permanent existence of a communist state in the Caribbean, or launch a military attack and take it out. "Our present view is that the latter course of action would be the only solution compatible with the security interests of the United States," deputy defense secretary Roswell Gilpatric had told the SGA at the time.[86] Now, three days after the disembarkation of the "tourists," the CIA's John McCone warned Kennedy that he thought the Soviets were preparing to install surface-to-air missiles. Though these could not hit the United States, they could take down a U-2—and McCone believed they might be a precursor to longer-range missiles.

McCone's colleagues, including Bob McNamara, mostly thought that he was paranoid, and that indulging in too much U-2 activity over Cuba might make the situation worse. Bob Stevenson, formerly of the Office of Inter-American Affairs, was asked that August to sit in on a National Intelligence Estimate of Cuba. He remembered later that "we all concluded, except one—the Air Force member took a footnote on it—we all concluded that the Soviets would not put missiles into Cuba. We just couldn't believe that they would be that stupid, is what it amounted to, and that the evidence was not conclusive."[87] Meanwhile, on 20 August, Jack Kennedy approved the first phase of Operation Mongoose's main invasion plan, aimed at isolating Cuba.

Days later, Mongoose's men organized a dramatic raid. Every Friday evening, various Cuban, Russian, Czech, Polish, and Chinese technicians met in the Blanquita Theatre in Miramar, Havana. Fidel Castro often attended. Afterward, they always went for drinks and dinner at the Hostel Icar, a large hotel with floor-to-ceiling windows looking out over the waterfront. On the night of 24 August, two low boats sent by the Cuban Revolutionary Student Directorate, one of the many exile groups working with the CIA, sailed under the Cuban radar. In Miami, they had been armed with a 20mm cannon, as well as a few rifles and pistols.

Still a few hundred yards out to sea, a spare fuel tank leaked all over the deck, right under the cannon. The men realized it might blow them up when they fired it, but felt they were too close to back out. In the illuminated windows of the Hostel Icar, they could see men in uniform milling about. They opened fire.

For five minutes, the exiles shot at the hotel with everything they had, shattering every pane of its glass frontage. "Their marksmanship was poor and they were pretty far out," said a Czech physician, who had been walking in the hotel's gardens. "But soon pandemonium ensued. Guests in nightgowns raced through the hotel. Panic seemed more dangerous than the effect of the raid."[88] The hotel's lobby was destroyed, but there were no serious injuries.

This raid, like many others, was planned by the JM/WAVE station in Miami. Three days later, on 27 August, Fidel sent Che Guevara and one of his own closest aides, Emilio Aragonés, to Moscow. In an atmosphere of such hostility with the United States, Fidel was more discomfited than ever by Khrushchev's insistence on keeping the missiles secret. "If our conduct is legal, if it is moral, if it is correct," Fidel asked Che to ask Khrushchev, "why should we do something that may give rise to a scandal?"[89]

Khrushchev was holidaying in the Crimea. In his absence, they were met by the Presidium chairman Leonid Brezhnev, and raised with him the question of missiles. "No, no, go and see Nikita," he said, "take the plane and go there, I don't want to know anything about this. Take it up with Nikita."[90]

The Cuban delegation flew to Yalta, and met Nikita on a pier on the shore of the Black Sea. Huddled in overcoats, both Che and Aragonés tried to persuade Khrushchev to make the deal public. Khrushchev insisted that to do so would only annoy the Americans, and might harm the Democrats' campaign for the midterm elections. After all, he said airily, when the United States learned that nuclear missiles were already in Cuba, it would have no choice but to accept it as a fait accompli.[91]

"You don't have to worry," Khrushchev said to Che. "There will be no big reaction from the US. And if there is a problem, we will send the Baltic Fleet."

"He was totally serious," remembered Aragonés. "When he said it, Che and I looked at each other with raised eyebrows. But you know, we were deferential to the Soviets' judgments, because, after all, they had a great deal of experience with the Americans, and their information was superior to what we had."[92]

Two days later, a U-2 flying over western Cuba took photographs of what appeared to be surface-to-air missile sites at Artemisa, sixty miles from San Cristóbal. John McCone was getting married that day, and departed afterward for a honeymoon in Saint-Jean-Cap-Ferrat, in the south of France. He left orders for daily U-2 overflights of Cuba, and demanded regular updates—contacting the agency five times from the Alpes-Maritimes.

On the last day of August, in McCone's absence, Jack Kennedy was briefed by a team from the CIA. He told them to put the information "back in the box and nail it tight." There were no more overflights while McCone remained in the south of France. "Everybody seemed to be rather relaxed about that," McCone remembered, of when he returned. "I was furious." Once he was back in Washington, more U-2s were sent, and this time revealed only antiaircraft missiles.[93] But the situation remained tense. If missiles capable of reaching the United States appeared in Cuba, it was American policy to go straight to war.

14

APOCALYPSE NOW?

★

ON 17 OCTOBER 1962, FOUR AMERICAN AIRCRAFT CARRIERS, TWENTY destroyers, fifteen troop carriers, and seventy-five hundred United States Marines made for the Caribbean island republic of Vieques. They were to mount an amphibious landing on the coral beaches, overthrow the dictator Ortsac, and impose democracy. The operation was supposed to last two weeks.

The approach of a hurricane postponed the invasion. In any case, it was only a game. Vieques was not a republic. It was an island municipality of Puerto Rico, and was often used for navy training exercises. As for the dictator Ortsac, it did not take a cryptologist to work out that spelling his name backward revealed the real-life target. Questioned by journalists, the information chief of the Department of Defense stoically insisted that Operation Ortsac had "nothing to do with any possible imminent action against Cuba."[1]

Operation Mongoose was achieving little, except to confirm to the Soviets the threat their Cuban protégés faced from the United States. That October alone, at least three separate CIA-sponsored terrorist groups from Miami would land on Cuban soil: one to blow up a tramway at a copper mine, one to attach a bomb to the hull of a Soviet ship, and one to sabotage a Cuban sugar transporter.[2] The counterrevolution was no closer. For months, the Joint Chiefs of Staff had been champing at the bit to invade. Operation Ortsac had been intended to impress the president. By the time the marines arrived in the Caribbean, though, the game had changed. On 16 October, the Americans found Khrushchev's hedgehog down their pants.

For weeks, there had been hard talk between the superpowers over Cuba. The United States Congress had declared its determination "to prevent by whatever means may be necessary, including the use of arms, the Marxist-Leninist regime in Cuba from extending, by force or the threat of force, its aggressive activities."[3] Khrushchev told a visiting member of

Kennedy's cabinet that the Soviet Union had armed Cuba and would continue to arm Cuba. "You have surrounded us with military bases," he observed. In March, new American nuclear bases had gone operational around the Soviet perimeter, in Turkey and Italy. The Soviets reserved their right to follow suit. The Soviet news agency, TASS, had issued a colorful statement on 11 September about "little heroic Cuba," valiant in the face of "the provocations the United States Government is now staging, provocations which might plunge the world into [the] disaster of a universal world war with the use of thermonuclear weapons."[4] That same day, Fidel Castro declared during a three-hour broadcast that if the United States tried to destroy the revolution in Cuba, it would be making its "last mistake." That oblique reference caught the attention of the CIA.[5]

There had been trouble all over the Caribbean since the summer. Though Kennedy had pulled back from an immediate invasion of Haiti, the marine mission in Port-au-Prince drew up a new plan for military intervention at the beginning of October. It included contingencies for the American occupation of the capital, riot control, and the arrival of a massive invasion force from Guantánamo Bay. The plan was supposed to be adaptable to any intervention: either unilateral or through the OAS, either in support of an internal Haitian faction or against a communist or Castroist invasion.[6]

In the Dominican Republic, elections were supposedly approaching—though a National Security policy directive from Washington stated that they would be delayed if it was "apparent that the results would be contrary to our interests."[7] The American-installed council of state was teetering. The two assassins of Trujillo on the council, Luis Amiama Tió and Tony Imbert, were drawing together to mount a coup. According to John Bartlow Martin, the president, Rafael Bonnelly, "seems discouraged, exhausted, nervous, worried. He is taking barbiturates and drinking a good deal." From exile in the United States, Joaquín Balaguer told the CIA he was having to restrain General Pedro Rodríguez Echevarría from heading back to the Dominican Republic and taking over. On 10 October, Amiama Tió said that the country could use "a little dictatorship."[8]

John McCone had been insisting since August that there were missiles in Cuba. On 12 September, the day after Fidel's speech, a CIA spy in Cuba saw a convoy of trucks and trailers, carrying cigar-shaped things, around sixty feet long, concealed under canvas tarpaulins. In a separate incident, Fidel's pilot was said to have got drunk in a Havana bar and bragged loudly that Cuba now had nuclear missiles. But firm evidence did not surface until a U-2 overflight on 14 October brought back photographs of a clearing in the woods near San Cristóbal, to the west of Havana. There were distinctive markings on the ground: four slashes, like the scratch of a colossal paw, along with tents, vehicles, and construction equipment.[9]

Early on the morning of 16 October, it fell to Mac Bundy to break the news to Jack Kennedy. The president was still in his pajamas, reading the morning papers. Bundy told him that Khrushchev had put missiles in Cuba, potentially capable of hitting targets in the United States.

"He can't do that to me!" exclaimed Kennedy. He sat on the edge of his bed, leafed through the U-2 photographs, and said, "We're probably going to have to bomb them."[10]

According to the Intelligence Board's analysis of the photographs, twenty-eight launch pads were under construction. There were mobile launchers in San Cristóbal and Guanajay. No warheads were to be seen. Kennedy put together an executive committee, known as Ex-Comm, to handle the crisis. The president wondered aloud what Khrushchev's motivation in sending missiles to Cuba could be. "But what is the advantage of that?" he asked. "It's just as if we suddenly began to put a major number of MRBMs [medium-range ballistic missiles] in Turkey. Now that'd be goddamn dangerous, I would think."

There was silence, and it fell to Mac Bundy to explain: "Well, we did, Mr. President."[11]

The American case against the Soviet missiles therefore sought to make a distinction between offensive and defensive weapons. There was no technical difference. The defense secretary, Bob McNamara, insisted they were distinguished by "purpose." That was open to interpretation. The Soviet Union considered the many NATO missiles aimed at it, including those in Turkey and Italy, to be offensive, and wanted them removed. "The only logical justification for our position, obviously one to which the Soviets and their allies could never agree, was that the U.S. and NATO were only devoted to preserving the status quo while the Soviet bloc was publicly committed to world domination," admitted Edwin Martin. "In this context of purpose our missiles were always defensive and theirs offensive. Exceptions did exist, of course, as when we interpreted 'status quo' as at a time in the past, not the present, which we certainly did in the case of Cuba."[12]

Still, the Americans were agreed that the Soviet missiles had to go. None of the options discussed by Ex-Comm was appetizing. John McCone pushed for an all-out invasion. One step down from that, Kennedy could order strategic air strikes against the missile sites. But it was not possible to guarantee that all the missiles would be taken out at first hit. If there were any left, they could be fired at American targets. There was also the danger that Soviet troops might be killed, provoking Moscow into escalating the conflict.

Bob McNamara, a man nicknamed "the computer" for his analytical mind, was much admired within the administration, but had a knack for rubbing the military brass the wrong way. According to one general, he brought up the air strike option with Curtis LeMay, the no-nonsense air force chief.

"Now, Curt," McNamara began, "we are pretty sure those are Russian technicians down there. I want to go in with an air strike. I don't want to kill any of those technicians but I would like to wound a couple. Can we do that?"

LeMay looked at him for a long time, and eventually said, "You must have lost your mind."[13]

The only voice in the Ex-Comm discussions seriously arguing for negotiation was that of Adlai Stevenson, who suggested withdrawing from Guantánamo Bay in exchange for demilitarization of Cuba, and offering an exchange of the American missiles in Turkey and Italy for the Soviet missiles in Cuba. Bobby Kennedy was so disgusted at Stevenson's apparent weakness he recommended replacing him as ambassador to the United Nations.

Jack Kennedy disagreed. "Now wait a minute," he was heard saying to Bobby. "Adlai showed plenty of strength and courage, presenting that viewpoint at the risk of being called an appeaser. . . . Maybe he went too far when he suggested giving up Guantanamo, but . . . I admire him for what he did."[14]

"I know that most of those fellows will probably consider me a coward for the rest of my life for what I said today," Stevenson said afterward, "but perhaps we need a coward in the room when we are talking about nuclear war."[15] Later, he vindicated himself in Kennedy's eyes with a showstopping performance at the United Nations, during which he unveiled the U-2 photographs and proved on the spot that the Soviet delegation was lying about the missiles.

The option of doing nothing at all about the missiles was mentioned a few times, including by Bundy and McNamara, but not loudly. Finally, there was the option of a naval blockade. Like the air strikes or an invasion, this would be an act of war and a violation of the United Nations Charter—but stopping and searching Soviet ships within a five-hundred-mile radius of Cuba was unlikely to kill anybody, which made it less provocative. Over the following days, the blockade and the air strikes emerged as the two most popular options in Ex-Comm.

The Kennedy administration attempted to keep the dramatic news of what had been found in Cuba, and what might be done about it, as quiet as possible. The president went ahead with a campaign trip to Chicago on 19 October. That night, though, Kennedy's adviser Ken O'Donnell said, "The President may have to develop a cold tomorrow." Lyndon Johnson, campaigning in Hawaii, accidentally used the same line to justify his early return to Washington. One newspaper inquired with Kennedy's press secretary about this epidemic of colds within the government.[16] Rumors were circulating in Washington of an imminent attack somewhere, but they were vague. The targets mentioned were Cuba, Berlin, or Haiti.[17]

On the morning of 20 October, the Joint Chiefs of Staff sent messages to American military commands worldwide, warning that tensions in Cuba—about which they were not specific—might call for military action soon. Trouble could break out anywhere: Turkey, Iran, Berlin. That very morning, trouble did break out in the Himalayas. China launched simultaneous attacks on the Himalayan extremes of India, at Ladakh in the west, and along the McMahon Line in the east. Still in the habit of forgetting about the Sino-Soviet split, the Kennedy administration did wonder whether China was acting in synchrony with the USSR, and if this was to be the great showdown: the all-out world war against communism that they had feared.[18] Fortunately, it was just a coincidence.

★

At noon Washington time on 22 October, it was announced that President Kennedy would be appearing on television at 7:00 PM to address the nation.

In Moscow, it was early evening. "They've probably discovered our missiles," said Khrushchev to his son, Sergei. But those missiles were defenseless, and could be taken out with an air strike—if the Americans could find them all. Discovery had come too soon. He called an emergency meeting of the Presidium.

"The thing is we were not going to unleash war," he said, his face flushed, his manner agitated. "We just wanted to intimidate them, to deter the anti-Cuban forces." At that moment, he realized what a mistake it had been not to listen to Fidel's pleas, and make public his agreement to arm the Cubans. "They can attack us," he said, "and we shall respond. This may end up a big war."[19]

Fidel, too, was preparing for a big war. Just as during the Bay of Pigs, he remained in Havana, and dispatched his three most important commanders to their usual regional posts: Che Guevara to Pinar del Rio, Juan Almeida to Santa Clara, Raúl Castro to Oriente. At 3:50 PM Havana time—4:50 PM in Washington—he placed the army on combat alert. At 5:35 PM—twenty-five minutes before Kennedy was due to speak—he declared a general combat alarm. All 400,000 of Cuba's armed combatants were mobilized: 100,000 troops, 170,000 reserves, and the rest militia and People's Defense units.[20] He also had the support of 43,000 Soviet troops, which the CIA had underestimated as 10,000.

"Good evening, my fellow citizens," said Kennedy, into the cameras ranged around him in the Oval Office. "This government, as promised, has maintained the closest surveillance of the Soviet military buildup on the island of Cuba. Within the past week, unmistakable evidence has established the fact that a series of offensive missile sites is now in preparation on that imprisoned island." He announced that all ships approaching Cuba would be subject to a naval quarantine—a softer word than blockade, but the same thing.

Though the Joint Chiefs of Staff continued to press Kennedy for air strikes, Ex-Comm had eventually gravitated toward the blockade because they could not be sure that there were nuclear warheads in Cuba yet. Preparations were being made for them, clearly, but there was a good chance that the nuclear devices themselves were still in transit to the island. "This was one of the great problems—whether the heads were there," said Edwin Martin, speaking in 1964. "If the blockade could stop heads from arriving it was more effective than if it couldn't."[21]

Dean Rusk, speaking in 1970, admitted: "We never saw an actual warhead on a missile, and we never saw a missile on a launcher ready for firing. My guess is that had we done so we probably would have struck with air any such missile that seemed to be in a position to fire."[22] He believed that the warheads were on the ships that turned around before they reached the blockade.

Furthermore, the Americans believed that Khrushchev would keep any nuclear weapons in Soviet hands. "I would think one thing that I would still cling to is that he's not likely to give Fidel Castro nuclear warheads," Bundy reassured Kennedy on 16 October. "I don't believe that has happened or is likely to happen."[23]

History must be grateful that the Americans did not know the truth. If they had, air strikes would have begun by the time Kennedy went on the air. A speech had already been drafted by Bundy for that eventuality.

Khrushchev would almost certainly have retaliated, and the "big war" would have been in motion.

The truth was that Cuba was full of nuclear warheads. There were thirty-six one-megaton warheads for the medium-range ballistic missiles; twenty-four one-megaton warheads for the intermediate-range ballistic missiles, which could hit Washington, D.C., the Panama Canal, and perhaps even New York City; eighty fourteen-kiloton warheads for cruise missiles, which could hit targets within thirty-five miles; a dozen smaller warheads for rockets; and six atomic bombs for Ilyushin-28 bomber planes.[24] Each of the cruise missile warheads alone was almost the same size as the Little Boy, the bomb dropped on Hiroshima. According to Carlos Lechuga, Cuba's ambassador to the United Nations, the heads of the Soviet troops in Cuba could fire them without Moscow's permission—and the heads of the Soviet troops in Cuba were working closely with Fidel and Raúl Castro. These missiles, defined as *tactical* rather than *strategic*, could not hit targets on the mainland of the United States, but they could certainly wipe out Guantánamo Bay and any nearby American aircraft carriers. The larger, strategic ballistic missiles could only be fired with authorization from Moscow.[25] But they constituted an arsenal capable of destroying huge swaths of the United States. If even a small part of it was fired, hundreds of thousands, even millions, could be killed.

The CIA report sent to Kennedy on the movement of Fidel's forces was vague: "Che Guevara reportedly has established a military command post at the town of Corral de la Palma in Pinar del Rio Province, and Raul Castro is alleged to have gone to Oriente Province—his usual post during previous military alerts." It was also misinformed. Che was fifteen miles from Corral de la Palma, overseeing Cuban and Soviet forces installing high-tech communications networks and living facilities in a network of interlinked caves deep in the lushly forested mountains. This Bond villain hideout was to function as the center of guerrilla operations in the long war he would direct against any American occupation.[26]

But it was Raúl who had the most important command. There was a cruise missile base at Mayarí, the Castros' home territory. It had already been ordered to prepare "to deliver a blow to the U.S. naval base at Guantánamo Bay." Raúl's intelligence network was working with the Soviets, delivering information on the precise marine deployments at Guantánamo Bay. The base was surrounded, and cruise missile launchers had been prepared. These were much more discreet than the large sites required for the ballistic missiles, and American U-2s had not spotted them amid the trees. Raúl made his headquarters in Santiago de Cuba, and toured the preparations for attack with the local Soviet commander. The nuclear warheads for the cruise missiles were already on their way from Mayarí.[27]

In Havana, Fidel watched as artillery moved into place along the elegant curve of the seaside promenade, and it was heaped with sandbags. Student militias helped to man the antiaircraft guns. Cylinders of barbed wire were unrolled along nearby beaches. He gave a defiant speech. "Castro reiterated his readiness to die with his people," the Canadian ambassador told the CIA, "but seems rather less concerned about whether they or anyone else remains alive."[28]

This was unfair. Fidel did not face annihilation lightly. But he understood what Nikita Khrushchev had not: that the missiles on his soil were not the salvation of Cuba but its death sentence. "Now, if the [Soviet] commanders were authorized to use tactical nuclear weapons, it goes without saying that in the event of an invasion we would have had nuclear war," he said. "What is a unit going to do if the country is being invaded and they have the tactical weapons? So I was convinced that an invasion would become a thermonuclear war."[29]

Had the United States launched an invasion straight off, as John McCone advocated, the Soviet commanders could have struck back with nuclear missiles. It is impossible to conceive of the United States responding to that with anything less than an all-out nuclear attack on Cuba. *Patria o muerte*—homeland or death—was about to face its ultimate test. If this was to be Calvary, Fidel was determined that he, and the Cuban people, would face death with honor and with dignity.

★

In a five-hundred-mile arc around Punta Maisí, on the easternmost tip of Cuba, the American naval blockade moved into place. Beneath the waters, Soviet nuclear submarines prepared themselves. Two ships from the Dominican Republic were the first to join the American quarantine line.[30]

"I believe strongly that the Americas must present a common front against the grave menace of the offensive nuclear weapons placed in Cuba by the Soviets, for continental security and the safeguard of humanity," François Duvalier wrote to Kennedy.[31] Ostentatiously, he placed all Haitian harbors and airfields at American disposal, put the Tontons Macoutes on high alert, and told the marine mission he was increasing air and sea patrols. Captain Charles Williamson was skeptical. The Haitian coastguard was dockbound anyway, and the country had no air combat capability. "Duvalier was merely striking a pose for the local and world news media," he wrote.[32] Nonetheless, two American ships did take advantage of his hospitality, and sent some marines ashore for a stroll along the beach. Papa Doc himself was not informed this was happening until the American troops actually marched beneath the foreign minister's windows. He panicked, began packing his belongings into his limousine, and prepared for a dash to the Colombian embassy.[33] Reassured that it was not an invasion, he did his best to capitalize on what his own commanders jokingly referred to as "Operation Stretchlegs" as a sign of American support for his regime. He repeated what he claimed to be Cuban rumors that the United States had nuclear weapons in Puerto Rico, Panama, and Haiti, and "insinuated that this canard somehow put Haiti in forefront of hemispheric defense," reported Raymond Thurston, the American ambassador. "I said it was our consistent policy to avoid confirming or denying presence of atomic weapons in this or that area but that there was no need for me to assure them there were not US atomic weapons in Haiti."[34]

The missile crisis bought Duvalier a further stay of execution. When the tension with Cuba began, a new action plan was immediately released, stating that "the kind of measures . . . which would assure Duvalier's departure by next May, are not acceptable to us at this time."[35] Now, Duvalier presented himself as a model of cooperation. Ambassador Thurston cabled to Dean Rusk, "We have taken advantage [of] Duvalier's self-described anticommunist position since onset of present Cuban crisis to raise with Foreign Minister certain questions relating to communist activities in Haiti."[36] But Papa Doc had taken advantage of the crisis, too, as another version of the action plan released after the crisis admitted. It had "permitted Duvalier to demonstrate his solidarity with the United States on this issue [anticommunism], and he is now projecting this to his people as implicit U.S. support for his regime."[37]

★

On the morning of 26 October, Nikita Khrushchev was given a gray folder filled with intelligence reports. As he skimmed through them, one caught his eye. It said that Kennedy was gearing up for a full amphibious invasion of Cuba, and the removal of Fidel Castro. When Khrushchev read it, according to his deputy foreign minister, Vasily Kuznetsov, "he dropped a load in his pants."[38]

The report was based on a conversation between two American journalists, overheard by a Russian bartender, at the National Press Club in Washington two evenings before. It was wrong; though invasion was an option under consideration, it had not been ordered. But the report prompted Khrushchev to dictate a hurried, emotional letter to Kennedy. In it, he insisted that the missiles had only been intended to defend Cuba—not to launch a first strike against the United States. If Kennedy promised not to invade Cuba and withdrew his fleet, this would all be over.

With the arrival of this letter, several of those in Ex-Comm thought they had already won. General LeMay was an exception, grunting that Khrushchev must think "we are a bunch of dumb shits, if we swallow that syrup."[39]

Khrushchev's letter had taken twelve hours to reach Kennedy, owing to the laborious process of translation and transmission then required. During those twelve hours, things moved on. The Soviet forces poised to attack Guantánamo Bay had been ordered to move to a new position, just fifteen miles from the base. Cruise missiles, which the local Soviet commanders could fire on their own authority, were maneuvered into their launch positions. Tropical rain had been bucketing down all day. On the other side of the perimeter, thousands of marines sat in their steamy, sodden trenches, unaware of the extraordinary danger that lurked beyond the barbed wire fence.[40]

Less than four hours after dispatching his letter to the American embassy, Khrushchev had received further information that an American attack on Cuba was not imminent after all. Reassured, he composed a second letter, more bullish in tone. "Your rockets are situated in Britain, situated in Italy and are aimed against us," he wrote. "Your rockets are situated in Turkey. You are worried by Cuba. You say that it worries you because it is a distance of 90 miles by sea from the coast of America, but Turkey is next to us. Our sentries walk up and down and look at each other. Do you consider that you have the right to demand security for your own country and the removal of those weapons which you call offensive and do not acknowledge the same right for us?"[41]

This was such a departure in tone from the previous letter that Mac Bundy would wonder whether Khrushchev might have been overthrown. In fact, it represented only a new confidence among the Soviets.[42] The game was back on.

★

On the afternoon of 26 October, Fidel Castro met General Issa Pliyev, the Soviet commander in Cuba. Fidel told Pliyev that he had decided to shoot down any American planes they could hit. He did not have access to the Soviets' surface-to-air missiles; it would have to be done with conventional weapons. "I told them that we had decided to fire against the low-level flights—those were the only ones we could reach," he remembered.

"These planes were, in effect, training daily on how they could destroy our weapons."[43]

Pliyev told him that the Soviet forces in Cuba were now ready for war. Neither was aware that Khrushchev now did not believe that an invasion was coming. Fidel himself was now convinced that American forces would land within seventy-two hours.

If that was so, Fidel knew Pliyev would strike back. He took the news to the rest of the Cuban leadership. Their meeting lasted until two in the morning. Though no record of that meeting has been released, the indication is that the other Cuban leaders must have been of the same mind as Fidel. On leaving the meeting, he went directly to see Aleksandr Alekseyev, and asked him to help draft in Russian a good-bye letter to Nikita Khrushchev.

Alekseyev provided beer and sausage, while Fidel went through at least ten versions of his letter. Both men were exhausted, and, though Alekseyev's Spanish was good, it was not perfect. Fidel was trying to phrase an idea both precise and delicate. Translating this into Russian would have been no easy task under any circumstances.

During one draft, Alekseyev asked directly if Fidel really meant what it seemed he did: that the USSR should launch a first nuclear strike against the United States.

"No," replied Fidel. "I don't want to say that directly, but under certain circumstances, we must not wait to experience the perfidy of the imperialists, letting them initiate the first strike and deciding that Cuba should be wiped off the face of the earth."[44]

Fidel wrote that he could see two possibilities in the American response: either air strikes or—less likely, but possible—a full invasion. In the event of a full invasion, he said, Khrushchev must not let concern for Cuba weaken his resolve.

"If . . . the imperialists invade Cuba with the goal of occupying it, the danger that that aggressive policy poses for humanity is so great that following that event the Soviet Union must never allow the circumstances in which the imperialists could launch the first nuclear strike against it.

"I tell you this because I believe that the imperialists' aggressiveness is extremely dangerous and if they actually carry out the brutal act of invading Cuba in violation of international law and morality, that would be the moment to eliminate such danger forever through an act of clear legitimate defense, however harsh and terrible the solution would be, for there is no other."[45]

This letter was intended as a declaration of Cuba's willingness to perform the supreme sacrifice. If the United States invaded, Cuba would be destroyed. But Cuba, Fidel was saying, was prepared to face that. If it happened, Khrushchev should have neither fear nor hesitation. Such a war would escalate, and the only option, as Fidel saw it, was to strike back hard and fast. To save the people of the Soviet Union from being annihilated at the next step, Khrushchev should, if Cuba were invaded, destroy the United States.

It was a shocking letter, and revealing. Fidel's reluctance to receive the missiles in the first place, and his repeated pleas that the deal be made public, had indicated that he understood the danger he was taking on by accepting Soviet nuclear weapons. Though he had reservations, he had accepted them anyway. He had also accepted the secrecy. By doing so, he had taken a terrible risk on the part of the Cuban people. The leaders of Britain, Turkey, Italy, and other countries who had accepted the missiles of superpowers had put their people on the front line of any potential nuclear war, too—but those leaders had not concealed this fact. When Fidel came to believe, on that dark, tense, drizzly night in Havana, that the hour really had come, and Cuba could be annihilated, he was explicitly prepared to let it happen. *Patria o muerte* was a proud cry when he made it for himself and for the men and women who willingly signed up to his cause. It took on a very different air when that pride drove him to put 7 million civilians in the line of fire.

Little did Fidel know that Khrushchev did not have the capacity to destroy the United States, except to some extent from Cuba. "The aim was to strengthen him [Khrushchev] morally, because I knew that he had to be suffering greatly, intensely," Fidel remembered. "I thought I knew him well. I thought I knew what he was thinking and that he must have been at that time very anxious over the situation."[46]

At twenty minutes to seven in the morning, Havana time, Fidel's letter went into the laborious transmission system. Alekseyev added a short cable summarizing the Cuban leader's thoughts as best he could. That cable took an hour to reach Moscow, and the information in it would not be relayed to Khrushchev for almost twelve hours. During those hours, the situation would change dramatically again.

That morning, 27 October, Major Rudolf Anderson climbed into his U-2 in Orlando, Florida, and set out to fly over military sites in Cuba. His mission, specifically, was to fly over the Guantánamo area and photograph Soviet and Cuban positions. The Pentagon and the CIA were unaware that nuclear cruise missiles had just been maneuvered into position within fifteen miles of the American base.

Anderson began filming as he approached Esmeralda, a known surface-to-air missile site halfway down Cuba's north coast. As usual, the Soviet air defense system in Camagüey was tracking him from the moment he entered Cuban airspace. He continued south-southeast to another site at Manzanillo, and then turned more sharply east over the Sierra Maestra to survey another at Santiago de Cuba. From Santiago, he flew over Guantánamo—almost certainly directly over the cruise missile deployments the Soviets had just finished putting up.

General Stepan Naumovich Grechko was the Soviet air force's head of military plans in Cuba. "Our guest has been up there for over an hour," he said to his deputy. "I think we should give the order to shoot [his plane] down, as it is discovering our positions in depth."

His deputy agreed. If the Americans saw the Soviets preparing to hit Guantánamo, the results could be disastrous. Grechko attempted to telephone General Pliyev, but could not reach him. Major Anderson's U-2 had already turned back toward Florida, and was approaching Nipe Bay. There were only minutes in which to make the decision.

"Very well," Grechko said. "Let's take responsibility ourselves."

At 10:16 Havana time, he sent an order to Camagüey to use two surface-to-air missiles, and shoot down the U-2.[47]

Three minutes later, Anderson was near the town of Banes, on the north coast of Nipe Bay. Without warning, two missiles zoomed up at him from among the trees. There was an explosion in the sky. Anderson was killed instantly. Smoldering parts of the U-2 crashed down into the forest.

Within the same hour, another American U-2 pilot, Chuck Maultsby, went off course in a surveillance mission from Alaska over the North Pole, and flew three hundred miles into Soviet airspace over the Chukotka Peninsula. Maultsby realized just how badly lost he was when he turned on the radio and heard balalaika music.[48] Soviet jets were scrambled to shoot him down. American fighters had also taken off, trying to guide him back. Maultsby made repeated Mayday calls over open radio asking for directions. Fortunately, he made his way back to Alaska intact, and both the Soviet and American planes returned to their bases.

"There is always some son of a bitch who doesn't get the word," moaned Kennedy.[49]

On the other side, the son of a bitch who hadn't got the word was General Grechko. "You have been precipitate in shooting the plane down while our negotiations with the U.S. authorities are progressing successfully," telegraphed an angry Marshal Rodion Malinovsky, Soviet minister of defense.[50] In fact, if Grechko was right that Anderson's U-2 had photographed cruise missile deployments around Guantánamo, shooting down the plane was a sensible military decision. Had those pictures been seen in Washington, they could well have prompted immediate air strikes or an invasion—and either of those would have killed a lot more people than shooting down one U-2.

Ex-Comm was considering exchanging American missiles in Turkey and Italy for Soviet missiles in Cuba (Kennedy was for it, but Bundy against) when news came through of Major Anderson's disappearance. In the event of a U-2 being shot down, it had been agreed already that the Pentagon would be authorized to take out a surface-to-air missile site. The Joint Chiefs of Staff were firmly in favor of air strikes on 29 October if the Soviets did not get on with dismantling the missile bases before then, and an invasion as early as 30 October.

"I'm not convinced yet of an invasion, because I think that's a bit much," Jack Kennedy replied. But he did order everyone to prepare for that eventuality. In one last attempt at negotiation, he wrote a final letter to Khrushchev. It offered to lift the blockade and pledge not to invade Cuba if the Soviet Union removed its missiles. Though no direct reference was made in the note to a swap for the missiles in Turkey or Italy, it did state that "the effect of such a settlement on easing world tensions would enable us to work toward a more general arrangement regarding 'other armaments,' as you proposed in your second letter."[51]

Losing the Turkish and Italian missiles would not, for the United States, represent a great sacrifice. They were considered all but obsolete, and Kennedy had considered removing them just two months before. But a host of concerns about looking weak, and making NATO look weak, obliged the president to keep the offer private. Bobby Kennedy was sent to deliver Kennedy's letter in person to the Soviet ambassador, Anatoly Dobrynin. He was to emphasize that the next twenty-four hours were crucial. If the Soviets did not start dismantling their bases, Jack Kennedy's hand would be forced to further action. Furthermore, Bobby was to say that Jack could not announce the removal of the missiles in Turkey and Italy, owing to pressures inside his administration and the United States' prestige with its allies. They would nonetheless be removed within "four or five months."[52]

By eight o'clock that evening, Bobby Kennedy was on his way to the Department of Justice, with his brother's last offer for peace in his hand.

★

A little less than two hours earlier—1:10 AM, Moscow time—Soviet foreign minister Andrei Gromyko had telephoned Nikita Khrushchev, and read him a summary of Fidel's letter.

"He proposed that to prevent destruction of our missile installations, we should immediately strike first, dealing a thermonuclear blow to the United States," Khrushchev remembered in his memoirs. "When this message was read aloud to us, we sat there in silence, looking at one another for a long time. It became clear at that point that Fidel absolutely did not understand our intentions."[53]

Despite all of Alekseyev's careful drafting, Khrushchev did not read the letter as a noble statement of Cuban self-sacrifice, and did not seem to understand that Fidel was advocating a nuclear response only in the event of a full invasion of Cuba. He thought that Fidel wanted him to bang his fist down on the big red button and nuke the United States there and then. Comrade Fidel seemed to have lost his mind—and Comrade Fidel was sitting on an island ninety miles from the United States, on top of a stack of Soviet nuclear weapons with the combined destructive power of four thousand Hiroshimas. As Edwin Martin, undersecretary of state for Latin American affairs, later put it, "Even under Soviet control there was serious risk of irresponsible Cuban initiatives, given the military's dominance in Cuba."[54] Soviet troops were outnumbered by Cubans under arms almost ten to one, but that hardly mattered. Fidel, Raúl, and Che were heroes, personal friends, and, above all, comrades to many of the Soviet commanders. They might not need to fight them. The full horror of the situation he had set up finally dawned on the Soviet premier. Khrushchev panicked, and summoned the Presidium to his dacha.

Oleg Troyanovsky, Khrushchev's special assistant for international affairs, was at the meeting. Fidel's letter was terrifying enough. Soon afterward, the message from Bobby Kennedy to Anatoly Dobrynin arrived, too. Dobrynin emphasized, said Troyanovsky, that "there were many hotheads in Washington who were demanding an attack against Cuba, and it was quite understandable that it was going to be difficult for the president to keep everything under control." Furthermore, they had a report that Kennedy was to address the nation again, at 5:00 PM Moscow time. "Everybody agreed that Kennedy intended to declare war, to launch an attack."[55]

Khrushchev saw that the only option was an immediate withdrawal of Soviet nuclear weapons from Cuba. There was no time to consult, or even inform, Fidel. In any case, Khrushchev stated in his memoirs, it had been Fidel's letter that forced the withdrawal.[56] With Fidel fixated, as he seemed to be, on a glorious death, Khrushchev could not risk an invasion pushing him over the edge.

At ten o'clock Washington time on the morning of 28 October, Radio Moscow broadcast the news that the Soviet missile sites in Cuba would be dismantled. In the White House, there was euphoria. The crisis was over. In public, Kennedy maintained dignity in his triumph. Only in private did he brag to his friends of his victory over Khrushchev—payback, many times over, for the Vienna conference: "I cut his balls off."[57]

In fact, though Jack Kennedy's coolheaded statesmanship throughout the crisis was justly heaped with praise at the time and has been ever since, it was Fidel Castro who had unwittingly forced the Soviets to take their missiles out of Cuba. And, when he found out, he was going to be furious.

★

That morning, the Cuban president, Osvaldo Dorticós, telephoned Aleksandr Alekseyev. He had just heard worrying news on the radio: the Soviets were removing the missiles from Cuba. Alekseyev told him not to fret. American radio, he said, was capable of saying anything. Dorticós replied that he was listening to Radio Moscow.

"I immediately imagined Fidel's reaction to the same news," wrote Alekseyev, "and felt myself the most unhappy person on the face of the earth."[58]

A journalist telephoned Fidel for confirmation. Fidel was in a meeting with Che Guevara, and the call was put through. He told the journalist that it was not true: Khrushchev would never back down. The journalist read him Khrushchev's statement. It was true.

"Fidel swore, as did I," remembered Che, "and to get rid of the tension he whirled around quickly and kicked the wall. A huge mirror hung in that spot. It was shattered by the impact and crashed in a noisy shower of glass."

"Son of a bitch!" shouted Fidel. "Bastard! Asshole! No *cojones*! *Maricón!*"[59]

Fidel had believed that this would be his—and Cuba's—apotheosis. Instead, it was a humiliation. Not only had he been deprived of his glorious death but, just as Cuba had passed from Spanish ownership to American care in 1898 without the consent of a single Cuban, so now had the United States and the Soviet Union settled the Cuban crisis without even bothering to tell him. Instead of being the greatest martyr in history, he was no more than a pawn: a little leader of a little country, whose fate would always be settled from on high, whether by Spain, the United States, or the Soviet Union.

"I would like to recommend to you now, at this moment of change in the crisis, not to be carried away by sentiment and to show firmness," wrote Khrushchev to Fidel that day. But Fidel was carried away by sentiment. "Countless eyes of Cuban and Soviet men who were willing to die with supreme dignity shed tears upon learning about the surprising, sudden and practically unconditional decision to withdraw the weapons," he replied. "Perhaps you don't know the degree to which the Cuban people was ready to do its duty toward the nation and humanity." Worse still, Khrushchev expected him to be grateful for being saved. "We knew, and do not presume that we ignored it, that we would have been annihilated, as you insinuate in your letter, in the event of nuclear war," Fidel went on. "However, that didn't prompt us to ask you to withdraw the missiles, that didn't prompt us to ask you to yield. Do you believe that we wanted that war? But how could we prevent it if the invasion finally took place?"[60]

The fury would never entirely abate. As late as January 1968, during a secret speech to the Cuban Central Committee, Fidel exploded when he read out Khrushchev's attempt to put a positive spin on the surrender, arguing that "Cuba was saved" and "Cuba lives."

"But Cuba had been alive and Cuba had been living, and Cuba did not want to live at the expense of humiliation or surrender; for that you do not have to be a revolutionary," Fidel shouted. "Revolutionaries are not just concerned with living, but with how one lives, living most of all with dignity, living with a cause, living for a cause."[61]

Across Cuba, Soviet symbols were ripped down and trampled upon. "*Nikita, mariquita, lo que se da no se quita*," sang schoolchildren. (Nikita, you little fairy, what you give you can't take back.)[62] The ballistic missiles had never been given to Cuba. But the Ilyushin-28 bomber planes, Fidel insisted, had been a gift. He was keeping them. American intelligence reported that Cuban troops were encircling Soviet bases on the island. It was possible he would keep them by any means necessary.

In return for his noninvasion pledge, Kennedy demanded that Cuba submit to weapons inspections. The secretary-general of the United Nations, U Thant, flew to Havana on 30 October to try to coax Fidel into admitting inspectors. He found both Fidel and Raúl dead set against, and disgusted with the USSR as well as the United States.

"What right does the United States have to ask this?" asked Fidel. "I mean, is this based on an actual right, or is it a demand by force, dictated from a position of strength?"

"This is my point of view: It is not a right," replied U Thant. "Something such as this could only take place with the approval and acceptance of the Cuban government."[63] In that case, Fidel decided, it would not take place. Inspectors were never allowed into Cuba. Consequently, the United States government never considered itself bound by Kennedy's noninvasion pledge—and, despite Khrushchev's pleading, that pledge was never registered with the United Nations.[64]

Khrushchev's deputy Anastas Mikoyan was sent back to Havana to talk to Fidel, but Fidel at first refused to see him. "It was very hard for us to receive the news at a time when we were beginning very thorny negotiations," the Cuban leader remembered. Eventually, they did talk, but Fidel was too angry to do much listening. "You offended our feelings by not consulting us," Che told Mikoyan. Moreover, "you effectively recognized the right of the USA to violate international law."[65] Back in Moscow, Mikoyan's wife died. In front of the Cubans, he wept—but he was not allowed back to the Soviet Union. The Kremlin forbade him to return until he had made some progress with Fidel.[66]

The Cubans did not consider the crisis over. "The situation here in Cuba is one of combat alert; the people await an attack on a war footing," Che Guevara wrote to a friend. "If we come to lose (which will happen after selling our lives very dear) people will be able to read in every nook of our island messages like those of Thermopylae. But, anyway, we are not studying our pose for a final gesture; we love life and we will defend it."[67] The Americans did not consider it over, either. Finally, with Washington threatening to destroy his Ilyushin-28s on the ground, Fidel relented, and agreed to give them back. The true end of the missile crisis came on the following day, 20 November, when Jack Kennedy returned American forces to their normal, peacetime levels of alert.

That same day, Bobby Kennedy advised Jack to make the noninvasion pledge of Cuba formal.[68] It was Jack who declined. Bobby was soon back in the hawks' nest, asking the CIA to draw up a new list of "possible actions which might be undertaken against Cuba."[69] Over the next few months, Jack continued to press the Joint Chiefs and Bob McNamara to keep the Cuban invasion contingency plans up to date.

According to the CIA, following the end of the crisis, the Cuban exiles in Florida were "depressed, heartsick, and convinced that the only hope is to provoke Castro 'into some mad action.'" They need not have feared for the commitment of the Kennedy brothers to their cause. Before the year was out, Jack Kennedy made a high-profile public appearance in Florida to accept the banner of Brigade 2506. "I can assure you that this flag will be returned to this Brigade in a free Havana," Kennedy told the audience.[70] During the crisis, the Kennedys had fallen out with Bill Harvey, the man in charge of the operation to kill Fidel Castro. Harvey thought this was because he had, at the climax of the crisis, told them to their faces: "If you fuckers hadn't fucked up the Bay of Pigs, we wouldn't be in this fucking mess."[71] But Operation Mongoose was not dead. In June 1963, Jack Kennedy would authorize a renewed CIA plan for covert sabotage and terrorism operations against Cuba.[72]

But Kennedy had learned from the crisis, and something in him changed. "He was no longer the Kennedy of 1959 or '60 who was basically, it seemed to me, a young man desirous of gaining power," said Chet Bowles. "Now he was anxious to use his power effectively and creatively."

Bowles saw Kennedy's affection for his daughter, Caroline, who had just turned five years old. "I know it may sound a little corny but our world doesn't matter much," the president remarked to him. "But I think Caroline's world does matter, and I am prepared to take every conceivable step to bring about a nuclear agreement with the Russians."[73] The missile crisis did achieve something, both for the Soviets and for the Americans. It reminded them of the consequences, if they could not find the road to peace.

PART FOUR

FALLOUT

15

PAPADOCRACY

★

ON 20 DECEMBER 1962, THE PEOPLE OF THE DOMINICAN REPUBLIC HAD gone to the polls for the first free election in their history. The far left boycotted it, but the far left was a negligible presence. Elected overwhelmingly was the moderate-left candidate, Juan Bosch of the Dominican Revolutionary Party.

Since his early escapades leading the Caribbean Legion, Bosch had become the most visible anti-Trujillo Dominican in exile. He had spent time in prerevolutionary Cuba, Venezuela, and Costa Rica, and formed along with Rómulo Betancourt and Luis Muñoz Marín the popular face of progressive democracy in the western hemisphere. His political and fictional writing had received widespread acclaim. As a speaker, he was simple and charismatic. His tall, dignified figure, with its expressive face and shock of pure white hair, had become immediately recognizable across Latin America. He won despite a concerted effort by the right-wing UCN, and by the Catholic church, to smear him as a Trujillista, a multimillionaire, and a communist: three things that it would be impossible to be simultaneously, and each of which he demonstrably was not.[1]

Shortly after the election, Betancourt was on an official visit to the United States. According to Edwin Martin, who was sitting alongside them at the top table of a White House dinner, Jack Kennedy asked Betancourt what he thought of Bosch. Betancourt replied, mildly, "He is a good novelist."[2] Though few members of the Kennedy administration claimed to have read Bosch's novels, this maxim made a deep impression upon them. It was repeated constantly; and, with repetition, Betancourt's sour grapes were transformed into all anyone in Washington needed to know about Juan Bosch.[3]

In January 1963, before his inauguration, it was Bosch's turn to visit the White House. First, he met Dean Rusk and the undersecretary of state, George Ball, and told them confidentially, "I want to be a key man in the fight against Fidel." A few days later, he had a meeting with Kennedy, and again the conversation turned to Cuba. Bosch congratulated Kennedy on the handling of the missile crisis, and noted that he had "unmasked Castro in the eyes of many Latin Americans." Kennedy remarked: "The Cuban problem may lead to war. I hope that war does not come to Latin America."[4]

Bosch was moved by Kennedy's words, and the seriousness with which he said them. "President Kennedy reacted as if war, the idea that war could reach America, not the United States, but Latin America, pained him personally. It hurt him as much as it could hurt me, a Latin American." He said later that he saw in Kennedy a "sensitivity, a rare, very masculine, very virile sensitivity. I would say that President Kennedy loved his country, the United States, as if the United States had been really a physical being, his mother, father or elder brother. And he had a guilt complex about what the United States may have done to the detriment of other countries in the past."[5]

Kennedy did care about the Dominican Republic, Edwin Martin remembered. He hoped that it might have the potential to shine as a beacon of the positive effects of American power. "There was a chance to remedy a wrong—the Marine occupation out of which Trujillo came. To establish a democracy in the Dominican Republic would be an enormous success to counter the Castro situation in Cuba."[6]

Behind the scenes, though, the Kennedy administration was already set against Bosch. Two days before the Dominican president-elect had met Rusk and Ball, the CIA had released an intelligence memorandum noting that "Bosch's reformist platform, his idiosyncrasies, and his opportunism, especially during his exile, have laid him open to allegations of pro-Communism." He was, it claimed, "a highly controversial figure . . . the possibility that he was secretly pro-Communist or a party member could not be ruled out."

There had been an awkward moment during another meeting, when the Americans started talking about the Alliance for Progress.

Bosch asked, "What is this AFP?"

"He seemed not to know anything about it," remarked Edwin Martin, crossly.

This probably said more about the Alliance for Progress than it did about Bosch, but was taken as confirmation of his supposed incompetence.[7]

John Bartlow Martin, Kennedy's ambassador to the Dominican Republic, had been a journalist with a vivid turn of phrase. As the representative of the United States, he did not moderate this style at all. Bosch, he wrote, "is devious, inclined by nature to dissemble and hide his real motives. He is vain; almost always refuses to admit error or weakness. He is sensitive and . . . accustomed to sympathetic, patient treatment of the kind usually reserved for a brilliant but willful [*sic*] child." Another American embassy official had moderated this view, noting that Bosch was in fact "an immensely likeable man with a real flair for dealing with people." But Martin's overblown words were more widely circulated, and biased those who met Bosch against him from the start. After their first meeting, Rusk and Ball had immediately condemned him as a ditherer, Ball claiming that he was "incapable of even running a small social club, much less a country in turmoil."[8] For all that the members of the Kennedy administration might talk about wanting a "decent democrat" in the Dominican Republic, their verdicts on Bosch implied that what they really wanted was another strongman.

Kennedy did not attend Bosch's inauguration in February 1963, but sent Lyndon Johnson and Edwin Martin. The American delegation drove into the capital from the airport. John Bartlow Martin, who stage-managed the visit, had already convinced himself that Johnson would be in mortal peril from Dominican communists. From the moment he met his colleagues off their plane, he was in a constant state of anxiety. On the way, the car had to cross a bridge next to a shantytown that, according to Edwin Martin, "was considered a haven for leftists."[9] A crowd had gathered to see the motorcade.

"When he saw this first big group, the Vice-President could not restrain his political instincts," remembered Edwin Martin; "he ordered the chauffeur to stop the car, jumped out, and started waving greetings, shaking hands, and kissing babies in full view of the shantytown only a hundred yards or so away." Back in the car, John Bartlow Martin became so worked up at the possibility that this cheerful crowd of ordinary Dominicans presenting their babies to Johnson might be bristling with Soviet-trained snipers that Edwin Martin said, "I feared a heart attack on the spot."[10] Fortunately, the only consequences of the stop were a few happy smiles, and plenty of glowing publicity for Johnson.

Bosch brought in a new democratic constitution, creating a secular state, protecting workers' rights, and giving rights to the Dominican electorate that it had never had before. He defended civil liberties, fought corruption, and reined in police violence while maintaining good public order. His fiscal policies were business-friendly. As part of public payroll cuts, he cut his own salary from $2,400 to $1,500 a month—and, uniquely among Dominican leaders until then, made no attempt to supplement it with graft. Even John Bartlow Martin, who did not like him at all, was forced to concede what he called the "indisputable fact" that Bosch's administration "may well have been the most honest in Dominican history, if not in Latin America."[11]

Some criticisms of Bosch's performance were valid. An attempt to introduce agrarian reform in the spring of 1963 almost drowned in bureaucracy. But the most common criticism of his regime from the Kennedy administration, and from John Bartlow Martin in particular, was that Bosch was soft on communism. He had allowed exiled leftists to return and enter politics, but refused to accept that this was a weakness. "I believe that, where there is true democracy, Communism should not be feared," he said. "If there had been a true democracy in Cuba, there would have been no possibility of establishing a Communist regime." Repeatedly, he insisted that the real threat came from right-wingers, who controlled the military and the police. Martin did not believe this, and alleged that Bosch "has been a deep-cover communist for many years." The cover must have been very deep. According to a CIA intelligence memorandum, Bosch said to artillery school graduates on 12 March that "there is only one dilemma [in Latin American politics] and it is quite clear: either democracy or Communism. And Communism means death, war, destruction, and the loss of all our possessions."[12]

The CIA concluded, "There is in fact no evidence that Bosch is himself a Communist—that charge is actually a matter of tenuous inference from the alternative charge, to which Bosch is indeed vulnerable." The alternative charge was that Bosch was thought to be so flimsy that the communists might overwhelm him. On that basis, the State Department said, "We believe that Bosch's present tolerance of communist activities in the Dominican Republic is a dangerous risk."[13] Juan Bosch did not realize it, but the end of his administration was already being preempted by the foreign government he trusted the most.

★

After the missile crisis, there was a subtle shift in American policy toward Cuba. The rhetoric had not changed much. "I don't accept the view that Mr. Castro is going to be in power in five years," Jack Kennedy told the American Society of Newspaper Editors in April. He said that he did not know how Fidel would go, but he did think that the United States would be seen to have played "a significant role." At the same time, though, the media were invited to notice a new joint Anglo-American policy of stopping armed invasions heading for Cuba. Television news crews were called to watch the United States Navy arrest an American and sixteen Cuban exiles in the process of launching a vigilante attack from the Bahamas. "We distinguish between those actions which advance the cause of freedom, and these hit-and-run raids which we do not feel advance the cause of freedom," said Kennedy, "and we are attempting to discourage these."[14]

Fidel Castro saw these efforts, and responded. During a ten-hour interview that spring with the American journalist Lisa Howard of ABC, he applauded the new efforts to halt exile raids. The CIA debriefed Howard afterward, and she emphasized that for economic reasons Fidel was "looking for a way to reach a rapprochement" with the United States. Her impression was that Che and Raúl remained opposed to any such move, but there were powerful voices for it—including Raúl Roa, the foreign minister, and René Vallejo, Fidel's personal physician, with whom Howard had a close relationship. According to Howard, Fidel indicated "that if a rapprochement was wanted President John F. Kennedy would have to make the first move."[15]

The chance of Kennedy making the first move was small, but Howard's observation that Fidel was squirming out of the Soviet embrace was accurate. Khrushchev noticed it, too. At the end of January, he had sent a rambling, thirty-one-page letter to Fidel, insisting that he visit the USSR to mend relations. "I have already told you, comrade Fidel, that there now exists, in our relations with you, a certain amount of resentment, and that this harms the cause, and naturally, harms Cuba and harms us," he wrote. "Allow me to tell you without beating around the bush: this harms our party and our country, but these difficulties cannot benefit you either."[16]

Fidel arrived in the Soviet Union on 25 April, very soon after his interview with Howard. He would spend six weeks visiting the canals of Leningrad, the tractor factories of Volgograd, the bazaars of Tashkent, and the frozen north of Murmansk. With Khrushchev, he embarked on a series of Ukrainian-style bonding activities: fishing, hunting, hiking, cross-country skiing. On several occasions, they visited armaments factories. Whenever Fidel expressed admiration for one weapon or the other, Khrushchev would loudly declare that some would be given to him as a gift—causing consternation among his aides, and landing Cuba afterward with a motley collection of odds and ends that did not work together. Nonetheless, it was all very flattering. On May Day, the two men appeared smiling side by side in Red Square, Moscow, in front of thousands of adoring Russians.[17]

After the parade, Khrushchev and Fidel retreated into the Kremlin for a celebratory lunch. All seemed to be going well, until the subject of the missile crisis came up. Within moments, the gigantic, hairy Cuban and the small, bald Ukrainian were shouting and swearing at each other over the table. The KGB's Nikolai Leonov, who had accompanied them for much of the trip, was so startled that he dropped a bottle of cognac. It smashed noisily on the floor.

There was a pause.

"In our country, a breaking glass can only mean happiness," said Khrushchev.

Fidel laughed, and the incident was over.

The two men later retreated to Khrushchev's official country residence at Zavidovo, just north of Moscow, and worked out the rest of their tension hunting wild boar. Afterward, Khrushchev placed before Fidel transcripts of the entire correspondence between himself and Kennedy during the missile crisis, and asked Leonov to translate all of it into Spanish, out loud.

Several hours later, an exhausted Leonov finished.

"Are you satisfied?" Khrushchev asked Fidel.

Fidel replied that he was. With that, the subject was closed.[18]

★

At first, the attacks in Haiti seemed random. They began at around the time of the missile crisis. In Port-au-Prince, several intellectuals and prominent members of society were beaten up for no reason. In Pétionville, a night watchman was crucified. Another night watchman, patrolling outside the public works building in the capital, was wrapped in barbed wire, and hung above his own shack to bleed to death. Soon, though, it became apparent that François Duvalier was extending a campaign of violence and intimidation to the whole of the Haitian people. Shipments of food and clothing, sent by international aid agencies, were deliberately obstructed at Haitian ports, while thousands starved and went seminaked in the streets. It became all but impossible to obtain an exit visa, after Duvalier decreed that every single one had to be personally authorized by him. His term as president was due to end in May 1963, but he did not look like a man preparing to leave office. Instead, he was shutting Haiti down.

Within the government, Zacharie Delva had risen to Duvalier's right hand. Delva was a former roadside snack cart owner from Gonaïves, who had become a Tonton Macoute leader and a powerful Vodou priest. He was interested only in the malignant applications of its rituals. Duvalier called him "Le Leader." Delva was thought to have been behind a wave of expulsions of Catholic priests since the missile crisis. He celebrated their departure by holding a Vodou ceremony on the steps of Port-au-Prince's Catholic cathedral, during which he sacrificed black pigs and drank their blood from a silver goblet.[19]

For several years, Haitian sources had been telling American diplomats that François Duvalier was mad. At the end of 1962, the Kennedy administration decided to find out for itself. A psychiatrist was given a cover story, and sent to Port-au-Prince. The American embassy arranged for him to have a private dinner with the unsuspecting Papa Doc. The results were unambiguous. "Duvalier is a psychopath," the psychiatrist reported; "there are unmistakable symptoms of paranoid megalomania. He is a very sick man."[20]

Others noticed it, too. The anthropologist Katherine Dunham described around the same time a "chemical change" that seemed to have taken place, affecting both Duvalier's physical capabilities and his personality. He had, she said, developed "a gray coloring which films a natural color and which, it is true, seemed to seep through his pores at our last encounter." She dismissed the rumor, then current in Port-au-Prince, that he was a zombie: "This was a man all right, but a man who had been extremely ill, physically, perhaps, and I had heard about that, but mostly morally and spiritually." He was, she said, "ill with the Faustian bargain and its price; and I see no difference when the changeover of chemistry and personality are made whether they are due to real or symbolic acts; the effect on man and society seems to be about the same."[21] According to the United States Marines commander in Haiti, Robert Heinl, the CIA bought space in the French magazine *Horoscope*, whose astrological forecast column Duvalier supposedly read, in an attempt to influence his thinking.[22]

Rumors began to circulate again that Duvalier was planning a genocide. In January 1963, Gerardo Blanco, the Dominican consul at Les Cayes, was found dead in his garden. His throat had been cut so violently that his head was barely attached. The machete work of a Tonton Macoute was not hard to identify. Blanco's alleged crime was accepting bribes to give Haitian mulattoes Dominican papers, allowing them to escape. It was reported that some Latin American embassies were charging up to $50,000 for the same privilege. The point of killing Blanco, though, was to send a message directly to Juan Bosch, who was calling publicly for the liberation of Haiti from Duvalier.[23]

According to a CIA report, several students were arrested for writing

DOWN WITH DUVALIER on walls, and distributing leaflets saying "Have confidence, Haitian people, the tyrannical regime of Duvalier is at an end." Thirty students and their families were arrested and tortured personally by Duvalier in the basement of the National Palace. The CIA found that at least one had been beaten to death.[24]

On 7 March, Dean Rusk cabled all the American ambassadors in Latin America, to ask what the governments to which they were accredited might think of "the actual landing of [U.S.] troops" in Haiti.[25] There was talk of a coup, masterminded by Clément Barbot. The CIA reported that Barbot planned first to kidnap and threaten to kill Duvalier's eleven-year-old son, Jean-Claude, but was talked out of it on the basis of probable international disapproval.[26] Barbot's group was thought to include Americans, and the embassy considered supporting him. Owing to his unsavory past, though, the ambassador Raymond Thurston reported to Dean Rusk, "I shall want to be pretty cagey at outset about commitments."[27] Many of the crucial names are still blacked out in declassified American documents. Until they are released, it is impossible to say for certain if Barbot really was the CIA's man or not.

Louis Déjoie's exiles, now training in the Dominican Republic with the apparent support of Juan Bosch, were also looking to overthrow Duvalier. There was a third group led by the exiled right-wing former dictator Paul Magloire, supported within Haiti by the former Cuban ambassador, Antonio Rodríguez Echazabal. "While Rodriguez ostensibly has broken with Castro, we cannot rule out possibility he may be playing a double game," warned a national security briefing. Nonetheless, of all the opposition groups in Haiti—and, when the State Department drew up a list of them, it ran to eleven pages—the Americans preferred the right-wing dictator, Magloire.[28]

Duvalier knew that the United States was preparing itself to withdraw recognition of his regime on 16 May, the day after his first term would expire. He let it be known, as the CIA put it, that "he could not care less if this happened." In private, expecting it to find its way to the CIA, he said that he was not a servant of the Americans and wanted them to stay out. "He said that in this respect Castro was right in his quarrels with the United States, and he planned to use Castro's tactics in dealing with the United States."[29]

A group of Haitian colonels began plotting in earnest. They went to the American embassy, asking for arms and support. Top-secret documents hint that a clandestine passing of arms to Haitian opposition figures—as to Dominican opposition figures during the last days of Trujillo—was considered.[30] But on 10 April, one day before the colonels were to launch their coup, Thurston formally told them that the United States could not at present help.

Undeterred, the colonels decided to raid Duvalier's own armory. News of the plot quickly reached Papa Doc's ears. He was convinced that the American embassy was responsible.[31] He summoned all his colonels to the National Palace. Most of them thought the better of that, and fled to the Brazilian embassy. The exception was Charles Turnier, a popular officer with a solid, pro-American record. Boldly, he went to the palace to face Duvalier. He was arrested, thrown into a holding cell at the Dessalines Barracks, and beaten up.

At dawn the following morning, 19 April, Turnier led a prison break. Wresting a pistol from a guard, he shot him, and freed several other political prisoners. They fled, and a few escaped. Turnier himself was shot and killed by an army sergeant as he ran. His body was left on the parade ground in front of the barracks, where for days it remained as a gruesome warning to others who might challenge the regime.[32]

Duvalier ordered a purge of the army. The lucky and the swift escaped into embassies. The rest were taken to Fort Dimanche, and many of those were never seen again. Raymond Thurston, at the end of his tether, cabled Dean Rusk to suggest that the time was right for the United States to send in the marines. He assured Rusk there was little chance of escalation, for the international communist presence in Haiti was nonexistent. The only threat was Cuba, and for Cubans to retaliate on behalf of Duvalier would be "suicidal." He concluded, "I think we can be sure Khrushchev would not get mixed up in this one."[33]

But American troops did not arrive. Instead, to celebrate his survival, Duvalier declared a Month of Gratitude, beginning on 22 April. Haitian exiles in the Dominican Republic flew over Port-au-Prince and dropped leaflets, exhorting what was left of the army to rise against "the gorilla Duvalier, the tyrant voudouist." According to one American sergeant, "Duvalier government announced it would shoot down all planes flying over territory (wonder what with) except Pan American." On 24 April, General Gérard Constant, the head of the army, went to the CIA for help in ousting Duvalier. Constant told the American agents that Duvalier had told him he had asked Fidel Castro for troops and arms to defend Haiti against invasion. The general, reported the CIA, "believes that Haiti is being turned into another Cuba."[34] It was not: as Thurston suspected, Fidel had no time for Papa Doc, and Papa Doc had no time for him. As usual, the allegations were designed to stoke American fears. Constant was hoping to prompt an intervention.

Amid the celebrations, on 26 April, a limousine was taking two of Duvalier's children, fourteen-year-old Simone and eleven-year-old Jean-Claude, to school. Two blocks from the National Palace, another car slowed down alongside the limousine. With perfect precision, three shots were fired. The driver and two Tontons Macoutes, the children's bodyguards, slumped down dead where they sat. The assassin did not fire on the children, who scrambled out and ran into the school, unharmed.

General Constant and Duvalier's physician, Jacques Fourcand, begged him to calm down, lest he have another heart attack. "The children aren't hurt," said Fourcand. "You have time for sober reflection."[35]

Sober reflection was not Duvalier's strong suit. Instead, he ordered sixty-five of his officers to be shot immediately without trial.[36] The Tontons Macoutes were unleashed. Guns cocked, they swaggered through Port-au-Prince, shooting and killing anyone whose car was the same make as the assassin's. Hundreds of civilians disappeared that day. By nightfall, bodies littered the streets.

The sharpest shot in the Haitian army had been one Lieutenant François Benoît, though he had been purged the previous week. In a blind fury, Duvalier became convinced—without evidence—that Benoît was the only man in Haiti capable of pulling off such a feat of shooting. The Macoutes went to look for Benoît. Twelve hours previously, he had escaped into the Dominican embassy. Instead, they went after his family. A squad arrived at the Benoît residence with submachine guns, and killed his father, his mother, a family friend, their servants, and their dogs, before setting fire to the house. Benoît's baby son, Gérard, perished in his cradle.

Benoît's wife was on her way to the school in which she taught. Literally minutes before the Macoutes swooped, she was tipped off, and soon made it into the Ecuadorean embassy. The Macoutes ransacked her school anyway, then went on to gut Benoît's brother's house. An elderly lawyer with no connection at all to François Benoît was brutally murdered, because he happened to be called Benoît Armand.[37]

The Macoutes soon extracted the fact that Benoît was under the protection of the Dominican embassy. Some headed for the ambassadorial residence. As his garden filled up with inflamed Macoutes, the terrified Dominican chargé d'affaires attempted to shoo them away. They formed an armed ring around the house. At the Dominican embassy itself, Duvalier's palace guard broke in and turned over two floors in search of Benoît and twenty-one other political asylum seekers. A secretary was menaced before the guard withdrew, leaving men on the perimeter to challenge anyone who tried to go in or out.

In Santo Domingo, Juan Bosch was livid. Describing the assault on the Dominican embassy and residence as "an invasion of our country," he ordered three thousand troops to the border, and the navy to sea.[38]

Coolly, Duvalier extended his terror to Dominicans and Americans. Scores of Dominicans were beaten up, or worse. A Dominican former boxer, in his late forties, was shot three times by the Macoutes. He pretended to be dead and, when they dumped him at the morgue, escaped. The first secretary of the American embassy was searched at gunpoint. Outside the embassy itself, a noise bomb was set off. A grenade was thrown at the house of a member of the United States Naval Mission.[39] Meanwhile, the gullible John Bartlow Martin sent alarming reports to Washington: Duvalier was being advised by Czechoslovakia and Poland, had signed a secret agreement with Czechoslovakia for economic aid, "promising in return to assist communist infiltration. . . . Rumors of deals between Duvalier and anti-Castro Cubans for naval bases in Haiti in hopes [of] provoking Castro invasion [of] Haiti."[40]

There was still a month to go before the date for which the United States had planned a possible intervention, but Kennedy realized it might not wait. The navy printed leaflets to be dropped over Haiti explaining the reasons for American intervention.[41] By 28 April, two thousand men of the Fourth Marine Expeditionary Brigade and the Caribbean Ready Amphibious Squad were in the Gulf of Gonâve, aboard the USS *Boxer*. Accompanying them were a Canadian destroyer, HMCS *Saskatchewan*, and the British HMS *Cavalier*. American helicopters were ready to be in Port-au-Prince within an hour of Kennedy's order.

Defiant in the face of this international fleet, Duvalier appeared before his public with his closest aides, including Jacques Fourcand and Luckner Cambronne. Fourcand delivered a violent speech, describing the United States as "a democracy of sluts." If the Americans made any attempt to topple Duvalier, he said, "blood will flow in Haiti like a river. The land will burn from the North to the South, from the East to the West. There will be no sunrise and no sunset, just one great flame licking the sky. There will be a Himalaya of corpses, the dead will be buried under a mountain of ashes. It will be the greatest slaughter in history."[42]

A jet landed at Port-au-Prince, containing several members of the Trujillo family. Duvalier welcomed them with much ceremony, checked them into the Hotel Excelsior, and gave them a luxury car. The Trujillos were mostly minor members of the family, but included two of Petán Trujillo's sons. It was said that Héctor Trujillo was on his way to join them.[43] Juan

Bosch's anger was now barely containable. Thurston pointed out to the State Department that Duvalier's motivation was not just to insult Bosch; "important consideration all along has been that each Trujillo visa has high price tag and Duvalier does need money for his goon squads."[44]

Bosch delivered a twenty-four-hour ultimatum to Duvalier, demanding the withdrawal of his men from the Dominican embassy, reparations, and a promise of better behavior in the future. The chief of the Dominican navy threatened to bomb Duvalier out of his palace, and remarked that "we can easily do again in 1963 what we did in 1844"—referring to the Dominican Republic's most famous military victory over Haiti.[45]

On the State Department's orders, John Bartlow Martin talked Bosch out of an immediate invasion, and pushed him to take the matter to the OAS. Reluctantly, Bosch agreed. Limply, the OAS asked both sides to take steps toward peaceful resolution, and offered to send a five-man investigating team. The team arrived on 30 April, and confirmed that the Macoutes had left the Dominican embassy. But Duvalier refused to give the asylum seekers inside it safe passage, insisting that seven of them, including Benoît, had been behind the attack on his children. To impress the investigators, he threw an impromptu carnival. Hastily assembled government floats paraded through streets still strewn with festering corpses from the Tontons Macoutes' exertions against Lieutenant Benoît. Bands played cheerful music, and the colorfully costumed performers smiled fixedly as they danced across dried splashes of blood. One hundred and fifty thousand of Port-au-Prince's citizens were forced to turn up and give their most convincing impressions of having a wonderful time. Large quantities of *clairin*, the traditional Haitian rum, were laid on by the government.[46]

In the middle of this ghoulish spectacular, the OAS team was received by Duvalier with a bodyguard of Tontons Macoutes. He sat in silence for an hour while they attempted to talk to him, then took them onto the balcony to view the carnival. Pointing at the USS *Boxer*, visible on the horizon, he said, "If the OAS claims the right to intervene because of repressive internal conditions, why don't they land troops in Alabama?"[47]

"I am the personification of the Haitian nation," Duvalier told his people. "I will keep power. God is the only one who can take it from me." He continued: "Bullets and machine guns capable of daunting Duvalier do not exist. They cannot touch me. . . . I am already an immaterial being." He finished with a cry: "No foreigner is going to tell me what to do!"[48]

Along the border between the Dominican Republic and Haiti, Juan Bosch had massed the Dominican armed forces: sixteen thousand troops, including a parachute company, well armed with tanks and jets. On the other side were four thousand poorly trained Haitian soldiers, plus at least ten thousand Tontons Macoutes. The *New York Times* estimated that the Dominicans would be in Port-au-Prince within four hours of setting foot in Haiti.[49]

By 7 May, the United States had evacuated all of its government dependents and nonessential civilians, and advised any other Americans in Haiti to flee. Sixteen hundred of them crammed themselves onto commercial jets. "Duvalier's black magic . . . which metamorphoses so easily into [Cuban] red magic, can no longer be accepted by us as a purely internal affair," opined the New York *Herald Tribune*. "And that is why we must take the bull by the horns and envision intervening 'now,' when it can serve our interests."[50]

Red magic was exactly what worried the State Department. In a briefing the next day, it said: "We believe that Fidel Castro will be strongly tempted to find some means of stepping into such a situation in order to bring about a solution favorable to his interests. We believe, too, that Haitian Communists—who, although few in number, constitute one of the better organized and technically adroit political groups in the country—would make every effort to play a determining role in any successor regime."[51] The CIA agreed, reporting that four ministers—Hervé Boyer, Clovis Désinor, Luckner Cambronne, and Jacques Fourcand—were planning to displace Duvalier on 15 May and declare a socialist state. "The ministers will then ask for Castro/Soviet-bloc assistance," it warned.[52] Juan Bosch had heard something similar, and told John Bartlow Martin that Duvalier himself would declare a socialist state on 16 May. If that happened, he said, the conflict would quickly become a "world problem," and he advised that the United States "do something" first. He suggested an invasion.[53]

These allegations of communism were evidently taken seriously, though they were being thrown around with abandon on every side. They should have been harder to believe. Duvalier had long demonstrated that he had no interest in socialism or communism, and neither did any of his cabinet. Far from supporting Duvalier, two of Haiti's genuine communist groups, both in exile in Cuba, broadcast daily over the radio that he was serving "the cause of Yankee imperialism."[54] Fidel Castro welcomed leftist exiles, but had long ceased actively cultivating Haitian invasion projects. Even if he could take Haiti, it was not clear why he would want to. "Do you really think the Soviets want to take over the world?" he said later. "Do you think that anybody is mad enough to want to take over the world? Why don't we give it to them? The world is a giant mountain of problems. . . . And Haiti is one lesson, right here in the Caribbean, right nearby. There are terrible social problems in Haiti."[55]

As 15 May approached, the American fleet remained in international waters, while the United States attempted to persuade Latin American governments to designate its marines as an inter-American force. Duvalier summoned a magician, and dressed himself in the robes of the Secte Rouge to place a death curse on Jack Kennedy. George Ball told senators in Washington that the president of Haiti was "in a rather psychotic state," lurking in the National Palace with "his hat pulled down over his ears and two guns on the table." The Dutch ambassador told Edwin Martin that five seats had been booked on a KLM flight from Curaçao to New York, Paris, and then Madrid in the names of François Duvalier, Simone Ovide Duvalier, two of their children, and Luckner Cambronne. The next day, the CIA reported that a Duvalier party had booked seats on a Pan American flight to Paris, and thence with Air France to Algeria. In Port-au-Prince, the besieged marine mission prepared to handle the potential chaos in a Duvalier-less Haiti the very next day.[56]

On the morning of 15 May, the Caribbean sun rose on an eerily quiet Port-au-Prince. During the night, the roadblocks had disappeared, but few ventured outside. Journalists were summoned to the National Palace just after lunch, and shown into the Yellow Room. Fresh pink roses garlanded every table. In the middle of this pretty scene, perfectly composed, was François Duvalier, conspicuously not on a flight to Paris, Curaçao, or anywhere else.

"Haiti will continue under my administration," he informed the journalists. "The country is calm and peaceful."

Duvalier took questions from foreign and Haitian correspondents. One asked whether Haiti would become a socialist state. "No! Absolutely no! Never!" he replied. And would he receive military aid from Cuba, or another communist country? "Absolutely no! Not either!" He praised the marine mission's technical assistance to his army, but chided it for attempting to influence Haitian political attitudes.[57] In New York, the Haitian consul-general collected $6,000 from the refund of Duvalier's air tickets, and told the press that the American government had manufactured the crisis. Duvalier, he said, had no plans to be communist or socialist.

That morning, Kennedy was still considering an invasion. "Seems to me we would be able to build some sort of a force that we could use as the excuse," he said to Dean Rusk. "In other words, the Bay of [Pigs], the Cuban thing, but to do it with a little more judgment."

Rusk suggested instead that they use Duvalier's dislike of the ambassador, Raymond Thurston, to strike a bargain, and get the men they believed to be communists out of his government. "After all, if he is asking us to change some top people, we might get across to him that if he gets rid of a couple of these bad eggs right next to him . . . we could pass both of them and start off on a fresh start."

"Yeah," replied Kennedy. "Alright."[58]

The United States decided not to invade. "We still had no alternative person or group ready to take over," said Edwin Martin. "The danger of a communist intervention seemed great. But more immediately we feared that the prime targets of the TTM, if so unleashed, or of urban mobs, would be the white personnel of the majority of the diplomatic missions and white businessmen or missionaries."[59] The Tontons Macoutes had been beating, torturing, and murdering black and mulatto people of all classes and occupations for years—hundreds in the last month alone. Martin's words are a stark reminder that this was not considered grounds for action.

On 16 May, Dean Rusk asked Martin what conditions would have to be met to restore cordial relations between Haiti and the United States. Two, Martin replied, were necessary: a constitutional, elected government, and the restoration of armed forces under American military guidance with the simultaneous disbanding of the Tontons Macoutes. Three more would be desirable: accepting restrictions on the use of economic aid, allowing all asylum seekers in foreign embassies to leave the country, and firing all "leftist" members of the cabinet. Even if Duvalier accepted all of these, Martin emphasized, he was still a bad lot. "He might still try to convert Haiti gradually or suddenly into a socialist state allied with Cuba and the Soviets."[60] Still obsessed with this absurd idea, the United States suspended diplomatic relations and economic aid on 17 May.

Duvalier's behavior was, to the Americans, incomprehensible. He was obviously not a decent democrat. Nor was he a military dictator in the familiar Latin American mold. His attitude toward the United States was a volatile and wholly unpredictable mixture of need, greed, wheedling, smoldering hatred, and open hostility. "I don't believe President Duvalier himself is a communist," said Raymond Thurston, "but he finds it useful to throw them in our face, and so far he seems to have them under control. We also know that the communists here maintain links with Castro in Cuba and with the international communist base in Mexico. . . . The longer it goes on, the better is the chance the Commies will get control."[61]

Duvalierism did not fit into conventional demarcations of politics, such as right and left. It was a distillation of all that had been powerful in Haiti's past—Vodou, black pride, nationalism—and all that had been malignant—ignorance, violence, and terror. Duvalier was not running a military junta, fascist dictatorship, communist state, or disciplined democracy. Haiti was something else. It was, as some observers called it, a Papadocracy.

Within a Papadocracy, Duvalier's actions made sense. The reason for the abrupt and complete loss of interest in war with the Dominican Republic or the United States was that Duvalier had belatedly discovered who had really attacked his children's limousine. It was not the unfortunate Lieutenant Benoît, whose presumed guilt had killed most of his family, and nearly started a war. The man responsible had been Duvalier's erstwhile closest ally and lifelong friend, Clément Barbot. Barbot himself now confessed to the crime in a letter to Duvalier. The shootings, he said, had been target practice.[62]

At fifty years old (seven past the average Haitian's life expectancy), and still in his physical prime, Barbot had assumed the status of a living legend. During those nightmarish months in Fort Dimanche, he was rumored to have experienced a religious awakening. Since then, he had been seen only at a Jesuit retreat and at confession.[63] It was said that he had repented of the sins he committed in Duvalier's name. Now, he was focused on one single goal: terrorizing and killing Duvalier.

From a base in the Port-au-Prince neighborhood of Martissant, Barbot declared an extraordinary private war against his former master. Over the following days, dozens of Macoutes would be shot in the streets. In one ambush, thirty Macoutes were killed. Barbot waited until their new captain, Jean Tassy, was away in Pétionville. Then he raided the armory of Fort Dimanche itself.

After a gruesome fashion, the former chief Macoute was enjoying himself. Barbot toyed with Duvalier. He even managed the feat, almost impossible in Haiti, of getting a telephone connection, and placed a direct call to Duvalier's office.

Don't drink your coffee, he told Duvalier. It has been poisoned.

"Clément," replied Duvalier, putting down the cup, "you will bring me your head."[64]

Finally, Tassy managed to track down Barbot's Martissant hideout. Some weapons were recovered, but the man himself was nowhere to be found. All Tassy saw was a black dog running away from the scene.

Haiti's gossip network lit up with the story. An obvious explanation was put forth: Barbot, the unkillable Macoute, must have magical powers. He could transform himself into a black dog. Duvalier, who knew the power of such stories and never missed an opportunity to engage with them, ordered that all black dogs be shot on sight.[65]

On 19 May, Barbot met Jerry O'Leary of the *Washington Star* in a straw hut on the edge of a field of sugarcane near Cazeau, six miles north of Port-au-Prince. The journalist remembered the former Macoute as "a handsome, slender man wearing only white underwear and carrying only a pistol. He showed me his marine-supplied weapons and pledged that his only aim was to rid Haiti of Duvalier."[66] Not until 1975 did O'Leary publish his allegation that, in May 1963, the United States Marine mission had supplied Barbot with small arms, ammunition, and grenades. The marines denied it.[67] O'Leary saw about a dozen rifles and revolvers in the cane field hideout, and Barbot told him that he was appealing to American contacts for more weapons. Papa Doc, Barbot told O'Leary, was a madman. "Duvalier is not a communist, a democrat, or anything else," he said. "He is an opportunist."[68]

Barbot hoped to bait Duvalier into reprisals, which might themselves trigger a full American invasion. Deliberately, he selected targets with American links.[69] He told O'Leary he was planning to blow up oil tanks at the Haitian-American Sugar Company (HASCO) the next day, attack three Tonton Macoute bases that had been set up in schools, and set fire to cane fields on both sides of Port-au-Prince.

O'Leary and a photographer spent the next evening with a group of United States Marines, watching for Barbot's chaos to begin. At 8:00 PM precisely, massive fires whipped through the cane fields on both sides of Port-au-Prince. From the city, blasts of gunfire and the echoes of explosions could be heard. The oil tanks at HASCO were spared, when the grenades Barbot's men threw at them failed to go off. The three Macoute bases were all successfully bombed. Raymond Thurston cabled to Dean Rusk that there were no figures available on how many were killed, but locals had reported hearing the screams of victims being loaded into ambulances.[70]

Despite all this, Duvalier had himself inaugurated as president again on 22 May. Juan Bosch was furious that Papa Doc was still in power, he told a visiting American diplomat. He felt thwarted by the fact that the United States had insisted on his calling in the OAS, rather than just invading, and said that the "US [was] now up [a] blind alley regarding Haiti."[71]

Just over a week later, on 3 June, the United States stumbled out of the blind alley and unexpectedly restored all diplomatic and economic relations with Duvalier's regime. Why it did so was—and is—a mystery. American officials stated blandly that good relations with Haiti were in the best interests of the United States. The conditions outlined by Edwin Martin to Dean Rusk had not been fulfilled. A rumor in the marine mission suggested that Duvalier had sent an emissary to President Charles de Gaulle of France, who had telephoned Kennedy and told him to leave Haiti alone.[72] This seems implausible; but, owing to the large number of documents remaining classified, there is no plausible explanation. Nonetheless, the restoration of relations was a fact. American warships sailed away from the Haitian coast. American cash flowed again into Haitian coffers. The Tontons Macoutes returned to their usual horrible activities, without censure. Duvalier remained president. He had won.

The next day, an article appeared in the *Washington Post* alleging that the United States had stopped Bosch from invading Haiti and toppling Duvalier. It upset Jack Kennedy. "Is this correct?" he wrote to Dean Rusk. "What instructions did we send to our Ambassador to the Dominican Republic? Did we in short 'intervene at least twice against positive steps to remove Duvalier from office with force of arms'?"[73]

Rusk replied that the State Department had indeed instructed Martin to call Bosch off. In a separate incident, sixty or seventy Haitian exiles who had been training in a secret camp in the Dominican countryside were disarmed and dispersed by the Dominican army. Rumors abounded that the United States had ordered the camp shut down, but, Rusk assured Kennedy, "we became privy to this operation only after it had been called off."[74]

Duvalier ordered the marine mission to leave, and declared Raymond Thurston persona non grata. A few days later, Thurston had a debriefing with the president in Washington.

"What next in Haiti?" asked Kennedy.

According to Edwin Martin, "Thurston responded that if Duvalier were not replaced in two or three years the condition of the people would make a communist takeover inevitable."[75] Thurston did emphasize, though, that the communists were not working with Duvalier. They hated him, too.

Back in Haiti, Clément Barbot's campaign of terror continued throughout June. But the collapse of American backing had rendered his cause hopeless. From his straw hut in Cazeau, he and his brother Harry, a pediatrician, planned a final suicide attack against Papa Doc. A peasant tipped off the Tontons Macoutes. On 14 July, the Macoutes arrived in Cazeau. They surrounded Barbot's hut, and poured gasoline. Torches were touched to the dry grass. The field burst into flame.

Choking on clouds of thick smoke, Clément Barbot, Harry Barbot, and three other men staggered out of the hut and into open ground. As soon as their forms became clear through the flames, the circle of Tontons Macoutes opened fire with machine guns. Afterward, graphic photographs of their bodies were released to the press. They did not convince everyone that Barbot was dead. According to *Time* magazine, even a week later, "black dogs on the street draw fearful sidelong glances."[76]

The new American ambassador, just arrived, was Glion Curtis. "Duvalierists [are] generally expected [to] breathe easier with death [of] Barbot and average Duvalier goon likely to be cockier than ever," he cabled gloomily to Rusk.[77]

On 26 July, the marine mission departed. One of its commanders, Charles Williamson, described Duvalier as "a third-rate dictator in a third-world country." He also noted, though, that Duvalier "began to treat the United States like a second-rate power—and got away with it."[78] Over the summer, a few exile raids were mounted from the Dominican Republic, allegedly supported by the CIA. All eventually foundered, complaining in several cases that American support had been too weak.[79]

Years later, Edwin Martin admitted that American efforts to oust Duvalier had been a failure: "It was a failure that in all the circumstances might have been swallowed more easily if we had not also been totally wrong in our prediction that if we failed in putting together an alternative government, we would be terribly busy in June dealing with a chaotic situation in Haiti, with a communist takeover possibly looming on the horizon," he admitted. "Instead, we had to watch Duvalier carry on without either a constitutional mandate or U.S. aid, faced with the weakest and most discouraged opposition of his term as president. We had to rethink U.S. policy from scratch."[80]

Once again, the United States government had allowed its largely fantastical fear of communism to distract it from the real dynamic of a revolution. The Haitian people suffered on under the rule of a psychopathic tyrant—one who now faced no internal opposition.

★

On 10 June 1963, Jack Kennedy stepped up at the American University in Washington to give a remarkable and brave speech. In it, he asked his fellow Americans to "reexamine our attitude toward the Soviet Union." The United States, he said, should try "not to fall into the same trap as the Soviets, not to see only a distorted and desperate view of the other side, not to see conflict as inevitable, accommodation as impossible, and communication as nothing more than an exchange of threats." Instead, he called for a "strategy of peace."[81]

The shift from the belligerent tone of his earlier speeches on the Soviet Union to a much more pragmatic and rational approach was not lost on

Nikita Khrushchev. A year later, Khrushchev told Bobby Kennedy that the American University speech "can be called courageous and more realistic than what the Soviet Union and other countries of the socialist world often heard from American shores."[82] It was possible to believe that this was the beginning of another thaw. Perhaps, if Kennedy were reelected in 1964, he would have a chance of making real progress toward ending the Cold War.

The American presidential elections were still a year away. In the meantime, Juan Bosch was in trouble in the Dominican Republic. Following the bizarre events in Haiti, he had said publicly that the military were putting pressure on him to leave office. On 20 September, there was a general strike, organized by business interests, and supported by the military and the Catholic church. Those bodies attempted to create a sense of public anger with Bosch, bringing peasants by the truckload into Santo Domingo for rallies of "Christian reaffirmation" against the communists.[83] Allegations that Bosch had opened the door to communism, and tolerated too much, poured forth.

On 22 September, John Bartlow Martin reported to the State Department that Bosch "is a lousy president . . . surrounded by too many incompetents, crooks, sycophants, and foolish relatives." He predicted that Bosch would shortly fall. The following day, he reported that it would be very shortly indeed: the military was planning a coup. Two American military attachés met the plotters, who promised to warn the United States when they intended to act.[84]

Bosch invited John Martin to one of the mansions formerly owned by the Trujillo family, on the coast outside Santo Domingo, on 24 September. He told Martin, "[The military is] going to kill me or overthrow me. Today."[85] He requested the protection of an American naval task force, like those that had been sent in November 1961 to oust the Trujillos, and in January 1962 to oust Balaguer.

"I asked," remembered Martin. "I transmitted the request and got an answer saying that they wouldn't send one except to prevent a Communist takeover. They wouldn't send it to prop up Bosch." George Ball's reply stated that, owing to "Bosch's incredibly poor performance," the United States could not "restrain" the Dominican military from taking over.[86]

The following day, the plotters, led by General Elías Wessin y Wessin, announced on the radio a state of siege. The democratic constitution was abolished. Communist parties were made illegal. Six right-wing parties were invited to set up a civilian junta. The United States cut diplomatic ties that afternoon and stopped aid, stating that the military's action would strengthen communism.[87]

Surprised by the lack of American support, the junta announced that the constitution was in force after all, and that a provisional government and free elections were on their way. The following days saw angry demonstrations against the coup. On 28 September, Juan Bosch and his wife were escorted to the presidential yacht, and sent back into exile.

Several Latin American leaders, including Luis Muñoz Marín of Puerto Rico, urged the United States to help restore Bosch to power. "We did not recommend it mainly because we felt U.S. military force would probably be required to overcome the resistance to be expected from the Dominican military," remembered Edwin Martin. In the Senate, Ernest Gruening of Alaska said that military force was exactly what the United States should use at such a moment, and that the charge that Bosch was "soft on communism" was the same one used by "any would-be dictator, scoundrel or crook who seeks U.S. support, recognition and U.S. financial aid."[88]

According to Edwin Martin, Bosch's fall was his own fault: "He listened to and seemed to sympathize with complaints made by leftist politicians, claiming to represent the poor. Probably some were Communists, probably most of them had some sort of political links with local communist groups. Thus the inexperienced Bosch failed to understand at all how as President, he should [create] . . . a steadily improving political, economic and social life for his people along AFP [Alliance for Progress] lines."[89]

With the Alliance for Progress in mind, Kennedy refused to recognize the Dominican junta until it committed to elections within the year. It offered to hold elections in the middle of 1965, almost two years away. Kennedy had lost the energy to fight yet another Caribbean battle, and by 1 November had settled on recognizing the regime anyway, on the grounds that it seemed both stable and anticommunist. Diplomatic relations would be resumed in December, with the junta then only promising elections at some point before 1966.[90]

It had been a year of coups in Latin America: Peru, Ecuador, Guatemala, the Dominican Republic, and, in October, Honduras. In three of those cases, Ecuador, the Dominican Republic, and Honduras, a constitutional government was replaced with a military dictatorship. This was not, from any angle, a good result for Kennedy's Latin American revolution.

"We face extremely serious problems in implementing the principles of the Alliance for Progress," Kennedy admitted. "It's probably the most difficult assignment the United States has ever taken on. . . . There are greater limitations upon our ability to bring about a favorable result than I had imagined."[91] It had been a difficult year for him, politically and personally. His approval ratings, a massive 83 percent after the Bay of Pigs, had sunk to 59 percent in the last few months. And, tragically, a son born that August to Jackie had lived for just two hours. For almost the entire duration of Patrick Kennedy's brief life, his father had held his hand. "He put up quite a fight," said the president quietly, as it was confirmed that Patrick was dead.[92]

Another new start was required. Still, Kennedy believed that Latin America might be the place for it. Whatever was happening elsewhere in the world, he told Rusk, Latin America "is the area of greatest danger to us."[93]

In September, following persistent lobbying by the journalist Lisa Howard, Kennedy had allowed secret preliminary talks between Carlos Lechuga, the Cuban ambassador to the United Nations, and Bill Atwood, an American journalist and diplomat. Cuba had responded warmly and pressed for more.[94]

At the end of October, Jean Daniel, a French journalist, writing for *L'Express*, met Kennedy in Washington. Daniel was scheduled to travel on to Cuba, and Kennedy saw him as a possible messenger. According to Arthur Schlesinger, the president spoke with unusual frankness. He had, he said, been thinking intensely about the Cuban Revolution.

"I believe that we created, built and manufactured the Castro movement out of whole cloth and without realizing it," Kennedy told Daniel. "I have understood the Cubans. I approved the proclamation which Fidel Castro made in the Sierra Maestra. . . . To some extent it is as though Batista was the incarnation of a number of sins on the part of the United States. Now we shall have to pay for those sins."

He asked Daniel to convey all this to Fidel. He also requested that Daniel return to Washington after his visit to Cuba. "Castro's reactions interest me," he said.[95] Daniel agreed. Soon afterward, he left for Havana. Soon after that, John F. Kennedy left for Dallas.

16

BAD NEWS

★

ON 22 NOVEMBER 1963, CIA SPECIAL AFFAIRS SECTION HEAD DESMOND FitzGerald was in Paris. The man he was to meet was Rolando Cubela. Cubela had been a member of the Cuban Revolutionary Directorate during the late 1950s, and fought alongside Che Guevara at the battle of Santa Clara. He seemed to be in and out of favor with the Cuban government, and had been trying to defect since the Bay of Pigs invasion. Two and a half months earlier, he had presented himself to the CIA in Brazil as a potential assassin. FitzGerald was meeting him to set up the murder of Fidel Castro.

Cubela had stated that he wanted to meet Bobby Kennedy personally, indicating that he knew enough about Operation Mongoose to know who was in charge. The request had been denied, but FitzGerald—a friend of both Kennedy brothers—told Cubela he spoke for Bobby.

FitzGerald gave Cubela a fountain pen fitted with a concealed needle, and filled not with ink but with Blackleaf 40. The toxin was designed to kill. Cubela was to return to Cuba, where the CIA had planned to deliver him a rifle as well. Before 22 November, though, counterintelligence agents within the CIA had doubts about Cubela. After his first contact two months earlier, a reporter for the Associated Press had spoken to Fidel Castro privately at a party in Havana. Fidel had told him he knew the American government was planning to kill him. "United States leaders should think that if they assist in terrorist plans to eliminate Cuban leaders, they themselves will not be safe," he said.[1]

Perhaps the timing of Fidel's remark was a coincidence. Perhaps Cubela was a double agent, and had told Fidel what was afoot. There was enough circumstantial evidence for the counterintelligence agent on FitzGerald's team to warn that Cubela was "insecure" before the meeting.

FitzGerald went ahead with the rendezvous anyway, but, when he left

Cubela, he was greeted with a piece of shocking news. His friend and president, John F. Kennedy, had just been shot.

★

It had been a beautiful Texas morning. A glamorous couple emerged from their plane at Love Field. They drove through Dallas surrounded by a motorcade, the chrome on their limousine gleaming in the midday sun. Two flags fluttered from the hood. The president and the first lady waved and smiled at the crowds as the limousine turned into Dealey Plaza and down Elm Street. Suddenly, the president seemed to grip his throat and lean forward. His wife turned to him. Then came the awful shot, that horrific, unforgettable moment. A flash of red. The president's head recoiled. Blood splashed over Jackie Kennedy's neat white gloves and pink wool suit.

Bobby Kennedy had just finished eating a tuna sandwich by the pool in the backyard of his home, Hickory Hill, in McLean, Virginia. His wife, Ethel, answered a call put through to the poolside telephone. It was J. Edgar Hoover, the director of the FBI. Jack Kennedy had been shot, but no one knew how serious it was. Ethel took her husband in her arms, and the two headed for the house, where Bobby made plans to fly to Dallas. He wondered, vaguely, who might have done it. "There's been so much hate," he said.[2] Then came the second call. Jack was dead.

At the moment the news broke, Fidel Castro was speaking to Jean Daniel of *L'Express*, who had conveyed to him Kennedy's message of possible reconciliation. During the meeting, the telephone rang with news of the president's shooting. "This is bad news," Fidel said to Daniel. "This is bad news."[3]

By contrast, François Duvalier was not sorry at all. He claimed to be the murderer. According to some colorful sources, on the morning of 22 November Papa Doc had stabbed his John F. Kennedy "voodoo doll" 2,222 times. That is probably not true, for voodoo dolls are not generally associated with Haitian Vodou; but Duvalier had put a death curse on Kennedy in May 1963, and he did consider twenty-two to be his lucky number. When the curse seemed to have worked that day, he was not at all surprised. He called for champagne, and sent the Tontons Macoutes out to organize public celebrations. They skipped through the streets, shouting, "Papa Doc may govern in peace, for his biggest enemy is gone!" There was a spontaneous carnival. The octogenarian Haitian intellectual Dantès Bellegarde wrote a commemorative pamphlet mourning Kennedy, and earned himself a beating by the chief of the Tontons Macoutes.[4]

Never have so many conspiracy theories sprung up around the death of one man than sprang up around the death of John F. Kennedy. There was no shortage of suspects. It was the communists. It was the Cuban exiles. It was the Secret Service. It was the FBI. It was the CIA. It was a rogue CIA conspiracy, led by David Atlee Phillips, Bill Harvey, and the JM/WAVE station in Miami. It was the CIA's counterintelligence chief, James Jesus Angleton. It was the bankers. It was the Israelis. It was the military-industrial complex. It was three suspiciously well-groomed tramps loitering by the grassy knoll. It was Kennedy's own bodyguard, firing at the assassin and hitting the president by mistake. It was Nikita Khrushchev. It was Sam Giancana. It was Jimmy Hoffa. It was Meyer Lansky. It was Santo Trafficante. It was the New Orleans mafioso Carlos Marcello. It was the right-wing oil magnate H. L. Hunt. It was François Duvalier and his sorcerers. Lee Harvey Oswald was a Soviet agent. He was a Cuban agent. He was an impostor. He was a communist stooge. He was a Mafia stooge. Jack Ruby was also a Mafia stooge. A KGB agent in New York said it was the KGB. The KGB said it was E. Howard Hunt. E. Howard Hunt said it was Lyndon Johnson. Lyndon Johnson said it was Fidel Castro. According to Bobby Kennedy, who had heard it from Pierre Salinger, Johnson really thought it was God: "He said that when he was brought up, he knew a young boy who wasn't very good, and the young boy ran into a tree on a bike, or something, and became crosseyed. And he thought that that was God's way of showing him and others that you shouldn't be bad, and this was retribution for being bad," Bobby remembered. "And then he said, in that context, that he thought because of President Kennedy's involvement in the assassination of Trujillo and [South Vietnamese President Ngo Dinh] Diem, that this was retribution—that his assassination in Dallas was retribution for that."[5]

On 29 November, Johnson told a group of his political friends that the assassination "has some foreign complications, CIA and other things. . . . We can't just [have] House and Senate and FBI people going around testifying [that] Khrushchev killed Kennedy or Castro killed him—we've got to have the facts." That same day, he telephoned the likes of Allen Dulles and the chief justice, Earl Warren, asking them to serve on an investigative commission. One of those he asked was Richard Russell, a Democratic senator from Georgia and an old friend of Dulles.

Russell said that he did not believe the Russians were involved, but "wouldn't be surprised if Castro—"

Johnson interrupted: "Okay, okay, that's what we want to know."[6]

That commission, which became known as the Warren Commission, would famously create more of a mystery than it solved. Concerned, still, with plausible deniability, and with the CIA's reputation, Allen Dulles made sure that the commission operated without any knowledge about the intricacy and extent of the Kennedy brothers' ties to the Mafia or the Cubans training in Miami, and without any knowledge of the secret war the Kennedys had been waging against Fidel Castro. The Warren Commission concluded that Lee Harvey Oswald was a lone gunman, acting alone.

Since then, every detail of Jack Kennedy's death and the circumstances around it has been questioned, and every frame of film scrutinized. The attention of countless experts, professional and amateur, has been focused obsessively upon the logistics, forensics, and physics of those few seconds in Dealey Plaza, and the knots and hoops of the massive web of connections surrounding it. Instead of a consensus, this investigation has delivered endless branching complexities. But the fact that there was, undoubtedly, a very large number of people and interests with a reason to seek Kennedy's death—and the fact that some of them may have seriously considered having him killed—does not prove that they were involved in the act itself. The fact that some of those people and interests arguably benefited from Kennedy's death does not prove that they were involved, either. The existence of irregularities in the initial investigation or Warren Commission report does not prove that everything in it is wrong—not even, necessarily, its conclusions. Human error and the inevitable confusion in people's perceptions and memories of traumatic events often give rise to inconsistencies. And the fact that many people and bodies, including the House Special Committee on Assassinations, which reviewed and critiqued the Warren Commission, believe there to have been a conspiracy does not prove that there was a conspiracy. The plural of opinion—even of educated and informed opinion—is not evidence.

"I'll tell you something that will rock you," Lyndon Johnson confided to the journalist Howard K. Smith in 1966. "Kennedy tried to get Castro—but Castro got Kennedy first."[7] If the Kennedy assassination were an event in a novel, it would be an irresistible twist: the Kennedy brothers spend tens of millions of dollars on dozens of schemes to kill Castro, but then, with one perfectly aimed, knockout blow, David slays Goliath. But there is no direct evidence that Fidel Castro, or any part of the Cuban government or secret services, was involved in Kennedy's assassination. There is an enormous patchwork of hints and possible coincidences, but they lend just as much, if not more, credibility to the theory that anti-Castro Cuban exiles, possibly in league with the Mafia, did it, as to the theory that pro-Castro Cubans did it.

Many years later, Raymond Garthoff, a special assistant in the State Department for Soviet bloc affairs, discussed with Fidel Castro the apparent inconsistency of Jean Daniel arriving with Kennedy's positive message to Fidel at the same time a poison pen was being given to Rolando Cubela. "There were contradictory strands in U.S. policy toward Cuba in 1963," Garthoff admitted, "but also, perhaps, it was one of those cases where the right hand did not know what the far-right hand was doing."[8] Fidel was sanguine about it: "Someone was giving someone a pen with a poison dart to kill me, exactly on the same day and at the same time that Jean Daniel was talking to me about this message, this communication from President Kennedy," he mused. "So you see how many strange things—paradoxes—have taken place on this Earth."[9]

The fact that Dulles and the CIA concealed from the Warren Commission the CIA's activities against Fidel Castro was a grave omission. "Because we did not have those links," explained the Warren Commission attorney Burt Griffin, "there was nothing to tie the underworld in with Cuba and thus nothing to tie them in with Oswald, nothing to tie them in with the assassination of the President."[10] It is the cover-up itself that has fueled the conspiracy theories. But the fact that the CIA covered up its own plots against Castro does not prove, or even substantiate, the theory that the CIA killed Kennedy, that Castro killed Kennedy, that the anti-Castro Cubans killed Kennedy, or that the Mafia killed Kennedy. All it proves is that the CIA was a shady organization determined to evade public accountability, and that is no surprise to anyone.

The CIA's files on Kennedy's assassination are due for declassification in 2029. Even after they are opened, the case may never be closed. The mystery has endured for so long, and has become so elaborate, that whatever emerges is unlikely to be believed by large numbers of people. The supporters of the Castro theory will not believe it was the Mafia; the supporters of the Mafia theory will not believe it was Castro; the supporters of the CIA theory will forever believe it was the CIA, because any evidence that emerges for any other theory might just be further evidence planted by the CIA to cover its own role; and none will believe that Lee Harvey Oswald was a lone gunman, acting alone.

In the early evening of 22 November, Air Force One landed in Washington. It was carrying Jack Kennedy's body, the distraught Jackie, still in her bloodstained pink suit, and the new president of the United States of

America, Lyndon B. Johnson, who had taken the oath of office onboard with Kennedy's shell-shocked widow at his side. Bobby was there to meet it, and was seen wiping his eyes, before he ran straight past Johnson to his sister-in-law. "He ran," Johnson said bitterly, "so that he would not have to pause and recognize the new President." Jackie Kennedy felt differently. "I think he is the most compassionate person I know," she said later of Bobby, "but probably only the closest people around him—family, friends, and those who work for him—would see that. People of private nature are often misunderstood because they are too shy and too proud to explain themselves."[11]

Soon after the assassination, Bobby spoke to John McCone of the CIA. "He wanted to know what we knew about it and whether it had been a Cuban or perhaps Russian hit," McCone remembered. "He even asked me if the CIA could have done it. I mentioned the mob, but RFK didn't want to know about it. I suspect he thought it was the mob. He said, 'They'—whoever 'they' were—'should have killed me. I'm the one they wanted.' He blamed himself because of all the enemies he'd made along the way and also because he'd advised his brother to go to Dallas."[12]

Bobby Kennedy had lost the brother he adored, and he had lost his position. Neither Johnson nor Bobby had ever bothered to conceal the contempt they felt for each other. Now, though, Johnson was in charge—and Bobby was out in the cold.

"Bobby at first acted as if he had been cut adrift and did not know quite what to try to do with himself in the years ahead," remembered his mother, Rose. By Thanksgiving, "he had reached a state, I suppose, of almost insupportable emotional shock."[13]

By the beginning of 1964, Bobby had regrouped enough of his energies to lobby for the vice presidency. There was no chance of his getting it. Though he had some supporters among die-hard Kennedy loyalists, they no longer held enough power to help him. Beyond that cabal, his short temper and arrogance had made him too many enemies. Johnson began dripping poison in journalists' ears about Fidel Castro being behind the plot to kill Kennedy, and Bobby being behind a plot to kill Fidel. Bobby, he told Leo Janos of *Time* magazine, "had been operating a damned Murder Incorporated in the Caribbean." He even took away Bobby's pet, Operation Mongoose, and had it destroyed. "We finally got sabotage stopped completely in April of 1964," remembered the CIA's Sam Halpern, "when we were able to convince President Johnson that we were wasting time and effort and money, and we were taking losses, and the other side was taking losses and it wasn't doing a damn bit of good." The operation's new plan to invade Cuba from the Dominican Republic was canceled. The CIA's efforts were redirected to Vietnam.[14]

Arthur Schlesinger was one of those die-hard Kennedy loyalists who supported Bobby. His remark that Johnson "thought that Latin America ended with Mexico" was something of an exaggeration.[15] But it is true that Johnson had neither much knowledge of the region, nor a great interest in it. He was led in much of his thinking by Tom Mann, a veteran of the Eisenhower administration, who ascended again to lead the State Department's Latin American policy. Mann still believed, as he had in the days of John Foster Dulles, that an enemy's enemy was a friend, and therefore that any regime in Latin America should be tolerated as long as it was staunchly anticommunist. He also believed that the Cuban Revolution could have been prevented had military aid to Batista been restored, and that to have done so would have been a good thing.[16] On that basis, relations with the junta in the Dominican Republic were restored on 14 December 1963.

In March 1964, Mann announced in a private speech to all ambassadors that the United States government would henceforth recognize and support Latin American governments on a case-by-case basis. The criteria for recognition and support were that a government encourage economic growth, protect American investments, abstain from interference in the internal affairs of other Latin American republics, and oppose the spread of communism. Absent from these criteria was any mention of social reform, progress, freedom, or democracy, or the Alliance for Progress.[17]

The Alliance had relied on involving and inspiring the Latin American democratic left. Even under Kennedy, though, the left in Latin America had been menaced and marginalized almost out of existence. Across the hemisphere, dictatorships were again on the rise—and dictators did not care for the Alliance's aims of democracy and reform.

Kennedy had put it to Latin America's strongmen that the soft revolution of the Alliance was the only alternative to violent revolution. On this, Che Guevara agreed with him. At the Punta del Este conference of August 1961, he too had stressed that "if there are not urgent measures to meet the demands of the people, the example of Cuba can take root in the countries of America."[18] The dictators spotted another way by which their overthrow could be avoided. They used Alliance funds for internal security, justified on grounds of ensuring stability—one of the Alliance's key aims. Several claimed that the internal threat from communism was the thing preventing them from establishing democracy, and accused Fidel Castro of sending communist agents to topple their regimes. Alliance cash, along with CIA and Green Beret manpower, went to support the development of paramilitary groups in countries like El Salvador, Guatemala, Colombia, and Paraguay. The paramilitary groups thus established went on to form the basis of the death squads that terrorized many Latin American countries in the second half of the twentieth century.[19]

Neither Johnson nor his successor, Dick Nixon, showed much interest in renewing the Alliance. In 1973, the committee that ran it was disbanded. It was almost universally judged to have been a failure.

★

Nikita Khrushchev had begun to lose his irrepressible energy. The two circuits he walked around his garden in the Lenin Hills every evening exhausted him. He had always worked late in the night, from multicolored folders spread out on the dining table or the bed. Now, he complained of eyestrain, and asked his assistants to read documents out loud to save him peering at the pages.

In April 1964, he celebrated his seventieth birthday in the dining room of his house in Lenin Hills: the same room in which the Presidium had met during the missile crisis. He insisted on receiving no presents—"Don't waste the people's money!"—but was ignored. The house was packed with Soviet luminaries. In particular, his son Sergei bitterly remembered, "Brezhnev smothered Father with the ritual kisses."[20]

Six months later, in October 1964, Khrushchev was ousted by Leonid Brezhnev and Alexei Kosygin. There was a grim meeting of the Presidium, at which Khrushchev was pilloried by everyone except the loyal Anastas Mikoyan.

"You used to behave yourself," said one. "Now, you're a changed man. . . . Stalin himself behaved more modestly than you do, Nikita Sergeyevich. . . . You're suffering from megalomania, and the illness is incurable."

After a round of such speeches, Khrushchev was permitted to speak. "These aren't tears of self-pity," he said, as they welled from his eyes. "The battle with Stalin's cult of personality was a big one, and I made a small contribution. You've already decided everything. I'll do what's best for the party."[21] The Presidium granted his "request" to retire. He was out.

Khrushchev was lucky, though he did not feel it. He was alive. He was allowed to keep his residence and a modest pension. Nonetheless, the severance of his familiar existence was hard to accept. Since his youth, he had been a proud and sincere member of the party, and a true believer in Marxism-Leninism. Now, he was introduced to Soviet communism's less pleasant side. His former colleagues were not permitted contact. He was delighted when Anastas Mikoyan telephoned to wish him a happy new year in 1965. The conversation was blameless, but Vladimir Semichastny, head of the KGB, sent a transcript to Brezhnev anyway. Mikoyan was called in for a dressing-down. He never saw Khrushchev again.[22]

Eventually, Khrushchev settled into a peaceable existence. Banned from drinking by his doctors, he nonetheless enjoyed staying up late with friends and singing Ukrainian folk songs.[23] He whiled away the Moscow nights to the sound of "I'd Take Up the Bandura" and "The Wide Dnieper Roars and Moans," while the Soviet apparatchiks went about scrubbing his memory from the public consciousness. He would die in 1971—not completely erased, but blurred out. He was denied a memorial in the Kremlin wall alongside the other leaders of the Soviet Union. Instead, his body would be interred in the cemetery at Novodevichy, the secluded, golden-domed convent outside Moscow, where the czars had once sent the awkward women they wanted to forget.

★

At the beginning of 1964, a mysterious Haitian arrived at Jack Kennedy's grave site in Arlington cemetery, just over the Potomac River from Washington, D.C. He took a pinch of earth from each corner of the grave. He unstoppered a flacon, and swished it around in the air above it. Finally, he plucked one dead flower from a wreath lying upon it. These talismans were carefully taken back to Port-au-Prince, and presented to François Duvalier. Papa Doc, it was said, needed the earth, the air, and the flower to summon Kennedy's soul, which he would then use to direct American foreign policy.[24]

Soon afterward, a new American ambassador, Benson Timmons, arrived in Port-au-Prince to resume relations. Duvalier kept him waiting for five weeks before agreeing to meet him. When Timmons finally met the president of Haiti, he was treated to a lecture on how much Duvalier had hated Jack Kennedy.

Timmons reassured Duvalier that things had changed. Lyndon Johnson had sent a message, expressing a new hope for "close cooperation and solidarity with the Government of Haiti." Friendly United States Navy visitors reappeared in the capital, and in Cap-Haïtien. The Inter-American Development Bank lent Duvalier another $2.6 million, intended for improvements to Haiti's water system. USAID gave him a $4-million investment guarantee for a new oil refinery. It seemed the spell had worked. Alternatively, the United States' change of attitude may have been connected to Duvalier's engagement of some powerful new lobbyists in Washington.[25]

Imbued with new confidence, Duvalier graciously permitted the

National Assembly to name him President for Life on 25 May, complete with the privilege of naming his own successor. A public vote followed three weeks later, asking Haitian voters if they wanted to ratify Duvalier's nomination. There was only one box to cross: yes. From a field of 2 million voters, Duvalier polled 2.8 million yes votes.[26] Though he was supposed to be aiming for cordiality, the American ambassador dodged the investiture ceremony. "If Dept [of State] has decided [to] clearly express its disapproval of Duvalier's president-for-life comedy (which I fully share), then I consider it best that I be ill on both June 22 and 23," Timmons cabled back to Dean Rusk.[27] Rusk telegraphed back the single word: "Agree."

Having ascended, in all but name, to the status of a king, Duvalier went about investing himself with divine right. In July, he had the Lord's Prayer rewritten. "Our Doc, who art in the National Palace for life, hallowed be Thy name by present and future generations. Thy will be done in Port-au-Prince as it is in the provinces. Give us this day our new Haiti and forgive not the trespasses of those anti-patriots who daily spit upon our country." There was a new catechism to go with it, which listed seven Duvalierist sacraments, and a new definition of extreme unction: "a sacrament instituted by the people's army, the civil militia, and the Haitian people . . . to crush with grenades, mortars, mausers, bazookas, flamethrowers and other weapons" the enemies of the state.[28] Duvalier had already been excommunicated, so the Catholic church had no sanction against this behavior. Unashamedly, he still attended services at Port-au-Prince's cathedral. The clerics did not want him there; but he always turned up with a phalanx of Tontons Macoutes, who guaranteed his admission, excommunication or no excommunication.[29]

The Americans were not impressed by any of this, but they and Duvalier were still dancing their old dance. Duvalier careered around, throwing moves with wild unpredictability, while the Americans attempted to work out whether it was better to ditch him or keep dancing, because the next man up might be even worse—perhaps even Fidel Castro. While the formal overtures of aid and military support continued, the CIA had apparently involved itself in anti-Duvalier exile groups training in the Dominican Republic. The Camoquins, named after a brand name for an antimalarial medication, were organized partly by the anti-Duvalier priests Jean-Baptiste Georges and Gérard Bissainthe. When their camp was raided by Dominican troops looking for communists, they found one copy of Che Guevara's *Guerrilla Warfare*—and a large stash of literature from the CIA and United States Information Agency. The Camoquins were allowed to continue their activities. In the early summer, they crossed the border south of Jimaní, and fought a few skirmishes with Tontons Macoutes.[30]

Rosalie Bosquet, known by her married name of Madame Max Adolphe, was the most notorious woman in Duvalier's administration, next to Mama Doc Simone Ovide Duvalier herself. Madame Max was the warden of Fort Dimanche, and head of the Fillettes Laleau, the all-female branch of the Tontons Macoutes. When the Camoquins foundered, Duvalier asked her to make a random list of twenty-one political prisoners in her charge. She did so. All were executed immediately, and the American embassy was informed that their deaths were a warning not to aid the anti-Duvalier rebels in the Dominican Republic. Madame Max was devastated. Foolishly, she had presumed Papa Doc meant to declare an amnesty, and had named twenty-one of her friends.

Duvalier had not finished. Across Haiti, there was another wave of beatings and arrests. In the countryside, two peasants were reported to have been crucified by the Tontons Macoutes. According to the *New York Times*, Duvalier personally finished off at least twenty prisoners in the basement of the National Palace, his good left hand supporting his arthritic right as he calmly shot them with his own revolver.[31]

On 5 August, a small boat landed at Dame-Marie, on the far tip of Haiti's southern peninsula. It contained thirteen young men: twelve mulattoes and one black. They called themselves Young Haiti. They had received modest funding from the CIA, and were trained at a Special Forces camp in North Carolina.[32] They were led by Guslé Villedrouin, the son of a Haitian colonel from Jérémie who had been killed during Duvalier's terror in May 1963. Villedrouin was twenty four years old, and a former member of the United States Air Force. Another member, Réginald Jourdan, had fought with Fidel Castro in the Sierra Maestra. Young Haiti's plan was consciously modeled on the *Granma* invasion of Cuba. Its men meant to wage a guerrilla war, and recruit peasants to swell their forces.

In Port-au-Prince, Duvalier noticed the parallel. "We mustn't forget that Castro began with little forays too," he said. "These things start small and end up out of control. Above all we must always guard against groups like these getting new recruits among the people." As the men of Young Haiti began their long march east, he took command of the military response. Meanwhile, five fighter planes were illegally exported from the United States to Haiti. The State Department, still working with Duvalier even though the CIA was working against him, raised no objection.[33] Soon, the men of Young Haiti were being bombed and strafed. On one occasion, they shot down a government plane.

Amid the torrential rains of hurricane season, the men of Young Haiti would hold out as guerrillas in open country for an impressive eighty-three days, and survive at least ten skirmishes with government troops. But, one by one, they were captured. When seven remained, Duvalier devised a plan to smoke them out of the mountains. He would take revenge on what was, for most of them, their hometown: Jérémie. He sent to Jérémie a notoriously brutal army lieutenant, José "Sonny" Borges, who had been fighting the Camoquins in the east; a top Fillette Laleau, Sanette Balmir; and one of his most feared Tontons Macoutes, Saint-Ange Bontemps. Bontemps was a psychopath, remembered for his role in defeating an earlier invasion from Cuba. During that invasion, he was said to have stabbed a young Cuban to death, withdrawn the bloody knife, and then, with relish, licked it clean.

Borges, Balmir, and Bontemps arrived in Jérémie prepared to terrorize the mulatto population. Shops were looted. Houses were burned. Hundreds were arrested. Some were stripped, and paraded through the streets. Most were beaten. A few were raped. The vilest punishments were reserved for the Drouin, Villedrouin, and Sansaricq families, whose scions were fighting in the hills.

On the evening of 19 September, the Sansaricqs were ordered into trucks by the Tontons Macoutes. They were driven to a clearing in the forest. The moonlight illuminated a shallow grave, which had already been dug in the soft ground. The children were crying and clinging to their mothers.

One old man, André Jabouin, had been brought along by the Macoutes as a civilian witness. "Give me the little girl," he asked them, indicating two-year-old Régine Sansaricq, the youngest of those arrested. "I'll say I adopted her."

"Listen, Jabouin, to be a Duvalierist you have to be bloodthirsty," snarled a Macoute. "Where is your manly courage?"

He drew his knife, and plunged it to the hilt into the two-year-old girl's chest.

Her mother, Louise, screamed. "Shit on all of you, you pack of dogs! You'll pay for your crimes one day. Pigs, cowards, filth—"

Shots rang out, and she fell. Sonny Borges booted her lifeless body into the grave.

Her sons Jean-Pierre and Stéphane, six and four, saw their mother die. Now, Stéphane was crying.

"Don't cry," said Borges. "I'll dry your eyes for you." He took Stéphane by the hand, and then slowly, deliberately, pushed his lit cigarette into the four-year-old boy's eye.

By the time the Macoutes finally left the clearing, all the Sansaricqs had been horribly mutilated, and lay dead or dying. An eventual investigation by Peter Benenson, a British lawyer who had recently founded the campaigning organization Amnesty International, concluded that the total death toll during the terror—which became known as the Vespers of Jérémie—ran into the hundreds.[34]

The remaining men of Young Haiti were trapped in a ravine on 26 October, near L'Asile. When they ran out of ammunition, they threw rocks at Duvalier's troops until they could fight no more. Afterward, three of the invaders' severed heads were sent to the National Palace, to be photographed for the next day's edition of *Le Matin*. The picture was published with the caption: "Dr. François Duvalier will fulfill his sacrosanct mission. He has crushed and will always crush the attempts of the opposition. Think well, renegades. Here is the fate awaiting you and your kind." The body of another invader, Yvan Laracque, was propped up on public display opposite an exit from the airport in Port-au-Prince, next to the sign that read WELCOME TO HAITI. After ten days, during which the sun turned the swollen corpse noxious and the flies swarmed, the Liberian ambassador protested that the sight of it was an offense to the dignity of all men of African descent. Duvalier finally permitted it to be removed and buried.[35]

Only two Young Haitians were left alive: Louis Drouin, twenty-eight years old, a mulatto, and Marcel Numa, twenty-one, the group's only black guerrilla. They were kept for weeks in Fort Dimanche, and subjected to the usual treatment.

On 12 November, Haiti's schools were closed. Hundreds of schoolchildren and peasants were taken by bus to the cemetery in Port-au-Prince. Two pinewood stakes were driven into the ground. Before the live audience, and rolling television cameras, Drouin and Numa were bundled out of a jeep and tied to the stakes. A French priest offered them the last rites, which they declined. Both men used their last moments to shout curses at François Duvalier. A nine-man firing squad lined up, and then—in front of the peasants, the children, and the cameras—opened fire with rifles and submachine guns. For weeks afterward, this macabre footage was repeated on Haitian television.[36]

State Department papers reveal little concern about, or even interest in, the gruesome scenes being played out in Haiti. After the Young Haiti invasion was defeated, Tom Mann requested a briefing from the department's inter-American affairs team. It came back on 23 November, titled "The Multiple Dilemma in Formulating U.S. Policy in Haiti." This report made no mention of the torture and murder of children in Jérémie, the hacked-off heads displayed at the National Palace, the mass slaughter of hundreds of university students and schoolchildren in August, the rumor that Duvalier was now said to be shooting up to three hundred people a month in his own basement, or the constant, desperate invasions by Haitian patriots, prepared to risk the most wretched fates imaginable for even the smallest hope of freeing their country from this monster. The main problem with Haiti, it suggested, was that the worsening despair might help communists. There was also another problem, distinctly secondary: that Haitian oppositionists, American citizens, and many Latin Americans considered American support of Duvalier to be immoral. On the other hand, it argued, "direct access to Duvalier is necessary in order to get maximum advantage for the U.S. from Haiti's vote and voice in international forums."

The report laid out four strategies. The United States could actively encourage the overthrow of Duvalier; it could work with him fully despite his shortcomings; it could maintain a presence but make its distaste for his style clear; or it could continue normal relations, but deny him endorsement and economic assistance. The last of these, it concluded, was "clearly the least unattractive of the alternatives open to the U.S."[37] Haiti's vote had already bought Duvalier an airport loan. It was still buying him the protection of the United States.

Throughout 1964 and 1965, Duvalier continued to push the limits of American tolerance. A rumor appeared in the *New York Times* that he intended to declare himself emperor. It was denied immediately by the Haitian government. Though the relevant telegram in the American national archives has been withdrawn from the State Department file for reasons of "national security," other telegrams in the same file indicate that the rumors were true; or at least true enough to be taken very seriously. The State Department scolded the Haitian ambassador in Washington after signs at a carnival in Port-au-Prince read VIVE FRANÇOIS PREMIER.[38]

The State Department was also exercised by the arrival in Port-au-Prince of an Egyptian businessman, Mohamed Fayed, and his apparent acceptance into the Duvalier inner circle. A new Fayed-Duvalier oil refinery was announced. There were persistent rumors that Fayed was to marry Duvalier's favorite daughter, Marie-Denise. "While Fayed may say this to all the girls, there nevertheless remains possibility that for his part Fayed is in earnest re his alleged plans for investment in Haiti and is seeking [to] strengthen his ties with Duvalier by dynastic marriage," reported Timmons. "Normally family relationships do not carry excessive weight with

Duvalier, as witness his execution early this year of his brother-in-law Lucien Daumec, but on other hand Duvalier has a strong protective feeling for his own children and this might extend to a son-in-law."[39]

Fayed caused further consternation by associating with George de Mohrenschildt, an oil geologist of Russian extraction living in Port-au-Prince. Mohrenschildt was briefly questioned by the Warren Commission, owing to an unlikely friendship he had struck up with Lee Harvey Oswald in Dallas shortly before Jack Kennedy's assassination. In 1977, he claimed that this association had been entered into at the request of the CIA. He then died of a gunshot wound in an apparent suicide on the day the House Committee on Assassinations telephoned him to arrange an interview.[40]

Fayed's sojourn in Haiti lasted six months, and ended in comedy. He sent a pot of "crude oil" provided to him by his Haitian contacts to London for analysis. His British associates examined it, and reported that it was in fact low-grade molasses. Fayed's Haitian partners had dug it out of an abandoned French-era sugar plantation.[41] Disgraced, Fayed fled Haiti, while Papa Doc threatened vaguely to have him murdered. Eventually, he ended up in London, where, under the name Mohamed al-Fayed, he would achieve considerable fame during his ownership of the department store Harrods. Marie-Denise Duvalier, who had never lacked for admirers, soon moved on to Max Dominique, a captain in her father's guard. Dominique's wife was paid $17,000 to divorce him, and the American embassy obligingly issued her with a nonimmigrant visa in her maiden name to remove her from the scene.[42]

The most commonly recurring theme of American correspondence on Haiti was still the quest for communism. Papa Doc made his position clear, in his own style. He arrested Jean-Jacques Dessalines Ambroise and his wife, Lucette Lafontant. Ambroise was a founding member of a genuine, though very small, Haitian communist party, the Popular Party of National Liberation. They were taken to the National Palace, and handed over to one of Duvalier's favorite torturers, Luc Désir. Ambroise was beaten until his bones were broken and his organs ruptured, then confined in a *cachot*—a cell so small he could not move—while he slowly died of his injuries. Lafontant was subjected to a series of tortures, including the hacking off of one of her breasts while she was still alive, before she, too, died on the floor of her cell.[43]

Such actions demonstrated clearly enough that Duvalier was not soft on communism. He was allowed to carry on.

★

Many of those involved in the Cuban Revolution had believed fervently that the island's sugar industry was the source of all its woes. Che Guevara, in particular, had taken this to heart. As chairman of the National Bank and minister of industry, he became obsessed with the idea that the sugar trade was slavery, and that Cuba must diversify. On a visit to Moscow, he had attempted to persuade the Soviets to help him set up metalworks and sheet steel factories. They were dumbfounded: Cuba had no coal or iron ore, nor a skilled labor force. "Che could not find arguments strong enough to convince them," remembered Nikolai Leonov. "They gave him more and more calculations showing that it would be anti-economic. The discussion lasted days. He insisted. He explained that this would help him create a working class and a market."[44]

At the time, Fidel Castro had expressed confidence in Che's ideas. After the Bay of Pigs, he had told the nation that other Latin American regimes were jealous of Cuba's economic policy. "They saw Che arrive at the National Bank and have complete success in his work," he had said on 23 April 1961. "And that brainy fellow [Che's predecessor at the bank, Felipe Pazos] whom everybody considered a great wise man on economic questions packed up and left the country after he had been dismissed from the National Bank. They assumed that without the aid of these 'brainy' gentlemen the country would fall apart. The opposite occurred, because those extremely brainy gentlemen were really at the service of imperialism, not the people. We replaced them with compañeros who are intelligent and who went there to work not for imperialism but for the people."[45]

Between 1961 and 1963, sugar production dived. It coincided with a drought. There was a 14 percent drop in the sugar area farmed, a 42 percent drop in the amount of cane processed, and a 33 percent drop in unit yield.[46] For the Cuban economy, this was an unprecedented disaster. It began to look as if those "brainy fellows" might have had a point after all.

Painfully honest as always, Che admitted publicly that there had been too much diversification. Now, he realized that sugar was the only crop that would bring Cuba decent returns. "At the outset of the Revolution many of us were not aware of this basic economic fact, because a fetishistic idea connected sugar with our dependence on imperialism and with the misery in the rural areas, without analyzing the real causes," he wrote. At an international summit, he went even further. "The suggestion of having a 15 per cent increase in agricultural production was simply ridiculous," he said. "In the distribution of income, we at first gave too much emphasis to the satisfaction of social necessities, paying more equitable wages and increasing employment, without sufficiently considering the condition of the economy. . . . The structure of our economy has still not changed after four years of revolution."[47]

Fidel never blamed Che, publicly or privately, for the Cuban economic meltdown. But the Argentine's star had long been dimming within the Cuban government. During his visit to Moscow in 1963, Fidel was persuaded that Cuba's sugar monoculture could be justified in a Marxist-Leninist context by the international division of labor according to resources and need. Fidel took increased Soviet aid, and with it Soviet economic advice. He began to reverse Che's policies.

Fidel's ideological flexibility was showing itself again. During 1963 and 1964, he dropped constant hints to the United States that he wanted to talk, and that he hoped for détente. Che, by contrast, was growing increasingly hard-line. As Raúl told Aleksandr Alekseyev, "If a day comes when Guevara realizes that he did something dishonest in relation to the revolution, he would blow out his brains." The comment was repeated to Che, who remarked bitterly, "Scruples are sometimes harmful for government figures."[48]

The early 1960s marked the high point of Chinese interest in the third world. Che had always admired Mao, and had stated a preference for Chinese communism in the past—even in front of the Soviets themselves, which, according to Sergei Khrushchev, "did not exactly do him any favors." He agreed with China that the Soviet Union's post–missile crisis policy of avoiding conflict with the United States was a dereliction of its internationalist duty.[49]

The Soviets had never liked Che, and when he enthused about Mao they liked him even less. Wayne Smith, formerly of the American embassy in Havana and later posted to the USSR, confirmed that in Moscow Che "came to be regarded as something of a bête noire, or, even worse, a Trotskyite."[50]

At the same time, Che had fallen out with his first and most important advocate, Raúl Castro. Havana gossip had it that the breaking point had come in the summer of 1962, when Raúl had tried and failed to persuade Khrushchev to make the Cuban missile deal public. Fidel, so the story went, remonstrated with his brother and insulted him by sending Che next. Though that may have caused a temporary upset, Che failed to persuade Khrushchev, too, which vindicated Raúl. The story is not a satisfactory explanation for the final ending of a seven-year friendship that had endured many greater trials. More important, perhaps, was the fact that Raúl had grown close to the Soviet armed forces and developed a fierce loyalty to Moscow. He was now often heard referring contemptuously to Che as "China's man."[51] The Sino-Soviet split was being echoed in Havana.

The discomfort Che felt spilled over into his personal life. He fought constantly with his wife, often over his rigid insistence on sticking to his principles. A friend saw them argue over whether or not she could take his official car to go shopping. "No, Aleida," he insisted. "You know the car belongs to the government, not to me. You can't use it. Take the bus like everyone else."[52] He insisted, too, that all the official gifts he received on his travels abroad be donated to training centers for Cuban youths. He had been given a large house in Havana, but it was, according to friends, almost empty. His study contained almost nothing except for portraits of Lenin, Simón Bolívar, and Camilo Cienfuegos.

Che usually disapproved of his friends' extramarital liaisons, so the fact that he had one himself at this point may have been a sign of his unhappy state. The evidence presented itself in 1964 in the form of a baby named Omar Pérez, named after the *Rubaiyat of Omar Khayyam*, which Che had given to the baby's mother, Lilia Rosa Pérez.[53]

Something had to be found for this lumpen revolutionary to do. In 1964, Fidel and Che came to the agreement that the latter should become a full-time roving ambassador. Traveling would keep him out of Cuba, and give him space away from his family; for, though Fidel constantly offered to send Aleida with him, Che usually preferred to travel alone. In Che's absence, Fidel renewed his appeals to the United States.

Lyndon Johnson responded with a firm line. There would be no dialogue with Cuba until Castro broke with the Soviet Union. "I was bothered by the hardness of our demands," said Wayne Smith, then on the Cuba desk at the State Department. "How could Castro break ties with the Soviet Union *before* reaching an accommodation with us? How could he renounce Soviet military assistance when he still faced a hostile United States? How could he renounce Moscow's economic aid without being certain of finding another benefactor? Obviously, he couldn't."[54]

Fidel's renewed overtures came at a pivotal moment. The OAS was to vote on the mandatory termination of all diplomatic and trade ties with Cuba. It had been an unpopular policy in the hemisphere ever since the Americans had first suggested it. Now, though, it had a chance of passing—because of a cache of apparently Cuban arms that had mysteriously appeared on a beach in Venezuela.

Rómulo Betancourt had been alleging for some time that all Venezuela's problems were the result of infiltration by Fidel Castro. In 1963, Kennedy had asked John McCone to look for evidence. Just before Kennedy's death, the cache of arms was discovered on a beach: mostly rifles with the Cuban coat of arms sanded off. The cache had ostensibly been left by the Cuban secret service for antigovernment guerrillas. The CIA had presented one rifle to Bobby Kennedy, who had shown it to Jack just before he departed for Dallas.[55]

It fell to Lyndon Johnson to release the story. There was an international scandal. Fidel replied that the cache had been planted by the CIA. Nikita Khrushchev backed him up. At the time, this was roundly scoffed at by the international press. But the press at the time knew nothing of the existence of Operation Mongoose, and had little idea of the lengths to which the Kennedy administration was prepared to go to damage Cuba. Since then, at least two former CIA men involved in the region at the time have implied that the arms were planted by the agency.[56]

The effect on the countries of Latin America was profound. Fifteen of them now supported the breaking of relations with Cuba. Only four—Mexico, Bolivia, Chile, and Uruguay—still opposed it. Some in the State Department believed that Fidel had chosen this moment to make his overture to sabotage that vote. "Imagine the confusion and the loss of momentum had we responded positively to Castro!" said one of Smith's colleagues. "We would never have gotten the Latin Americans back together again in a united front against Castro."[57]

Later in life, Smith conceded that perhaps Fidel's overture had been a ploy. "Still, I wonder why we did not at least send a secret emissary to sound Castro out," he wrote. "We could have done so without delaying the vote in the OAS. . . . I think we at the working level would have been more inclined to do so if we had known about the Kennedy-Castro communications and been aware of the seriousness with which Kennedy treated the matter. We were not aware. Only years later did I find out about Jean Daniel's mission and about Bill Atwood's conversations in New York. When I learned of them, my immediate reaction was to wish we had weighed Castro's overtures of 1964 as carefully as Kennedy had obviously weighed those of 1963."[58]

★

Meanwhile, Che had begun his wanderings. He appeared at the United Nations in New York in December 1964, railed publicly against imperialism in the Congo, and was nearly stabbed by a would-be assassin on Second Avenue. He sent a message of support to the activist Malcolm X, who was also agitating against the war in the Congo.

From New York, he went on to Algeria, then toured Africa: Mali, Congo-Brazzaville, Guinea, Ghana, and Dahomey. He made a trip to China and then returned, via Paris, to Africa: Tanzania and Egypt. In Cairo, he visited

Gamal Abdel Nasser, whom he had first met in 1959. Nasser thought Che seemed unhappy. Was everything well between him and Fidel? he asked. Che replied distantly that he had many questions that he could not answer.[59]

Che's interest in spreading the Cuban Revolution across the world was developing into a secret plan, with Fidel's support, to bring Cuban guerrillas to the Congo. At his final African engagement, in Algiers, he gave a wildly inflammatory speech at a conference. Addressing the African and Asian delegates as "brothers," he told them it was the duty of the whole socialist world to fight imperialism. He demanded that the developed socialist countries share what wealth they had freely with the third world, and then launched a full-frontal attack on the Soviet Union's "immoral" exploitation of the low prices accepted by third-world producers for raw materials. "If we establish that type of relationship between the two groups of nations," he said, "we must agree that socialist countries are, to a certain extent, accomplices to imperialist exploitation."[60]

This was an unashamedly Chinese line, and both the Chinese and Soviet observers in the audience noticed it. As for Fidel, in principle he agreed with Che that the Soviets should be doing more to help third-world wars of liberation. But Che had made his speech at an inopportune moment. Fidel's hopes of détente with the United States had foundered. To save Cuba from starvation, he was obliged to rebuild the relationship with Moscow. It was not an easy task anyway, owing to his own inability to toe the Soviet line for more than a few weeks at a stretch. But Che had publicly insulted the Soviet Union, and that put the whole deal in danger.

Three weeks later, on 15 March 1965, Che landed back on the tarmac at Havana. He was met by Aleida, and by Fidel and Raúl Castro. Conspicuously, there was no press conference. From the airport, he was taken away for forty hours of secret talks with Fidel, Raúl, and others.

No eyewitness has ever revealed what went on in those meetings. The best evidence comes from what Che's bodyguard, one Argudín, told Che's aide, Daniel Alarcón Ramírez, known as Benigno; and what Célia Sánchez told the journalist Carlos Franqui.

"Shit, I'm worried," Argudín said to Benigno, during a break from his duties. "I overheard a very big argument between *el Fifo* [Fidel] and Che."

"What about?"

"They were discussing Chinese policy and discussing another Soviet leader."

Benigno mentioned a few Soviet names.

"No," replied Argudín, "it was the one that's already dead. The one they call Trotsky, and they said to Che that he was a Trotskyist. Raúl said that. Raúl was the one who said he was a Trotskyist, that his ideas made it clear that he was a Trotskyist."

According to Argudín, Che was enraged. He looked like he was about to attack Raúl, and was shouting, "You're an idiot, you're an idiot." He looked at Fidel for support. Fidel gazed back, impassively.[61]

Carlos Franqui adds that Fidel, too, had berated Che for his irresponsible speech in Algiers. "Guevara acknowledged that what they said was true, that he had no right to say that on behalf of Cuba, that he accepted his responsibility, but that that was his way of thinking and he could not change it," he remembered. "That they should not expect a public self-criticism, or any private apology to the Soviets, and with his Argentine humor he said that the best would be for him to punish himself, that he would go and cut sugarcane."[62]

Argudín said that Che stormed out of the room, slamming the door behind him. He repaired to the sanatorium in the hills at Topes de Collantes, in the Sierra del Escambray. High among thick, hummingbird-filled rain forests of mahogany and eucalyptus, Che spent a week enduring the crippling asthma attacks that panic had often brought on. His life inside the Cuban government was over. It was not at all clear what he could do next.

17

ANOTHER CUBA

★

ON 24 APRIL 1965, SEVENTEEN-YEAR-OLD LUCI JOHNSON WAS CROWNED queen at the annual Azalea Festival in Norfolk, Virginia. Watching proudly was her father, Lyndon Johnson, the president of the United States. The Johnson family had planned to spend that weekend at Camp David.[1] Then came the dramatic news. Revolution had broken out in the Dominican Republic.

"I had been concerned about the Dominican Republic from the day I took office, and indeed well before that time," remembered Johnson in his memoirs. "The Dominicans had lived for thirty years under the iron-fisted rule of dictator Leonidas Trujillo."[2] The dictator had been Rafael Trujillo. Perhaps the unfamiliarity of double-barreled Spanish surnames had prompted Johnson's mistake. Since Juan Bosch's fall in 1963, the Dominicans had endured the undemocratic rule of a junta. The power behind it was General Elías Wessin y Wessin, a hotly pro-American right-winger. Its civilian face was Donald Reid Cabral, a half-Scottish former car dealer from Santo Domingo. Reid Cabral was also hotly pro-American—the Dominicans called him "El Americanito," while the Americans knew him as "Donny Reid"—and right-wing.[3]

The International Monetary Fund demanded that Reid Cabral follow its experimental austerity measures. He complied with everything it suggested, and in doing so created massive unemployment and disastrous shortages in social provision. Consequently, the poor hated him. He also attempted to do something about the Dominican Republic's corruption. That was a worthy cause, but Reid Cabral achieved little—apart from annoying the elites who enjoyed the benefits of that corruption. The rich started hating him, too. He also attempted military reform, peppering the ranks with officers trained in the United States, and cutting defense spending. In doing so, he kicked away yet another prop from beneath his shaky power base, for the military hated to be interfered with. To maintain himself in power, he was obliged to reinstitute Trujillo-style death squads. By early 1965, the only significant support he had was that of the American government. A secret CIA poll revealed that, among the Dominican electors, approval for Donny Reid was running at 5 percent.[4]

In January, a broad Dominican exile coalition in Puerto Rico signed a pledge to invade their homeland and restore democracy. Juan Bosch was at the helm. Standing alongside his center-left Dominican Revolutionary Party (PRD) was the center-right Christian Social Reformist Party (PRSC), and some dissenting conservatives. Neither Bosch nor any other member of the coalition requested support from any of the three Marxist parties in the Dominican Republic, and on more than one occasion their offers of help were actually declined.[5] Eventually, the coalition would become known as the Constitutionalists. Its conservative and military opponents would be known as the Loyalists.

At the end of March, it was reported that Reid Cabral might postpone the elections planned for that year.[6] In any case, with both Joaquín Balaguer (who had commanded around half the public's support in the CIA's secret poll) and Juan Bosch (who had commanded a quarter) in exile, there appeared to be no chance of achieving a legitimate popular government by the ballot box. The Constitutionalists scheduled a revolution for January, but at the last minute rearranged it for 26 April 1965. Two days before that, the Dominican chief of staff, General Marcos Rivera Cuesta, attempted to arrest four of the military leaders involved in the planned rebellion. But General Rivera had not brought enough men to pull off the arrest. The military leaders turned on Rivera, taking him prisoner instead.

This forced an early start to the revolution and sent both the Constitutionalists and the Loyalists into a muddle. The news was broken on lunchtime radio, which was the first either Reid Cabral or the revolution's civilian leader, José Rafael Molina Ureña, had heard of it. The United States was similarly surprised. Its ambassador, Tapley Bennett, was in Washington. Many of the embassy staff were at a conference in Panama; air attaché Thomas Fishburn was playing golf with the Dominican air force chief, General Emilio de los Santos; and the naval attaché was, ironically, on a dove-shooting trip with Tony Imbert, one of the assassins of Trujillo. Reid Cabral spent the afternoon trying to muster support among the generals, but so profoundly had he annoyed them over the preceding year that the only one who would listen was Wessin. Even he could not be persuaded to stand up for his puppet, though he was, uniquely among the generals, inclined to fight the revolution.[7] Early the next morning, Donny Reid resigned.

Faced with almost no opposition, and supported by several senior military leaders, the Constitutionalists easily took the presidential palace. One of their leaders, Colonel Francisco Caamaño, a stout, balding thirty-two-year-old with a thin mustache and a commanding gaze, talked the guards into joining the revolution and had them arrest their own officers.[8] The generals suggested that a new military junta be appointed, which they would control. But the Constitutionalists, committed to civilian government and the return of Juan Bosch, would not consider it.

At half past four that afternoon, jets of the Dominican air force swooped low over the old center of Santo Domingo, and opened fire on the presidential palace. Unexpectedly, a Loyalist fightback had begun. But it had not come out of nowhere. It had come out of the American embassy. According to a cable that the acting head of the embassy sent to the State Department that day, "Our attachés have stressed to the three [Loyalist] military leaders, Rivera, de los Santos and Wessin, our strong feeling everything possible should be done to prevent a Communist take-over."[9] At this point, the Loyalists were not promised American military support; but it is plain that they had American moral support. The suggestion that a communist takeover might be in the offing, meanwhile, seems to have been a case of Chinese whispers. Earlier that morning, Loyalist generals had expressed to the American embassy their unsupported opinion that a few communist agitators may have been among the Constitutionalist ranks.

That afternoon, from the poor neighborhoods and the rich—but mostly the poor—ordinary men and women had turned out to celebrate the fall of Reid Cabral's junta. As the planes of their own air force zoomed overhead, the mood changed, and the people began to build barricades. Over the next few days, between four and five thousand civilians would spontaneously join the Constitutionalists in battle against the generals. Meanwhile, at the presidential palace, Molina assumed the provisional presidency, and named Caamaño minister of the interior. In practice, Caamaño was also directing rebel operations, for Molina's chosen defense minister had at that moment been stricken by an attack of hepatitis.

In Washington, the Chinese whispers continued. A telegram that went from the White House situation room to Lyndon Johnson at Camp David that day said the rebellion was led by PRD leaders who were "identified with the party's left wing" and "have been suspected of ties to the extreme left." Instead of Bosch, it suggested, the answer would be to bring back the Americans' preferred man, former Trujillo vice president Joaquín Balaguer. "Balaguer is firmly anti-Communist and enjoys the support of some of the country's best people," it said. "We could cooperate with him, as we have in the past."[10]

Alarming reports of looting, gun battles, piles of bodies in the streets, and twelve-year-old boys toting automatic weapons were telegraphed back to Washington by its excitable embassy. The Loyalists, headquartered at the San Isidro air base, retained control over the air force and the tank regiments of the army. "We are going to have to really set up that government down there, run it and stabilize it some way or another," Johnson told Tom Mann over the telephone that morning. "This Bosch is no good."

"He's no good at all," agreed Mann. "And if we don't get a decent government in there Mr. President, and we get another Bosch, it is just going to be another sinkhole."[11]

The one thing worse than another sinkhole was another Cuba. By 27 April, Johnson believed, "control of the rebel movement was increasingly in the hands of the rebel officers and the three major Communist parties in the Dominican Republic—one oriented toward Moscow, another linked to Castro, and a third loyal to Peking. None of these parties was extremely large but all were well armed, tightly organized, and highly disciplined."[12] This was an extraordinary overstatement. The three Marxist parties in the Dominican Republic were tiny, poorly organized, and bitterly divided. They had been excluded from the planning of the revolution, and were not invited to join it now, though some of their members tagged along anyway. They were the Popular Socialist Party (PSP), created by Trujillo in the 1940s, and now nominally loyal to Moscow; the Popular Dominican Movement (MPD), a splinter from the PSP that also had close links in its early years with Trujillo and his son Ramfis, now calling itself Marxist-Leninist, though it had attempted to ingratiate itself with Peking; and the 14 June Movement (1J4), similar to the 26 July Movement in Cuba. As recently as 1962, the 1J4 had been allied with the right-wing National Civic Union (UCN). Nonetheless, it was the only one of these parties that was not to some degree a creation of the Trujillo family. It did have historical links to Castro's Cuba, though its spell of conservatism had done nothing to nurture them. 1J4 had been permitted to train some young Dominican guerrillas in Cuba, though according to one of the Dominicans their training was "worthless." It had focused on mountain operations, and the fight in Santo Domingo would be urban.[13]

On the morning of 27 April, Mann told Johnson that, though Bosch himself was probably not a communist, he was surrounded by them, and they were "much smarter than he is."[14] That day, the Loyalists resurged, besieging the Constitutionalists on land, sea, and air. Santo Domingo descended into all-out war. Tanks rolled out from San Isidro over the Duarte Bridge, and into the narrow colonial streets of the city center, automatic fire blasting ancient plaster from buildings that had stood since the days of Columbus. That afternoon, Caamaño, Molina, and others went to the American embassy and requested that the United States mediate, to end the fighting and find a peaceful settlement.

Ambassador Bennett bluntly refused to help. He told Caamaño and Molina that the Constitutionalist rebels were in league with the communists. As such, he argued, they had no right to mediation. Instead, the Constitutionalists must offer total surrender.[15]

Caamaño and Molina were shocked. Not only were they not communists, but they had been actively anticommunist. Their support base ranged from democratic left to democratic right, and included much of the country's business elite. Their stated and sincere aim was to restore civilian government and hold free elections.[16]

Repeatedly, the United States expressed neutrality, but its actions spoke differently. The Constitutionalists had not bargained for taking on a superpower as well as the Loyalist forces, and were now presented with a horrifying choice. They could scuttle, or they could stand and fight the United States of America. Several members of the provisional government scuttled, heading into the usual Latin American embassies. From his office in the smashed and broken remains of the palace, Molina said he would rather die than betray the Dominican people; but he was abandoned by his own supporters, and was forced out that afternoon.[17]

The American line pushed the Constitutionalists farther to the left. With the departure of those moderate leaders who did not want to take on the United States, some leftist civilians who had joined the revolution were given the opportunity to rise up the ranks. But it was still by no means communist-dominated, or even communist-inclined. Caamaño, who now emerged as the leader, had a background as far from communism as it was possible to imagine. His father, one of Trujillo's generals, had coordinated the Parsley Massacre back in 1937. He himself had trained in the United States with the marines, and had for the previous year headed the pro-American junta's riot police. Now, quite unexpectedly, this scion of the extreme right was the democratic left's only hope.

Caamaño, and his fellow colonel Ramón Montes Arache, returned to the battlefield to fight on. In the streets of Santo Domingo that afternoon, and on the crucial Duarte Bridge, they fought hand to hand with their former brother officers. Untrained civilians under their command ambushed and blew up Loyalist tanks. Despite the Loyalists' superior firepower, the Constitutionalists had the large majority of the people on their side. By seven o'clock that evening, after a day of guerrilla fighting, they again held the capital.

The Constitutionalists seemed to be heading for victory. But the Loyalists had recourse to a higher authority. By 28 April, ships full of United States Marines were already anchored just off the Dominican coast. The CIA, too, was operating in full support of the Loyalist cause.

Antonio Martínez Francisco, a wealthy businessman and secretary-general of Bosch's PRD, had sought asylum in the Mexican embassy after Bennett had refused mediation. That morning, he was telephoned by Arthur Briesky, the second secretary at the American embassy, and asked to return there for an important discussion. He agreed, and a car arrived. In it were a Loyalist colonel and a CIA agent, who pulled a gun on him.

Martínez was taken to San Isidro, where, he said, he met Briesky, the American air attaché Fishburn, and a group of Loyalist generals. Shaking with such uncontrollable fear that he could not drink the coffee they offered him, he was forced to read an appeal over the radio asking the Constitutionalists to surrender their weapons.[18] The CIA had selected three obscure colonels from the army, navy, and air force to run the country, led by Colonel Pedro Bartolomé Benoit of the air force. Benoit requested the assistance of United States troops. But by this point the American intelligence services were beginning to put together a truer picture of what was going on, and it had transpired that only two of the Constitutionalist leaders had any hint of left-wing associations in their backgrounds. This was not enough to justify an intervention, so Bennett told Benoit that he could not request marines unless American lives were in danger.

"Regarding my earlier request," Benoit promptly replied, "I wish to add that American lives are in danger."[19]

"It's just like the Alamo," Johnson told the National Security Council back in Washington. "Hell, it's like if you were down at that gate, and you were surrounded, and you damn well needed somebody. Well, by God, I'm going to go—and I thank the Lord that I've got men who want to go with me, from McNamara right on down to the littlest private who's carrying a gun."[20]

Johnson did not trouble himself with the legal prerequisites of the United Nations or the OAS. The OAS held the principle of nonintervention dear. Conventions signed by the United States at Montevideo and Buenos Aires required that any such action on the part of any member state went through its council. But the OAS's sensibilities were not high on the list of Johnson's priorities. He summed up his feelings about that organization with the memorable phrase: "It couldn't pour piss out of a boot if the instructions were written on the heel."[21] Late that night, while the first five hundred Marines were deploying, Johnson summoned Republican congressional leaders Everett Dirksen and Gerald Ford to the White House. So eager was the president to share his achievement that he did not even take the time to change out of his pajamas. He told them, "I have just taken an action that will prove that Democratic presidents can deal with Communists as strongly as Republicans."[22]

In Johnson's mind, in Mann's mind, in Bennett's mind, and in the minds of the CIA and American military command, the idea that the Dominican revolution was communist had been implanted at the very beginning, and could not be dislodged. But the operation had to be presented publicly as an intervention to save American lives and property. "Your announced mission is to save U.S. lives," the Joint Chiefs of Staff informed the invasion force. "Your unannounced mission is to prevent the Dominican Republic from going Communist. The President has stated that he will not allow another Cuba—you are to take all necessary measures to accomplish this mission."[23] While still in the United States, the Eighty-second Airborne received orders that they were to support the Loyalist cause. The Constitutionalists were described to them as Castro-supporting communists.[24]

A total of twenty-three thousand American troops would arrive in the Dominican Republic by 17 May—almost half the number then deployed in Vietnam. Vietnam was almost seven times the size of the Dominican Republic, and had a population ten times the size. By the State Department's own figures, there were only around one thousand American citizens in the Dominican Republic on 30 April. There were three or four thousand lightly armed rebels. Operation Power Pack, as the Dominican action was known, was a massive intervention, involving paratroopers of the Eighty-second Airborne as well as the marines. It was supported from the earliest days by a full psychological warfare team and the CIA. The war was not confined to Santo Domingo: Dean Rusk suggested that covert intelligence teams be sent in green helicopters to every part of the country to hunt down communists, under the pretense of offering food, medical assistance, and evacuation for foreign nationals.[25]

"I think that there were some questions raised as to whether or not we needed that much force," remembered Cyrus Vance, then deputy secretary of defense. "I don't think there was any dispute on the desirability of that action initially, but there was considerable dispute both within and without the government on the question of acting before the OAS met." But as Johnson told Mann on the day the action began, he did not "want the rebels to win; he had just about lived down the Bay of Pigs and he [did not] want Mr. Mann to get him involved in another spot like that."[26] The lesson of the Bay of Pigs, as he read it, was that military interventions in the Caribbean required overwhelming force.

The following day, 29 April, Admiral William Raborn, the new director of the CIA, telephoned Johnson and told him that "Castro-trained guerrillas" had pushed aside the "slightly pink" Bosch people and taken over: "In my opinion this is a real struggle mounted by Mr. Castro."

"How many Castro terrorists are there?" asked Johnson.

"Well," replied Raborn, "we have positively identified eight of them."[27]

That day, despite still only having eight names confirmed, the American government released a list of fifty-three that it claimed were those of Castro-trained communists in the Constitutionalist ranks. American journalists investigated the list, and quickly found that some of the claimed "communists" were listed twice, were in prison, or were not even in the Dominican Republic. On a television colloquy soon after the events, Dan Kurzman of the *Washington Post* said: "I found that of the three [names on the list] who were supposed to have been given jobs by the Caamaño government, one turned out to be a die-hard conservative, another was a naval officer known to be a conservative, and another—"

"One of them was ten years old," interrupted Tad Szulc of the *New York Times*.

"No, let's not exaggerate," said Kurzman. "He was fifteen years old, and he'd never had an official job."[28]

The first signs of doubt in Washington poked through on 30 April. Bob McNamara telephoned Johnson, and told him in strong terms that he thought the president should not publicly blame communists for the revolution. The reason, he said, was that Johnson would have "a pretty tough job proving that the Inter-American system was being menaced by powers outside the republic."

"We all know they are," said Johnson. "What is wrong with my saying it?"

"You would have a hard time proving to any group that Castro has done more than train these people, and we have trained a lot of people and he has trained a lot of people," said McNamara; "to say you as President [have] personal knowledge that powers outside the hemisphere are trying to subvert this government or those people, I don't think you are in a very strong position to say that."

Johnson asked if the CIA could document Castro's involvement. McNamara replied that he thought not. Some rebels may have trained in Cuba, but there was no evidence that Castro had directed the training.[29]

That same day, the State Department prepared its legal defense. The military intervention had violated the charter of the OAS, among other treaties. That charter stated that a sovereign state's territory "may not be the object, even temporarily, of military occupation or of other measures of force taken by another State, directly or indirectly, on any grounds whatever." The only legal argument that the State Department could come up with was to emphasize that the military action "was not for the purpose of intervening in any Dominican affairs, whether internal or external, but was limited to the purpose of protection of human lives."[30]

This position was far from watertight. The OAS charter's use of the phrase "on any grounds whatsoever" meant that the occupiers' motive was legally irrelevant, even if it were humanitarian. In any case, the argument was abjectly undermined by the department's own files. Communications to and from Santo Domingo since 25 April had focused overwhelmingly on the threat of a communist takeover, and barely mentioned the need to protect human lives.[31] Conscious of this, Dean Rusk directed the embassy in Santo Domingo to find "fresh information" linking the PRD "with communist influence and violence."[32]

Johnson had only approached the OAS on 29 April, a day after sending troops. Now, he invited the three "wise men" of Latin America, Rómulo Betancourt, Pepe Figueres, and Luis Muñoz Marín, to Santo Domingo, in the hope that they would try to talk the Constitutionalists into a solution the United States could tolerate. Washington was still publicly professing neutrality when it came to the choice between Bosch and Wessin, though that day Tap Bennett accused Bosch of "mouthing vicious propaganda and playing communist game from safe refuge in Puerto Rico."[33] According to reliable newswires, American forces were advancing in front of Wessin's troops.

Meanwhile, at the United Nations, Adlai Stevenson was experiencing an unpleasant case of déjà-vu. He had been obliged to present the American case on 29 April. The Brazilian mission officer told him frankly that the case was poor, even in terms of protecting lives; citizens living in another country were there at their own risk, and could not be taken to provide an automatic excuse for armed intervention. "He said this type of US intervention completely destroyed our image in Latin America and throughout the world," Stevenson wrote to Rusk.[34] Meanwhile, the Cuban foreign minister wrote to United Nations secretary-general U Thant calling the intervention aggressive, and the USSR requested a meeting of the Security Council to consider "the armed interference by the United States in the internal affairs of the Dominican Republic."[35] On 3 May, the United States was obliged to block a Soviet-sponsored resolution calling for the withdrawal of troops. "Nothing has caused me as much trouble since the Bay of Pigs," Stevenson wrote sadly to Arthur Schlesinger, "and it goes on and on."[36] According to his friends, defending the Dominican intervention troubled him more than anything else he had been required to say at the United Nations in defense of his country. He would himself later remark that it took a year off his life.[37]

Just when it looked like things could get no worse, Johnson sent to Santo Domingo Kennedy's former amateur ambassador, John Bartlow Martin. By Martin's own admission, when he arrived on 30 April he did not know who Francisco Caamaño was. He spent that evening consulting his old friend Tony Imbert. Within forty-eight hours, he had made up his mind that Caamaño was a "dangerous man," and the sort of natural leader who "could become [a] Dominican Castro." Instead, he suggested, Imbert should take over the government.[38]

American forces were advancing from two fronts on the rebel bases. Caamaño contacted Bosch in Puerto Rico, and told him that it looked like the Americans meant to start an all-out attack. Bosch told him that Americans would not do such a thing. Caamaño should avoid firing on American troops unless they advanced into rebel territory, and talk to Martin.[39] Martin put heavy pressure on the Loyalist generals, and managed to broker a cease-fire.

On the face of it, this was a positive achievement. It probably prevented a full-scale pitched battle between American troops and rebels, which would have cost hundreds, perhaps thousands, of lives. But it was to the strategic disadvantage of the Constitutionalists, who had held the upper hand. Furthermore, even just a few hours after the cease-fire was signed, American commanders began to use it to play a double game. Over the next few days, whenever Constitutionalist cells sniped at forces entering their territory, the United States government (including Johnson himself) publicly denounced each incident as a major violation of the cease-fire and evidence of Caamaño's perfidy. At the same time, American commanders found it convenient to assume that United States troops were not covered by the cease-fire, and authorized massive military operations against the Constitutionalist effort.[40] The next day, Martin contacted Bosch, and reassured him that Washington had not, as he feared, "double crossed him," denying reports of an American bias toward the Loyalist cause. On 2 May, Martin told the Associated Press that the revolution was now under "the complete domination of Castro Communism."[41]

"What began as a popular democratic revolution committed to democracy and social justice very shortly moved and was taken over and really seized and placed into the hands of a band of Communist conspirators," Johnson elaborated that day. "Our goal in keeping the principles of the American system is to help prevent another Communist state in this hemisphere, and we would like to do this without bloodshed or without large-scale fighting."[42]

For those attempting at the time to piece together the American government's reasoning, the speech revealed an inconsistency. If, as Johnson put it, the revolution had at first been popular, democratic, and committed to social justice, it was a mystery why the United States had not then supported it.[43]

Even publicly, the American mission had now crept from protecting American lives to defending the hemisphere from communism. For the member states of the OAS, this confirmed their widespread mistrust of the American intervention. The next day, Rómulo Betancourt berated Dean Rusk at length for what he said was being perceived as "another case of unilateral intervention, with no collective backing." He also told Rusk that the Venezuelan embassy in Santo Domingo was reporting that the Constitutionalists were dominated by democratic groups, not communists.[44]

Martin went to San Juan that day to talk to Bosch, who insisted that the revolution had nothing to do with Castro or communism. This, he reported to Rusk, indicated that Bosch was "completely out of touch with reality." Bitterly, Martin observed, "[Bosch] has been turning anti-American, especially since I publicly labeled his movement communist-dominated."[45]

On 3 May, still at war, the Constitutionalists convened a national assembly in line with the constitution they wanted to restore. It was made up of a broad selection of balanced political interests. It included Bosch's PRD, the right-wing UCN, the Christian Social Reformists, and members of the military. Tap Bennett described this convention as a "lame effort [to] present specious image of responsible movement observing constitutional processes," and assured Dean Rusk that he and Martin were attempting to put together their own provisional junta, which would obviously be better.[46]

It was now apparent that the United States meant to choose the provisional president, regardless of what the Dominicans thought. Rómulo Betancourt warned Rusk that Wessin was not an appropriate candidate, for he had already been rejected by the people.[47] Rusk had already realized that Washington's fondness for Wessin was best concealed, and had the day before asked Bennett to tell Wessin that it was "neither in his interest or ours for him to become over-identified with U.S. at this point." He added, "It would be particularly helpful if he could be persuaded to stop playing the 'Star Spangled Banner' over San Isidro Radio Station."[48]

"We are not the aggressor in the Dominican Republic," insisted Johnson on 4 May. "Forces came in there and overthrew that government and became aligned with evil persons who had been trained in overthrowing governments and in seizing governments and establishing Communist control." Then he tried yet another reframing of his actions: the intervention as a peacekeeping mission. "Our Ambassador reported that they were marching a former policeman down the streets and had threatened to line a hundred up to a wall and turn a machinegun loose on them. With reports of that kind, no President can stand by."[49] Reports of that kind—and worse—had been coming out of Haiti on a weekly basis since 1957, and three presidents had found it possible to stand by. Only Jack Kennedy had come close to intervening against François Duvalier.

At the beginning of 1965, Bobby Kennedy had become a senator, taking the New York seat from his brother Jack's old foe Ken Keating. On 6 May, he gave an understated speech against Johnson's policy, drafted by Arthur Schlesinger. In it, he noted, "our objective must surely be not to drive genuine democrats in the Dominican revolution into association with the communists."[50] Two days later, Bennett was obliged to report to Rusk that the moderate Dominican politicians hiding out in the Colombian embassy, including the former Constitutionalist leader, Molina, and a former ambassador to the United States, Enriquillo del Rosario, agreed with Bobby Kennedy. "Molina kept insisting communists would have had no chance without bombing [from 25 to 28 April, at the United States' behest] and American opposition to constitutional government," Bennett reported. The Dominicans, he admitted, were "extremely bitter and enthusiastically place all blame on US, claiming Washington misinformed by embassy."[51]

By then, Martin had composed his new junta, though he had had trouble persuading respectable politicians to join it. Alongside his preferred military man, Tony Imbert, and the CIA's, Pedro Bartolomé Benoit, three obscure civilians had been sworn in on 7 May. Dean Rusk alerted Martin and Bennett that the American legal case for intervention had now shifted to justify the new focus on staying in Santo Domingo for what Martin estimated would be at least six months. The State Department now claimed it was acting within the OAS charter, and argued that articles 15 and 17 of that charter "did not preclude United States' placing armed forces in Dominican Republic for humanitarian purpose of saving lives." It even invoked the Punta del Este agreement from 1962, which Rusk was fully aware he had only forced through by bribing François Duvalier with an airport loan, to justify the intervention. That agreement, State argued, urged its members to take steps against "the continued intervention in this hemisphere of Sino-Soviet powers."[52]

To the OAS, the American government alleged Soviet and Chinese involvement, which it claimed gave it the power to act unilaterally. To the United Nations Security Council, it insisted that the Dominican Republic issue was one of internal "regional security," and therefore should be handled by the OAS.[53] In reality, as McNamara had already observed, there was little chance of pinning responsibility for Dominican communists on the Soviet Union or China. The State Department's hopes had briefly been raised by reports like that in *El Caribe* the same week. The newspaper alleged that the police had found boxes of grenades, explosives, and ammunition when raiding Constitutionalist posts in the city, all of which had Chinese writing on them. Eagerly, the Department of Defense investigated; but a few days later it was obliged to report internally that "actually, there were no Chinese markings, but several of the boxes had 'Made in Japan' stamped on them." The "grenades" and "bombs," it transpired, were fireworks—which, the department helpfully clarified, "make a flash-bang when shot into the air. These so-called bombs could also be the reason for many explosions heard in many areas, [which] never cause any damage."[54]

"In the early stages I think there was a general feeling in Washington that there was a substantial Communist presence," admitted Deputy Defense Secretary Cyrus Vance. "But I think as time went on and more information became available, people realized that this perhaps was not the fact."[55] Those people did not include Johnson himself, who even in his memoirs insisted that the communist threat had not been overstated, and "at least 1,500" of the four or five thousand armed civilians on the Constitutionalist side were members of communist parties or sympathizers. When the operation in Santo Domingo picked up remarkably few of the supposed Castro agents and Cuban-trained communists that he had feared, the president blamed faulty intelligence.[56] By late May, the CIA was insisting that "Communists did, in fact, clearly dominate the rebel movement between 28 April and 2 or 3 May," but admitted that since 4 May they seemed to have vanished.[57] In the absence of communists, the president tried to demonstrate to an increasingly doubtful public that he had acted in defense of American and Dominican lives when ordering the invasion. This culminated in a remarkable press conference, at which he claimed that before American troops arrived on 28 April,

> some fifteen hundred innocent people were murdered and shot, and their heads cut off, and six Latin American embassies were violated and fired upon over a period of four days before we went in. As we talked to our ambassador to confirm the horror and tragedy and the unbelievable fact that they were firing on Americans and the American Embassy, he was talking to us from under a desk while bullets were going through his windows and he had a thousand American men, women, and children assembled in the hotel who were pleading with their President for help to preserve their lives.[58]

This was fantasy. Neither American nor any other press reports, nor even the imaginative briefings Johnson received from the embassy in Santo Domingo, claimed that any embassies had been attacked, let alone the American embassy. No American civilians were hurt before the intervention. Around fifteen hundred people had indeed been killed in the first few days of the uprising; but almost all of them were civilians living in poor neighborhoods that had been bombed by the Loyalist air force, supplied with fuel, and egged on by the American government and military.[59] Johnson was ultimately responsible for the deaths he was now claiming justified his intervention. And, contrary to what Johnson repeatedly insisted, there was not even one verified case of beheading. This headline-grabbing claim caused him particular trouble. The president was reduced to telephoning Tap Bennett and pleading, "For God's sake, see if you can find some headless bodies."[60]

Still, Operation Power Pack had made François Duvalier happy. The American ambassador in Port-au-Prince reported that Papa Doc was completely in favor of Johnson's action. "Duvalier favors an authoritarian regime in Dom Rep, as far to right as possible, on assumption it would be friendly toward him or at least neutral," he wrote.[61] Soon afterward, Duvalier reminded Johnson that "peace and stability are contingent upon prosperity," and therefore the United States government, "assisted by international banking institutions dedicated to economic development," ought to send him more money. He also informed the embassy that the east of Haiti was now full of communists—ones that, no doubt, would prove extremely expensive to remove.[62]

John Bartlow Martin's man, Tony Imbert, was put in charge of the junta on 7 May. A week later, his troops began Operación Limpieza—Operation Cleanup—in Santo Domingo's Constitutionalist northern barrios. According to José Moreno, a Jesuit priest who observed the operation, American troops were overtly supporting Imbert, logistically and strategically.[63] The Constitutionalist defense was now in the hands of Caamaño, his steadfast ally Colonel Montes Arache, and their 120 largely civilian guerrilla units.

On the afternoon of 16 May, as the Caribbean rains pattered down, Moreno and a friend went into the rebel zone. "When we crossed Checkpoint Charlie at Avenida Bolívar," he wrote, "I began to fear that I might never return alive." Rebels manned machine guns in doorways and on rooftops around Independence Park. Down El Conde, the main street of the old town, there were armed rebels at every intersection. A jeep drew up and out climbed André de la Rivière, a French mercenary, with an assault rifle slung around his shoulders. La Rivière had fought in Indochina and Algeria, and had been sent by the Haitian opposition leader Louis Déjoie to assassinate François Duvalier in 1961.[64] Since the attempt had failed, he had been running a training camp for Haitians in the Dominican countryside. His graduates included members of Young Haiti, the invasion force that had recently attempted to topple Duvalier. Now, he was advising the Constitutionalists. Together, la Rivière and Moreno stood on a corner, while the Frenchman complained at length about the papal nuncio having asked him if he was a communist. In fact, he had been expelled from the French army some years before for right-wing tendencies, and *Paris-Match* reported that he had lately cooperated with the CIA.[65]

By this point, though the OAS had grudgingly approved the American action, it had in doing so lost face with the people of Santo Domingo. During Operación Limpieza, Tap Bennett reported that OAS-marked cars were being booed in the streets, and rebels waved banners saying, ONU sí, OEA NO (UN yes, OAS no)—a slogan that was widely repeated across the Dominican Republic.[66] At the United Nations, the Cubans and Soviets continued to push the issue, but, as the State Department put it in one memo, "we are trying to create a stalemate in which no resolution will be passed in the UN."[67]

Lyndon Johnson sent the lawyer Abe Fortas, an old friend, to Puerto Rico, in the hope that Bosch could be persuaded to concede. Fortas got nowhere. "This fellow Bosch is a complete Latin poet-hero type and he's completely devoted to this damn constitution," he told Johnson. Mac Bundy went next, to the Dominican Republic and Puerto Rico, and through him Johnson sent a message for Caamaño: "Tell that son of a bitch that unlike the young man who came before me I am not afraid to use what's on my hip." Bundy, in fact, soon came to the conclusion that the communist threat had been overstated.[68] Further, he argued, the provisional government would need to include Constitutionalists, perhaps even in the presidential role. In this, he faced the unflinching opposition of Tom Mann back in Washington, who had already tried and failed to bribe Caamaño to defect, and would only consider Loyalist rule.[69]

The fighting dragged on through June. In July the Constitutionalists accepted, without much enthusiasm, a provisional government under Héctor García Godoy. "We could not win, but they could not overcome us either," Caamaño told the people, in a stirring resignation address from the Ozama Fort. "It is true that we had to yield, but the invader who came to destroy our revolution had also to bend before the courage of our people. . . . But most important of all: there has been a democratic awakening in our national consciousness—an awakening against coups d'état and against administrative corruption, nepotism, and interventionism."[70] The Dominican revolution did not die quietly; and neither, it turned out, would Caamaño.

The American occupation ended in September. Juan Bosch was permitted, finally, to return. Criticism of Johnson's intervention continued. In an article for the *New York Times Magazine*, titled "How Many Dominican Republics and Vietnams Can We Take On?" Senator Frank Church argued that the United States had "downgrade[d] freedom by equating it with the absence of Communism; we upgrade a host of dictatorial regimes by dignifying them with membership in what we like to call the 'Free World.'"[71]

"Underlying the bad advice and unwise actions of the United States was the fear of another Cuba," said Senator Bill Fulbright. "The specter of a second Communist state in the Western hemisphere—and its probable repercussions within the United States and possible effects on the careers of those who might be held responsible—seems to have been the most important single factor in distorting the judgment of otherwise sensible and competent men."[72] Johnson never forgave Fulbright for this speech and was so angry that he banned the senator from state ceremonies and the use of an official jet.

Johnson continued to defend Operation Power Pack. To his mind, it demonstrated that a leftist revolution could be defeated if the United

States acted quickly, decisively, and on a massive scale. The experience in Santo Domingo would inform the later interventions in Grenada militarily, and in Nicaragua and El Salvador strategically. It would form the basis for what came to be called "shock and awe." From Washington, Power Pack appeared to be, as John Hay had said of the Spanish-American conflict over Cuba sixty-seven years before, a "splendid little war." But a leading authority on Dominican history, Professor Howard Wiarda, wrote that "if one were looking for a single day that one could identify as the day the United States lost the Cold War in Latin America, and throughout the Third World," that day would be 28 April 1965, when the marines landed in Santo Domingo. And, as the journalist David Halberstam put it, both Johnson's administration, and those that came after, would soon discover an unpleasant truth: "not all countries were as easy to get out of as the Dominican Republic."[73]

★

The drama in the Dominican Republic had overshadowed a new mystery in Cuba. Che Guevara had vanished. He had not been seen since 20 March, five days after his arrival back in Cuba. The only clue to go on was a letter he had sent to his mother, Celia de la Serna, in Argentina. He had told her he was leaving the government. He meant to spend a month cutting cane, and would then work in a factory for five years, to understand industry. He finished the letter with a warning that she should not travel to Cuba for any reason at all.

Frightened, la Serna replied on 14 April, advising her son to leave the country. "If all roads in Cuba have been closed to you, for whatever reason, in Algiers there's a Mr. Ben Bella who would appreciate your organizing his economy, or advising him on it; or a Mr. Nkrumah in Ghana who would welcome the same help," she wrote. "Yes, you'll always be a foreigner. That seems to be your permanent fate."[74] Uncharacteristically, Che did not respond to this message.

On 30 April, Fidel and many other leaders went to cut cane, in one of their regular demonstrations of revolutionary participation. Che was nowhere to be seen, and by now Cuba was alive with gossip about his whereabouts. "The only thing I can tell you is that Major Guevara will always be where he is most useful to the revolution," said Fidel to the assembled newsmen.[75]

Meanwhile, Celia de la Serna fell ill and died, without knowing what had happened to her son. There were many rumors. According to a report sent to Tony Imbert's office in Santo Domingo, Che had arrived in the

Dominican Republic on 25 April, and signed into the Ambassador Hotel under the name Oscar Ortiz. Later, he moved to Caamaño's sector. During one of the battles between Loyalists and Constitutionalists that spring, Che Guevara was shot down in a Santo Domingo street. His body was identified as Ortiz.

Imbert believed this story for several weeks, but it had been planted by the Cuban security services as a diversion.[76] Finally, in July, Che arrived in Dar es Salaam, Tanzania. He gave no indication as to what had happened during those few months, though several private letters he sent to his family and friends before he left Cuba survive. They were all written as good-byes. To his parents, he wrote: "I have loved you very much, but I haven't known how to express my affection. I'm extremely stiff in my behavior, and I believe there were times when you didn't understand me, but, believe me now, understanding me wasn't easy."

To his five legitimate children, Hildita, Aleidita, Camilo, Celia, and Ernesto, he said that they should endeavor to grow up "like good revolutionaries." "Above all, always be able to feel deeply any injustice committed against anyone in any part of the world. It's a revolutionary's most beautiful quality."[77]

But his most passionate letter of all was that to Fidel, resigning as a minister, a major in the army, and even as a Cuban citizen. "My only serious fault is not to have trusted you more, from the first moments in Sierra Maestra, and not to have understood quickly enough your qualities as leader and revolutionary," he wrote. "I have lived through marvelous days and, at your side, I felt the pride of belonging to our people during the bright and sad days of the Caribbean crisis. . . .

"If my final hour comes under distant skies, my last thoughts will be for this people and especially for you."[78]

He continued on to the Congo, to bring revolution to the heart of Africa.

18

ZOMBIES

★

AT THE END OF 1965, BOBBY KENNEDY ARRANGED A MEETING WITH State Department officials to discuss a tour he was planning of Latin America. He asked them what he should say about the Dominican intervention.

"No one asks about that any more," said Jack Hood Vaughn, the assistant secretary of state for Latin American affairs.

"Well, you and I don't talk to the same Latins," Kennedy replied, "because that's all they ever ask me." Kennedy offered him a bet that it would be one of the first three questions he heard in Latin America.

Vaughn took the bet. "If they *do* ask you," he added, "you can always tell them what your brother said about Cuba."

The room seemed suddenly to have filled with ice. Bobby was famous for his ability to transfix those who crossed him with a subzero stare. According to an aide who was present, this one could "wither tree branches a hundred miles away."

"Which comment of *President Kennedy*'s was that, Mr. Vaughn?" Kennedy asked.

Vaughn mumbled something about the United States not allowing another Cuba in the hemisphere.

"I hope you are not quoting President Kennedy to justify what you did in the Dominican Republic," Kennedy said.[1]

When he arrived in Latin America, Bobby Kennedy immediately won the bet with Vaughn. "I saw much progress and much retrogression as well," he said publicly. "Military coups, stagnating economies, unchecked population growth, tiny islands of enormous privilege in the midst of awful poverty: These, and the smarting wound caused by the U.S. intervention in the Dominican Republic, posed serious threats to the Alliance's bold hope."[2]

In Peru, he was photographed in a slum, kicking a football around with some children in streets running with sewage. Afterward, he got back into his car with Dick Goodwin, his brother Jack's former aide, who had accompanied him on the trip.

"These people are living like animals," he snapped, "and the children—the children don't have a chance. What happened to all our AID money? Where is it going?"

Goodwin told him that the AID money was still in the United States, held up while an oil dispute was being settled.

Kennedy sat back in his seat, an expression of disgust on his face. "Wouldn't you be a communist if you had to live there?" he asked Goodwin. "I think I would."[3]

Thirteen years earlier, another privileged young man had had an identical revelation when he visited the copper and sulfur mining country around Chuquicamata, Chile. He met a peasant couple who were dirt poor, and shivering in the freezing conditions. They told him they were communists, though the communist party was illegal. "It's a great pity that they [the government] repress people like this," the young man had written. "Apart from whether collectivism, the 'communist vermin,' is a danger to decent life, the communism gnawing at his entrails was no more than a natural longing for something better, a protest against persistent hunger transformed into a love for this strange doctrine, whose essence he could never grasp but whose translation, 'bread for the poor,' was something he understood and, more importantly, that filled him with hope."[4]

That young man had been Che Guevara. Witnessing Latin America's poverty had made a profound impact on his life. Now, it would make one on Bobby Kennedy's.

When Kennedy returned to the United States, he appeared on the TV program *Meet the Press* and said that American policy had to change. "If all we do . . . [is] associate ourselves with those forces which are against subversion and against Communism," he said, "then I think it is self-defeating and will be catastrophic." Finally, Bobby Kennedy began to reject the idea of a global communist conspiracy. He emphasized that there were differences between the USSR, China, and Cuba. He acknowledged that "anti-American sentiments are not necessarily the same as pro-Communism or subservience to our enemies."[5] He admitted some of his mistakes and those of the CIA that he was prepared to say he had known about. He wanted to regenerate the Alliance for Progress.

The following year, Kennedy broke with Lyndon Johnson's administration over the events in Vietnam. "All that boy has done since I became

President," Johnson growled, "is snipe at me. He's been running for office since I was sworn in."[6] Increasingly, it looked like Bobby might indeed run for the presidency. But there was more to that ambition than the familiar insatiable Kennedy appetite for power. Something inside Bobby seemed to have changed, and found meaning. This, after all, was the erstwhile attack dog of Jack Kennedy's foreign policy: a man who had wanted to fake bombings of American bases and embassies to start wars in Cuba and the Dominican Republic; a man who had masterminded a terrorist campaign in Cuba, and suggested extending it to American soil; a man who, quite possibly, had planned the murders of foreign leaders, and certainly their violent removal from office.

Since then, Bobby Kennedy had been on a personal journey. Now, he was a leading white supporter of the fight for civil rights. He was a stern critic of American misdeeds in Latin America and Southeast Asia. He was being reborn as the champion of the disenfranchised. By 1966, Bobby Kennedy was in the process of becoming, as Arthur Schlesinger described him, "the voice of American reason and conscience."[7] It was an astonishing transformation. And, as far as can be told—which, with his papers still closed to researchers, is not very far—it seemed to be genuine.

★

In May 1966, an election was held in the Dominican Republic, pitting Juan Bosch against Rafael Trujillo's former puppet, Joaquín Balaguer. The United States preferred Balaguer. An American intelligence estimate admitted Bosch would have the anti-American vote, but noted: "At the same time, many Dominicans will recognize that, without US economic aid and its steadying influence exercised through the OAS and the IAPF [the Inter-American Peace Force established in the Dominican Republic], no solutions to the country's grave political and economic problems are possible. Many such people will vote for Balaguer despite a possible distaste for the Yankee presence." Hints in the archives point to the United States government adding its financial support covertly to Balaguer's campaign, which cost an extravagant $13 million. As the national security adviser Walt Rostow wrote to Johnson, "nothing should be spared which will not be counterproductive to get out the rural vote."[8] The rural police and the Dominican military openly campaigned for Balaguer.

The campaigning was conducted in an atmosphere of extreme violence, especially in the countryside. Bosch supporters were beaten, and on some occasions tortured and murdered. Balaguer campaigners drove around in trucks, announcing through loudspeakers that their candidate was "the American choice."[9] Threatened by assassination, and unable to rely on police protection, Bosch was forced to conduct his campaign mostly over the radio.

At the polls themselves, there were allegations and denials of electoral fraud against Bosch. Either way, the campaign had ruined his chances. When the result came in, Balaguer had won with 56 percent of the vote. Bosch came in second, with 39 percent. The pro-Castro party, IJ4, commanded less than 1 percent.[10]

In power, Balaguer was the recipient of bounteous generosity from the north. During his first two and a half years in office, the American government gave him over $132 million in economic assistance, either grants or loans on favorable terms. It also bought 700,000 tons of Dominican sugar at two cents per pound over the world market price, giving the country an extra $28 million annually. Balaguer created tax-free industrial zones for American companies, froze wages for Dominican workers, and fenced in the trade unions. Much of the political opposition was exiled. Trujillistas crept back into power, and Balaguer's regime soon developed its own poor record on human rights. During his first two terms, between 1966 and 1974, more than three thousand left-wing political figures and activists were murdered.[11]

Faced with extermination, the Dominican left started to congregate in Cuba. Francisco Caamaño, the unlikely hero of the revolution, was sent to London as a military attaché. In 1967, he vanished. Secretly, he too made his way to Cuba. The pin-striped suit of a London diplomat was discarded in favor of combat fatigues. The United States Marine–trained scion of the right was going to join up with Fidel Castro.

After a few months of training in Cuba, Caamaño resurfaced in press photographs, lean, strong, and inevitably having grown an impressive beard. With the Cuban army training them, the rebels planned an imitation of the *Granma* expedition. "They changed the principal characters," explained one of Caamaño's guerrillas, Manuel Matos Moquete: "Caamaño in the place of Fidel, Amaury [Germán Aristy] in the place of Frank País; changed also were the scenes of action: Dominican Republic in the place of Cuba; Santo Domingo, in that of Oriente province; the Cordillera Central, in that of the Sierra Maestra."[12]

To the disappointment of the Dominicans, Fidel offered little more than quiet hospitality and moral support. "Caamaño did not understand, when he went to Cuba, that the Cubans could no longer act like they had under Che," Matos Moquete said. "The guerrilla wave had passed. Cuba was moving toward a policy of coexistence with its neighboring states, as it had always wanted."[13]

In February 1973, Caamaño and nine men would land in the southwestern Dominican Republic, at Playa Caracoles. He survived for some weeks, skirmishing with Balaguer's forces, before being wounded, captured, and summarily executed.[14] It was a doomed attempt, but a brave one. Today, Caamaño is commemorated in the Dominican Republic as a national hero: a man who lost his life standing up to a foreign-backed dictatorship.

There was no chance of Balaguer and Castro developing a constructive relationship, but François Duvalier liked the new Dominican president. Balaguer had the exiled Haitians who had been plotting in the Dominican Republic rounded up, bound hand and foot, and delivered back to Papa Doc at gunpoint. Full diplomatic relations were soon reestablished between the two countries. Balaguer and Duvalier signed another cane-cutting deal, whereby the latter sent the former twenty thousand Haitian cane cutters every year to work on Dominican plantations. Duvalier received $1 million, plus a bonus of $10 per cane cutter, and held back $1 of every $15 in their pay packets.[15]

Ramfis Trujillo was sentenced in absentia to thirty years' hard labor for his involvement in the murders of political prisoners during his brief and unofficial rule. Hard labor was one of the things Ramfis would never do. Under Balaguer, his former close associate, the Dominican Republic did not pursue him. He remained in gilded exile in Spain until, at the end of 1969, he crashed his car into another, driven by the Duchess of Albuquerque. She was killed instantly. Ten days later, Ramfis too died of his injuries, lamented by almost no one.[16]

★

From Dar es Salaam, Che Guevara arrived in the Congo with Cuban troops. They joined up with some former supporters of murdered Congolese leader Patrice Lumumba, hoping to establish guerrilla bases and spread Cuban-style revolution.

It was a disaster. In addition to his perpetual asthma, Che was soon struck down with fever, and with a spell of diarrhea that lasted for several months. The Congolese troops did not take to him, nor to the training schedule he attempted to impose. He lost his temper, and shouted at them in faltering French. "I told them that I would put dresses on them and make them carry yucca in a basket (a female occupation) because they were worthless, and worse than women," he wrote in his diary. "I preferred to form an army with women rather than have individuals of their category. As the translator interpreted my outburst to Swahili, all the men looked at me and cackled with laughter with a disconcerting ingenuousness."[17]

"Shit, Che, nobody knows what the hell we're doing here," remarked Emilio Aragonés, who had been stationed with him. In October 1965, eight weeks into his illness and deeply depressed, he was told that Fidel Castro had just made public the private letter he had written to him before leaving Cuba, reading it out during a speech.

Che leaped up from the log on which he had been sitting. "Say that again, say that again," he said. "How was that?" He began pacing around, swearing curses: "Shit-eaters," he said, "they are imbeciles, idiots."

"We started to move away," remembered his aide Benigno, "because when he was upset we used to leave him alone like a lion, we didn't want to cast a shadow. Nobody wanted to be around because we had already had the experience of seeing him angry."[18]

The public release of his farewell letter, Che believed, made it impossible for him ever to return to Cuba. It also caused problems among his men: "the comrades see me as a foreigner among Cubans, as when I started out in the Sierra many years before," he wrote in his diary. "Many things that had been shared were now lost. . . . This separated me from the troops."[19]

The adventure in the Congo soon fizzled out. Che went to Eastern Europe and began to consider again a hope he had long nurtured of returning to his own country, Argentina.

This put Fidel in a panic. Che would, he knew, be hunted down and killed if he went home. "There was an ongoing struggle with Fidel to keep [Che] from going to Argentina," remembered Victor Dreke, who had accompanied Che to the Congo.[20] Instead, Fidel tried to persuade Che to return to Cuba, but he would not. The revolutionary had to be found another revolution.

Fidel insisted that it was Che himself who chose Bolivia, but the evidence suggests that it was an idea developed by both men. In May 1966, Fidel met Mario Monje, the first secretary of the Bolivian communist party.

"Listen, Monje," Fidel had said, "there is a mutual friend of ours who wants to return to his country, and I ask you personally to choose the people who will protect this man. No one can doubt his rank as a revolutionary. He wants to return to his country. This has nothing to do with Bolivia."[21]

Monje knew it was the legendary Che Guevara he was being asked to accept. Overawed, he agreed.

Che arrived in Bolivia on 7 November 1966, and was soon made to feel unwelcome. Monje came to see him on New Year's Eve. The two squabbled over which of them should lead the struggle, Che describing Monje as "at first evasive and then treacherous." Even beyond Monje, the Bolivian leadership failed to demonstrate overwhelming delight at Che's presence, and seemed to know neither what to do with him nor with any revolution he might engender.

In Cuba a decade before, the rebels in the Sierra Maestra had been able to cling to a real sense that they spoke with the national will, and that they were riding a wave of history. In Bolivia, a wider network of practical support or even popular enthusiasm did not materialize. Deep in the jungle, painfully isolated, Che's band was being eaten alive by mosquitoes and *boro* flies. The men and women were obliged to hunt and scavenge for a meager diet of wild animals, catfish, parrots, and palm hearts. Within five months, they had to start eating their own horses. They suffered from malaria, edema, and exhaustion.

Fidel sent occasional, formal-sounding messages. In his diary, Che faithfully recorded every one. During the early months of 1967, the guerrillas began to skirmish with the Bolivian army. But morale was low, and Che's troops were weak. By June 1967, Che recorded that the situation was improving; yet still he had only twenty-four men, one of whom was badly injured, and no peasant recruits. When the United States announced that it was sending advisers to Bolivia, he wrote hopefully, "Perhaps we are witnessing the first episode in a new Vietnam." But the situation in Bolivia resolutely failed to make any such impact on the international media.

"I turned 39 [today] and am inevitably approaching the age when I need to consider my future as a guerrilla," he wrote on 14 June, "but for now I am still 'in one piece.'" He spent the day by a campfire in the jungle, eating stew and waiting for news from a party sent ahead to cut a trail. His asthma was now sometimes so bad it prevented him from sleeping. By September, the government forces—complete with their new advisers, sent by the CIA to hunt Che down—were closing in. Che heard over the radio that the president offered 50,000 pesos ($4,200) for information leading to his capture: "one crazy journalist thinks that US $4,200 is too little money, considering what a menace I am."[22]

In the middle of the day on 8 October, Che's guerrillas got into another skirmish with the army on the ridges of a ravine, the Quebrada del Yuro. They fought until the light went out of the sky. Che was shot in the calf of his left leg. Finally, he was captured, and taken to the town of La Higuera. He was kept in a school, tied up, for a day, while it was decided what to do with him. Felix Rodríguez, a CIA agent, arrived.

Che would not answer to an interrogation, but Rodríguez told him he just wanted to exchange views. He tried to get Che to "speak badly about Fidel," but his captive refused to play along. Che noticed that Rodríguez was not Bolivian, and asked him if he was Cuban or Puerto Rican. Rodríguez confirmed that he was Cuban. More than that, he had been a member of Brigade 2506, and was a veteran of the Bay of Pigs invasion.

"Ha," was Che's only reply.

Finally, the verdict came. Mario Terán, a warrant officer, approached Che with a semiautomatic rifle.

Dark eyes looked up to meet his.

"I know you've come to kill me," said Che. "Shoot, coward, you are only going to kill a man."[23]

Terán hesitated for a moment, then fired, aiming at Che's arms and legs. It was supposed to appear that the guerrilla had died in combat. Che did not cry out, but writhed silently with the pain. Terán fired again, this time aiming at Che's chest. Eventually, Che Guevara died there on the dusty floor.[24] His final hour, as he had predicted, had come under distant skies: in a schoolroom, in a village, in the backwoods of a country that had rejected his revolution, and for whose cause he had little enthusiasm.

Afterward, his body was taken by helicopter to the nearby town of Vallegrande. It was washed. The hair and beard were combed and trimmed. It was dressed in a clean pair of trousers, and laid out on a table, to be photographed and shown to the world. Che's glazed eyes were left open in death. The half-naked body, surrounded by his captors, covered with wounds and scratches; the tousled hair and beard; the beatific expression: every aspect of the photographs recalled the deposition from the cross. Just as, in 1919, the photograph of the dead guerrilla hero Charlemagne Péralte exhibited by the United States Marines had appeared to the Haitian people as an incarnation of Jesus of Nazareth, so too was Che, in death, called the Christ of Vallegrande. Just as in the case of Charlemagne Péralte, these photographs of a dead guerrilla had a radically different effect on Latin American public opinion than that which their makers had intended.

Back in Washington, Walt Rostow received the news of Che's death with satisfaction. His mood was visibly elated when he summoned his staff. "Gentlemen," he said. "I have very important news. The Bolivians have executed Che." He paused for effect. "They finally got the son of a bitch. The last of the romantic guerrillas."[25]

In death, Che would at last secure what he never fully had in life: Fidel's wholehearted admiration and respect. "Few times in history, perhaps never before, has a figure, a name, an example become a universal symbol so quickly and with such impassioned force," said Fidel. "This is because Che embodies, in its purest and most selfless form, the internationalist spirit that marks the world of today and that will characterize even more the world of tomorrow."[26]

While Che lived, Fidel had always kept him at arm's length. The Argentine had great courage and energy, but even greater integrity. The integrity was the problem. Throughout his short life, Che had always put his principles, however impossible, before the fundamental urge to win, and keep winning. In the cockpit of Caribbean politics, that could never work. While Che had lived, his integrity had been irritating and distracting. Only after his martyrdom did it appear noble.

Che seemed to be worth more dead than alive, not only to Fidel, but to radical politics. The photographs of the Christ of Vallegrande stunned the world. But it was Alberto Korda's picture of Che's living, lupine, hard-set face staring defiantly from beneath his signature beret at the funeral for the victims of the *Coubre* explosion that became the icon. That picture, which for years had hung as a single print on Korda's studio wall, was rediscovered in 1967. It found its way onto the cover of a reissue of Che's *Guerrilla Warfare*, and was soon adopted by American protesters demonstrating against the war in Vietnam and in favor of civil rights. Ultimately, "Heroic Guerrilla" would become the most reproduced photograph of all time, making Che Guevara's probably the most famous face in the history of the world. Millions of people have held it aloft on banners, worn it on T-shirts, daubed it on walls, referenced it on album covers, printed it on mugs and key rings and bags—though few of them have known much about the man himself. Che has become a universal symbol of revolution, without context. For a man who spent his life searching for a context in which to start his revolution, it was poetic justice.

★

Che's death removed one of the greatest sources of friction between Fidel and the Soviet Union, and allowed Cuba to retire from third-world adventurism. That had been bad news for Caamaño, but it was necessary if Fidel was to patch up relations with the Soviet Union.

Since the missile crisis, Fidel had been intermittently rude to Moscow. He had formed independent alliances with the pro-Chinese communist states North Korea and North Vietnam in 1966. He had published a treatise rejecting Soviet thinking on Latin America in 1967, and accused the Soviet Union of having ties to the region's oligarchs.[27] In 1967, the Soviet premier, Aleksei Kosygin, had traveled to Havana for a summit of the Latin American Solidarity Organization, and attempted to persuade Fidel to tone down his anti-Soviet rhetoric. Fidel refused, and deliberately pushed through a resolution deploring the role of the USSR in persuading Venezuelan communists to give up their armed struggle. Poison-pen editorials about Fidel and Che began to appear in *Pravda* and *Kommunist*. "Although propagandists for these revolutionaries sometimes, to give the appearance of being Marxists, speak of the role of the masses," read one, "their arrogant disregard for any form of struggle except armed struggle is all too clear."[28]

Now, though, Fidel's only option for survival was to get back in with the Soviets. The Cuban economy was in tatters. The island was stricken by fuel and food shortages. Its own sugar production could not compensate. Cuba's pact with China had fallen apart in 1966. The prospect loomed of Fidel's old foe Richard Nixon entering the White House—which raised the possibility of another invasion, or at least renewed hostility from the United States. Though the last few anti-Castro guerrillas surviving in the Sierra del Escambray had been taken out in 1967, the threat of counter-revolution had not disappeared, as an attempt that year, known as Project Nassau, reminded the Cuban state.[29]

Project Nassau was an ambitious plan led by far-right interests, and developed in the United States. It was directed by Fulgencio Batista's former crony Rolando Masferrer, and the American arms dealer Mitchell WerBell, an eccentric character with a waxed mustache and strong CIA connections. WerBell had also appeared during the Dominican revolution, on the Loyalist side, and would be treated by the United States Army in Vietnam with equivalent rank to a senior officer. Also involved was the Haitian priest Jean-Baptiste Georges, who back in the early 1950s had been François Duvalier's landlord. He was not on the extreme right, but was desperate to see Duvalier fall.

This unlikely coalition sought to strike first at Haiti, and remove Duvalier. Haiti would then function as a base, from which the project would launch a larger attack on Cuba. "This Papa Doc—wait until I get him—I'll crack his balls like hazelnuts," growled Masferrer.[30] As if the plan was not madcap enough, its makers invited a CBS camera crew to Miami to film a documentary of their efforts. This revolution would be televised.

The show soon spiraled out of control. During filming, one Cuban exile trainee guerrilla was shot in the eye on camera. He sued CBS for

$1 million, though the claim was later settled for much less. The television producers realized that they were mixed up in something beyond their control. Betraying something of their naïveté about the state of affairs in the Caribbean, they believed they were blowing its cover when they informed the CIA about the project. It is unlikely that the agency was surprised. It was sponsoring various anti-Duvalier and anti-Castro plans at the time, including Haitian Resistance, an exile group led by Paul Magloire, Daniel Fignolé, and Louis Déjoie, aiming at an invasion in 1968. It is not clear whether the CIA's interests extended to Project Nassau, though it had worked with Masferrer and WerBell in the past. Eventually, Project Nassau fell apart, and its headquarters were raided by customs authorities.[31]

In August 1968, Warsaw Pact tanks rolled into Czechoslovakia, where the government had attempted liberalizing reforms in defiance of Soviet policy. This was the sort of action guaranteed to elicit a vicious condemnation from Fidel. His staff trooped to a meeting shortly after the news broke, confidently expecting to witness a lengthy and stinging diatribe about Soviet imperialism.

But Fidel seemed nonchalant. He shrugged. "Well, the Soviet Union has done the right thing," Adolfo Rivero, a member of the PSP, remembered him as saying.

"It was kind of a surprise," Rivero continued. "We all expected a big blast against the Soviet Union, and it never came. Maybe he was thinking: 'Let's keep good relations with the Soviet Union, because they are the only thing keeping me in power.' The United States would never sympathize with him, and if he lost the Soviet Union he would have lost the only real ally he had."[32]

As the tall, bearded figure swept out, his aides were left in a state of shock. In view of his past, though, they should not have been. His decision to support the Prague Spring was, like all his important decisions, pragmatic. Fidel Castro had survived this long by playing the game of Caribbean politics better than anyone else. And he meant to survive for a good deal longer yet.

★

In March 1968, Robert F. Kennedy declared that he would run for president. Shortly afterward, Lyndon Johnson announced that he would not seek reelection. The prospect of another Kennedy presidency drew closer, with a transfigured Bobby now pushing a progressive line.

During Kennedy's campaign, he took Dick Goodwin to lunch, and asked him to describe his impressions of Che Guevara. Goodwin did so. Afterward, Bobby thought for a moment.

"You know, sometimes I envy the bastard," he said. "At least he was able to go out and fight for what he believed. All I ever do is go to chicken dinners."[33]

Across much of the world, 1968 was a year of violence. On 4 April, it fell to Bobby himself to announce the assassination of Martin Luther King to a predominantly black crowd in Indianapolis.

"For those of you who are black and are tempted to be filled with hatred and mistrust of the injustice of such an act, against all white people, I would only say that I can also feel in my own heart the same kind of feeling," he said. "I had a member of my family killed, but he was killed by a white man." It was the first time he had commented publicly on Jack's death.

"What we need in the United States is not division," he continued; "what we need in the United States is not hatred; what we need in the United States is not violence and lawlessness, but is love and wisdom, and compassion toward one another, and a feeling of justice toward those who still suffer within our country, whether they be white or whether they be black."[34] His words were driven by obvious feeling. The crowd, though distraught, applauded and whooped approval.

Two months later, Bobby Kennedy won the California primary, and moved a step closer to the Democratic presidential nomination. A new Kennedy era seemed set to dawn. That night, 5 June, at a quarter past midnight, he walked with an entourage through the pantry of the Ambassador Hotel in Los Angeles. An apprentice jockey called Sirhan Sirhan stepped out and opened fire with a revolver. Six people were shot, including Bobby. Three bullets struck him. One more passed through the fabric of his jacket. He lost consciousness on the floor, amid a chorus of screaming and crying all around him.

"Tonight this Nation faces once again the consequences of lawlessness, hatred, and unreason in its midst," Lyndon Johnson said on television that night, as Bobby Kennedy lay in the Good Samaritan Hospital, doctors fighting to save his life. "It would be wrong, it would be self-deceptive, to ignore the connection between that lawlessness and hatred and this act of violence." Referring to the assassinations of Jack Kennedy and Martin Luther King, and the attempt on Bobby, he continued: "those awful events give us ample warning that in a climate of extremism, of disrespect for the law, of contempt for the rights of others, violence may bring down the very best among us." It was an echo of Bobby's own speech on the death of King. But in place of passion was the stern tone of authoritarianism.

That night, Johnson paced around the Oval Office, unable to focus. Repeatedly, he telephoned the Secret Service, from the telephone installed under the table, and asked, "Is he dead yet?"[35] Early on the morning of 6 June, he was. Ironically, Bobby Kennedy—once the fiercest of his brother Jack's warmongers—had become, by the time of his death, the United States' best hope for peace.

★

François Duvalier had not survived as president of Haiti through any form of merit. Papadocracy had pushed the country into despair. In 1946, Haiti's external debt had been $4 million. By 1971, it would be $52 million. Around 80 percent of aid and loans granted to Haiti during Duvalier's presidency was stolen. By the late 1960s, workers' pay was long in arrears. Many Haitians could not find work in the first place. The International Commission of Jurists, based in Geneva, estimated Duvalier's annual income from the treasury alone at $10 million. The nation's gold and foreign currency reserves had been plundered, from a surplus of $900,000 in 1960 to a deficit of $11.3 million in 1965. Eighty percent of Haiti's qualified professionals had fled in the first six years of Duvalier's rule. By 1970, there would be more Haitian doctors in either Montreal or New York City than there were in Haiti.[36]

Duvalier sustained himself by deals with the Mafia. Having lost out in Cuba, the mob was looking for another Caribbean location for its casinos. Though Port-au-Prince, with its open sewers, barefoot street children, and armed bands of zombielike Tontons Macoutes in mirrored shades did not look much like a tourist paradise, the Mafia considered that there was potential for gated resorts. Furthermore, it developed a lucrative deal selling arms and ammunition to Duvalier. "He was worse than any crime boss I ever met," said Vincent Teresa, a New England mafioso, of Papa Doc, "and I've met more than a few."[37]

Aside from its continuing relationships with the United States and the Dominican Republic, Haiti was isolated. As a State Department officer told the marine commander Robert Heinl the same year, "As far as most members of the O.A.S. are concerned, Haiti might as well be in Africa, or on the moon, they have no involvement."[38]

In 1966, Graham Greene's Haitian novel, *The Comedians*, was published. Duvalier, though not a character in it, was a constant and malevolent presence, who liked to watch his victims die at the hands of the

Tontons Macoutes. The Macoutes themselves were portrayed as a rogue army bent on torture and killing. Luckner Cambronne's enterprising work on raising funds for Duvalierville was mentioned, as was Duvalierville itself. "On the flat shoddy plain between the hills and the sea a few white one-room boxes had been constructed, a cement playground, and an immense cockpit which among the small houses looked almost as impressive as the Coliseum," wrote Greene. "They stood together in a bowl of dust which, when we left the car, whirled around us in the wind of the approaching thunderstorm; by night it would have turned to mud again." There was a description of the attack on François Benoît for his supposed shooting of the Duvalier children's guards. Clément Jumelle's funeral was re-created, complete with its daylight hijack by the Macoutes and their stealing of the corpse, and reassigned to a fictional government minister. The CIA's "very direct route to Papa Doc" was asserted by one character, Dr. Magiot. "Papa Doc is a bulwark against Communism," observed Magiot. "There will be no Cuba and no Bay of Pigs here."[39]

Duvalier was upset. "The book is not well written," he told the Port-au-Prince newspaper *Le Matin*. "As the work of a writer and journalist, the book has no value." Critics disagreed, and Greene denied any exaggeration in his portrait of Haiti and its tyrant: "Impossible to deepen that night."[40]

Unabashed, Duvalier published a brochure, *Graham Greene Démasqué—Finally Exposed*, in French and English. It described Greene as "a liar, a cretin, a stool-pigeon . . . unbalanced, sadistic, perverted . . . the shame of proud and noble England . . . a spy . . . a drug addict . . . a torturer." "The last epithet has always a little puzzled me," Greene admitted. "*The Comedians*, I am glad to say, touched him on the raw."[41]

Alongside such slander against Greene, the brochure was full of glossy photographs of Duvalierville and other shining examples of Haiti's modernity and sophistication. Unfortunately, these photographs fitted the descriptions written by Greene, provoking hilarity in the embassies that received the brochure. Angrily, Duvalier withdrew his publication. When, in 1967, a Hollywood film adaptation of *The Comedians* was released, it was banned in Haiti. Duvalier's ally Balaguer ensured that it was not shown in the Dominican Republic, either.

Despite the scandal, the pope announced in 1966 that the Vatican was keen to improve relations with Papa Doc. Native Haitian bishops were installed; through them, the Catholic church assured Duvalier of "[its] entire collaboration in the political, economic and social domain." Duvalier's excommunication was lifted, and in a solemn ceremony he was reconnected to the Christian god. With a nod to both the Vatican and the

Americans, Duvalier confirmed that his policy was the "defense of Christian civilization against atheist materialism and the ideological intolerance of leveling and inhumane communism."[42] Two of his daughters married that year: Marie-Denise made it legal with Max Dominique, and Nicole married Luc-Albert Foucard, the tourism minister and brother of Duvalier's private secretary and mistress, Francesca Foucard Saint-Victor.

The happy family image did not last long. Duvalier's sixtieth birthday fell on 14 April 1967. Haitians were obliged to celebrate with a special carnival. Luc-Albert Foucard organized the four-day party. It included poetry readings (mostly from Papa Doc's own works), a military parade, and a troupe of beauty queens shipped in from Miami and the Dominican Republic.

On the second day of festivities, the trouble started. During the carnival parade, while the floats were passing by the National Palace, a massive bomb went off. It had been hidden inside an ice cream cart. Another exploded under a tap-tap, on which a group of musicians had been playing a specially composed merengue in honor of Papa Doc.[43]

Duvalier suspected that Max Dominique, Marie-Denise's husband, was responsible. In the middle of the night on 8 June 1967, he summoned nineteen senior officers, including Dominique and the chief of staff, Gérard Constant, to the National Palace. They were kept waiting for two hours before being loaded onto a truck. Sensing that her father was taking her husband to his death, Marie-Denise followed at a discreet distance in her Thunderbird, her submachine gun stowed under the seat. The truck drove in the direction of Fort Dimanche.

At the fort, the truck came to a halt in the pitch black of the rifle range. Its headlights illuminated nineteen stakes standing upright in the ground. Nineteen fellow staff officers were already tied to them. The men tied to the stakes were, one and all, loyal Duvalierists, and close friends of Max Dominique. They included Sonny Borges, the torturer from Jérémie; Captain Harry Tassy, who was rumored to have impregnated Duvalier's daughter Simone but refused to marry her; and a young male officer who was said to have seduced Duvalier's son, Jean-Claude.

Each of the newly arrived officers, including Dominique, was given a rifle loaded with a single bullet. Duvalier gave the order. They must shoot to kill their friends. There was no time to think or question. "Fire!" barked Papa Doc. Nineteen fingers squeezed nineteen triggers. Nineteen bullets found their targets. Not a single shooter had to reload. Not a single victim survived.[44]

Two weeks later, Duvalier decided he had not gone far enough, and should also kill Max Dominique. Duvalier's wife, Simone Ovide, and Marie-Denise are said to have begged for Dominique's life on their knees. Marie-Denise agreed to take her husband into exile. She and Dominique boarded a plane. As it soared up off the runway, Papa Doc kept his eyes on it. Almost absentmindedly, he gave a signal. Dominique's two bodyguards and his chauffeur were shot where they stood, on the airfield.

The president returned to his palace and went alone to his office, where he leafed miserably through old family photographs. He telephoned several close aides in tears, bewailing the loss of his daughter. Later, he ranted at his wife, for persuading him not to shoot Dominique. He had Dominique's father, Alexandre, seized and thrown into Fort Dimanche, and cabled to the son, "Give me back my daughter and I will give you back your father."[45] Dominique refused. His father would die in prison.

Duvalier's moping and raging continued unabated, until his wife threatened to leave him and join the Dominiques in exile. Then he lost his temper completely, and leaped at her, fists flying. His portly fifteen-year-old son, Jean-Claude, grabbed his spitting, howling little father, manhandled him roughly into a side room, and locked the door. For three hours, the president stewed, before he pressed the emergency alarm to summon the Tontons Macoutes to free him. When they arrived, he treated them to an oration on Mama Doc's wickedness, claiming that the better-bred likes of Eva Perón would never have behaved so shabbily toward their husbands.[46]

"As for the Communists, Haiti is one of the few Latin American countries on which they seem to have no designs," opined *Time* magazine loftily in 1967; "it is too helplessly backward even for them." This did not stop Duvalier killing communists wherever he could find them, or pretend to have found them. During 1968 and 1969, he murdered large numbers of Haitian patriots, and attacked the offices of Haiti's tiny Unified Party of Haitian Communists in Port-au-Prince, Pétionville, and Cap-Haïtien. Twenty people were slaughtered, and their corpses hung up at Fort Dimanche to impress the public and the Americans. The International Commission of Jurists cast doubt on Duvalier's commitment to any particular ideology, concluding that "the systematic violation of every single article and paragraph of the Universal Declaration of Human Rights seems to be the only policy which is respected and assiduously pursued in this Caribbean Republic."[47]

This did not bother Richard Nixon's new administration in the United States, which on entering office in 1969 embarked on a warming of relations with Duvalier's Haiti. It sent a new ambassador, Clinton Knox, who announced that Haiti required more aid. Duvalier was delighted, and Knox did not even appear to be embarrassed when he was unofficially described as an honorary Tonton Macoute. New York governor Nelson Rockefeller visited, and was received by Duvalier with friendly handshakes. The precise nature of Duvalier's various health problems was a state secret; but the president was so ill by then, said Rockefeller, that he had had to hold him up in front of the photographers. Papa Doc suggested that Haiti could provide a reservoir of manual labor for the United States, more convenient than the sweatshops of Asia.[48]

To everyone's surprise, Marie-Denise returned home for Christmas in 1969, and reconciled with her father. Max Dominique was pardoned. He too returned with their baby, named Alexandre after his murdered paternal grandfather. Marie-Denise fired her father's mistress as his private secretary, and took over herself.[49]

Duvalier's health was failing, and it looked like he would probably name Marie-Denise as his successor. There was another heart attack, and a stroke. By the end of the year, he publicly promised Haiti "a young leader," and on 3 January 1971 a national newspaper, *Le Nouveau Monde*, published its opinion that "a Duvalier should one day succeed a Duvalier." The National Assembly amended the constitution to remove the requirement that the minimum age for a president was forty years. A public holiday was declared for 22 January, and on that day Duvalier appeared on the balcony of the National Palace with his teenage son.

"He will succeed me not only as Chief of State, but as Chief of the Duvalierist Revolution," said Papa Doc. "Good luck, my son, Jean-Claude Duvalier."[50] The old man reached up and placed his hands on the shoulders of his massive boy. A cheer rose from the crowd.

In true democratic fashion, there was a national referendum a month later to confirm Jean-Claude's succession. It produced the truly democratic result of 2,391,916 votes for Jean-Claude, and none against.[51] On 8 March, Duvalier met Clinton Knox, to plan for the handover. The United States would support the succession. Luckner Cambronne was now appointed head of the council of ministers, and effective regent for Jean-Claude. Tension was high: the sidelined Marie-Denise Duvalier would not go anywhere without her submachine gun, even taking it with her when she walked the palace corridors.

The bedridden Duvalier called his top military men into his chamber, to address them. "My government has not been what I wanted it to be," he said shakily. "I've had to do things, things that weren't what I set out to do." Then the tears came. "My mission is at an end. I'm about to die. I know that choosing Jean-Claude was not the best option, but I did it because I wanted to guarantee the security of those who have taken such heavy responsibilities on my behalf."[52]

As the sun dipped in the sky on 21 April 1971, François Duvalier slipped peacefully away. A houngan came to perform the traditional Vodou ceremony, sending his spirit to Guinée. He drew a cross the size of Duvalier's body on the floor, and then clambered atop the corpse itself, exhorting Papa Doc's soul to leave. Several of those present swore that, just at the moment the soul departed, Duvalier's head gave a little twitch.[53]

For three days, Papa Doc lay in state, guarded by twenty-two Tontons Macoutes and twenty-two soldiers. Haitians, Dominicans, and Americans alike had long feared that Duvalier's death, when it came, would spark a revolution. It did not. Crowds milled around outside the National Palace, but remained calm. Nonetheless, the Dominican Republic's border troops were put on full alert, and American planes and ships patrolled. As *Time* magazine noted, "The U.S. is worried that Fidel Castro, who has been more bellicose than usual in recent weeks, may seize upon Duvalier's death as an opportunity to stir up trouble in Haiti."[54] But Fidel, too, stayed quiet.

The United States went further than just guarding against a Cuban invasion. The Duvalier family feared the return of thousands of exiled Haitians from Miami. During Jean-Claude Duvalier's swearing-in as President for Life, immediately after his father's death, United States Navy warships guarded the coast, and kept the returning Haitians out.[55]

Duvalier was buried on 24 April, the feast day of Baron Samedi. It was a hot and breezeless day. A mass was offered by the Catholic archbishop. A separate oration described Papa Doc as "the messiah." One hundred and one guns fired a salute, church bells rang out, and the coffin was drawn to the cemetery through streets festooned with flowers. Ambassador Knox was seen to be wearing on his lapel emblems of loyalty to Papa Doc and the new ruler, Jean-Claude, Baby Doc.[56] The cortège was heavily guarded—but many, even among the guards, believed that a high Vodouist like Duvalier would not die quietly. According to *Le Monde*, some guards stationed along the route scattered at the approach of his coffin, fearing that he might peek out.[57]

"Duvalier has *zombified* his country," former Haitian diplomat Rémy Bastien wrote from exile in 1966. "According to folklore, the *zombi* must be fed salt in order to regain his facilities. When Duvalier goes, who will feed salt, the salt of life to a whole nation?"[58]

Haiti was not fed salt. Instead, it was passed from Doc to Doc. François Duvalier left behind him a trail of wreckage and misery. Somewhere between thirty thousand and sixty thousand Haitians had been murdered directly by the state during his rule—hundreds, allegedly, by his own hand. Hundreds of thousands had fled. Of those who remained, one in twenty was a Tonton Macoute.[59]

In 1986, when Baby Doc Jean-Claude Duvalier was finally removed from office, his personal fortune was estimated at $450 million, and his mother Simone Ovide's at $1.15 billion.[60] Throughout the thirty years of François and Jean-Claude Duvalier's rule, Haiti was the poorest nation in the western hemisphere. It still is.

★

Even well before the Cuban Missile Crisis, the Washington-based administrations that dealt with Fidel Castro, Rafael Trujillo, and François Duvalier had concluded that Castro was the most dangerous of these leaders, and that Cuba was the one of their three countries that did not count as part of the "free world." Edwin Martin, assistant secretary of state for inter-American affairs under John F. Kennedy, described Trujillo's regime as "harsh" and Duvalier's as "brutal," but concluded: "The worst dictatorial regime was, of course, that of Castro in Cuba. Under him the people enjoyed neither democracy nor any improvement in well-being."[61] If those are the criteria, it is impossible to construct a serious argument contending that Castro was the worst of the three.

Fidel Castro's half century at the helm of Cuba provokes passions of a rare intensity, both for and against. He took over from a dictatorship, promising democracy and liberation. Cuba ended up a totalitarian state, administered largely through the armed forces. Hundreds of thousands of people left the island. The economy was wrecked. But these things also happened in Haiti and the Dominican Republic. From any point of view, Castro's Cuba was less murderous, less violent, less corrupt, more economically and socially egalitarian, immensely healthier and better educated, and less racist than either Duvalier's regime or Trujillo's. None of these men was a democrat in the sense of holding free and fair elections, though all claimed to speak with the authentic voice of their nations. At some points, each of them did, though from what little reliable information there is on free political opinion in any of these countries it is clear that Castro had by far the largest and most consistent popular support.

The Trujillo and Duvalier regimes were among the most kleptocratic, sadistic, repressive, and murderous in the entire twentieth century—a century that, tragically, provided plenty of competition. The State Department knew what was going on in these countries. And yet the idea that Fidel Castro was the worst of these leaders took hold and stuck, regardless of the evidence—and the bodies—piling up.

"Many criticisms have been leveled at the CIA for its activities during the 1950s and 1960s, especially in the field of covert action," admitted Dick Bissell, the agency's deputy director for plans at the time. "Having rethought this policy many times since then, I am convinced that the agency acted in the government's best interest in attempting to preserve the highly desired principle of democracy. From today's perspective, many episodes might be considered distasteful, but during the Eisenhower and Kennedy years the Soviet danger seemed real and all actions were aimed at thwarting it."[62] But though it talked a good game about preserving democracy, the actions of the CIA, and the United States government as a whole, consistently undermined and attacked democracy throughout Latin America and the Caribbean. This was at least as true, and arguably even more true, under the Democratic presidencies of Kennedy and Johnson as it had been under the Republican presidency of Eisenhower.

By the late 1960s, the main focus of American concern had shifted from the Caribbean to Southeast Asia. No lessons had been learned. In the Dominican Republic, the United States continued to support a corrupt and repressive regime. In Haiti, it supported something even worse. In Cuba, Fidel Castro came to rely on three things for his legitimacy: the economic support of the Soviet Union, the personal affection many Cubans continued to have for him, and the aggressive attitude of the United States against him. This last was perhaps the most important. The American embargo against Cuba, known in Cuba as *el bloqueo* (the blockade), must go down as one of the most agonizingly drawn-out mistakes in foreign policy history. Analysts may debate how many of Cuba's economic problems are the result of the embargo, and how many are the fault of its own government. Whatever the truth, the embargo certainly allowed the Cuban government to claim that almost any misfortune that befell the country could be blamed upon the American government. Internationally, Washington's contention that its embargo was based on a principled concern for human rights and democracy did not wash; the United States continued to trade openly and freely with any number of countries whose records on human rights and democracy were far worse than Cuba's. Slamming the door on Cuba made the United States look petty, undignified, and hypocritical—and, by contrast, allowed Fidel to look decent, open-minded, and righteous, even when he was none of those things. Not only did fifty years of *el bloqueo* fail to dislodge Fidel Castro; it made him a legend. All

Fidel had to do was stand firm as the United States attacked him, taking the blows, and refusing to back down. In the process, he became an icon to millions around the world—notably, an icon not of communism, but of a far more enduring anti-Americanism.

The American politicians who oversaw the secret war were neither stupid nor evil. On the contrary, most of them were highly intelligent, and filled with good motives. The United States of America was founded on the fine principles of life, liberty, and the pursuit of happiness, of all men being equal, of colonialism being inimical to freedom, and of it being the right of the people of a nation to organize their government as they see fit. Many of the politicians who ran this war believed sincerely that they were acting in accordance with these principles. They saw communism as the enemy of everything for which the United States stood. From their efforts emerged the fundamental problem of declaring war on an idea. With all the money, all the weapons, and all the most sophisticated torture techniques in the world, it is not possible to control ideas; still less, if one does not understand the ideas one means to control.

American politicians rarely understood why Latin Americans might be attracted not just to communism, but to an alliance with the Soviet Union. They saw anti-Americanism as a product of Soviet influence, though in reality it was the other way around. They could not see why anti-American feeling was so deep and so widespread in Latin America. Democrats criticized Republicans for wielding American power to negative effect in the region. They hardly ever questioned the United States' right to wield power over the hemisphere in the first place. Perhaps because the United States was a nation founded on strong anti-imperialist principles, successive administrations developed a culture of denial about the reality of how its power was used, and how it was perceived. They believed too strongly that the United States was incapable of being an empire to be able to see that Latin Americans were responding to it as colonized peoples always respond to imperial domination: either by bowing and scraping their way to a position of patronage, or by taking up arms and fighting to the death.

The logic of the duck test may be applied. The United States may not have been wearing a label that said "empire." But from the point of view of Cuba, Haiti, and the Dominican Republic it looked like one and acted like one, and when it opened its beak it even quacked like one.

The young senator John F. Kennedy warned in 1958: "If we take our Western Hemisphere friends for granted—if we regard them as worthy of little attention, except in an emergency—if, in patronizingly referring to them as our own 'back yard,' we persist in a 'Papa knows best' attitude, throwing a wet blanket on all of their proposals for economic co-operation and dispatching Marines at the first hint of trouble—then the day may not be far off when our security will be far more endangered in this area than it is in the more distant corners of the earth to which we have given our attention."[63] Four years later, his prophecy was fulfilled—by him.

The secret war in the Caribbean destroyed any hope of freedom and democracy in Cuba, Haiti, and the Dominican Republic. It toppled democracies. It supported dictators. It licensed those dictators' worst excesses. It financed terrorism. It set up death squads. It turned Cuba communist, and kept it communist for half a century. It did massive and permanent damage to the international reputation of the United States. It nearly triggered a nuclear holocaust. The fact that this war began, and was run, with good intentions is not a mere historical curiosity. It may be one of the most important lessons of our age.

A NOTE ON NAMES

★

The Dominican Republic and Cuba are both part of the Spanish-speaking Latin America. French is the language of the elite in Haiti. Most Haitians speak Kreyòl, blending French with various West African languages and influences from Spanish and English. Haitian Kreyòl was only formally transliterated after the events covered by this book. At the time, it was written in various ways, largely derived from French, and was known by its old spelling, Creole. The old spellings have been left unmodernized in the text.

The Dominican Republic and Haiti make up the island of Hispaniola, whose name in English comes from Christopher Columbus's name for it, Isla Española. It is sometimes romantically referred to by the names its pre-Columbian inhabitants gave it, Ayiti or Kiskeya (Quisqueya in Spanish). In this book, Hispaniola has been preferred for familiarity. Under colonial rule, the Dominican Republic was known as Santo Domingo and Haiti as Saint-Domingue. The capital of the Dominican Republic is also Santo Domingo, except from 1936 to 1961, when it was renamed Ciudad Trujillo. Historically appropriate names have been used at every point in this book. As a result, some confusion may arise over whether Santo Domingo is a city or a country. It is hoped that the context makes this clear. To complicate matters further, there is also an Anglo-Caribbean island nation called Dominica, which is not affiliated to the Dominican Republic. It does not feature in this story.

The word *America* is used here to refer to the continents. The country sometimes known by that name is always called *the United States.* Citizens of the United States are referred to as *Americans*, rather than by the term preferred in Latin America, *North Americans* (*norteamericanos*), which might be thought to include Canadians.

Titles, such as president or general, and the names of prominent buildings and organizations, such as the National Palace of Haiti and the Dominican or Cuban Popular Socialist Party, have usually been Anglicized in the text for the convenience of the reader. Exceptions have been made when the names themselves are particularly resonant: Great General Trujillo would not have the same ring as Generalissimo Trujillo, Fort Dimanche loses its evocative menace if rendered as Sunday Fort, and it would be bizarre to call the Tontons Macoutes Uncle Knapsacks.

The syncretic religion of Haiti is commonly known to English-language speakers as Voodoo. Academic writers call it Vodu, Vodoun, Voudou, Vaudoun, Vadoux, and other variations. In this book, it is Vodou, the spelling used by Haiti's Bureau of Ethnology in the mid-twentieth century. The spelling Voodoo might have been preferred for familiarity, but it is often used by non-Haitians to refer pejoratively to various forms of witchcraft, and has acquired lurid associations. Vodou refers exclusively to the religion.

The racial terms used in the text reflect those preferred by Cuban, Haitian, and Dominican writers of the 1950s and 1960s, most commonly *black* and *white*. *Mulatto*, denoting mixed race, is dated in the Anglophone world, but was used freely in the Caribbean at the time.

It is characteristic of Latin American and particularly Cuban politics to refer to leaders even formally by their first names or nicknames: Fidel (Castro), Raúl (Castro), Che (Ernesto Guevara). Rafael Trujillo, on the other hand, was almost never referred to as Rafael. He was always Trujillo, if not El Benefactor or one of his other titles. François Duvalier was often called Papa Doc, a name he himself invented. It is impossible to impose consistency on the names in this text without running into absurdity: to call Fidel, Raúl, and Che by the names F. Castro, R. Castro, and Guevara throughout would require either a tin ear for Cuban political culture or a trenchant determination to ignore it in favor of Anglophone convention.

Russian and Chinese place and personal names have been transliterated without perfect consistency, but with a nod to the forms common in the documentary sources of the 1950s and 1960s: Nikita Khrushchev rather than Nikita Kruschev, Peking rather than Beijing. Some of these, especially the Chinese transliterations, are old-fashioned, but they give an authentic flavor of the time.

NOTES

★

Abbreviations

ARCHIVES

BP	British Pathé film archive. Available at http://www.britishpathe.com/
FAOH	The Foreign Affairs Oral History Collection of the Association for Diplomatic Studies and Training, Library of Congress. Available at http://rs6.loc.gov/ammem/collections/diplomacy/index.html
FRUS	Foreign Relations of the United States. An ongoing series published by the Office of the Historian, Department of State, Washington, D.C.
HLMP	Herbert L. Matthews Papers, Butler Library, Columbia University, New York
JFKL	John F. Kennedy Presidential Library and Museum, Boston, Massachusetts
USNA	United States National Archives, College Park, Maryland

PERSONAL NAMES

AWD	Allen Welsh Dulles
DDE	Dwight David "Ike" Eisenhower
EGS	Ernesto "Che" Guevara de la Serna
FCR	Fidel Castro Ruz
FD	François "Papa Doc" Duvalier
FDR	Franklin Delano Roosevelt
JCD	Jean-Claude "Baby Doc" Duvalier
JFD	John Foster Dulles
JFK	John Fitzgerald "Jack" Kennedy
LBJ	Lyndon Baines Johnson
NSK	Nikita Sergeyevich Khrushchev
RCR	Raúl Castro Ruz
RFK	Robert Francis "Bobby" Kennedy
RMN	Richard Milhous "Dick" Nixon
RLT	Rafael Leónidas Trujillo Molina

The Secret War

1. RFK and FCR in Breuer, *Vendetta!*, p. 4.
2. Lyman Lemnitzer to Robert McNamara, 13 March 1962, in White, *The Kennedys and Cuba*, p. 113.
3. See chapter 13, "Throwing a Hedgehog Down Uncle Sam's Pants."
4. Detzer, *The Brink*, p. 195; Dobbs, *One Minute to Midnight*, p. 257; unnamed housewife in Detzer, *The Brink*, p. 167.

5. Blight et al., *Cuba on the Brink*, p. 412, disagrees strongly that the object was Berlin. The present author does not think it was, either, though Berlin may have been part of NSK's motivation. See chapter 13, "Throwing a Hedgehog Down Uncle Sam's Pants."
6. JFK in Fursenko and Naftali, *Khrushchev's Cold War*, p. 339.
7. Graham Greene, foreword, in Diederich and Burt, *Papa Doc*, p. viii; Espaillat, *Trujillo*, p. x.
8. *Small Wars Manual Fleet Marine Reference Publication 12–15*, U.S. Marine Corps.

1. The Entrails

1. FCR to Luis Conte Agüero, in Matthews, *Revolution in Cuba*, p. 67.
2. FCR, March 1954, in Franqui, *Diary*, p. 71.
3. Franqui, *Diary*, pp. 67–76; for JFK's cigars, see Pierre Salinger, "Kennedy, Cuba and Cigars," *Cigar Aficionado*, Autumn 1992.
4. Williams, *From Columbus to Castro*, pp. 42–44.
5. Ibid., pp. 237–41; David Geggus, "The Haitian Revolution," in Knight and Palmer, *The Modern Caribbean*, pp. 21–23.
6. Abbott, *The Duvaliers and Their Legacy*, p. 11.
7. Price-Mars, *So Spoke the Uncle*, pp. 47–48; Arthur, *Haiti*, p. 18; Rémy Bastien, "Vodoun and Politics in Haiti," in Courlander and Bastien, *Religion and Politics in Haiti*, pp. 42–43. As with all history preserved through oral traditions, there is some debate over whether the Bois Caïman ceremony is fact or in some part folk legend. French and Haitian accounts of it fit accurately with Pétro Vodou rituals of the time, and the evidence does point to Boukman triggering the revolution with a meeting in that place on that date. See the discussion at http://www.webster.edu/~corbetre/haiti/history/revolution/caiman.htm.
8. David Brion Davis, "Impact of the French and Haitian Revolutions," in Geggus, *The Impact of the Haitian Revolution*, pp. 7–8; John Adams in Pezzullo, *Plunging into Haiti*, p. 52.
9. FCR, 15 April 1954, in Franqui, *Diary*, p. 76.
10. James, *The Black Jacobins*, pp. 73–75.
11. Charles Leclerc, 17 September 1802, in Williams, *From Columbus to Castro*, p. 254.
12. Jean-Jacques Dessalines in Richardson, *The Caribbean in the Wider World*, p. 170.
13. FCR, 15 April 1954, in Franqui, *Diary*, p. 76.
14. Logan, *Haiti and the Dominican Republic*, p. 99.
15. Thomas Jefferson to the Marquis de Lafayette, 30 November 1813, in Westad, *The Global Cold War*, pp. 10–11. Westad's chapter titled "The Empire of Liberty" is an excellent explanation of the evolution of a distinctive American imperial ideology.
16. John Quincy Adams to the House of Representatives, 4 July 1821.
17. James Monroe, 2 December 1823.
18. Arthur, *Haiti*, pp. 21–22.
19. Nicholls, *From Dessalines to Duvalier*, p. 25; Jean-Jacques Acaau in Heinl and Heinl, *Written in Blood*, p. 181, and see p. 203n.
20. Logan, *Haiti and the Dominican Republic*, p. 40.
21. Carlos Manuel de Céspedes in Francisca López Civeira, "Relaciones controversiales y la construcción del partido revolucionario Cubano en Estados Unidos," in Lorini, *An Intimate and Contested Relation*, p. 13.
22. José Martí in Ferguson, *Makers of the Caribbean*, p. 46. FCR quoted Martí's letter in the Second Declaration of Havana, 4 February 1962.
23. Jenks, *Our Cuban Colony*, p. 42.
24. John Hay in Rojas, *Essays*, p. 25.
25. Benjamin, *The United States and the Origin of the Cuban Revolution*, p. 61.

26. Franklin W. Knight, "Cuba: Politics, Economy, and Society, 1898–1985," in Knight and Palmer, *The Modern Caribbean*, pp. 170–71.
27. Theodore Roosevelt in Williams, *From Columbus to Castro*, p. 422; Crandall, *Gunboat Democracy*, p. 9.
28. Theodore Roosevelt, 6 December 1904, in Logan, *Haiti and the Dominican Republic*, p. 54; see also Welles, *Naboth's Vineyard*, vol. 2, pp. 617–23.
29. Lippmann, "Vested Rights and Nationalism in Latin-America," p. 356. Bahía Honda was relinquished in 1912 for larger area at Guantánamo; in 1925, the United States gave up its claim to the Isle of Pines.
30. Theodore Roosevelt in Grandin, *Empire's Workshop*, p. 24; William Howard Taft, 1912, in Pearce, *Under the Eagle*, p. 17. The full story of the National City Bank's adventures in Haiti is an extraordinary one, but could fill a book by itself. Parts are told in Blancpain, *Haïti et les États-Unis*; Davis, *Black Democracy*; Logan, *Haiti and the Dominican Republic*; Diederich and Burt, *Papa Doc*; and other sources in the selected bibliography.
31. Woodrow Wilson in Logan, *Haiti and the Dominican Republic*, p. 118.
32. Blancpain, *Haïti et les États-Unis*, p. 32; Davis, *Black Democracy*, p. 153; Logan, *Haiti and the Dominican Republic*, p. 123.
33. Heinl and Heinl, *Written in Blood*, p. 381; report of Pierre Girard, French ambassador, to M. Delcassé, French minister of foreign affairs, 31 July 1915, in Blancpain, *Haïti et les États-Unis*, pp. 54–55.
34. Logan, *Haiti and the Dominican Republic*, pp. 130–31.
35. Abraham F. Lowenthal, "The United States and the Dominican Republic to 1965: Background to Intervention," *Caribbean Studies* 10, no. 2 (July 1970): 34.
36. Logan, *Haiti and the Dominican Republic*, pp. 61–63.
37. Herbert J. Seligmann, "The Conquest of Haiti," *Nation* 111, no. 2871 (10 July 1920): 35.
38. Pezzullo, *Plunging into Haiti*, p. 79.
39. Chapman, *Jungle Capitalists*, pp. 84–85; Richard H. Immerman, *John Foster Dulles: Piety, Pragmatism, and Power in U.S. Foreign Policy* (Wilmington, DE: Scholarly Resources Books, 1999), pp. 6–7.
40. Lewis S. Gannett, "The Conquest of Santo Domingo," *Nation* 111, no. 2872 (17 July 1920): 64; italics Gannett's.
41. Garner, *American Foreign Policies*, p. 87, citing the *New Republic*, 26 January 1927, p. 266; Johnson, *The Sorrows of Empire*, p. 192.
42. Spector, *W. Cameron Forbes*, pp. 39–42; Edwin L. James, *New York Times Magazine*, 11 July 1926, p. 1; in Garner, *American Foreign Policies*, p. 216.
43. Casuso, *Cuba and Castro*, p. 30.
44. Knox in Williams, *From Columbus to Castro*, p. 464.
45. Philip Guedalla, 1927, in Garner, *American Foreign Policies*, p. 70.

2. Good Neighbors

1. Logan, *Haiti and the Dominican Republic*, p. 68; Crassweller, *Trujillo*, pp. 25–33; Wiarda, *The Dominican Republic*, p. 35.
2. Crassweller, *Trujillo*, pp. 33–36.
3. John Gunther, "Hispaniola," *Foreign Affairs* 19, no. 4 (July 1941): 768.
4. Friedman, *Nazis and Good Neighbors*, p. 74.
5. Espaillat, *Trujillo*, p. 24.
6. Lawrence de Besault, *President Trujillo: His Work and the Dominican Republic* (n.p.: Washington Publishing, 1936), p. 29. As quoted in Galíndez, *The Era of Trujillo*, p. 16n.
7. Charles Curtis to State Department, 1930, in Crassweller, *Trujillo*, p. 212; Galíndez, *The Era of Trujillo*, pp. 12–15.

8. Souchère, *Crime à Saint-Domingue*, pp. 86–87; Hicks, *Blood in the Streets*, p. 12; Crassweller, *Trujillo*, pp. 69–71.
9. State Department message in Abraham F. Lowenthal, "The United States and the Dominican Republic to 1965: Background to Intervention," *Caribbean Studies* 10, no. 2 (July 1970): 47; Galíndez, *The Era of Trujillo*, pp. 16–17; Logan, *Haiti and the Dominican Republic*, p. 70.
10. Galíndez, *The Era of Trujillo*, p. 20; Crassweller, *Trujillo*, pp. 89–91.
11. Galíndez, *The Era of Trujillo*, pp. 188–89; Wiarda, *The Dominican Republic*, p. 41; Souchère, *Crime à Saint-Domingue*, pp. 104–5; for the wondrous tale of Pega Palo, see Espaillat, *Trujillo*, pp. 45–51.
12. Galíndez, *The Era of Trujillo*, pp. 26, 167.
13. Truman Capote, *Answered Prayers: The Unfinished Novel* (London: Hamish Hamilton, 1986), p. 27.
14. Oscar Michelena in Hicks, *Blood in the Streets*, p. 51; see also Crassweller, *Trujillo*, pp. 110–11.
15. Galíndez, *The Era of Trujillo*, p. 29; Taber, *M-26*, p. 22; BP: PM2963, 24 August 1933; BP: PM0733, 21 August 1933; Sumner Welles in Taber, *M-26*, pp. 23–24; see also Benjamin, *The United States and the Origin of the Cuban Revolution*, p. 88.
16. Franklin W. Knight, "Cuba: Politics, Economy, and Society, 1898–1985," in Knight and Palmer, *The Modern Caribbean*, p. 174; there is a fuller account in Schmitz, *Thank God They're on Our Side*, pp. 75–83.
17. FDR in Schmitz, *Thank God They're on Our Side*, p. 74, BP: PM0462, 1933.
18. Pezzullo, *Plunging into Haiti*, pp. 79–80.
19. Grandin, *Empire's Workshop*, pp. 34–35.
20. Norman Armour to Sumner Welles, 7 November 1934, in Heinl and Heinl, *Written in Blood*, p. 491.
21. RLT in Hicks, *Blood in the Streets*, p. 106.
22. Hicks, *Blood in the Streets*, p. 108; Abbott, *Haiti*, p. 49; Crassweller, *Trujillo*, pp. 154–56.
23. Hicks, *Blood in the Streets*, p. 109; Diederich and Burt, *Papa Doc*, pp. 40–41.
24. RLT in Quentin Reynolds, introduction, in Hicks, *Blood in the Streets*, p. vi.
25. Galíndez, *The Era of Trujillo*, p. 207.
26. Hicks, *Blood in the Streets*, pp. 122–23; Diederich and Burt, *Papa Doc*, pp. 43–44.
27. Diederich and Burt, *Papa Doc*, pp. 42–43; Galíndez, *The Era of Trujillo*, pp. 205–8, 223; Logan, *Haiti and the Dominican Republic*, p. 146; Abbott, *Haiti*, p. 50; Hamilton Fish in Hicks, *Blood in the Streets*, pp. 125, 128; see also ibid., pp. 130, 144.
28. Galíndez, *The Era of Trujillo*, p. 38 and n. Published editions of FRUS have shed no light on this claim.
29. *Listín Diario* in Galíndez, *The Era of Trujillo*, p. 38.
30. Galíndez, *The Era of Trujillo*, p. 39; see also Wiarda, *The Dominican Republic*, p. 45.
31. Crassweller, *Trujillo*, p. 80.
32. Friedman, *Nazis and Good Neighbors*, pp. 74–75; Gunther, "Hispaniola," p. 771; see also Hicks, *Blood in the Streets*, pp. 211–12.
33. BP: PM1015, 19 June 1939; Galíndez, *The Era of Trujillo*, pp. 212–15; Caballero, *Latin America and the Comintern*, p. 53.
34. Blas Roca, *Fundamentos del Socialismo en Cuba*, in Goldenberg, *The Cuban Revolution and Latin America*, p. 118.
35. Diederich and Burt, *Papa Doc*, p. 35; Ferguson, *Papa Doc, Baby Doc*, p. 33; Michael Largey, *Vodou Nation: Haitian Art, Music and Cultural Nationalism* (Chicago: University of Chicago Press, 2006), pp. 192–94.
36. Unnamed source in Diederich and Burt, *Papa Doc*, p. 44.

37. Abbott, *Haiti*, p. 55.
38. Diederich and Burt, *Papa Doc*, p. 48.
39. Ibid., pp. 45–46. Some of the correspondence can be read in Crassweller, *Trujillo*, pp. 160–62.
40. Diederich and Burt, *Papa Doc*, p. 55; Heinl and Heinl, *Written in Blood*, pp. 526–28.
41. James Byrnes to Harry S. Truman, March 1946, in Schmitz, *Thank God They're on Our Side*, p. 155.
42. Franqui, *Diary*, p. 41; Rolando Masferrer in Hinckle and Turner, *The Fish Is Red*, pp. 250–51.
43. Matthews, *Revolution in Cuba*, p. 42; Detzer, *The Brink*, p. 20.
44. FCR in Franqui, *Diary*, pp. 1–2.
45. FCR himself has admitted this. See Rice, *Rhetorical Uses*, pp. 123–24.
46. Matthews, *Revolution in Cuba*, p. 40; Detzer, *The Brink*, pp. 20–21; Balfour, *Castro*, pp. 26–27. See also La Cova, *The Moncada Attack*, pp. 18–19 and ff.; La Cova's book is passionately anti-FCR.
47. Balfour, *Castro*, p. 26.
48. FCR in Franqui, *Diary*, p. 109. See also FCR in Blight et al., *Cuba on the Brink*, pp. 181, 231. Sutton, *The Caribbean as a Subordinate State System*, part 1, p. 16; Matthews, *Revolution in Cuba*, pp. 45–46; Franqui, *Diary*, p. 41; Ameringer, *The Caribbean Legion*, p. 56; Phillips, *Cuba*, pp. 242–43.
49. FCR in Franqui, *Diary*, pp. 12–14; Matthews, *Revolution in Cuba*, p. 46; Roy R. Rubottom, 13 February 1990, FAOH.
50. Reid-Henry, *Fidel and Che*, p. 48.
51. Alex Pompez in Paterson, *Contesting Castro*, p. 51. This story has been fiercely debated.
52. FD in Diederich and Burt, *Papa Doc*, p. 58.
53. Memorandum of a conversation between Val Washington and William Wieland, 8 June 1959, USNA: RG 59, entry 3148, box 2, Haiti.
54. Logan, *Haiti and the Dominican Republic*, p. 152.
55. Westad, *The Global Cold War*, p. 118; Halle, *The Cold War as History*, p. 237; Harry S. Truman, 12 March 1947.
56. CIA, "Soviet Objectives in Latin America," 1 November 1947, in Westad, *The Global Cold War*, p. 146; Anthony P. Maingot, "Caribbean International Relations," in Knight and Palmer, *The Modern Caribbean*, p. 261.
57. JFD in Immerman, *The CIA in Guatemala*, p. 10; Westad, *The Global Cold War*, p. 55; Joseph Stalin in Prizel, *Latin America Through Soviet Eyes*, p. 1; Andrew and Mitrokhin, *The Mitrokhin Archive II*, p. 27.
58. Galíndez, *The Era of Trujillo*, pp. 61–64, 235; Souchère, *Crime à Saint-Domingue*, p. 109; Crassweller, *Trujillo*, pp. 218–20.
59. George Kennan in Crandall, *Gunboat Democracy*, p. 17.
60. Reid-Henry, *Fidel and Che*, p. 56.
61. BP: PM2589, 1952.
62. FCR in Taber, *M-26*, p. 30.
63. FCR in Matthews, *Revolution in Cuba*, p. 33.
64. Memorandum of conversation between Willard L. Beaulac and Miguel Angel de la Campa, 22 March 1952, FRUS 1952–54, vol. 4, p. 869; Bonsal, *Cuba, Castro, and the United States*, p. 11.
65. DDE in Brendon, *Ike*, p. 205; Dockrill and Hopkins, *The Cold War*, p. 57.
66. Schlesinger, *A Thousand Days*, p. 205; Brendon, *Ike*, pp. 229–30; Chapman, *Jungle Capitalists*, p. 128; Garthoff, *A Journey Through the Cold War*, pp. 41–42.
67. Schmitz, *Thank God They're on Our Side*, p. 180.

3. Quacking Like a Duck

1. Record of conversation, 25 July 1953, FRUS 1952–54, vol. 4, p. 897.
2. Balfour, *Castro*, p. 37; Matthews, *Revolution in Cuba*, p. 51.
3. FRUS 1958–60, vol. 4, p. 310.
4. Andrew and Mitrokhin, *The Mitrokhin Archive II*, p. 34.
5. Antolín Falcón in Franqui, *Diary*, p. 54.
6. RCR in Matthews, *Revolution in Cuba*, p. 53.
7. Balfour, *Castro*, p. 38.
8. Boris Luis Santa Coloma in Franqui, *Diary*, p. 57.
9. FCR in Matthews, *Revolution in Cuba*, p. 55.
10. Taber, *M-26*, pp. 32–41; Matthews, *Revolution in Cuba*, pp. 56–58; La Cova, *The Moncada Attack*, pp. 92–99. La Cova disputes many of the usual details of the story as it is conventionally told, such as the exact place of Renato Guitart's death. La Cova rightly criticizes the conventional story for having been mythologized to some extent to build a positive image of the Cuban Revolution, but his account suffers equally from the opposite tendency.
11. Abel Santamaría via Haydée Santamaría, in Matthews, *Revolution in Cuba*, pp. 59–60; see also Franqui, *Diary*, pp. 60–61.
12. According to FCR, in Santamaría, *Moncada*, p. 111. There are photographs in the modern museum at the Moncada Barracks showing the extent of the tortures. The extent of the tortures is disputed by La Cova, *The Moncada Attack*, pp. 164–46.
13. Jesús Montané in Taber, *M-26*, p. 14.
14. Franqui, *Diary*, p. 61; García, *Veintiseis*, pp. 113–14. The story, repeated by FCR during his subsequent trial, that Haydée Santamaría was presented with her brother's eyeball by a torturer during these interrogations is almost certainly apocryphal.
15. Haydée Santamaría in Matthews, *Revolution in Cuba*, p. 64.
16. Matthews, *Revolution in Cuba*, p. 58.
17. Taber, *M-26*, pp. 41–45; Matthews, *Revolution in Cuba*, p. 62.
18. Record of a conversation between John L. Topping and Aurelio Concheso, Washington, 1 September 1953, FRUS 1952–54, vol. 4, p. 899.
19. PSP statement in Matthews, *Revolution in Cuba*, p. 50; see also George Volsky, "Cuba," in Szulc, *The United States and the Caribbean*, p. 99.
20. Juan Almeida in Matthews, *Revolution in Cuba*, p. 63.
21. Taber, *M-26*, pp. 45–47; Matthews, *Revolution in Cuba*, p. 64. Reid-Henry, *Fidel and Che*, pp. 74–77, reconstructs part of what may have been the original speech.
22. DDE to Jenner, 30 November 1953, in Brendon, *Ike*, p. 242; Dockrill and Hopkins, *The Cold War*, pp. 56–60.
23. Andrew and Mitrokhin, *The Mitrokhin Archive II*, pp. 27–28.
24. Alexander Wiley in Immerman, *The CIA in Guatemala*, pp. 102–3. See also JFD in Rabe, *Eisenhower and Latin America*, p. 30.
25. Richard Patterson in Immerman, *The CIA in Guatemala*, p. 102.
26. RLT in Galíndez, *The Era of Trujillo*, p. 236.
27. See FRUS 1952–54, vol. 4, pp. 933–42.
28. Schmitz, *Thank God They're on Our Side*, pp. 193–94; Anderson, *Che Guevara*, p. 122.
29. Jorge Ubico in Grose, *Gentleman Spy*, p. 369.
30. See Goldenberg, *The Cuban Revolution and Latin America*, p. 71.
31. William Prescott Allen to DDE, in Grose, *Gentleman Spy*, p. 369.
32. Grose, *Gentleman Spy*, pp. 368–69.
33. John E. Peurifoy in Weiner, *Legacy of Ashes*, p. 107; and in Brendon, *Ike*, p. 284. See

also Schmitz, *Thank God They're on Our Side*, p. 195; Rabe, *Eisenhower and Latin America*, p. 47.

34. Weiner, *Legacy of Ashes*, pp. 108–9; Grandin, *Empire's Workshop*, p. 44.
35. Guillermo Toriello and JFD in Immerman, *The CIA in Guatemala*, pp. 147–48. See also Rabe, *Eisenhower and Latin America*, pp. 51–52.
36. Westad, *The Global Cold War*, pp. 146–48; Weiner, *Legacy of Ashes*, p. 112; Brendon, *Ike*, pp. 284–85.
37. For various legends of EGS's adventures in Guatemala, see Chapman, *Jungle Capitalists*, p. 143; Grose, *Gentleman Spy*, pp. 383–84.
38. Anderson, *Che Guevara*, pp. 17–18.
39. Ibid., p. 35.
40. Miriam Urrutia, in ibid., p. 36.
41. EGS in Franqui, *Diary*, p. 21.
42. Rojo, *My Friend Che*, p. 25. Rojo's book, as noted by EGS's first wife in Gadea, *Ernesto*, pp. xiii–xv, claims more intimacy with EGS than he really had. It does nonetheless contain some useful and accurate insights. To be fair, Gadea also claims more intimacy with EGS than she really had. See Anderson, *Che Guevara*, p. 775.
43. Rojo, *My Friend Che*, pp. 40–41; see also Franqui, *Diary*, p. 23.
44. Anderson, *Che Guevara*, p. 120; Gadea, *Ernesto*, p. 4; Rojo, *My Friend Che*, pp. 40–41, 50–51.
45. EGS in Anderson, *Che Guevara*, p. 152.
46. Gadea, *Ernesto*, pp. 40–41.
47. Anderson, *Che Guevara*, p. 572.
48. Castañeda, *Compañero*, p. 73.
49. Gadea, *Ernesto*, p. 56.
50. Phillips, *The Night Watch*, p. 54. Castañeda, *Compañero*, p. 74, casts some doubt on this story on the basis that there is no trace of the file in the CIA's archives. Phillips may have invented the story. On the other hand, the CIA's archives are notoriously incomplete.
51. RLT, 12 August 1954, in *El Caribe*, in Galíndez, *The Era of Trujillo*, p. 75n.
52. Galíndez, *The Era of Trujillo*, pp. 219, 227.
53. Diederich and Burt, *Papa Doc*, pp. 66–67; Abbott, *Haiti*, pp. 60–61. Machiavelli's classic treatise was also a favorite across the border. "I doubt that Trujillo had ever read Machiavelli," admitted Arturo Espaillat, the Benefactor's security chief. "I had. In Machiavelli's 'The Prince' I had found the key to many of Trujillo's own political actions and precepts." Espaillat, *Trujillo*, p. x.
54. Paul Magloire in Diederich and Burt, *Papa Doc*, p. 68; Harold Courlander, "Vodoun in Haitian Culture," in Courlander and Bastien, *Religion and Politics in Haiti*, pp. 6–7.
55. Federico G. Gil, "The Kennedy-Johnson Years," in Martz, *United States Policy in Latin America*, p. 6; JFD in Schmitz, *Thank God They're on Our Side*, p. 185.
56. Bonsal, *Cuba, Castro, and the United States*, p. 13; Rabe, *Eisenhower and Latin America*, p. 87; RMN in Logan, *Haiti and the Dominican Republic*, p. 74; Diederich and Burt, *Papa Doc*, p. 69.
57. RCR in Reid-Henry, *Fidel and Che*, p. 101.
58. FCR, 4 April 1954, in Franqui, *Diary*, p. 75.
59. FCR to Natalia Revuelta, n.d., in Fernández, *Castro's Daughter*, p. 66.
60. Matthews, *Revolution in Cuba*, p. 43; Taber, *M-26*, p. 48; Franqui, *Diary*, pp. 81–82; Castro, *Prison Letters*, pp. 30–31, 49–50.
61. Bonsal, *Cuba, Castro, and the United States*, p. 13.
62. FCR, 7 July 1955, in Franqui, *Diary*, p. 90.

4. Comrades

1. Rojo, *My Friend Che*, p. 70.
2. Gadea, *Ernesto*, p. 90.
3. EGS in ibid., p. 99. Castañeda, *Compañero*, pp. 82–83, points out that FCR and EGS might have met earlier briefly, but this was their first significant encounter; Lucila Velázquez, in Castañeda, *Compañero*, p. 84.
4. FCR in Paterson, *Contesting Castro*, p. 19; see also Taber, *M-26*, p. 52, Guevara, *Guerrilla Warfare*, p. 121.
5. Anderson, *Che Guevara*, p. 184; Guevara, *Guerrilla Warfare*, p. 46; Alberto Bayo in Balfour, *Castro*, p. 46.
6. Anderson, *Che Guevara*, pp. 194–95.
7. EGS in ibid., p. 180.
8. FCR in Gadea, *Ernesto*, p. 126; EGS in Anderson, *Che Guevara*, p. 191; Gadea, *Ernesto*, p. 156.
9. Bonsal, *Cuba, Castro, and the United States*, p. 11; Paterson, *Contesting Castro*, pp. 34–41. The average rural per capita income in Cuba in 1958 was $91.25.
10. López-Fresquet, *My Fourteen Months with Castro*, p. 10, quotes the statistics as 11 percent and 4 percent, respectively.
11. Sartre, *Sartre on Cuba*, p. 12.
12. Bonsal, *Cuba, Castro, and the United States*, p. 15; Paterson, *Contesting Castro*, pp. 38–40.
13. Terrence George Leonhardy, 29 February 1996, FAOH.
14. Andrew and Mitrokhin, *The Mitrokhin Archive II*, p. 34; Anderson, *Che Guevara*, pp. 206, 445n.
15. Grose, *Gentleman Spy*, pp. 419–20; NSK in Andrew and Mitrokhin, *The Mitrokhin Archive II*, p. 5.
16. Khrushchev, *Khrushchev Remembers*, pp. 15–17, 22–23, 44; Tompson, *Khrushchev*, pp. 15–16.
17. Khrushchev, *Khrushchev Remembers*, p. 320; Fursenko and Naftali, *Khrushchev's Cold War*, pp. 15–17.
18. Fursenko and Naftali, *Khrushchev's Cold War*, p. 23; Dockrill and Hopkins, *The Cold War*, p. 63.
19. Fursenko and Naftali, *Khrushchev's Cold War*, p. 35; Halle, *The Cold War as History*, pp. 341–42.
20. Mao Tse-tung in Taubman, *Khrushchev*, p. 339.
21. Balfour, *Castro*, p. 45; Franqui, *Diary*, p. 104.
22. Franqui, *Diary*, p. 107.
23. Castañeda, *Compañero*, pp. 92–93; EGS in Anderson, *Che Guevara*, p. 199. Emphasis Che's.
24. FCR in Franqui, *Diary*, p. 105.
25. Song to Fidel, in Guevara, *Venceremos!*, p. 25.
26. FCR in Guevara, *Reminiscences*, p. 39.
27. Logan, *Haiti and the Dominican Republic*, pp. 153–54; Ferguson, *Papa Doc, Baby Doc*, pp. 35–36; Heinl and Heinl, *Written in Blood*, p. 565; Péan, *Haïti*, pp. 157–58; Espaillat, *Trujillo*, pp. 55–58. Espaillat alleges that FCR backed Prío's deal with FD, but there is no corroborating evidence to support this.
28. Heinl and Heinl, *Written in Blood*, pp. 538–40; Diederich and Burt, *Papa Doc*, p. 70.
29. Diederich and Burt, *Papa Doc*, pp. 74–75.
30. Paterson, *Contesting Castro*, p. 33; Matthews, *Revolution in Cuba*, p. 71. Prío claimed in a 1974 interview that the sum was $100,000. Hinckle and Turner, *The Fish Is Red*, p. 9.
31. The KGB official was Yuri Paporov. Anderson, *Che Guevara*, p. 203.

32. Diederich and Burt, *Papa Doc*, p. 73; Bonsal, *Cuba, Castro, and the United States*, p. 15. The chief of police, General Rafael Salas Cañizares, would later die of his injuries.
33. Franqui, *Diary*, p. 114.
34. Espaillat, *Trujillo*, p. 139.
35. Paterson, *Contesting Castro*, pp. 32–33; Reid-Henry, *Fidel and Che*, p. 149.
36. EGS interviewed by Lisa Howard, *Issues and Answers*, ABC, 22 March 1964, box 27, HLMP.
37. EGS in Gadea, *Ernesto*, p. 156.
38. Faustino Pérez in Franqui, *Diary*, p. 121.
39. FCR, "In Tribute to Che," 18 October 1967, in Guevara, *Reminiscences*, p. 16.
40. Taber, *M-26*, pp. 54–60; Franqui, *Diary*, pp. 121–24; Sartre, *Sartre on Cuba*, p. 17; Guevara, *Reminiscences*, pp. 40–41.
41. Juan Manuel Márquez and Faustino Pérez in Franqui, *Diary*, p. 124.
42. Faustino Pérez in Matthews, *Revolution in Cuba*, p. 72.
43. FCR in Taber, *M-26*, p. 19.
44. Guevara, *Reminiscences*, p. 41.
45. Guevara, *Venceremos!*, p. 360.
46. EGS in Reid-Henry, *Fidel and Che*, p. 154; and in Franqui, *Diary*, p. 125; see also Guevara, *Reminiscences*, pp. 43–45.
47. Taber, *M-26*, pp. 63–66.
48. FCR, "A Necessary Introduction" (1968), in Guevara, *The Bolivian Diary*, p. 17; Franqui, *Diary*, p. 126.
49. Taber, *M-26*, pp. 65–66; Guevara, *Reminiscences*, p. 47; Matthews, *Revolution in Cuba*, p. 70; Guevara, *Guerrilla Warfare*, p. 5.
50. FCR in Balfour, *Castro*, p. 48; Guevara, *Reminiscences*, p. 52; Anderson, *Che Guevara*, p. 216.
51. Franqui, *Diary*, p. 137; Guevara, *Venceremos!*, p. 362; Guevara, *Guerrilla Warfare*, p. 53.
52. Detzer, *The Brink*, p. 23.
53. EGS in Franqui, *Diary*, p. 139; Anderson, *Che Guevara*, p. 236.
54. *Schweizer Illustrierte Zeitung*, 25 March 1957, box 36, HLMP; Phillips, *Cuba*, pp. 300–301.
55. Franqui, *Diary*, p. 146.
56. Russell H. Fitzgibbon, epilogue, in Galíndez, *The Era of Trujillo*, p. 269; Crassweller, *Trujillo*, pp. 329–31.
57. Espaillat, *Trujillo*, p. 42.
58. Oral History Project interview with Juan Bosch by Lloyd N. Cutler, Spring 1964, p. 7, JFKL.

5. "A Lot of Fuss by a Bunch of Communists"

1. Faure Chomón in Franqui, *Diary*, p. 159.
2. Phillips, *Cuba*, p. 305; the shooting was wrongly reported as an accident. "Order Is Restored in Havana After Revolt Costing 45 Lives," *Miami News*, 14 March 1957.
3. Bonsal, *Cuba, Castro, and the United States*, p. 17; see also *Bohemia*, 28 May 1957.
4. Heinl and Heinl, *Written in Blood*, p. 539.
5. Logan, *Haiti and the Dominican Republic*, pp. 153–54; BP: PM2874, 1957.
6. Daniel Fignolé and Jean Beauvoir in Abbott, *Haiti*, pp. 66–67.
7. Heinl and Heinl, *Written in Blood*, pp. 546–47.
8. Gerald Drew in Abbott, *Haiti*, p. 68.
9. Souchère, *Crime à Saint-Domingue*, pp. 24–25; editor's preface in Galíndez, *The Era of Trujillo*, p. xi.
10. Crassweller, *Trujillo*, pp. 317–18.

11. Editor's preface in Galíndez, *The Era of Trujillo*, p. xii; Logan, *Haiti and the Dominican Republic*, p. 74; Rabe, *The Most Dangerous Area in the World*, p. 35; Crassweller, *Trujillo*, pp. 315–16.
12. Crassweller, *Trujillo*, pp. 319–21.
13. Souchère, *Crime à Saint-Domingue*, pp. 60–61; Rabe, *The Most Dangerous Area in the World*, p. 35; Espaillat, *Trujillo*, pp. 166–69; Manuel de Irujo, "The Disappearance of Professor Galindez," *Science and Freedom*, no. 6, August 1956, p. 5.
14. Souchère, *Crime à Saint-Domingue*, p. 63.
15. FCR in Taber, *M-26*, p. 11.
16. Paterson, *Contesting Castro*, p. 86.
17. According to Enrique Meneses, who reported on the barbudos for *Paris-Match*, FCR considered having the men shave in March 1958. They were to occupy towns, and he believed clean-shaven men would make a better impression. Meneses claims to have convinced him otherwise, on the grounds that the beards made for better photographs. Meneses, *Fidel Castro*, p. 57.
18. Taber, *The War of the Flea*, pp. 32–33; FCR in Franqui, *Diary*, p. 181.
19. Taber, *The War of the Flea*, p. 30; Guevara, *Guerrilla Warfare*, p. 53.
20. Taber, *The War of the Flea*, pp. 31–32; Miller, *The Lost Plantation*, p. 8.
21. Robert A. Stevenson, 19 September 1989, FAOH.
22. Smith, *The Fourth Floor*, pp. 15–16.
23. Ibid., pp. 19–21; see also Phillips, *Cuba*, pp. 327–28.
24. Paterson, *Contesting Castro*, p. 95.
25. Terrence George Leonhardy, 29 February 1996, FAOH.
26. Diederich and Burt, *Papa Doc*, pp. 4–10; Heinl and Heinl, *Written in Blood*, pp. 548, 555n.
27. FD in Diederich and Burt, *Papa Doc*, p. 8.
28. Lundahl, *Politics or Markets?*, p. 270; Heinl and Heinl, *Written in Blood*, p. 566; Ferguson, *Papa Doc, Baby Doc*, pp. 38–40.
29. Martin, *Kennedy and Latin America*, pp. 232, 262n.
30. Heinl and Heinl, *Written in Blood*, p. 555n.
31. Ibid., p. 566; Abbott, *Haiti*, p. 77; Diederich and Burt, *Papa Doc*, pp. 98–99; Williamson, *The U.S. Naval Mission to Haiti*, p. 12.
32. Heinl and Heinl, *Written in Blood*, p. 565; Lundahl, *Politics or Markets?*, p. 265; Ferguson, *Papa Doc, Baby Doc*, pp. 38–40; Diederich and Burt, *Papa Doc*, p. 103.
33. Lundahl, *Politics or Markets?*, p. 265; FD in Diederich and Burt, *Papa Doc*, pp. 99–100.
34. Espaillat, *Trujillo*, p. 57; Heinl and Heinl, *Written in Blood*, p. 561; Lundahl, *Politics or Markets?*, p. 287; Diederich and Burt, *Papa Doc*, pp. 103–4.
35. Lundahl, *Politics or Markets?*, p. 284.
36. Abbott, *Haiti*, pp. 78–80; Heinl and Heinl, *Written in Blood*, p. 566; Péan, *Haïti*, pp. 194–95.
37. FD in Sapène, *Procès à: Baby Doc*, p. 159; Heinl and Heinl, *Written in Blood*, pp. 571–72.
38. Phillips, *Cuba*, p. 329.
39. George Smathers in Paterson, *Contesting Castro*, p. 52. See Heymann, *RFK*, p. 13, for Palm Beach gossip about Rose Kennedy and Earl Smith's relationship. JFK himself had allegedly been involved with Earl Smith's much younger wife, Florence, prior to Smith's marriage.
40. Kennedy, *Times to Remember*, p. 136; Hersh, *The Dark Side of Camelot*, pp. 14–15; Leaming, *Jack Kennedy*, p. 38.
41. Joseph Kennedy Sr. in Leaming, *Jack Kennedy*, p. 59.
42. Joseph Kennedy Jr. to Joseph Kennedy Sr., 2 November 1940, in ibid., p. 97.

43. Leaming, *Jack Kennedy*, pp. 118–19.
44. Ibid., p. 120.
45. Sander Vanocur in Kennedy, *Times to Remember*, p. 437.
46. Leaming, *Jack Kennedy*, pp. 196–97.
47. Reminiscences of Theodore C. Sorensen (1977), John F. Kennedy Project, Columbia University Oral History Research Office Collection, New York, pp. 2–3.
48. Reminiscences of Dwight D. Eisenhower (1967), Eisenhower Administration Project, Columbia University Oral History Research Office Collection, New York, pp. 66–67.
49. Goldenberg, *The Cuban Revolution and Latin America*, pp. 157–58.
50. Carlos Franqui to Frank País, April 1957, in Franqui, *Diary*, p. 176.
51. FCR to Jules Dubois, 1958, in George Volsky, "Cuba," in Szulc, *The United States and the Caribbean*, p. 102, and Franqui, *Diary*, p. 320; in Goldenberg, *The Cuban Revolution and Latin America*, p. 164; and in Meneses, *Fidel Castro*, p. 62.
52. RCR to FCR, January 1958, in Franqui, *Diary*, p. 282.
53. FCR in Meneses, *Fidel Castro*, pp. 61–62.
54. Embassy in Cuba to State Department, 3 March 1958, FRUS 1958–60, vol. 6 (Cuba), pp. 46–47.
55. RCR to Jules Dubois, July 1958, in Franqui, *Diary*, p. 385.
56. See, for example, Earl Smith to Department of State, 20 February 1958, FRUS 1958–60, vol. 6, p. 29. There are scores of further examples in the State Department's records.
57. Smith, *The Closest of Enemies*, p. 15.
58. FCR, 28 January 1958, in Franqui, *Diary*, p. 283; Oscar H. Guerra to Department of State, 21 February 1958, FRUS 1958–60, vol. 6, p. 32.
59. Heinl and Heinl, *Written in Blood*, pp. 566–67; Williamson, *The U.S. Naval Mission to Haiti*, p. 12; Espaillat, *Trujillo*, pp. 58–59. Espaillat mistakenly suggests that Kébreau died soon afterward; in fact, he lived until 1963. Like RLT, FD sometimes capriciously reinstated his enemies. Kébreau would later serve as Haiti's ambassador to Italy.
60. Abbott, *Haiti*, pp. 80–81; Raymond Thurston to Department of State, 17 January 1962, National Security Files, box 103, JFKL.
61. Williamson, *The U.S. Naval Mission to Haiti*, p. 12.
62. Paterson, *Contesting Castro*, pp. 140–41.
63. Taber, *The War of the Flea*, p. 31.
64. FCR to EGS, 25 March 1958, in Franqui, *Diary*, p. 293.
65. Paterson, *Contesting Castro*, p. 131.
66. Memo from the director of the Office of Middle American Affairs to the assistant secretary of state for inter-American affairs, 10 January 1958, FRUS 1958–60, vol. 6, p. 6.
67. Paterson, *Contesting Castro*, pp. 59–60, 125–26.
68. FCR in Franqui, *Diary*, p. 299.
69. Crassweller, *Trujillo*, p. 346.
70. FRUS 1958–60, vol. 6, p. 208.
71. Paterson, *Contesting Castro*, p. 143.
72. Fulgencio Batista, 6 April 1957, in ibid., p. 140.
73. Phillips, *Cuba*, p. 352; FCR to Celia Sánchez, 16 April 1958, in Franqui, *Diary*, pp. 300–301.
74. In Phillips, *Cuba*, p. 352.
75. Fulgencio Batista in Paterson, *Contesting Castro*, p. 144.

6. "The Minds of Unsophisticated Peoples"

1. Benjamin, *The United States and the Origins of the Cuban Revolution*, p. 139.
2. Nixon, *RN*, p. 186.

3. Nixon, *Six Crises*, p. 202; *RN*, pp. 186–88; *Six Crises*, p. 204.
4. Grandin, *Empire's Workshop*, pp. 54–55; Nixon, *RN*, p. 189.
5. Nixon, *RN*, pp. 190–91.
6. "The Guests of Venezuela," *Time*, 26 May 1958.
7. Paterson, *Contesting Castro*, p. 152; Grandin, *Empire's Workshop*, pp. 54–55.
8. Nixon, *RN*, p. 191; William P. Snow to JFD, 15 May 1958, FRUS 1958–60, vol. 5, p. 237.
9. Franqui, *Diary*, p. 340.
10. 22 May 1958, FRUS 1958–60, vol. 5, p. 240.
11. 19 June 1958, ibid., p. 29.
12. DDE, 22 May 1958, in Schmitz, *Thank God They're on Our Side*, p. 213; and Stephen G. Rabe, "The Caribbean Triangle: Betancourt, Castro, and Trujillo and U.S. Foreign Policy, 1958–1963," *Diplomatic History* 20, no. 1 (Winter 1996): 58.
13. JFK in Rabe, *The Most Dangerous Area in the World*, p. 12.
14. Logan, *Haiti and the Dominican Republic*, p. 72.
15. Ferguson, *Papa Doc, Baby Doc*, pp. 38–40; Heinl and Heinl, *Written in Blood*, p. 567; Lundahl, *Politics or Markets?*, p. 268; Sapène, *Procès à: Baby Doc*, p. 158; Nicholls, *From Dessalines to Duvalier*, pp. 230–31.
16. Gerald A. Drew in Williamson, *The U.S. Naval Mission to Haiti*, p. 19.
17. FCR to Celia Sánchez, 5 June 1958, in Franqui, *Diary*, p. 338.
18. RCR to Vilma Espín and René Ramos Latour, 12 June 1958, in ibid., p. 335.
19. Taber, *The War of the Flea*, p. 34; Paterson, *Contesting Castro*, pp. 160–61.
20. Manuel Fajardo in Franqui, *Diary*, pp. 356–57.
21. Park Wollam in Paterson, *Contesting Castro*, p. 163.
22. Paterson, *Contesting Castro*, pp. 160–64. The commander at Guantánamo Bay was Rear Admiral Robert B. Ellis.
23. AWD in FRUS 1958–60, vol. 6, p. 122.
24. Earl Smith in Paterson, *Contesting Castro*, p. 168; 12 July 1958, FRUS 1958–60, vol. 6, p. 151.
25. Paterson, *Contesting Castro*, p. 168.
26. BP: PM2902, 1958; Smith, *The Fourth Floor*, p. 144; Earl Smith to JFD, 9 July 1958, FRUS 1958–60, vol. 6, p. 135.
27. Arleigh Burke to Joint Chiefs of Staff, 10 July 1958, FRUS 1958–60, vol. 6, p. 140.
28. Phillips, *Cuba*, pp. 356–57.
29. Taber, *The War of the Flea*, p. 34; Detzer, *The Brink*, p. 23; C. Allan Stewart, deputy director of Office of Middle American Affairs, to William P. Snow, deputy secretary of state for inter-American affairs, 24 July 1958, FRUS 1958–60, vol. 6, p. 163.
30. Terrence George Leonhardy, 29 February 1996, FAOH; Paterson, *Contesting Castro*, p. 157.
31. As remembered by Oleg Daroussenkov, in Blight and Kornbluh, *Politics of Illusion*, p. 36. See also Anderson, *Che Guevara*, pp. 252, 273.
32. FCR in Blight et al., *Cuba on the Brink*, p. 284.
33. Andrew St. George in Hinckle and Turner, *The Fish Is Red*, p. 59. See also Paterson, *Contesting Castro*, p. 64; see also FRUS 1958–60, vol. 6, p. 132.
34. Al Cox and Robert Reynolds in Weiner, *Legacy of Ashes*, p. 179.
35. Paterson, *Contesting Castro*, p. 63.
36. Espaillat, *Trujillo*, p. 67.
37. Duvalier, *Mémoires*, p. 87.
38. Heinl and Heinl, *Written in Blood*, pp. 567–69; Ferguson, *Papa Doc, Baby Doc*, p. 41; Abbott, *Haiti*, pp. 82–85; Diederich and Burt, *Papa Doc*, pp. 113–19.
39. Conversation in Abbott, *Haiti*, p. 85.

40. Williamson, *The U.S. Naval Mission to Haiti*, p. 21.
41. 12 September 1958, in ibid., p. 22.
42. Heinl and Heinl, *Written in Blood*, p. 587.
43. FD, 5 August 1958, in ibid., pp. 575–76.
44. Paterson, *Contesting Castro*, p. 188.
45. Memorandum of a conversation between Earl Smith and Andrés Rivero Agüero, 15 November 1958, FRUS 1958–60, vol. 6, p. 253; Earl Smith to State Department, 22 October 1958, FRUS 1958–60, vol. 6, p. 241.
46. Bonsal, *Cuba, Castro, and the United States*, p. 20.
47. Smith, *The Closest of Enemies*, p. 34.
48. National Security Council, 30 October 1958, FRUS 1958–60, vol. 6, pp. 244–45.
49. Bonsal, *Cuba, Castro, and the United States*, p. 22; Paterson, *Contesting Castro*, p. 196.
50. Espaillat, *Trujillo*, p. 141.
51. Phillips, *Cuba*, p. 384.
52. Bonsal, *Cuba, Castro, and the United States*, p. 22.
53. Rabe, "The Caribbean Triangle," pp. 59–60.
54. Zsa Zsa Gabor and Gerold Frank, *My Story: Written for Me by Gerold Frank* (1960; London: Pan Books, 1962), pp. 252–66, sketches some of Ramfis's exploits in the United States. Gabor, an ex-fiancée of Porfirio Rubirosa, claims to have introduced Ramfis to Hollywood.
55. Henry Dearborn, 8 May 1991, FAOH; Vega, *Eisenhower y Trujillo*, p. 3; special report by the Operations Coordinating Board to the National Security Council, 26 November 1958, Annex B, in FRUS 1958–60, vol. 5, p. 59.
56. Val, *La dictature de Duvalier*, p. 48; Heinl and Heinl, *Written in Blood*, p. 574; Ferguson, *Papa Doc, Baby Doc*, p. 44; Diederich and Burt, *Papa Doc*, p. 130.
57. EGS and Camilo Cienfuegos, 6 December 1958, in Franqui, *Diary*, p. 464.
58. Castañeda, *Compañero*, p. 132; Aleida March in Anderson, *Che Guevara*, pp. 356, 361.
59. March, *Evocación*, p. 60.
60. AWD in National Security Council, 23 December 1958, FRUS 1958–60, vol. 6, p. 302; Eisenhower, *Waging Peace*, p. 521.
61. FCR to EGS, 26 December 1958, in Castañeda, *Compañero*, p. 137.
62. EGS in ibid., p. 135. Castañeda notes that Fulgencio Batista alleged that EGS had bribed the train to surrender, and Eloy Gutiérrez Menoyo has alleged there was a deal. But it seems entirely plausible that Batista's forces would have surrendered, as they so often did during the revolution.
63. Paterson, *Contesting Castro*, p. 221; Rabe, "The Caribbean Triangle," p. 60.
64. Smith, *The Fourth Floor*, p. 184; FRUS 1958–60, vol. 6, pp. 323–29.
65. Terrence George Leonhardy, 29 February 1996, FAOH.
66. Smith, *The Fourth Floor*, pp. 185–86; Greene, *Ways of Escape*, p. 214; Paterson, *Contesting Castro*, p. 38; see Phillips, *Cuba*, p. 309, for a description of Ventura.
67. Phillips, *The Night Watch*, p. 77.
68. Smith, *The Fourth Floor*, pp. 185–86; Espaillat, *Trujillo*, pp. 142–43; Crassweller, *Trujillo*, p. 344; BP: PM2764, 1959; Greene, *Ways of Escape*, p. 214.
69. Smith, *The Closest of Enemies*, p. 37; Paterson, *Contesting Castro*, pp. 54, 224–25; Charles Higham, *Errol Flynn: The Untold Story* (London: Granada, 1980), p. 381.
70. The figure of 803 men comes from Williams, *From Columbus to Castro*, p. 481. Williams estimates that adding other groups to M-26-7 still amounted to fifteen hundred at most. In 1963, FCR claimed that he had had fewer than five hundred men on the day of victory.

7. "Not Red, But Olive Green"

1. FCR in Crassweller, *Trujillo*, p. 346; Miller, *The Lost Plantation*, p. 8.
2. George Raft in Smith, *The Closest of Enemies*, p. 40; Smith, *The Fourth Floor*, pp. xv–xvi.
3. Phillips, *Cuba*, p. 397; Smith, *The Closest of Enemies*, p. 40.
4. Miller, *The Lost Plantation*, p. 8; see also López-Fresquet, *My Fourteen Months with Castro*, p. 65; Phillips, *Cuba*, p. 401.
5. Franqui, *Diary*, p. 504.
6. Gadea, *Ernesto*, p. 171. "For all this, I prefer you to live" has been substituted here for the confusingly translated line in the English-language edition of Gadea's book, which is rendered as "Because of all this, I want you always." The Spanish original, in Gadea's own words, was "Por todo esto prefiero que estés vivo." See Hilda Gadea, *Che Guevara: Años decisivos* (Mexico City: Aguilar, 1972), p. 202.
7. Phillips, *Cuba*, pp. 405–6.
8. Earl Smith to State Department, 9 January 1959, FRUS 1958–60, vol. 6, p. 350.
9. JFD to DDE, 7 January 1959, FRUS 1958–60, vol. 6, p. 347; Bonsal, *Cuba, Castro, and the United States*, p. 36; BP: PM2930, 1959.
10. Miller, *The Lost Plantation*, pp. 8–9.
11. Park Wollam to Department of State, 14 January 1959, FRUS 1958–60, vol. 6, p. 358. The Santiago police chief was Bonifacio Haza Grasso.
12. Bonsal, *Cuba, Castro, and the United States*, p. 36.
13. Miller, *The Lost Plantation*, p. 10.
14. BP: PM1567, 2 February 1959; Detzer, *The Brink*, p. 31; FRUS 1958–60, vol. 6, p. 367. Earl Smith reported that Miró Cardona did, in fact, have a sore throat, but it was universally thought that his resignation was political.
15. FCR in FRUS 1958–60, vol. 6, p. 381; see also BP: PM1567, 29 January 1959.
16. Chronology of U.S.-Cuba relations, National Security Files, box 46, JFKL; Castañeda, *Compañero*, p. 143.
17. FRUS 1958–60, vol. 6, p. 382.
18. Stephen G. Rabe, "The Caribbean Triangle: Betancourt, Castro, and Trujillo and U.S. Foreign Policy, 1958–1963," *Diplomatic History* 20, no. 1 (Winter 1996): 63; Jake Esterline in Weiner, *Legacy of Ashes*, p. 181.
19. Franqui, *Diary*, pp. 429–30; Christian Herter, 6 January 1959, FRUS 1958–60, vol. 6, p. 344.
20. Smith, *The Closest of Enemies*, p. 34; Robert A. Stevenson, 19 September 1989, FAOH; Paterson, *Contesting Castro*, p. 248.
21. Taubman, *Khrushchev*, p. 492. Anderson, *Che Guevara*, pp. 414–15, argues that Soviet interest in Cuba also began in mid-1958. The Soviet Union was then in contact with the PSP, and the PSP was in contact with M-26-7, but there is no evidence that the Soviet Union saw a Cuba headed by FCR as of any interest at all until the very last week of 1958, and no evidence that it considered any form of alliance until the visit of Anastas Mikoyan to Havana in the spring of 1960.
22. Fursenko and Naftali, *Khrushchev's Cold War*, p. 295.
23. Khrushchev, *Memoirs*, vol. 3, p. 315.
24. Castañeda, *Compañero*, p. 153.
25. Smith, *The Closest of Enemies*, p. 51.
26. FRUS 1958–60, vol. 6, p. 356.
27. William Wieland to Roy R. Rubottom, 18 February 1959, USNA: RG 59, entry 3148, box 2, Cuba.
28. Phillips, *Cuba*, p. 417; see also FRUS 1958–60, vol. 6, p. 418.

29. Phillips, *Cuba*, p. 417.
30. FRUS, 1958–60, vol. 5, p. 80; also vol. 6, pp. 397–98.
31. Hinckle and Turner, *The Fish Is Red*, pp. 59–60. The CIA station chief was Jim Noel.
32. FRUS 1958–60, vol. 6, p. 387; William Wieland to Roy R. Rubottom, 18 February 1959, USNA: RG 59, entry 3148, box 2, Cuba.
33. FCR in Castañeda, *Compañero*, p. 157; ibid., p. 139; USNA: RG 59, entry 3148, box 2, Cuba.
34. Robert A. Stevenson, 19 September 1989, FAOH.
35. Bonsal, *Cuba, Castro, and the United States*, p. 55.
36. FCR in López-Fresquet, *My Fourteen Months with Castro*, p. 49.
37. Fursenko and Naftali, *Khrushchev's Cold War*, p. 296; FRUS 1958–60, vol. 6, p. 396.
38. Castañeda, *Compañero*, p. 147.
39. Lyonel Paquin in Abbott, *Haiti*, p. 93.
40. William Wieland, 23 March 1959, USNA: RG 59, entry 3148, box 2, Haiti. It was alleged by the American marine commander in Port-au-Prince at the time that FD had Major Claude Raymond organize a secret deal with FCR to bring an end to the radio broadcasts (Heinl and Heinl, *Written in Blood*, p. 573). If that is true, it would have been profoundly out of character for FCR, who was in early 1959 passionately committed to the cause of felling dictatorships across the Caribbean region.
41. Memo of meeting between Val Washington, William Wieland, Allan Stewart, and John Calvin Hill, 11 February 1959, USNA: RG 59, entry 3148, box 2, Cuba.
42. Abbott, *Haiti*, p. 93; Diederich and Burt, *Papa Doc*, pp. 131–35.
43. Heinl and Heinl, *Written in Blood*, p. 628n.
44. John Calvin Hill, 29 January 1959, USNA: RG 59, entry 3148, box 2, Haiti. Hill mentioned Jules Blanchet as someone whose background caused him doubts.
45. Diederich and Burt, *Papa Doc*, pp. 138–39; Heinl and Heinl, *Written in Blood*, p. 573; Abbott, *Haiti*, pp. 94–95.
46. FD in Heinl and Heinl, *Written in Blood*, p. 577; Sapène, *Procès à: Baby Doc*, p. 84.
47. John Calvin Hill, 1 April 1959, USNA: RG 59, entry 3148, box 2, Cuba.
48. Rojo, *My Friend Che*, p. 178.
49. EGS in Castañeda, *Compañero*, p. 145; Reid-Henry, *Fidel and Che*, p. 211.
50. Eisenhower, *Waging Peace*, p. 523.
51. BP: PM2716, 1959.
52. Robert A. Stevenson, 19 September 1989, FAOH.
53. RMN, April 1959, in Nixon, *RN*, p. 202. See FCR's reaction in Blight et al., *Cuba on the Brink*, p. 178.
54. Bender, *Cuba vs. United States*, p. 13.
55. FCR in López-Fresquet, *My Fourteen Months with Castro*, p. 106.
56. Robert A. Stevenson, 19 September 1989, FAOH.
57. López-Fresquet, *My Fourteen Months with Castro*, p. 107.
58. Unnamed CIA agent in ibid., p. 110. López-Fresquet calls him "Frank Bender," which was the usual alias of the CIA's Gerald Droller, also known as Gerry Drecher, later closely involved in the Bay of Pigs invasion.
59. López-Fresquet, *My Fourteen Months with Castro*, pp. 111–12.
60. Robert A. Stevenson, 19 September 1989, FAOH. Rufo López-Fresquet says the argument happened in Houston, Texas, not Dallas.
61. Philip Bonsal via Whiting Willauer, in Hugh Thomas, "Cuba vs America," *New Statesman*, 21 December 1962. See also Bonsal, *Cuba, Castro, and the United States*, p. 59.
62. Magdoff, *The Age of Imperialism*, pp. 1465–67. Magdoff quotes Thomas Balogh, *The Economics of Poverty*, outlining the process by which the IMF supported what Balogh

called *neo-imperialism* on the part of the American government in the 1950s and 1960s.

63. The figures were 66 percent of exports ($527.8m) and 70 percent of imports ($546.9m). Bender, *Cuba vs. United States*, p. 5.
64. Bonsal, *Cuba, Castro, and the United States*, pp. 43–45.
65. Ibid., p. 42.
66. Guevara, *Guerrilla Warfare*, pp. 129, 131.
67. Robert A. Stevenson, 19 September 1989, FAOH.
68. Williams, *From Columbus to Castro*, pp. 481–82.
69. Castro, *Fidel Castro Speaks*, p. 74.
70. JFD via AWD, May 1959, in Grose, *Gentleman Spy*, p. 461.
71. Fursenko and Naftali, *Khrushchev's Cold War*, p. 24; Westad, *The Global Cold War*, pp. 69–70.
72. Williamson, *The U.S. Naval Mission to Haiti*, p. 58; Ferguson, *Papa Doc, Baby Doc*, p. 42; Abbott, *Haiti*, pp. 96–97.

8. "Our Real Friends"

1. USNA: RG 59, entry 3148, box 2, Haiti; Williamson, *The U.S. Naval Mission to Haiti*, p. 64; Heinl and Heinl, *Written in Blood*, pp. 574, 628n; Diederich and Burt, *Papa Doc*, pp. 105, 142–43.
2. 8 July 1959, in Williamson, *The U.S. Naval Mission to Haiti*, p. 67.
3. Abbott, *Haiti*, pp. 97–98; Diederich and Burt, *Papa Doc*, p. 148.
4. Williamson, *The U.S. Naval Mission to Haiti*, p. 66.
5. Crassweller, *Trujillo*, p. 353.
6. USNA: RG 59, entry 3148, box 2, Haiti.
7. Abbott, *Haiti*, pp. 104–5.
8. The author is indebted to Dr. Monal Wadhera for this analysis.
9. Abbott, *Haiti*, p. 97; FRUS 1958–60, vol. 5, p. 819.
10. Crandall, *Gunboat Democracy*, p. 47; Crassweller, *Trujillo*, p. 348.
11. Crassweller, *Trujillo*, p. 366; Ramfis Trujillo in John Bartlow Martin, report on the Dominican Republic, President's Office Files: Countries, box 115a, JFKL.
12. Crassweller, *Trujillo*, p. 357.
13. Espaillat, *Trujillo*, p. 156; Stephen G. Rabe, "The Caribbean Triangle: Betancourt, Castro, and Trujillo and U.S. Foreign Policy, 1958–1963," *Diplomatic History* 20, no. 1 (Winter 1996): 60.
14. FRUS 1958–60, vol. 5, p. 290.
15. Roy R. Rubottom, 8 July 1959, in ibid., p. 297.
16. Background paper, State Department, 7 August 1959, in ibid., pp. 322–26.
17. Crassweller, *Trujillo*, pp. 353–54.
18. Roy R. Rubottom in conversation with Marcos Falcón Briceño, 9 July 1959, FRUS, 1958–60, vol. 5, p. 299.
19. BP: PM2732, 1959; BP: PM1591, 3 August 1959; Andrew and Mitrokhin, *The Mitrokhin Archive II*, p. 35.
20. Quoted in Espaillat, *Trujillo*, p. 150.
21. Espaillat, *Trujillo*, p. 152.
22. Conversation in López-Fresquet, *My Fourteen Months with Castro*, pp. 137–38.
23. Espaillat, *Trujillo*, pp. 154–60.
24. Government memo, 20 July 1959, USNA: RG 59, entry 3148, box 2, Cuba.
25. See Warren Commission, *Report*, p. 370.
26. Betty Sicre in Lee Server, *Ava Gardner: Love Is Nothing* (2006; London: Bloomsbury,

2007), pp. 377–78; Lorenz, *Marita*, pp. 22–23. Lorenz's memoirs are not a reliable source, but Gardner's biographer considers the story to be plausible.

27. George Volsky, "Cuba," in Szulc, *The United States and the Caribbean*, p. 120.
28. William J. Bonthron in Williamson, *The U.S. Naval Mission to Haiti*, p. 70.
29. Diederich and Burt, *Papa Doc*, p. 146.
30. Heinl and Heinl, *Written in Blood*, pp. 574–75 and 628–29n.
31. Williamson, *The U.S. Naval Mission to Haiti*, p. 73.
32. FRUS, 1958–60, vol. 5, pp. 818–19.
33. FD in Heinl and Heinl, *Written in Blood*, p. 576.
34. Richard M. Morse, "Haiti, 1492–1988," in Morse, *Haiti's Future*, p. 8.
35. Memorandum of a conversation between Val Washington and William Wieland, 8 June 1959, USNA: RG 59, entry 3148, box 2, Haiti.
36. FD, 5 October 1959, in Williamson, *The U.S. Naval Mission to Haiti*, p. 78.
37. Williamson, *The U.S. Naval Mission to Haiti*, pp. 67, 368n.
38. Brendon, *Ike*, p. 371.
39. Khrushchev, *Memoirs*, vol. 3, p. 167.
40. Ibid., pp. 134–35. The translation used in Taubman, *Khrushchev*, p. 428, is harsher, and says that the capitalists did look exactly like their caricatures, except for the pigs' snouts.
41. Marilyn Monroe in Taubman, *Khrushchev*, p. 430.
42. NSK and Frank Sinatra in ibid., p. 431; see also Khrushchev, *Memoirs*, vol. 3, pp. 108–9; Fursenko and Naftali, *Khrushchev's Cold War*, p. 233.
43. NSK in Brendon, *Ike*, p. 378.
44. George Kistiakowsky in ibid., p. 379.
45. Eisenhower, *Waging Peace*, p. 439; Taubman, *Khrushchev*, pp. 437–39.
46. Taubman, *Khrushchev*, p. 532.
47. Aleksandr Alekseyev in Andrew and Mitrokhin, *The Mitrokhin Archive II*, p. 35; see also Taubman, *Khrushchev*, p. 542.
48. López-Fresquet, *My Fourteen Months with Castro*, p. 130.
49. DDE in Paterson, *Contesting Castro*, p. 3.
50. Gadea, *Ernesto*, p. 173.
51. López-Fresquet, *My Fourteen Months with Castro*, p. 57.
52. Smith, *The Fourth Floor*, p. 203.
53. Robert A. Stevenson, 19 September 1989, FAOH.
54. Translation of memorandum no. 100 from French embassy in Havana, 14 July 1961, USNA: RG 59, entry 3148, box 8, Cuba—Miscellaneous, July–August 1961.
55. López-Fresquet, *My Fourteen Months with Castro*, p. 58.
56. Guevara, *Guerrilla Warfare*, p. 6; Castañeda, *Compañero*, p. 72.
57. Bonsal, *Cuba, Castro, and the United States*, p. 6; Special National Intelligence Estimate, 29 December 1959, FRUS 1958–60, vol. 5, p. 414.
58. Dean Acheson to Herbert Matthews, 21 December 1959. Cataloged correspondence, HLMP.
59. Research Institute report, 1 August 1959, USNA: RG 59, entry 3148, box 2, Cuba.
60. López-Fresquet, *My Fourteen Months with Castro*, p. 59.
61. FCR to Wayne Smith, in Balfour, *Castro*, pp. 67–68.
62. Crassweller, *Trujillo*, p. 422.
63. Ibid., p. 425.
64. Henry Dearborn, 8 May 1991, FAOH.
65. FRUS 1958–60, vol. 5, p. 89.
66. Joseph Farland to John Calvin Hill, 1 December 1959, USNA: RG 59, entry 3148, box 2, Dominican Republic.

67. Espaillat, *Trujillo*, p. 3.
68. Juan Perón in Crassweller, *Trujillo*, p. 382.
69. Crassweller, *Trujillo*, p. 384.
70. Espaillat, *Trujillo*, p. 3.
71. Ibid., pp. 4–5; Henry Dearborn, 8 May 1991, FAOH; Crassweller, *Trujillo*, pp. 386–87; Logan, *Haiti and the Dominican Republic*, pp. 72–73. Vega, *Eisenhower y Trujillo*, p. 95, points out that this story differs in several retellings.
72. RLT in Crassweller, *Trujillo*, p. 394.
73. Weiner, *Legacy of Ashes*, p. 180.
74. Grose, *Gentleman Spy*, pp. 493–94; Blight and Kornbluh, *Politics of Illusion*, pp. 83–84.
75. DDE in Brendon, *Ike*, p. 385.
76. Guevara, *Guerrilla Warfare*, p. 136.
77. J. C. King in Grose, *Gentleman Spy*, p. 494. King had changed his mind on the usefulness of eliminating RCR and EGS: see Blight and Kornbluh, *Politics of Illusion*, pp. 83–84.
78. Carter, *Covert Action*, pp. 64–65.
79. Richard Bissell, "What We Are Doing in Cuba," quoted by AWD, in Weiner, *Legacy of Ashes*, p. 181.
80. RLT in Crassweller, *Trujillo*, p. 430.
81. Gonzalez, "The United States and Castro," p. 727; FCR in Bender, *Cuba vs. United States*, p. 16.
82. Rabe, *Eisenhower and Latin America*, p. 131.

9. "A Crusade to Save Free Enterprise"

1. DDE in Brendon, *Ike*, p. 384.
2. Eisenhower, *Waging Peace*, pp. 527–30.
3. López-Fresquet, *My Fourteen Months with Castro*, p. 174.
4. Anastas Mikoyan in Andrew and Mitrokhin, *The Mitrokhin Archive II*, p. 36.
5. Bonsal, *Cuba, Castro, and the United States*, p. 16.
6. Memorandum of a conversation between E. M. Bernstein and Felipe Pazos, 12 August 1959, USNA: RG 59, entry 3148, box 2, Cuba.
7. Nikolai Leonov in Andrew and Mitrokhin, *The Mitrokhin Archive II*, p. 28.
8. John Calvin Hill, 23 February 1960, USNA: RG 59, entry 3148, box 3, Cuba 1960, January–June.
9. Smith, *The Closest of Enemies*, p. 55.
10. Lester Mallory to Douglas Dillon, 24 February 1960, USNA: RG 59, entry 3148, box 3, Cuba 1960, January–June.
11. FCR in Anderson, *Che Guevara*, p. 464; Sartre, *Sartre on Cuba*, p. 142.
12. "Remember *La Coubre*," *Time*, 14 March 1960; Miller, *The Lost Plantation*, pp. 39–40; FCR in Blight et al., *Cuba on the Brink*, p. 180.
13. BP: PM2952, 1960; FCR in Fursenko and Naftali, *Khrushchev's Cold War*, p. 301.
14. The French outfit said to be responsible was La Main Rouge. USNA: RG 59, entry 3148, box 3, Cuba 1960, January–June.
15. In line with his communist beliefs, Korda received and claimed no royalties from *Guerrillero Heroico*. He did, however, sue a picture agency and an advertising agency when it was used to advertise a brand of vodka. EGS was opposed to the excessive consumption of alcohol. Korda received an out-of-court settlement of $50,000, which he donated to the Cuban health-care system.
16. Robert A. Stevenson, 19 September 1989, FAOH.

17. Christian Herter in Brendon, *Ike*, p. 387.
18. Reminiscences of Dwight D. Eisenhower (1967), Eisenhower Administration Project, Columbia University Oral History Research Office Collection, New York, 1967, pp. 66–67.
19. Eisenhower, *Waging Peace*, p. 533.
20. NSK in Andrew and Mitrokhin, *The Mitrokhin Archive II*, p. 36; Fursenko and Naftali, *Khrushchev's Cold War*, p. 302.
21. William Wieland to John Calvin Hill, 23 March 1960, USNA: RG 59, entry 3148, box 3, Cuba 1960, January–June.
22. John Calvin Hill to Lester Mallory of ARA, 11 April 1960, in ibid.
23. Edwin N. Clark to DDE, re: "U.S. Plan for Trujillo's Retirement," 13 April 1960, USNA: RG 59, entry 3148, box 4, Dominican Republic: Gen. Edwin N. Clark.
24. Policy planning staff, 13 April 1960, in Stephen G. Rabe, "The Caribbean Triangle: Betancourt, Castro, and Trujillo and U.S. Foreign Policy, 1958–1963," *Diplomatic History* 20, no. 1 (Winter 1996): 66.
25. RMN, Douglas Dillon, and initiative by Christian Herter to DDE, all 14 April 1960, in Schmitz, *Thank God They're on Our Side*, p. 231.
26. Grose, *Gentleman Spy*, p. 480; Bissell, *Reflections of a Cold Warrior*, pp. 127–28.
27. C. Douglas Dillon, 28 April 1987, FAOH.
28. NSK in Grose, *Gentleman Spy*, p. 484; Taubman, *Khrushchev*, pp. 456–57, points out that NSK was obliged to reveal this news when one of his subordinates accidentally revealed Powers's survival in earshot of Llewellyn Thompson.
29. DDE in Brendon, *Ike*, p. 391; Weiner, *Legacy of Ashes*, p. 185.
30. Grose, *Gentleman Spy*, p. 490; C. Douglas Dillon, 28 April 1987, FAOH.
31. Harold Macmillan in Brendon, *Ike*, p. 392.
32. NSK and Anastas Mikoyan in Taubman, *Khrushchev*, pp. 447, 468.
33. Aleksandr Alekseyev in Andrew and Mitrokhin, *The Mitrokhin Archive II*, p. 37; see also Taubman, *Khrushchev*, p. 542; Khrushchev, *Memoirs*, vol. 3, p. 317.
34. Williamson, *The U.S. Naval Mission to Haiti*, pp. 116–17; Diederich and Burt, *Papa Doc*, p. 150.
35. FD, 21 June 1960, in Diederich and Burt, *Papa Doc*, pp. 151–52; see also Lundahl, *Politics or Markets?*, p. 275.
36. Lundahl, *Politics or Markets?*, pp. 275–76; Williamson, *The U.S. Naval Mission to Haiti*, p. 124.
37. Diederich and Burt, *Papa Doc*, p. 152; Reid-Henry, *Fidel and Che*, p. 232.
38. Russell H. Fitzgibbon, epilogue, in Galíndez, *The Era of Trujillo*, p. 273; Crassweller, *Trujillo*, pp. 415–16.
39. Vega, *Eisenhower y Trujillo*, p. 106; RLT in Crassweller, *Trujillo*, p. 416.
40. Crassweller, *Trujillo*, p. 312; Rabe, "The Caribbean Triangle," p. 64.
41. Several unflattering cartoons of Betancourt produced by RLT's press can be found in Vega, *Kennedy y los Trujillo*, and Vega, *Eisenhower y Trujillo*.
42. J. C. King and Henry Dearborn in Rabe, *Eisenhower and Latin America*, p. 158.
43. National Security Council meeting, 25 July 1960, in Schmitz, *Thank God They're on Our Side*, p. 231; FRUS 1958–60, vol. 5, pp. 807–8.
44. RLT in Espaillat, *Trujillo*, p. 125.
45. Anthony P. Maingot, "Caribbean International Relations," in Knight and Palmer, *The Modern Caribbean*, p. 267; FCR, "Report to the Cuban People on the Victory at Playa Girón," 23 April 1961, in Castro and Fernández, *Playa Girón*, p. 160.
46. In "Trying to Topple Trujillo," *Time*, 5 September 1960.
47. Rabe, "The Caribbean Triangle," p. 68.

48. Henry Dearborn in ibid., p. 69.
49. Hersh, *The Dark Side of Camelot*, p. 196.
50. Henry Dearborn, 8 May 1991, FAOH.
51. In Andrew and Mitrokhin, *The Mitrokhin Archive II*, p. 38.
52. NSK in Fursenko and Naftali, *Khrushchev's Cold War*, p. 306.
53. Garthoff, *A Journey Through the Cold War*, p. 48.
54. Andrew and Mitrokhin, *The Mitrokhin Archive II*, pp. 38–39.
55. Fursenko and Naftali, *Khrushchev's Cold War*, p. 306.
56. FRUS 1958–60, vol. 5, p. 447.
57. Sartre, *Sartre on Cuba*, pp. 119–20, 132.
58. BP: PM2970, 28 July 1960. A year previously, a State Department report similarly quoted FCR saying, "If anything should happen to me, I warn you you will have my more violent brother to contend with." FCR in Research Institute report, 1 August 1959, USNA: RG 59, entry 3148, box 2, Cuba.
59. Clément Barbot in Nicholls, *From Dessalines to Duvalier*, p. 220; Williamson, *The U.S. Naval Mission to Haiti*, p. 123.
60. Diederich and Burt, *Papa Doc*, p. 153; Nicholls, *From Dessalines to Duvalier*, p. 217; Heinl and Heinl, *Written in Blood*, p. 585.
61. FRUS 1958–60, vol. 5, p. 446.
62. Heinl and Heinl, *Written in Blood*, pp. 583–84; Abbott, *Haiti*, p. 106; Diederich and Burt, *Papa Doc*, pp. 158–62; Nicholls, *From Dessalines to Duvalier*, p. 223; Val, *La dictature de Duvalier*, pp. 67–68; Duvalier, *Mémoires*, p. 69.
63. Williamson, *The U.S. Naval Mission to Haiti*, p. 139.
64. Bissell, *Reflections of a Cold Warrior*, p. 144.
65. Schlesinger, *Robert Kennedy*, pp. 482–84; Hersh, *The Dark Side of Camelot*, pp. 162–63, 167; Heymann, *RFK*, p. 265.
66. Jacob Esterline in Kornbluh, *Bay of Pigs Declassified*, p. 265; see also Jacob Esterline in Blight and Kornbluh, *Politics of Illusion*, p. 85; Bissell, *Reflections of a Cold Warrior*, p. 157.
67. Hersh, *The Dark Side of Camelot*, p. 164. The agents included David L. Christ, who—unknown to the Cubans—was the CIA's most senior audio operative. They languished in a Cuban prison until the Kennedy administration secured their release on 21 April 1963.
68. Detzer, *The Brink*, pp. 2–5. Detzer adds, "Maybe it was his beard." The question was raised by some whether FCR had intended all along to stay in the Theresa, historically associated with African American politics and culture. It seemed he had been in touch with its management before he left Cuba.
69. Khrushchev, *Memoirs*, vol. 3, p. 271; Westad, *The Global Cold War*, p. 174.
70. Halle, *The Cold War as History*, p. 390.
71. Grose, *Gentleman Spy*, p. 513.
72. Weiner, *Legacy of Ashes*, pp. 189–90.
73. Paterson, *Contesting Castro*, pp. 208–9; Weiner, *Legacy of Ashes*, pp. 185–87.
74. Richard Bissell in Mosley, *Dulles*, p. 467.
75. Ibid.
76. Ibid., p. 466.
77. Jacqueline Kennedy in Grose, *Gentleman Spy*, p. 491.
78. Hersh, *The Dark Side of Camelot*, pp. 173–74; Grose, *Gentleman Spy*, p. 495; Hinckle and Turner, *The Fish Is Red*, pp. 109–10; Phillips, *The Night Watch*, p. 91.
79. JFK, 15 December 1958 at a Democratic dinner, San Juan, Puerto Rico, in Kennedy, *The Strategy of Peace*, p. 136; ibid., p. 132; JFK, 1 January 1960, in ibid., p. 7.
80. Halberstam, *The Best and the Brightest*, p. 27.
81. JFK in the *Atlantic Monthly*, February 1961, p. 6; from a review of B. H. Liddell Hart's

Deterrent or Defense, Saturday Review, Fall 1960; JFK in Rabe, *The Most Dangerous Area in the World*, p. 14.
82. Dockrill and Hopkins. *The Cold War*, p. 77.
83. Nixon, *Six Crises*, p. 354.
84. Grose, *Gentleman Spy*, pp. 508–9; Hersh, *The Dark Side of Camelot*, p. 181.
85. Robert F. Kennedy Oral History, vol. 1, pp. 40d–e, Oral History Program, JFKL; Grose, *Gentleman Spy*, p. 512; Hersh, *The Dark Side of Camelot*, pp. 170–71; Wyden, *Bay of Pigs*, pp. 66–67. Bissell gave varying and sometimes contradictory accounts of his relationship with JFK and the Bay of Pigs operation, which are detailed by Hersh.
86. Patterson in Hersh, *The Dark Side of Camelot*, p. 177.
87. In Hersh, *The Dark Side of Camelot*, pp. 179–80.
88. Halberstam, *The Best and the Brightest*, pp. 28–29.

10. Regime Change

1. RLT in Oral History Project interview with William Pawley by Raymond Henle, 4 April 1967, Herbert Hoover Presidential Library.
2. Henry Dearborn to State Department, 5 September 1960, USNA: RG 59, entry 3148, box 4, Dominican Republic Letters.
3. Oral History Interview with Chester Bowles, 1 July 1970, p. 49, JFKL.
4. Leaming, *Jack Kennedy*, p. 259.
5. Harold Macmillan in ibid., p. 220; Rose Kennedy in Salinger, *P.S.*, p. 84; see also Kennedy, *Times to Remember*, p. 349.
6. Nixon, *RN*, p. 224.
7. Wyden, *Bay of Pigs*, pp. 44–45; Hersh, *The Dark Side of Camelot*, p. 131 and ff.; Summers, *Official and Confidential*, pp. 268–70. Dallek, *John F. Kennedy*, pp. 294–96, dismisses the allegations, though without a great deal of evidence.
8. Kennedy, *Times to Remember*, p. 349; Salinger, *P.S.*, p. 85; Salinger, *John F. Kennedy*, p. 10.
9. Kennedy, *Times to Remember*, p. 349.
10. Jacob Esterline in Weiner, *Legacy of Ashes*, p. 191.
11. Miller, *The Lost Plantation*, p. 125.
12. Ibid., p. 145; Sartre, *Sartre on Cuba*, pp. 98–99; EGS in Sartre, *Sartre on Cuba*, p. 94.
13. FCR's opponents in the Cuban exile community have been at pains to point out that there was a considerable resistance to the revolution at this time. There was, but all the available data—from international observers on the ground and from U.S. intelligence—indicates that if FCR had held a genuine election at the beginning of 1961, he would have won by an overwhelming majority. See Jorge Domínguez in Blight and Kornbluh, *Politics of Illusion*, p. 79.
14. National Intelligence Estimate, December 1960, in Bissell, *Reflections of a Cold Warrior*, pp. 160–61.
15. Bissell, *Reflections of a Cold Warrior*, p. 160.
16. Miller, *The Lost Plantation*, pp. 63, 169.
17. EGS in Rojo, *My Friend Che*, p. 102.
18. NSK in Abel, *The Missiles of October*, p. 19; James J. Wadsworth in BP: PM3000, January 1961.
19. Eisenhower, *Waging Peace*, p. 613.
20. Williamson, *The U.S. Naval Mission to Haiti*, p. 142; Diederich and Burt, *Papa Doc*, pp. 164–65.
21. DDE in Bissell, *Reflections of a Cold Warrior*, p. 161; DDE in Stephen G. Rabe, "The Caribbean Triangle: Betancourt, Castro, and Trujillo and U.S. Foreign Policy, 1958–1963," *Diplomatic History* 20, no. 1 (Winter 1996): 70.

22. Martin, *Kennedy and Latin America*, p. 211; Briefing paper on the Dominican Republic, National Security Files, box 66, JFKL.
23. Robert F. Kennedy Oral History, vol. 2, p. 163, Oral History Program, JFKL; Garthoff, *A Journey Through the Cold War*, pp. 132–33; Schlesinger, *Robert Kennedy*, p. 422; see also Arthur Schlesinger in Blight and Kornbluh, *Politics of Illusion*, p. 63.
24. Adolf Berle in Rabe, *The Most Dangerous Area in the World*, p. 22; Adolf Berle in Lucien S. Vandenbroucke, "The 'Confessions' of Allen Dulles: New Evidence on the Bay of Pigs," *Diplomatic History* 8, no. 4 (Fall 1984): 372.
25. Report to the president-elect of the Task Force on Immediate Latin American Problems, 4 January 1961, in Schmitz, *Thank God They're on Our Side*, p. 244.
26. Eisenhower, *Waging Peace*, p. 614.
27. DDE in memorandum on conference between President Eisenhower and President-Elect Kennedy, 19 January 1961, President's Office Files: Special Correspondence, box 29a, JFKL; transfer meeting notes in Weiner, *Legacy of Ashes*, p. 197.
28. In Salinger, *P.S.*, p. 90.
29. Halberstam, *The Best and the Brightest*, p. 41.
30. Laing, *Robert Kennedy*, p. 140; Oral History Project interview with Adolf Berle, 6 July 1967, p. 20, JFKL.
31. Kennedy, *Times to Remember*, p. 364; RFK in Guthman, *We Band of Brothers*, p. 88.
32. Oral History Project interview with Chester Bowles, 2 February 1965, p. 17, JFKL.
33. Garthoff, *A Journey Through the Cold War*, p. 121; Higgins, *The Perfect Failure*, pp. 85–86. JFK's secretary of the treasury, C. Douglas Dillon, and DDE's former defense secretary, Thomas Gates, were among those who blamed JFK's dismantling of the DDE security apparatus directly for the Bay of Pigs fiasco.
34. JFK in *Atlantic Monthly*, February 1961, p. 6.
35. Memorandum on United States–Haitian relations, 30 January 1961, National Security Files, box 103, JFKL.
36. FD to JFK, 18 January 1961, translated 24 January 1961, National Security Files, box 103, JFKL.
37. Dean Rusk in Heinl and Heinl, *Written in Blood*, p. 590.
38. Williamson, *The U.S. Naval Mission to Haiti*, pp. 148–50; Logan, *Haiti and the Dominican Republic*, p. 155; Heinl and Heinl, *Written in Blood*, pp. 580–81.
39. Adolf Berle to Dean Rusk, 14 February 1961, USNA: RG 59, entry 3148, box 9, Haiti.
40. Robert A. Stevenson, 19 September 1989, FAOH.
41. Memorandum of discussion on Cuba, 28 January 1961, National Security Files, box 35a, JFKL.
42. Allen Dulles in Grose, *Gentleman Spy*, p. 518.
43. Joint Chiefs of Staff report in Freedman, *Kennedy's Wars*, pp. 131–32; see also Bissell, *Reflections of a Cold Warrior*, p. 166.
44. Williamson, *The U.S. Naval Mission to Haiti*, pp. 151–52.
45. Devine to Scott, 25 January 1961, USNA: RG 59, entry 3148, box 9, Dominican Republic—Miscellaneous.
46. Oral History Project interview with Adolf Berle, 6 July 1967, p. 55, JFKL.
47. Kennedy, *Times to Remember*, p. 355.
48. Lem Billings in Heymann, *RFK*, p. 243.
49. Espaillat, *Trujillo*, p. 183.
50. Robert F. Kennedy Oral History, vol. 3, p. 243, JFKL.
51. Hersh, *The Dark Side of Camelot*, pp. 197–99.
52. Henry Dearborn, 8 May 1991, FAOH.
53. Briefing paper on the Dominican Republic, National Security Files, box 66, JFKL.
54. Dean Rusk to JFK, 15 February 1961, National Security Files, box 66, JFKL.

55. Henry Dearborn, 22 March 1961, in Rabe, *The Most Dangerous Area in the World*, p. 38.
56. Leaming, *Jack Kennedy*, p. 258.
57. Robert Maheu in Hersh, *The Dark Side of Camelot*, p. 203; Richard M. Bissell in Vandenbroucke, "The 'Confessions' of Allen Dulles," p. 374n.
58. Hersh, The *Dark Side of Camelot*, p. 205; Freedman, *Kennedy's Wars*, p. 138.
59. Rojo, *My Friend Che*, pp. 100–101.
60. Freedman, *Kennedy's Wars*, p. 138.
61. Immerman, *The CIA in Guatemala*, pp. 194–96.
62. Oral History Project interview with Dean Rusk, 19 February 1970, vol. 1, p. 89, JFKL.
63. JFK, 11 March 1961, in White, *The Kennedys and Cuba*, p. 20; JFK in Grose, *Gentleman Spy*, p. 519; Kornbluh, *Bay of Pigs Declassified*, p. 259.
64. AWD in Vandenbroucke, "The 'Confessions' of Allen Dulles," p. 369; and in Grose, *Gentleman Spy*, p. 522.
65. Jacob Esterline in Kornbluh, *Bay of Pigs Declassified*, p. 261.
66. JFK, "Preliminary Formulations of the Alliance for Progress," presidential address for Latin American diplomats and members of Congress, 13 March 1961.
67. Rabe, *The Most Dangerous Area in the World*, p. 149.
68. Williams, *From Columbus to Castro*, pp. 484–85; Rabe, *Eisenhower and Latin America*, pp. 148–49; Guevara, *Venceremos!*, p. 158.
69. According to Richard Neustadt. Oral History Project interview with McGeorge Bundy, March 1964, p. 152, JFKL.

11. "One of the Most Ridiculous Things That Has Ever Occurred in the History of the United States"

1. McGeorge Bundy to JFK, 15 March 1961, in Freedman, *Kennedy's Wars*, p. 136; and in Hersh, *The Dark Side of Camelot*, p. 211. Emphasis Bundy's.
2. Richard M. Bissell, response to Lucien S. Vandenbroucke, "The 'Confessions' of Allen Dulles: New Evidence on the Bay of Pigs," *Diplomatic History* 8, no. 4 (Fall 1984): 378; and Bissell, *Reflections of a Cold Warrior*, p. 170.
3. Castro and Fernández, *Playa Girón*, p. 102; Sartre, *Sartre on Cuba*, pp. 136–42.
4. Jacob Esterline in Kornbluh, *Bay of Pigs Declassified*, p. 263.
5. Phillips, *The Night Watch*, pp. 101–2.
6. Bissell, response to Vandenbroucke, "The 'Confessions' of Allen Dulles," p. 379.
7. Arthur Schlesinger in Blight and Kornbluh, *Politics of Illusion*, p. 65.
8. Arthur Schlesinger to JFK, 31 March 1961, President's Office Files: Countries, box 114a, JFKL.
9. Chester Bowles to Dean Rusk, 31 March 1961, in White, *The Kennedys and Cuba*, p. 23; William Fulbright to JFK, in Halberstam, *The Best and the Brightest*, p. 497.
10. FCR, 8 April 1961, in Blight and Kornbluh, *Politics of Illusion*, p. 88.
11. Castro and Fernández, *Playa Girón*, p. 62.
12. Blight and Kornbluh, *Politics of Illusion*, pp. 84–87.
13. Wyden, *Bay of Pigs*, pp. 156–57; Adlai Stevenson in Martin, *Adlai Stevenson*, p. 624.
14. Oral History Project interview with Theodore Sorensen, 6 April 1964, p. 17, JFKL.
15. Erneido Oliva in Johnson, *The Bay of Pigs*, p. 74.
16. JFK in Goodwin, *Remembering America*, p. 174.
17. FD in Heinl and Heinl, *Written in Blood*, p. 586; see also State Department report in Péan, *Haïti*, p. 210n.
18. Oral History Project interview with Chester Bowles, 1 July 1970, pp. 61–62, JFKL.
19. JFK in Bissell, *Reflections of a Cold Warrior*, p. 183; BP: PM3028, 1961, Phillips, *The Night Watch*, p. 109. Some sources have this as "Alert! Alert! Look well at the rainbow.

The first will rise very soon," and attribute it to E. Howard Hunt, but Phillips claimed it in his own memoirs. See Hinckle and Turner, *The Fish Is Red*, p. 87.

20. BP: PM3028, 1961; Leaming, *Jack Kennedy*, pp. 246–47; Freedman, *Kennedy's Wars*, pp. 135, 141; Phillips, *The Night Watch*, p. 105; Wyden, *Bay of Pigs*, pp. 175–76.
21. Phillips, *The Night Watch*, p. 106. Emphasis Phillips's.
22. Oral History Project interview with Dean Rusk, 19 February 1970, vol. 1, p. 95, JFKL.
23. Crassweller, *Trujillo*, pp. 430–31; Hersh, *The Dark Side of Camelot*, pp. 197–99.
24. Rabe, *The Most Dangerous Area in the World*, pp. 38–39; Robert Murphy in Espaillat, *Trujillo*, p. 15.
25. FCR, 16 April 1961. In Castro and Fernández, *Playa Girón*, pp. 53–55.
26. JFK in Leaming, *Jack Kennedy*, p. 247.
27. Charles Cabell to Maxwell Taylor, 9 May 1961, in White, *The Kennedys and Cuba*, pp. 28–29.
28. Jack Hawkins and Jacob Esterline in Bissell, *Reflections of a Cold Warrior*, p. 185; Major General George Reid Doster in Wyden, *Bay of Pigs*, p. 202.
29. Allen Dulles in Grose, *Gentleman Spy*, p. 520.
30. Allen Dulles and Robert Amory in ibid., p. 526 and n; see also Bissell, *Reflections of a Cold Warrior*, p. 179.
31. Alfredo Durán in Blight and Kornbluh, *Politics of Illusion*, p. 70.
32. Wyden, *Bay of Pigs*, pp. 136–37.
33. Castro and Fernández, *Playa Girón*, p. 103; Wyden, *Bay of Pigs*, pp. 218–19.
34. Testimony of José Ramón Fernández, in Castro and Fernández, *Playa Girón*, p. 113.
35. William Robertson in Wyden, *Bay of Pigs*, p. 229; Freedman, *Kennedy's Wars*, pp. 142–43.
36. Testimony of José Ramón Fernández, in Castro and Fernández, *Playa Girón*, pp. 107, 110; see also Wyden, *Bay of Pigs*, pp. 248–50.
37. Erneido Oliva in Johnson, *The Bay of Pigs*, p. 135.
38. Andrew and Mitrokhin, *The Mitrokhin Archive II*, p. 39.
39. Bissell, response to Vandenbroucke, "The 'Confessions' of Allen Dulles," p. 378.
40. FCR, "The Order to Battle," 17 April 1961, in Castro and Fernández, *Playa Girón*, pp. 71–72.
41. Blight and Kornbluh, *Politics of Illusion*, pp. 96–97.
42. McGeorge Bundy to JFK, 18 April 1961, National Security Files, box 35a, JFKL.
43. NSK to JFK, 18 April 1961, in White, *The Kennedys and Cuba*, p. 32; JFK to NSK, 18 April 1961, in ibid., p. 34.
44. Arleigh Burke, memorandum, 18 April 1961, in White, *The Kennedys and Cuba*, p. 33; conversation in Freedman, *Kennedy's Wars*, p. 144, from Vandenbroucke, *Perilous Options*, p. 46. See also Bissell, *Reflections of a Cold Warrior*, p. 189.
45. In Leaming, *Jack Kennedy*, p. 249.
46. Salinger, *John F. Kennedy*, p. 42.
47. Leaming, *Jack Kennedy*, p. 250.
48. José Ramón Fernández, in Wyden, *Bay of Pigs*, p. 263.
49. Conversation in Johnson, *The Bay of Pigs*, p. 177.
50. EGS in Rojo, *My Friend Che*, p. 129; see also Gadea, *Ernesto*, p. 174.
51. Joseph Kennedy in Kennedy, *Times to Remember*, p. 372; Allen Dulles in Nixon, *RN*, p. 233; Phillips, *The Night Watch*, p. 109.
52. JFK in Nixon, *RN*, pp. 234–35.
53. Chester Bowles, 20 April 1961, in White, *The Kennedys and Cuba*, p. 37.
54. Halberstam, *The Best and the Brightest*, p. 87.
55. Oral History Project interview with Chester Bowles, 1 July 1970, pp. 65–66, JFKL.
56. Chester Bowles, 20 April 1961, in White, *The Kennedys and Cuba*, p. 37.

57. RFK to JFK, 19 April 1961, in ibid., p. 36.
58. Oral History Project interview with McGeorge Bundy, March 1964, p. 121, JFKL; JFK in Schlesinger, *A Thousand Days*, p. 234.
59. Robert F. Kennedy Oral History, vol. 1, p. 58, JFKL.
60. Samuel Halpern in Blight and Kornbluh, *Politics of Illusion*, p. 139.
61. JFK, 21 April 1961, in Leaming, *Jack Kennedy*, p. 251.
62. Grose, *Gentleman Spy*, p. 530.
63. JFK in Bissell, *Reflections of a Cold Warrior*, p. 191; Mrs. Allen Dulles in Vandenbroucke, "The 'Confessions' of Allen Dulles," p. 366.
64. Chester Bowles, 22 April 1961, in White, *The Kennedys and Cuba*, pp. 43–44. According to Dick Goodwin, Bowles's loss of office was a direct result of his criticism of the Bay of Pigs. Goodwin, *Remembering America*, p. 187.
65. CIA memorandum, 9 May 1961, in White, *The Kennedys and Cuba*, pp. 54–55.
66. Testimony of José Ramón Fernández, in Castro and Fernández, *Playa Girón*, p. 126.
67. Unnamed Cuban exile in Espaillat, *Trujillo*, p. 109.
68. The estimate was made by Hugh Thomas. See Blight and Kornbluh, *Politics of Illusion*, p. 11. Vandenbroucke, *Perilous Options*, p. 44, says that 200,000 were corralled in sports stadia, theaters, and ballparks in Havana alone. It is not clear from Vandenbroucke's piece what evidence exists for such a high figure.
69. Smith, *The Closest of Enemies*, p. 72.
70. Andrew and Mitrokhin, *The Mitrokhin Archive II*, p. 39.
71. Alfredo Durán in Blight and Kornbluh, *Politics of Illusion*, pp. 111–12.
72. Vega, *Kennedy y los Trujillo*, p. 13.
73. FCR and José Peréz San Román in Johnson, *The Bay of Pigs*, pp. 280–81.
74. JFK in Goodwin, *Remembering America*, p. 186.
75. Nixon, *In the Arena*, p. 336; JFK in Hersh, *The Dark Side of Camelot*, p. 209; Leaming, *Jack Kennedy*, pp. 251–52.
76. Douglas MacArthur in Stanley Weintraub, *15 Stars: Eisenhower, MacArthur, Marshall: Three Generals Who Saved the American Century* (New York: Free Press, 2007), p. 499; and in JFK, memorandum, 28 April 1961, President's Office Files: Special Correspondence, box 31, JFKL.
77. Photograph, Castro and Fernández, *Playa Girón*, p. 206.
78. FCR, May Day speech, 1 May 1961, in ibid., pp. 228–29.
79. George Volsky, "Cuba," in Szulc, *The United States and the Caribbean*, p. 106.
80. Khrushchev, *Memoirs*, vol. 3, p. 320.
81. FCR, "Report to the Cuban people on the Victory at Playa Girón," 23 April 1961, in Castro and Fernández, *Playa Girón*, p. 181.
82. Walt Rostow to JFK, 21 April 1961, in Hersh, *The Dark Side of Camelot*, p. 220.
83. Oral History Project interview with McGeorge Bundy, March 1964, pp. 23, 27, JFKL.

12. The Death of the Goat

1. Crassweller, *Trujillo*, pp. 434–35.
2. CIA cable in Hersh, *The Dark Side of Camelot*, p. 199.
3. McGeorge Bundy to JFK, 2 May 1961, National Security Files, box 66, JFKL.
4. Frank Devine to Wymberley Coerr, 8 May 1961, USNA: RG 59, entry 3148, box 9, Dominican Republic—Miscellaneous.
5. "Dominican Situation Report," 8 May 1961, National Security Files, box 66, JFKL.
6. Memo to McGeorge Bundy, n.d. (circa 5 May 1961), National Security Files, box 66, JFKL.
7. Heinl and Heinl, *Written in Blood*, p. 588.
8. Unnamed State Department official in Diederich and Burt, *Papa Doc*, p. 231.

9. Nicholls, *From Dessalines to Duvalier*, p. 231; Diederich and Burt, *Papa Doc*, pp. 169, 344–45; Péan, *Haïti*, p. 386. Some sources say Alexis was tortured to death. Others say he was shot by an army lieutenant. The evidence is not conclusive. See, for instance, Eddy Arnold Jean, *L'itinéraire romanesque de Jacques Stephen Alexis* (Port-au-Prince: Editions Haïti Demain, 2007), pp. 41n, 42; Mudimbe-Boyi Mbulamwanza, *L'oeuvre romanesque de Jacques-Stephen Alexis, écrivain haïtien* (Lubumbashi-Kinshasa: Editions du Mont Noir, 1975), p. 12.
10. Williamson, *The U.S. Naval Mission to Haiti*, pp. 164–65; Heinl and Heinl, *Written in Blood*, p. 591.
11. Henry Dearborn, 8 May 1991, FAOH.
12. JFK in Rabe, *The Most Dangerous Area in the World*, p. 39.
13. Henry Dearborn to Frank Devine, 2 May 1961, USNA: RG 59, entry 3148, box 9, Dominican Republic—Letters.
14. Henry Dearborn, 8 May 1991, FAOH.
15. Rabe, *The Most Dangerous Area in the World*, p. 39.
16. Espaillat, *Trujillo*, p. 18.
17. Crassweller, *Trujillo*, pp. 437–39; Espaillat, *Trujillo*, p. 19.
18. Espaillat, *Trujillo*, pp. 19–20.
19. Henry Dearborn, 8 May 1991, FAOH.
20. Dominican government statement in Espaillat, *Trujillo*, p. 21; Rabe, *The Most Dangerous Area in the World*, p. 40.
21. Robert F. Kennedy Oral History, vol. 1, p. 65, JFKL.
22. Schlesinger, *A Thousand Days*, p. 289.
23. Freedman, *Kennedy's Wars*, p. 4; see also Dallek, *John F. Kennedy*, pp. 398–99.
24. The author thanks Dr. Monal Wadhera, who carried out a blind analysis of the available details of JFK's medical history.
25. JFK in Dobbs, *One Minute to Midnight*, p. 318; Leaming, *Jack Kennedy*, p. 258.
26. Leaming, *Jack Kennedy*, pp. 264–69; Taubman, *Khrushchev*, p. 494.
27. Khrushchev, *Khrushchev Remembers*, p. 458; see also Khrushchev, *Memoirs*, vol. 3, p. 296.
28. JFK confided this off the record to Herbert Matthews, who only revealed it after JFK's death. Herbert L. Matthews, lecture, Notre Dame, 10 November 1964, box 27, HLMP. See also memorandum of the Vienna discussions in White, *The Kennedys and Cuba*, p. 60.
29. Memorandum of the Vienna discussions, in White, *The Kennedys and Cuba*, p. 60. See also Fursenko and Naftali, *Khrushchev's Cold War*, p. 361.
30. Robert F. Kennedy Oral History, vol. 8, p. 630, JFKL; Martin, *Kennedy and Latin America*, p. 403.
31. JFK and James Reston in Halberstam, *The Best and the Brightest*, pp. 96–97.
32. Alfredo Lebron, 31 May 1961, USNA: RG 59, entry 3148, box 9, Dominican Republic (Chronology).
33. Crassweller, *Trujillo*, p. 444.
34. Ibid., p. 446.
35. Oral History Project interview with Chester Bowles, 1 July 1970, p. 48, JFKL.
36. Rabe, *The Most Dangerous Area in the World*, p. 40.
37. Halberstam, *The Best and the Brightest*, p. 89; Oral History Project interview with Chester Bowles, 1 July 1970, p. 49, JFKL.
38. Abraham F. Lowenthal, "The United States and the Dominican Republic to 1965: Background to Intervention," *Caribbean Studies* 10, no. 2 (July 1970): 35; Espaillat, *Trujillo*, p. 17.

39. Interview in Santo Domingo, October 2008. Name withheld by author.
40. Henry Dearborn, 8 May 1991, FAOH.
41. Leaming, *Jack Kennedy*, p. 281.
42. JFK in Schlesinger, *A Thousand Days*, p. 598; see also Henry Dearborn, 8 May 1991, FAOH.
43. Dick Goodwin to McGeorge Bundy, 8 June 1961, National Security Files, box 66, JFKL; Rabe, *The Most Dangerous Area in the World*, p. 41.
44. See, for example, Goodwin, *Remembering America*, p. 152.
45. Robert A. Stevenson, 19 September 1989, FAOH.
46. Espaillat, *Trujillo*, p. xiii.
47. Crassweller, *Trujillo*, pp. 137–41.
48. Martin, *Kennedy and Latin America*, p. 260n.
49. "Courses of Action in the Dominican Republic," 17 June 1961; State Department to John Calvin Hill, 3 August 1961; and "Courses of Action in the Dominican Republic," 17 June 1961; all in National Security Files, box 66, JFKL.
50. John Bartlow Martin, report on the Dominican Republic; Joaquín Balaguer statement, 8 July 1961; both in President's Office Files: Countries, box 115a, JFKL.
51. "Popular Dominican Movement," n.d. (July 1961), National Security Files, box 66, JFKL; John Bartlow Martin, report on the Dominican Republic, President's Office Files: Countries, box 115a, JFKL.
52. John Calvin Hill to State Department, 24 July 1961, National Security Files, box 66, JFKL.
53. John Calvin Hill to State Department, 31 July 1961, in ibid.
54. John Calvin Hill to State Department, 1 August 1961, in ibid.
55. John Bartlow Martin in Heinl and Heinl, *Written in Blood*, p. 596; Diederich and Burt, *Papa Doc*, p. 171; Abbott, *Haiti*, p. 103; Williamson, *The U.S. Naval Mission to Haiti*, p. 199.
56. Heinl and Heinl, *Written in Blood*, pp. 578–79; Ferguson, *Papa Doc, Baby Doc*, pp. 46–47; Diederich and Burt, *Papa Doc*, p. 173.
57. Martin, *Kennedy and Latin America*, pp. 234–35.
58. Dean Rusk to State Department, 2 June 1961, in Rabe, *The Most Dangerous Area in the World*, p. 50.
59. "Castro/Communist Penetration in the Dominican Republic," 17 August 1961, USNA: RG 59, entry 3148, box 9, Dominican Republic—Miscellaneous.
60. Andrew and Mitrokhin, *The Mitrokhin Archive II*, p. 40.
61. Italian embassy report, 26 July 1961, USNA: RG 59, entry 3148, box 8, Cuba—Various Reports; Andrew and Mitrokhin, *The Mitrokhin Archive II*, pp. 43–45.
62. CIA paper, undated [circa August 1961], in White, *The Kennedys and Cuba*, pp. 62–63.
63. NSK in Detzer, *The Brink*, p. 154.
64. EGS in Rojo, *My Friend Che*, p. 119.
65. EGS in Ernesto Che Guevara, "Cuba and the 'Kennedy Plan,'" *World Marxist Review* 5, no. 2 (February 1962): p. 28; C. Douglas Dillon in Rabe, *The Most Dangerous Area in the World*, p. 32.
66. Unnamed Brazilian diplomat in Goodwin, *Remembering America*, p. 195.
67. EGS in ibid., p. 196.
68. Goodwin, *Remembering America*, pp. 197–99.
69. Richard Goodwin to JFK, 22 August 1961, USNA: RG 59, entry 3148, box 8, Cuba—Miscellaneous, July-August 1961; Goodwin, *Remembering America*, pp. 198–202; George Volsky, "Cuba," in Szulc, *The United States and the Caribbean*, p. 109.

70. Goodwin, *Remembering America*, pp. 207–8.
71. In September 1963, Carlos Lechuga, Cuba's ambassador to the UN, met the American diplomat William Atwood for preliminary talks. Atwood was not a member of the Kennedy administration, but he was its representative. Castañeda, *Compañero*, p. 242.

13. Throwing a Hedgehog Down Uncle Sam's Pants

1. Review of Operation Mongoose, 18 January 1962, in White, *The Kennedys and Cuba*, p. 88; Sherman Kent to AWD, 3 November 1961, in ibid., p. 75.
2. Edward Lansdale in Heymann, *RFK*, p. 258; Rafael Quintero in Blight and Kornbluh, *Politics of Illusion*, p. 121.
3. Richard Bissell in Shesol, *Mutual Contempt*, p. 128; Samuel Halpern in Blight and Kornbluh, *Politics of Illusion*, p. 117.
4. Memorandum on Operation Mongoose, 2 February 1962, in White, *The Kennedys and Cuba*, pp. 100–105.
5. Detzer, *The Brink*, pp. 34–35; Ray Cline in Heymann, *RFK*, p. 260.
6. CIA memo, 8 August 1962, in Dobbs, *One Minute to Midnight*, pp. 17–18.
7. Unnamed CIA official in Detzer, *The Brink*, p. 35; Robert F. Kennedy Oral History, vol. 3, p. 281, JFKL; Rafael Quintero in Blight and Kornbluh, *Politics of Illusion*, p. 127.
8. Rafael Quintero in Blight and Kornbluh, *Politics of Illusion*, p. 120.
9. Samuel Halpern in ibid., p. 116.
10. Robert F. Kennedy Oral History, vol. 3, p. 281, JFKL.
11. Unnamed CIA agent in Heymann, *RFK*, p. 259.
12. Castro and Fernández, *Playa Girón*, p. 83n; Higgins, *The Perfect Failure*, p. 55.
13. Hersh, *The Dark Side of Camelot*, pp. 187–89.
14. Leaming, *Jack Kennedy*, p. 308.
15. JFK, November 1961, in Schlesinger, *Robert Kennedy*, p. 492.
16. McGeorge Bundy and Robert McNamara in ibid., p. 498; JFK in Shesol, *Mutual Contempt*, p. 127.
17. Summers, *Official and Confidential*, p. 290.
18. McGeorge Bundy in Detzer, *The Brink*, p. 37.
19. Higgins, *The Perfect Failure*, pp. 152–53; Hinckle and Turner, *The Fish Is Red*, p. 104.
20. Chester Bowles, May 1961, in Halberstam, *The Best and the Brightest*, p. 88.
21. Ramfis Trujillo in Gleijeses, *The Dominican Crisis*, p. 37.
22. John Bartlow Martin in Chester, *Rag-Tags, Scum, Riff-Raff, and Commies*, p. 25; and in Schmitz, *Thank God They're on Our Side*, p. 249.
23. Roger Hilsman, 20 September 1961, National Security Files, box 66, JFKL.
24. BP: PM2601, 23 October 1961.
25. María Martínez to Ramfis Trujillo, n.d., in Gleijeses, *The Dominican Crisis*, p. 45.
26. Ramfis Trujillo, 26 October 1961, in ibid., p. 41.
27. María Martínez to Ramfis Trujillo, n.d., in ibid., p. 45.
28. Oral History Project interview with Teodoro Moscoso, 18 May 1964, pp. 20–25, JFKL.
29. Gleijeses, *The Dominican Crisis*, p. 46; Rabe, *The Most Dangerous Area in the World*, pp. 42–43; Crassweller, *Trujillo*, p. 446.
30. "Where the Money Went," *Time*, 23 November 1962; Wiarda, *The Dominican Republic*, p. 41.
31. Dean Rusk in Abraham F. Lowenthal, "The United States and the Dominican Republic to 1965: Background to Intervention," *Caribbean Studies* 10, no. 2 (July 1970): 35.
32. Lowenthal, "The United States and the Dominican Republic to 1965," p. 35; BP: PM2611, 7 December 1961; BP: PM2607, 14 December 1961.

33. JFK to John Calvin Hill, 16 December 1961; Joaquín Balaguer in John Calvin Hill to secretary of state, 19 December 1961; both in National Security Files, box 66, JFKL.
34. Gleijeses, *The Dominican Crisis*, pp. 55–64.
35. Chester, *Rag-Tags, Scum, Riff-Raff, and Commies*, pp. 26–28.
36. JFK in "Verdict on Santo Domingo," *Time*, 11 November 1966.
37. Duvalier, *Mémoires*, pp. 315–18; Heinl and Heinl, *Written in Blood*, pp. 578–79; Ferguson, *Papa Doc, Baby Doc*, pp. 46–47; Diederich and Burt, *Papa Doc*, p. 184.
38. Robert Newbegin to Dean Rusk, 6 November 1961, National Security Files, box 103, JFKL.
39. Oral History Project interview with Raymond Thurston by Dennis J. O'Brien, 9 June 1970, p. 20, JFKL.
40. Martin, *Kennedy and Latin America*, p. 234; Oral History Project interview with Raymond Thurston by Dennis J. O'Brien, 9 June 1970, p. 18, JFKL.
41. Raymond Thurston to Department of State, 17 January 1962, National Security Files, box 103, JFKL.
42. Williamson, *The U.S. Naval Mission to Haiti*, p. 199.
43. Schlesinger, *A Thousand Days*, pp. 607–8; Rabe, *The Most Dangerous Area in the World*, p. 51; Heinl and Heinl, *Written in Blood*, p. 589. The Heinls give the "breakfast" sum as $2.25. The twelve nations that could be relied on to vote with the United States were Colombia, Costa Rica, the Dominican Republic, El Salvador, Guatemala, Honduras, Nicaragua, Panama, Paraguay, Peru, Uruguay, and Venezuela. See also Ferguson, *Papa Doc, Baby Doc*, pp. 42–44; Martin, *Kennedy and Latin America*, pp. 201, 239; Logan, *Haiti and the Dominican Republic*, p. 155; Federico G. Gil, "The Kennedy-Johnson Years," in Martz, *United States Policy in Latin America*, pp. 21–22.
44. Raymond Thurston to secretary of state, 28 January 1962, National Security Files, box 103, JFKL.
45. Oral History Project interview with Raymond Thurston by Dennis J. O'Brien, 9 June 1970, p. 21, JFKL.
46. JFK in Halberstam, *The Best and the Brightest*, p. 84; Dockrill and Hopkins, *The Cold War*, p. 84.
47. Marshal Kirill Moskalenko in Taubman, *Khrushchev*, p. 537.
48. Detzer, *The Brink*, pp. 48–49; Leaming, *Jack Kennedy*, pp. 328–29.
49. Via Sergei Khrushchev, in Blight et al., *Cuba on the Brink*, p. 130.
50. 20 February 1961, USNA: RG 59, entry 3148, box 8, Cuba—Miscellaneous, January–February 1961.
51. Park Wollam to departments, 25 September 1961, USNA: RG 59, entry 3148, box 8, Cuba—Miscellaneous, September–December 1961.
52. Department of State statement, 22 January 1962, in Bender, *Cuba vs. United States*, p. 21.
53. Taubman, *Khrushchev*, p. 534.
54. FCR in Detzer, *The Brink*, p. 25.
55. Castañeda, *Compañero*, p. 209; Reid-Henry, *Fidel and Che*, p. 244.
56. Author's interview with Adolfo Rivero, January 2010.
57. EGS in Castañeda, *Compañero*, p. 212.
58. George Volsky, "Cuba," in Szulc, *The United States and the Caribbean*, p. 103; Hugh Thomas, "Mao's Cuba," *New Statesman*, 2 November 1962; Ernst Halperin, "The Castro Regime in Cuba," *Current History* 51, no. 304 (December 1966): 356–59; Fursenko and Naftali, *Khrushchev's Cold War*, p. 427.
59. Khrushchev, *Khrushchev Remembers*, p. 461; NSK in Taubman, *Khrushchev*, p. 541; Fursenko and Naftali, *Khrushchev's Cold War*, p. 431.

60. NSK in Taubman, *Khrushchev*, p. 535. The quotation appears, in a slightly different translation, in Khrushchev, *Memoirs*, vol. 3, pp. 325–26.
61. J. Edgar Hoover in Heymann, *RFK*, p. 267; Summers, *Official and Confidential*, p. 291.
62. RFK, 9 May 1962, in Shesol, *Mutual Contempt*, p. 129; Heymann, *RFK*, p. 267.
63. Kirk LeMoyne Billings in Heymann, *RFK*, p. 268.
64. Edward Lansdale, December 1961, in Dobbs, *One Minute to Midnight*, p. 154.
65. Wyden, *Bay of Pigs*, p. 110n.
66. Richard Helms in Shesol, *Mutual Contempt*, p. 129; Richard Goodwin in Hinckle and Turner, *The Fish Is Red*, p. 109; unnamed CIA official in Mosley, *Dulles*, p. 473n.
67. Salinger, *John F. Kennedy*, p. 127; review of Operation Mongoose, 20 February 1962, in White, *The Kennedys and Cuba*, p. 106; Blight et al., *Cuba on the Brink*, pp. 18–19.
68. Fursenko and Naftali, *Khrushchev's Cold War*, p. 435.
69. NSK in Taubman, *Khrushchev*, p. 545; Blight et al., *Cuba on the Brink*, pp. 77–78.
70. FCR, speaking in 1992, in Lechuga, *Cuba and the Missile Crisis*, pp. 24–25; see also Taubman, *Khrushchev*, p. 545; FCR in Blight et al., *Cuba on the Brink*, p. 83.
71. Vitali Korionov in Anderson, *Che Guevara*, p. 527.
72. Edwin Martin acknowledged this in his memoirs. Martin, *Kennedy and Latin America*, p. 443.
73. Robert Heinl in Raymond Thurston to Dean Rusk, 1 August 1962, National Security Files, box 103, JFKL; Oral History Project interview with Raymond Thurston, 9 June 1970, p. 23, JFKL.
74. State Department memo of Goodwin/Thurston/JFK meeting, n.d. (circa June 1962), National Security Files, box 103, JFKL.
75. Raymond Thurston to Dean Rusk, 15 June 1962; and Raymond Thurston to secretary of state, 11 August 1961; both in National Security Files, box 103, JFKL.
76. Abbott, *Haiti*, p. 108.
77. Martin, *Kennedy and Latin America*, p. 242.
78. See, for example, "The Situation in Haiti," 7 August 1962, National Security Files, box 103, JFKL.
79. Raymond Thurston to Dean Rusk, 1 August 1962, National Security Files, box 103, JFKL; Williamson, *The U.S. Naval Mission to Haiti*, p. 239; Raymond Thurston to Dean Rusk, 8 August 1961, National Security Files, box 103, JFKL.
80. Raymond Thurston to Dean Rusk, 8 August 1961; Robert Heinl to Dean Rusk, 9 August 1962; both in National Security Files, box 103, JFKL.
81. Miscellaneous notes on Haiti, 9 August 1962; Raymond Thurston to Dean Rusk, 17 August 1962; both in ibid.
82. Raymond Thurston to secretary of state, 21 August 1962; CIA information telegram, 23 August 1962; both in ibid.
83. CIA information telegram, 21 September 1962, in ibid.
84. Raymond Thurston to secretary of state, 30 September 1962, in ibid.
85. Detzer, *The Brink*, pp. 56–58.
86. Roswell Gilpatric to the Special Group (Augmented), 28 June 1962, in White, *The Kennedys and Cuba*, p. 121.
87. Detzer, *The Brink*, p. 63; Robert A. Stevenson, 19 September 1989, FAOH.
88. Hinckle and Turner, *The Fish Is Red*, pp. 131–32; Detzer, *The Brink*, pp. 36–37.
89. FCR in Blight et al., *Cuba on the Brink*, p. 85.
90. Leonid Brezhnev in Castañeda, *Compañero*, p. 227.
91. Lechuga, *Cuba and the Missile Crisis*, p. 31.
92. Emilio Aragonés in Taubman, *Khrushchev*, p. 553; Blight et al., *Cuba on the Brink*, p. 351.
93. JFK in Leaming, *Jack Kennedy*, p. 349; John McCone in Schecter and Deriabin, *The*

Spy Who Saved the World, p. 333; Abel, *The Missiles of October*, pp. 20, 25; Detzer, *The Brink*, p. 64.

14. Apocalypse Now?

1. Arthur Sylvester in Abel, *The Missiles of October*, p. 97.
2. Dobbs, *One Minute to Midnight*, pp. 23–24, 61–62, 211–12; Detzer, *The Brink*, p. 145. The tramway mission was led by Eugenio Martinez, later one of the burglars at Watergate.
3. 3 October 1962, in Bender, *Cuba vs. United States*, p. 21.
4. NSK to Stewart Udall, 6 September 1962, in White, *The Kennedys and Cuba*, pp. 153–54; TASS statement, *New York Times*, 12 September 1962, in Roberta Wohlstetter, "Cuba and Pearl Harbor: Hindsight and Foresight," *Foreign Affairs* 43, no. 4 (July 1965): 702–3; Detzer, *The Brink*, p. 66.
5. CIA memorandum, 12 September 1962, National Security Files, box 46, JFKL.
6. Williamson, *The U.S. Naval Mission to Haiti*, p. 244.
7. National Security Policy directive, September 1962, in Rabe, *The Most Dangerous Area in the World*, p. 44.
8. John Bartlow Martin to State Department, 10 October 1962, National Security Files, box 67, JFKL.
9. Detzer, *The Brink*, pp. 70–71, 91; Abel, *The Missiles of October*, pp. 26–33.
10. JFK in Leaming, *Jack Kennedy*, p. 355; and in Taubman, *Khrushchev*, p. 529.
11. JFK and McGeorge Bundy in May and Zelikow, *The Kennedy Tapes*, p. 100.
12. Martin, *Kennedy and Latin America*, pp. 441–42.
13. Conversation in Detzer, *The Brink*, p. 130.
14. JFK via Kenneth O'Donnell, in Detzer, *The Brink*, p. 159; see also Martin, *Adlai Stevenson*, p. 724.
15. Adlai Stevenson in Detzer, *The Brink*, p. 159.
16. Kenneth O'Donnell in Abel, *The Missiles of October*, p. 86; Detzer, *The Brink*, p. 153.
17. Karl E. Meyer, "Solidarity in Washington," *New Statesman*, 26 October 1962.
18. Abel, *The Missiles of October*, p. 88.
19. NSK in Dobbs, *One Minute to Midnight*, p. 32; and in Taubman, *Khrushchev*, p. 561.
20. Lechuga, *Cuba and the Missile Crisis*, p. 49.
21. Oral History Project interview with Edwin Martin, 20 May 1964, pp. 35–36, JFKL.
22. Oral History Project interview with Dean Rusk, 19 February 1970, vol. 1, p. 119, JFKL.
23. McGeorge Bundy in May and Zelikow, *The Kennedy Tapes*, p. 99.
24. Dobbs, *One Minute to Midnight*, p. 58. Dobbs credits the cruise missiles with a range of 110 miles (180 kilometers). The figure of 60 kilometers comes from Lechuga, *Cuba and the Missile Crisis*. See also Fursenko and Naftali, *Khrushchev's Cold War*, p. 440, for more figures on Soviet deployment in Cuba.
25. Lechuga, *Cuba and the Missile Crisis*, p. 48.
26. CIA memorandum, 26 October 1962, National Security Files, box 46a, JFKL; Dobbs, *One Minute to Midnight*, pp. 80–82.
27. Soviet order, 8 September 1962, in Dobbs, *One Minute to Midnight*, p. 125; ibid., pp. 126–27.
28. BP: PM1735, 1 November 1962; Ambassador Kidd in CIA memorandum, 27 October 1962, National Security Files, box 46a, JFKL.
29. FCR in Blight et al., *Cuba on the Brink*, p. 111.
30. Gleijeses, *The Dominican Crisis*, p. 70.
31. FD to JFK, 23 October 1962, National Security Files, box 103, JFKL.
32. Williamson, *The U.S. Naval Mission to Haiti*, p. 250.
33. Heinl and Heinl, *Written in Blood*, p. 592.

34. Raymond Thurston to Dean Rusk, 23 November 1962, National Security Files, box 103, JFKL.
35. "Haiti—Plan of Action," 16 October 1962, National Security Files, box 103, JFKL. The ellipsis is a short, blacked-out section, which perhaps defines the type of measures suggested or the person or body who suggested it.
36. Raymond Thurston to Dean Rusk, 12 November 1962, National Security Files, box 103, JFKL.
37. "Revised Action Plan (Haiti)," 20 January 1963, in ibid.
38. Vasily Kuznetsov in Taubman, *Khrushchev*, p. 568.
39. May and Zelikow, *The Kennedy Tapes*, p. 491; Curtis LeMay in Dobbs, *One Minute to Midnight*, p. 165.
40. Dobbs, *One Minute to Midnight*, pp. 178–81; Detzer, *The Brink*, p. 233.
41. NSK to JFK, 27 October 1962, National Security Files, box 47, JFKL.
42. McGeorge Bundy in May and Zelikow, *The Kennedy Tapes*, p. 509; Taubman, *Khrushchev*, pp. 569–70.
43. FCR in Blight et al., *Cuba on the Brink*, p. 107.
44. FCR in Taubman, *Khrushchev*, p. 572.
45. FCR to NSK, 26/27 October 1962, in Blight et al., *Cuba on the Brink*, p. 509.
46. FCR in ibid., p. 109.
47. Dobbs, *One Minute to Midnight*, pp. 236–37.
48. Ibid., p. 260.
49. JFK in Detzer, *The Brink*, p. 246.
50. Rodion Malinovsky in Lechuga, *Cuba and the Missile Crisis*, p. 74.
51. JFK in May and Zelikow, *The Kennedy Tapes*, p. 566; JFK to NSK, 27 October 1962, in ibid., p. 604.
52. RFK in May and Zelikow, *The Kennedy Tapes*, p. 608.
53. Khrushchev, *Memoirs*, vol. 3, p. 341.
54. Martin, *Kennedy and Latin America*, p. 443.
55. Oleg Troyanovsky in Blight et al., *Cuba on the Brink*, p. 74.
56. Khrushchev, *Memoirs*, vol. 3, p. 341.
57. JFK in Taubman, *Khrushchev*, p. 581.
58. Aleksandr Alekseyev in ibid., p. 781n.
59. EGS in Rojo, *My Friend Che*, p. 134; FCR in Taubman, *Khrushchev*, p. 579. "No *cojones!*" means "No testicles!" and "*Maricón!*" is a homophobic insult, equivalent to "faggot."
60. NSK to FCR, 28 October 1962, in Blight et al., *Cuba on the Brink*, p. 510; FCR to NSK, 31 October 1962, in ibid., p. 517; FCR to NSK, 31 October 1962, in ibid., p. 518.
61. FCR, January 1958, in Blight et al., *Cuba on the Brink*, p. 190.
62. Castañeda, *Compañero*, p. 229.
63. U Thant in Lechuga, *Cuba and the Missile Crisis*, p. 102; see also FCR in Blight et al., *Cuba on the Brink*, p. 218.
64. JFK to NSK, 14 December 1962, in White, *The Kennedys and Cuba*, pp. 296–98.
65. FCR in Blight et al., *Cuba on the Brink*, p. 219; EGS in Reid-Henry, *Fidel and Che*, p. 274.
66. Abel, *The Missiles of October*, p. 195; see also Khrushchev, *Memoirs*, vol. 3, pp. 342–43; CIA memorandum, 1 November 1962, National Security Files, box 46a, JFKL.
67. EGS to Anna Louise Strong, 19 November 1962, in Castañeda, *Compañero*, p. 231n.
68. Ex-Comm meeting, 20 November 1962, in White, *The Kennedys and Cuba*, p. 286.
69. RFK in Paterson, *Contesting Castro*, p. 261.
70. CIA memorandum, 1 November 1962, National Security Files, box 46a, JFKL; JFK in Meneses, *Fidel Castro*, p. 158.
71. William Harvey in Dobbs, *One Minute to Midnight*, p. 155.

72. White, *The Kennedys and Cuba*, p. 301, and see documents pp. 308, 321, 330–31.
73. JFK in Oral History Project interview with Chester Bowles, 2 February 1965, p. 27, JFKL.

15. Papadocracy

1. Gleijeses, *The Dominican Crisis*, pp. 82–85.
2. Rómulo Betancourt in Martin, *Kennedy and Latin America*, p. 217.
3. It is, for example, echoed by Arthur Schlesinger as "Bosch was essentially a literary figure, better as a short story writer than as a statesman." Schlesinger, *A Thousand Days*, p. 600.
4. Juan Bosch in Martin, *Kennedy and Latin America*, p. 214; and in memorandum of conversation, 10 January 1963, National Security Files, box 66, JFKL; JFK in Oral History Project interview with Juan Bosch by Lloyd N. Cutler, Spring 1964, p. 6, JFKL.
5. Oral History Project interview with Juan Bosch by Lloyd N. Cutler, Spring 1964, pp. 2–3, JFKL.
6. Oral History Project interview with Edwin Martin, 20 May 1964, p. 45, JFKL.
7. Martin, *Kennedy and Latin America*, p. 261n.
8. CIA memorandum, 2 January 1963, National Security Files, box 66, JFKL; George Ball in Rabe, *The Most Dangerous Area in the World*, p. 45.
9. Martin, *Kennedy and Latin America*, p. 218.
10. Ibid.
11. John Bartlow Martin in Gleijeses, *The Dominican Crisis*, p. 89.
12. Oral History Project interview with Juan Bosch by Lloyd N. Cutler, Spring 1964, p. 6, JFKL; John Bartlow Martin, January 1963, in Rabe, *The Most Dangerous Area in the World*, p. 46; Juan Bosch in CIA intelligence memorandum, 7 June 1963, National Security Files, box 66, JFKL.
13. CIA intelligence memorandum, 7 June 1963; William H. Brubeck to McGeorge Bundy, 4 June 1963; both in National Security Files, box 66, JFKL.
14. JFK, 19 April 1963, in Martin, *Kennedy and Latin America*, p. 195; and in BP: PM2647, 4 April 1963.
15. Lisa Howard, 1 May 1963, in Schlesinger, *Robert Kennedy*, p. 542.
16. NSK to FCR, 31 January 1963, in Castañeda, *Compañero*, p. 230.
17. BP: PM2659, 1963; PM2651, 1963.
18. Taubman, *Khrushchev*, pp. 597–98. NSK himself gave a lengthy and rather one-sided account of his discussions with FCR in Khrushchev, *Memoirs*, vol. 3, pp. 343–49.
19. Nicholls, *From Dessalines to Duvalier*, p. 224; Abbott, *Haiti*, pp. 106–7.
20. Unnamed psychiatrist in Hinckle and Turner, *The Fish Is Red*, p. 237.
21. Dunham, *Island Possessed*, pp. 164–65.
22. Heinl and Heinl, *Written in Blood*, p. 632n.
23. Ibid., p. 595; Diederich and Burt, *Papa Doc*, p. 196; Robert D. Tomasek, "The Haitian-Dominican Republic Controversy of 1963 and the Organization of American States," *Orbis* 12, no. 1 (Spring 1968): 302.
24. Heinl and Heinl, *Written in Blood*, p. 595; CIA information telegram, 14 February 1963, National Security Files, box 103, JFKL.
25. Dean Rusk to embassies, 7 March 1963, National Security Files, box 103, JFKL.
26. CIA information telegram, 24 March 1963, in ibid.
27. Raymond Thurston to Dean Rusk, 15 March 1963, in ibid.
28. "Haiti—Current Situation," n.d. (March 1962) and list of current opposition groups in Haiti, April 1963; both in ibid.
29. CIA information telegram, 10 April 1963, in ibid. The CIA report added, "There was

no indication that the president meant to use communist tactics or ally himself with the Sino-Soviet bloc." The most alarming thing in the report was arguably the fact that the CIA still considered there to be such a thing as the Sino-Soviet bloc, seven years after the split between China and the Soviet Union had begun, and two after it had become public.

30. Raymond Thurston to Dean Rusk, 20 April 1962, National Security Files, box 103, JFKL.
31. CIA information telegram, 18 April 1963, in ibid.
32. Heinl and Heinl, *Written in Blood*, p. 596; Abbott, *Haiti*, pp. 108–10; Diederich and Burt, *Papa Doc*, p. 199. Heinl's and Abbott's versions do not record Turnier's escape, and Diederich and Burt claim it was government propaganda, but it is documented in several CIA, embassy, and other information telegrams in National Security Files, box 103, JFKL.
33. Raymond Thurston to Dean Rusk, 20 April 1963, National Security Files, box 103, JFKL.
34. Abbott, *Haiti*, pp. 108–10; Charles Bushey, diary, 22 April 1963, in Williamson, *The U.S. Naval Mission to Haiti*, p. 307; CIA information telegram, 25 April 1963, National Security Files, box 103, JFKL.
35. Jacques Fourcand in Abbott, *Haiti*, p. 110.
36. "Breaking the Spell," *Time*, 3 May 1971; see also Raymond Thurston to Dean Rusk, 30 April 1963, National Security Files, box 103, JFKL, which implies the total shot may have been as high as ninety.
37. National Security Files, box 103, JFKL; Heinl and Heinl, *Written in Blood*, p. 597; Abbott, *Haiti*, p. 110; Ferguson, *Papa Doc, Baby Doc*, pp. 44–45; Williamson, *The U.S. Naval Mission to Haiti*, p. 309. There is some confusion in the National Security Files as to whether Mme Benoît was eventually murdered or not.
38. Juan Bosch in "The Worst of Neighbors," *Time*, 10 May 1963.
39. Raymond Thurston to Dean Rusk, 6 May 1963; and Raymond Thurston to Dean Rusk, 27 April 1963; both in National Security Files, box 103, JFKL.
40. John Bartlow Martin to secretary of state, 26 April 1963, National Security Files, box 67, JFKL. The reports were made to Martin by Lieutenant Colonel Roger Alvarez, an anti-Duvalier Haitian.
41. Naval message, 27 April 1963, National Security Files, box 103, JFKL.
42. Jacques Fourcand in Heinl and Heinl, *Written in Blood*, p. 598.
43. John Bartlow Martin to secretary of state, 26 April 1963, National Security Files, box 67, JFKL.
44. Raymond Thurston to Dean Rusk, 18 April 1962, National Security Files, box 103, JFKL.
45. Tomasek, "The Haitian-Dominican Republic Controversy of 1963 and the Organization of American States," pp. 294–95; Army Staff Communications message, 29 April 1963, National Security Files, box 103, JFKL.
46. Tomasek, "The Haitian-Dominican Republic Controversy of 1963 and the Organization of American States," pp. 295–96; Diederich and Burt, *Papa Doc*, p. 213.
47. FD in Abbott, *Haiti*, p. 111.
48. FD in "The Worst of Neighbors."
49. Tomasek, "The Haitian-Dominican Republic Controversy of 1963 and the Organization of American States," pp. 296–97.
50. Williamson, *The U.S. Naval Mission to Haiti*, p. 326; BP: PM2653, 9 May 1963; *Herald Tribune* in Abbott, *Haiti*, p. 111.
51. "Short-term Prospects for Haiti and Possible U.S. Courses of Action," Department of State, 8 May 1963, National Security Files, box 103a, JFKL.

52. CIA information telegram, 9 May 1963, in ibid.
53. Juan Bosch in John Bartlow Martin to Dean Rusk, 14 May 1963, National Security Files, box 104, JFKL.
54. In Gérard R. Latortue, "Tyranny in Haiti," *Current History* 51, no. 304 (December 1966): 351.
55. FCR in Blight et al., *Cuba on the Brink*, p. 272.
56. Heinl and Heinl, *Written in Blood*, pp. 592, 601; George Ball in Rabe, *The Most Dangerous Area in the World*, p. 53; Martin, *Kennedy and Latin America*, p. 245; CIA information telegram, 14 May 1963, National Security Files, box 104, JFKL.
57. FD in Heinl and Heinl, *Written in Blood*, p. 601, and in Raymond Thurston to Dean Rusk, 15 May 1963, National Security Files, box 104, JFKL; Martin, *Kennedy and Latin America*, pp. 247–48.
58. JFK and Dean Rusk, 16 May 1953, Presidential Recordings (transcript of dictabelt 19a), JFKL, in Péan, *Haïti*, p. 322n.
59. Martin, *Kennedy and Latin America*, p. 248.
60. Ibid., p. 249.
61. Raymond Thurston in Heinl and Heinl, *Written in Blood*, p. 618.
62. "The Living Dead," *Time*, 26 July 1963.
63. Diederich and Burt, *Papa Doc*, p. 201.
64. FD in Heinl and Heinl, *Written in Blood*, p. 602; "The Living Dead."
65. Williamson, *The U.S. Naval Mission to Haiti*, p. 321; Diederich and Burt, *Papa Doc*, p. 222.
66. Jerry O'Leary in Williamson, *The U.S. Naval Mission to Haiti*, p. 332.
67. Heinl and Heinl, *Written in Blood*, p. 632n.
68. Clément Barbot in ibid., p. 603.
69. Raymond Thurston to Dean Rusk, 20 May 1963, National Security Files, box 104, JFKL.
70. Williamson, *The U.S. Naval Mission to Haiti*, pp. 332–33; Raymond Thurston to Dean Rusk, 21 May 1963, National Security Files, box 104, JFKL.
71. Ambassador to Bogotá (Freeman) to Dean Rusk, 24 May 1963, National Security Files, box 104, JFKL.
72. Diederich and Burt, *Papa Doc*, p. 237; Williamson, *The U.S. Naval Mission to Haiti*, p. 336.
73. JFK to Dean Rusk, 4 June 1963, National Security Files, box 104, JFKL.
74. Dean Rusk to JFK, 7 June 1963, in ibid.
75. Martin, *Kennedy and Latin America*, p. 250.
76. "The Living Dead"; see also Heinl and Heinl, *Written in Blood*, p. 603.
77. Glion Curtis to Dean Rusk, 15 July 1963, National Security Files, box 104, JFKL.
78. Williamson, *The U.S. Naval Mission to Haiti*, pp. 348–49.
79. Tomasek, "The Haitian-Dominican Republic Controversy of 1963 and the Organization of American States," p. 302; Rabe, *The Most Dangerous Area in the World*, pp. 53–54. See also, for instance, Glion Curtis to Dean Rusk, 5 August 1963; CIA information telegram, 8 August 1963; and CIA information report, 29 August 1963, all in National Security Files, box 104a, JFKL.
80. Martin, *Kennedy and Latin America*, p. 251.
81. JFK, 10 July 1963, in Garthoff, *A Journey Through the Cold War*, p. 165.
82. NSK to RFK, 29 June 1964, Oral History Project, JFKL.
83. Moreno, *Barrios in Arms*, pp. 17–20; Gordon K. Lewis, "The Politics of the Caribbean," in Szulc, *The United States and the Caribbean*, p. 29.
84. John Bartlow Martin to State Department, 22 September 1963, National Security Files, box 66, JFKL; Martin, *Kennedy and Latin America*, p. 220.

85. Juan Bosch in Chester, *Rag-Tags, Scum, Riff-Raff, and Commies*, p. 39.
86. John Bartlow Martin in Robert F. Kennedy Oral History, vol. 4, p. 308, JFKL; George Ball in Chester, *Rag-Tags, Scum, Riff-Raff, and Commies*, p. 39.
87. Martin, *Kennedy and Latin America*, p. 222.
88. In ibid., pp. 224, 261n.
89. Ibid., pp. 219–20.
90. Rabe, *The Most Dangerous Area in the World*, p. 47.
91. JFK, 1963, in Federico G. Gil, "The Kennedy-Johnson Years," in Martz, *United States Policy in Latin America*, p. 17.
92. Goldman, *The Tragedy of Lyndon Johnson*, p. 14; Leaming, *Jack Kennedy*, p. 387.
93. JFK to Dean Rusk, 29 October 1963, in Rabe, *The Most Dangerous Area in the World*, p. 151.
94. Castañeda, *Compañero*, p. 242; Blight et al., *Cuba on the Brink*, pp. 238–39.
95. JFK in Schlesinger, *Robert Kennedy*, p. 553.

16. Bad News

1. FCR in Hinckle and Turner, *The Fish Is Red*, p. 191; see also Edward Jay Epstein, "The Plots to Kill Castro," *George*, June 2000; Schlesinger, *Robert Kennedy*, pp. 547–48.
2. RFK in Laing, *Robert Kennedy*, p. 182.
3. FCR in Schlesinger, *Robert Kennedy*, p. 556; see also interview with FCR in Tad Szulc Papers, box 1, JFKL.
4. Val, *La dictature de Duvalier*, p. 34; Sapène, *Procès à: Baby Doc*, pp. 91–92; Gold, *Best Nightmare on Earth*, p. 141; Heinl and Heinl, *Written in Blood*, p. 629n.
5. Robert F. Kennedy Oral History, vol. 4, p. 323, JFKL. Dallek, *Flawed Giant*, p. 136, quotes part of this and adds, "Since JFK had no direct connection to either killing [of Trujillo or Diem], it made the assertion all the more galling to RFK." In fact, RFK does not say that JFK was not involved in those killings in the Oral History transcript. The fact that neither he nor John Bartlow Martin, interviewing him, makes such a comment might itself be seen as a point of interest.
6. In Grose, *Gentleman Spy*, p. 542.
7. LBJ said this to several people. See, for instance, in Dallek, *Flawed Giant*, p. 53.
8. Raymond Garthoff in Blight et al., *Cuba on the Brink*, p. 283.
9. FCR in ibid., pp. 237–38.
10. Burt Griffin in Summers, *Official and Confidential*, p. 326.
11. LBJ in Dallek, *Flawed Giant*, p. 50; Jacqueline Kennedy in Laing, *Robert Kennedy*, p. 183.
12. John McCone in Heymann, *RFK*, pp. 359–60.
13. Kennedy, *Times to Remember*, pp. 422–23.
14. LBJ in Shesol, *Mutual Contempt*, p. 134; Samuel Halpern in Blight and Kornbluh, *Politics of Illusion*, p. 117; Hinckle and Turner, *The Fish Is Red*, p. 238.
15. Arthur Schlesinger in Federico G. Gil, "The Kennedy-Johnson Years," in Martz, *United States Policy in Latin America*, p. 23.
16. Carolyn M. Shaw, "The United States: Rhetoric and Reality," in Legler et al., *Promoting Democracy*, p. 74; Gleijeses, *The Dominican Crisis*, p. 124.
17. Schmitz, *Thank God They're on Our Side*, pp. 265–66.
18. EGS in Rabe, *The Most Dangerous Area in the World*, p. 32.
19. Grandin, *Empire's Workshop*, pp. 48–49, 95–96; Frank O. Mora, "Paraguay: From the *Stronato* to the Democratic Transition," in Jeanne A. K. Hey, *Small States in World Politics: Explaining Foreign Policy Behavior* (Boulder, CO: Lynne Rienner, 2003), p. 19.
20. Khrushchev, *Khrushchev on Khrushchev*, pp. 52–53.

21. Dmitry Polyansky in Taubman, *Khrushchev*, p. 14; NSK in ibid., p. 15.
22. Khrushchev, *Khrushchev on Khrushchev*, pp. 197–98.
23. Ibid., pp. 199, 325.
24. Heinl and Heinl, *Written in Blood*, p. 593, and 631n for Carter.
25. LBJ to Benson Timmons, 8 April 1964, in ibid., p. 608; Logan, *Haiti and the Dominican Republic*, p. 156.
26. Abbott, *Haiti*, p. 120; Diederich and Burt, *Papa Doc*, p. 282.
27. Benson Timmons to Dean Rusk, 19 June 1964, USNA: RG 59, Central Foreign Policy Files, 1964–66, POL-15-1, box 2264.
28. Ferguson, *Papa Doc, Baby Doc*, p. 49; Nicholls, *From Dessalines to Duvalier*, p. 233.
29. Norman Warner to Department of State, 17 December 1965, USNA: RG 59, Central Foreign Policy Files, 1964–66, POL-15-1, box 2264.
30. Heinl and Heinl, *Written in Blood*, p. 604; Diederich and Burt, *Papa Doc*, pp. 290–91.
31. Abbott, *Haiti*, p. 120; Heinl and Heinl, *Written in Blood*, p. 605; Diederich and Burt, *Papa Doc*, p. 294.
32. Diederich and Burt, *Papa Doc*, pp. 242, 257, 265.
33. FD in Abbott, *Haiti*, p. 123; Diederich and Burt, *Papa Doc*, p. 300.
34. Heinl and Heinl, *Written in Blood*, pp. 605–7; Abbott, *Haiti*, pp. 122–29; Chassagne, *Bain de sang*, pp. 14–25; Péan, *Haïti*, pp. 121–25.
35. Ferguson, *Papa Doc, Baby Doc*, pp. 47–48; Abbott, *Haiti*, p. 122; Diederich and Burt, *Papa Doc*, pp. 304–5; "A Warning to Renegades," *Time*, 27 November 1964.
36. Heinl and Heinl, *Written in Blood*, pp. 605–7; Abbott, *Haiti*, pp. 128–32; "A Warning to Renegades."
37. Kennedy Crockett, "The Multiple Dilemma in Formulating U.S. Policy in Haiti," 23 November 1964, USNA: RG 59, Central Foreign Policy Files, 1964–66, POL-15-1, box 2264.
38. Benson Timmons to Dean Rusk, 23 March 1965; Dean Rusk to Benson Timmons, 5 March 1965; both in USNA: RG 59, Central Foreign Policy Files, 1964–66, POL-15-1, box 2264.
39. Benson Timmons to Dean Rusk, 10 November 1964, in ibid.
40. Warren Commission, *Report*, pp. 282–83; Gold, *Best Nightmare on Earth*, pp. 131–32; Summers, *Official and Confidential*, p. 329; Hinckle and Turner, *The Fish Is Red*, p. 210.
41. Tom Bower, *Fayed: The Unauthorised Biography* (London: Macmillan, 1998), pp. 20–25.
42. Norman Warner to Department of State, 23 November 1965, USNA: RG 59, Central Foreign Policy Files, 1964–66, POL-15-1, box 2264.
43. Abbott, *Haiti*, p. 136.
44. Nikolai Leonov in Castañeda, *Compañero*, p. 184.
45. FCR, "Report to the Cuban people on the Victory at Playa Girón," 23 April 1961, in Castro and Fernández, *Playa Girón*, pp. 167–68.
46. Williams, *From Columbus to Castro*, p. 483.
47. Ernesto Che Guevara, "The Cuban Economy: Its Past, and Its Present Importance," *International Affairs* 40, no. 4 (October 1964): 593; EGS, 14 July 1963, in Williams, *From Columbus to Castro*, p. 488.
48. RCR and EGS in Reid-Henry, *Fidel and Che*, p. 279.
49. Sergei Khrushchev in ibid., p. 245; Westad, *The Global Cold War*, p. 164; Prizel, *Latin America Through Soviet Eyes*, pp. 9–11.
50. Smith, *The Closest of Enemies*, p. 44.
51. RCR in Anderson, *Che Guevara*, p. 597.
52. EGS in Rojo, *My Friend Che*, p. 143.

53. Castañeda, *Compañero*, pp. 264–65.
54. Smith, *The Closest of Enemies*, p. 88.
55. According to Richard Helms, in Rabe, *The Most Dangerous Area in the World*, p. 107.
56. The agents were Joseph Burkholder Smith and Philip Agee. Rabe, *The Most Dangerous Area in the World*, p. 107.
57. Unnamed State Department official in Smith, *The Closest of Enemies*, p. 88.
58. Smith, *The Closest of Enemies*, p. 90.
59. Reid-Henry, *Fidel and Che*, p. 319.
60. EGS in Anderson, *Che Guevara*, pp. 624–25.
61. Benigno in Castañeda, *Compañero*, p. 296.
62. Carlos Franqui in ibid., p. 297.

17. Another Cuba

1. Johnson, *The Vantage Point*, p. 187.
2. Ibid., p. 188.
3. Pearce, *Under the Eagle*, pp. 62–65.
4. Crandall, *Gunboat Democracy*, p. 54; Chester, *Rag-Tags, Scum, Riff-Raff, and Commies*, pp. 42–45.
5. Moreno, *Barrios in Arms*, pp. 23–24.
6. "Nobody's Yes Man," *Time*, 26 March 1965.
7. Moreno, *Barrios in Arms*, pp. 32–34; Theodore Draper, "The Dominican Intervention Reconsidered," *Political Science Quarterly* 86, no. 1 (March 1971): 15–16.
8. J. I. Quello and N. Isa Conde, "Revolutionary Struggle in the Dominican Republic and Its Lessons," *World Marxist Review* 8, no. 12 (December 1965): 76.
9. In Draper, "The Dominican Intervention Reconsidered," p. 6.
10. FRUS 1964–1968, vol. 32, pp. 59–60.
11. Ibid., p. 62.
12. Johnson, *The Vantage Point*, p. 193.
13. Manolo González in Moreno, *Barrios in Arms*, p. 58.
14. Thomas Mann in FRUS 1964–1968, vol. 32, p. 65.
15. Michael J. Kryzanek, "The Dominican Intervention Revisited: An Attitudinal and Operational Analysis," in Martz, *United States Policy in Latin America*, p. 142; Moreno, *Barrios in Arms*, pp. 27–29; Chester, *Rag-Tags, Scum, Riff-Raff, and Commies*, p. 64.
16. See FRUS 1964–68, vol. 32, pp. 69–70, for Tapley Bennett's version of the meeting.
17. Gleijeses, *The Dominican Crisis*, pp. 242–43.
18. Ibid., p. 254; Moreno, *Barrios in Arms*, pp. 31–32. Moreno was told this story both by Martínez and by a Loyalist general.
19. Pedro Bartolomé Benoit in Pearce, *Under the Eagle*, p. 63.
20. LBJ in Goldman, *The Tragedy of Lyndon Johnson*, p. 395.
21. LBJ in Schlesinger, *Robert Kennedy*, p. 691.
22. LBJ in Kryzanek, "The Dominican Intervention Revisited," in Martz, *United States Policy in Latin America*, p. 140; Chester, *Rag-Tags, Scum, Riff-Raff, and Commies*, p. 80.
23. Joint Chiefs of Staff message in Crandall, *Gunboat Democracy*, p. 70.
24. Kryzanek, "The Dominican Intervention Revisited," in Martz, *United States Policy in Latin America*, p. 141.
25. Dean Rusk to Santo Domingo, 1 May 1965, USNA: RG 59, Central Foreign Policy Files, 1961–63, POL-23-9, box 2126.
26. Cyrus Vance, 3 November 1969, FAOH; LBJ paraphrased in FRUS 1964–1968, vol. 32, p. 74.
27. LBJ and William Raborn in FRUS 1964–68, vol. 32, pp. 89–90; see also Dean Rusk in Crandall, *Gunboat Democracy*, p. 71.

28. In Goldman, *The Tragedy of Lyndon Johnson*, pp. 396–97.
29. LBJ and Robert McNamara, 30 April 1965, in FRUS 1964–68, vol. 32, p. 109.
30. Leonard C. Meeker, "Legal Basis for United States Actions in the Dominican Republic," 30 April 1965, USNA: RG 59, Central Foreign Policy Files, 1961–63, POL-23-9, box 2126.
31. See, for example, Dean Rusk to Santo Domingo, 29 April 1965, 2:26 PM, USNA: RG 59, Central Foreign Policy Files, 1961–63, POL-23-9, box 2126; dozens of similar examples may be found in the same files.
32. Dean Rusk to Santo Domingo, 1 May 1965, in ibid.
33. Tapley Bennett to Dean Rusk, 29 April 1965, in ibid.
34. Adlai Stevenson to Dean Rusk, 29 April 1965, in ibid.
35. In Martin, *Adlai Stevenson*, p. 845.
36. Adlai Stevenson to Arthur Schlesinger, in ibid., p. 844.
37. Martin, *Adlai Stevenson*, pp. 842–44.
38. Moreno, *Barrios in Arms*, pp. 36–37; John Bartlow Martin in Dean Rusk to embassies in Caracas and Lima, 2 May 1965, USNA: RG 59, Central Foreign Policy Files, 1961–63, POL-23-9, box 2126.
39. Chester, *Rag-Tags, Scum, Riff-Raff, and Commies*, pp. 90–91.
40. Ibid., p. 92.
41. State Department to embassies, 1 May 1965, USNA: RG 59, Central Foreign Policy Files, 1961–63, POL-23-9, box 2126; USNA: RG 59, Central Foreign Policy Files, 1961–63, POL-23-9, box 2127.
42. LBJ, 2 May 1965, in Crandall, *Gunboat Democracy*, p. 71.
43. Draper, "The Dominican Intervention Reconsidered," p. 4.
44. Record of meeting, USNA: RG 59, Central Foreign Policy Files, 1961–63, POL-23-9, box 2127.
45. John Bartlow Martin in Tapley Bennett to Dean Rusk, 4 May 1965, in ibid.
46. Tapley Bennett to Dean Rusk, 5 May 1965, in ibid.
47. Record of meeting, in ibid.
48. Dean Rusk to Tapley Bennett, 2 May 1965, USNA: RG 59, Central Foreign Policy Files, 1961–63, POL-23-9, box 2126.
49. LBJ, 4 May 1965, in Crandall, *Gunboat Democracy*, p. 73.
50. Chester, *Rag-Tags, Scum, Riff-Raff, and Commies*, p. 111; see also Schlesinger, *Robert Kennedy*, p. 691; RFK in Crandall, *Gunboat Democracy*, p. 72.
51. USNA: RG 59, Central Foreign Policy Files, 1961–63, POL-23-9, box 2128.
52. Dean Rusk to embassies, 8 May 1965, in ibid.
53. "The Dominican Republic Issue in the United Nations Security Council," 12 May 1965, USNA: RG 59, Central Foreign Policy Files, 1961–63, POL-23-9, box 2129.
54. General Linvill to Admiral Moorer and General Wheeler, 16 May 1965, USNA: RG 59, Central Foreign Policy Files, 1961–63, POL-23-9, box 2126.
55. Cyrus Vance, 3 November 1969, FAOH.
56. Johnson, *The Vantage Point*, p. 200; Westad, *The Global Cold War*, p. 152.
57. CIA memo, 27 May 1965, in Crandall, *Gunboat Democracy*, p. 60.
58. LBJ, 17 June 1965, in Johnson, *The Johnson Presidential Press Conferences*, p. 326.
59. Chester, *Rag-Tags, Scum, Riff-Raff, and Commies*, p. 259.
60. LBJ in Andrew and Mitrokhin, *The Mitrokhin Archive II*, p. 31. Alternatively, "I want you to go down there [to Santo Domingo] and see if you can find some of those people who were beheaded." Dallek, *Flawed Giant*, pp. 266–67.
61. Benson Timmons to Dean Rusk, 12 May 1965, USNA: RG 59, Central Foreign Policy Files, 1961–63, POL-23-9, box 2129.
62. FD to LBJ, 3 June 1965, USNA: RG 59, Central Foreign Policy Files, 1964–66, POL-15-1, box 2264; Val, *La dictature de Duvalier*, p. 53.

63. Moreno, *Barrios in Arms*, pp. 36–37.
64. Diederich and Burt, *Papa Doc*, pp. 174–75.
65. Moreno, *Barrios in Arms*, pp. 71, 141. On 15 June 1965, while driving a car in Santo Domingo, La Rivière was shot in the jugular and killed by U.S. Marines.
66. Tapley Bennett to LBJ, 16 May 1965, USNA: RG 59, Central Foreign Policy Files, 1961–63, POL-23-9, box 2126.
67. State Department memo for McGeorge Bundy, 12 May 1965, USNA: RG 59, Central Foreign Policy Files, 1961–63, POL-23-9, box 2129.
68. Abe Fortas, record of a telephone conversation, 16 May 1965, 12:30 PM. In Westad, *The Global Cold War*, pp. 151–52; LBJ in Halberstam, *The Best and the Brightest*, p. 644; McGeorge Bundy in Chester, *Rag-Tags, Scum, Riff-Raff, and Commies*, pp. 263–64.
69. Cyrus Vance, 3 November 1969, FAOH; Chester, *Rag-Tags, Scum, Riff-Raff, and Commies*, p. 131.
70. Francisco Caamaño in Moreno, *Barrios in Arms*, pp. 44–45.
71. Frank Church in Schmitz, *Thank God They're on Our Side*, pp. 289–90.
72. William Fulbright, Senate speech, 15 September 1965, in Crandall, *Gunboat Democracy*, p. 89.
73. Kryzanek, "The Dominican Intervention Revisited," in Martz, *United States Policy in Latin America*, pp. 151–53; Howard Wiarda in Chester, *Rag-Tags, Scum, Riff-Raff, and Commies*, p. 252; Halberstam, *The Best and the Brightest*, p. 81.
74. Celia de la Serna to EGS, 14 April 1965, in Rojo, *My Friend Che*, p. 174.
75. FCR in ibid., p. 176.
76. Rojo, *My Friend Che*, pp. 182–83.
77. EGS to parents; EGS to children; both in ibid., p. 182.
78. EGS to FCR, n.d. 1965, in ibid., pp. 180–81; Guevara, *Venceremos!*, p. 411.

18. Zombies

1. Halberstam, *The Unfinished Odyssey*, p. 46; Shesol, *Mutual Contempt*, p. 279. The aide quoted was Adam Walinsky.
2. Kennedy, *To Seek a Newer World*, p. 63.
3. RFK in Shesol, *Mutual Contempt*, p. 280.
4. Guevara, *The Motorcycle Diaries*, p. 78.
5. RFK in Shesol, *Mutual Contempt*, p. 282; Kennedy, *To Seek a Newer World*, p. 90n.
6. LBJ in Halberstam, *The Unfinished Odyssey*, p. 37.
7. Arthur Schlesinger in Kennedy, *Times to Remember*, p. 439.
8. Intelligence estimate in Crandall, *Gunboat Democracy*, p. 91; Rostow to LBJ, 10 May 1966, in ibid., p. 92. See also Pearce, *Under the Eagle*, pp. 62–65.
9. Chester, *Rag-Tags, Scum, Riff-Raff, and Commies*, pp. 230–31.
10. Ibid., pp. 244–51; Gleijeses, *The Dominican Crisis*, pp. 281, 300; Juan de Onis, "The Hispanic Caribbean," in Szulc, *The United States and the Caribbean*, p. 168; Crandall, *Gunboat Democracy*, p. 90.
11. Chester, *Rag-Tags, Scum, Riff-Raff, and Commies*, pp. 272–73; Michael J. Kryzanek, "The Dominican Intervention Revisited: An Attitudinal and Operational Analysis," in Martz, *United States Policy in Latin America*, pp. 145–46.
12. Matos Moquete, *Caamaño*, p. 135.
13. Ibid., p. 163.
14. Gleijeses, *The Dominican Crisis*, p. 299.
15. Val, *La dictature de Duvalier*, p. 72; Abbott, *Haiti*, pp. 138–39, 142; Ferguson, *Papa Doc, Baby Doc*, pp. 53–54.
16. Galíndez, *The Era of Trujillo*, p. 194n.

17. EGS in Anderson, *Che Guevara*, p. 661.
18. Castañeda, *Compañero*, pp. 300, 317–18. There is a milder account in Reid-Henry, *Fidel and Che*, p. 342.
19. EGS in Castañeda, *Compañero*, p. 317.
20. Victor Dreke in Reid-Henry, *Fidel and Che*, p. 345.
21. FCR in Castañeda, *Compañero*, p. 335.
22. Guevara, *The Bolivian Diary*, 31 January 1967, p. 78; 14 July 1967, p. 191; 13 April 1967, p. 130; 14 June 1967, p. 171; 12 September 1967, p. 234.
23. Felix Rodríguez and EGS in Anderson, *Che Guevara*, pp. 736, 739.
24. Fidel Castro, "A Necessary Introduction" (1968), in Guevara, *The Bolivian Diary*, pp. 29–30; Anderson, *Che Guevara*, p. 739.
25. Walt Rostow in Halberstam, *The Best and the Brightest*, p. 197.
26. Castro, "A Necessary Introduction," in Guevara, *The Bolivian Diary*, pp. 13–14.
27. Wayne S. Smith, "Castro, Latin America, and the United States," in Martz, *United States Policy in Latin America*, pp. 291–92.
28. *Kommunist*, 1968, in Prizel, *Latin America Through Soviet Eyes*, p. 15.
29. Westad, *The Global Cold War*, pp. 213–14; Prizel, *Latin America Through Soviet Eyes*, pp. 14–15; Rojas, *Essays*, p. 136.
30. Rolando Masferrer in Hinckle and Turner, *The Fish Is Red*, p. 233.
31. Sapène, *Procès à: Baby Doc*, p. 94; Hinckle and Turner, *The Fish Is Red*, pp. 250–59; Diederich and Burt, *Papa Doc*, pp. 374–75.
32. Author's interview with Adolfo Rivero, January 2010.
33. RFK in Goodwin, *Remembering America*, p. 530.
34. RFK, 4 April 1968.
35. LBJ in Shesol, *Mutual Contempt*, pp. 455–56.
36. Heinl and Heinl, *Written in Blood*, pp. 612, 615; Ferguson, *Papa Doc, Baby Doc*, pp. 57–59; Robert D. Crassweller, "Darkness in Haiti," *Foreign Affairs* 49, no. 2 (January 1971): 321; Gérard R. Latortue, "Tyranny in Haiti," *Current History* 51, no. 304 (December 1966): 353.
37. Vincent Teresa in Hinckle and Turner, *The Fish Is Red*, p. 248.
38. In Latortue, "Tyranny in Haiti," p. 352.
39. Graham Greene, *The Comedians* (1966; Geneva: Heron Books, 1981), pp. 173, 246.
40. FD in Abbott, *Haiti*, p. 141; see Greene, *Ways of Escape*, p. 232; Greene, *The Comedians*, p. 2.
41. Greene, *Ways of Escape*, p. 232.
42. Archbishop François Wolff Ligondé in Nicholls, *From Dessalines to Duvalier*, p. 226; FD, June 1966, in Sapène, *Procès à: Baby Doc*, p. 109.
43. "Birthday Blowout," *Time*, 28 April 1967; Heinl and Heinl, *Written in Blood*, p. 616.
44. Crassweller, "Darkness in Haiti"; Abbott, *Haiti*, p. 145; Diederich and Burt, *Papa Doc*, pp. 370–71.
45. FD in Heinl and Heinl, *Written in Blood*, p. 617.
46. Diederich and Burt, *Papa Doc*, pp. 372–73.
47. "Birthday Blowout"; International Committee of Jurists, September 1967, in Heinl and Heinl, *Written in Blood*, p. 615.
48. Ferguson, *Papa Doc, Baby Doc*, pp. 54–55; Sapène, *Procès à: Baby Doc*, p. 119.
49. Abbott, *Haiti*, pp. 152–54.
50. FD in Heinl and Heinl, *Written in Blood*, p. 623.
51. Ferguson, *Papa Doc, Baby Doc*, pp. 56–57; Heinl and Heinl, *Written in Blood*, p. 624.
52. FD in Abbott, *Haiti*, p. 159.
53. Heinl and Heinl, *Written in Blood*, pp. 624–25.
54. "Breaking the Spell," *Time*, 3 May 1971.

55. Richard M. Morse, "Haiti, 1492–1988," in Morse, *Haiti's Future*, pp. 8–9; Nicholls, *From Dessalines to Duvalier*, p. 239.
56. Ferguson, *Papa Doc, Baby Doc*, pp. 56–57; Abbott, *Haiti*, p. 163.
57. *Le Monde*, 28 April 1971, in Sapène, *Procès à: Baby Doc*, p. 193.
58. Rémy Bastien, "Vodoun and Politics in Haiti," in Courlander and Bastien, *Religion and Politics in Haiti*, p. 66.
59. Abbott, *Haiti*, p. 162.
60. Ibid., pp. 138–39; Lundahl, *Politics or Markets?*, p. 302.
61. Martin, *Kennedy and Latin America*, p. 3.
62. Bissell, *Reflections of a Cold Warrior*, p. 142.
63. JFK, 15 December 1958, in Kennedy, *The Strategy of Peace*, p. 136.

SELECTED BIBLIOGRAPHY

★

Abbott, Elizabeth. *Haiti: The Duvaliers and Their Legacy*. London: Robert Hale, 1991.

Abel, Elie. *The Missiles of October: The Story of the Cuban Missile Crisis, 1962*. 1966; new edition, London: Macgibbon and Kee, 1969.

Ameringer, Charles D. *The Caribbean Legion: Patriots, Politicians, Soldiers of Fortune, 1946–1950*. University Park: Pennsylvania State University Press, 1996.

Anderson, Jon Lee. *Che Guevara: A Revolutionary Life*. London: Bantam Press, 1997.

Andrew, Christopher, and Vasili Mitrokhin. *The Mitrokhin Archive: The KGB in Europe and the West*. London: Allen Lane, 1999.

———. *The Mitrokhin Archive II: The KGB and the World*. London: Allen Lane, 2005.

Arthur, Charles. *Haiti: A Guide to the People, Politics and Culture*. London: Latin American Bureau; New York: Interlink Books, 2002.

Balaguer, Joaquín. *Memorias de un cortesano de la "Era de Trujillo."* 1988; Madrid: Impresos y Revistas, 1989.

Balfour, Sebastian. *Castro*. 1990; second edition, Harlow, Essex: Longman, 1995.

Bender, Lynn-Darrell. *Cuba vs. United States: The Politics of Hostility*. Second edition. San Juan, Puerto Rico: Inter American University Press, 1981.

Benjamin, Jules R. *The United States and the Origin of the Cuban Revolution: An Empire of Liberty in an Age of National Liberation*. Princeton, NJ: Princeton University Press, 1990.

Benson, Thomas W. *Writing JFK: Presidential Rhetoric and the Press in the Bay of Pigs Crisis*. College Station: Texas A&M University Press, 2004.

Bissell, Richard M., Jr., with Jonathan E. Lewis and Frances T. Pudlo. *Reflections of a Cold Warrior: From Yalta to the Bay of Pigs*. New Haven, CT: Yale University Press, 1996.

Blancpain, François. *Haïti et les États-Unis, 1915–1934: histoire d'une occupation*. Paris: L'Harmattan, 1999.

Blight, James G., Bruce J. Allyn, and David A. Welch. *Cuba on the Brink: Castro, the Missile Crisis, and the Soviet Collapse*. Lanham, MD: Rowman and Littlefield, 2002.

Blight, James G., and Peter Kornbluh, eds. *Politics of Illusion: The Bay of Pigs Invasion Reëxamined*. Boulder, CO: Lynne Reinner, 1998.

Blouet, Olwyn M. *The Contemporary Caribbean: History, Life and Culture Since 1945*. London: Reaktion Books, 2007.

Bonsal, Philip W. *Cuba, Castro, and the United States*. Pittsburgh, PA: University of Pittsburgh Press, 1971.

Brendon, Piers. *Ike: The Life and Times of Dwight D. Eisenhower*. London: Secker and Warburg, 1987.

Breuer, William B. *Vendetta! Fidel Castro and the Kennedy Brothers.* New York: John Wiley and Sons, 1997.
Butler, Smedley Darlington. *The Letters of a Leatherneck, 1898–1931.* Edited by Anne Cipriano Venzon. New York: Praeger, 1992.
Caamaño Grullón, Claudio. *Caamaño: Guerra Civil 1965.* Santo Domingo: Claudio Caamaño, 2007.
Caballero, Manuel. *Latin America and the Comintern, 1919–1943.* Cambridge: Cambridge University Press, 1986.
Calder, Bruce J. *The Impact of Intervention: The Dominican Republic During the U.S. Occupation of 1916–1924.* Austin: University of Texas Press, 1984.
Carter, John J. *Covert Action as a Tool of Presidential Foreign Policy: From the Bay of Pigs to Iran-Contra.* Lewiston, NY: Edwin Mellen Press, 2006.
Castañeda, Jorge. *Compañero: The Life and Death of Che Guevara.* Translated from the Spanish by Maria Castañeda. London: Bloomsbury, 1997.
Castro, Fidel. *Fidel Castro Speaks.* Edited by Martin Kenner and James Petras. 1969; London: Allen Lane, 1970.
———. *My Life.* Edited by Ignacio Ramonet. Translated by Andrew Hurley. London: Allen Lane, 2007.
———. *The Prison Letters of Fidel Castro.* Edited by Ann Louise Bardach and Luis Conte Agüero. 1959; New York: Nation Books, 2007.
Castro, Fidel, and José Ramón Fernández. *Playa Girón.* New York: Pathfinder, 2001.
Castro, Juanita. *Fidel y Raúl, mis hermanos: la historia secreta.* With María Antonieta Collins. Doral, FL: Aguilar, 2009.
Casuso, Teresa. *Cuba and Castro.* Translated from the Spanish by Elmer Grossberg. New York: Random House, 1961.
Célestin, Clément. *Compilations pour l'histoire.* 4 vols. Port-au-Prince: N. A. Theodore, 1957–60.
Chapman, Peter. *Jungle Capitalists: A Story of Globalisation, Greed and Revolution.* Edinburgh: Canongate, 2007.
Chassagne, Albert D. *Bain de sang en Haïti: les Macoutes opèrent à Jérémie en 1964.* New York: Albert D. Chassagne, n.d. [circa 1986].
Chester, Eric Thomas. *Rag-Tags, Scum, Riff-Raff, and Commies: The U.S. Intervention in the Dominican Republic, 1965–1966.* New York: Monthly Review Press, 2001.
Courlander, Harold, and Rémy Bastien. *Religion and Politics in Haiti: ICR Studies 1.* With a preface by Richard P. Schaedel. Washington, DC: Institute of Cross-Cultural Research, 1966.
Crandall, Russell. *Gunboat Democracy: U.S. Interventions in the Dominican Republic, Grenada, and Panama.* Lanham, MD: Rowman and Littlefield, 2006.
Crassweller, Robert D. *Trujillo: The Life and Times of a Caribbean Dictator.* New York: Macmillan, 1966.
Dallek, Robert. *Flawed Giant: Lyndon Johnson and His Times, 1961–1973.* Oxford: Oxford University Press, 1998.
———. *John F. Kennedy: An Unfinished Life, 1917–1963.* London: Allen Lane, 2003.
Davis, H. P. *Black Democracy: The Story of Haiti.* London: George Allen and Unwin, 1929.
Delince, Kern. *Les forces politiques en Haïti: manuel d'histoire contemporaine.* Paris: Éditions Karthala; Plantation, FL: Pegasus Books, 1993.
DePalma, Anthony. *The Man Who Invented Fidel: Castro, Cuba, and Herbert L. Matthews of the New York Times.* New York: Public Affairs, 2006.
Detzer, David. *The Brink: Cuban Missile Crisis, 1962.* London: J. M. Dent and Sons, 1980.

Diederich, Bernard, and Al Burt. *Papa Doc: Haiti and Its Dictator.* London: Bodley Head, 1970.
Dobbs, Michael. *One Minute to Midnight.* 2008; London: Arrow Books, 2009.
Dockrill, Michael L., and Michael F. Hopkins. *The Cold War, 1945–1991.* 1998; second edition, Basingstoke: Palgrave, 2006.
Dunham, Katherine. *Island Possessed.* 1969; Chicago: University of Chicago Press, 1994.
Duvalier, François. *Mémoires d'un leader du tiers monde: mes négociations avec le Saint-Siège ou, Une tranche d'histoire.* Paris: Hachette, 1969.
———. *Oeuvres essentielles.* Third edition. Port-au-Prince: Presses Nationales d'Haïti, 1968.
Eisenhower, Dwight D. *Waging Peace: The White House Years, 1956–1961.* 1965; London: Heinemann, 1966.
Epstein, Edward Jay. *Inquest: The Warren Commission and the Establishment of Truth.* London: Hutchinson, 1966.
Espaillat, Arturo R. *Trujillo: The Last Caesar.* Chicago: Henry Regnery, 1963.
Estrada, Ulises. *Tania: Undercover with Che Guevara in Bolivia.* Melbourne: Ocean Press, 2005.
Ferguson, James. *Makers of the Caribbean.* Guadeloupe: Institut de Coopération Franco Caraïbe; Kingston: Ian Randle, 2005.
———. *Papa Doc, Baby Doc: Haiti and the Duvaliers.* 1987; Oxford: Basil Blackwell, 1989.
Fernández, Alina. *Castro's Daughter: An Exile's Memoir of Cuba.* Translated by Dolores M. Koch. New York: St. Martin's Press, 1998.
Foss, Clive. *Fidel Castro.* 2000; Stroud, UK: Sutton, 2006.
Franqui, Carlos. *Diary of the Cuban Revolution.* Translated by Georgette Felix, Elaine Kerrigan, Phyllis Freeman, and Hardie St. Martin. 1976; English-language translation, New York: Viking Press, 1980.
———. *Family Portrait with Fidel: A Memoir.* Translated by Alfred MacAdam. New York: Random House, 1984.
Freedman, Lawrence. *Kennedy's Wars: Berlin, Cuba, Laos, and Vietnam.* Oxford: Oxford University Press, 2000.
Friedman, Max Paul. *Nazis and Good Neighbors: The United States Campaign Against the Germans of Latin America in World War II.* Cambridge: Cambridge University Press, 2003.
Fursenko, Aleksandr, and Timothy Naftali. *Khrushchev's Cold War: The Inside Story of an American Adversary.* New York: W. W. Norton, 2006.
Gaddis, John Lewis. *The Cold War: A New History.* 2005; London: Penguin Books, 2007.
Gadea, Hilda. *Ernesto: A Memoir of Che Guevara.* Translated from the Spanish by Carmen Molina and Walter I. Bradbury. London: W. H. Allen, 1973.
Galeano, Eduardo. *Open Veins of Latin America: Five Centuries of the Pillage of a Continent.* Translated by Cedric Belfrage. 1971; London: Serpent's Tail, 2009.
Galíndez, Jesús de. *The Era of Trujillo: Dominican Dictator.* Edited by Russell H. Fitzgibbon. 1956; Tucson: University of Arizona Press, 1973.
Galván, William. *Minerva Mirabal: historia de una heroína.* Santo Domingo: Biblioteca Taller, 1997.
García, Horacio, ed. *Veintiseis.* Havana: Editorial de Ciencias Sociales, 1970.
García-Pérez, Gladys Marel. *Insurreción y Revolución, 1952–1959.* Havana: Ediciones Unión, 2006.
Garner, James Wilford. *American Foreign Policies: An Examination and Evaluation of Certain Traditional and Recent International Policies of the United States.* New York: New York University Press, 1928.

Garthoff, Raymond L. *A Journey Through the Cold War: A Memoir of Containment and Coexistence*. Washington, DC: Brookings Institution Press, 2001.

Geggus, David P., ed. *The Impact of the Haitian Revolution in the Atlantic World*. Columbia: University of South Carolina Press, 2001.

Geyelin, Philip. *Lyndon B. Johnson and the World*. London: Pall Mall Press, 1966.

Gleijeses, Piero. *The Dominican Crisis: The 1965 Constitutionalist Revolt and American Intervention*. Translated by Lawrence Lipson. Baltimore: Johns Hopkins University Press, 1978.

Gold, Herbert. *Best Nightmare on Earth: A Life in Haiti*. 1991; London: Flamingo, 1994.

Goldenberg, Boris. *The Cuban Revolution and Latin America*. London: George Allen and Unwin, 1965.

Goldman, Eric F. *The Tragedy of Lyndon Johnson*. 1968; London: MacDonald, 1969.

Gonzalez, Edward. "The United States and Castro: Breaking the Deadlock." *Foreign Affairs* 50, no. 4 (July 1972).

Goodwin, Richard N. *Remembering America: A Voice from the Sixties*. Boston: Little, Brown, 1988.

Grandin, Greg. *Empire's Workshop: Latin America, the United States, and the Rise of the New Imperialism*. 2006; New York: Henry Holt, 2007.

Greene, Graham. *Ways of Escape*. Toronto, Canada: Lester and Orpen Dennys, 1980.

Grose, Peter. *Gentleman Spy: The Life of Allen Dulles*. 1994; London: André Deutsch, 1995.

Guevara, Ernesto "Che." *The Bolivian Diary: Authorized Edition*. With an introduction by Fidel Castro and preface by Camilo Guevara. 1968; Melbourne: Ocean Press, 2006.

———. *Guerrilla Warfare*. 1961; London: Penguin Books, 1969.

———. *The Motorcycle Diaries: Notes on a Latin American Journey*. Translated by Alexandra Keeble. London: Fourth Estate, 2004.

———. *Reminiscences of the Cuban Revolutionary War*. Translated by Victoria Ortiz. 1968; London: Penguin Books, 1969.

———. *Venceremos! The Speeches and Writings of Ernesto Che Guevara*. Edited by John Gerassi. London: Weidenfeld and Nicolson, 1968.

Guthman, Edwin. *We Band of Brothers*. New York: Harper and Row, 1971.

Halberstam, David. *The Best and the Brightest*. 1972; London: Pan Books, 1974.

———. *The Unfinished Odyssey of Robert Kennedy*. New York: Random House, 1968.

Halle, Louis J. *The Cold War as History*. London: Chatto and Windus, 1967.

Heinl, Robert Debs, Jr., and Nancy Gordon Heinl. *Written in Blood: The Story of the Haitian People, 1492–1995*. Revised and expanded by Michael Heinl. Lanham, MD: University Press of America, 1996.

Hersh, Seymour. *The Dark Side of Camelot*. 1997; London: HarperCollins, 1998.

Heuman, Gad. *The Caribbean*. London: Hodder Headline, 2006.

Heymann, C. David. *RFK: A Candid Biography of Robert F. Kennedy*. London: William Heinemann, 1998.

Hicks, Albert C. *Blood in the Streets: The Life and Rule of Trujillo*. New York: Creative Age Press, 1946.

Higgins, Trumbull. *The Perfect Failure: Kennedy, Eisenhower, and the CIA at the Bay of Pigs*. New York: W. W. Norton, 1987.

Hinckle, Warren, and William W. Turner. *The Fish Is Red: The Story of the Secret War Against Castro*. New York: Harper and Row, 1981.

Hunt, E. Howard. *Undercover: Memoirs of an American Secret Agent*. 1974; London: W. H. Allen, 1975.

Immerman, Richard H. *The CIA in Guatemala: The Foreign Policy of Intervention*. Austin: University of Texas Press, 1982.

Jagan, Cheddi. *The West on Trial: My Fight for Guyana's Freedom*. London: Michael Joseph, 1966.

James, C. L. R. *The Black Jacobins: Toussaint L'Ouverture and the San Domingo Revolution.* With an introduction and notes by James Walvin. 1938; London: Penguin Books, 2001.

Jenks, Leland Hamilton. *Our Cuban Colony: A Study in Sugar.* New York: Vanguard Press, 1928.

Johnson, Chalmers. *The Sorrows of Empire: Militarism, Secrecy, and the End of the Republic.* 2004; London: Verso, 2006.

Johnson, Haynes, with Manuel Artime, José Peréz San Román, Erneido Oliva, and Enrique Ruiz-Williams. *The Bay of Pigs: The Invasion of Cuba by Brigade 2506.* 1964; London: Hutchinson, 1965.

Johnson, Lyndon Baines. *The Johnson Presidential Press Conferences.* Introduction by Doris Kearns Goodwin. 2 vols. New York: Earl M. Coleman Enterprises, 1978.

———. *The Vantage Point: Perspectives of the Presidency, 1963–1969.* 1971; London: Weidenfeld and Nicolson, 1972.

Kennedy, John F. *The Strategy of Peace.* Edited by Allan Nevins. London: Hamish Hamilton, 1960.

Kennedy, Robert F. *To Seek a Newer World.* 1967; London: Michael Joseph, 1968.

Kennedy, Rose Fitzgerald. *Times to Remember: An Autobiography.* London: Collins, 1974.

Khrushchev, Nikita Sergeyevich. *Khrushchev Remembers.* Translated and edited by Strobe Talbott, with an introduction, commentary, and notes by Edward Crankshaw. Boston: Little, Brown, 1970.

———. *Memoirs of Nikita Khrushchev.* Edited by Sergei Khrushchev. 3 vols. Providence, RI: Thomas J. Watson Institute for International Studies; University Park: Pennsylvania State University Press, 2007.

Khrushchev, Sergei. *Khrushchev on Khrushchev: An Inside Account of the Man and His Era.* Edited and translated by William Taubman. London: Little, Brown, 1990.

Klein, Woody. *All the Presidents' Spokesmen: Spinning the News—White House Press Secretaries from Franklin D. Roosevelt to George W. Bush.* Westport, CT: Praeger, 2008.

Knight, Franklin W., and Colin A. Palmer, eds. *The Modern Caribbean.* Chapel Hill: University of North Carolina Press, 1989.

Kornbluh, Peter, ed. *Bay of Pigs Declassified: The Secret CIA Report on the Invasion of Cuba.* New York: New Press, 1998.

La Cova, Antonio Rafael de. *The Moncada Attack: Birth of the Cuban Revolution.* Columbia: University of South Carolina Press, 2007.

Laing, Margaret. *Robert Kennedy.* London: MacDonald, 1968.

Las Casas, Bartolomé de. *A Short Account of the Destruction of the Indies.* Edited and translated by Nigel Griffin, with an introduction by Anthony Pagden. London: Penguin Books, 1992.

Leaming, Barbara. *Jack Kennedy: The Making of a President.* London: Weidenfeld and Nicolson, 2006.

Lechuga, Carlos. *Cuba and the Missile Crisis.* Translated by Mary Todd. Melbourne: Ocean Press, 2001.

Legler, Thomas, Sharon F. Lean, and Dexter S. Boniface, eds. *Promoting Democracy in the Americas.* Baltimore: Johns Hopkins University Press, 2007.

Lenin, Vladimir Ilyich. *Imperialism: The Highest Stage of Capitalism: A Popular Outline.* Introduction by Norman Lewis and James Malone. 1916; London: Junius Publications, 1996.

Levilain, Guy Viêt. *Cultural Identity, Négritude and Decolonization: The Haitian Situation in the Light of the Socialist Humanism of Jacques Roumain and René Depestre.* New York: American Institute for Marxist Studies, 1978.

Lippmann, Walter. "Vested Rights and Nationalism in Latin-America." *Foreign Affairs* 5, no. 3 (April 1927).

Logan, Rayford W. *Haiti and the Dominican Republic.* Oxford: Oxford University Press, 1968.
López-Fresquet, Rufo. *My Fourteen Months with Castro.* Cleveland: World Publishing, 1966.
Lorenz, Marita, with Ted Schwarz. *Marita: One Woman's Extraordinary Tale of Love and Espionage from Castro to Kennedy.* New York: Thunder's Mouth Press, 1993.
Lorini, Alessandra, ed. *An Intimate and Contested Relation: The United States and Cuba in the Late Nineteenth and Early Twentieth Centuries/Una relación íntima y controvertida: Estados Unidos y Cuba entre los siglos XIX y XX.* Florence: Firenze University Press, 2005.
Lundahl, Mats. *Politics or Markets? Essays on Haitian Underdevelopment.* London: Routledge, 1992.
Maclean, Betsy, ed. *Haydée Santamaría.* Melbourne: Ocean Press, 2003.
Magdoff, Harry. *The Age of Imperialism: The Economics of U.S. Foreign Policy.* New York: Monthly Review Press, 1969.
March, Aleida. *Evocación.* Havana: Fondo Editorial Casa de las Américas, 2007.
Marquis, John. *Papa Doc: Portrait of a Haitian Tyrant, 1907–1971.* Kingston, Jamaica: LMH Publishing, 2007.
Martí, José. *Inside the Monster: Writings on the United States and American Imperialism.* Translated by Elinor Randall et al. Edited by Philip S. Foner. New York: Monthly Review Press, 1975.
Martin, Edwin McCammon. *Kennedy and Latin America.* Lanham, MD: University Press of America, 1994.
Martin, John Bartlow. *Adlai Stevenson and the World: The Life of Adlai E. Stevenson.* Garden City, NY: Doubleday, 1977.
Martz, John D., ed. *United States Policy in Latin America: A Quarter Century of Crisis and Challenge, 1961–1986.* Lincoln: University of Nebraska Press, 1988.
Matos Moquete, Manuel. *Caamaño: la Última Esperanza Armada.* 2000; Santo Domingo: Publicaciones Matos Moquete, 2005.
Matthews, Herbert L. *Revolution in Cuba: An Essay in Understanding.* New York: Charles Scribner's Sons, 1975.
May, Ernest R., and Philip D. Zelikow, eds. *The Kennedy Tapes: Inside the White House During the Cuban Missile Crisis.* Cambridge, MA: Belknap Press of Harvard University Press, 1997.
Meneses, Enrique. *Fidel Castro.* Translated by J. Halcro Ferguson. 1966; London: Faber and Faber, 1968.
Miller, Warren. *The Lost Plantation: The Face of Cuba Today.* London: Secker and Warburg, 1961.
Mills, C. Wright. *Listen, Yankee: The Revolution in Cuba.* 1960; New York: Ballantine Books, 1961.
Moreno, José A. *Barrios in Arms: Revolution in Santo Domingo.* Pittsburgh, PA: University of Pittsburgh Press, 1970.
Morse, Richard M., ed. *Haiti's Future: Views of Twelve Haitian Leaders.* Washington, DC: Wilson Center Press, 1988.
Mosley, Leonard. *Dulles: A Biography of Eleanor, Allen, and John Foster Dulles and Their Family Network.* London: Hodder and Stoughton, 1978.
Nicholls, David. *From Dessalines to Duvalier: Race, Colour and National Independence in Haiti.* Cambridge: Cambridge University Press, 1979.
Nixon, Richard M. *In the Arena: A Memoir of Victory, Defeat, and Renewal.* New York: Simon and Schuster, 1990.
———. *RN: The Memoirs of Richard Nixon.* London: Sidgwick and Jackson, 1978.
———. *Six Crises.* London: W. H. Allen, 1962.

Organisation Extérieure du Parti Unifié des Communistes Haïtiens. *Haïti sous Duvalier: terrorisme d'état et visages de la résistance nationale.* N.P.: PUCH, n.d. [1973].
Parry, J. H., P. M. Sherlock, and A. P. Maingot. *A Short History of the West Indies.* Fourth edition. London: Macmillan, 1987.
Paterson, Thomas G. *Contesting Castro: The United States and the Triumph of the Cuban Revolution.* New York: Oxford University Press, 1994.
Péan, Leslie J.-R. *Haïti: économie politique de la corruption. Tome IV: L'ensauvagement macoute et ses conséquences (1957–1990).* Paris: Maisonneuve and Larose, 2007.
Pearce, Jenny. *Under the Eagle: U.S. Intervention in Central America and the Caribbean.* London: Latin America Bureau, 1981.
Pérez, Louis A., Jr. *A Guide to Cuban Collections in the United States.* New York: Greenwood Press, 1991.
———. *Historiography in the Revolution: A Bibliography of Cuban Scholarship, 1959–1979.* New York: Garland Publishing, 1982.
———. *Intervention, Revolution, and Politics in Cuba, 1913–1921.* Pittsburgh, PA: University of Pittsburgh Press, 1978.
Pérez, Louis A., Jr., and Rebecca J. Scott, eds. *The Archives of Cuba/Los archivos de Cuba.* Pittsburgh, PA: University of Pittsburgh Press, 2003.
Perkins, Dexter. *The United States and the Caribbean.* 1947; revised edition, Cambridge, MA: Harvard University Press, 1966.
Pezzullo, Ralph. *Plunging into Haiti: Clinton, Aristide, and the Defeat of Democracy.* Jackson: University of Mississippi Press, 2006.
Phillips, David Atlee. *The Night Watch.* 1977; London: Robert Hale, 1978.
Phillips, R. Hart. *Cuba: Island of Paradox.* New York: McDowell, Oblensky, n.d. [1959].
Price-Mars, Jean. *So Spoke the Uncle.* Translated and introduced by Magdaline W. Shannon. 1928; Washington, DC: Three Continents Press, 1983.
Prizel, Ilya. *Latin America Through Soviet Eyes: The Evolution of Soviet Perceptions During the Brezhnev Era, 1964–1982.* Cambridge: Cambridge University Press, 1990.
Rabe, Stephen G. *Eisenhower and Latin America: The Foreign Policy of Anticommunism.* Chapel Hill: University of North Carolina Press, 1988.
———. *The Most Dangerous Area in the World: John F. Kennedy Confronts Communist Revolution in Latin America.* Chapel Hill: University of North Carolina Press, 1999.
Reid, Michael. *Forgotten Continent: The Battle for Latin America's Soul.* 2007; updated edition, New Haven, CT: Yale University Press, 2009.
Reid-Henry, Simon. *Fidel and Che: A Revolutionary Friendship.* London: Sceptre, 2009.
Reynolds, Edward. *Stand the Storm: A History of the Atlantic Slave Trade.* London: Allison and Busby, 1985.
Rice, Donald E. *The Rhetorical Uses of the Authorizing Figure: Fidel Castro and José Martí.* New York: Praeger, 1992.
Richardson, Bonham C. *The Caribbean in the Wider World, 1492–1992: A Regional Geography.* Cambridge: Cambridge University Press, 1992.
Rodríguez, Juan Carlos. *The Bay of Pigs and the CIA.* Translated by Mary Todd. Melbourne: Ocean Press, 1999.
Rojas, Rafael. *Essays in Cuban Intellectual History.* London: Palgrave Macmillan, 2008.
Rojo, Ricardo. *My Friend Che.* Translated by Julian Casart. New York: Dial Press, 1968.
Salinger, Pierre. *John F. Kennedy, Commander in Chief: A Profile in Leadership.* New York: Penguin Studio, 1997.
———. *P.S., A Memoir.* New York: St. Martin's Press, 1995.
Santamaría, Haydée. *Moncada: Memories of the Attack That Launched the Cuban Revolution.* Translated and introduced by Robert Taber. Secaucus, NJ: Lyle Stuart, 1980.

Sapène, Raymond. *Procès à: Baby Doc (Duvalier père et fils)*. Châtelaudren: S. E. F. Philippe Daudy, 1973.
Sartre, Jean-Paul. *Sartre on Cuba*. 1961; Westport, CT: Greenwood Press, 1974.
Schecter, Jerrold L., and Peter S. Deriabin. *The Spy Who Saved the World: How a Soviet Colonel Changed the Course of the Cold War*. 1992; London: Brassey's, 1995.
Schlesinger, Arthur M., Jr. *Robert Kennedy and His Times*. London: André Deutsch, 1978.
———. *A Thousand Days: John F. Kennedy in the White House*. 1965; London: Mayflower-Dell, 1967.
Schmitz, David F. *Thank God They're on Our Side: The United States and Right-Wing Dictatorships, 1921–1965*. Chapel Hill: University of North Carolina Press, 1999.
Shacochis, Bob. *The Immaculate Invasion*. 1999; London: Bloomsbury, 2000.
Shesol, Jeff. *Mutual Contempt: Lyndon Johnson, Robert Kennedy, and the Feud That Defined a Decade*. New York: W. W. Norton, 1997.
Smith, Earl E. T. *The Fourth Floor: An Account of the Castro Communist Revolution*. 1962; Washington, DC: Selous Foundation Press, 1991.
Smith, Wayne S. *The Closest of Enemies: A Personal and Diplomatic Account of U.S.–Cuban Relations Since 1957*. New York: W. W. Norton, 1987.
Sorensen, Theodore C. *Kennedy*. London: Hodder and Stoughton, 1965.
Souchère, Elena de la. *Crime à Saint-Domingue: L'affaire Trujillo-Galíndez*. Paris: Éditions Albin Michel, 1972.
Spector, Robert M. *W. Cameron Forbes and the Hoover Commissions to Haiti, 1930*. Lanham, MD: University Press of America, 1985.
Summers, Anthony. *Official and Confidential: The Secret Life of J. Edgar Hoover*. London: Victor Gollancz, 1993.
Sutton, Paul K. *The Caribbean as a Subordinate State System, 1945–1976*. Hull: Department of Politics, University of Hull, 1980.
Sweig, Julia E. *Inside the Cuban Revolution: Fidel Castro and the Urban Underground*. Cambridge, MA: Harvard University Press, 2002.
Szulc, Tad, ed. *The United States and the Caribbean*. Englewood Cliffs, NJ: Prentice-Hall, 1971.
Taber, Robert. *M-26: Biography of a Revolution*. New York: Lyle Stuart, 1961.
———. *The War of the Flea: The Classic Study of Guerrilla Warfare*. With a foreword by Bard E. O'Neil. 1965; New York: Brassey's, 2002.
Taubman, William. *Khrushchev: The Man and His Era*. London: Free Press, 2003.
Thomas, Hugh. *Cuba, or, The Pursuit of Freedom*. 1971; updated edition, New York: Da Capo Press, 1998.
Tompson, William J. *Khrushchev: A Political Life*. 1995; Basingstoke: Macmillan, 1997.
Torres Cairo, Carlos. *Alberto Korda: Diario de una Revolución*. Valencia: Ediciones Aurelia, 2006.
Torres Cairo, Carlos, and Saúl Corral López. *Girón: los días gloriosos de una batalla, The Glorious Days of the Bay of Pigs Battle*. Valencia: Ediciones Aurelia, 2007.
———. *Raúl Corrales: Cuba, la imagen y la historia*. Valencia: Ediciones Aurelia, 2006.
Val, Jacques. *La dictature de Duvalier*. Paris: La Pensée Universelle, 1971.
Vandenbroucke, Lucien S. *Perilous Options: Special Operations as an Instrument of U.S. Foreign Policy*. Oxford: Oxford University Press, 1993.
Vega, Bernardo. *Eisenhower y Trujillo*. Santo Domingo: Fundación Cultural Dominicana, 1991.
———. *Kennedy y los Trujillo*. Santo Domingo: Fundación Cultural Dominicana, 1991.
Warren Commission. *Report of the President's Commission on the Assassination of President John F. Kennedy*. Washington, DC: United States Government Printing Office, 1964.

Weiner, Tim. *Legacy of Ashes: The History of the CIA*. With a new afterword. 2007; New York: Anchor Books, 2008.

Welles, Sumner. *Naboth's Vineyard: The Dominican Republic, 1844–1924*. 2 vols. New York: Payson and Clarke, 1928.

Westad, Odd Arne. *The Global Cold War: Third World Interventions and the Making of Our Times*. Cambridge: Cambridge University Press, 2005.

White, Mark J., ed. *The Kennedys and Cuba: The Declassified Documentary History*. Chicago: Ivan R. Dee, 1999.

Wiarda, Howard J. *The Dominican Republic: Nation in Transition*. London: Pall Mall Press, 1969.

Williams, Eric. *From Columbus to Castro: The History of the Caribbean, 1492–1969*. London: André Deutsch, 1970.

Williamson, Charles T. *The U.S. Naval Mission to Haiti, 1959–1963*. Annapolis, MD: Naval Institute Press, 1999.

Wyden, Peter. *Bay of Pigs: The Untold Story*. London: Jonathan Cape, 1979.

Yaffe, Helen. *Che Guevara: The Economics of Revolution*. Basingstoke: Palgrave Macmillan, 2009.

ACKNOWLEDGMENTS

★

I would like to thank all the superb archivists and librarians at the institutions in which I researched and wrote this book. These have included the John F. Kennedy Presidential Library and Museum in Boston, Massachusetts, where I would especially like to thank Stephen Plotkin; the National Archives of the United States, College Park, Maryland; the Butler Library, Columbia University, New York, where special thanks go to Tara Craig, Caronae Howell, Jennifer Lee, and Dawn Whitehead; the Hispanic Reading Room at the Library of Congress, Washington, D.C., particularly Joan F. Higbee and Katherine McCann; Craig G. Wright of the Herbert Hoover Presidential Library, who provided expert assistance online; the British Library in London; and the sublime London Library.

I have benefited from the support of an exceptionally talented and creative transatlantic editorial team. At Simon & Schuster in London, I would like to thank my editor Mike Jones; and Emma Ewbank, Hugo de Klee, Reginald Piggott, Rory Scarfe, Katherine Stanton, and Sue Stephens. At Henry Holt in New York, I would like to thank my editor Gillian Blake; and Marjorie Braman, Nicole Dewey, Lisa Fyfe, Vicki Haire, and Allison McElgunn. At McClelland & Stewart in Toronto, I would like to thank my editor Anita Chong; and Ruta Liormonas and Doug Pepper. I would also like to thank all the sales people, distributors, buyers, and bookshop staff who have worked and are working with this book: you do a great job, and it's very much appreciated. At my literary agency, AP Watt, I would like to thank my agent Natasha Fairweather, and Emily Kitchin, Rob Kraitt, Linda Shaughnessy, and Donald Winchester. I would also like to thank Richard Foreman, my publicist, for far too many late nights.

Thanks to everyone who gave up their time to speak to me, passed on contacts or information, or simply discussed ideas. In particular: Jad Adams, Helen Atsma, Nora Bensahel, Tina Brown, Jimmy Burns, Jean-Michel Caroit,

Svetlana Chervonnaya, Aruna Dahanayake, Edward Jay Epstein, Yolette Etienne, Andrew Gordon, John Gordon IV, Daniel Green, James Hoge, Sergei Khrushchev, Hal Klepak, Nekita Lamour, Dominic Lieven, Alexander van Praag, Angel Rabasa, Adolfo Rivero, Paraag Shukla, Roberto Solera, Sergio Solera, Vicente Solera-Deuchar, Monal Wadhera, Maddie West, Beryl Williams, Peter Wilson, and Xun Zhou.

I submitted requests to talk to Fidel and Raúl Castro, the two most significant characters from this narrative remaining alive at the time of writing, but no interview was granted. I also submitted a request to talk to Jean-Claude Duvalier, and received no response. Though I would have welcomed the opportunity to hear any of the protagonists' opinions firsthand, I had intended from the beginning that this book would rely principally on the documents, memoirs, oral histories, and news reports set down as closely as possible to events in the 1950s and 1960s. The point of my research was to uncover what the people on all sides thought and did at the time, not to hear how any particular individual might have reassessed or rationalized what happened in the half century since then. Of course, I am very grateful to those who did talk to me, including those few who prefer not to be named. "I am still scared of Trujillo," one former Dominican dissident said to me under the trees in Parque Colón, the traditional meeting place for political discussions in Santo Domingo. "You can tell me that his body is dead, but his system, his influence, is alive. I will never believe that he is not waiting around a corner for me."

Travels in pursuit of this story have taken me all over the world: not only around Cuba, Haiti, and the Dominican Republic, but to Buenos Aires, Mexico City, Berlin, Moscow, New York, Washington, D.C., Boston, Miami, and back home to London. Thanks to everyone who has been of help on this epic and wonderful journey. In Haiti, I would particularly like to thank Kristie van de Wetering, Tanya Merceron, and Ruthchel Nelson, as well as Amy Barry, Lys Holdoway, and the team at Oxfam GB. In the Dominican Republic, I am eternally grateful to Elizabeth Mavrikis and her family at the Coco Boutique Hotel, who drove the streets of Santo Domingo at midnight through hurricane floods to find the passport I had dropped in a puddle after a purgatorial bus ride from Port-au-Prince. It was a privilege to get to know Cuba, Haiti, and the Dominican Republic, three proud and fascinating countries. Though much in this story speaks of the worst times in their histories, I have found Cubans, Haitians, and Dominicans themselves to be unfailingly generous and hospitable. After writing this book, I believe less than ever that people get the government they deserve.

Special thanks to Gretchen Elkins and Claire Sheedy for the use of their beautiful apartment in New York, which made the research I did there even more of a pleasure. Extra-special thanks to my *Red Heat compañeros*: Kati Hajibagheri, Dora Napolitano, Tim Robey, and Lucy Whitaker, who traveled with me at various points, and Adi Bloom and Eugénie von Tunzelmann, whose ongoing intellectual support, and brilliant and incisive comments on the first draft of this manuscript, were invaluable. Finally, as always, to my parents, Carol Dyhouse and Nick von Tunzelmann, whose love makes everything possible.

This book is dedicated to my late grandfather, John Dyhouse. Born in colonial Burma but raised in a slum in Birmingham, he made a fortune, and then spent it taking his grandchildren to see the world. Thanks to him, I was fortunate enough to visit ten Caribbean nations before I was even sixteen years old, as well as parts of Africa, Asia, the Americas, and Europe. John's love of adventure, his enthusiasm for meeting new people in new places, and his sense of humor were irrepressible. I remember him with great fondness and gratitude, and, thanks to his habit of giving cocktails a Caribbean twist with overproof rum, a slight headache.

INDEX

★

ABOUT THE AUTHOR

© Andrew Whitehurst

ALEX VON TUNZELMANN is the author of *Red Heat* and *Indian Summer*. She was educated at Oxford and lives in London.